Of Gifted Voice

Praise for the Book

'Keshav Desiraju's magnificent biography of M.S. Subbulakshmi reveals to us the musician beyond the performer, the person beneath the phenomenon. Based on many years of primary research, it pays equal attention to the life and to the music, while richly illuminating the wider social and cultural history of the time. This is a superb book, which in its subtlety, sensitivity and depth, is entirely worthy of its remarkable subject.'

– Ramachandra Guha, *biographer and historian*

'To even think of peeking into the shadows and tragedies lurking behind the extraordinary life, personality and music of an artiste as celebrated and revered as M.S. Subbulakshmi would take immense courage. To be able to do so with an analytical vigour and candour that neither attempts to sensationalize nor be overcritical is the almost impossible task that the author has achieved.'

– Shubha Mudgal, *musician*

'A most engaging book focusing on M.S. Subbulakshmi's greatest gift to the world: her luminous, classical music. We have front row seats with Keshav Desiraju in MS's concerts through the decades; through his meticulous research, we get to know the texture of the programmes, the songs and the order in which she sang them in the different venues, and get to know the musicians who accompanied her. Beyond the well-known persona of M.S. Subbulakshmi is the consummate musician, and Keshav Desiraju's book introduces us to this artiste.'

—Vasudha Narayanan, *distinguished professor, Department of Religion, University of Florida*

'*Of Gifted Voice* is about the genius, beauty and tragedy of M.S. Subbulakshmi's life, but, above all, it is about music. It is an account so rich, knowledgeable, accessible and engrossing that it made no difference that I knew nothing about Carnatic music when I started reading the book. After finishing it, I wanted to listen to every piece it describes.'

— Anuradha Roy, *novelist*

'Keshav Desiraju sensitively stitches together a scholarly narrative of an artiste the world reveres as he locates the life of MS in a world culturally rich yet socially complex, bringing the reader closer to understanding how women performers have navigated through considered identities, nationalism, modernity and reform. This book is a remarkable sadhana that will inspire artistes and richly inform the reader of this gifted voice and her mysterious world.'

— Vidya Shah, *musician*

'In *Of Gifted Voice*, Keshav Desiraju has produced the definitive M.S. Subbulakshmi biography — a wise, elegant and fascinating book that considers her life, her music and her stature in equal measure. It is difficult to imagine anyone better placed to chronicle MS's life than Keshav, who has followed and studied her music for decades, and who is able to write about her with both passion and balance. This is an indispensable book for any aficionado of classical music.'

— Samanth Subramanian, *journalist and biographer*

Of Gifted Voice

THE LIFE AND ART OF
M.S. SUBBULAKSHMI

KESHAV DESIRAJU

HarperCollins *Publishers* India

First published in hardback in India in 2021 by
HarperCollins *Publishers*
A-75, Sector 57, Noida, Uttar Pradesh 201301, India
www.harpercollins.co.in

2 4 6 8 10 9 7 5 3 1

Copyright © Keshav Desiraju 2021

P-ISBN: 978-93-9032-754-6
E-ISBN: 978-93-9032-755-3

The views and opinions expressed in this book are the author's own and the facts are as reported by him, and the publishers are not in any way liable for the same.

Keshav Desiraju asserts the moral right
to be identified as the author of this work.

All rights reserved. No part of this publication may be reproduced, stored in a retrieval system, or transmitted, in any form or by any means, electronic, mechanical, photocopying, recording or otherwise, without the prior permission of the publishers.

Typeset in 11.5/15.2 Linden Hill at
Manipal Technologies Limited, Manipal

Printed and bound at
Thomson Press (India) Ltd.

MIX
Paper
FSC™ C010615

This book is produced from independently certified FSC™ paper to ensure responsible forest management.

S
1920–1983

DRR
1916–1989

Contents

A Note on Style	ix
Acknowledgements	xiii
Preface	xvii
1. Sangita Vadya Vinodini	1
2. Shanmukhavadivu	32
3. A Child of Her Times	53
4. The Move to Madras	64
5. Sadasivam	78
6. The Politics of Language	98
7. Meera	122
8. MS: The Growth of the Name	135
9. Maestra: The Great Concert Years	155
10. Sangitha Kalanidhi	181
11. The Singer of Chants	202

12. Subbulakshmi	221
13. The Years of Retirement	248
14. Bharat Ratna	268
15. A Life	284
Notes	311
Appendix I: Dramatis Personae	409
Appendix II: Some Notes on Songs	430
Glossary	451
Bibliography and Suggested Readings	463
Index	475
Index of Songs	491
About the Author	500

A Note on Style

THERE can be a problem with Indian names written in English. All proper nouns have been used, insofar as can be established, as they have been conventionally spelt. *Kalki* R. Krishnamurthi and J. Krishnamurti had the same given name, spelt differently in English. This is true of other names as well. Viswanathan, Vishwanathan and Visvanathan are the same name, spelt differently, as are Subrahmanyam, Subramaniam and Subramanian. The name Subbulakshmi itself is often written as Subbalakshmi or Subbulaxmi. Likewise, Shanmukhavadivu could be, and often is, written as Shanmugavadivu, with no significant loss of meaning. This is to do with transliteration from the Tamil.

Some names are written in English in a manner which seems elegant to me. For instance, I have used Carnatic instead of Karnatic, Karnatik or Karnatak, though I will admit that I would write *karnataka sangeetam*. I also write 'Minakshi' though the name is often written as 'Meenakshi'. Subbulakshmi's film is always *Sakuntalai* though I have written the name as Shakuntala when referring to the character. Likewise, Mira, though the film is always '*Meera*'.

The trinity have had their names spelt in a variety of ways. Tyagaraja has been called Thyagaraja, Thiagaraja and Thyagarajar, and in moments of rapture, 'Iyer-val'. Syama Sastri has been Shyama Sastri and Shyama Shastri and Muthusvami Dikshitar has been Muttuswami Dikshitar, Muddusvami Dikshitar, Muthuswami Dikshithar and sometimes Muthusvami Diksita. I have used Tyagaraja, Syama Sastri and Muthusvami Dikshitar. I have used Svati Tirunal but he could also become Swati, or Swathi, Thirunal.

Some famous musicians, and persons well known in public life, and especially in south India, are often referred to by their initials. Thus, MS, GNB and MLV. Others were always referred to by one distinctive part of their full names. Hence *Chembai* Vaidyanatha Bhagavathar, *Ariyakudi* Ramanuja Iyengar, *Musiri* Subramania Iyer, *Semmangudi* Srinivasa Iyer and *Lalgudi* G. Jayaraman. R. Krishnamurthi, founder and editor of *Kalki*, was likewise always Kalki. Sometimes honorifics become part of a person's name. T. Dhanam can be T. Dhanammal, simply Dhanammal or 'Vina' Dhanammal. Subbulakshmi herself was called Kunja in her mother's home, Kunjakka by younger members of her husband's home and Kunjamma by close friends.

In transcribing names of songs and ragas, I have not used diacritical marks. Thus, Sankarabharanam instead of śamkarābharaNa, Shanmukhapriya instead of ṣaNmukhpriya and 'Hiranmayim Lakshmim' instead of 'hiraNmayīm laksmīm'. Most references to songs are in the '*Opening words of song*'/Raga format, such as '*Tulasi jagajjanani*'/Saveri or '*Vara Narada*'/Vijayasri.

Some words in Indian languages are now so commonly used that I have not used italics: bhakti, bhajan, devadasi, mrdangam, ghatam and raga. I have, however, used italics for *ragam-tanam-pallavi*, *neraval*, *svara*, *abhang*, *kirtana*, *kriti* and other purely musical terms. All these terms are explained in the Glossary.

The cities of Chennai, Mumbai and Kolkata have been referred to as Madras, Bombay and Calcutta if the reference in the text relates to a time before the name was changed.

A Note on Style

There are many titles awarded to musicians and composers, and these are often used while referring to them. Readers will find the title *Sangitha Kalanidhi* recurring frequently, the title awarded by The Music Academy, Madras, at Chennai every year to the president of the annual conference and concerts. I have used the spelling *Sangitha* because that is what the Music Academy uses; the word could be, and is, spelt also as Sangeeta, Sangeetha or Sangita.

Acknowledgements

THIS book was written through the year 2017, but it has been in gestation for very much longer than that. This was always a book I was going to write.

I owe many early learnings and insights to P.V. Sankara Bhagavathar of Matunga, Bombay, Chingleput Ranganathan and Gautam R. Desiraju.

Several members of Subbulakshmi's family and intimate circle have shared memories. Seetha Ravi and Gowri Ramnarayan have been extremely generous with their time. V. Shrinivasan has given me ready access to his very large collection of photographs. Lakshmi Natarajan at *Kalki* allowed me access to the magazine's photo archive. I am also grateful to S. Tyagarajan, K. Rajendran and K.R. Athmanathan. I hope they will like this book.

I have also greatly benefited from conversations with V. Swaminathan, C.B. Srinivasan, R. Subbulakshmi and S. Vijayalakshmi. I am grateful to the late M.K. ('Ramesh') Ramasubramanian for showing me an important letter.

Readers of this book will realize early on that it has not been easy to locate many primary sources in researching this biography of Subbulakshmi. She would certainly have had music notebooks. It is known that she kept a diary, never failing to write a daily entry. Gowri Ramnarayan's biography, *MS and Radha* (Wordcraft, 2012), even includes a photograph of the entry for 12 June 1966, along with the information that Subbulakshmi maintained a diary 'every day since the 1940s'. It has not proved possible to trace these notebooks or diaries. It is, of course, true, as A.N. Wilson says in *Victoria* (New York: Penguin Press, 2014, p. 12), while deploring the destruction of many of Queen Victoria's papers by her children after her passing, 'that just because a letter or a diary has been burned does not mean it was either sinister or even especially interesting'. Even so, the personal papers of a public figure cannot be without their points of value.

Researching at the British Library, London, is always a joy, but it was made the more pleasurable by Nasreen Munni Kabir's warm and cheerful hospitality. Munni, thank you. Anuradha Roy and Nandini Mehta, both formidable editors, read this book in draft and made important and useful comments. It is a pleasure to thank them. Sriram V. has been extremely kind in sharing his considerable knowledge of facts and events. V. Navaneeth Krishnan has been generous with his knowledge of Subbulakshmi's recordings, concerts and photographs. To both of them, my thanks.

Despite the enormous commitments on his time, A.R. Venkatachalapathy patiently read me through the correspondence of T.K. Chidambaranatha Mudaliar. I am grateful to him.

I am grateful to Shyama Warner, who read the manuscript in entirety and made many valuable suggestions. All editorial infelicities which remain are entirely my responsibility.

At HarperCollins, Siddhesh Inamdar has been consistently supportive. I am grateful both to him and to Antony Thomas for their courtesy with a first-time author.

Several friends have helped in the writing of this book, with information, suggestions, hospitality, translations and leads. I am happy to be able to thank A.S. Panneerselvam, Amitabha Bhattacharya,

Acknowledgements

Amrit Srinivasan, Amrita Patel, Annalakshmi Chellam, Arvind Kumar Sankar, Bandana Mukhopadhyay, C.V. Krishnaswami, Hemalatha Murli, Indira Gopal, Janaki Nathen, K. Eswar, Kanakalatha Mukund, Kezevino Aram, M.A. Siddique, Michele Ferenz, Mrinal Pande, N. Ram, N.L. Rajah, Nachiket Patwardhan, Nirmala Sundararajan, Padma Sugavanam, R. Champakalakshmi, R.K. Shriram Kumar, R. Veezhinathan, Rajiv Menon, Ravi Chellam, S. Annapurna, S. ('Musiri Thyagu') Thyagarajan, Sandeep Bagchee, Seemantini Apte, Subhashini Parthasarathy, T.M. Krishna, Tara Murali, Usha Krishnan, V.B. Srinivasan, V.K. Shankar, V.S. Sambandan, Vasudha Narayanan, Virginia Danielson and Yadav Murti Sankaran. I apologize in advance to anyone whose name I have inadvertently left out.

Over many years now, several friends have been constantly encouraging: Anant Jani, David Grewal, Girindre Beeharry, Iswar Hariharan, Keshava Guha, Lakshmi Vijayakumar, Madhav Khosla, Prabha Sridevan, Prashant Upadhyaya, Radhika Khosla, Rohini Somanathan, Rupert Snell, Salila 'Bulani' Raha, Samanth Subramanian, Shanta Guhan, Shozeb Haider, Soumitra Pathare, V. Senthil Kumar and Vandana Gopikumar. I am delighted to be able to say to them that the book is done.

Some friends have passed on. I owe much to Ann Shankar, D.L. Rao, Janaki Krishnan, K.V. Ramanathan, Sita Narasimhan, V. Ranganayaki, Vasudha Dhagamwar and Vimala and B.D. Pande.

Much of the research for this book was done in the libraries and archives at the British Library, London, the *Hindu*, Chennai: the India International Centre, New Delhi; the James A. Rubin Collection of South Indian Classical Music, Eda Kuhn Loeb Music Library, Harvard University; the Madras Institute of Development Studies, Chennai, the Music Academy, Madras, at Chennai; the Nehru Memorial Museum and Library, New Delhi; the Roja Muthiah Library, Chennai; the Sangeet Natak Akademi, New Delhi; and at the State Government Archives, Chennai. I am grateful to them all. I must also recognize the good people who maintain the site www.sangeethapriya.org and the TAG Digital Archives at the Music Academy, Madras, at Chennai. The magazine *Sruti*, published from October 1983, has also been an essential source of information.

This book would not have been actually written were it not for Ramachandra Guha and his infectious enthusiasm, and his constant urging that I begin to write. I have learnt much from him over very many years and am glad of the chance to be able to say so. Sujata and Ram, my thanks.

My sisters Srilata Iyer and Sucharita Ranganathan have over sixty years given gladly and unstintingly of their time and affection. This book is an inadequate token of gratitude. Srilu and Mani, Suma and Rangu, my thanks.

My brief meetings with Subbulakshmi over many years were always with Gopalkrishna Gandhi or through his intervention. But this is the least of what I owe. I am grateful for his constant presence. Tara and Gopal, my thanks.

My parents did not live to see this book, or much else in my life. From her I learnt the meaning of duty; from him I learnt the meaning of goodness, and it is to their memory that this book is dedicated in remembrance, with respect and with very much love.

Preface

कलावती कमलासन युवती कल्याणम कलयतु सरस्वती[1]

'O Sarasvati, beautiful and young, with eternal youth, thou who art seated upon a lotus flower, work good for us!'

(Opening words of Muthusvami Dikshitar's composition *'Kalavati'* in the raga Kalavati)

ALL lives are a mixture of character and destiny[2] but it is only in some lives that character is so sharply etched and in which destiny plays so dramatic a role as to make the life itself immortal. M.S. Subbulakshmi is one of these immortals.

M.S. Subbulakshmi has been portrayed in various ways, as a musician who sought and achieved an all-India appeal, as a philanthropist and benefactor of noble causes, as an icon of high south Indian style, as a woman of piety and devotion, and as a friend and associate of the good and the great. But while she was all of these, she was first and foremost a classical musician of the highest order, and it is as such that her life's work must be assessed. 'And after all these years, despite her saintly persona and many avatars, it is the music by which we remember her.'[3]

Indeed, that is how she identified herself.[4] This task is not particularly easy, especially given how long her career was and how significantly her style and presentation changed over the years. It was said of the singer Ariyakudi Ramanuja Iyengar (1890–1967) that he 'bestrode the concert stage of Karnatak [sic] music for a little more than half a century – a dangerously long period for any but the greatest artist'.[5] This is true as well of Semmangudi Srinivasa Iyer (1908–2003), but these two pre-eminent Carnatic musicians, over their very long performing careers, stayed within the bounds of the course they set for themselves early on. This was not the case with Subbulakshmi.

It was a life lived in the public glare; it was a life whose most private moments were carefully obliterated. In her very last years, in a private conversation with an acquaintance, she observed, 'I do not wish to speak untruths but much of the truth of my life is better unsaid.'[6] In the same conversation she said, 'I have been condemned to fame.' And even of the person who was accessible to the outsider, and of the truths which could be said, there were many. 'There is, therefore, an early Subbulakshmi, and a mid-course Subbulakshmi, a Subbulakshmi of the screen, a Subbulakshmi of the *sabhas*, a Subbulakshmi of fun and frolic and laughter, a Subbulakshmi, sublime, serene and sacred. Each Subbulakshmi is real, essential.'[7] And in each of these roles, she was nothing but utterly true. If she completely absorbed the Tamil Brahmin ethic in her manner and style, a trait for which she is now mocked by some, she was, to others such as the poet Hoshang Merchant, Mira personified.

> *You have bodied ecstasy,*
> *Who will find the singer in the song*
> *Or ever sift you from the seer?*[8]

Subbulakshmi's was a life of extraordinary achievement, especially so for a woman of her times. She was without formal education and without resources and identified by society only as belonging to the devadasi, or courtesan, tradition, but she had unimaginable talent and iron determination. It is widely held that she was an uncommonly modest woman, who rarely expressed an opinion and was easily led, but there is equally no doubt that she knew what she had and had the ambition to achieve what she wanted.

For all her attainments, Subbulakshmi never regarded herself as a feminist icon of any sort. In a foreword to a book of translations of the saint-poet Mira, she observed, very conservatively, 'At a time when so much is said about the liberation of women the world over, it is good to think of a woman whose soul wanted to liberate itself and merge with the Lord.'[9] She always purveyed the impression of traditional conservatism, and insofar as she ever expressed herself on the subject, she was generally of the view that the enormous ability and power of women, *strishakti*, needed to be curbed and kept in control, preferably by men.

For all the magnificence of her art, we still have no real idea of the person. From a shadowy childhood and tumultuous youth, Subbulakshmi grew into a phenomenon. Recent biographies have followed the standard version, of a powerful voice which shone briefly in films and then surrendered itself to devotional worship and to the cause of the nation; but it is hard not to conclude that the creation of the phenomenon, which transformed a tradition and exalted an art, did not in the process also lead to the snuffing out of a personality, of a spirit and of an extraordinary presence. This is clearly the stuff of tragedy.

1

Sangita Vadya Vinodini

संगीत वाद्य विनोदिनी...

(*'She who delights in song'*, from Muthusvami Dikshitar's *'Hiranmayim Lakshmim sada bhajami'* in the raga Lalita)

THE Carnatic music tradition is of relatively recent origin but it has drawn, over the centuries, from a complex mix of religion, ritual practice, social structures and notions of what constituted entertainment. It is a complicated subject, with many regional variations spread over time but it is clear that the musical tradition arose from a meeting of extant musical forms and practice and the Hindu notion of bhakti, or literally, service of the chosen deity.[1]

The earliest texts, from the mists of antiquity, are the Vedas, commonly dated to the third century BC, themselves probably the result of the philosophical speculations of the hordes of people migrating into the plains of upper India from the West over 200–1500 BC.[2] Many of the Vedas relate to forms of worship and ritual and many are in praise of nature. 'These Vedas ... are the productions of a race as yet in infancy, struggling in the dark to give expression to its religious emotions. The first gods which the Hindus worshipped were nothing but the forces of nature personified, Agni, the god of fire, Indra, the god of the sky, Varuna, the god of rain.'[3] Of the four principal Vedas, the *Sama Veda* is, to this day, sung.[4]

These texts were composed in Sanskrit, which the migrants brought with them, by priests who assumed the highest position in the hierarchical categorization of society that evolved over time. Religious practice evolved, moving from a Vedic worship of nature to a more sophisticated worship of a personal, and then an impersonal god. Several broad strands of philosophical teaching are identified, which – along with the Vedic texts and related texts such as the Upanishads and the Bhagavad Gita, itself a part of the vast epic Mahabharata – formed the bulk of Indian religious and philosophical explorations.

In a parallel movement, the Sanskrit of the religious texts was used in literature, drama and poetry, with Kalidasa of the fifth century AD regarded as among the greatest poets of his time.[5] Tamil writings of the Sangam era – the first three centuries after Christ – testify to the existence of lively cultural and literary traditions and an exposure of the people of these coastal areas to trade, and to the outside world.[6]

It has been suggested that the general peace and political stability that prevailed over the subcontinent from the third century onwards led, in time, to more attention being paid to matters of the spirit, with the production of large collections of texts and devotional hymns, often identifiable as poetry, set to metre and meant for musical performance.[7] These texts were further developed by Sankara (AD 788–820) and his brothers in spirit Ramanuja (1017–1137[?]) and Madhva (1238–1317) who through their interpretation of the texts provided the foundations for Hindu religious practice; many texts attributed to them, such as the *Saundaryalahari* of Sankara, are recited or sung to this day, as are long classic texts, such as the *Sri Vishnu Sahasranamam*.

All this activity can, however, be regarded as well within the Brahminic fold with the principal language being Sanskrit and the principal exponents from the priestly castes. At the risk of oversimplifying some fairly intense developments, it can be argued that the use of other languages as a medium of expression of devotion, and often by persons not belonging to the priestly castes, marked the first great explosion of bhakti. The *Bhagavata Purana* of the tenth century specifically identifies *kirtana*, or singing, as one of the nine forms of bhakti, and what happened over the next few centuries can be seen as a great surge of devotional worship.

Scholars are divided on whether the works of the vernacular poets, writing not in Sanskrit but in the rich, and ancient, languages of the subcontinent, should alone be regarded as the core of the bhakti movement or whether the older religious texts in Sanskrit should also be included. This difference of opinion is linked to the question of whether the vernacular revolution was indeed against high Sanskritic dogma, much as the earlier teachings of Gautama Buddha and Mahavira can be said to be a revolt. It is relevant that at some politically charged moments, the issue arises of whether or not the works of the mystic Sufi poets are in the broad stream of bhakti. Whatever the disputations among the experts, what is indisputable is that great works of devotional literature survive from these centuries across India and have contributed vastly to the musical tradition of the area.

The Sanskritist and musicologist V. Raghavan promoted the view that waves of bhakti moved northwards from the south of the subcontinent.[8] The Alwars wrote in Tamil in praise of Vishnu, the '*Divyaprabandham*', verses which may have been sung 'with raga and tala by temple minstrels at Srirangam'. Andal, of the ninth century, from the Vaishnavite tradition, is credited with the '*Tiruppavai*'. The Nayanars (or Nayanmars) in the Tamil country were Saivite poets, such as Sundarar of the eighth century, whose *tevaram* songs may have been 'originally sung to ancient Indian melodic patterns'. Tamil hymns of the ninth-century Saivite poet Manikkavacakar may have been sung. The Kannada country saw Virasaivas such as Basava, Allamaprabhu and Akka Mahadevi and, later, dasas such as Purandaradasa and Kanakadasa.

A little to the north, in the Marathi-speaking area, were Jnanadev (thirteenth century), Namdev (thirteenth century) and Tukaram (sixteenth century), whose kirtan singing 'resulted in collections of thousands of *abhang* hymns'.[9] Still further north were Narsi Mehta, writing in Gujarati in the fifteenth–sixteenth century, and Mira in sixteenth-century Rajasthan. Nanak in fifteenth–sixteenth-century Punjab and Lal Ded in fourteenth-century Kashmir were at the very north of India. Moving into the plains of the Ganga, there are Kabir of the fifteenth century and Tulsidas of the sixteenth–seventeenth century, both in the Benares region, and Surdas and Raskhan, both of the sixteenth century and writing in Brajbhasa.[10] In Raghavan's reading, waves of bhakti spread further to the east over the fifteenth–sixteenth centuries, through Vidyapati in Bihar, Sankaradeva in Assam and Chaitanya in Odisha. Slightly earlier than these poets were Jayadeva in Odisha in the twelfth century and Annamacharya in the Telugu area near Tirupati in the fifteenth century, bringing the great arc of bhakti back to the Tamil country in the deep south of India.

For all that this is a fascinating theory, opinion is divided on how far these saint-singers were actually the 'great integrators' of Raghavan's speculations. For the most part, they were not at all from the mainstream traditions of worship and art music but often from the marginalized, subaltern and lower caste groups and, far from being integrators, were actually dissenters. For one thing, many of them were women – Mira, Andal, Janabai, Lal Ded – whose literary output survives in history and in contemporary performance.

Integrators or not, the popular songs of the bhakti singers, set to tune and metre, became the vehicle of devotional music. A good example is the *bhajana sampradaya* tradition in the deep south, with its roots in Marathi kirtan singing.[11] At the same time, it has been suggested that the 'classicization of the devotional song – the north Indian *pada* and the south Indian *kirtana* – probably started in the fourteenth century when the refrain, called Dhruva in north India and *pallavi* in south India, was placed at the beginning of the compositions as the first theme or musical idea'.[12] The *kirtana* and the *kriti* – terms we will come across often – refer to two important types of composed songs in the Carnatic tradition. The *kirtana* is a simple, devotional piece, often with many verses set to the same tune, and suitable for group singing. The *kriti* is a more sophisticated form.

There are other points of interest. It has been suggested that the nature of bhakti itself changed with the introduction of musical forms as the vehicle of expression, with the strong intellectual tradition of the Alwars and Andal being replaced by the pure adoration of Mira and Namdeo.[13] It is also possible that it was through the return of the bhakti tradition to the south that Hindi first became understood outside north India.[14] Through these various movements over centuries, we can trace the evolution of devotional literature from the earliest speculations by philosophers and savants on questions of identity, on duality between the Self and the divine and on the means to personal salvation, to texts used in daily worship of particular gods and goddesses by householders, and, in due course, in performance in more secular spaces.

In a country as diverse as India, it is hard, and not necessarily meaningful, to speak of culture as if it were a single dominant ethos. There are many strands, of greater or lesser antiquity, with many different peoples representing or projecting the main elements of a culture, with a binding feature across them being the sense that the cultural tradition of a people represented what to them was both beautiful and good. In most cases, this included both musical representation and the practice of a belief system but, as at least one musicologist has pointed out, the development of a musical tradition within the framework of religious belief required 'not only a body of priests who knew what they are doing but a body of musicians who knew what is being done'.[15]

It was in this context that musicologists and grammarians were at work. Bharata's *Natya Sastra* (first century AD) is traditionally regarded as the original musical text, the precursor to the *Sangita Ratnakara* of Sarangadeva (1210–47) of Devagiri in what is now south Maharashtra, the text from which both the Carnatic and the Hindustani traditions seek validation. This work identified the seven *svaras*, and the twenty-two *srutis*,[16] the different groupings of which resulted in different ragas, each with a 'distinct and recognizable melodic flavour or character'[17] and ranks with the earlier *Natya Sastra* in making no differentiation between north and south India.[18] Subsequent works of musical grammar developed these themes;[19] at the same time, there was a great deal of musical composition, though it is not immediately clear that these composed pieces were set to anything that would be recognized today as music, or whether these were pieces composed to be chanted.

It is in the fifteenth century that musicologists have placed the growth 'of the music of the Karnataka Desa as a distinct variant of the larger Indian musical tradition ... specific to the area lying between the Krishna and the Kaveri'.[20] This region was under the intermittently hostile rule of the Hoysalas and the Kakatiyas of the Deccan and the Cholas, Cheras and Pandyas of the Tamil region. But despite hostilities between warring rulers, a tradition of temple worship, pilgrimage and devotional poetry and singing was established. Telugu, Kannada and Marathi were widely used and Tamil, of course, had a much older history of poetry. Sanskrit was still in use as the language of culture. Vijayanagar, in what is now north Karnataka, is associated with the establishment of the south Indian musical tradition, based on ragas as melodic entities.

Musicologists and lay listeners alike have grappled with the idea of a raga. At a very basic level, it is a scale of notes. A set of notes has an identity but it is left to the performing musician to give that identity character. Not every set of notes will necessarily work either on the concert platform or as a listening experience. Composed pieces attempt to determine the usages permitted within any set of notes identified as a raga and with every rendition a raga grows, both in the musician's understanding and in the public imagination.[21]

It is commonplace today for the Hindustani and Carnatic systems of music to be regarded as the 'classical' music of north and south India; what is undeniable is that two different traditions grew, not all at once, and over a long period, but deriving from the same basic material. It is not even clear that the term 'Carnatic' originated as referring to the geographical south of India, or the region now identified as Karnataka, or whether its roots lie in the Sanskrit *karna* or 'ear', with *karnataka* meaning that which is haunting to the ear. For that matter, there is no specific reason to link the term 'Hindustani' with the geographic north given that the Mughal empire, 'Hindustan', which so identified itself extended into the far south of the peninsula.

Hindustani and Carnatic music alike are based on raga, though the ragas are handled differently, with different accents on the notes, and different styles of improvisation. In performance today, they provide different musical experiences but there are common origins. For one, there is the vocabulary. Identical or similar words are used, even if they do not mean the same thing anymore, such as *alap/alapana*, *raag/raga*, *svara*, *sruti*, *tanpura/tambura*, *mridang*/mrdangam, *taan/tanam*, and so on. There are the names of raag/ragas such as Bhairavi, Saranga, Kalyan/Kalyani, Hindolam, Todi, Khamaj/Khamas, Jhinjhoti/Jenjuti, Kafi/Kapi, Abhogi, Kalavati, Kedara. These words have come down over centuries, several have geographical connotations and many are used in the same broad context, even if the ragas they refer to are quite different. Several ragas are performed in both traditions even if with different names and with different emphases; Bhoop/Mohana, Malkauns/Hindolam and Mian-ki-Todi/Subhapantuvarali are familiar examples.

Most importantly, both systems continue to use the same set of notes, the twenty-two *srutis* mentioned earlier, even if the structure of the ragas built using these and their rendering is quite different.

It is, of course, true that there are broad underlying principles. A sensitive critic has defined these as the three unities of Indian music: the use of the drone to keep the pitch, the unity of mood and atmosphere in raga rendering, subject to the melodic laws of the raga and the constant flow of rhythm.[22] An understanding of these notions helps in an appreciation of a Hindustani or Carnatic music performance.

Interestingly, Hindustani music has a well-established theory and system by which ragas are associated with different times of the day and night; Carnatic music makes no such differentiation.

While 'Hindustani songs' have been popular in south India since the nineteenth century, no recognizably Carnatic musical form, with the possible exception of *svaraprasthara*, or the play of seven *svaras* or musical syllables during extemporization of a line in a song, has been adopted by Hindustani musicians. However, there have been exchanges of ragas with each other, for instance Brindavanasaranga, Jaunpuri, Dhanasri, Tilang and Bagesri from the north being readily used in the south.[23] In the reverse direction, Charukesi, Simhendramadhyamam, Vachaspati, Kiravani and Hemavati, all recognizably Carnatic ragas, are performed in the Hindustani style. A linked issue, to which we will turn, is the performance of the bhajan as a concert item.

Too much should not be made of the similarities between the systems. It is routine for nationalist leaders to aver that Hindustani and Carnatic music 'were basically the same and were "Bharateeya Sangeet" to the core' or even for senior musicians to hold that the two systems were 'brothers from the same stock', but such generalizations need not be taken seriously.[24] One feature will immediately strike a contemporary listener. The Hindustani tradition focuses on raga rendition as the centrepiece of any recital, with the words of a *bandish* receiving perfunctory attention; the Carnatic tradition has given pride of place to the composed piece, or *kriti*, many of which are rendered in a recital without raga elaboration.

The *kriti* itself has been seen as the template, 'the means of fixing the traditional form of a raga',[25] an elaboration of the scales to a demonstrable example of what the raga should look and sound like. The *kriti* was the accompaniment to dance, and so served an important purpose in laying down the beat. It has been suggested that the manner of singing, the speed, the emphases, the articulation of words were all linked, in the first place, to the need to harmoniously accompany a dancer performing any particular piece, leading in time to determining the nature of the vocal performance itself. '*Gamaka* in a *raga* is like *abhinaya* in a dance.'[26] This led in time to the much greater emphasis given to the formal structure of a raga in the south Indian tradition, with careful notation of the phrases appropriate for any raga, and an emphasis on naming and identifying ragas.

The overwhelming majority of composed pieces, *kritis* and others, currently in vogue in the Carnatic tradition are religious in content and can and do play a role in ritual worship. Even where the text of a Hindustani *bandish* is non-secular, the reference is purely nominal. It is not that the Carnatic song tradition is only chanting; the lyrics are always subservient to the melody but it is the lyrics which give body to the performed piece. The association of the repertory of the Carnatic tradition with temples – and organized worship – and the identification of musical excellence with greater devotion, are issues which will continue to occupy us.

An inescapable conclusion is that Carnatic music as it is known and practised today is identifiably Hindu – even perhaps identifiably Brahmin – music in a way in which Hindustani music is not. It is not just that in every generation there have been outstanding Muslim performers in the Hindustani tradition; the emphasis is overwhelmingly on raga and the expression of emotion through raga and only very slightly on the particular texts which may be taken up for elaboration.

Many influences have come to bear on the musical traditions of north India. 'Hindustani music has quite obviously been open to influences from all over the high hinterland of Asia Minor, Arabia, Mesopotamia, Slavic Russia, Tibet and China. This had its own positive and progressive impact and even today many of the important musicians of Hindustani music are Muslim and their vocalists in no way think it incongruous or heretical to be singing hymns and love lyrics in praise of Hindu deities.'[27] It would, however, be simplistic to hold, as at least one scholar has done, that with the coming to the subcontinent of Islam a 'delicate Moslem superstructure with fine curves was given to the robust body of Hindu music. The south, untouched by Islam, kept up and developed the older and more traditional style.'[28] South India was not untouched by Islam, and Hindustani music was and is not necessarily non-Hindu in manner and style.

There are then the questions of what is classical and what is not, and whether the classical is necessarily the more sophisticated, of whether antiquity alone bestows classicism, of whether the use of a 'classical' language like Sanskrit makes a musical form classical and whether, and if so how, a vernacular form is in any manner a lesser form. There are the questions of whether the classical is the traditional, and what the traditional is, or how, if they do, either of these differ from the artistic. Scholars have noted that Indian musicology did not originally prefer the term classical, using instead *marga*, music of great antiquity from the time of the Vedas, and *desi*, or more contemporary art music. However, in contemporary practice, *marga* has come to mean major, canonical, classical and *desi*, regional or local.

There is also the interesting question of the *purpose* of musical understanding, and the belief that music, along with the other art forms such as dance, poetry and painting, can provide a composite emotional and even spiritual experience. Different modes of artistic expression are seen, by some at least, as 'different pathways leading to a single goal, the goal being the organization of all human faculties toward the devotion of god and the experience of divine reality. This was an extraordinary ideal and like many ideals frequently honoured in the breach, but its supremacy was unchallenged by any others.'[29]

Religion, ritual and performance; these three features continue to remain interlinked, even if the links are disputed. The notion that musical experience was, and must be, part of spiritual evolution is difficult to comprehend and remains a contested area for some performers and listeners, but it is the notion on which tradition and heritage essentially rest.[30]

Thanjavur is the heart of Carnatic country.[31] For over a thousand years, the town and its surrounding areas, in the delta of the Kaveri, has been dominated by the Brihadiswara Temple (AD 1010) built by Rajaraja Chola at the height of Chola domination of the south. The temple is a public space and temple practice and ownership of agricultural lands have contributed to the accumulation of great riches.

The region came, at some stage, under the rule of the Telugu-speaking Nayaks of Vijayanagar. Their language and cultural richness proved to be of no little significance for the later growth of the Carnatic repertory. With the fall of Vijayanagar (1565) and the decline of Nayak rule, Thanjavur came under the rule of the culturally vibrant, Marathi-speaking Marathas. Interestingly, Telugu continued to be the language of the Maratha courts, in addition to Marathi, in this heart of the Tamil country. Since May 1992, Thanjavur has been recognized by UNESCO as a World Heritage Zone, a meeting place of the richness of the Tamil, Telugu, Kannada and Marathi cultures. Thanjavur was by no means the only pilgrim centre in the area. There was the temple at Chidambaram (twelfth and thirteenth centuries), again an expression of high Chola style, dedicated to Siva manifested as the sky, the *akasa-lingam*, worshipped as Nataraja, the primordial dancer. There were again the various temples at Kanchipuram, to Sri Kamakshi (originally fifth century), and her consort Ekamreswara (seventh century), dedicated to Siva worshipped as a manifestation of the earth, the *prithvi-lingam*. Famously, at Madurai was the great temple to Sri Minakshi (believed orginally to be of sixth century and rebuilt in the seventeenth century). Then there was Tiruchirappalli/Srirangam with the Sri Ranganathaswami Temple (sixth–ninth centuries), perhaps the most famous temple to Vishnu in the south. In addition, the Tamil country boasted a host of temples of great antiquity and legend, such as at Tirunelveli, Kumbakonam and Tiruvannamalai.

Students of the works of Muthusvami Dikshitar, to whom we will come shortly, will be familiar with the large number of his songs, composed on the presiding deities at very many temples, both the grand and the lesser known, and the wealth of geographical, iconographic and other local details they contain. These temples played a dominant role in the daily life of the people in the surrounding region and maintained large establishments.

It was in the prosperous and fertile Thanjavur region, under the peaceful rule of the Maratha rulers that the next great works of Carnatic grammar were written: Govinda Dikshitar's *Sangita Sudha* (1614) and his son Venkatamakhin's *Caturdandi Prakasika* (mid seventeenth century).[32] These works attempted to define the ragas known and sung at the time and to place them within a structure of parent and derived ragas. A descendant, Muddu Venkatamakhin, drew on earlier work identifying the twenty-two *srutis* and set in place the system of seventy-two *melakarta* ragas, a work of statistical neatness which has remained the basis of the raga structure of Carnatic music, though it has led to endless debate on the notion of 'artificial' ragas.

It is entirely likely that very few songs existed in Muddu Venkatamakhin's time which were set to music in any of the ragas defined by him, and it is a mark of his imagination that he saw that this is what the ragas *could* look, and sound, like. The entire issue is complicated and in time, with the publication of further works of grammar such as Govinda's *Sangraha Chudamani*, the proposition was well established that parent, or *janya*, ragas could have derivative, or *janaka*, ragas.[33]

We know something of the range of musical composition of this time and the lives of Jayadeva, Annamacharya (1408–1503/1507), Purandaradasa (1485–1565) and Ksetragna, also Kshetrayya (mid seventeenth century), all of whose works are still sung, albeit in musical structures set by musicians of succeeding generations. What is interesting is that there is much in these works, other than those of Purandaradasa, which can only be described as erotic where adoration of the chosen deity is often expressed in the most open declaration of carnal love.

We will come to Narayana Tirtha (1580–1660) (or 1650?–1750?) and Bhadracala Ramadas (1620–88), great devotees of Krishna and Rama respectively, and many of whose compositions still exist, and to Sadasiva Brahmendra (xxxx–1714/1755). There were again composers who were not primarily regarded as devotional poets but whose names remain; these include Sarangapani (1680–1750), Marimuthu Pillai (1712–87), Pachhimiriyam Adiappier and Margadarsi Sesha Iyengar (both eighteenth century).

The real explosion was still to come, and when it came, nothing was to remain the same in the practice and performance of Carnatic music, in its defining features, or in its ideals of what constituted wholesome music. Syama Sastri (1762–1827), Tyagaraja (1767–1847) and Muthusvami Dikshitar (1775–1835) – now revered as the trinity – were great masters who, over their lifespans, formalized the use of raga and the nature of compositions and effectively created the modern Carnatic repertory. In the words of a broad-brush identification of their styles,

> (t)he art of composition took a new shape and attained fresh life in their hands. Of the three, Tyagaraja's songs are noted for the varied moods and ideas of devotion and the poetic expression of these; those of Muthusvami Dikshitar for their scholarly tenor and the fullness

of the exposition of the melodic forms; both were prolific in their creative activity. Syama Sastri, who composed a limited number, distilled into his pieces the quintessence of the melody and rhythm, the setting and pattern of the latter imparting a unique quality to his compositions.[34]

Another critic has observed grandly, if somewhat meaninglessly, that these composers were called the trinity 'in analogy to the three Facets of Godhead'.[35]

This is not a universally accepted position. The art critic Sadanand Menon observes, 'Bhakti was about humanism. The trinity was a backlash against its egalitarian core; it laid the ground for a Brahminical resurgence.'[36] It is quite possible that the upper caste origins of the trinity and their education in Sanskrit and orthodox ritual practice led them towards a particular type of composition. It is possible that the life and work of the three, as aggressively promoted by an upwardly mobile Brahmin elite, 'belittles the significance of others including a number of non-Brahman composers'.[37] However, it is open to debate whether this actually militated against the relatively less vigorous, less structured nature of compositions by the bhakti poets, who were women and men of all castes. It is relevant that the nature of the compositions of the trinity made them more suited to the concert platform than to the more public spaces where bhakti singers lived.

Syama Sastri, Tyagaraja and Muthusvami Dikshitar were recognized early as being different from, and more definitively influential than, other musicians of their time. A record in 1887 identified 'Tyagayya, Shama Sastri and Trivaloor Dixita' among a small list of 'Principal Musicians of Note'.[38] A 1905 record, obviously written by a person of Telugu extraction, observes that 'Theethchithulu, Thiagarajayya, Syama Sastrulu were the three great masters of Music of the age'.[39]

The musical legacy of these masters was protected and promoted by their disciples. Tyagaraja had a host of disciples, many recognized as composers in their own right and many more as performing artistes. Several schools arose, each of which promoted its version of Tyagaraja *kritis*, with their varying oral and notated forms. A hundred songs of Tyagaraja were published as early as 1859, some with and some without notations.

Muthusvami Dikshitar's brother's descendants, led by the musicologist Subbarama Dikshitar, formed the principal line of musical descent along with the four dance-master brothers Ponnayya, Chinnayya, Vadivelu and Sivanandam, 'Natya Vadiwaloo' and 'Natya Shivanantha' in the 1887 reference above. The line included Tambiappan Pillai, Koranadu Ramaswami Pillai, Vallalarkoil Ammani, Tiruvarur Kamalam[40] and Tirukkadaiyar Bharati.

Syama Sastri's principal disciple was his son Subbaraya Sastri, a student also of Tyagaraja, but there were also Dasari, Porambur Krishnayyar and Sangita Svamin. Subbaraya Sastri's line of students included Tirugnana Mudaliar and Kanchipuram Dhanakoti Ammal, her sister Kamakshi Ammal and her daughters Kuppammal and Ramu Ammal – the 'Dhanakoti Daughters'. Interestingly, not all of these students of the trinity were of Brahmin origin, and the women were of the community of devadasis, a theme which will recur.[41]

Three broad features mark the immediate post-trinity period. The first is the complex web of relationships, either of family, marriage or discipleship, between composers, performers and students, till the shift of the geographical locus of the performing tradition to Madras, which occurred in the late nineteenth and early twentieth centuries, roughly over 1850–1920.

Another feature is the continued importance of *Harikatha* as the dominant mode of performance, and one with considerable mass appeal. Stories from the mythological works and the lives of saints were often the theme for these events where a principal performer, sometimes with an orchestra and chorus, told the story and sang songs. There was a considerable element of humour in these tellings, essentially to hold audience interest, but they were exercises in spiritual teaching and in inculcating religious practices within the household. *Harikatha* was primarily evangelical; it was meant to spread devotion through the stories of saints and mythological tales. Music was a secondary, if essential, consideration, with an emphasis on quick, lively renderings. The introduction of several 'Hindustani' ragas is attributed to *Harikatha*.[42]

Most accounts of the development of this popular art form recognize the Marathi influence, through the Maratha court at Thanjavur, of the *kirtana* tradition at the shrine in Pandharpur. Thanjavur Krishna Bhagavathar (1847–1903) and Tiruppazhanam Panchapakesa Sastrigal (1868–1924) were popular performers, and several of the early twentieth-century singers had a considerable reputation as performers of *Harikatha*.[43] The importance of *Harikatha* for later developments is that it was a public performance, accessible to all, and in a language understandable to all. It has been suggested that it 'was the most popular performance space in South India' before the growth of the towns.[44] Significantly, there were popular women performers of *Harikatha*, C. Saraswathi Bai (1892–1974) and Banni Bai (1912–99) being the most famous.

A third feature is the complete absence in the record of this period of women composers. If women were composing songs, they were doing so entirely within their homes. Even in contemporary times, there are very few women composers and possibly none credited with the description of *vaggeyakara* given to composers of both the lyric and the tune of a song. The songs written by women survive only in bhakti poetry.

By 1900, the time was ripe for a great performing tradition to be established. We know more about the men and women who were helping to build the tradition, who derived their authority from the work of the trinity; men and women whose gifts equalled the opportunities created by history and society. Contemporaries of the trinity, even if their works have not achieved the same spread, include Iraiyaman Tampi (1782–1856), Ghanam Krishna Iyer (1790/1799–1854), Vina Kuppayar (1798–1860), Kavikunjara Bharati (1810–96) and Gopalakrishna Bharati (1811–96). A junior contemporary of the trinity, Svati Tirunal Rama Varma, Maharaja of Travancore, (1813–46) has achieved much greater recognition than his peers.

The next generation of composers included Nilakantha Sivan (1839–1900), Pallavi Seshayyar (1842/46–1905/08/09), Patnam Subramania Iyer (1845–1902), Mysore Sadasiva Rao (1805?–85), Ramanathapuram Srinivasa Iyengar (1860–1919), Lakshmana Pillai (1864–1959), Annamalai Reddiar (1865–91), Dharmapuri Subbarayar (1864–1927), Mysore Vasudevacharya (1865–1961), Tirupati Narayanaswami Naidu (1873–1912), Harikesanallur Muthiah Bhagavathar (1877–1945) and Mayuram Viswanatha Sastri (1893–1958).

It was not just that an impressive body of composed pieces and musical practice was being built, the spaces where music could be performed were also expanding. The renowned philosopher and art historian Ananda Coomaraswamy wrote as late as 1917 that '...(t)he art music of India exists only under cultivated patronage, and in its own intimate environment ... It is the chamber music of an aristocratic society where the patron retains musicians for his own entertainment and for the pleasure of the circle of his friends; or it is temple music where the musician is the servant of God. The public concert is unknown, and the livelihood of the artist does not depend upon his ability and will to amuse the crowd'.[45] But times were changing. Historians have noted the shift away from the patronage of the performing arts by temples and courts and somewhat exclusive salons. 'At the beginning of the twentieth century the world of courtly patronage was nearly gone.'[46] And if 'intimate settings like the royal court, the *jhalsa-ghar* or the elite salons of patron-connoisseurs'[47] were disappearing, *sabhas* were beginning to appear, or clubs meant primarily to promote popular entertainment, in newly prosperous towns.

The coastal city of Madras was not known for its musical traditions or for any sort of history of music, even at a time when Tanjore, Puducota, Tinnevelly, Mysore, Vijayanagaram, Bobbili, Bellary were celebrated, or even the Malayalam-speaking area of Malabar.[48] It was, however, the leading city of the province and the seat of power and it was to Madras that men flocked in search of education, employment and opportunities.[49]

Sociologists have studied the processes by which established traditions move across geographies, and of how people carry with them the shared memories and customs of what was once home.[50] It has been suggested, for instance, that cultural performances fall into six types: folk, ritual, popular, devotional, classical and modern urban.[51] Madras, in particular, as an urban space receiving a large number of migrants from the hinterland, did not have traditional performance spaces and the establishment of such spaces – the *sabhas* – was to have a radical impact on the content and nature of the performance, and on access to musical entertainments.

The first wave of migrants to the cities were primarily the merchants and dubashes – agents for the British – most of whom were from the non-Brahmin castes.[52] The educated professionals, many of whom were Brahmin, seeking salaried or office employment, or service with the government or as lawyers, constituted the second wave. This is important in the context of the alleged takeover of the entire performing space by the upper castes, a theme to which we will return. They were the new elites, interested in making a mark in public life in general, and not necessarily only in the promotion of the performing arts.

The Madras Mahajana Sabha, set up in 1884, and in itself an offshoot of the mid-century 'Madras Native Association', was a club of prosperous professional men from Brahmin and other castes.[53] The Tondaimandalam Sabha and the Bhaktimarga Prasanga Sabha set up in the 1850s in Madras were only the first of many associations specially connected with culture and art. The Poona Gayan Samaj opened its Madras chapter in 1883, its activities limited to discussions and publications.[54] The Sri Parthasarathi Swami Sabha, the Muthialpet Sabha, the Jagannatha Bhakta Sabha, the Sri Sarada Gana Sabha, the Mylai Sangeetha Sabha and the Rasika Ranjani Sabha were all forerunners to the four most sturdy of them all, the Music Academy set up in 1928, the Indian Fine Arts Sabha set up in 1932, the Adyar Academy of the Arts (later Kalakshetra) set up in 1935 and the Tamil Isai Sangam set up in 1943.[55]

The performing tradition, in the immediate post-trinity period, is well documented, with such prominent names as Maha Vaidyanatha Iyer (1844–93), Madurai Pushpavanam Iyer (late 1880s?–1920?), 'Vina' Dhanam, also Dhanammal (1866–1938) and 'Vina' Seshanna (1852–1926). Things began to change in the early twentieth century. The musician Jon Higgins has suggested that possibly the most fundamental change was in the identity of the (upper caste, male) performing musician.

> Under royal patronage the court musician was responsible to God and to his patron, normally in that order. Music was understood principally as an expression of the artist's devotion to his *ista devata* or personal deity, and only in this context was it to be experienced as art or entertainment. However, once patronage entered the public domain their role as *bhagavathars* (or singers of religious music) retained only nominal importance, being overshadowed by the more secular, and significantly more profitable, role of popular entertainer.[56]

With the acceptance of the notion of a musical concert as an entertainment, which took place in a secular space, major changes began to occur in the nature of musical performances. By the 1930s, the trend was for organized concerts by a principal musician with accompanists, often in *sabhas* and other public spaces – a concert pattern largely inspired by Ariyakudi Ramanuja Iyengar. There was a distinction made between 'classical' and other pieces, with pride of place given to the great compositions of Syama Sastri, Tyagaraja and Muthusvami Dikshitar.

The easy availability of printed versions of songs, often with notation, and of musical exercises suitable for teaching increased the currency of these compositions. Books reduced the dependence on the oral tradition, often located only within the performing families. The *Gayakaparijatam* published by the Singaracharyulu brothers in the early 1880s, for instance, includes in addition to *svara* exercises and twenty-seven *varnams*, thirty *kritis* of Muthusvami Dikshitar, nine of Syama Sastri and twenty-five of Tyagaraja.[57]

The Music Academy did much to promote rigour, to document standard versions of songs and to establish recognized versions of raga *laksana*. The scholar Lakshmi Subramanian has suggested that the *sabhas* were responsible for attempting to lay down the rules of performance and of concert aesthetics while at all times being respectful of tradition and of what was perceived as authentic. She suggests further that the canonization of Tyagaraja has its origins in the growth of the Madras *sabhas*.

All this was considered a substantial improvement over the largely provincial entertainments of the previous century, though it must be admitted that the earlier traditions had validation and relevance within their contexts.

The Carnatic repertory was growing and had powerful foundations. The nature of performance was changing, secular spaces for performance were being identified and the focus of attention was moving away from the Tamil hinterland to Madras. Upper-caste men continued to dominate the performance space, but there was another very important development. Over this same period, the practice of classical music was moving from being the highly exclusive preserve of families traditionally wedded to the arts, and performed largely by women from these families, to being a more generally accessible tradition.

Caste was all. It was the accepted principle that 'under the caste system, people inherit from their parents their place in the social and spiritual hierarchy, their occupation and their level of spiritual purity'.[58] Caste was the determinant of access to education, to language, literature and poetry, to ritual practice, to the temples and halls where music was performed and to leisure time.

The traditional categories of *periya melam* and *chinna melam*, or greater and lesser musical traditions, were the two dominant forms of musical performance and were caste- and gender-based hierarchies. The *periya melam* included wind and percussion instruments, led by the nagasvaram,[59] and including the drone, drum, cymbals and conch, each of which were played by men of a designated caste.

The *chinna melam* tradition included the dancing girls, devadasis, their male dance masters and their particular dance repertoires. The devadasis had specific linkages to the temple establishments, which gave them protection and employment and scholars have traced their existence to as early as the eleventh century.[60] The core of the musical tradition was represented by neither *melam*, but by the singing *bhagavathars*, invariably Brahmin men.

Vocalists and instrumentalists were differentiated from percussionists, and performers from teachers. Upper-caste men could be, and were, composers and, predominantly, performers. As performers they were usually vocalists as wind instruments were forbidden to them. The only women in this network of musicians were devadasis, women performers of varying castes, their occupation binding them together. The scholar Vasudha Narayanan reminds us that 'in southern India, the dynamic creativity in the production and performance of classical dance and song seems to have been confined to male Brahmins and courtesans'.[61]

The crucial determinants of who a devadasi was can be simply stated.[62] She sang or danced. She may or not have had a formal relationship with a local temple. She was probably unmarried, even if she was in a relationship as an offshoot of her duties in the temple. She had no particular caste status, even if she had a patron of high caste. She was prominent in the community where she lived, and with a certain measure of social sanction, if not ready acceptance, and was invited, and even welcomed, at ritually auspicious occasions. Since, in a patrilineal society, 'she lived outside of the institution of human marriage', her children identified themselves only as her children. And, if she did not enjoy the comfort, conjugality and companionship which marriage afforded, at least in theory, and in a time when women at all levels of society were bound by patriarchal norms, she was usually more literate than other women, more adept at handling money, could acquire rights to lands and properties and could adopt children.

Devadasis were not always, or only, dancers though a great deal is known of the elaborate ritual practices that went into the training of the 'dancing girls'. 'Some of them were dedicated to the temple, some served at the local ruler's pleasure, (and) some were simply born into matriarchal families associated with the arts.'[63] It was not an association which could be casually assumed. Years later, the dancer Balasaraswati, speaking of the rigours of a devadasi's training, recalled her grandmother Dhanammal's chastisement, *'Vidyadharanam na sukham na nidra'*, 'For students there can be no comfort, no sleep.'[64] Their sons and brothers were often percussionists and nagasvaram players, and routinely married women of other caste groups. Some devadasi women, who were not dedicated, could, and did, marry.

It was an ambiguous situation. The honoured status granted to the devadasi as *nityasumangali*, 'a woman married in perpetuity and free from the taint of widowhood (since god-husbands do not die) simultaneously denied her the status of a wife to ordinary men'.[65] This is a charitable view. A more cynical view has been expressed: 'As far as historical data goes, we can discern both in the north and south of the country, and at all levels of society, a great public attraction for a female performer who can, through song and dance, deal with the great moral ambivalence in Indian society about the physicality of love and sex'.[66]

It is only in 1948 that the term *isai vellalar* was introduced to describe the diffuse community of devadasis with the accompanying idea that everyone whose hereditary occupation was music and dance belonged to that particular caste.[67] The term 'vellalar' was applied to persons of an agricultural community and the prefixing of the term 'isai' or 'music' suggested that their position within society, in the caste hierarchy, was at least as high as that of the numerically much larger vellalars.

South India was by no means unique in its practice of ritual dedication of women to temples and ritual worship, and through this to the performing arts. Wherever such a tradition prevailed, it was primarily an effort to contain female sexuality within a structure of ritual worship 'and thereby rendering it benign and beneficial to state and society'.[68]

Aside from the connections to the temples, the practice of women dedicated to the arts privileged the right of wealthy, upper-class men to appreciate and enjoy music and dance performances. Not all the practitioners of these arts were great artistes, with an instinctive understanding of the muse, and not all their patrons had necessarily any sense of the arts, but that was not the point.[69]

That devadasis had a literary tradition is well documented. Davesh Soneji writes of a Ceylon-based devadasi who wrote an account of her times and her kin, a narrative which includes these remarkable words. 'It is a history of those noble women who attained great fame by mastering the three branches of the Tamil language – literature, music and theatre. It is a history of those wise women who wore virtue as an ornament and grew prosperous on account of their piety. It is also the history of women who suffered on account of their lack of virtue'.[70]

The existence of such a social arrangement was widely known even in the West. The term 'devadasi' appears in European literature as early as 1713. There is a detailed record of a group of Telugu-speaking devadasis, or *bayaderes*, in French, from Tiruvendipuram, near Pondicherry – Tilammal, Ammani, Rangam, Sundaram and Vaidam, the last only six years old – who visited Paris in 1838 and gave *twenty-six* performances. They attracted the attention of Theophile Gautier, poet and dance critic, who later adapted Kalidasa's *Sakuntalam*, a theme to which we will return, for his own ballet *Sacountala*. 'The very word bayadere,' wrote Gautier, 'evokes notions of sunshine, perfume and beauty...'.[71]

The practice came under attack from the 1830s onwards, when the artistic achievements of a devadasi began to be stigmatized and her connections to a temple criticized. However, it is likely that even when there was no formal dedication signalling the beginning of a contractual relationship of a devadasi with the temple and the deity, some form of private ceremony within the home was still performed almost up until the time it was outlawed, in 1947.[72]

Lakshmi Subramanian has observed that there was a huge difference in the position of women dedicated to the temples and living on temple grants and those women maintained by wealthy, and often cultivated, men. She suggests that some of these women in the latter category actually flourished and perfected their art and that *kulaparampara*, or family tradition, ensured that the performing arts were protected as an art form over the generations. Amrit Srinivasan has noted, 'The devadasi's alliances with men of the patron class were not only accepted publicly but were considered proper to her life and work, even recommended for artistic and professional development.'[73]

With all this, the system was stacked against the women of the devadasi communities, and in course of time it was *their* supposed immorality which became the main reason for the 1947 legislation.[74] Public opinion was against them. 'Whatever be the origin of devadasis, or temple girls, the system of prostitution, to which it has given rise, is vicious and requires to be put down. It has been opposed by all champions of social purity and has already been suppressed by law in the Madras Presidency.'[75]

That the devadasi community constituted a class of skilled professionals cannot be doubted and as Davesh Soneji has argued, with the passing of the Madras Devadasi (Prevention of Dedication) Act, 1947, 'an entire community of performers was disenfranchised, socially, politically, economically and culturally'.[76] Another acerbic scholar writes of the fate of devadasi women after 1948, 'Once assertive and accomplished women, now artistically suspect, financially straitened, socially outcaste by their original patrons.'[77] David Shulman, recognizing the role of Tamil- and Telugu-speaking courtesans, 'active both in royal venues and in the great temples' in keeping the heritage alive, writes even more forcefully that the 1947 prohibition by the British Raj of the dedication of women to temples was 'one of their last, and particularly destructive, acts in India'.[78]

Periya melam, which primarily, if not solely, involved men of the isai vellalar community playing the nagasvaram, also declined following the passing of the temple traditions which assured them of both livelihood and artistic performance.[79]

On balance, though, and understanding that many women suffered when their customs and traditions were made unlawful, it has to be recognized that the tradition was deeply flawed. There was no particular status in concubinage, and the much-vaunted agency of professional courtesans may only have been a way of asserting such independence and dignity as they could salvage out of a fundamentally iniquitous arrangement. That the arts flourished as they did is a tribute to the character and spirit of the women, and men, who did not have other opportunities.

Women practitioners who were not from the traditional devadasi families were only seen from the 1930s onwards. It was relatively simpler for women who sang; the radio and the gramophone record gave them many opportunities and even when they sang on stage it was not necessarily a performance meant for the eye alone. It took a little longer for women from caste Hindu families to appear publicly as dancers, in performances that depended critically on their attractiveness on stage. As late as 1935, Rukmini Devi's (1904–86) public performance was received, by some at least, with outrage.

The issue continues to be debated. A contemporary writer has held, for instance, 'Carnatic music, for almost a century now, the preserve of urban Brahmin men – whether as composers, singers, musicians, accompanists or listeners – in Chennai and other artistic capitals of southern India.' She goes on to explain the argument that

> what is now considered classical Carnatic music and what is now called Bharatanatyam classical dance were both originally the provenance of women, especially temple dancers and courtesans, and of non-Brahmin 'holding communities' like the isai vellalars. These groups were sidelined and their art forms taken over by socially dominant Brahmin practitioners and patrons, who cleansed the music and dance of their vernacular, erotic, demotic and popular character, and reinvented them as classical, religious, refined and urbane. The temple courtyard and the noisy village square gave way to the *kutcheri* and the sophisticated concert hall as performance spaces, which closed their door to ordinary people.[80]

These contentious issues will recur[81] and it is useful to recall that the debate really centres around four issues: the transformation of the content and repertoire from the vernacular to the classical, the relocation of spaces for performance from the public to the private, the expropriation of the art form by upper-caste men and the loss of agency by devadasi women.[82] None of these statements is fully accurate.

It would be incorrect to say that the content and repertoire was *entirely* erotic or popular; if we accept that bhakti in all its forms gave the motivation to the composition of musical pieces, there is much that is religious in what was being performed. It cannot be denied that listening to a *padam* of Kshetrayya sung, or sung to the accompaniment of *abhinaya*, can be a deeply spiritual experience, provided it is well done. The point is not that the text of a *padam* can be read as erotic; the point is whether or not it is being done with any grace.

The question of relocation and expropriation by upper-caste men is more complicated. The simple point is that the role played by Brahmin priests and non-Brahmin merchants, agriculturists and landlords in sponsoring the performance of music and dance and in offering patronage to traditional performers was taken over by men with some education who migrated to the towns and cities. These men were usually upper caste as only they had easy access to education in those restrictive times, and it was they who, in order to promote in their new environment the entertainments of their villages, set up the ubiquitous *sabhas*. It would be incorrect to presume that there was a conscious attempt to expropriate or to disempower the vernacular castes; persons belonging to the performing tradition really only needed a patron and if upper-caste men were setting up spaces for performance in the cities, there was no lack of musicians or dancers willing to appear on those platforms.

There were other difficult issues. A music or dance performance is not necessarily better for being performed in a village square, or for being performed by a member of the 'holding community'. It is a peculiar proposition that an art form, or the art form we are concerned with here, was itself compromised by being performed by the upper castes and that the true repository of all that was good in the form were the subaltern castes. Even assuming that the statement was made for effect, it is hard to agree with the view that upper-class domination of the performance space was 'stifling genuine growth'.[83]

Even more contentious is the question of agency. Admittedly, women of the devadasi community had agency insofar as it related to their ability to perform an art form, but it is necessary to ask at what price this agency was acquired. And in any case, the whole notion of caste-based employment militates against the notion of human rights, whether it is employment as a priest or as a temple dancer.

It is interesting that while similar trends can be noticed in the context of the performance of Hindustani music, passions have not been so inflamed. For a start, there were both Hindu and Muslim singers, with well-defined notions of gharanas, schools of music, which began to be identified from the nineteenth century onwards. A gharana was often identified by region and a senior musician representing the gharana took on students who may or may not have been from his family or even his stated religion. However, the important feature of the gharana was not just the bond of discipleship but the distinctive style and manner of rendition which could differ radically between gharanas.

As in the south, women performers who belonged exclusively to matrilineal communities devoted to the practice of music and dance, were professional entertainers, or *tawa'ifs*. It was accepted that women performed lighter forms such as *thumri* and were not encouraged to perform the more serious forms such as *dhrupad* or *khayal*. There was no association of any sort with a temple or with ritual worship and while the term courtesan can be broadly used, it appears that over the centuries at least ten categories of female entertainers, including devadasi, were identified, with varying degrees of connection to the arts, to the temples and to the world of entertainment.[84]

The *tawa'if* was a cultivated soul and it has been said that 'the morals and manners and distinctiveness of Lucknow culture and society were sustained by courtesans'.[85] She was reasonably prosperous and probably owned property and paid taxes. However, the *bai*, or *baiji*, to use another term, who could be Hindu or Muslim, or sometimes, complicatedly, both, could not, like her south Indian counterpart, easily marry and was generally dependent on a patron's whims.

Interestingly, north Indian *tawa'ifs*, often Muslim by faith, appear to have lived in Madras, where they were called *kanchen*. They flourished right until the late nineteenth century, their fortunes declining with changing times and growing public sentiment against such entertainments.[86]

With the growth and development of urban centres, particularly Bombay, rich traders and businessmen became patrons of music, with their private salons and drawing rooms. Communities of women performers referred to by the quaint appellation of 'songstresses' moved to Bombay and other cities, both courtesans from northern and central India and devadasis from Goa and neighbouring areas.[87] Some songstresses may have performed at their own rooms, in establishments similar to 'Vina' Dhanammal's in Georgetown in Madras. In time, as in the south, music clubs were established. The Parsi Gayan Uttejak Mandali, set up in 1870, may have been the first formal club followed by the Poona Gayan Samaj in 1883 and the Saraswat Gayan Samaj in 1896.

A lively tradition of song and dance was established, and along with it the accepted view that the women artistes were, in all effect and practice, prostitutes. Women from 'non-traditional' backgrounds began to learn public performance of music, and not only of semi-classical forms, only after India's independence in 1947 'when upper-caste Hindu women increasingly dislodged an earlier generation of *baijis*', a transformation 'that might succinctly be labelled as "*bai*" to "*tai*"'.[88]

It is against this background that we must recognize the monumental role played by women of the devadasi community in keeping the art form alive. '*Vidyasundari*' Bangalore Nagaratnamu, sometimes Nagaratnammal, was a stalwart representative of the devadasi clan, famed as much for her knowledge of Sanskrit and the scriptures as for her devotion to the memory of Tyagaraja. Then there were Coimbatore Thayi,[89] Kanchipuram Dhanakoti Ammal and her sisters, Doraikannu and her daughter Mylapore Gowri Ammal, Tiruvallaputtur Kalyani and her daughters Jeevaratnam and Rajalakshmi, famed as the 'Kalyani

Daughters'.[90] There are others whose names still live, including Kumbakonam Balamani, Pandanallur Jayalakshmi,[91] Thanjavur Kamalambal,[92] Kumbakonam Bhanumathi and her cousin Varalakshmi, Madras Vanajakshi, Tanjavur Kanakamala, Mannargudi Meenakshi,[93] Srirangam Nagaratnam, Tiruvidaimarudoor Bhavani, Tiruchendur Shanmukhvadivu, Salem Godavari,[94] and Tiruvarur Rajayi.

Some of these women achieved popularity, and even a degree of fame, as performing artistes and some were under the protection of royalty,[95] but by and large their lives were limited not only by the lack of opportunities, but by a crippling dependence on the whims of fickle patrons, *mirasdars* and 'minors', traders, politicians and businessmen, musicians and priests. The *thumri* singer Naina Devi, herself of orthodox Brahmo stock, has written of the *tawa'ifs* that '... a woman despite her brilliant accomplishments was never really secure. Unless she was very lucky, the caprices of a patron, the fickleness and dishonesty of a lover, not to forget silently creeping old age, would get her in the end.'[96]

Tanjavur Dhanam, who grew with age and proficiency in her art to be hailed as 'Vina' Dhanammal, is among the better-documented women of her profession. Dhanammal claimed a musical lineage from each of the trinity through the schools of Syama Sastri's grandson Annaswami Sastri, Tyagaraja's student 'Vina' Kuppayar and Muthusvami Dikshitar's student Suddhamandalam Tambiappan Pillai. A well-known photograph shows her staring stonily, even angrily, into the distance, a hard, unyielding face, not beautiful but commanding.[97] She and her daughters T. Rajalakshmi (1885–1957), T. Lakshmiratnam (1888–1940), T. Jayalakshmi (Jayammal) (1890–1967) and T. Kamakshi (1892/3–1953) constituted a prominent devadasi clan. There are formal studio photographs of the mother and her four daughters and their children, one taken around 1914 and one around 1936.[98]

Dhanam was the daughter of Sundarammal,[99] the daughter of Rukmini, the daughter of Kamakshiammal, the daughter of Papammal. So did the professional dancers and musicians of the time define themselves, their lineage and their tradition. Indeed, it is not inaccurate that Aniruddha Knight, the son of Dhanalakshmi Shanmukham Knight, the daughter of Balasaraswati, the daughter of Jayammal, the daughter of Dhanammal, claims to be a ninth-generation musician and dancer.

Tanjavur Dhanam's roots were deep in the musical traditions of the Kaveri. From her family lineage, she inherited songs in the genre of semi-erotic *padams* and *javalis*. Her grandmother Kamakshiammal moved the family to Madras around 1857 but Dhanam stayed true to her tradition of performance. The salon was her natural home, the cultivated man about town her preferred audience, the songs of the trinity and love poetry in Telugu, some written in tribute to her by Dharmapuri Subbarayar, her repertoire of choice. She was recognized in her lifetime as a great artist but not one who cared much for promoting herself. More poignantly, 'Vina' Dhanammal, honoured as she was for her lineage as much as for her art, died, as did many of her clan, a courtesan in poverty and bereft of patronage.[100]

There were countless others, musicians and dancers of greater or lesser talent, more or less graced by luck and circumstance, with or without the ability to control their lives, women known only by their town and for their art. The greatest of them was Madurai Shanmukhavadivu Subbulakshmi.

2

Shanmukhavadivu

ఏమని నే నీ మహిమ దెలుపుదు (న)మ్మ [1]

(*'Mother, how do I fathom your greatness?'*,
from Subbaraya Sastri's *kriti* in the raga Mukhari)

MADURAI is famed in legend and history, one of the oldest continuously inhabited cities of the world, the seat of successive generations of kings of many clans, the site of temples and monasteries, a thriving business and pilgrimage centre, with a flourishing citizenry. We have a description from 2,000 years ago:

> The sun, worshipped by the whole world, arose to the music of morning birds that dwell in suburban gardens, among shimmering ponds and fields where a rich, ripe harvest waved in the wandering breeze. At sight of the sun, the lotuses opened in the lakes and pools. Through the morning haze it woke from their sleep the people of the proud city ... (t)he thunder of the morning drums and the sound of the conch arose in the morning air from the sacred temple of Shiva the three eyed, or Vishnu who displays a bird on his standard, of

Baladeva holding his plough, and of young Murugan whose banner bears a cock. The chanting of prayers was heard in the homes of the priests, conversant with celestial law, and in the palace of the ever-victorious king.[2]

In those very early times, the Greek historian and ambassador Megasthenes (350 BC–290 BC) wrote of Madurai,[3] as did the scholar Ptolemy (first century), who described 'Madoura' as a well-known trading emporium.[4] The traveller Ibn Battuta (1304–68/9? 1377?) visited Madurai, married locally and is said to have disliked the place intensely.[5] A historian of south India cites early Tamil texts which held that 'when the wise balanced the city of Madurai against the rest of the world in their imagination, they pronounced the city to be superior in excellence'.[6]

The Madurai region came successively under the rule of the Pandyas, the Cholas, the Pandyas again in the late thirteenth century, the Khiljis and the Tughlaqs from the distant north and then from the late fourteenth century, peaceably under the Vijayanagar kings who gave way in time to the Maratha Nayak rulers who at some point conceded power to the East India Company. This extremely concise history cannot disguise the fact that Madurai was a great prize. The great temple to Minakshi, the oldest parts of which are traced to the thirteenth century, may not have existed at the time when Madurai was already a flourishing pilgrimage spot but today it is the heart of the city, a vast compound containing concentric squares, the major part of which was built by Tirumala Nayak (1623–60).[7] The larger of the temples is dedicated to her consort Siva in the form of Sundaresvara, but the reigning presence is that of Minakshi, 'she whose eyes are as shapely as the contours of a fish',[8] a dark image, purportedly of jade,[9] with a parrot on her hand.[10] 'The temple is the hub around which the city revolves, and it has always been so. From the early days of the Pandyas onwards no ruler dared rule without first seeking legitimacy from the temple's prime deity, Minakshi'.[11]

Ritual worship in the temple would not have been possible without an elaborate temple establishment of priests, officials, accountants, cooks, flower sellers, water carriers and every other sort of service providers including musicians, drummers and dancing girls. Women in this last category were 'mostly recruited from the Vellalar and Mudaliar castes, but they effectively formed a distinct, partly endogamous caste, and many dancers' daughters became dancers, while their sons became temple musicians'.[12] The conditions within which devadasi women lived and worked were begging to be abused.[13] English opinion was broadly of the view that the whole business was an abomination. Missionaries regarded it as their duty to save young girls from the perils of dedication to temples.[14]

An official gazette published in 1868 is full of scorn.

> The dasis, dancing girls ... are each of them married to an idol when quite young and judging from appearances their stony husbands would seem to be by no means incapable of performing the most important of marital duties. The male children ... have no difficulty in acquiring a decent position in society. The female children are generally brought up to the trade of the mothers but are occasionally raised by irregular marriages with low-caste men to a better kind of life.[15]

And finally J.H. Nelson, MA, informs us witheringly that ' [a]s a rule the dasis of Madura are very deficient in good looks, and very bad dancers'.

Whatever their attractions, or the lack of them, this community of professional women was large enough. The 1850–51 census of the 'Madura' district enumerated 1,963 dasis from a population of 17,44,587.[16] A 'Mahometan' population of 34,165, a 'Brahman' population of 32,593 and a vellalan population of 164,801 were all dutifully recorded, as were details of at least ninety-four other castes. It was not only the dasis who vexed Mr Nelson, MA so. 'The few so-called Brahmans to be found in the district at the present time are all of more or less doubtful origin. The Brahmans who officiate in the great pagodas at and near Madura are reputed to be of very impure blood; whilst those of Rameshwaram are said to be the result of connections such as Manu could scarcely have contemplated in his most despairing moods'.

A subsequent gazette, edited by Francis in 1906, makes no reference to dasis and has no census enumeration of them, suggesting that by this time they were no longer recognized in any significant number as being a caste-based occupational group. It is possible that by this time the merchant and landlord classes had taken over from the temple establishments the responsibility for supporting the dasi community.

Subbulakshmi was born in Madurai on 16 September 1916, the daughter of 'Vina' Shanmukhavadivu, the daughter of Akkammal. As her title indicates, Shanmukhavadivu was primarily a *vainika*, though her mother Akkammal was among the earliest of woman violinists.[17] A citation made towards the end of her life states that Shanmukhavadivu's father was one M.S. Swaminathan,[18] described as an erudite connoisseur. It has been suggested that a grandmother or grand-aunt was a performer of *sadir*, or traditional dance.[19]

A horoscope cast according to the Hindu tradition circulates on the Internet; the astronomical details are presumably correct for the time of birth given, though the provenance of this time is now unclear. The date corresponds to *Bhadrapada Panchami, Krishna paksha*, the fifth day in the month of Bhadrapada, with the waning moon in Aries, passing through the constellation Arietis, or *Bharani nakshatra* in the *Mesha rasi* according to Hindu nomenclature. In later life, Subbulakshmi believed implicitly in astrological predictions.[20]

The name is Lakshmi's, 'that of the goddess of the good and the beautiful',[21] but what of the prefix? In her memoirs, 'Sister' R.S. Subbalakshmi, a child widow who became the face of social reform in south India, recalled that when she was a child no one explained the meaning of her name to her and she presumed they were just sounds without any meaning. As a young adult, she learnt that *subba*, or *subbu*, meaning auspicious or fortunate, was a corruption of the Sanskrit *shubha*.[22] Years later, the Hindi film *Meera* announced its lead actor, in the Devanagari script, as Shubhalakshmi.

Shanmukhavadivu lived in a small house on Hanumantharayan Koil Street, a narrow lane hardly a hundred yards from the west gate to the temple. The house still stands, a narrow and steep staircase leading to the living area upstairs, the downstairs room now occupied by a busy optician's establishment.[23] It was not an affluent household; it was not even reasonably provided for. There were other family members in the vicinity, and recalled as being very respectable people, and even prosperous. Among these was Shanmukhavadivu's sister, or cousin, Shanmukhasundari, believed to have been as fair as the white jasmine, the *jaji*, and hence, Jajima.

Paternal responsibility was never acknowledged though Subbulakshmi herself, in her later years, referred to Subramania Iyer, a lawyer of Madurai, as her father and even reminisced affectionately about him. This version has been generally accepted in biographical accounts which followed, with most suggesting that the matter be allowed to rest as this was what Subbulakshmi either believed or wanted to believe or was said to want to believe.[24]

The matter is, however, not quite that simple, if only for the reason that till 1974, when the fact of the existence of one Subramania Iyer and his place in Subbulakshmi's life was sprung onto a curious public, the accepted, if unspoken, version was that Subbulakshmi was the child of the fantastically gifted vocalist Madurai Pushpavanam Iyer.

Every detail about the life of Pushpavanam, as he was always referred to, is hazy. He was born in the late 1880s or very early 1890s, the younger brother of Madurai Ramaswami Iyer, the father of *Sangitha Kalanidhi* Madurai Mani Iyer (1912–68). There is a photograph of the brothers and their very young wives, Pushpavanam and Sundarathammal (or Sundarambal) and Ramaswami Iyer and Subbulakshmi taken around 1914, as suggested by the presence of the infant Mani Iyer, on his uncle's lap.[25] The infant was born in 1912 and we have the detail that Pushpavanam Iyer was married on 6 February 1914. They were evidently men who took themselves seriously and are very elegantly dressed for the camera and Pushpavanam, in particular, is a handsome man.

There is ample testimony to Pushpavanam Iyer's musical prowess and a record of his being a disciple of Ettayapuram Ramachandra Ayyar (1846–1915), himself from the musical line of Muthusvami Dikshitar's brother Balusvami Dikshitar. A sharp, if somewhat quixotic, *rasika* R. Rangaramanuja Ayyangar (1901–80) writes expansively that the world of Carnatic music has not seen since a 'musician, man or woman, whose voice made even the remotest approach to Pushpavanam's in sweetness, carrying power, flexibility and majesty ... What an intoxicating voice ... responding readily with incredible ease and grace to the surging crescendo of ravishing sophisticated music conjured up from a highly imaginative mind!'[26]

Semmangudi Srinivasa Iyer, who was even younger, recalled attending his concerts and 'a wonderful voice marked by power and sinuous beauty'.[27] Tales are told of Pushpavanam's renderings of *'Vatapi'*/Hamsadhwani, *'Ksheerasagarasayana'*/Devagandhari, *'Akshaylingavibho'*/Sankarabharanam, *'Sri Subramanyaya namaste'*/Kambhoji, *'Nagumomu'*/Abheri and of *'kavadichindu'*.[28] Sri Chandrasekhara Saraswati, the then senior pontiff of Kanchi, known as Paramacharya, later to become a significant influence in Subbulakshmi's life, is believed to have heard Pushpavanam Iyer sing at Kumbakonam on 3 October 1916.[29] Late in life, *Sangitha Kalanidhi* Papanasam Sivan (1890–1973) recalled a 1912 concert of Pushpavanam Iyer with Malaikottai Govindaswami Pillai (1878–1931) on the violin, and both Azhaganambi Pillai (1863?–1926?) and Pudukkottai Dakshinamurthi Pillai (1875–1936) on the mrdangam.[30]

The presence of accompanying artistes so much senior to him in age and standing suggests that Pushpavanam was a recognized star.

Pushpavanam's career, brilliant, and even meteoric, was, sadly, very short, and it is commonly believed that his end was the result of general dissipation and drunkenness.[31] There is no agreement on when he eventually died. One version is that the end came in 1920 or thereabouts, in Thanjavur, while under the care of a friend Mahadeva Rao. An appreciation published in 1938 says, somewhat vaguely, that he died 'about twenty years ago'.[32] Rangaramanuja Ayyangar, however, is firmly of the view that Pushpavanam Iyer was born in 1885 and died in August 1917, on the Vinayaka Chaturthi day.[33] This event would have been on 21 August 1917. An article published in 1921 suggests similarly that Pushpavanam Iyer had died a few years earlier.[34] The understanding within Pushpavanam's family, however, is that he died at the age of twenty-eight and that he lived till his daughter Rajam, born in 1917, was about two or three.

More importantly, his widow Sundarathammal, who was widowed at 17, but lived on to pass away in 1978, recalled her husband saying to her that he had another daughter, slightly older than Rajam, born to Shanmukhavadivu. Her recollection of the exact words spoken to her by her husband at the birth of their daughter Rajam was '*Angeyum ponnnu thaan*', or translated very literally, 'there also, only a girl'.[35]

This appears to have been an open secret within the family, and was common knowledge within Tamil society at several levels.[36] It has been recently written that Madurai Pushpavanam Iyer was a close friend of Shanmukhavadivu, but this interesting detail is followed by a very unlikely account of Pushpavanam being accompanied on his visits by his young nephew Mani, in itself an improbable occurrence, and the two children Mani and Subbulakshmi playing musical games together.[37] It is, of course, likely that Subbulakshmi and Mani Iyer knew each other in childhood, but not when Pushpavanam Iyer was still calling. Rajam's son recalls the astonishing resemblance between Subbulakshmi and Rajam, their near-identical faces, the similarity in their voice and manner, the frizzy hair and the comfort and familiarity with which Subbulakshmi greeted Rajam and her children on their visits to her.[38] There is a reference in print, admittedly in a somewhat lowbrow film magazine, in 1944, stating that Subbulakshmi was the daughter of the dasi Shanmukhavadivu and the celebrated Pushpavanam Iyer, who was also the father of Rajam.[39]

Shanmukhavadivu is believed to have been a competent enough vina player, the student of Karur Venkatarama (or Venkataramana) Bhagavathar (dates unclear), with a limited style and repertoire; senior *vidvans* of her time appear to have noticed her playing and encouraged her, most particularly Tirukkodikaval Krishna Iyer (1857–1913), later a teacher of Semmangudi Srinivasa Iyer, and the Karaikudi brothers, *Sangitha Kalanidhi* Karaikudi Sambasiva Iyer (1888–1958) and his elder brother Karaikudi Subbarama Iyer (1883–1936), both very distinguished *vainikas*.[40] She was a regular performer at wedding concerts, but there is no indication of her daughter's phenomenal musical ability. A gramophone record of her playing 'Rama nee samanam evaru'/ Kharaharapriya while also singing the *sahitya* circulates on the Internet. The sharp plucking of the strings and the near absence of any *gamaka* in the singing are both remarkable.[41] And her looks were unremarkable, whereas her daughter, from early adulthood to the end of her days, was a legendary beauty.

Shanmukhavadivu already had a son Sakthivel, born in 1912. She had a second daughter, Vadivambal, born in 1925. A charming photograph exists of Shanmukhavadivu and her daughters probably taken around 1930.[42] Subbulakshmi, even if very young, is wearing a sari and Vadivambal is a little child in a skirt. Madurai Pushpavanam Iyer's family does not believe that he was father to either of the other two of Shanmukhavadivu's children. This is certainly true in the case of Vadivambal who, quite simply, was too young to have been his daughter.

It is, of course, possible that there was a Subramania Iyer in Shanmukhavadivu's life; the historian Lakshmi Subramanian credits him with contacts in Madras, which facilitated Shanmukhavadivu's concert engagements.[43]

Subbulakshmi was not unaware of Pushpavanam Iyer's name and reputation. Her biographer T.J.S. George cites a reference in her correspondence in the late 1930s with *Sangitha Kalanidhi* G.N. Balasubramaniam (1910–65), of whom more anon, to the early death of the 'immortal' Pushpavanam. In a late, and very unusual, interview she regretted the fact that she was too young to appreciate the music of 'three giants, Ramanathapuram (Poochi) Srinivasa Iyengar, Madurai Pushpavanam Iyer and Konerirajapuram Vaidyanatha Iyer (who) strode the South Indian music world like colossuses'.[44] It is, however, a matter of bewildered speculation as to why Subbulakshmi, late in life, unquestionably one of the greatest performing artistes of her generation, should have acknowledged an obscure mofussil lawyer as her father rather than, as was widely believed, the greatest musician of *his* generation. This secret she has taken with her to the great beyond.

Subbulakshmi spoke very little of her early years, or not at least outside her immediate family circles. Almost certainly she would have attended music and dance performances but '... she never talked about those days, or those experiences'.[45] There is a long and charming recollection published very late in her lifetime but it is strangely neutral in its key elements.[46] These could be anyone's memories. There is her own recollection of a passing sadhu spotting her in the temple and predicting a great future, but these are the type of stories which improve in constant retelling.[47] One recollection which is of significance is of her listening to a young Saraswathi Bai performing *Harikatha* on a nationalist theme.

In the narrow lanes around the Minakshi temple in Madurai is the small upstairs room in a dwelling on Chokkanatha Street where Sri

Ramana Maharshi in 1896, then a lad of sixteen, had his realization of death. It is possible that Subbulakshmi was aware of what was already a spot famed in the devotional literature surrounding the saint, though there is no way of saying now whether she had visited the place. It is, literally, a few minutes' walk from her mother's door.

One of Subbulakshmi's biographers has written of the rich musical atmosphere in Shanmukhavadivu's home during Subbulakshmi's childhood.[48] Among the stalwarts who visited and may even have taught mother and daughter one or more songs were Ariyakudi Ramanuja Iyengar, nagasvara *vidvan* Madurai Ponnusamy Pillai (1877–1929) and Pudukkottai Dakshinamurthi Pillai.

Seithur Sundaresa Bhattar and Madurai Srinivasa Iyengar are often mentioned as Subbulakshmi's earliest teachers but it is hard to come by any information about them. Subbulakshmi's recollection is that Srinivasa Iyengar taught her for a brief while, up to the stage of *varnam*, before leaving town, and dying. Given that she was recording by 1926, this must have been the early 1920s.[49] Most of what is known of Seithur Sundaresa Bhattar comes from his long-term association as student and violin accompanist of Kanchipuram Naina Pillai (1888/89?–1934), himself a disciple of Ettayapuram Ramachandra Bhagavathar, whom we have already recognized as a teacher of Pushpavanam Iyer. Seithur Sundaresa Bhattar was, along with Shanmukhavadivu, a student of Karur Venkatarama Bhagavathar.[50] He was active for many more years and was, as late as 1945, playing the violin on All India Radio, Madras.[51]

The composer and lyricist Madurai Bhaskara Das (1892–1952) noted in his diaries that Shanmukhavadivu had, during the 1920s, lived for a while in Ettayapuram; presumably her daughters were with her. He notes in 1930 and 1931 that he was composing and teaching 'gramophone songs' to the young Subbulakshmi, again presumably a preparation for a career as a singing actor, and that she had paid him ₹5 per song.[52] A character called Buffoon Chinnabhaskar worked as an intermediary, carrying the songs to Shanmukhavadivu's home. We can only presume that he played comic roles on the Tamil stage.[53]

In an unusual recollection made in 1965, Subbulakshmi spoke of how she trained her voice in those early years, practising for hours, with and without the accompaniment of the tambura, the drone, with a view to ensuring that the harmony between voice and drone was always maintained.[54]

It is still recalled in Madurai that Subbulakshmi sang, as a very young child, in the home of Judge Subramania Iyer of the Madras High Court, on the occasion of an *upanayana* ceremony in that family.[55] There is a reference to Subbulakshmi singing at the hundred-pillared Rockfort temple in Tiruchirappalli in 1927, at a concert organized by F.G. Natesa Iyer (1880–1963), later to be her co-star in *Sevasadanam*. Natesa Iyer's daughter recalls that Subbulakshmi was accompanied by T. Chowdiah (1895–1967) on the violin and Pudukkottai Dakshinamurthi Pillai on the mrdangam. 'MS sang superbly and won the hearts of the listeners.'[56] Another version dates the recital to February 1929, a version which gains in accuracy from the detail that after the recital a Muslim listener raced out to buy a gold medal as a gift for the young artiste.[57]

There is a reference to Subbulakshmi learning Mira bhajans from S.V. Venkataraman, later to be the highly successful music director of her film *Meera*, while still living with her mother in Madurai.[58] He may have taught her two bhajans, the tunes of which were later used by him for two of her film songs.[59] A more substantial account is that of G. Venkatachalam, impresario and aesthete, who first met Subbulakshmi in 1929 when she came to Bangalore to record for HMV, and when she 'gave a benefit recital to a packed house of music lovers'.[60] Venkatachalam observes, 'for a girl of thirteen she had the will of a woman of forty, and for a gay, light-hearted child of song, she was a bit self-willed and stubborn'. This is not the Subbulakshmi the world came to know later.

The 1920s was not a good time to be a woman musician trying to develop her art. Here is an extraordinary diatribe entitled 'Notes on Music. Women singers' by one C.R. Srinivasa Iyengar, BA, which gives some idea of the scorn in which they were held as serious performing artistes.[61] As an example of *babu* English it is unmatched. For high dudgeon, it is unequalled.

> As to the material that makes up a concert, the tradition of the hoary past as embodied or illustrated by such master singers as the Lakshminarayana sisters (Yenadi) or Dhanam of Madras is too good to be lost or disfigured. The quintessence of music is not as present-day exponents would have it, Raga, *pallavi*, but pieces (*keerthanas*), the master pieces of immortal composers that 'on the stretched forefinger of all time sparkle forever'. Raga and *pallavi* forsooth. As they operate upon them now, I would rather welcome the delectable pair of cholera and famine, plague and pestilence, Scylla and Charybdis, Satan and Beelzebub. Your *keerthana* contains in itself every essential of good music – raga, *bhava*, and *tala* (melody, emotion and measure). It is a miniature world of music.
>
> Without fear or favour, prejudice or prepossession, one can conscientiously affirm that the ladies' concerts preserve to a very considerable extent the time-honoured traditions of the past; though I am forced to remark that the lady singers of recent years fall off from the path of rectitude and bow the knee to Baal and his priests. They have abjured the tambura and replaced it with the braying harmonium with its 'equal temperament of unequal notes'. They have the infection of the *swara*-juggling and long winded raga *alapana*; they too ape the men in pitching upon a particular raga as the victim of the day (not a large field to choose from though, seeing that Todi, Bhairavi, Kalyani, Shankarabharanam and Kambhoji are the subjects invariably brought up for vivisection) and bleeding it white; they are almost as good or as bad as the men in tearing the

doomed *pallavi* to tatters until nothing is left of it but the name; a lady singing a *pallavi* recalls to me the picture of a dog trained to walk on its hind legs – it is ungainly, uncouth, unseemly and uncalled for. Her native element is *keerthanams*, and *padams*, or erotic pieces. It is her birthright, of which no power in heaven, earth or hell can deprive her. A man crooning a *padam* and a woman banging away at a *pallavi* are two of the most repulsive sights under the sun. Let us give it a decent burial, this interminable anaconda of raga and the bristling porcupine of a *pallavi*; let us bury it deep and let its echoes be heard no more in the land of the living or the dead.[62]

One wonders which hapless *pallavi*-attempting woman musician had provoked this; but the message is clear: a devadasi should sing 'women's songs'.[63] Erotic pieces were her birthright. And while our acerbic critic did concede that the courtesan singers were 'more presentable and behave more pleasantly in society'[64] he continued to rail in the columns of the *Hindu* against women singers, as for instance in a 1925 series of articles called 'Music and Sex', most of which is unprintable.[65]

The early twentieth century saw many recording companies establish shop in Madras and being significantly more interested in recording women than men. Over 500 women are believed to have been recorded in different languages by such companies as HMV, Columbia, Broadcast, Odeon and Twins and about *half a million* actual plates released.[66] The *baijis*, songstresses, of the north and the women of the devadasi families in the south were the obvious first port of call for enterprising record manufacturers. 'All the female singers were of course from the caste of the public women, and in those days it was practically impossible to record the voice of a respectable woman. The songs and dances were passed on by word of mouth from mother to daughter. They began public appearances at the age of ten to twelve years. The clever ones went up to the top and sometimes travelled all over the country in great demand at the wedding feasts of the wealthy'[67]. The cynicism implicit in this remark says something of the wretched circumstances of devadasi life.

The earliest women to have been recorded in the south were probably 'Miss Dhanakoti', 'Danakoti and Sister, Conjeevaram'[68] and 'Miss Nagaratnam' in 1905 but a much better recording is available for Salem Godavari (died 1911), 'Miss Lokamba', 'Miss Vanajatchi', 'Miss Bavani Sani', Sundari and Varalakshmi, Shanmuga Vadivoo Tiruchendur, 'Misses Gangaratnam and Manickam' and 'Veena Dhanam's daughters', all of whom were recording from 1909 onwards.[69] Coimbatore Thayi (1872–1917) is listed as having recorded eighty-seven different pieces over a four-day session in 1910. From the north Gauhar Jan (1873–1930), Zohrabai Agrewali (1868–1913) and Janki Bai Ilahabadi (1880–1934) were very widely recorded.[70]

There were several others, now forgotten, such as Ganamohini of whom it was patronizingly said that she 'is the finest musical product of the Andhra province, and it is no wonder since she received her training in Madras'[71] and T. Girijambal whose music was described as 'a fine combination of charming and naïve provincialism, well-grounded theory and art and attractive theme [sic] that never tries the people to whom it appeals'.[72] One 'Miss T.N. Manickam' is described as 'ever pleasant to hear, with her distinct individuality'. Ranjitha Bushani comes in for praise as does 'Miss Satyavathi Bai (Cocanada), a singer and *Harikatha* exponent, for her 'beautiful and expressive voice, ready reception and retentiveness'.[73]

Subbulakshmi's earliest recordings from 1924, when she was eight, or possibly from 1926, are '*Marakatavadivu*', an Arunagirinathar's composition in Senchurutti[74] (Jenjuti) and '*Uttukuliyinile*', a ragamalika composition.[75] The second piece is not available but the first is a loud and sprightly rendering, that of a child, but a confident and bold child. The musician T.M. Krishna notes that her 'voice is already fast-moving, with the ability to render speedy phrases with aplomb. Her musical accent is natural and free; there is nothing contrived in the way her voice negotiates the twists and turns of the composition.'[76]

More recordings followed in these early years, of Tamil and Telugu songs; these include several Tyagaraja songs not heard in her concerts in later years such as *'Elavatarame'*/Mukhari, *'Ninnu vina gati'*/Balahamsa, *'Tulasi jagajjanani'*/Saveri, *'Paraloka bhayamu'*/Mandari, *'Vidajaladura'*/Janaranjani, *'Korisevimpa'*/Kharaharapriya and *'Sri Raghukula'*/Huseni.[77] These early recordings include, in 1930, the evergreen *'Krishna nee begane baro'*/Yamunakalyani. There is also a reference to a 1931 recording of a Tamil song, *'Ella arumaigalum peravendum iraiva'*.[78]

For all their stuffiness, the music critics of the newspapers recognized genius when they heard it. Of 'Miss Veena Dhanam Ammal' it was written, 'We cannot afford to miss anything that comes from this talented musician' and likewise of 'Miss K.B. Sundarambal' that as sung by her 'anything is sweet, telling and welcome'.[79] Of particular interest is a review of a recording of the fourteen-year-old D.K. Pattammal (1919–2009), and despite the pomposity which passed for high literary style in those days, it is worth reading in full.

> D.K. Pattammal is the best type of the amateur singer of our times just crossing the border-land leading over to, not exactly professionalism, but music of a high quality that goes along with classic models. It is a very rare specimen of voice, fresh and untainted, pure and healthy, even as nature had fashioned it, to which she adds correctness and accuracy of rendering after the lights of the present-day music. Of course the two pieces that the management has selected to place before the public are but an earnest of what is to come, considerably higher in quality and worthy of acceptation.[80]

The critic has rightly seized on the two attributes always associated with Pattammal, the pure quality of her voice and the correctness of her style. And, truly, four generations of listeners did find her 'worthy of acceptation'.

Madurai at this time was a hotbed of nationalist activity. Both the Justice Party and the Indian National Congress, the two leading nationalist parties of which we will hear more, were active and M.K. Gandhi (1869–1948) visited Madurai on 26 March 1919, the first of six recorded visits.[81] It is unclear what impact any of this had on Shanmukhavadivu though it is fascinating to think that she may have heard of Gandhi's third visit, in September 1921, when he stayed on West Masi Street, a street parallel to Hanumantharayan Koil Street. This particular visit is famous in Gandhi lore as the time when he gave up all other forms of formal clothing in favour of the loincloth and made his first public appearance in his new attire. It is not readily known whether the Mahatma visited the shrine of Minakshi on his first visit in 1919, as the records are contradictory, but he did visit the shrine on his last visit, in 1946, making a point of the fact that the temple was now open to people of all castes.[82] Sarojini Naidu (1879–1949), poet, nationalist and devoted follower of the Mahatma, later to be a patroness of Subbulakshmi, spoke at a public meeting in Madurai in October 1922, of Gandhi and his message.[83]

Even if we do not now know of what the political developments of the time meant to Shanmukhavadivu and her daughter, we know that they were travelling for concerts, in and around Madurai. A *rasika* from Devakottai recalls a recital at Chhathiram Somasundaram Chettiar's house in 1926, when Subbulakshmi received, along with a sari and fruits and flowers, the grand sum of ₹5.[84] T. Sadasivam (1902–97), whom we will meet again, spoke of a concert in Trivandrum in 1929 or 1930.[85] The distinguished mrdangam *vidvan* Palghat Mani Iyer (1912–81), recalled that he had first heard Shanmukhavadivu and Subbulakshmi performing together at the Nellai Chandra Vilas Hotel in Tirunelveli.[86] It is possible that Subbulakshmi gave what may have been her first 'benefit' recital in 1929 or shortly thereafter in aid of the Madurai Diraviyam Thayumanavar Hindu College at Tirunelveli, with tickets sold at ₹100, an occasion when she may have been gifted a pair of diamond earrings by a fan.[87]

We still know comparatively little about the many accomplished and popular women musicians and dancers in the south, of the generations prior to Subbulakshmi. The names which have survived include 'Vina' Dhanam, Bangalore Nagaratnamu (1878–1952),[88] Rukmini Devi Arundale, C. Saraswathi Bai, Madras Lalithangi (1907–55) and K.B. Sundarambal (1907–80). Saraswathi Bai, who was probably among the very first of the Brahmin women to perform publicly, learnt, from a very early age, Sanskrit, Hindustani music, the art of *Harikatha* and the skill of performance.[89] In her old age she took to the stage once more to read the citation when Subbulakshmi was awarded the title of *Sangitha Kalanidhi*.

Madras Lalithangi, daughter of Perumalkoil Narayanamma, famed for her voice and vast repertoire, was among the musicians most associated with reviving the compositions of Purandaradasa.[90] Kodumodi Balambal Sundarambal was a stage and film actor, famed for her powerful singing voice, who continued to appear in mythological films till late in life. Sundarambal was a unique character who is still remembered for her role in and as *Avvaiyar*.[91] In a fascinating aside, the film historian Randor Guy tells us that many years later when both Sundarambal and Subbulakshmi were known as film actors, the possibility of a film starring both of them was raised though, sadly, the film *Valli Thirumanam* was never made.[92]

The world of Hindustani music saw in these generations, women of such standing as Ravi Varma's muse and model Anjanibai Malpekar (1883–1974), and the fabulous *Surasri* Kesarbai Kerkar (1890–1977), among the greatest musicians of the twentieth century – legendary disciple of Alladiya Khan (1855–1946) – famed for her spectacular voice

Shanmukhavadivu

and style. 'Scrupulousness, fastidiousness and a lofty disdain of public approval remained the hallmarks of her personality and music.'[93] Other names are those of Alladiya Khan's other great disciple *Ganatapasvini* Mogubai Kurdikar (1904–2001),[94] Hirabai Barodekar (1905–89), hailed as '...amongst the most distinguished and popular Hindustani vocalists of the 20th century, and almost certainly the most melodious female voice heard in recent times',[95] and Siddheshwari Devi (1903–77), a particular friend of Subbulakshmi.

In her own time, Subbulakshmi had several women contemporaries in the world of music and dance, all of whom enjoyed varying degrees of popularity and even fame. For a start, there were Dhanammal's granddaughters, Brinda, Muktha and Balasaraswati. *Sangitha Kalanidhi* T. Brinda (1912–96), daughter of T. Kamakshi, was a student of Kanchipuram Naina Pillai and of senior musicians within her family. She always had a following of *rasikas* who admired her distinction and rigour and she was famed as much for her renderings of *padam* and *javali* as for her sharp tongue. Strangely for a musician steeped in the notion of *kulaparampara*, Brinda taught for several years at the College of Carnatic Music, Madras. Her sister T. Muktha (1914–2007) was her partner for many years and became a much-loved teacher. *Sangitha Kalanidhi* T. Balasaraswati (1918–84), daughter of T. Jayammal, was a close friend of Subbulakshmi, insofar as she was allowed to make and keep friends; her talent and her achievements rivalled Subbulakshmi's and no account of dance in India is complete without recognizing her remarkable presence.

Other contemporaries of Subbulakshmi included Rajam Pushpavanam (1917–91), daughter of Madurai Pushpavanam Iyer, and N.C. Vasanthakokilam (1919–51), a popular and charismatic singer who died young. More significantly, there was *Sangitha Kalanidhi* D.K. Pattammal, respected as much for her learning as for the quality of her music. An extraordinary musician of the same generation, if inadequately recognized, was Philomena Thumboochetty (1913–2000), trained on the violin in London and Paris and hailed for her stylish technique.[96]

Mrinalini Sarabhai (1918–2016), born to south Indian aristocracy, was the leading dancer of that generation from outside the courtesan tradition and did much to take south Indian dance beyond the south.

All these women were born in the decade of the 1910s as was, from the north, the distinguished Gangubai Hangal (1913–2009), renowned vocalist of the Kirana gharana and disciple of Sawai Gandharva (1886–1952), described as a symbol of 'the true grit of tradition as well as that of uncompromising values'.[97] From the north Karnataka region she learnt Carnatic music briefly in early childhood before realizing that her gifts lay elsewhere.[98] Roshanara Begum (1917–82), a kinswoman of Hirabai Barodekar, and Begum Akhtar (1914–74), both sang for films but were famed for their elaborate concert styles.[99] Malka Pukhraj (1912–2004) was a ghazal singer of great repute.

Of Subbulakshmi's many contemporaries from the world of films, Kanan Devi (1916–92), who came 'from the professional class of entertainers in Bengal' was said to have had 'three unfailing attributes, looks, histrionic talent and a golden voice'.[100] Vasundhara Devi (1917–88) came from a more conventional background but that possibly made it more difficult for her to enter film, where her appearances are still remembered.[101] Shanta Apte (1916–64), later to be the heroine of Subbulakshmi's film *Savitri*, was the toast of the 1940s with several hit films. Vinjamuri Anasuya Devi (1920–2019) and her sister Vinjamuri Seetha Devi (1923–2016) were hugely popular Telugu folk singers.

The star of the generation subsequent to Subbulakshmi was undoubtedly *Sangitha Kalanidhi* M.L. Vasanthakumari (1928–90), Lalithangi's daughter, and the greatest creative imagination the world of Carnatic music has seen in the last century, but also included C.P. Radha (born 1935) and R. Jayalakshmi (1934–2014), cousins who were the daughters of sisters, referred to always as Radha Jayalakshmi as if they were one. Students of T.R. Balasubramaniam – himself a student of *Sangitha Kalanidhi* G.N. Balasubramaniam – they were very popular concert artistes through the 1950s and 1960s, and were admired for their vivacious style and repertoire; however, their concert career came to a very abrupt end in the late 1970s even as the careers of other women singers singing together took off.[102] Also of this generation was Srirangam Gopalaratnam (1939–93),[103] a student of *Sangitha Kalanidhi* S. Pinakapani (1913–2013), who along with other students of her guru, constituted the vanguard of Andhra music.[104] We should also note the career of the nagasvaram player Madurai Ponnutayi (1929–2012), who was not indeed the first woman to play that difficult instrument but certainly the best among them.[105] The Hindustani musicians of this succeeding generation to Subbulakshmi's included Girija Devi (1929–2017), of whom it was said that it 'was not her voice alone that made her the kind of phenomenon she was, but her life and art, that raised the standard of the genre (*thumri*) which was looked down upon as "semi-classical"'.[106] Then there were Prabha Atre (born 1932), *Ganasaraswati* Kishori Amonkar (1932–2017), daughter of Mogubai Kurdikar, she whose '... music carries the very pulse beat of genius',[107] the reclusive Annapurna Devi (1927–2018), daughter and disciple of Ustad Allauddin Khan (1862–1972),[108] and Sharan Rani (1929–2008), from a conservative Delhi family, who was Allauddin Khan's disciple and one of the first women to play on the sarod.

Famously, this is the generation of Lata Mangeshkar and Asha Bhosle. Lata Mangeshkar was born in 1929, and after a lifetime of singing 'playback' for films has possibly the best-known female voice in India. A biographer writes of her, 'Lata Mangeshkar's fame in the world of Indian music is unrivalled. Unlike many stars whose celebrity status distances them from ordinary people, admiration for her is highly personalized because she is intimately linked to the emotions of millions of people through her songs. No bond could be stronger.'[109] Her sister, and possible rival, Asha Bhosle (born 1933) has sung even more songs than Lata. 'The two, Asha and Lata, have been performing contemporaries for full forty years now. Through those two score years, if Lata brooks no equality, the truth is that Asha, too admits no superiority. At long last, Asha's impact is her very own, if Lata is Lata, so is Asha Asha.'[110]

The world of dance saw Shanta Rao (1930–2007), Indrani Rahman (1930–99), Vyjayantimala (born 1933) and the iconic Kamala (born 1934).[111] Several of these women, including Kishori Amonkar, Vyjayantimala and Girija Devi, were, many decades later honoured with the M.S. Subbulakshmi Centenary Award.[112]

These, then, were the women who performed in Subbulakshmi's time, and before and since, the women with whom she had to compete in the world of mass entertainment. For longer or shorter periods of time, whatever the medium of their expression, they captivated their audiences. Writing years later G. Venkatachalam selected six artistes to represent India at a hypothetical *world* music festival: Roshanara and Kesarbai for Hindustani music; Subbulakshmi and Pattammal for the Carnatic; and Kamala Jharia and Kanan Bala for popular songs. All these women enjoyed fame, and even greatness. It was to take a while before women were seen as comparable to their brother musicians but it is a mark of Subbulakshmi's unique presence, good fortune and genius that, almost from the very beginning, she held her own.

3

A Child of Her Times

పరమేశ్వరి సుందరేశు రాణి బాలాంబ మధుర వాణి[1]
(*'Goddess of the universe, consort of the beautiful Siva,*
sweet-voiced child...'
from Syama Sastri's Mayamma in the raga Ahiri)

SUBBULAKSHMI was born at a time of extraordinary developments in the life of the nation, a time when the nationalist cause was gaining strength and when fundamental changes were taking place in society. Women were particularly impacted and it is worthwhile to look at the changes which were taking place.

There was, first of all, the call of nationalism, the demand for freedom and, starting from 1915, the exceptional impact of Gandhi. The rise of nationalist feeling around the country, starting with the establishment of the Indian National Congress in 1885, was fuelled by the growth in English education and consequently the movement of educated, upper-caste men to urban settlements. These men sought, understandably enough, to recreate the traditional entertainments of their past, a trend which the historian Lakshmi Subramanian has called the 'intervention of a new urban western educated elite that endeavored to relocate classical music from the court and temple to the secular arena'.[2]

But there were also efforts to justify and validate the nationalist cause in the name of a great and ancient tradition. The Indian National Congress recommended the convening of 'All India Music Conferences', the first of which was held in Baroda in 1916 with V.N. Bhatkhande, the foremost musicologist of the day, declaring that 'the great nation will sing one song'. The establishment of the Music Academy in Madras in 1927 was likewise a decision taken by one of the committees of the Congress.

Secondly, and linked to the call for freedom, was the notion that the soul of India vested in its womenfolk and in their tremendous capacity for sacrifice. Odd as this may seem today, it was a very widely held view. Conservative Hindu society accepted that the proper place for a woman was the home and that marriage and motherhood was for women 'the normal life'. It was their lot to flourish within the domestic sphere. Sarvepalli Radhakrishnan (1888–1975) held that '[t]here is nothing more attractive than modesty, nothing more shining than shyness in a woman'.[3] Rabindranath Tagore (1861–1941), writing in his middle years, held that 'the domestic world has been the gift of God to women'.[4] He is also credited with the view that 'Woman is endowed with the passive qualities of chastity, devotion and power of self-sacrifice in a greater measure than man.'[5]

Gandhi, who did more than any other to change the lives of Indian women in the twentieth century, believed in a separation between the domestic, female spaces and the wider world of men.[6] Contrariwise, it was Gandhi who drew thousands of women into the public arena by exhorting them to join the nationalist cause and even go to jail if necessary, but that was from a conviction that it was 'their acquired habits of deference, acceptance, and patience' which made them ideal satyagrahis.[7]

Somewhere in all this was the deeply held view that women were spiritually superior to men and that their chastity held them at all times to the path of true conduct. Gandhi, in particular, believed that 'the experience of pregnancy and motherhood especially qualified women to spread the message of peace and non-violence. If they could endure labour pains, they could endure anything.'[8]

Gandhi, who first encountered devadasis in Cocanada (now Kakinada) in April 1921,[9] was affected by the condition of 'fallen women', not that he was particularly sympathetic to their situation.[10] To him 'devadasi' was 'a euphemism for prostitutes'.[11] 'We also have in the South the immoral and inhuman institution of Devadasis.'[12] He was equally concerned with the condition of underage wives and child widows and regarded spinning as the one constructive activity which women could undertake. Even enlightened opinion endorsed the view that it was pure womanhood that kept alive the soul of India. 'India in every generation has produced millions of women who have never found fame, but whose daily existence has helped to civilize the race, and whose warmth of heart, self-sacrificing zeal, unassuming loyalty and strength in suffering, when subjected to trials of extreme severity, are among the glories of this ancient race'.[13]

A third, great strand in the public debates within society centred around social reform. Till well into the 1920s, the daughters of the caste Hindu families in south India were married very young, before puberty and quite often to men many years older than themselves. They had very little by way of schooling and were taught not to have many expectations beyond marriage, religious observances and motherhood. Widowhood was a fate to be dreaded. Remarriage was almost impossible. A widow's lot was very hard to bear and, indeed, shaven-headed widows could be seen in Madras till well into the 1960s.[14]

Social reform in India originated in Bengal through the efforts of Raja Ram Mohan Roy (1772–1833) and Ishwar Chandra Vidyasagar (1820–91). But it was the teachings of Sri Ramakrishna (1836–86) and Vivekananda (1863–1902) that impacted south India as well. One of the consequences of the steadily increasing migration to the cities was a recognition that sisters and daughters needed a better deal, what a scholar has referred to as the 'growing awareness amongst the Madras elite of the urgent need to alter those Hindu sacerdotal customs that comprehensively defined and regulated women's lives from childhood to death'.[15] Even if it did not use the language of human rights, the move towards social reform in India did stem from a basic understanding that 'in all human beings, irrespective of sex, the same drama of the flesh and the spirit, of finitude and transcendence takes place'.[16]

Lastly, there was the growth in formal education for women. Schooling for girls had begun in the Tamil districts as early as the 1820s, but these schools rarely saw upper-caste or upper-class girls. It was generally regarded as 'unbecoming for a Brahmin girl to attend school and learn English'.[17] An 1822 survey recorded that only girls from devadasi families were in schools. A school for Muslim girls was started in Madurai in 1815 by an American Mission. In 1836, a day school run by a Mrs Eckhard reported sixty-five non-Christian students, of which not a single one was Brahmin; ten were devadasis and the others were Vellalas, Naidus, Pallans and Parayans. In 1870, of the approximately 15 million women in the Tamil districts, a little over 10,000 were enrolled in something resembling modern schools. In 1881-82, a survey revealed 23,860 girls in schools, and further roughly 14,000 in co-educational schools, in the Madras Presidency.

Even as late as 1917, it was stated at a public meeting at Kothamangalam in Ramnad that only 1 per cent of the female population in the Madras Presidency knew how to read and write.[18] Even if Subbulakshmi herself had next to no formal schooling, through this period there were schools for girls in Madurai. The American Mission ran several Hindu Girls Schools. A Town High School of Madurai, later the Sethupathi High School, was set up for boys and girls in 1889. The Saurashtra Sabha of Madurai ran primary schools.

Higher education for women began later but even so women's colleges, often with missionary support, began to be established in the early years of the twentieth century. The Madurai Girls Boarding School began teachers' training in 1876. The Sarah Tucker College,

Palayankottai, the Presentation Convent College, Vepery and the St. Mary's Presentation Convent College, Black Town, in Madras, had an aggregate strength of ten women each.[19] By 1911-12, there were nineteen women's colleges in the Presidency.

We have noted, then, four broad trends which impacted on the lives of women: the rise of nationalism, the celebration of Indian tradition and values, the call of social reform and the growth of education for girls and women. British rule in India was sought to be justified on many grounds, not the least of which was the argument that the subcontinent was rife with anarchy and chaos, and in the grip of barbaric social customs. The lamentable situation of women in caste Hindu society was seen as a sign of the degraded cultural traditions of society at large. The nationalist reaction to this was to seek to achieve independence not just as an economic or political goal but as a way of establishing the cultural, moral and spiritual superiority of India, and of the countries of the East. Built into this argument was the notion that the pursuit of material interests, which necessarily involved trade, commerce and other dealings with the Western world, was the domain of the male while 'the home in its essence must remain unaffected by the profane activities of the material world, (with) women as its representation'. It may be necessary for India to develop, earn her independence and look to the West for modern learning and scientific excellence, but the essence of India lay in her inner core, 'the worlds of custom, tradition, the arts and women'.[20]

Nowhere was this made more clear than in the public outcry following the publication in 1927 of Katherine Mayo's *Mother India*, a tract which focused on the abominable situation of Indian women and on child marriage, early maternity and the brutal treatment of widows.[21] Starting with Gandhi, everyone condemned *Mother India*, and particularly prominent women in public life. Sarojini Naidu, herself hailed as 'the most outstanding Indian woman of her generation, ... a liberal thinker, a literary artist, a social reformer and a political fighter', took the position that Indian women, given their spiritual superiority and innate capacity for sacrifice, were capable of redeeming themselves from the evils to which they were subject.[22] Speaking some years before the Mayo crisis, Sarojini Naidu had declaimed, 'Woman makes the nation, on her worthiness or unworthiness, weakness or strength, ignorance or enlightenment, her cowardice or courage lie folded the destiny of her sons.'[23] She made this subject the theme of her Kamala lectures at the University of Calcutta in 1928, though the text of her exact words is now not available.

Two other important trends, especially for the Tamil country, and particularly for the practice of the performing arts, must be noted. The songs and writings of *Mahakavi* Subramania Bharati (1882–1921), 'the herald of the Tamil renaissance', resounded widely wherever Tamil was spoken, and he was firmly of the view that the war against imperialism had to be carried out along with the struggle for women's emancipation.[24] Bharati was a fiery nationalist. He translated *Bande Mataram* and wrote popular songs of freedom; he was deeply devout and wrote verses to the Mother Goddess.[25] His very positive attitudes towards women, among other influences, fed into the Dravidian movement and its early emphasis on women's emancipation.

Periyar E.V. Ramaswami Naicker (1879–1973) had no time for social reform attempted within the structures of patriarchal societies. Nothing less than destruction of existing norms would do. Periyar encouraged widow remarriage and education for girls; he questioned 'the basic pillars of patriarchy, like the monogamous family and the norms of chastity prescribed for and enforced upon women'.[26] He spoke of the rights of women to divorce and abortion and condemned caste rules regarding marriage and social conduct. Under his leadership, the Suyamariathai Iyakkam, or Self-Respect Movement, conducted over 8,000 marriages over 1929–32 alone. Every year at the Self-Respect Conference, a Women's Conference was held, as for instance in Madurai in 1938.

These powerful voices, bringing into public discourse the notions of family, monogamy, chastity, caste and empowerment bring us to that other great social movement of the times, the anti-*nautch* movement, as it was commonly, if tastelessly, called. One name, above all others, stands out. Muthulakshmi Reddy (1886–1968), a doctor and the daughter of a devadasi, Chandra of Pudukkottai, fought relentlessly for the cause. Following the *Mother India* scandal, she had a public resolution passed denying that Indian womanhood as a whole was in a state of slavery, superstition, ignorance and degradation as claimed by Katherine Mayo but which asked for early steps to prohibit child marriage, early parenthood, enforced widowhood, dedication of girls to temples and 'commercialized immorality'.[27] Another scholar has noted that Dr Reddy's cause received support from 'Anglo-Indian' legislation which encompassed the spread of disease, the regulation of brothels and the formal registration of prostitutes – an exercise which routinely, and unhappily, registered devadasi women as prostitutes.[28]

Another name which needs to be remembered is that of Moovalur Ramamirtham Ammaiyar (1883–1962). Born to the devadasi tradition, she broke away from it, married of her choice, entered political life, met Gandhi in 1921 and later joined Periyar Ramaswami Naicker's movement. Her 1936 novel, *Mosavalai allathu mati pettra mainer*, or 'The Treacherous Net of the Dasis, or a Minor grown wise', is not of any particular literary value ('sickeningly didactic') but was timely and effective and 'helps to understand why the devadasi system was abolished'.[29] A woman character in this novel says these remarkable words, '... to get rid of the devadasi system, it is first necessary to destroy the puranas, the agamas, the smritis, the religion and even god himself. They are at the bottom of the system. If they are destroyed there won't be any justification for the whole caste and crowd of the devadasis.'

It would be incorrect to presume that the community of devadasis was broadly supportive of Muthulakshmi Reddy's cause. Devadasi *sangams* in several places opposed the move, and Bangalore Nagaratnamu lent her support, the broad argument being – even if the devadasis did not themselves articulate it in these words – that colonial and native conceptions of the practice varied significantly. What was regarded as immoral conduct to a 'western' cast of mind, and in the Indian Penal Code of 1861, did not, in the local imagination, necessarily constitute deviant behaviour.[30] Indeed, the argument went, devadasi women were professional artistes of repute, free to pursue their creativity and their art. The battle continued till 1947, when the legislation abolishing the practice was passed.

The issue has been studied extensively; there is a nationalist/ modernist view, there is a feminist view and there is a moralist view, and the debate, if no longer relevant, has recently resurfaced on social media.[31]

With the disintegration of their world, women of the devadasi communities were on their own, and had to seek a future either through marriage or employment with theatre groups and the like.[32] Their children were rapidly assimilated into caste society, leaving no trace of the *chinna melam* tradition from which they sprung. It is not necessary to mourn the passing of the institution, but it is necessary to recognize that much damage has been done to the devadasi heritage by the loose use of the term in film and in popular writing. 'Devadasi was a celebratory reference to artistic and religiously significant women, who later became victims of men. The word itself does not need to be discarded, its abusive usage needs to be challenged.'[33]

Another factor which influenced the tradition of the practice and performance of music was the interest shown by Western visitors and thinkers, many of theosophist persuasion.[34] This need not be overemphasized, but the establishment in 1886 of the world headquarters of the Theosophical Society in Madras has meant, over the years, that theosophy itself is much better known in south India than almost anywhere else in India or even in the wider region.

It is not easy to describe the nature of theosophy. The original writings are dense and unapproachable, but the essence appears to be the existence of one supreme truth, an understanding to be found in the teachings of Hinduism and other ancient faiths such as Buddhism and Zoroastranism. This One Truth was known to great teachers of the past, who may, in the conception of the theosophists, still take the form of Masters, or occult beings. Among the educated English men and women who came to the Theosophical Society in Madras were those who believed in a once golden Hindu age, with the arts of that religious tradition assuming a 'spiritual' dimension. This fed neatly into the argument that the upper castes, usually Brahmins, and the ones to whom theosophy had the greatest appeal, were the hereditary custodians of the highly spiritual music of the region. It also fed into the nationalist argument that India was a great and ancient land whose cultural traditions were far more rooted than anything in the West. This need not detain us here, but the point is that this sort of attention to the form could only have encouraged the aspirational migrants from the hinterland in their attempts to establish spaces for musical performance wherever they settled.

Clearly, there were many forces at work. The cause of nationalism and an independent India required a public recognition of India's rich cultural traditions, and much of the tradition of performance belonged to women. Nationalism required that women play an equal role in the struggle and needed to be educated for this purpose. However, traditional society relegated women to spaces outside the public sphere by not just exalting the domestic space as being somehow purer than the outside world, but also by denying women the opportunity for education, employment or negotiating the public space. There was some disquiet surrounding the fact that while women may have been the repository of the performing tradition, there was the taint of a perceived lack of chastity.

All this came to a head starting with the 1920s, precisely the time when south India was answering the call of Gandhi, the time when women's education, including higher education, was being taken seriously and a time when women musicians and dancers were beginning to recognize spaces outside the temple and the salon. Subbulakshmi, whose first recordings date to 1926, was a child of these revolutionary times.

The public controversy surrounding the marriage of Rukmini Devi (1904–86) in 1920 to George Arundale (1878–1945) is worth recalling if only because it reflects many of the issues raised by nationalism, modernity, social reform and women's engagement with the world. Such a controversy would hopefully be considered ridiculous today. However, at the time it did become a very public cause with the prestigious *Hindu* newspaper weighing in powerfully, if ultimately fruitlessly, against the marriage.

Rukmini Devi was sixteen, the daughter, and one of eight children, of a Tamil Brahmin family deeply involved in theosophy. Very soon after her father's death in late 1919, her marriage to the forty-one-year-old George Arundale, an English educationist and disciple of Annie Besant, was announced. There was an outburst of righteous indignation with the *Hindu* ponderously opining, almost certainly wrongly, that such a union would be 'irregular in law as it would be inadvisable socially'.[35] The family was divided, the public inflamed. Public meetings in Conjeevaram,[36] Tiruvannamalai and Tiruppur condemned the developments.[37] Annie Besant was attacked for encouraging the match.[38] George Arundale gave what was seen to be a commitment to withdraw from his intentions but which turned out to be only a notice of postponement.[39] The couple had ultimately to marry quietly in Bombay on 27 April 1920.

This matter tells us much about how society regarded women and their situation. It did not seem to occur to anyone, least of all the *Hindu*, that this was an entirely private matter. For a start, there was no notion of privacy or of individual rights. Leaders of public opinion fumed at the idea of a minor contemplating marriage, quite ignoring the fact that it was still entirely common at the time for women in caste Hindu households to be married before puberty. It appears that the one single fact that so provoked society was the fact that a woman had expressed a choice; this apparent loss of control was more than could be borne.

Subbulakshmi's marriage, twenty years later, though potentially controversial, did not arouse any similar public reaction. It is a measure of how society had evolved over two decades.

It is also interesting that Rukmini Devi Arundale went on to become a legend even if, at least to some in the world of the performing arts, she will always be a symbol of upper caste, and particularly Brahmin, appropriation of the dance form. Kalakshetra, the institution she set up, was from early on commended, by the *Hindu* no less, for its services to Indian art, dance and music.[40] And decades later, at the time of the Arundale centenary, his varied services to India, in education, in the arts and in its spiritual development were richly praised.[41]

4

The Move to Madras

ఏమందునే ముద్దు బాలామణికి, నేన..[1]

('*What shall I say to this charming girl..?*'
from Dharmapuri Subbarayar's *javali* in the raga Khamas)

IT is unclear exactly when Shanmukhavadivu and Subbulakshmi made the move to Madras. Late in 1931 they were still in Madurai, as we learn from the entries in Madurai Bhaskara Das's diaries.[2] The young girl's appearance at the Kumbakonam Mahamakham in February 1932 is well known, arranged as it was by the lawyer-turned-film director K. Subrahmanyam (1904–71), later to introduce Subbulakshmi to the films.[3] Late in life, Semmangudi Srinivasa Iyer recalled hearing her sing in Kumbakonam and this may well have been the occasion.[4]

It is possible that, emboldened by the success of that appearance, mother and daughter ventured further out to Madras. One of Subbulakshmi's biographers recalls her performing at the Music Academy, Madras, on 1 January 1932, when she 'sang the full gamut of a concert repertoire, something that was seldom expected of a female vocalist', and apparently standing in for Ariyakudi Ramanuja Iyengar, who had cancelled his recital.[5] There is no other confirmation of this.

T.T. Krishnamachari (1899–1973), later to become one of Subbulakshmi's well-placed patrons, was present at a concert at Saundarya Mahal by the young girl, which he incorrectly believed was in August 1931. Many years later he recalled, 'The singer on the stage was a tinily built young girl. But on her face, I could see a radiance (prakasam).'[6]

It was around this time that Subbulakshmi was taken by her mother to see 'Vina' Dhanammal. Shanmukhavadivu herself was presented as a young girl to the senior *vainika* – who is believed to have blessed her with the gift of musically gifted children.[7] One of Subbulakshmi's early recordings in 1932 was the *javali*, '*Emandune muddu balamani*'/ Kapi by Dharmapuri Subbarayar, whose attachment to Dhanammal was widely known. It is a matter of speculation whether the still young Subbulakshmi made the connection. It is not easy to separate fact from fiction in all the accounts of the young (or, for that matter, at any time) Subbulakshmi but this meeting is one that she herself formally acknowledged. In her presidential address to the Music Academy, Madras, in December 1968, Subbulakshmi said, 'I recollect the late Vina Dhanammal to whose house in Egmore my mother took me when I was a young girl. After hearing me sing Dhanammal said, "This girl has a bright future." Those words still ring in my years.'[8]

The mrdangam *vidvan* Pudukkottai Dakshinamurthi Pillai, who accompanied her at the Rockfort concert in 1927, was also important in advancing Subbulakshmi's career at this time in her life, a time of which we know very little.[9] More than sixty years later, in a rare interview, Subbulakshmi chose to remember him and none other when asked as to which masters had inspired her.[10]

Shanmukhavadivu and Subbulakshmi are said to have stayed on Tana Street in Purasawalkam[11] and later at Big Street, Triplicane. It is not clear what happened to the still very young Vadivambal. Indeed, there is very little now known even of what mother and daughter were doing in Madras outside of stray concert appearances. We have earlier noted the report in a film magazine, in 1944, that Shanmukhavadivu and her daughters had been living under the protection of one Lakshmanan Chettiar.[12] This may well refer to this period. Lakshmanan Chettiar, a prominent banker of Devakottai, is better remembered for having been murdered in 1943 on the Trivandrum Express.[13] There is a reference that Subbulakshmi, as a young woman, heard Kesarbai Kerkar sing in Madras but it has not been possible to substantiate this.[14]

However, about the first performance for which there is still a definite record is on 28 December 1933, at the Saundarya Mahal hall on Govindanaicken Street, under the auspices of the Indian Fine Arts Society, where 'Miss M.S. Subbulakshmi performed with the accompaniment of Miss Shanmuga Vadivoo on the veena and Mr Gururajappa of Mysore (Brother of Mr T. Chowdiah) on the violin.'[15] This may well have been the concert T.T. Krishnamachari remembered. It is also known that Subbulakshmi sang at the Indian Fine Arts Society as early as 1932.[16]

The Indian Fine Arts Society was established by wealthy members of the Telugu-speaking Arya Vaisya community and one C.Y. Anjaneyulu Chetty, in particular, arranged for a concert by Subbulakshmi in his grand Chetpet residence, Clanstephan, even prior to her 28 December recital. It is known that a grateful Subbulakshmi, over the years, always sang at weddings in Chetty's family.[17] The Society usually held its events at the more revered Gokhale Hall but appears to have moved Subbulakshmi's concert to the Saundarya Mahal in deference to the wishes of Annie Besant who had ruled that the Gokhale Hall could not be used for performances by women of the courtesan class.[18] It is reported that she sang at the Music Academy in 1933 but there is no record of this in the printed programme.[19]

From around the time the Madras *sabhas* came into being, a tradition was established of a music and dance 'season' every December. Over the years, the tradition has flourished with ever-increasing numbers of performances and a dazzling range of titles awarded to celebrated performers; the annual season of the Music Academy in 1931 is the first for which we have some record. C. Saraswathi Bai, the *Harikatha* exponent was a serious candidate for the presidency of the sessions, and if she had been so recognized would have been remembered as the first woman to have been awarded the *Sangitha Kalanidhi*. In the event male prejudice held the day. As it happens, Saraswathi Bai's achievement in performing from a public platform in 1909 when she was but seventeen is insufficiently recognized today.

Subbulakshmi's friendship with Balasaraswati probably began around this time. There is a famous photograph, frequently reproduced, of the two of them wearing men's pajamas, striped, and pretending to smoke cigarettes, possibly of the candy variety.[20] It is important to date this photograph accurately, but there are only straws in the wind. Balasaraswati herself told the friend to whom she gave her copy of the photograph that it was taken at the Taj Mahal Hotel in Bombay and her biographer Douglas Knight dates it to 1937.[21] However, both girls are very young, with their features still not fully formed. Could it have been before 1936, the year Subbulakshmi met Sadasivam and Balasaraswati became R.K. Shanmukham Chetty's partner, when both were still in their late teens? Or could this have been the trip to Bombay when T. Sadasivam escorted Subbulakshmi on the train journey, an event frequently mentioned in accounts of their relationship? We have the detail that Balasaraswati and her cousins were part of a programme in Bombay where Subbulakshmi was performing.[22]

Decades later, the photograph, taken out of context, keeps being used as a prop for social media excitement on what constitutes women's rights. 'Legends Balasaraswati and M.S. Subbulakshmi pose in this secret teenage defiance studio picture from 1937' shrieks a Twitter post in 2017.[23]

One question though continues to tease. Who exactly took the photograph?

Even by 1932, when she was only fourteen, Balasaraswati had already performed publicly in Madras under the auspices of the Indian Cultural Bureau and had been awarded the title of *Gana Saraswati* by the Indian Fine Arts Society.[24] Kalki R. Krishnamurthi (1899–1954), always just Kalki, wrote appreciatively of her understanding of the *padam*, 'Krishna nee begane baaro', and her interpretation on stage. By the time she was sixteen, she had performed in Calcutta and Benares.[25]

An important development in 1931 was the dance performance on 15 March 1931 in a public, and modern space by the Kalyani Daughters, Jeevaratnam and Rajalakshmi, the daughters of Tiruvalaputtur Kalyani (1873–1938).[26] This performance took place at the Gana Mandir and was facilitated by the reformist lawyer, aesthete and dancer, E. Krishna Iyer (1897–1968). 'The event was poorly attended and did not even create a ripple, but there is scarcely any doubt that it is one of the most important events in the entire history of Indian dance.'[27] It is possibly this performance which Rukmini Devi Arundale saw and which drove her to Mylapore Gowri Ammal (1892–1971) to learn the form.[28]

The Kalyani Daughters performed again at the 1932 season, on 1 January 1933, as did Varalakshmi (1918–37) and Saranayaki, the granddaughters of Kumbakonam Gowri, on 28 December 1933. A member of the audience raved, 'Three superb hours of perfect art and most enjoyable music.'[29] A public recital by Dhanammal on 16 July 1933 was widely advertised, where men could get the best seats for a rupee but women only the second-best seats at half a rupee.[30] It was at this very time, on 25 August 1933 to be precise, that a precocious and already world-travelled thirteen-year-old, Ravi Shankar (1920–2012), found himself at one of Dhanammal's famous Friday soirées, his first introduction to the music of south India.[31] Varalakshmi and her niece

Bhanumati (1922–2006) performed in the 1934 season, while in the 1935 season there were dance recitals by Balasaraswati, Sabaranjitham and Nagaratnam of Panthanallur, and music by Lalithangi, readily recognized by critics as a serious musician.[32] In 1936, and frequently in the years following, Muktha and Brinda sang to the accompaniment of their sister Abhiramasundari's violin. Dhanammal played vina on 30 December 1936 (with loudspeaker arrangement as the notice carefully notes). The courtesan musicians were respected within their sphere, and Varalakshmi's passing in November 1937 was marked by the Music Academy with a full-page photograph in its journal.[33]

Rukmini Devi broke the myth that women from upper-caste homes could not learn dance. Till that time, even if music was permitted to be learnt and performed, dance, in caste households, was still regarded as beyond the pale. Music could always be disguised as part of ritual worship and the repertoire provided enough to satisfy the most conservative elements. Dance was a visual form which called attention to the female form; it recognized the erotic, it legitimized longing, even if for a god, and was hence unacceptable for the daughters of caste households who were expected to marry and establish caste households in their turn.

Rukmini Devi as the daughter of an intellectually highbrow Brahmin theosophist family and as the wife of an Englishman had, or assumed, the authority to flout society's norms. It may be too much to say that she made dance 'acceptable as *an art form* (italics added) to society' but she certainly made it an acceptable accomplishment for women to seek and acquire. She understood that traditional dancers were themselves caught in a web which was not of their making. 'Society is more responsible than the Devadasi for the corruption that nearly destroyed the art.'[34]

Rukmini Devi changed everything; costume, stage decor, concert planning, the nature and composition of music accompaniment and the manner of teaching.[35] When she set up the International Academy of the Arts in 1936, several prominent citizens of Madras lent support, among them Kalki, who had at that time probably not yet met Subbulakshmi.[36] The Academy grew into Kalakshetra in 1940 and stands testimony to Rukmini Devi's determination. Over the years, despite the rise to prominence of many dancers and many schools, and despite a serious repositioning of the devadasi heritage,[37] the Kalakshetra *bani* has flourished.[38]

It was in these years that the term Bharatanatyam was coming into vogue, as a replacement for the more traditional *sadir*, a change in nomenclature still rued by those who mourn the passing of the devadasi communities.[39]

Not everyone was pleased with these developments.[40] Balasaraswati, who has always been posited as a counter-representative of the subaltern – and now dispossessed – tradition, is credited with a remark, which is almost certainly true, in response to Rukmini Devi that 'upper-caste women have taken up our profession and they have left us only their art'.[41] Women like Balasaraswati were fighting for what they had, for that was all that they had. Rukmini Devi could afford to flout convention; Balasaraswati could not. Subbulakshmi managed to reject one set of conventions and exchange them for another.[42]

These questions of agency, and change and expropriation, and the loss of hereditary rights, continue to be discussed. It is important to remember that up until the 1930s there was a revealing difference between the performance of music and the performance of dance. Dancers were always devadasi women. The appropriation, if that is the term we must use, of the dance form happened very quickly in the 1930s.[43] There was no parallel process in the performance of music, no takeover by persons who were hitherto unconnected with performance. Up until the early part of the twentieth century, vocalists were mainly upper-caste men, or devadasi women. As new spaces for performance opened up, the performing musicians continued, largely, to be upper-caste men. Male

The Move to Madras

vocalists who were not Brahmin, or upper caste, were known but were not, either before or after the rapid growth of urban performing spaces, particularly influential. Devadasi singers did move their establishments to the newly growing cities but their performances were still mostly in private salons.

Instrumentalists and percussionists were better placed, and Dwaram Venkataswami Naidu (1893–1964), Tirupamburam Swaminatha Pillai (1898–1961),[44] Chittoor Subramania Pillai (1898–1975) and T. Chowdiah (1895–1967), all graced as *Sangitha Kalanidhi*, and perhaps the most famous of all, T.N. Rajarathinam Pillai (1898–1956) – all of them enjoyed considerable eminence. Rajarathinam Pillai in particular, poised on the cusp between *periya melam* and 'Carnatic music', enjoyed great status, though he was never allowed to forget his caste identity as an *isai vellalar*, not that he would have, from what we know, wanted to do so. The art of percussion, always open to the non-Brahmin castes, and to the brothers and sons of devadasi singers and dancers, produced Palani Subramania Pillai (1908–62).

The scholar Sriram V. has called attention to the role that could have been played, had he lived, by the legendary Kanchipuram Naina Pillai.[45] Ariyakudi Ramanuja Iyengar, with his distinctive ideas on concert pattern could, in some limited sense, be identified with the 'new' music of the 1930s onwards. Naina Pillai was his near-exact contemporary, of substantial musical lineage and much influence. What if he had lived longer? Could he have achieved the same status? Could he have established a musical tradition outside the Brahmin fold?

Through the 1930s, the Music Academy settled into its role as the leader of the Madras 'season'. More women were beginning to appear on its stage, notably 'Miss D.K. Pattammal' in 1935, the first in what was a near-uninterrupted chain of season appearances at the Music Academy for the next fifty years.[46] There is a story of an early 1930s appearance by Subbulakshmi in Madurai where the audience included a very young Pattammal. A confidante recalls, and she could have only heard the story from Subbulakshmi, Pattammal's focused attention on how the only slightly older musician was going about her business. There is no independent confirmation of this encounter but both of them were singing publicly at that time. Pattammal's first recorded appearance is of 1933 and as early as 1936 she had Kalki commend her rendition of Muthusvami Dikshitar's songs and predict a bright future for her.[47]

Subbulakshmi participated as an observer in the concerts held in the 1934 season of the Music Academy, Madras. There is a well-known photograph of Subbulakshmi, Shanmukhavadivu and Lalithangi taken on this occasion, none looking as if even remotely aware that their names would live forever. It is not so well known that Subbulakshmi also sang at this season, on 2 January 1935, her first 'season' appearance at the Music Academy.[48] She had sung earlier that season at the Indian Fine Arts Society on 29 December 1934. The incumbent President of the Music Academy declared in 1987 that Subbulakshmi's first Academy appearance was at the 1935 season but the concert is not listed in the published list even if the back cover of the 1935 souvenir does advertise gramophone records of 'Miss Subbulakshmi'.[49] She did not perform at the Music Academy's annual festival till 1938 but the 1936 souvenir has her again, unnamed, in an advertisement for G.K. Vale, the society photographers.[50] Souvenirs for both 1936 and 1937 have her on the back cover in advertisements for her own long-playing records.

A friend recalls Subbulakshmi singing at the Theosophical Society in the early 1930s. This same friend also recalls Subbulakshmi, Pattammal and Vasanthakokilam all visiting her home, though not possibly all at the same time, to learn and improve their Telugu pronunciation.[51] Another reference is to a marriage concert in Trivandrum in 1936[52] and a recital in Tenkasi in about 1936.[53] At this distance, such vague references are all that survive.

The Move to Madras

The young Rajam Pushpavanam (1917–91) had moved by this time from Thanjavur to Madras. She was a student of the violinist Parur Sundaram Iyer (1891–1974) and of her cousin Madurai Mani Iyer and had recorded as early as 1930. Interestingly, the inveterate diarist Varadachariar had heard 'Rajam Pushpavanam's sophisticated voice' in 1938.[54] This once feted singer came from a rich musical heritage. Her father's reputation would still have been remembered and the young Rajam did become very popular, and at a very young age. Oddly, she was never to perform at the Music Academy.

It is always said that D.K. Pattammal was the first Brahmin woman to have sung publicly but, insofar as these achievements mean anything, it is possible that the young Rajam was there before her. Rajam appears to have been both bold and enterprising. She had toyed with the possibility of acting and was a serious contender for the lead role in the 1936 film *Vasantha Sena*; in 1937, when she could not have been more than twenty, she had composed music for a Tamil film *Rajasekharan*.[55] And she was one of four women in Madras with a driving licence. By all accounts, she was a very wealthy woman, earning well from a thriving concert career.[56] There is reason to believe that she and Subbulakshmi knew each other in these early days in Madras, when Rajam was the more prosperous, the better-known performer, and the more outgoing.

It was an exciting time in the performing space. Ariyakudi Ramanuja Iyengar, Chembai Vaidyanatha Bhagavathar (1896–1974), Chittoor Subramania Pillai, Musiri Subramania Iyer (1899–1975) and Maharajapuram Viswanatha Iyer (1896–1970) commanded their audiences. Semmangudi Srinivasa Iyer, Madurai Mani Iyer and G.N. Balasubramaniam were their acknowledged successors. There were many women jostling for attention, not least among them D.K. Pattammal, Rajam Pushpavanam and N.C. Vasanthakokilam, but as a *rasika* of the times noted, half a century later, 'MS challenged them all for the attention and affection of music buffs ... The initials

MS spelt the magic of music ... the joy of listening to MS was an experience in itself.'[57]

A significant development of this time and one which would play an important role both in Subbulakshmi's later career and in the social context in which music was performed and appreciated was the coming of the radio. The Madras Radio Club was founded in 1924 and would broadcast from prominent public spots. 'Twice every week, after 5.30 p.m., the beaches of Marina, Santhome and the High Court would resound with the reverb of amplified radio broadcasts of music, and 10-minute lectures.'[58] The Madras Corporation Radio, which was set up in 1930, likewise set up relaying outlets in public places. 'Six loudspeakers were installed at the Marina, Robinson Park, People's Park and the High Court Beach, to be operated in the evenings.'[59] When this was absorbed into All India Radio on 16 June 1938, the inaugural concert was given by a nineteen-year-old D.K. Pattammal. Radio clubs, which started in the mid 1920s in Bombay, Calcutta, Madras, Rangoon and Karachi, had a limited reach and were essentially 'trying to relieve the after-dinner tedium of gymkhana life with brief interludes of music'.[60] The Indian Broadcasting Company was set up in 1927, and collapsed in 1935, to be revived as All India Radio (AIR) in 1936.

Many of the ills which have beset public broadcasting in India over the decades date back to these early days; the lack of capacity to cater to the wide range of languages and cultural interests, the inability of very poor people to buy radios and the stultifying effect of state control.[61] 'The record of All India Radio in those pre-Independence days is not a distinguished one. In fact it was a rather pathetic one.'[62] For all that, broadcasting spread quickly and AIR, which began broadcasting from Delhi, Bombay and Calcutta, opened stations in Madras, from June 1938, and from Lahore and Peshawar to be followed by Dacca and Trichy. The Madras station was regarded as a success and an unnamed bureaucrat noted loftily that it had '... in the short period of its working, familiarized listeners with the Carnatic style of music, till then unknown on the air. Listeners have now begun to wonder if there is any more left and whether south Indian music is not for ever destined to remain the petrified classic it has come to be at present'. The bureaucrat was not, however, very hopeful and held that for all its intellectualism, the Carnatic form was assured only of 'an abiding though limited future'.[63]

This was a wrong conclusion. It is true that the reach of the radio was not extensive. Even several years after the coming of radio, in January 1942, it was somewhat proudly being announced that 1,42,125 persons owned radios in British India.[64] The number of such people within the reach of the Madras and Trichy stations would have been pitifully low, but the number of people performing on this new medium was very impressive. Particularly large numbers of women, who may not have either wanted to perform publicly or who may not have had the chance to do so, were performing on the air. Not all of them belonged to the courtesan tradition. Music was always being taught within caste Hindu homes, and even as far abroad as Bombay and Calcutta, but it was radio which opened up the performing space for amateur singers and vina players. For reasons not very clear, radio seems to have assumed greater respectability than the gramophone record industry.

The names of the women performing on radio make fascinating reading and in themselves tell a story. Over the years 1939–45, to give only a very small sample, there were A.R. Pankajavalli, Nagambujam, Thillai Ammal of Chidambaram, T. Chandrammal of Mysore, Sengamalavalli Ammal, Balamba and Sugandi, Nanjangud Nagaratnam, Mallavarapu Jayalaxmi, G. Subhadramma, Vydehi Vijiaragavan, K. Bala Tripurasundari Ammal (vina and vocal), Meenakshi and Sulochana, A.R. Sundaram, Rajayee of Pandanallur, C. Sundarasaradamma, Miss M.A. Krishnaswami Iyengar, Gowri Ramunni Menon, Janamma David, S. Adilakshmi Ammal of Panruti, Kamala and Vimala, T. Ramathilakamma, Saranayaki Ammal, M.R. Syamala (vina and vocal), Miss A. Mathews, Nappinai Rangarajan, T.R. Navaneetham (flute), V. Vanibai, Tirumullaivayil Rajeswari, M.S. Tripurambal,

K. Anasuya, S. Kousalya Ramakrishna Reddy, Rukmini Rajagopalan, T.V. Kumudini, Krishnaveni Radhakrishnan (vina), Parvathi Kailasapathy, Ramanathapuram Devakunjari, Shanmuga Vadivoo of Tiruchendur, Kamalini Sitharam, V. Perundevi, Bhagirathi Narasimhan, Karaikkal S. Sundarakamakshi, Sundari Tampi, Sushila Achyutaraman and Parassala Ponnammal.

Some names feature more regularly than others. Lalitha Venkataram, S. Chellammal, C.S. Rajam, Choodamani, Hamsaveni Sisters, Leela and Sarojini, even if they are not remembered now, were regular performers.[65] Some musicians such as T. Suryakumari, Vasundhara Devi and K.B. Sundarambal, were obviously popular because of their records; the same is true of Subbulakshmi, Pattammal, Vasanthakokilam and Rajam Pushpavanam whose records were played nearly every week. Dhanammal's recordings were frequently aired and occasionally, recordings by 'Shanmuga Vadivoo' of Madurai of *tanam* and *'Sivadikshapari'*/Kuranji. Of Subbulakshmi's recordings, the film songs were broadcast often as also *'Saraguna'*/Kedaragaula, *'O Jagadamba'*/Anandabhairavi, *'Vadera daivamu'*/Pantuvarali, *'Manasa etulo'*/Malayamarutam *'Ennaganu'*/Pantuvarali, *'Manamuleda'*/Hamirkalyani and *'Elavataram'*/Mukhari.

Of particular interest are recordings of Hindi bhajans, of which there is no other trace now, such as *'Ek sahara tera'*, *'Nainan gungat me'* and *'Main nirgunia'*.[66] These songs had entered Subbulakshmi's repertoire at a very early stage in her career and before she became familiar with the *Ashrama bhajanavali*, the prayer book used in Gandhi's ashrams. There is an intriguing reference to a recording by Subbulakshmi of a song in Megharanjani, now untraceable.[67] There are references to recordings of Tamil songs which then disappeared from her concert lists; *'Enakkum Iru padam'*, termed as a Ramayana ragamalika, *'Endan idadu'*, *'Adaravatravar'* and *'Unnuruvam'* are examples.[68]

Saraswathi Bai sang regularly on the radio as did Pattammal and Brinda and Muktha. On occasion, Brinda alone played the vina. Her sister T. Abhiramasundari also played solo violin recitals. Though the Dhanammal school is reputed for its slow renderings, the radio programmes invariably include a very long list of songs for the time available. Of particular interest is a recital by Dhanammal's daughter T. Lakshmiratnam on 6 March 1939, shortly before her death, called 'Songs we are forgetting'. It is an enticing list of songs made the more poignant by the fact that some have indeed disappeared from the concert platform.[69]

The radio continued to play a very important role in popularizing classical music and over the years the National Programme of Music and the annual Akashvani Sangeet Sammelan contributed hugely to this. With the cassette and CD revolution and with the availability of music of all types on the Internet, radio has lost its pre-eminence and even its relevance; but in its time it built many reputations and made many careers.[70]

Another quaint, but very popular, presence from the late 1930s onwards was that of the bands, successors to those maintained by the Maratha rulers of Thanjavur in the early nineteenth century. In a spectacular welter of key elements from Indian and English group performance traditions, these bands played items from the Carnatic repertoire, *tevarams*, Tyagaraja *kritis* and the like on Western instruments.

> The Nathamuni band was similar in size to the band in Thanjavur (approximately ten players), on clarinet, Eb soprano clarinet, Eb alto saxophone, cornet, trombone, possibly baritone horn, euphonium, bagpipes, tavil, and talam. Doubled instruments included saxophone but may have also included euphonium or cornet as well. The band also included a bass instrument (apparently a low brass horn such as a tuba) which is played with great skill.[71]

The men playing these instruments were most often from the communities that provided nagasvaram players, and all performances were outdoors, on the Marina Beach and elsewhere.

5

Sadasivam

पुराणपुरुषं पुरान्तकं शंकराभरण भासमानदेहम्.[1]

('*O primordial being, destroyer of the tripuras, whose body shines with auspicious ornaments*'.
From Muthusvami Dikshitar's '*Sadasivam upasmahe*' in the raga Sankarabharanam)

SUBBULAKSHMI met T. Sadasivam on 30 June 1936; it is more appropriate to say that it was on this day that T. Sadasivam met Subbulakshmi.[2] Later in life, he would reminisce that the meeting was fated, that a sage in the Himalaya had predicted that a woman of great qualities would shortly enter his life.[3] That this prediction was made while he was on pilgrimage with his wife Parvati and elder daughter Radha only makes it poignant.[4]

T. Sadasivam's story has been told many times and often in his own words. He was born on 4 September 1902, the seventh of the sixteen children of Tyagarajan and Mangalammal, and had some education, even if he did not complete his schooling, and certainly considerable fluency in Tamil and English. He was energetic and enthusiastic and was imprisoned in the Vellore jail for his participation in the freedom struggle; his prison experiences were often recalled by his intimates.

Sadasivam took some effort to erase his past before he met Subbulakshmi and it is unclear now when he married Apitakuchamba, the daughter of one Gopala Subramaniam, and known always as Parvati in her husband's home. Their elder daughter Radha was born on 11 December 1934 and their younger daughter Vijaya on 20 August 1938.

Parvati's given name, traditionally Saivite, of the goddess at Tiruvannamalai, has an interesting derivation of '...the powerful female deity, "Apitakuchamba", or "the goddess with the undrunk breast". It is a celebration of womanhood without any need to be apologetic about not having succumbed to the reproductive cycle.'[5]

Nothing in Subbulakshmi's life, over the nearly seventy years still ahead of her, was to remain the same. Sadly, the same was to be true of Parvati, though she had but four years left. Even Subbulakshmi's most sympathetic biographer has admitted that Parvati's options more or less vanished when her husband met the girl from Madurai.[6] She appears to have been a simple girl from a small town, probably born around 1915 and married around 1931 or 1932. Her flower-like beauty is remembered in family circles but it was not enough. Nothing in her background or experience had prepared her for what now faced her. A contemporary author has reminded us that '(t)he most common form of companionship in the world is the bad marriage' and this was Parvati's inevitable fate.[7]

Sadasivam was fascinated by Subbulakshmi; what will always be a matter of speculation is what it was in her that appealed to him. With the benefit of hindsight it appears that to him what always mattered the most was the potential she represented for fame and which, it must be acknowledged, he was able to perceive. It will always stand to his credit that he broke from convention, that he offered Subbulakshmi marriage and that he protected her with everything he had, but it is unclear what else he offered her. There has been much hagiographic writing surrounding this high-profile couple. Their mutual admiration of each other, their shared religious observances, her ready willingness to comply with his demands on- and off-stage, their sense of family, these and more have been much aired;[8] but it has never been suggested that theirs was a romantic relationship.

It is hard, and not particularly pleasant, to speculate on what fate might have dealt Subbulakshmi had Sadasivam not crossed her path. More film roles, perhaps, but this path would not have been without its perils. Throughout her life, she gave the impression of extreme vulnerability and even a mother's protection may not have been of much use to a single woman seeking a future in the world of mass entertainment. The sad life of the gifted N.C. Vasanthakokilam or the failed career of Rajam Pushpavanam indicate what might have been.

Of course, even without Sadasivam, Subbulakshmi's formidable talent may well have ensured that she achieved distinction as a classical musician; but without Subbulakshmi, Sadasivam would have been long forgotten.

The Trivandrum Sisters[9] sang at the 1937 season, as did Brinda and Muktha, with sister Abhiramasundari on the violin, a recital described by a listener as 'faultless, flawless music and the sweetest for years'.[10] Even a professional critic was impressed, if clumsy in his expression.

> The indolent grace of Muthuswamy Dikshitar's hymn to Tyagaraja and the Sun God and the eternal youth of Gaula and Sourashtram were vividly brought out. In between was Tyagaraja's magnificent paean *'Darinitelusu'* ... Between the handiwork of giants jostled in Brovasamaya of the minor composer from Karur. The Tamil padam in Begada Yarukkakilum was beautiful ... The performance concluded with some light Hindustani music.[11]

Muthuratnambal of Tinnevelly, granddaughter of Nallanayakam, performed Bharatanatyam. Dhanammal played, in what must have been one of her last public performances, on 28 December 1937, a recital, described as 'divine', that included '*Vinapustakadharini*', '*Sadhincene*', '*O Jagadamba*', '*Tulasidalamulace*' and '*Angarakam*' – all songs Subbulakshmi sang often in her middle years.[12]

It was around the time Subbulakshmi met Sadasivam that she began filming for *Sevasadanam*. The film world was not new for her. Shanmukhavadivu herself had acted in *Sangeetha Lava Kusa* (1933); it does seem, however, that though this film had a staggering sixty-plus songs, Shanmukhavadivu may not have sung any of them seeing as she was cast as a washerwoman.[13] Even so, it could not have been an easy decision for the young girl; acting in films was still mildly disreputable, and not a profession for women from respectable families. Historians of film have noted that Durga Khote (1905–91) and Devika Rani (1908–94), two of the earliest stars of the Hindi film, were always promoted as having come from 'good families'.[14] It is, of course, possible that as Subbulakshmi had not yet joined the ranks of respectability, these considerations did not arise.

The gramophone record, the radio and the talking film, each dramatically changed the reach of musical performance. The arrival of the sound cinema enabled an easy transfer of singing stars from the drama theatre to the screen.[15] Touring talkies were known in the Tamil country from 1905 onwards; it was a very popular medium and 108 silent films are believed to have been made but the Tamil cinema dates itself to the silent film *Keechaka Vadham* in 1916, with *Kalidas* in 1931 being the first musical.[16] Both *Bhakta Prahlada* in Telugu, produced in 1931, and *Srinivasa Kalyanam* in 1934 claim to be the first south Indian 'talkie'. Once the technique was learnt, there were a large number of talkies with thirty-six produced in Tamil in 1936 alone.

The lawyer-director K. Subrahmanyam was quick to recognize the potential of the new medium and the tremendous potential of singing stars.[17] His first film *Pavalakkodi* (1934) had fifty-five songs with Papanasam Sivan as lyricist. Subbulakshmi was by no means the first of the Tamil singing stars. Her namesake S.D. Subbulakshmi (1918–87),

K. Subrahmanyam's second wife, was the star of *Pavalakkodi* and T.P. Rajalakshmi (1911–64) in *Kalidas* (1931) may have been the first singing star.[18] Dasari Ramatilakam (1905–52) was another very well-known singer, dancer and actor who, starting with the Telugu *Chintamani* in 1933, went on to star in several other mythological films.[19]

Subrahmanyam, who directed mythological films, and also films with a social message, gave Subbulakshmi her first film *Sevasadanam*. There is a mildly salacious story that he had intended to cast Subbulakshmi, in her first film role, in the mythological story of Vipranarayana; however as this would have involved her wearing a costume, or the lack of one, as befitted a temple dancer in a Tamil film, she is believed to have refused.[20] It is recalled that over the year and a half of film shooting, around late 1936 to early 1938, K. Subrahmanyam housed Subbulakshmi and, presumably, her mother, in the first floor of the house where his own wife S.D. Subbulakshmi lived and that it was during this time that Sadasivam's courtship was conducted.[21] Years later, it was recalled of Subrahmanyam that 'at a time when South Indian films were a photographic version of crude stage plays, he took it away from its shackles and set it on a course which combined art with idealism'.[22] The film's co-star was the very young Saridey Varalakshmi (1927–2009), whose musical skills were sufficiently impressive for her to have been cast alongside the already popular Subbulakshmi.[23]

The novel by Munshi Premchand (1880–1936) is set in Benares, now Varanasi, and was first written in Urdu in 1917 'under the titillating title *Bazaar-e-husn* or the "Bazaar of beauty"'. It was recast in Hindi in 1918 'under the sober and uninspiring title Sevasadan or the "house of service"'.[24] A Tamil translation by the social worker S. Ambujammal (1899–1984) was serialized in *Ananda Vikatan*.[25] The tale itself is somewhat tedious and preachy, but the theme of the film was cutting quite close to home.[26] A young Brahmin girl married to a much older man, who ill-treats her, leaves him to become a professional singer, with all the probabilities of that decision, and subsequently reforms to set up a school for the girl children of women in a similar situation. Three and a half hours into the film the repentant, but still old, husband returns to her. The film does not exist anymore and very little remains other than unflattering photographs of Subbulakshmi gazing into a mirror, scowling on a swing and carrying a badminton racket.

The magazine *Filmindia*, edited by the flamboyant Baburao Patel (1904–82) of Bombay, carried a full-page photograph in its April 1938 issue of 'Miss M.S. Subbulakshmi, known as "Nightingale of the South" in Sevasadan'.[27] The film was released on 2 May 1938 under the banner of Madras United Artists Corporation and Chandraprabha Cinetone, Madras, of which the latter may already have passed into Sadasivam's ownership. *Ananda Vikatan* reviewed it at length, and for all we know, Sadasivam may have written or at least motivated the review. 'M S Subbulakshmi did not disappoint us with her fantastic songs.'[28] *Filmindia* found it too long but did concede that 'Miss M.S. Subbulakshmi has given beautiful music though she has sung too many songs.'[29] More astutely the paper noted, 'Subbulakshmi who happens to be a favourite will prove a great factor in the success of the picture' but could not help the condescending comment that the film would do well 'in the Tamil districts'.[30] Kalki Krishnamurthi was cautious in his appreciation, commending the music but not the acting.[31]

N.D. Varadachariar saw it twice, opining the first time that it was 'a Tamil talkie far above current Tamil standards', though his second experience was of 'a very exhausting picture of over four hours' duration'.[32] However, its high point was ten songs which included seven by Papanasam Sivan and Pallavi Gopala Iyer's '*Needu charana*'/Kalyani and Bhadracala Ramdas' '*Ennaganu*'/Pantuvarali, both concert staples of Subbulakshmi's later years, the latter being performed even sixty years later.[33] It also had a variation on the lively '*Syama sundara*'/Tilang, originally taught to her in Madurai by Narayan Rao Vyas and '*Guha saravanabhava*'/Simhendramadhyamam, popularized by Saraswathi Bai.

Indeed, the music scholar Sriram V. believes that Saraswathi Bai herself was a role model to the young Subbulakshmi.[34]

But if *Sevasadanam* had its artistic problems, the musician-critic Gowri Ramnarayan sees in it an experience which made the young Subbulakshmi recognize that 'charity can empower people'.[35] Both Sumati, the protagonist of the film, and Subbulakshmi, the actor playing the role, discover that giving of oneself can be ennobling.

The photograph of Subbulakshmi, reproduced in *Filmindia*, and autographed by her in English, is interesting only in that with no schooling whatsoever she should have learnt to write in a cursive script. In a late recollection, Sadasivam's daughter Vijaya noted that Subbulakshmi could speak Telugu and Kannada in addition to her native Tamil, and that her earliest learning may even have been in the now forgotten *grantha* script. Vijaya also recalled that Subbulakshmi attended the Good Shepherd Convent along with Radha and her, in the early 1940s, in order to learn English from one Mother Cecilia.[36]

Dhanammal died in 1938, playing the vina at her select gatherings, despite illness, almost till the end.[37] The civil servant and music critic S.Y. Krishnaswamy wrote years later of 'the simplicity of distilled grandeur' of her music and of how *rasikas* of old '... went on a Friday evening to a narrow street in Georgetown, climbed the ill-lit stairs to a partly covered terrace and listened with bated breath but unwhispering humbleness to a blind old lady, playing on the veena and singing in accompaniment'.[38] A contemporary wrote, 'A greater loss never befell art in decades and perhaps, she will not have her peer for years and years.'[39]

It is difficult to assess her life's work at this distance of time based only on a few recordings which still survive as curiosities and which could sound strange and unaccented to the modern ear.[40] Years later, her granddaughter Balasaraswati said of her, 'She set an ideal of richness and subtlety of emotional expression that shines like a lamp before those who have heard and appreciated her music.'[41] Another distinguished musician said, more than sixty years after the event, of a 1930 recital by Dhanammal, 'I had not heard Veena music of that kind before, nor have I heard it since.'[42] A similar tribute came from a musicologist of the north, writing, almost certainly, of Dhanammal: 'In 1914 I heard a great woman veena player of the South ... The old lady's fingering was most accurate and she had a dignity which I have seldom found in others.'[43] In a whimsical but deeply felt tribute, Kalki Krishnamurthi, who had worshipped at her Friday soirées, observed that Dhanammal in the world of music would be remembered as would be in their respective worlds the names of Kamban, Asoka, Napoleon and Tyagaraja![44]

What specifically were the highlights of Dhanam's musical style and how was she different from the trends of the day? Lakshmi Subramanian spends considerable time on trying to understand her vina technique.[45] Her style depended absolutely on the composed piece and her art lay in its sensitive understanding and interpretation. This was as true of devotional compositions of the trinity as of love poetry. Composed pieces could be embellished with raga *alapana*, an elaboration of the raga, though this was usually brief, or with *tanam*, an extension of raga elaboration using highly accentuated phrases. The mood was always slow and reflective. There was no gimmickry, no flashiness, no aggressive demonstration of *laya*, but instead a refined performance which to Dhanammal represented the best of a woman's art.[46]

Tanjavur Dhanam's death was widely, and publicly, mourned, with memorial meetings held across the region.[47] The diarist Varadachariar writes of a memorial meeting with a 'hundred minutes of splendid music by all the granddaughters of Dhanam'.[48] Possibly the most thoughtful tribute was paid ten years after her death by *Sangitha Kalanidhi* T.V. Subba Rao in powerful words, some extracted here.

Dhanam was no composer but only a musician. She learnt from the most authentic sources and ... could render various varnas, *svarajatis*, *tillanas* in a style that combined both grace and power. *Padams* and *javalis* were her forte ... She had the benefit of contact with the greatest musicians of her times and assimilated their peculiar excellences ... She thus combined not only the noblest elements of a hoary tradition but every variety of contemporary merit. Her play was thus the epitome of all that is good in music. To practise the instrument as well as to sing after the manner of Dhanam is to cultivate the true beauty and grace of Carnatic music.[49]

Sixty years later, much the same language could have been used about Subbulakshmi. She, in her time, became the epitome of all that was good in music.

There were other interesting goings-on at this time. The accounts are sketchy and the dates are confusing, but somewhere after Subbulakshmi's meeting with Sadasivam in 1936 and before the release of *Sevasadanam*, Shanmukhavadivu appears to have returned hastily to Madurai with her daughter with a view to securing Subbulakshmi's future in the time-honoured way of her community, possibly involving an association with a notable from Ramnad.[50] The daughter seems to have revolted and fled, alone, to Madras to Sadasivam's protection, possibly early in 1938.

That one decisive journey would never be retraced. 'Shanmugavadivu [sic] was not spurned, as much as just, simply, left behind. Subbulakshmi was the moon that left the earth behind. It had to. Sadasivam triggered the counter-gravity and stabilized the new orb in its own utterly unique space.'[51] That Parvati was alive and in residence, and pregnant, was a matter of detail.[52] The police were involved, and the courts, but Subbulakshmi did not leave Madras, or Sadasivam's house.[53]

These tensions may have died down when it was obvious that she would never return to Madurai, a prospect facilitated by the fact that Parvati, who had left for her father's place for the birth of her second daughter was not to return. It is not even very clear where Vijaya's birth took place in August 1938 but it was possibly in Kulithalai, near Karur.[54] It is equally unclear when exactly Parvati died, but it was possibly early in 1940, said to be of a scorpion bite.

All versions of the story suggest that the child Radha was with Subbulakshmi since 1938, and while it is improbable that Parvati would have abandoned a small child, what seems most likely is that she left leaving Radha in the care of a woman to whom she had already developed an attachment. Radha Viswanathan is always said to have 'begun' her musical career at the age of four, in 1938, when she sat alongside, and possibly sang with, Subbulakshmi. It must be recorded that by all accounts, not least those of Radha and Vijaya themselves, Subbulakshmi gave herself totally to the demands of motherhood. She disliked their being referred to as her step-daughters and for a time saw the rest of her life as being devoted only to home and family.[55]

Through this time, Subbulakshmi was aware of her precarious position, not just as another member of Sadasivam's household but in society in general. For all purposes, she was still, in conventional society, a member of a lower caste and was bound, in the opinion of those who gave themselves the right to rule on such matters, to conduct herself in the manner prescribed. A visit to Bombay in 1939 is known where the young Subbulakshmi, a guest at a Brahmin house, was required to wash the plate on which she ate her meals, a wholesome practice but not one that was expected of other members of the household.[56] Such cruelties were not uncommon. The venerable Gangubai Hangal, late in life, full of age and honours, still recalled singing at a Congress event in Belgaum in 1924 in Gandhi's presence, but her more dominant recollection was of fearing being asked to sit separately to eat and to wash her dishes after eating.[57]

Subbulakshmi's Music Academy recital in 1938, the year Ariyakudi Ramanuja Iyengar presided over the festival, is the first for which we have full concert details. In time she was to give thirty-three 'season' concerts from that stage.[58] Her own presidency was to come in 1968 and the last season appearance was in 1978, with those forty years effectively containing her most sustained contribution to the art of performance.

The concert began with the Bhairavi *varnam* '*Viriboni*', always a favourite, and included '*Sri Maha Ganapati*'/Gaula (which surfaced again in the 1977 Carnegie Hall recital), a few Tyagaraja songs not often heard in later years,[59] '*Ma Ramanan*'/Hindolam and another great favourite '*Needu charana*'/Kalyani, both making the transition from *Sevasadanam* to the concert platform and finally, and almost inevitably, a *ragam-tanam-pallavi* elaboration in Sankarabharanam. There were a multitude of smaller pieces listed, including a *javali*, *tevaram*, *tiruppugazh*, *padam*, Hindustani song and national songs.

Interestingly, Subbulakshmi's late afternoon concert was followed by G.N. Balasubramaniam's night concert, with lightning striking Madras twice the same evening. Balasubramaniam's first Academy appearance had been in the previous season. Reviewing both concerts for his magazine, Kalki highlighted the two main features of Subbulakshmi's music being her voice and the way she used it.[60]

The 'sweet voiced' D.K. Pattammal, now well-established as a regular concert performer, and not yet twenty, won praise for her Music Academy concert in the 1938 season, with Kalki rightly identifying *visranti* or repose as a distinguishing feature of her music.[61] She was already known for complicated *pallavis*, with this recital having a major Todi.[62] Incidentally, Pattammal sang for films. Her patriotic song in K. Subrahmanyam's 1939 hit film *Thyaga Bhoomi* with lyrics by Kalki and music by Papanasam Sivan made her famous and she continued to sing playback through the 1940s.[63] Pattammal's association with Sivan extended over the decades and she sang many of his songs on screen and on stage.[64]

Other young women performers like Vasundhara Devi were also getting noticed. Varadachariar said of her, 'Vasundhara, who acts and sings better than any South Indian I have seen so far.'[65] Her Hindustani music won even Kalki's grudging approval[66] and her records of both Hindustani and Tamil songs were played frequently on radio. The 1939 season at the Music Academy also featured music by Her Highness the Princess Manku Thampuran of Cochin and dance by Miss Lakshmi and Miss Kalanidhi. The two dancers went on to achieve considerable distinction, Lakshmi Shankar as a Hindustani vocalist and Kalanidhi Narayanan as a teacher of dance, specifically *abhinaya*.

The 1938 season saw a young nineteen-year-old N.C. Vasanthakokilam win a prize at the Academy.[67] By all accounts a tempestuous and charismatic artiste, Vasanthakokilam did not perform again at the Music Academy's seasons until 1946 but she was an enormously popular and successful singer.[68] Kalki wrote appreciatively of her singing and of her strong voice being suitable both for radio and for the stage.[69] Her recordings sold well and she gave frequent concerts for the rest of her short life at the Tyagaraja *aradhana* at Tiruvaiyaru.[70]

Vasanthakokilam is an enigmatic character who, had she lived longer and had better luck with the men in her life, may well have continued to draw the same record audiences that Subbulakshmi did, though she may not have aspired, from what little we know of her, to the same conservative lifestyle that became Subbulakshmi's lot.[71] To start with, there was the matter of the name change. At a time when women from traditional families were struggling with coming to terms with modernity, and when marriage may or not have been an option for them, Kamakshi, daughter of Nagapattina Chandrasekhara Iyer, of Irinjalakuda, Kerala, walked out of a marriage, joined the films, and took the name N.C. Vasanthakokilam, with its deliberate suggestion of devadasi origins.

Somewhere in the 1930s, Subbulakshmi made a highly successful 'first' appearance in Bangalore. T. Chowdiah may have had something to do with this, and possibly accompanied her on the violin.[72] Decades later, a *rasika*, in happy remembrance of that occasion, contributed to a new institution in Subbulakshmi's name.[73]

Sakuntalai, Subbulakshmi's second film, is known now only for its very pretty and tuneful duets but has been described as '[t]he finest film of 1941'.[74] Directed by the maverick American director Ellis R. Dungan (1909–2001) and produced by Chandraprabha Cinetone, it had lyrics by Papanasam Sivan, which were set to music by Thuriayur Rajagopala Sarma (1905–86), both big names in the world of classical performance.[75] T. Sadasivam was credited with the dialogue, though it has been suggested that this was a front for a more serious writer who did not wish to be publicly associated with screenplay writing.

Ellis Dungan recalled late in life that he was approached in 1939 to direct 'a film for M.S. Subbulakshmi and her *Kalki* magazine publisher husband, T. Sadasivam'.[76] Since the marriage did not take place till July 1940 this suggests that Subbulakshmi and the still-married Sadasivam were regarded as a couple by those in the business, and also that Sadasivam was quite in control of any professional decision Subbulakshmi came to take. There is a recollection that the garland worn by Shakuntala in the ashram scenes was kept by Sadasivam and placed around Subbulakshmi's neck every day before shooting commenced.[77] All this makes the involvement of G.N. Balasubramaniam as the film's hero Dushyanta much the more curious.

The choice of Kalidasa's most famous play, a love story, is interesting. Shakuntala is the embodiment of modesty, as befits a child of an ashram, but she is also the daughter of an *apsara*, a celestial courtesan. And in the words of a contemporary scholar, Dushyanta is 'an ideal man and king. Dushyanta is so integrated, his passions so well aligned with his understanding of morality, he cannot act, nor even think inappropriately, his very attraction to Shakuntala must mean she cannot be an ascetic woman.'[78]

The story of Shakuntala, told in Sanskrit, is but a link in the much larger tradition. In her magical exploration of the theme, the Sanskritist Wendy Doniger points out that cutting across cultures and centuries we have tales of forgetful and wayward kings, exploited, if clever, heroines, unacknowledged children, and recognition finally arising out of the production of a ring, quite often through the intermediation of a fish.[79] In all these tellings, the basic theme is passion, betrayal, abandonment and reunion.

G.N. Balasubramaniam was not a great actor, but he was a charismatic and wildly popular musician and had acted in at least two films, *Bhama Vijayam* and *Sati Anasuya*. He plays a surprisingly endearing Dushyanta, not that *Filmindia* thought so. As the contemporary poet Arundhathi Subramaniam writes,

A man with wine-dark eyes who knows
Of the velvet liquors and hushed laughter
In curtained recesses[80]

The inescapable truth is that Subbulakshmi and her co-star were thrown together through the shooting of the film, and this partnering gave rise, at least on her side, to great love. Her biographer T.J.S. George, who has had access to a selection of her letters written in this period, is in no doubt on this score, as no one can be who reads even the extracts, presumably in translation, selectively presented by him. It is not known when the two met but it seems that Sadasivam accepted G.N. Balasubramaniam as the film's hero only with reluctance, though this is possibly more because he feared Balasubramaniam's popularity with the public would eclipse that of Subbulakshmi, and not because he expected anything more to be happening. In any case, the film is billed as her film, with Balasubramaniam getting a mention only in the list of the cast. What is even more curious is that the dialogue for which Sadasivam took all credit is fairly intimate and the happy on-screen pairing of the two musicians quite obvious for all to see. The duets '*Manamohananga*' and '*Premayil*' will live as long as film music lives but, in the event, the strong-willed Subbulakshmi who fled her mother's home chose the prestige and protection of Sadasivam's name.

Over the next twenty-five years, Subbulakshmi and G.N. Balasubramaniam lived and worked in the same space. There is evidence that she met socially with members of his family. His student T.R. Balasubramaniam was one of Radha's early teachers. Subbulakshmi was a leading performer when G.N. Balasubramaniam presided over the annual concerts at the Music Academy in December 1958. There is no evidence that there was any connection between them, but she could not have forgotten him.

Decades later, after Subbulakshmi's passing, a senior *vidvan* who had taught her a few songs reminisced that she had always 'a soft corner' for Balasubramaniam.[81] In a 1972 interview, and assuming as we must that her replies were written by Sadasivam, she spoke appreciatively of musicians who 'gave body and shape to the present concert pattern' and included in this list Ariyakudi Ramanuja Iyengar, Maharajapuram Viswanatha Iyer, Musiri Subramania Iyer, Madurai Mani Iyer and G.N. Balasubramaniam.[82] Many years later, the family of G.N. Balasubramaniam even proudly announced that Subbulakshmi and Sadasivam had attended a wedding in the family.[83] And in another odd reference, Balasubramaniam's daughter recalled that Sadasivam had once described her father as a perfect gentleman.[84]

Sakuntalai was keenly anticipated and finally released in December 1940 and did well with Subbulakshmi '...on her way to becoming a legend, (playing) the title role. She was no great actor, but her beauty, rare charisma and fascinating voice impressed everyone without exception.' Even *Filmindia*, which otherwise trashed the film, held that 'M.S. Subbulakshmi, because of her musical talents and her intense popularity all over the South, is easily the biggest drawing card in the picture.'[85]

The duets were, of course, popular, but connoisseurs went to see the film for Balasubramaniam's Kambhoji *viruttam* and the song in Kuntalavarali.[86] Many viewers went to see the comedy scenes. The posters screamed, 'Kokilagana M.S. Subbulakshmi, The Siren Star of the South in the matchless Tamil musical *Sakuntalai* supported by the master mirth makers N.S. Krishnan T.S. Durairaj, T.A. Mathuram.'[87]

Not all viewers were impressed. The acerbic N.D. Varadachariar fussed, 'The Tamil screen will never improve unless we have there a different set of actors – or is it that the Tamil genius abhors the histrionic art?'[88] A safe conclusion is that the acting was not up to much but then the acting was not meant to be the point.

It is interesting that though Subbulakshmi was well known, she was by no means the only aspiring star in Madras, or even the only star with that name. The Madras United Artists Corporation had featured one G. Subbulakshmi, a singer with many popular long-playing records to her credit,[89] in *Baktha Chetha*, where her co-star was Papanasam Sivan. The corporation was about to begin shooting *Ahimsa Sakthi* with S.D. Subbulakshmi.[90] Singing on the radio were a V. Subbalakshmi, a P.L. Subbalakshmi, a J. Subbulakshmi and, a few years later, a K. Subbulakshmi. There was a T.S. Subbulakshmi playing the flute. And then again, there was Subbulakshmi of Trivandrum.[91]

Our Subbulakshmi was also performing. There is a record of a ninety-minute radio recital on 16 May 1939 with some songs not heard in later years, '*Tattvamariya*'/Ritigula, '*Kapali*'/Mohana, '*Vallagada*'/Sankarabharanam, '*Ma ramanan*'/Hindolam, '*Meevalla*'/Kapi, '*Vandinam*'/

Todi, 'Paramukham'/Kharaharapriya, 'Karuna'/Hemavati, 'Andavanae'/ Shanmukhapriya, a *padam* in Saveri, a ragamalika, something described as 'a light song' and finally 'a boquet [sic] of miscellanies'.[92] In ninety minutes this must have been a brisk business.

Shooting for the film did not prevent her from presenting what, from the thoughtful choice of songs, was an outstanding recital at the Music Academy in the 1939 season, a concert which raised record funds.[93] The fare, which began with a now unknown *varnam* in Natakuranji, included some pieces which never left her repertoire such as 'Meevalla'/ Kapi, which was still being presented by her sixty years later, 'Mariyada gadayya'/Bhairavam and 'Needu charana'/Kalyani, both repeated from the previous year and most famously 'Ennaganu Rama bhajana'/Pantuvarali.

However, there are songs in that concert that vanished from her stock: Dikshitar's 'Chintayama'/Bhairavi, Trivadi Duraiswami Iyer's 'Elagu daya vachu'/Sankarabharanam, Tyagaraja's 'Nadasudha'/Arabhi and Kavikunjara Bharati's *Ivanaro*/Kambhoji. There were other Tamil songs, Sivan's 'Thamasamen'/Todi and 'Kapali'/Mohana and Muthiah Bhagavathar's sprightly 'Jalandhara'/Valaji, all leading up to a *ragam-tanam-pallavi* in Shanmukhapriya. Interestingly, two songs from this concert, 'Chintayama'/Bhairavi and 'Ivanaro'/Kambhoji, were presented by G.N. Balasubramaniam in his Music Academy concert the previous year.[94] It is tempting to speculate that Subbulakshmi learnt them from him.

It is necessary to look carefully at these early concerts. They reflect a very close attention to presenting a growing repertoire, a matter to which she paid less and less attention as she grew older. Even by this time, she was beginning to repeat herself at the same location. Kalki Krishnamurthi observed cannily of her 30 December 1939 recital that while many features of her singing, the voice projection, the *alapanas*, choice of songs and even the *tukkadas* were the same as of a few years earlier, she managed to infuse a freshness into them.[95] This is a gift on which she fully capitalized. One endearing feature of this concert needs to be better known. Subbulakshmi was so lost in her music that she concluded '*Needu charana*', a piece in Kalyani and then began a Kalyani *alapana* again. Such a thing would never have been allowed to happen in the Sadasivam years. And another important conclusion one can draw from these early concerts is that Subbulakshmi had not yet begun to think of herself as a devotional singer.

By the time *Sakuntalai* was completed and well before its December 1940 release, Subbulakshmi and Sadasivam were married on 10 July 1940. The details of this ceremony have been recounted often. The marriage was registered under the Special Marriages Act, with K. Srinivasan (1887–1959) of the *Hindu* and M.S. Venkataraman (1902–67), a civil servant and distant relative, as witnesses. K. Srinivasan was an active promoter of Pattammal and Sundarambal as well and the patronage of the *Hindu* counted for something. M.S. Venkataraman was a friend of film director K. Subrahmanyam and knew Subbulakshmi from *Sevasadanam* days. Their families were close and Subbulakshmi even sang at the wedding celebrations of his eldest daughter just days before her own.[96] The formal registration of the marriage was followed by a very small affair at the temple in Tiruneermalai, then a distant suburb of Madras, now completely absorbed into Chennai, even if the papers reported the presence of 'a distinguished gathering'.[97] Kalki Krishnamurthi and his wife were, according to one account, present as also *Rasikamani* T.K. Chidambaranatha Mudaliar (1882–1954), a connoisseur and aesthete.[98]

The involvement of such grandees of upper-caste Madras society was presumably to silence mutterings of any sort, this having less to do with the origins of Sadasivam's new bride than with the haste with which the proceedings were being conducted, so soon after Parvati's passing. Ellis Dungan took a well-known photograph of the garlanded couple.[99] A photograph taken by one V.I. Neelakantan featured in the *Illustrated*

Weekly of India published out of Bombay, aimed at the upper class, non-south Indian reader with the caption 'Popular Music Star Married'.[100]

Soon after the wedding, the newly-wed couple are known to have travelled to the parental home of Sadasivam's first wife and brought back with them a motherless, and sadly neglected, Vijaya, who is known to have always been grateful for this act.[101]

The Isai Vellalar Sabha in Kumbakonam honoured Subbulakshmi with the title *Isaivani* in 1940 and in doing so recognized one of their own.[102] Presented by Semmangudi Srinivasa Iyer and the violinist *Sangitha Kalanidhi* Kumbakonam Rajamanickam Pillai (1898–1970), it was an honour Subbulakshmi treasured.[103] In hindsight, it is odd that Sadasivam should have allowed this public tribute by this particular *sabha* but perhaps in those early days any attention was welcome.

In the same month, December 1940, that *Sakuntalai* was released, Subbulakshmi had another high-profile billing at the Music Academy's season concert, including being featured on the cover of the Conference Souvenir and Concert Programme,[104] but the historian Sriram V. has discovered that the recital was cancelled owing to differences between the management of the Academy and the artiste's husband. Such events were to recur. Over the years, *sabha* organizers learnt the hard way that Sadasivam was at all times to be kept happy. The success of the film probably gave him the sense of entitlement to do as he did.

As an exercise in mapping Subbulakshmi's concert style, however, the bill of fare of the aborted concert makes good reading. '*Sarasiruha*'/Nata, '*Vinayakuni*'/Madhyamavati and '*Mamava pattabhirama*'/Manirangu were to recur often in later years, but Syama Sastri's '*Marivere*'/Anandabhairavi disappeared. She was at that time under the influence of Papanasam Sivan, represented by two famous songs, '*Kana Kann kodi*'/Kambhoji and '*Paramukham*'/Kharaharapriya, though these were not to remain favourites. Muthiah Bhagavathar's enchanting '*Vijayambike*'/Vijayanagari was listed followed by a *ragam-tanam-pallavi* in Todi.

We know very little of Vadivambal's activities during these times. At the time of Subbulakshmi's marriage, she would still have been in her very early teens. There is a photograph taken at Muthiah Bhagavathar's house in Trivandrum of Shanmukhavadivu and her daughters with Muthiah Bhagavathar, his wife, the child Radha and others.[105] Mother and daughters seem cheerful and happy, and from the similarity to other photographs, we can reasonably date this to 1940. There is another photograph of Sadasivam with Subbulakshmi and her siblings, all four of them wearing garlands and posing for the camera.[106] Whatever the bad blood following Subbulakshmi's escape from Madurai to Madras, some sort of peace must have been established, post marriage, at least for the photograph.

For Subbulakshmi, the decade ended on a high. She had successfully left Madurai, and the compunctions of family, behind her. Of Joseph Conrad and his abandoning Poland for the English-speaking world, Maya Jasanoff writes, 'You could spend your whole life in the place where you were raised or you could leave and never come back.'[107] Subbulakshmi was by now a recognized star, with two high-profile films to her account. She had been hailed as *Kokilagana* and had made a mark as a serious concert artiste with crowd-pulling *sabha* appearances. She had comprehensively reinvented herself by marriage into upper-caste society and, at twenty-four, had acquired a partner who saw her as his life's mission. But she never 'came back' to Madurai.

As G.N. Balasubramaniam said to her, albeit as Dushyanta to Shakuntala, '*Nee patta mahishi aahapore*', 'You are going to become a great queen.'[108]

6

The Politics of Language

அலைமகள் கலைமகள் பணி கீர்வாணி[1]

('*Sweet-voiced friend of Lakshmi and Sarasvati!*',
from Papanasam Sivan's '*Devi neeye thunai*' in the raga Kiravani)

THE years immediately after marriage were very busy. Sadasivam and R. Krishnamurthi had set up a new paper, '*Kalki*',[2] and Sadasivam's new wife was persuaded to go before the camera again to raise funds for this venture. In the event, Subbulakshmi invested ₹20,000 towards twenty shares in the paper; significantly, fifteen of these were in her husband's name and five in the name of Kalki Krishnamurthi.[3]

Savitri was released in 1941 and involved an extended stay of nine months in Calcutta where the film was shot. Subbulakshmi's lifelong friendship with Narayani (Chinnani) Mahadevan (1920–2014) began at this time, and included frequent correspondence and visits to each other's houses.[4] Till the end of her days, a photograph taken at that time would be at Subbulakshmi's side, of the musician and her friend.[5]

It is not easy to track down a version of the film today though there is a record of Subbulakshmi attending a screening in Chennai in March 1997.[6] The lyricist for many of the songs was again Papanasam Sivan, a composer of great repute, many of whose songs became staple items in Subbulakshmi's concert repertoire. At least one of Subbulakshmi's songs, '*Aggini Endrariyaro*', a ragamalika in Kedaragaula, Hemavati and Saveri can be found on the Internet as well as a few of the songs of Shanta Apte, the Marathi actor, who, indeed, played the title role. Subbulakshmi was cast as Narada, the celestial minstrel, and her songs included '*Bhajare Gopalam*'/Hindolam and '*Bruhi Mukundeti*'/Kuranji, which survived the film and entered the Carnatic repertory. This was a popular role for women and there were others who played Narada, particularly Vasanthakokilam, twice, and T. Suryakumari.[7] Even G.N. Balasubramaniam had played Narada on screen, twice, in *Bhama Vijayam* (1934) and *Sathi Anasuya* (1937).

The casting of Shanta Apte is interesting. For one, she was, at the time, much the bigger star, a larger-than-life character who was well known for her theatrics, on and off screen. Born, like Subbulakshmi, in 1916, she appeared in her first film at sixteen and was hugely successful as a singing star by the time she was twenty. She had learnt music from one Narayan Rao Thite even if she had had no lessons in acting.[8] One of her famous roles, in *Kunku*, was, rather like Subbulakshmi's in *Sevasadanam*, as the young bride of a much older man. In 1942 itself, just as *Savitri* was released, she was playing the role of an activist urging a group of tribal people to agitate against a set of forest contractors led by her husband, a very different comment on harmonious marital relations from the story of Satyavan and Savitri. But Shanta Apte was unlucky; her career ended and she died before she was fifty.[9]

Her preoccupation with *Savitri* notwithstanding, Subbulakshmi performed at the Music Academy at its 1941 season, the unpleasantness of the previous year having been forgotten, and the Academy even repeating the honour of featuring Subbulakshmi on the cover of the Concert Souvenir and Concert Programme. It is the first recorded instance of her singing the ubiquitous '*Vatapi Ganapatim*' of Muthusvami Dikshitar in Hamsadhwani, which she sang at the Academy the next year as well, innumerable times again and in her last major public appearance in 1997. Syama Sastri's *'Brovavamma'*/Manji was presented, and again in 1942, but did not survive in her longer-term repertoire. There were three songs of Papanasam Sivan, *'Deviyai pujai'*/Kamavardhini, *'Paramukham'*/Kharaharapriya and *'Ma daya'*/Vasanta, and it is pleasing to speculate that she learnt at least two of them on the sets of *Savitri*. Two songs of Tyagaraja, *'Ela ni daya radu'*/Athana and *'Kaddanuvariki'*/Todi led on to a *ragam-tanam-pallavi* in, inevitably, Sankarabharanam.

There is a record of a Gokhale Hall concert in 1942, with Kalki writing appreciatively of Subbulakshmi's Kharaharapriya and Sankarabharanam, at the very location where a scant eight years earlier she had not been allowed to perform.[10] The 1942 Music Academy concert saw some new songs but favourites such as *'Ennaganu'* in Pantuvarali were already beginning to reappear. *'Sabhapati'* in Abhogi and *'Pakkala nilabadi'* in Kharaharapriya, never to leave Subbulakshmi's repertory, were newly presented and finally a *ragam-tanam-pallavi* in Mayamalavagaula. Speculating only on the basis of the few concert lists available, it is clear that here was constant learning, even at times of personal turmoil and professional commitments. This speaks of great discipline and diligence. Among the senior musicians who over the 1940s taught Subbulakshmi, *Sangitha Kalanidhi* Mazhavarayanendal Subbarama Bhagavathar (1888–1951) stands out; he taught Subbulakshmi the art of *pallavi* singing.[11] In a late recollection to a confidante, she remembered Subbarama Bhagavathar as the teacher she loved the most.[12]

Subbulakshmi's first meeting with Gandhi was on a visit to Sevagram in 1941.[13] In her own recollection of this meeting, sixty years later, she sang Sankarabharanam for him, noting with some wonder, happily and gratefully but improbably, that he had known that her rendering of that raga was quite famous.[14]

The Ashrama Bhajanavali used in Gandhi's ashrams was the source of many of the bhajans which became a part of Subbulakshmi's repertoire. Of particular importance is 'Vaishnava jana to', which she sang over many years to a tune set by one Cambridge-educated Vaidyanathan.[15] This song, interestingly, was not her property alone and Gandhi's liking for it may have had something to do with its popularity. Pattammal sang it in Sindhubhairavi,[16] as did Ariyakudi Ramanuja Iyengar[17] and, most surprising of all, Brinda and Muktha.[18] K.S. Narayana Iyengar (1903–59), Mysore Asthana Mahanataka Veena (Gottuvadyam) Vidwan, recorded the Sindhubhairavi version played on the gottuvadyam, the instrument now called chitraveena. Then there is a rendering by the actress-singer Amirbai Karnataki (1906–65). Lata Mangeshkar's version, set to raga Misra-Khamaj, is possibly the best known outside south India, if lacklustre. Contemporary musicians continue to sing it set to this basic tune.[19] A much-publicized version sung by singers from over 124 countries was released in 2018, again using the same Misra-Khamaj. A version sung in the qawwali style by Pakistani singers is available on the Internet.

'Vaishnava jana to' is a hymn with a continuous presence in the collective memory of the subcontinent. It is a simple verse with a powerful message of brotherhood. Gandhi's own translation of this hymn is workmanlike.[20]

> He is a Vaishnava who identifies himself with others' sorrows and in so doing has no pride about him. Such a one respects every one and speaks ill of none. He controls his speech, his passions and his thoughts. May his mother be blessed. He is equi-disposed towards all, has no desires, regards another's wife as his mother, always speaks the truth and does not touch other people's property. He labours neither under infatuation nor delusion and withdraws his mind from worldly things; he is intent on Ramanama; his body is his sacred shrine for pilgrimage; he is no miser and is free from

cunning and he has conquered passions and anger. Narasaiyo says: His presence purifies his surroundings.[21]

Subbulakshmi recorded her version along with the other staple of the Gandhian establishment, 'Raghupati Raghava Rajaram'.[22] Throughout her career, she sang it with aplomb, often as the opening piece of a concert of devotional items, as in her Gandhi centenary concert relayed on All India Radio on 2 October 1969.

Subbulakshmi sought out and sang songs that were known across India. In the early 1940s, she recorded with Dilip Kumar Roy; the record has 'Vande Mataram' on one side and the Bengali 'Dhano dhanya pushpa bhora' on the other.[23]

⁂

Subbulakshmi's fame was spreading. In 1941, when she was still only twenty-five, she was felicitated in Bangalore by Sir C.V. Raman and presented a silver tea set by Lady Lokasundari Raman.[24] Earlier that year, she had appeared in a *sabha* concert in Calcutta[25] and shortly thereafter had her portrait unveiled in Vellore by the president of the Madras Music Academy, no less, who noted that she was 'an outstanding personality among vocal musicians (with) a voice of exquisite sweetness and power' and one with 'a fine and accurate sense of rhythm'.[26] These are extraordinary honours for one so young.

Madras was affected by Second World War, and the early months of 1942 saw an out-migration of over 200,000 persons.[27] Several government offices were moved inland, and fear of Japanese attack led to panic, but things settled down by May 1942. It is not immediately clear if and how this impacted the cultural scene. Several prominent musicians, Musiri Subramania Iyer, Madurai Mani Iyer, the Alathur brothers, Saraswathi Bai and others, left Madras for safer places up-country.[28] Subbulakshmi continued to draw record crowds through this period. A contemporary account jokingly calls for police presence at her next recital after what appears to have been chaotic scenes at an earlier one where a thousand people turned up at a venue which could only accommodate 500.[29]

It was at this time that Subbulakshmi, the popular film and concert artiste, became involved in the politics of the day, through an issue that drew in language, cultural identity, caste, music and political representation. This was the call for the promotion of *Tamil Isai*. It was at once a movement for cultural sub-nationalism and a struggle for control over the *sabhas* of Madras, newly developed institutions which offered tremendous potential for the exercise of patronage. The issues involved can be identified easily enough.

The art and practice of Carnatic music was centred in the Tamil-speaking country, amongst a largely Tamil-speaking public. The substantial bulk of what was emerging as the Carnatic repertory was in Telugu and Sanskrit, not least because of the songs composed by the trinity. Tamil is among the most ancient of Indian languages with poetry, drama, devotional verses and other literary forms as in Telugu and Sanskrit, but Telugu songs predominated in the musical repertory, songs meant for musical performance. It is convenient to assume that from the time of the trinity onwards, and thanks to their disciples, their joint body of work in Telugu and Sanskrit set the norm for what was suitable for musical performance. Tyagaraja was writing in his native Telugu but Syama Sastri and Muthusvami Dikshitar did not use their native Tamil and instead chose Telugu, the language of the Nayak court at Tanjore, and Sanskrit, the language of classical poetry and scripture.

These three composers were, in the manner of their times, highly educated men. This was due in the most part to their Brahmin ancestry and the consequent access this gave them to Sanskrit scriptural texts and to ritual practices in temples, conducted always in Sanskrit. Their joint body of work is almost exclusively religious in theme and word. While all three of them were supremely gifted musicians with a superior sense of poetry, metre, rhetoric, literary embellishment, the use of language and of the listener's ear, they were also deeply devout men of more than ordinary spiritual attainments.

The consequence of all this was that their lives' work, already set to alien tongues, was easily identified with upper-caste orthodoxy. This may not have been anyone's intention but post the trinity, the dominant ethos within the world of Carnatic music was Brahmin, with appeal to Brahmin sensibilities. This was a departure from an earlier practice where there was, or so it is believed, greater professional intermingling between people involved in the form and the practice of the arts, whether Brahmin priests and composers or non-Brahmin singers and dancers, dance teachers or instrumentalists of all castes.

With Tamil finding itself outside the fold of the repertory, and with non-Brahmins finding themselves outside the fold of the cognoscenti, it was perhaps inevitable that resentment set in among Tamil people living in their own region being pushed to the margins of the dominant cultural expression of that very region. There were other aggravating features. Traditionally, the practice of music and dance was restricted to certain communities and even if these communities did not cohere to any one caste grouping, all of them were regarded as not of the upper castes. The performing arts were a subaltern profession, a situation under threat of upper-caste appropriation. At the same time, there were signs that the government would act to prohibit the professional activities of devadasi women, the anti-*nautch* movement, and which would, indeed, lead in 1947 to the passing of law on the subject. So not only were the Tamil speakers marginalized by the content and the practice, existing practitioners from among them were being stigmatized as immoral or worse. At the same time, upper-caste women were entering the world of dance and music, secure in their access to the best of the tradition.

Even more aggravating was the growth of new spaces for the performance of music and dance. The temple courtyards, which were accessible to all, and the private salon which, even if not readily accessible, was the domain of the independent professional woman, were being replaced by the city *sabhas*; and while these at least should have been secular spaces, they were in reality clubs for expatriate Brahmins, newly removed from the villages. The men, for it was usually men, who migrated from the villages and small towns to Madras were able to establish themselves as successful professionals because their upper-caste background had given them the education and the opportunities to do so. 'Colonial Madras carved out significant, highly visible domains of Tamil Brahmin privilege, particularly in the civil service, the courts, education and prestige professions.'[30]

The *sabhas* had their own problems with each other. The Music Academy set up in 1928, the Indian Fine Arts Society set up in 1932 and the Mylai Sangeetha Sabha, a defunct association resurrected by Subbulakshmi's husband Sadasivam in 1942, were always squabbling, but this was more to do with patronage and finances than anything else. They were, after all, competing for the attention, and the money, of the same people. To the larger world outside Mylapore,[31] they were all the same, symbols of upper-caste chauvinism, likely to appropriate all that was best in local tradition, and bent on denying access to the subaltern, the vernacular and the original keepers of the arts. Indeed, there was no way this charge could be denied. The Mylai Sangeetha Sabha, in its efforts to draw custom, put out a somewhat impertinent advertisement saying that the Sabha 'has been started in response to the increasing demands from the intelligent public for classical concerts'.[32]

There was a political undertone to much of this. The roots of Dravidian politics in the last century lie in the Justice Party, set up in 1916, a rallying point for non-Brahmin interests. Its main opposition was from the Congress party, dominated by educated professionals, many of whom Brahmin, and was a successful force in Tamil politics till, in due course, it was absorbed into the Self-Respect Movement of E.V. Ramaswami Naicker and later, in 1944, into the Dravidar Kazhagam, the forerunner of the political parties which dominate Tamil Nadu today.

A scholar has noted that 'the rejection of Sanskrit, seen as the language of ritual, and English, as the language of colonial opportunity, went hand-in-hand with Tamil as the true language of self-respect'.[33] So there was political support, even if not always expressed, for the popular view that Brahmin interests were supplanting non-Brahmin interests in the matter of cultural heritage and influence. Equally, as another scholar has noted, while the claims for *Tamil Isai* being made by a non-Brahmin elite had political backing, there was a serious divergence of views between the strong atheist traditions of the Dravidian movement and the ethos of *Tamil Isai*, which had issues not with the non-secular content of songs in the Carnatic repertory but only with the language.[34]

Matters came to a head with the first *Tamil Isai* conference, organized by Rajah Sir Annamalai Chettiar (1881–1948), business magnate and patron of the arts, in 1941, where a call was given for the promotion of Tamil songs. Annamalai Chettiar was a worthy champion for the cause, and widely respected. An enormous volume in tribute, of over 1,100 pages, was produced for his sixtieth birthday in 1941, including a Sanskrit poem composed by Saraswathi Bai.[35]

The establishment responded loftily that music was beyond language and more prosaically that even if one wanted to perform in Tamil, there were no songs of any value that were available. Much of the glory surrounding the trinity stems from the belief that they were *vaggeyakaras*, persons who composed both the words and the music for their works. Even assuming that Tamil texts were available for performance, they would need to be set to tune before they could be presented on the stage. And possibly with malice unintended, the Music Academy went on to honour the distinguished Andhra violinist Dwaram Venkataswami Naidu as *Sangitha Kalanidhi* at the annual festivities in December 1941 – the first time a Telugu-speaking Andhra musician had been so chosen.[36]

With a view to addressing the question more resolutely, Annamalai Chettiar set up the Tamil Isai Sangam on 19 June 1943, a *sabha* like the

Music Academy and other *sabhas*, which would provide a platform for the Tamil cause.[37]

This entire matter bristles with real and perceived inconsistencies. C. Rajagopalachari (1878–1972), always known as Rajaji, and Kalki Krishnamurthi, patron and friend respectively, of Sadasivam and Subbulakshmi, both members of Madras' Brahmin elite, were strongly aligned to the movement for *Tamil Isai*. T.T. Krishnamachari, later a patron and intimate of Subbulakshmi and Sadasivam was at that time closely identified with the establishment and not overly inclined to promote Subbulakshmi. Balasaraswati's partner Sir R.K. Shanmukham Chetty (1892–1953) was firmly with the *Isai* movement, as was *Rasikamani* T.K. Chidambaranatha Mudaliar.[38]

Several senior musicians, mainly instrumentalists or percussionists, closely associated with the Music Academy and other *sabhas*, did not belong to the Brahmin fold. Senior Brahmin singers such as Ariyakudi Ramanuja Iyengar routinely sang Tamil songs, often unforgettably so, but did not side with the *Tamil Isai* activists. There is in the record a letter of Kalki Krishnamurthi to Ariyakudi Ramanuja Iyengar urging him to begin his concerts with a Tamil *pasuram* even if he continued with Tyagaraja after that.[39] Ariyakudi did not oblige; many years later at a public function he said that 'whatever he was today he owed to Sri Thyagaraja'.[40] Several publicly bemoaned the lack of Tamil compositions in concerts.[41] Tyagaraja unwittingly ended up as the focus of the ire of the *Tamil Isai* protagonists even as many of them expressed great regard for his songs.

The inevitable conclusion is that while the movement as it swelled from the ground was genuine enough, the one fact that brought matters to a head, and which demanded that people stand up and be counted, was the growth of the *sabhas* and the possibilities of greater influence, riches and standing in society.

Subbulakshmi cast her lot with the Tamil Isai Sangam. The interesting question is why she chose to do so. It would have been entirely appropriate for her to feel sympathy for the cause, but equally it could be argued that the establishment camp is where she wanted to be, having just secured the protection of a Brahmin husband and the approbation of the larger fold. We can, unfortunately, rule out the possibility that this was entirely her own decision and she is herself on record saying that she did as Sadasivam directed her to; he may have been influenced by Rajaji and more immediately, by Chidambaranatha Mudaliar and Kalki. It is also the case that Sadasivam was always fighting with *sabha* managers and he may have assessed, correctly, that he had much greater bargaining power with a newly set up Sangam if he could offer his wife's presence on their stage.

In any case, Subbulakshmi set upon a determined course of action. Through 1943, she toured the south and Ceylon intensively, singing Tamil songs, many of which were sourced by Kalki and Chidambaranatha Mudaliar. She sang the songs of Suddhananda Bharati and of her old friend Madurai Bhaskara Das, which in addition to being in Tamil were on nationalist themes.[42] Interestingly, N.C. Vasanthakokilam was an enthusiastic supporter of the movement, though she is not often recalled as such.[43] Subbulakshmi was willing to sing at the Music Academy in the 1943 season but did not do so owing to a disagreement between the Academy and Sadasivam on the Tamil songs she meant to sing. The Tamil Isai Sangam, though, gave her a wonderful audience and raised goodly funds from the concert.

In the event she was not seen at the Music Academy in 1944, 1945 and 1946. This too is strange. Subbulakshmi could easily have sung at both venues. She would have drawn crowds anywhere and there were indeed ten musicians in the 1943 season, including G.N. Balasubramaniam, a bigger star than her, who sang at both places. It is quite possible that her boycott of the Music Academy was part of some plan of Sadasivam to force the Music Academy to beseech her presence. And this is indeed what happened some years later, when Subbulakshmi sang at the 1947 season at the Music Academy. Intriguingly, when this happened Sadasivam gave the Music Academy all the funds he had raised for his Mylai Sangeetha Sabha.[44]

With the establishment of the Tamil Isai Sangam and of an annual season as in other *sabhas*, the passion ran out of the movement. Another reason could be the unavailability of a solid repertory of songs in Tamil, on par with what the trinity had produced, to sustain and enliven a healthy concert style. Tamil musicians were reduced to singing either the songs of inferior composers or indifferently tuned religious verses. The Sangam has, however, over the past decades, remained a focus for Tamil music and many contemporary musicians have indeed considerably livened the Tamil concert repertory.

A very interesting development, which needs more study, is the use of raga and Tamil lyrics in the Christian liturgy. This only highlights the case of the proponents of Tamil Isai that the use of the language would increase the spread of the musical form. An equally important point, of course, is that there is nothing in the theory and grammar of Carnatic raga structures that limits their use to Hindu devotional themes.[45]

Subbulakshmi's entry into Madras society brought many remarkable changes in her life. The couple appear to have made a home initially in Kilpauk. There are letters written by Subbulakshmi in 1942 with a stylish letterhead. One reads M S SUBBULAKSHMI CARE T SADASIVAM and another, M S SUBBULAKSHMI SADASIVAM, both with a postal address of Landons Road, Kilpauk, Madras, and an address for telegrams of Kokila, quite the necessary accoutrements for an ambitious professional seeking opportunities.[46]

The household moved shortly to a much grander residence, set in almost three acres, again in Kilpauk, originally Sladen Gardens and now, reflecting the purposes of its new owner, Kalki Gardens.[47] The property was bought in Subbulakshmi's name, and for the first time in her life she was a wealthy woman, a woman of property.[48] For nearly forty years, this was a prized address. Subbulakshmi and her ambitious husband were host to musicians, journalists, politicians, self-proclaimed saints and godmen, and the Madras elite. 'Literary and musical celebrities flocked to [his home-cum-office], as did businessmen and industrialists. Sadasivam's khadi and MS' silks made an amazing combination. His sandal-paste fragrance and her imported perfumes, his laughter, her smile were an enchantment...'[49]

Subbulakshmi is hardly likely to have met Rajaji socially before her marriage, but post-1940 his was a lasting and fundamental presence in her life, right till the very end, when she cancelled her Christmas Day recital at the Music Academy in 1972 on account of his illness; he passed away that same evening.[50] *Rasikamani* T.K. Chidambaranatha Mudaliar was another major presence in the lives of the Sadasivams, writing often, and affectionately, from his home in Tenkasi to both of them. As a friend has observed, 'The girl from Madurai was breathing a different air altogether.'[51]

Even if she were comparatively new to the company she was now keeping, she was famous and much in demand. Mrinalini Sarabhai recalled that at the time of her wedding in 1942, she had planned only a simple ceremony with Subbulakshmi singing at the function.[52] In the event this did not happen, but there were many other society weddings where she was singing, in the families of judges, Indian Civil Service officers and wealthy businessmen, not to mention up-country gentry.

Amongst the many prominent members of the social and cultural elite, one whose presence in Subbulakshmi's life we have noted and whose influence came to matter greatly was certainly Kalki R. Krishnamurthi. A well-regarded journalist, freedom fighter, littérateur and widely read novelist, Kalki was at the *Ananda Vikatan* magazine with Sadasivam.[53] He wrote political propaganda, music, dance and film reviews, biographies, film scripts and had translated Gandhi. Sadasivam and he had met as early as 1921, both united in their love for the songs of Subramania Bharati, their chosen vocation of journalism, their devotion to Gandhi in the cause of khadi and in their service of Rajaji. It was a relationship of opposites drawn together in common purpose. It cannot be forgotten that Sadasivam was, at least for the record, Krishnamurthi's employer, but as a sympathetic friend has noted, 'Krishnamurti [sic] wrote the word, Sadasivam published it. The ink was Krishnamurti's, the imprint, Sadasivam's. Krishnamurti was the bullion, Sadasivam the mint. Krishnamurti was the river, Sadasivam the turbine. The result, naturally, was electric.'[54]

Given this degree of intimacy, Kalki would have been a close observer of the goings-on and there is reason to believe that he may have ensured that Sadasivam proposed marriage.[55] Kalki wrote four short stories related to the situation of women of the devadasi community, a subject that both interested and pained him. The women protagonists of these starkly melodramatic stories usually lead sad and unhappy lives and gender injustice moved the author. Kalki was influential in matters musical. His reviews, which were widely read, were cutting and to the point. He would not tolerate cant and big names meant nothing to him. And he was influential with the radio as a member of the Advisory Committee of AIR Madras.[56]

Subbulakshmi respected Kalki's musical knowledge.[57] It is quite possible that she did not get this quality of perceptive criticism from Sadasivam. She might well have got it from G.N. Balasubramaniam but that story was petering out at exactly this time. Kalki wrote songs for her to sing. As early as 1940, she had recorded '*Kandadun kando*' and '*Malai polutinile*'. There were a few other songs written for her and the songs for *Meera*, the 1945 film, constituted the most significant contribution.

Interestingly, neither Kalki nor his wife Rukmini were overawed by Subbulakshmi.[58] He was close to D.K. Pattammal and promoted her assiduously. A song Kalki wrote for Pattammal, '*Poonkuyil koovum*' was a great hit with the public.[59] Subbulakshmi knew this song but never performed it in public, recognizing it as Pattammal's property. Another of his favourites was K.B. Sundarambal. Kalki was close to Vasanthakumari and, indeed, was a witness at her wedding in 1951, the other witness being Kasturi Srinivasan, a witness also to Subbulakshmi's wedding. In these curious ways did the Madras elite cling together.

Links between the Sadasivam and Kalki families were strengthened with the 1949 marriage of Kalki's daughter Anandhi with Sadasivam's nephew Ramachandran and later, after Kalki's passing, in 1957 with the marriage of his son Rajendran with Sadasivam's daughter Vijaya.

Close to the end of his life, Kalki spoke on Subbulakshmi's behalf at a felicitation event. 'She was not vain enough to think,' he said, 'that the title had been bestowed on her for her musical talents ... She felt that the title was awarded perhaps in recognition of the services she had been rendering to public causes through her music.'[60] This is debatable but the warmth of the remark cannot be mistaken. And as Kalki Krishnamurthi neared his untimely end, he requested Subbulakshmi to sing for him; sitting at his bedside, two days before the end, she sang the *viruttam* '*Orutaram Saravanabhava*'.[61]

Most importantly, Subbulakshmi appears to have recognized that Kalki Krishnamurthi always treated her with dignity and respect. He admired her, he may even have been fond of her, but he did not covet her. To Subbulakshmi this was his greatest strength. And many years later, on the occasion of the Kalki centenary, Subbulakshmi emerged from her reclusive widowhood to sing what is possibly the most exquisite song he wrote for her, '*Katrinilae varum geetam*'.[62]

Subbulakshmi's long and distinguished, even unparalleled, career as a performer who supported worthy causes began in the 1940s.

Sadasivam's involvement in the national cause had brought him close to Rajaji; his canny perception of the public arena led to two developments, both enormously significant in shaping Subbulakshmi's public image as a national figure. As a sharp critic has noted, 'If the nation had a voice, Sadasivam at least thought he knew what it sounded like.'[63]

The first was the announcement, in 1944, that she would give five benefit concerts in aid of the Kasturba Gandhi Memorial Fund. The great public grief at Kasturba's passing, in prison, led to the establishment of the Fund, and many national leaders were associated with raising funds for the cause.[64] The Mahatma himself agreed to chair the national committee with the lawyer Alladi Krishnaswami Iyer (1883–1953) chairing the Madras Committee.[65] Subbulakshmi's offer to give five free concerts 'two in the city and three in the mofussil were [sic] gratefully accepted'. She was clearly a star for around this time the papers reported her return from a 'glorious and triumphant tour of North India'.[66]

The second was, of course, the film *Meera*, to which we will return.

The Kasturba Gandhi Memorial Fund recitals were not, in the event, the first benefit recitals which Subbulakshmi gave. 'Kokilagana Isaivani Srimati M.S. Subbulakshmi' sang on 18 June 1944 in the Town Hall, Bangalore, for the Bangalore Gayana Samaja[67] and there may have been other recitals, but the Memorial Fund recitals themselves, held over July–September at Madras, Tiruchirappalli, Madurai, Coimbatore and Thanjavur captivated the public mind, and caught the Mahatma's attention. The concerts certainly served their purpose. The concerts at Madras and Madura [sic] raised ₹12,367 and ₹15,006 respectively, handsome amounts for the time, with the series of five concerts between them raising ₹1 lakh.[68]

This was the beginning of a long innings as a performer for charity. Over the years, large numbers of educational, religious and cultural institutions were supported by Subbulakshmi's munificence. 'Smt.

Subbulakshmi is not only an artiste and devotee but a great humanitarian in making her art the instrument of relieving the distress of the people. She has responded graciously whenever there is a call for raising funds for public institutions, whether it is in the south or north.'[69] Indeed, even in the remaining four years of the 1940s, there were another twenty-six benefit recitals as they came to be called, of which twenty were for educational institutions.[70] A 1946 benefit recital, for instance, in aid of the National College at Tiruchirappalli raised the not insignificant sum of ₹40,000.[71]

That ubiquitous Carnatic institution, the *sabha*, was flourishing over this period, despite the divide caused by the *Tamil Isai* movement. A quick survey of the papers for 1944 show repeated advertisements for music recitals at the Mylai Sangeetha Sabha, the Thyagabrahma Gana Sabha, the Sri Parthasarathy Swami Sabha, the Egmore Dramatic Society and the Rasika Ranjani Sabha. And if Subbulakshmi was rapidly moving ahead to become the leader of the pack, several other women artistes were prominently featured in the city's halls. Pattammal was singing, of course, and for charity and to raise funds for public causes,[72] but so too were N.C. Vasanthakokilam, and Rajam Pushpavanam the only two singers who had the potential to rival Subbulakshmi and, if the fates had been less wilful, to overtake her.[73] Vasanthakokilam, in particular, consciously followed Subbulakshmi's example and was even called an 'MS duplicate'.[74] She released many records, sang often on the radio, acted in films, six of them over the 1940s; 'Whatever MS did, she did.'[75]

'Maduragana Miss N.A. Sundaram of Madras'[76] and M.P. Doraikannu Ammal of Mayavaram were performing. Sundaram appears to have been very popular and was singing in aid of various worthy causes.[77] From the photographs in the papers it seems that Subbulakshmi, Rajam Pushpavanam and N.A. Sundaram all adopted the same look; it is a matter of speculation of who was copying whom.

Rajam Pushpavanam, the daughter of Madurai Pushpavanam Iyer, was well known on the *sabha* circuit and had recorded quite widely. A strong-willed woman, she married young and had children, and was regarded as a singer who would go very far. This happy prospect was not to be. She stopped singing in about 1943 following the sudden death of her eldest child, and after unsuccessfully attempting a return to the stage after her husband's passing in 1950, she gave up performance and retired to teaching and occasional radio programmes.[78]

It is a matter of speculation of how this impacted Subbulakshmi's career. There were obvious similarities between them, and their voices and styles of singing, and Rajam had the advantage of an acknowledged musical pedigree, but with the lack of any family support or an ambitious husband such as both Subbulakshmi and Pattammal had, her concert career languished. Rajam Pushpavanam lives in the happy memories of her students, as a charming, ever-smiling woman, always well-dressed and well-groomed, with a plentiful store of songs. She continued to learn from her cousin Madurai Mani Iyer, to whom she was close, and from Justice T.L. Venkatarama Iyer, more famous as Pattammal's mentor.[79] At this distance of time, perhaps, all one can say is Rajam was simply unlucky.

K.B. Sundarambal, whom even the fastidious N.D. Varadachariar called 'a superb musician with an enslaving, rapturous voice'[80] was at the height of her success, famed for her devotional and patriotic songs.[81] The gramophone companies were discovering new singing stars, and wedding concerts, a uniquely south Indian creation, became the rage. One particular wedding, in a highly placed family, appears to have cleaned out the market with performances by Subbulakshmi, Ariyakudi Ramanuja Iyengar, G.N Balasubramaniam, Saraswathi Bai, Balasaraswati, Tiruvavaduthurai Rajarathnam Pillai, Veeraswami Pillai and others. The programme was even announced in the papers for the edification, doubtless, of those who were not invited to the festivities.[82]

Lalithangi was performing frequently. At her relatively young passing in 1955, senior *vidvans* recalled her musical gifts and vast repertoire, and the fact that she had even learnt *padams* from 'Vina' Dhanammal. It was said of Lalithangi what was always said of her daughter, that she was 'a generous and kind hearted woman'.[83] With the coming of the radio, she was featured often in broadcasts of Purandaradasa songs[84] and was a star in what was a very special event on radio, a performance of the *Gita Govinda* where she sang as Radha to G.N. Balasubramaniam's Krishna and D.K. Pattammal's *sakhi*.[85] The feature included a full seventeen of Jayadeva's *ashtapadis*. Vasanthakumari later recalled that it was at the rehearsals for this programme that she, as a young twelve-year old, met G.N. Balasubramaniam for the first time, later to be her celebrated teacher.[86]

'Kumari Vasanta' was becoming recognized on the radio, singing alone, as early as in December 1938[87] and in January 1942,[88] or with her mother in June 1944 and in January, March and May 1945.[89] Mother and daughter issued records together.[90] An elegant letterhead exists, for *Ganakalabhushani Lalithangi and Vasanta Kumari, Musicians*. They sang together in Delhi and Simla in 1940. Vasanthakumari's first major appearance was in Bangalore in 1941, with T. Abhiramasundari on the violin and Hamsa Damayanti on the mrdangam.[91] There is a record of an appearance at the Music Academy in the 1943 season during the demonstration sessions.[92] The Rasika Ranjani Sabha announced a recital on 28 June 1944, starting at the odd time of 5.25 pm, of Lalithangi and her daughter Vasanthakumari; this may well have been one of the earliest public recitals in Madras of this renowned artiste.[93] Her first appearance at the Music Academy was on 30 December 1944, billed, at the age of sixteen, as 'Srimathi M.L. Vasanthakumari'; in the same season she appeared at the Tamil Isai Sangam.[94] A recital in November 1946,[95] another during the 1946 season which 'took the listeners by storm'[96] and *sabha* concerts in November 1947[97] were all reported in the press.

Other names are found in the record though these singers have now left no trace; P.A. Periyanayaki both acted in films and issued records[98] and Alamelu Mangal of Bombay had high-profile appearances[99] as did the 'Ambur Sisters', Amirthavalli and Sundaravalli.[100] Balam Ramamurthi won first prize at the Music Academy's competition in 1945[101] and, indeed, one Miss Hemamalini, daughter of 'C.K. Vijayaraghavan, Esq., I.C.S.' was actually performing dance.[102]

Interestingly, women singers were often accompanied on the violin and mrdangam by other women. T. Abhiramasundari was, of course, playing for her sisters on the violin, but so were Komalavalli and M.S. Pattammal.[103] Sethu Bai, Kanakambujam, Hamsa Damayanti and Ranganayaki were mrdangam artistes.[104] There is a record of Savitri Ammal who played the gottuvadyam, and T.R. Navanitam and Kesi, both of whom performed on the flute.[105] Early radio recitals, in 1945, by Radha and Jayalakshmi are recorded,[106] in what was a long innings of singing for radio. Concerts of 'C.P. Radha and R. Jayalakshmi' were advertised,[107] and, at least in one recital, with Balasaraswati's brother T. Ranganathan (1925–87) on the mrdangam.

For Subbulakshmi's friend Balasaraswati, the 1940s were a troubled period.[108] She was always proud, and outspoken, about her devadasi heritage and resented the assumptions made in upper-caste society of the character and way of life of women of her community. She had first danced at the Music Academy in 1935 and was a regular feature for the rest of the decade but did not appear on that stage between 1942 and 1949. It is quite possible that while her art had its devoted following, the wider audience was looking for more excitement on stage.

A devotee wrote mournfully to the *Hindu* of an occasion where '... during the earlier part of the evening the unappreciative part of the audience openly and noisily protested against the singing of

Balasaraswathi [sic] and Jayamma and effectively stopped them when they were just getting into form. The dissenters had no better respect for the "abhinaya" that followed either but showed better discretion by walking out. The treat that was afforded to the rest of the gathering will be fresh in their mind for a long time to come'.[109]

There is a record of a tour of Ceylon in 1944 (where the posters screamed clumsily, if accurately, *The Greatest Exponent of the Classical art of South India and Well Known danseuse acclaimed to be the unrivalled Queen of the Art*).[110] Balasaraswati was still young, she knew she was a great artiste, she knew she came from a splendid heritage of performance, but she now faced ill-health, stigma, discrimination and neglect.[111] Women of her mother's generation were still assured of their designated place in society and her contemporaries and cousins Brinda, Muktha and Abhiramasundari, for all that they were negotiating more modern spaces, accepted society's diktat. But Balasaraswati was different; she saw no reason to be embarrassed by her heritage, and this inevitably caused grief. Subbulakshmi, of course, had crossed borders altogether.

Subbulakshmi had soon become the prominent name and face in Madras, and was working the *sabhas*, for all that she was not singing at the Music Academy. The Tamil audiences were apparently welcoming of musicians from the north. 'Music, such as was given by Roshanara or Bismillah, appealed to them as well as Ramanuja Iyengar or Subbulaxmi [sic].'[112] What is more significant is the bracketing, even if in a private record, of two Carnatic artistes of distinct generations, the fifty-three-year-old Ariyakudi Ramanuja Iyengar and the twenty-seven-year-old Subbulakshmi, the leading male and the leading female singers of the day. The tension this pairing created would recur.

The chain of benefit recitals had taken off. Subbulakshmi sang for the Mylai Kapaliswarar Rangagopuram renovation in December 1946,[113] for the Coimbatore Congress Building Fund in January 1948,[114] for the

Vidyadayini High School, Suratkal[115] and for the Nadar Saraswathi High School, Theni, both in March 1948.[116] This last event had the best tickets priced as high as ₹250, a not insignificant sum for the time, and for Theni.

There were, of course, wedding recitals and regular *sabha* appearances. 'Miss Not this Enchanting Performance' screamed an advertisement enticingly for a Chidambaram recital in November 1946, adding helpfully that 'Orders for reservation are pouring in'[117]. This is a four-hour recital a devoted listener likened to the blessing of Nataraja himself.[118] And new records were being released: Kalki's *'Vandadum Solai'* in 1946 ('The Queen of Music, Sterling Performance by Isaivani Kokilagana Srimathi M.S. Subbulakshmi'), and *'Arul Purivai'* and other songs in March 1948.[119] Both Subbulakshmi and Pattammal issued records of the songs of Bharati, in aid of the Bharati Memorial being constructed in Ettayapuram, a venture with which Kalki was closely associated.[120] If HMV came out with flashy advertisements[121] for Subbulakshmi's *'Deivatamizh nattinilae'* and *'Thavavum Palithathamma'*, Columbia pushed Pattammal singing 'two Bharathi songs in ecstatic style', *'Chinnam chiru kiliye'* and *'Thondru nigazhntha'*.[122]

It was not only in Madras that Subbulakshmi was well known. The existing record speaks of concerts in the south, in Trivandrum and Alappuzha, in Lalgudi, Chidambaram, Tiruchirappalli, Ootacamund, Bangalore and Mysore and in distant Patna, Benares, Calcutta and Delhi. A young admirer of those days recalled years later the huge excitement in south Indian circles in Delhi whenever Subbulakshmi visited, and the thrilling possibility of a sight, even from a distance, of the bejewelled, silk-clad beauty.[123] Decades later, at the passing of a distinguished *rasika*, his son recalled, 'He gazed in smitten devotion as a blossoming MS captivated a generation of boys like him with her voice and beauty alike'.[124] An appearance at All India Music Conference in 1944 in Bombay 'transformed a local reputation into a nation-wide one'.[125] The 'entrancing, celebrated nightingale Subbalakshmi [sic]' was again welcomed at a benefit performance in May 1945 in Matunga, the south Indian enclave within cosmopolitan Bombay.[126]

She returned to Bombay, and Matunga, in April 1946, with T. Chowdiah as the violin accompaniment, Kalpathi Ramanathan on the mrdangam and Alangudi Ramachandran on the ghatam for a recital in aid of the Sri Thyagabrahma Mahotsava Sabha Centenary Celebration.[127] This was a gala event for while the public could get in for as little as ₹2, rising up to ₹25 for what were the best seats, patrons and donors could, and almost certainly did, pay ₹250. Should they have wished, tickets could be bought in advance at many locations, including 'The Madras Brahmins Coffee Hotel, next to Post Office, Matunga.'

This recital was reviewed extensively by Kalki Krishnamurthi.[128] His reviews of Subbulakshmi's music in earlier years were always complimentary but not extravagant and occasionally even sharp; but times had changed.[129] He went into raptures over the Bombay recital where Subbulakshmi began with the *pancharatna kriti 'Sadhincene'*/Arabhi and went on to Pantuvarali, Sankarabharanam, Kharaharapriya and a *pallavi* in Todi. The lighter songs at the end included his own composition *'Katrinilae'* from the film *Meera*. The Hindustani vocalist Omkarnath Thakur was in the huge, and hugely appreciative, crowd.

Another critic claimed that the 'evening rose to a great height of classical Karnataki [sic] music' with a 'cosmopolitan gathering of about 6,000 in the specially constructed "pandal" and the overflow crowd of about 3,000 in the open ground surrounding it appreciatively enjoy [sic] the programme of South Indian music intermingled with the occasional Hindustani devotional song'.[130] This is a revealing statement. The intermingling of the 'occasional Hindustani devotional song' became increasingly the case with Subbulakshmi's concerts over the years, and this was not a trend which was uniformly appreciated. What is interesting is that even as early as 1946, before the Hindi version of *Meera*, and before her identification as a devotional singer, she had begun to sing songs from outside the main classical Carnatic tradition. The

The Politics of Language

evening concluded with the presentation to the artiste of a portrait of Kasturba Gandhi, a portrait which still hangs, over seventy years later, in what was Subbulakshmi's last home, in Kotturpuram, Chennai.

A report on a May 1947 recital in Delhi reads, 'Big guns in politics and Delhi society attended the function'.[131] Oddly, and sadly, the presence of politicians, businessmen and other socially prominent people, with or without any sense of musical appreciation, was a feature of Subbulakshmi's concerts to which Sadasivam was obsessively attached. Those who were close to him thought this was an endearing aspect of his personality; others were embarrassed. She was far greater than most of the Very Important Person(s) whose presence he craved, but he did not seem to know this.

And, indeed, very many years later, in the late autumn of Subbulakshmi's life, a worthy contemporary was believed to have asked who she was to comment on Subbulakshmi's music when it had found favour with such as Gandhi, Rajaji and Nehru.[132]

7

Meera

एक तू ही अब धनी हमारे कृष्ण नट नागर![1]

('Benefactor, ours,
You alone now are,
Krishna,
Dancing into our lives
With the bounty of your enchantment'. From a song in *'Meera'*.
Lyrics by Narendra Sharma.)

IF the Kasturba Memorial Fund recitals were the first of Sadasivam's successful projections of Subbulakshmi on the national scene, his second venture, without any doubt, surpassed all his expectations. This was *Meera*. In what can only be regarded as a directorial coup, Sadasivam cast Subbulakshmi, finally and irrevocably, into a role she played for the rest of her life.

The story of Mira is rich with love and longing, with poetry and song, and it is a story which is known throughout India and not just in her native desert lands in the north-west of modern India. She was probably born in 1498 in the Rajput clan called Rathore and married in 1516 into the Sisodiya clan. Rajput women were bound by ancient codes of chastity and obedience and Mira conformed to these but she was, in her mind, bound to none other than Krishna and found her companions not in the palace but in spaces where worship took place and where devotees of all castes mingled.[2] Widowhood, banishment and pilgrimage became her lot and around 1546, if legend is to be believed, she became one with the idol at Dwaraka. What is more likely is that she disappeared into the country to avoid the royal emissaries sent from her husband's family in Chittorgarh.[3] Mira's poems are songs of longing but they are not songs of desire as are, for instance, the *padams* of Kshetragna, which Subbulakshmi was also to sing.

The decision to cast Subbulakshmi in a film on Mira was taken as early as October 1943; the film *Meera*, Subbulakshmi's last, appeared in Tamil in 1945.[4] Kalki Krishnamurthi wrote the dialogue and S.V. Venkataraman composed the music for the twenty and more songs. Ellis Dungan was recalled, still a successful director of many Tamil films without knowing a word of the language – a decision which surely paid off.[5] Unusually for the time, it was decided to shoot 'on location' and the entire party proceeded to the north.[6]

The songs are still familiar and include the immortal '*Katrinilae varum geetam*', in the raga Ratipatipriya, a tune borrowed from Sheela Sarkar's '*Toot gayi man bina*', a song of which it has been said, 'Words cannot do justice to this tune that straddles the classical with the popular.'[7] Other hits were '*Giridhara Gopala*' in a soaring Mohana, '*Maravene*', set to the tune of the *javali* '*Chelinenetlu*'/Pharaz, '*Ennadu ullame*' and the *viruttam* '*Udal Uruga*'.[8] Curiously, this was not the first time the story of Mira was told on the south Indian screen. There is a record of a Tamil *Meera Bai* produced in 1936 with T.V. Rajsundari Bai in the title role and a Telugu *Meerabhai* in 1940 with Indira. These films have vanished as have the stories of their leading ladies.

The decision to remake the film in Hindi was Sadasivam's who, through this one move, wittingly gave Subbulakshmi the superb opportunity not just to play the role of a singer and poet, who was also a saint, but to display this to all of India. He may even have sensed that

Meera would be a money spinner. In the first few months alone after the late 1945 release, Subbulakshmi received ₹83,050 as film royalties and ₹6,550 as royalties on the sale of records, large sums for the time. She appears to have been persuaded to set up a trust fund for her husband's nephews and daughters from royalties to be received in the future.[9]

This early identification with the bhakti tradition shaped Subbulakshmi's later career as a performing artiste. She was never any more to be just a singing star with an appealing screen presence. A student of bhakti has observed, 'As the film became famous and Subbulakshmi's own reputation as a bhakta began to grow, this Tamil version of Meerabai was transposed "back" into Hindi.'[10] *Meera*, in both versions, for all its lack of sophistication, is compellingly watchable.[11] Subbulakshmi's entrance on screen in both the Tamil and Hindi versions is in a sequence where the child Mira, played by Sadasivam's elder daughter Radha, singing *'Nandabala'* becomes, to the frenzied background of bells and cymbals and a full-blown orchestra, the adult Mira singing *'Murali mohana'*! For all its theatrics, it is unforgettable.[12]

And it must be admitted that Subbulakshmi brings passion to her playing of Mira. Over thirty years later, the role was played on film again by the popular actor Hema Malini 'with the cool composure of the righteous', to quote the biographer of Ravi Shankar who composed the music of the film. Subbulakshmi's was a very different Mira.[13]

The late 1947 release was aggressively promoted and ran to packed halls.[14] 'Chandraprabha Cinetone's "Meera" starring the Nightingale of India, beautiful Subbulakshmi in the title role is scheduled for early release in Bombay. Subbulakshmi's name is a household word in India, for her fame has gone far and wide' raved one paper.[15] The following week, the paper again asserted, 'A rare and delightful treat awaits ardent filmgoers and lovers of music in Chandraprabha Cinetone's highly ambitious devotional "Meera", starring celebrated Kokilagana Subbulakshmi, the acknowledged Queen of Indian song in the title role',[16] and finally, on the day of the release itself, reported that the 'eagerly awaited devotional "Meera" starring the famous South Indian nightingale Shreemati M.S. Subbulakshmi in the title role will be released with great éclat at a gala premier at the Central today'.[17]

This was only the build-up. On release, the reviewer was ecstatic.

> Subbulakshmi shines as actress and songstress in the title role of Meera. A singer of outstanding merit and an actress of great histrionic ability (she) plays the celebrated Queen of Mewar with a high degree of sincerity which brings the royal devotee to pulsating life on the screen ... She proves an ideal choice for stellar role for no artiste could have done better justice to the bhajans, padas and devotional hymns composed by the poetess Meera. Golden cascades, gorgeous melody well up from Kokilagana Subbulakshmi's slender throat as she renders with consummate artistry the exquisite hymns which hold you spellbound and entranced, particularly the bhajan at the finale which is a brilliant tour de force.

The critic notes though, with some honesty, that the 'film is boring when she is not on the screen'.[18]

But if all this was Sadasivam's organizing ability at work, the film drew 'unprecedented crowds of ardent film goers and lovers of Indian music'.[19] An imaginative, if shrewd, directorial decision was to have Sarojini Naidu introduce the artiste on screen. 'Sm. M.S. Subbulakshmi has rightly earned a glowing tribute for her voice of liquid gold from Sm. Sarojini Devi, the poetess-daughter of Mother India.'[20] In her characteristically eloquent way, and speaking 'of set purpose' in English, Mrs Naidu hailed the fact that "India in this generation had produced so supreme an artiste". And Subbulakshmi was then only thirty-one.

The grand premiere in Delhi was held in the presence of Prime Minister Nehru and Governor-General Mountbatten and Lady

Mountbatten. Over seventy years later, a member of the audience recalled the singer's 'great and beautiful voice'.[21]

Not everyone was as charitable. The January 1948 issue of the popular *Filmindia* had a full page colour photograph of Subbulakshmi and one of Radha, taken from the film and three other photographs of Radha but the review of the film was itself mixed. Ellis Dungan is dismissed as an unknowing 'white director', Sarojini Naidu mocked for her grandiose manner and poor Nagiah, the actor playing the lead male role, dismissed as 'a round shouldered potato'.[22] But even *Filmindia* had to concede that 'Subbulakshmi sings beautifully'.[23]

As we have seen, Subbulakshmi's *Meera* was not the first time the story was told on film. At the very time of the release of her film, another Hindi film *Meerabai* was running in cinema halls in Bombay, starring an actor called Neena 'as only she can bring a new freshness and appeal to the songs of Meera'.[24] Vani Jairam sang to music composed by Ravi Shankar for the Hindi film we have noted earlier.[25] The songs of Mira have always drawn women singers. Lata Mangeshkar,[26] Juthika Roy[27] and Kishori Amonkar,[28] the stars of the film, semi-classical and classical worlds have all sung her. And the songs of Subbulakshmi's film, which easily made the transition to her concert repertoire, stayed with her till the very end. Indeed, Subbulakshmi felt that Mira never left her. 'Travelling in Brindavan, Mathura, Dwaraka and Rajasthan for the film, I felt that Meera was alive and could never die. How could she, when what she sang was as timeless as the blue of the sky and the sea?'[29]

Meera was Subbulakshmi's last brush with films,[30] and as a contemporary film-maker has reminded us, what we are left with is 'the young, innocent, porcelain-skinned, perfectly-chiselled Meera who sang in perfect pitch'.[31] This image has lasted decades. There are letters from T.K. Chidambaranatha Mudaliar in 1950 with talk of travelling to

Bombay for a film shooting, and of the need to preserve Subbulakshmi's art in this way, but we do not have an idea of what this venture could have been.[32] There is further evidence that Subbulakshmi expected to make two more films in 1951 and 1952, essentially to raise funds for *Kalki*, but these plans did not materialize, probably because funds for *Kalki* were found elsewhere.[33] Some years later, there was talk that she was the first choice of the director of the 1960 hit *Hum Dono* to sing 'Allah tero naam'. In the event nothing came of this, perhaps fortuitously. The lyrics by Sahir Ludhianvi may well have appealed to Subbulakshmi but her voice would have been much too strong for the somewhat lugubrious song which was finally sung by Lata Mangeshkar.[34]

Meera became popular outside India as well. As early as 1951, it was shown in The Netherlands, where the story of Mira, intriguingly, was well known.[35] Subbulakshmi sang the bhajans of Mira for the rest of her life, all taken from the film to the concert platform. As it happens, almost none have survived her on the concert platform, or none in the highly mannered way in which she presented them.[36] There were some songs which were recorded but did not make it to the final screen version; 'More aangan mein murali bajao re' is one such, a charming song never presented on stage but which circulates on YouTube.[37]

A very significant exception of a bhajan which was not from the film but which became the piece most associated with her was 'Hari tum haro'. The story of how this piece was learnt and sung, in October 1947, for the Mahatma's birthday, has been repeated often, and tediously, but what is not so well known is Gandhi's reaction, for it was for him that it was sung. Maniben Patel, an intimate of the Gandhi establishment, recorded the Mahatma's comments in her diary, 'Her voice is exceedingly sweet ... To sing a bhajan is one thing; to sing it by losing oneself in god is quite different.'[38]

Gandhi's own translation of this often-sung verse is not so widely known.

> O God, Thou deliverest Thy servants from difficulties.
> Thou savedst Draupadi's honour by extending her garment infinitely
> For Thy devotee Thou becamest man.
> Thou destroyedst Hiranyakashipu; didst not tolerate him.
> Thou savedst the sinking elephant and pulled him out of the water.
> Says Mira the servant and beloved of Giridhar:
> Where there is grief there is the cry of distress (sent to heaven).[39]

An appealing story is told by Subbulakshmi's adopted son Tyagarajan of how she, in response to a question from him on how the bhajan was tuned using a piano, simply 'sat down on the piano stool and started playing Durbari, then she sang *Hari tum haro*', accompanying herself on the piano'.[40]

The year 1947 was a time of turmoil, soon to become a time of horror. Madras was not so affected by the convulsions of Partition but Subbulakshmi could not but have been aware of the national scene. Independence, when it came to India on 15 August 1947, was marked with celebration and rejoicing. The newspapers proudly announced a recital by Subbulakshmi on AIR Trichy ('You should not miss this enjoyable programme of the Independence Day celebrations'). It was, of course, business as usual for most people with the same newspapers advertising toilet soap ('Kanan Devi keeps her skin clear and lovely with Lux Toilet Soap') and construction material ('Construct your house of Independence with Dalmia Cement'). There is also a stern, and somewhat poignant, notice by Delhi Rationing, 'Are You Leaving For Pakistan? If so, please do not forget to surrender your Ration Cards (Food and Cloth) at your Circle Rationing Office or at the Delhi Railway Station.'[41]

Shortly after the terrible killings in Calcutta in August 1947, Gandhi moved to Delhi, the scene of sectarian violence. 'Amidst all the torments, visitors, invited and uninvited, flocked to Birla House to see him, thirty-one-year-old M.S. Subbulakshmi, among them. At the evening prayer there, when the "Ramdhun" was to start, Gandhi said to her, "*Subbulakshmi tum gao, tum shuru karo*".'[42] The historian Lakshmi Subramanian points out that Gandhi had more than just a passing acquaintance with the singer with a fine voice. 'He pointed out in the 6 December 1947 prayer meeting that while she was new in Delhi, her music had all the signs of complete involvement and it was this quality that mesmerized people. He urged some of his follower to give her more space in Delhi and encourage her to sing and perform in the city'.[43]

Immediately after Gandhi's assassination on 30 January 1948, the song '*Hari tum haro*' was broadcast on the radio. The story is told most poetically by a contemporary writer. 'And then, even as Gandhi's corporeal frame awaits co-mingling with the elements, the "daughter of Madurai's goddess Meenakshi", muse of all devotion and only maestro of her kind, Subbulakshmi, listens to her own voice singing to all humankind the song of Mewar's daughter Mirabai seeking a deliverance for humanity from fear, from pain'.[44]

Gandhi's ashes were sent across the country for public homage and immersion. Subbulakshmi was among those at the airport in Madras when the ashes were received.[45] An eyewitness recalls Subbulakshmi standing for hours by the urn containing the ashes and singing, with tears flowing[46] and later, of her singing '*Vaishnava Jana to*' as the ashes were being taken for immersion.[47] Subbulakshmi, Pattammal, Vasanthakokilam and Tiruppugazh Mani[48] sang on the radio in a special commemorative programme and a special half hour of Subbulakshmi's bhajans was broadcast at a time when memorial meetings were being held across the state.

The release of *Meera* was, of course, a huge event in Subbulakshmi's professional life, but there was no letting up from the routine, which was singing concerts. The rift over Tamil Isai was over and Subbulakshmi made a grand comeback at the Music Academy on 28 December 1947. T. Chowdiah accompanied her on the violin, as he was to do for a while. The concert saw '*Rama nannu brovaravemako*'/Harikambhoji and '*Sarojadalanetri*'/Sankarabharanam, both to reappear at the UN concert eighteen years later, admittedly with many in-between appearances. There were two other Tyagaraja songs, '*Meevalla*'/Kapi and '*Ela ni daya radu*'/Athana, Dikshitar's '*Subramanyena*'/Suddhadhanyasi[49] and a *ragam-tanam-pallavi* in Kiravani. The concert also included Svati Tirunal's '*Kripaya palaya*'/Charukesi, which suggests that she had begun learning from Semmangudi Srinivasa Iyer, who was at that very time busy setting the lyrics of Svati Tirunal to appropriate raga and *tala* settings.

Early in 1949, on 27 March to be exact, Subbulakshmi sang in New Delhi, at a benefit recital where the prime minister was present, for the Madrasi Education Society. The story of Nehru's description of Subbulakshmi as the Queen of Music has been told often, and very pedantically, but his presence is worth noting. A devoted member of the audience recalled in a letter to his family that the prime minister said, 'I am a prime minister. But I stand before a queen – the queen of great art, music. I pay my humble homage to her.'[50]

Jawaharlal Nehru was not allowed, though, to get away with posing as a patron of the arts,[51] and given that his eye for a beautiful face was well known,[52] the critic of *Shankar's Weekly* noted archly that

> (i)t was a revelation to many that our Prime Minister has an ear for music, when Panditji, being present at Shreemati M.S. Subbulakshmi's recent song recital at Y.M.C.A., New Delhi, declared his keen appreciation of Karnatic music. He went on to say that he was haunted not only by the voice, but by the face of the Melody Queen of Madras. Indian classical singers, as we see them, contort their faces while they control their voices, so-much-so that we are usually inclined to close our eyes when we hear them sing. In the case of Shreemati Subbulakshmi, however, we see and hear at the same time, combining visual with aural entertainment.[53]

The gala continued. The *Hindu* recorded, for instance, that a 'large and distinguished gathering' attended a benefit music concert given by her in aid of the South Indian Journalists' Federation, and which raised ₹47,000 for that organization.[54] Subbulakshmi's generosity was hailed as being as great as her popularity. Kasturi Srinivasan, always a friend, said he 'was introduced to her music fifteen years ago by the late Keerthanacharya C.R. Srinivasa Iyengar and ... ever since then I have been following her progress and it is no wonder she has attained eminence in the musical world. May God bless her with long life.'

Subbulakshmi was everywhere. The 1948 annual issue of *Swatantra* carried Subbulakshmi's picture on its cover and a rapid pace of wedding concerts had begun. But for all her fame, Subbulakshmi still needed to consolidate her position. There were many other attractive and popular women singers appearing on the Madras platforms. Vasanthakokilam was singing, and Pattammal, Vasanthakumari and K.B. Sundarambal.[55] Vasanthakumari's film career was taking off.[56] Pattammal too had a career in film music, starting with *Thyaga Bhoomi* in 1939 all the way until the early 1950s and was famed for her patriotic songs.[57] Radha and Jayalakshmi were well established on the concert scene by 1951.[58] The old guard was still ably represented by Brinda and Muktha.[59]

Through this time in the late 1940s, Sadasivam's daughter Radha was seen often performing dance along with Kalki's daughter Anandhi. Their dance career began in 1945[60] and did not last very long, but they were students of Vazhuvoor Ramaiah Pillai, later to become famous as the teacher of Kamala,[61] who did much to popularize the form with the daughters of the Brahmin elite of Madras. It is possible that Radha was his first student.[62]

The young girls danced on 28 September 1947[63] and again on 1 January 1948 with Subbulakshmi singing the *padas*. The fare included popular Tamil numbers such as '*Thaye Yashoda*'/Todi, '*Yenpalli kondirayya*'/, '*Kalai thookki*'/Yadukulakambhoji and the lilting '*Ghanashyam aaya re*' from the Hindi *Meera*. Interestingly, Subbulakshmi was well trained in *abhinaya*, and was able to guide her wards.[64] Radha performed alone at Vani Mahal on 25 December 1949, after Anandhi's marriage to Sadasivam's nephew Ramachandran, and also gave benefit performances for the Vidyodaya School on 11 February 1950, in Bombay in August 1950 and in Bangalore in January 1951, but her dance career faded away in the face of competition. 'Kumari Vaijayanthimala [sic] of "Life" fame' was performing dance[65] as were Lalitha, Padmini and Ragini[66] and Kamala.[67] Chandralekha, in later life a significant presence on the Madras cultural scene, made her Madras debut in April 1952.[68] Tara Chaudhuri, now forgotten, but then hailed as 'India's premier dancer,'[69] was a frequent visitor to Madras, as was Shanta, the striking student of Pandanallur Meenakshisundaram Pillai.[70]

Subbulakshmi's benefit concert drive continued to be busy. Bombay was a regular stop on her travels. A benefit recital in December 1947 in aid of the South Indian School raised the stupendous sum of ₹98,000. A later recital in April 1948, to raise funds for a Gandhi memorial, was expected to draw a crowd of 50,000 and raise a sum of ₹2 lakh.[71] She sang in the Sevasadan grounds, Nagpur, in February 1946 in aid of the Madras Girls' School Building Fund.[72] There is a record of another benefit concert in Nagpur in March 1949, for the building fund of the Central College for Women, which raised what was for then the very large sum of ₹35,000. 'We have never heard such music in Nagpur before. Subbulakshmi is not a singer. She is a musical miracle.'[73] Sadasivam was feted no less than his wife. 'The discovery, growth and spread of the reputation and talents of Subbulakshmi are entirely due to Mr Sadasivam (who) was like the person who tended the wick in the lantern. He was the person who regulated the flow of Subbulakshmi's great gifts.'[74] With all this, it is not in the least surprising that his head turned, but it is significant that the anonymous reporter recognized her overwhelming talent.

A recital in December 1948 at the Rajaji Hall in Chennai in aid of the Tiruvallikeni Women's School raised ₹40,000.[75] She sang at the

Tower Talkies in Tanjore for the Rotary Maternity Fund[76] and for the Congress Exhibition at Exhibition Grounds in Madras on 3 January 1950.[77] A 'Grand Music Programme by Kokilagana Isaivani Srimathi M.S. Subbulakshmi' was announced[78] for 1 January 1950 as was a benefit concert for the Ambur Hindu High School Building Fund on 21 January 1950 in, no less, 'a specially erected pandal at the Hindu High School compound, Ambur, North Arcot'.[79] With the best seats going at ₹200, Ambur was doing quite well.

Subbulakshmi was much in demand at society weddings, and while other leading musicians such as Ariyakudi Ramanuja Iyengar, G.N. Balasubramaniam and Semmangudi Srinivasa Iyer were available, often with close links to particular regions and particular families, a performance by 'MS' was the icing on the cake.[80]

Several high-profile appearances notwithstanding, Subbulakshmi did not perform at the Academy season in 1948, 1949 and 1950, even if she sang at the Tamil Isai Sangam on 27 December 1949. It has been suggested that Sadasivam perceived a slight to his wife from the Academy's administration, a slight that took several years to resolve. It was only in 1951 that she reappeared on that platform.

Subbulakshmi had not only escaped from Madurai; she had been quite spectacularly thrust into orbit. Vadivambal, her younger sister, did not have the same chance. Somewhere along the way, she attracted the attention of a wealthy bon vivant from Coimbatore, a fact that was common knowledge.[81] She continued to live in Madurai till her death, possibly of double pneumonia,[82] in early November 1947, when she was twenty-two[83] and at the exact time that *Meera* was being aggressively launched.[84] The singer Ananthalakshmi Sadagopan, who was Madurai based, recalled Vadivambal as talented and beautiful and who both sang and played the vina.[85] This memory was also shared by Sadasivam's niece who lived in his house and would have seen Vadivambal.[86] There is another recollection that 'she was even more beautiful than MS' but there are tantalizingly few verifiable details.[87] A recording survives, attributed unambiguously to M.S. Vadivambal.[88] It is a voice at once strong and powerful, but unpolished and raw. It is a strangely adult voice; the songs recorded are '*Kairatnama*' in Punnagavarali and '*Theyilai Thothathile*' in Jenjuti.[89] It is not even clear whether Vadivambal was being trained for any sort of musical career. And, in any case, she was very soon dead.

The 1940s ended triumphantly for Subbulakshmi. She had established herself as a classical singer, as a devotional singer, a benefactress of noble causes and as a singing star on the screen, a musician with a voice 'of real grandeur'.[90] Her decision to renounce films was seen as an act of self-denial and years later she was hailed as 'a rare example of an artiste who renounced films when at her peak'.[91] But if she left the world of films, her four-film career set the pace for a dazzling concert career.

Years later, a commentator shrewdly observed that while she may have been 'far removed from the tinsel world of glamour, too feminine, mild-mannered and modest to be paced in a cinema crowd', her later success was closely linked to 'the pious roles she played, upholding some of the ideals set for the Indian woman, enhancing the parts with the wealth of her music and the richness of her voice'.[92] She was the toast of Madras and moved easily in high society and as Sarojini Naidu said in the film, '...(e)very child in India has heard of Subbulakshmi for the beauty of her voice, the magic of her personality, the gracious charity of her heart; but in the North she is still to be known to be loved, to be honoured, to be cherished as one of the greatest artistes in India'.[93]

Madurai was well behind her. She now belonged to India.

8

MS: The Growth of the Name

చక్కని రాజమార్గములుండగా సందుల దురనెలా ఓ మనసా...?[1]

('*When there's a straight royal highway to travel, why do you duck down the side-streets, O heart?*',
translation by William J. Jackson of the *pallavi* of Tyagaraja's '*Tsakkani rajamargamu*' in the raga Kharaharapriya)

THE 1950s were, in hindsight, years of consolidation and of Subbulakshmi's rapid rise as one of India's leading classical singers, with an ever-growing repertoire. *Sangitha Kalanidhi* Musiri Subramania Iyer (1899–1975), always the teacher Subbulakshmi acknowledged publicly, was a personal friend of the Sadasivams. Musiri, as he was always called, was a hugely successful concert artiste over the 1930s and 1940s and went on to be a much sought-after teacher and well-respected principal of the College of Carnatic Music, as it was then known.[2]

It is not easy to track the full list of the songs which Musiri taught Subbulakshmi, but they included some which she presented extremely often such as '*Rama Rama gunaseema*'/Simhendramadhyamam, '*Durusuga*', '*Anjaneya*' and '*Muruga Muruga*' in Saveri, '*O Rangasayee*' and '*Tiruvadicharanam*' in Kambhoji, '*Sri Chandrasekhara yatindram*'/

Sankarabharanam and '*Manju nigar*', of the type called *kavadichindu*, devotional verses in Tamil in praise of the deity at Tiruttani. Not so frequently heard were '*Sri Kumara*'/Athana, '*Janani pahi*'/Suddhasaveri and '*Devi Jagajjanani*'/Sankarabharanam. It is also clear from listening to recordings of Musiri's concerts that she learnt *alapana* and *neraval* from him.

A very important learning from Musiri was the '*Melakarta Ragamalika*' of Maha Vaidyanatha Iyer (1844–93), which he had himself learnt from *Sangita Kalanidhi* T.S. Sabhesa Iyer (1872–1948), a disciple of Vaidyanatha Iyer, himself a disciple of Manambuchavadi Venkatasubbayyar (1803–62), a direct disciple of Tyagaraja. It is possible that this great composition was actually learnt and kept aside till some years later, when Semmangudi Srinivasa Iyer, who had learnt it from *Sangita Kalanidhi* Umayalpuram Swaminatha Iyer (1867–1946),[3] another disciple of Maha Vaidyanatha Iyer, reintroduced it into Subbulakshmi's repertoire. The *Melakarta Ragamalika* as presented by Subbulakshmi is quite different from the version presented by Musiri himself in concerts, tighter and more compact, and this is possibly the influence of her other teacher, Semmangudi.[4]

Semmangudi famously said that he chose not to present the composition himself in his recitals and asked Subbulakshmi to do so because it was only in her voice that he found the pristine clarity that the song demanded. A piece of luminous intensity, it was first presented by Subbulakshmi in six segments in her annual season concert at the Music Academy over 1968–76[5] and subsequently released as a commercial recording in 1989. After every Academy presentation, the extracts would appear, usually in her Madras concerts, doing much to give the piece greater currency.

Mayavaram V.V. Krishna Iyer (1901?–57) was another professional teacher and one-time concert artiste who added substantially to the stock of Subbulakshmi's songs, teaching both her and Radha. Side by side with intensive learning, the decade of the 1950s saw Subbulakshmi at her busiest, with *sabha*, wedding and benefit concerts. The partial list available gives details of thirty-six benefit recitals over the decade.[6]

There was an astute image change around the mid 1950s. The chintzy prints disappeared, as did the single plait. Across India it is still possible, particularly among more conservative communities, to identify the religion, caste and economic status from the manner in which women dress. This was very much more the case at the time of Subbulakshmi's entrance into the wider world. A contemporary writer has got very quickly to the point.

> For many, M.S. epitomized the Tamil Brahmin aesthetic: straight parting; slightly oiled hair pulled back into a braid or a chignon adorned with Madurai jasmine flowers; bright red *bindi*; Kanjeevaram silk saris in jewel tones with poetic names borrowed from nature such as peacock blue, onion skin pink, mango yellow, parrot green; star-shaped diamond earrings; the all-important diamond nose rings – a solitaire on one nostril, and a triumvirate on the other; at least two necklaces, including the long, hanging *mangalsutra*; bangles on both hands – a mixture of tingling glass bangles interspersed with gold ones; a simple plain blouse that matched the sari – none of the mirror-work or designer blouses, the blouse cut close to the neck without a deep back; the sari *pallu* worn around the neck; anklets; toe rings for sure; a heady fragrance from a combination of jasmine flowers, sandalwood oil moisturizer and herbal hair oil; and lips red from the betel leaf that is chewed after lunch. [M.S. wore lipstick too]. This sensuous aesthetic – can you imagine, not one of your senses is left unattended? – is what M.S. modelled. It is how Tamil Brahmin women of that era dressed.[7]

Intimates have written of her impeccable grooming, her fastidiousness in all things related to her appearance, her delicate table manners, her love of flowers, and of perfumes.[8] For a woman from a background as humble as hers, she had extraordinary style and, in time, came to represent high south Indian style.[9] An endearing detail of Subbulakshmi's glorious concert years 'was in being one of the few people to have had a colour named after her. MS blue was the name given to a distinctive shade of blue, inky, yet iridescent and shot through with black and green highlights, that was used in saris woven specially for her.'[10]

The concert lists of Subbulakshmi's annual appearances at the Music Academy in 1951, 1952, 1953 and 1955 are revealing.[11] These were still recitals where she had not begun toying with the conservative concert pattern into which she was groomed. There are stray pieces which occur and are not heard again, or are not heard again with any degree of frequency, such as *'Sita manohara'*/Ramapriya, *'Kala kanthi'*/Nilambari in 1951, *'Santana Rama'*/Hindolavasanta and *'Tappagane'*/Suddhabangala in 1953 and *'Mamava sada'*/Kanada and *'Eduta nilacite'*/Sankarabharanam in 1955. However, the favourites predominated: *'Vidulaku'*/Mayamalavagaula, *'Rama nannu brovaravemako'*/Harikambhoji, *'Kamalambike'*/Todi, *'Sabhapatikku'*/Abhogi, *'Gopanandana'*/Bhushavali, *'Sarasaksha'*/Pantuvarali, *'Pakkala nilabadi'*/Kharaharapriya, *'Janani'*/Ritigaula, *'Hariharaputram'*/Vasanta, *'Sarojadalanetri'*/Sankarabharanam, *'Rangapura vihara'*/Brindavanasaranga, *'Vatapi'*/Hamsadhwani and *'Durusuga'*/Saveri.

These songs stayed at the core of her repertoire for the next twenty years; four of them were presented in the UN Concert of June 1966, by which time they had attained the high polish that repeated performance had given them. The 1951 recital even included *'Sadasivam upasmahe'*/Sankarabharanam, a masterpiece resurrected in her *Sangitha Kalanidhi* recital in 1968. More predictably, Sankarabharanam figured in all four years, a fall-back option guaranteed to draw applause. *Ragam-tanam-pallavi* was presented in Kharaharapriya, Bhairavi and Sankarabharanam, reliable concert staples which Subbulakshmi repeated often, at least as long as she was still presenting this distinctive form.

The Ariyakudi concert pattern, and the impact it has had on the teaching of music, on performance style and on the enlightenment of the audience have been and are subjects of lively discussion. The growth of the *sabhas*, and the introduction of the *sabha kachheri*, the ticketed performance, had major implications for concert style and pattern. Ariyakudi Ramanuja Iyengar, always 'Ariyakudi', seized the moment and pioneered a brisk concert style that catered both to knowledgeable *rasikas* and new listeners.

Concerts of the old style went on for five hours and more with only a few songs but with very extensive raga development and long *ragam-tanam-pallavi* suites.[12] They may even have included short breaks to enable the invariably upper-caste performers attend to their obligatory devotions. The concert pattern popularized by Ariyakudi required a singer to commence the recital with a *varnam*, followed immediately by a few fast, even racy, *kriti* renderings, followed by longer songs, some with brief raga *alapana*, and some to which *kalpana svara* was added as an embellishment. Several songs of Tyagaraja lend themselves to this end. Ariyakudi further laid down that the main raga taken up for *tanam* and *pallavi* should be a *ghana raga*, which for the present can be defined as substantial, and easily understood by the audience. Where a comparatively rare raga was selected, its characteristic features were to be introduced at the very start of the rendering, a point on which Subbulakshmi was known to have views. The second half of the recital, which would include one or even two percussion interludes, would consist of *padam, javali, tevaram, tiruppugazh, ashtapadi, tillana, stotram*, a selection of the fairly wide range of miscellaneous compositions available within the Carnatic repertoire. Some of these forms call for a considerable degree of musical prowess and it would be mistaken to classify all of them as 'light'.

It should be noted that the pre-composed piece with its defined structure and lyrics, and the possibility it affords for extemporization is an ideal focal point both for the performer and the listener. Every composition is set to raga and *tala*, with its emotional content, *bhava*, deriving from the meaning of the text and performer's understanding of that text. And it was in structuring a concert around the pre-composed pieces, *kriti*, *varnam*, *padam* and the like, that Ariyakudi Ramanuja Iyengar decisively ensured that all aspects of what was to him a wholesome musicality were properly represented.

The Ariyakudi *margam* served him very well. Some years before his passing, a critic observed, 'I cannot think of anyone who has so consistently dominated the concert platform over such a long period, a period of over fifty years over which he lived and worked and sang, steadfast and severe, a little outside current fashions strengthening the Karnatik tradition in his own unobtrusive, untheatrical way, enlarging our repertoire and with it our musical horizons'.[13] Another critic was more blunt. 'There have been greater musicians, nadopasakas, but Ariyakudi was the greatest master of the art and craft of the modern concert platform.'[14]

According to the historian Lakshmi Subramanian, Ariyakudi's innovations in concert format were intended to 'quicken the concert tempo with shorter performances and a balanced selection of compositions'. She correctly notes that, 'the decision to stay with the medium and fast tempo, in marked contrast to the slower movement adopted by musicians in the north, became an important marker of the Karnatik [sic] style'. She suggests also that contemporary audiences were not as comfortable with the more 'classical' pieces as they were with 'love songs, nationalist poetry and Tamil devotional lyrics', all of which found place in the new concert pattern.[15]

The critic 'Aeolus' thought that Ariyakudi Ramanuja Iyengar made the presentation of music 'vigorous, individual and mass-centred. He brought verve in the place of virtuosity, variety in the place of monotony, imagination in the place of idiosyncrasy and tempo in the place of tedium.'[16] Even allowing for the critic's love of alliteration and bombast, there is substance in what he says for the Ariyakudi legacy lives to this day. But for all its attractiveness, the Ariyakudi style's emphasis on the brisk and the short can also be seen as the one single reason which limits the appeal of classical Carnatic music for connoisseurs of the Hindustani style, where musicians spend years learning the nuances of rendering a raga. A style which depended substantially on song-rendering effectively encouraged a large number of amateur singers to mount the concert platform.

A more serious, even unfortunate, consequence of the dominance of the Ariyakudi-concert style is the conflation, in the public mind, of the obviously upper-caste style and manner of Ramanuja Iyengar with the identification of what should have been public spaces, the *sabhas*, as private clubs for Brahmin enthusiasts. What in musical terms should simply have been a way of presenting a repertory, and which could well have served its purpose till it was replaced by another equally widely accepted form of presentation, has been seen, at least by some, as yet another means of asserting caste dominance.

Subbulakshmi was by now, even as early as 1950, very well known in Delhi and elsewhere. In the course of a longer piece fussing about the general neglect of all things south Indian in the capital, a columnist stressed, '...and, finally, all Madrasis are not stenographers. Just in case a reminder is needed, Radhakrishnan, Subbalakshmi [sic], Pothan Joseph, Rukmini Arundale and C.V. Raman all came from Madras'.[17] Precisely.

In 1954, the year when the government instituted a scheme of national awards, Subbulakshmi was awarded the Padma Bhushan.[18] This was a matter of rejoicing, and she had publicly been accorded precedence over Kamaladevi Chattopadhyaya, Rukmini Devi, Balasaraswati and Ariyakudi Ramanuja Iyengar, who were awarded the Padma Bhushan in 1955, 1956, 1957 and 1958 respectively. Many years later, this was followed, in 1975, by the Padma Vibhushan and finally in 1998 by the Bharat Ratna.

The annual Radio Sangeet Sammelan programmes broadcast on All India Radio were begun in 1954. The 1955 season of the Sammelan was a splendid affair with the Carnatic style justly represented by great artistes of several generations.[19] Ariyakudi Ramanuja Iyengar led the team along with vocalists Maharajapuram Viswanatha Iyer, Semmangudi Srinivasa Iyer, G.N. Balasubramaniam, Madurai Mani Iyer, M.M. Dandapani Desigar, Alathur Srinivasa Iyer and Alathur Sivasubramania Iyer and a young K.V. Narayanaswamy. The instrumentalists included Karaikudi Sambasiva Iyer and K.S. Narayanaswami on the vina, T.N. Rajarathnam Pillai on the nagasvaram, Dwaram Venkataswami Naidu on the violin and T. Viswanathan on the flute. T. Jayammal and T. Balasaraswati sang *padams*, an imaginative choice for a radio concert, and finally there were Vasanthakumari, Pattammal and Subbulakshmi.

Subbulakshmi and Palghat Mani Iyer were selected in 1956 by the Sangeet Natak Akademi as Musicians of the Year; years later, she would go on to be elected to a Fellowship of the Akademi.[20] She was given a splendid send-off at the Madras Central station with large crowds of cheering friends. A particularly sensitive tribute was paid to her on the occasion of the Akademi award. 'It has been given to Subbulakshmi to give us the beauty, the joy, the pristine glory of music.'[21] Her recital on this occasion included Subbaraya Sastri's '*Ninnu vina*' in Kalyani, a lively and engaging song not otherwise known in her repertoire. The other songs were more usual: '*Naneke badavanu*'/Behag and '*Rangapuravihara*'/Brindavanasaranga and two of her more popular bhajans, '*Bhajore Bhaiyya*' and '*Kahan re pathik kahan*'.[22]

Her closeness to Jawaharlal Nehru, and over the years to his family, meant a great deal to Subbulakshmi. Her first meeting with him was possibly in December 1947 at the Delhi release of *Meera*. She would frequently speak of how he regarded her, born in 1916 to Indira's 1917, as his elder child, *mootta kuzhandai*, and the Sadasivam family may even on occasion have stayed at Teen Murti House, the prime minister's official residence.[23] We have also noted the March 1949 concert where the prime minister was present. A better-known meeting between Subbulakshmi and Jawaharlal was at the 29 November 1953 recital in aid of the Ramakrishna Mission. This was the second occasion when he described her as the queen of song.[24] Recalling the event decades later, a veteran journalist wrote of what he saw as '...a deep friendly relationship between a man and a woman without a trace of sensuousness' with the prime minister going on to the stage as the audience was dispersing to hold the artiste's hand in tribute.[25]

Yet another meeting was at the ceremony on 5 October 1955 when the foundation stone for the present auditorium of the Music Academy was laid.[26] Here again, the prime minister repeated before a packed audience, for the third time, the by-now clichéd line about Subbulakshmi being the queen of song. This closeness did not go unnoticed and the humorous journal, *Shankar's Weekly*, in its put down of the prime minister's favourites, awarded M. Subbulakshmi [sic] the award of Ram Bandhu, Second Class and the Rani-ki-Jhansi, Second Class.[27] The entire list of awards is actually very funny and says something about the spacious 1950s in newly independent India when no one was above being taken down a notch.

That particular concert in aid of the Music Academy's building ruffled many feathers, especially those of more senior musicians who felt they had been overlooked on such a momentous occasion. It is reported that Subbulakshmi's sometime friend G.N. Balasubramaniam helped in cooling passions, on the very practical argument that the Academy was best served by choosing the performer whose concert would raise the most funds through ticket sales.[28]

A recording is to be found on the Internet of Subbulakshmi singing at a religious event at Anandashram in Kerala in September 1955. This is of interest only because it is about the first recording there is after *Meera*.

'*Vatapi*'/Hamsadhwani, '*Sogasuga*'/Sriranjani and '*Teliyaleru*'/Dhenuka are sung exceedingly fast. It now appears that this may have been the style at the time though not, fortunately, for much longer.

The 1950s were the years when Subbulakshmi's peers were performing widely and receiving acclaim. Vasanthakokilam had passed on in 1951, at the very young age of thirty-two.[29] She was singing till quite near to her end by which time it had probably also become evident that Subbulakshmi was racing ahead.[30] Rajam Pushpavanam had stopped performance but Pattammal had acquired a fine reputation for her rich and stately expositions, and had sung briefly, and successfully, for films. Vasanthakumari's first Music Academy appearance was in the 1954 season but she was already a sensation and had been hailed as *Sangeetha Vani*. Her silken voice was ideal for films and she was an extremely successful playback singer, but she was primarily a classical performer, a disciple of G.N. Balasubramaniam, and much in demand both at *sabhas* and at weddings, even as early as 1951.[31]

More women singers were being recognized. C. Saroja and C. Lalitha, R. Vedavalli and Sikkil Neela and Sikkil Kunjumani, all later to follow Subbulakshmi's path to the *Sangitha Kalanidhi*, made their appearance in the Music Academy in the 1959 season, as did Mani Krishnaswami in 1960. Another appearance in the 1959 season was of V. Ranganayaki, disciple of Namakkal Sesha Iyengar, singer for Balasaraswati during much of the 1950s and later a distinguished musicologist.

Balasaraswati was performing in Madras and elsewhere. It was said of her performance in Delhi, shortly after Shanmukham Chetty's passing, when she did not have connections in the capital, that '...her royal status, regality in every line of her dominated the whole hall the minute she started dancing. She was beyond analysis for she was Dance itself. True genius is rarely come by these days but when it does is unmistakably recognizable to all who have eyes to see.'[32] But this was on the stage.

Despite a long association of almost twenty years, and a child, the notice in the *Hindu* of 6 May 1953 of Shanmukham Chetty's death merely states that he was survived by his wife and three daughters. Such were the indignities of devadasi life.

By the end of the decade of the 1950s, Subbulakshmi was reaching the peak of her powers, but if her days were packed with *sabha* and wedding recitals, there is no doubt that something of a sameness had begun to set in. Four commercial recordings are available of concerts from this time: at Bhavani, Erode, in 1956; the Music Academy recital of December 1956; a recital in Ceylon/Sri Lanka in 1958; and a 1960 recital at the Rasika Ranjani Sabha. Two other recitals, at the Bharathi Gana Sabha in June 1958 and the Rasika Ranjani Sabha in September 1958 are available at a music archive in Chennai. These concerts bear study.

The first thing that strikes a listener today is the overall briskness and speed. These are representatives of the Ariyakudi pattern at its most popular, the emphasis being on racy numbers, fast *alapanas*, torrential *svaraprasthara*, and song piled upon song. Subbulakshmi was not alone in this matter. A recording is available of Vasanthakumari's Music Academy season recital in 1955; a rapid succession of songs, with delightful, quicksilver *alapanas*; possibly this is what was expected.[33] In the Bhavani concert where Subbulakshmi had her standard accompanists of the time, R.K. Venkatarama Sastri on the violin, Umayalpuram Kothandarama Iyer on the ghatam and V. Nagarajan on the mrdangam, a quick *Viriboni*/Bhairavi *varnam* led on to Tyagaraja's '*Dinamanivamsa*'/Harikambhoji, Muthusvami Dikshitar's '*Ramanatham*'/Kasiramakriya, Svati Tirunal's sprightly '*Vande sada Padmanabham*'/Navarasakannada, Patnam Subramania Iyer's '*Sankalpamettido*'/Kharaharapriya – a song which disappeared from her later repertoire – several already overexposed songs, '*Sri Kamakoti*'/Saveri, '*Arta piravi*'/Sankarabharanam,

'*Sambho Mahadeva*'/Bauli and '*Paadalum*'/Suddhasaveri, all leading up to *ragam-tanam-pallavi* in Todi.

What is most intriguing is that the identical list of songs was presented by Subbulakshmi at her Music Academy appearance in the 1958 season. Even given that her husband had his own definite ideas on which songs would attract audience applause, this does appear a bit extreme. That Subbulakshmi was capable of inspired improvisation was in no doubt; that she should have been made, machine-like, to repeat herself can only be regarded as unfortunate.

The Music Academy concert at the 1956 season followed the same pattern as the Bhavani concert. The recital began with racy versions of '*Angarakam*'/Surati, '*Rama nannu brovaravemako*'/Harikambhoji and '*Sarasaksha*'/Pantuvarali followed by '*Saranam saranam*'/Saurashtra, two more Tyagaraja *kritis*, '*Ksheenamai*'/Mukhari and '*Dhyaname*'/Dhanyasi and going on through '*Sarojadalanetri*'/Sankarabharanam and '*Hariharaputram*'/Vasanta to a *ragam-tanam-pallavi* in Bhairavi. The post *pallavi* fare included the Nadanamakriya *padam* Paiyyada. All known and to be repeated often. The commercially released version of this concert includes, almost certainly wrongly, Syama Sastri's Todi *svarajati*.

The commercially released version of Subbulakshmi's 1958 recital for the Sri Ramakrishna Mission, Jaffna, also appears suspiciously like a combination of recitals. With R.K. Venkatarama Sastri on the violin, V. Nagarajan on the kanjira and Umayalpuram Kothandarama Iyer on the ghatam, Subbulakshmi raced through '*Era napai*'/Todi, '*Rama nannu*'/Harikambhoji, '*Eppadi manam*'/Huseni, and '*Kanjadalayatakshi*'/Kamalamanohari all leading up to longer presentations of Bhairavi, Kambhoji and Kalyani. The Kambhoji piece, Papanasam Sivan's '*Kadirkamakandan*' is noteworthy in that it addresses the deity at the great shrine to Siva in southern Sri Lanka. The *ragam-tanam-pallavi* in the original recital was probably in Todi, in keeping with the concert practice Subbulakshmi followed that the *varnam* and the main *ragam* are the same, though the commercial release includes a *ragam-tanam-pallavi* in

Shanmukhapriya and other miscellaneous items borrowed from another recital, possibly also in Sri Lanka.

The Bharathi Gana Sabha recital of June 1958 is unexceptional in its choice of songs, which included 'Rama nannu brovaravemako'/Harikambhoji, 'Birana brova'/Kalyani, 'Sri Kamakoti'/Saveri, 'Gopanandana'/Bhushavali, 'Darini'/Suddhasaveri, 'Sarojadalanetri'/Sankarabharanam, 'Sri Parvati'/Bauli, 'Rangapura vihara'/Brindavanasaranga and a *ragam-tanam-pallavi* in Kharaharapriya. Despite the complete lack of novelty, it makes for a very good listening experience. The Rasika Ranjani Sabha recital of September 1958 repeats many of these songs and includes 'Sri Sukra bhagavantam'/Pharaz, 'Tsakkani raja margamu'/Kharaharapriya and a *ragam-tanam-pallavi* in Todi.

The Music Academy recital during the 1959 season is not available commercially but the list of songs suggests the same broad trend: 'Ennaganu'/Pantuvarali, never to leave her active repertoire, 'Sri Kantimatim'/Desisimharava, 'Nannu palimpa'/Mohana, 'Durusuga'/Saveri, 'Sankaracharyam'/Sankarabharanam and a *ragam-tanam-pallavi* in Bhairavi. The recital is possibly also the first time Subbulakshmi presented Svati Tirunal's 'Bhavayami Raghuramam'/ragamalika.

The Music Academy, at its annual conference in December 1957, selected the violin *vidvan* from Mysore, T. Chowdiah (1895–1967), the son of a devadasi dancer Sundaramma of Hassan,[34] to chair the proceedings and receive the title of *Sangitha Kalanidhi*. Mysore was the flavour of the season. Jayachamaraja Wodeyar (1919–74), the maharaja, and a composer of some distinction, opened the proceedings and *Sangitha Kalanidhi* Mysore K. Vasudevacharya gave away the awards at the *sadas* on 1 January 1958 at the P.S. High School grounds. Subbulakshmi was known to sing the songs of both the maharaja and of Vasudevacharya with aplomb; but the occasion was special to her for another reason: Shanmukhavadivu was selected to receive a certificate of merit at the *sadas*. The citation, in a few surprisingly well-chosen words, dwelt on the significant details of her life, her parentage, her tradition, her learning and her greatest achievement.[35]

> Born in 1889 of a family devoted to music; daughter of Sri M.S. Swaminathan and the violinist Akkammal; had her first training in vocal music under Karur Sri Venkataramana Bhagavathar; took to the Veena later and began giving Veena recitals in her fifteenth year; has given numerous recitals and gained the appreciation of the public and the approbation of the veteran *vidwans*; trained her daughter Srimati M.S. Subbulakshmi and gave many recitals along with her young daughter of gifted voice.

Subbulakshmi received the award on behalf of her mother.[36] G.N. Balasubramaniam was also on stage, reading the citation for another award winner, the past ever silently casting a glow on the present. She had sung at the same location the previous day, a fine recital of her middle years. The trinity was well represented, even if with familiar offerings: '*Kamalambike*'/Todi and '*Kanjadalayatakshi*'/Kamalamanohari, '*Gnanamosagarada*'/Purvikalyani, '*Nagumomu*'/Abheri, '*Evarimata*'/Kambhoji and '*Palintsu Kamakshi*'/Madhyamavati. The often-sung '*Sri Kamakoti*'/Saveri and an unusual Svati Tirunal composition, '*Kala kanthi*'/Nilambari, led to a *ragam-tanam-pallavi* in Kalyani.

A recital of 1 January 1960, which circulates on the web but is not available commercially, continues with the trend set during the 1950s. With R.K. Venkatarama Sastri on the violin, V. Nagarajan on the mrdangam and Alangudi Ramachandran on the ghatam, and Vijaya Rajendran singing with her, Subbulakshmi begins with a sprightly *varnam* in Kalyani and runs through the stock songs of the time: '*Rama nannu brovaravemako*'/Harikambhoji, '*Sarojadalanetri*'/Sankarabharanam and '*Rangapuravihara*'/Brindavanasaranga, and other favourites such as

'*Birana brova*'/Kalyani, '*Sri Kamakoti*'/Saveri, '*Gopanandana*'/Bhushavali, '*Ka Va Va*'/Varali and a *ragam-tanam-pallavi* in Kharaharapriya. Everything about the recital is fast, glittering and predictable.

The Rasika Ranjani Sabha recital in 1960, where Subbulakshmi was accompanied by M.S. Gopalakrishnan on the violin, T.K. Murthy on the mrdangam, Umayalpuram Kothandarama Iyer on the ghatam and Pudukkottai Mahadevan on the morsing, rests — like every other concert of the time — on flashy displays of vocal prowess. '*Viriboni*'/Bhairavi, '*Jagadanandakaraka*'/Nata and Svati Tirunal's '*Devadeva kalayami*'/Mayamalavagaula were followed by *alapanas* for '*Sri Kantimatim*'/Desisimharava and '*Sri Kamakoti*'/Saveri. Other often-heard pieces led up to '*Akshayalingavibho*'/Sankarabharanam and later to a *ragam-tanam-pallavi* in Simhendramadhyamam.

The Music Academy season concert in the same year, 1960, was very similar in structure with '*Viriboni*'/Bhairavi and a *ragam-tanam-pallavi* in Kharaharapriya between them containing a Mayamalavagaula, a Pantuvarali, a Sankarabharanam and Syama Sastri's Yadukulakambhoji *svarajati*. This is what the public liked, popular songs, racy *alapanas*, slightly over-fast *svaraprasthara* and at all times an electrifying pace. Ten years later, the pace had reduced considerably and that was Subbulakshmi at her most mellow and most reposeful. But that was still in the future.

Visits to Delhi continued to be frequent. There is a record of a 1958 concert which she concluded with the national anthem[37] as also of a recital at a wedding in a politician's home in Delhi in August 1959. A Vigyan Bhavan recital in aid of the Kashmir Relief Fund was widely reviewed with one sharp critic noting that one 'of the dangers to which a great musician with a popular following is exposed is the resulting dilution in his or her art',[38] clearly a reference to Subbulakshmi's endless repetition, presented in order to secure audience applause. The critic was not quite done. 'M.S. Subbulakshmi finds herself in this predicament today. People think of her as Meerabai, as Gandhiji's favourite singer but not as a classical singer the like of whom we may not hear for another decade or so.' One can indeed sympathize with the critic who notes with some sorrow that, 'the pity of it all was that last evening she was in magnificent form'.

A critic in 1961 regretfully noted Subbulakshmi's advancing years.[39] At forty-five she was hardly decrepit but such was the criticism of the time. Yet another critic waited 'with some trepidation' for a concert in New Delhi, the unease stemming from the likelihood, duly confirmed, of a concert which was a mish-mash of genres and languages, 'two rounds of Hindi bhajans interrupting the Karnatak [sic] fare with '*Vaishnava Jana to*' and a Rabindra geet thrown in for good measure'.[40] While conceding that 'though long-established in the front rank of artists she hasn't ceased to grow', the critic also mourned that 'a similar variety programme during her last appearance in Delhi a year ago ... had been dismal'.[41] It was left, at one of these concerts, for Vice President Radhakrishnan to rise to Subbulakshmi's defence by observing that since she had become a national symbol she needed perforce to satisfy many tastes.[42] There is reason to believe that Subbulakshmi herself was not at ease with the makeover to her presentational style. Many years later, a fellow musician noted, 'While her singing was appreciated by the crowd, deep inside she always had the yearning to sing and achieve greater heights through singing in a more classical style which may not always have a mass appeal.' But by this stage of her career, whatever influence she may have had over the content of her concerts had completely disappeared.[43]

Most of Subbulakshmi's *sabha* concerts of the 1950s included a *ragam-tanam-pallavi* suite, a somewhat stylized presentation, and often prized as the centrepiece of a traditional music recital. This presentation calls for a development of the *raga*, as in *alapana*, followed by further development in the form of *tanam*, or accelerated phrases using the word 'anantam' or variations thereon. The pre-composed *pallavi* comes then, often set to tricky *tala* structures, and sung in various speeds with *neraval* and several rounds of *kalpana svaras*. A neat description of the exact nature of this form is available in an American source.[44] It is a presentation which calls upon an artiste's imagination and the ability to improvise. It calls for complete control over *laya* and it is about the only recognized form in the classical repertory where raga is privileged over *sahitya*.

Subbulakshmi sang *ragam-tanam-pallavi* often for the major part of her career, at least over the period 1940–70, and this fact is insufficiently recognized. It is true that in her later career, when the mood was overtly 'popular devotional', she gave up the practice, but for the better part of her concert life she was a traditionalist. This matter arises frequently with Subbulakshmi always being compared poorly, and unfairly, to Pattammal. She may not have sung this form as consistently as Pattammal, and neither of these singers was as adept and ingenious in *ragam-tanam-pallavi* as Vasanthakumari, but the record speaks for itself. A popular website has recordings of at least twenty *ragam-tanam-pallavi* renderings and these have been studied in some depth by a distinguished *vainika*, a student, incidentally, of T. Brinda who came from a tradition where *ragam-tanam-pallavi* was not performed at all.[45] It is interesting, and again somewhat sad, that not singing a *ragam-tanam-pallavi* suite has never been held in the case of Brinda to indicate a lack of *vidvat* and always so held in the case of Subbulakshmi.

When Pattammal and Subbulakshmi began their concert careers in the early 1930s, there were no practising women musicians from whom they could learn the art and style of *ragam-tanam-pallavi*, if one discounts such performers as the one we came across earlier, who was demolished by the learned critic in the *Hindu*. It is not even very clear where they learnt the form. *Tanam*, for instance, which is an extension of raga rendering using characteristically accelerated phrases, is a skilled art. In a lecture-demonstration on the raga Todi, Vasanthakumari observed that *tanam* was best sung by male singers, as that had its own '*gambhiram*' or solidity, but added modestly that women were also now singing *tanam*.[46] Semmangudi Srinivasa Iyer is reported to have said of Subbulakshmi that he had never heard a woman musician sing *tanam* better. Great masters can be allowed backhanded compliments, but the point remains that this was a diligently acquired skill. Years later, *Sangitha Kalanidhi* R. Vedavalli wrote appreciatively of Subbulakshmi's correct use of the syllables meant for *tanam* and of the possibility that her skill in *tanam* grew out of her experience in playing the vina.

Subbulakshmi stuck to a few ragas when she presented a *pallavi* suite, Todi, Sankarabharanam, Shanmukhapriya, Kharaharapriya, Kalyani, Bhairavi and Kiravani being the most common, with Kambhoji following. In her early concert years, she generally stayed with the convention of a *varnam* and *pallavi* being in the same raga. There are stray *pallavis* in Hemavati, Begada, Mohana, Mayamalavagaula, Dhanyasi, Dharmavati, Simhendramadhyamam and Saveri. This is a relatively small number and reflects the same tendency as was known with Subbulakshmi's song renderings, to stick to a limited, and highly finished, set of songs, out of a considerably larger, and enviable, repertoire. The question of why a musician of such gifts should have been so consistently risk-averse will continue to occupy us. It is not that she was unequipped. A story is recounted of the early 1950s when Subbulakshmi learnt from the mrdangam *vidvan* Palani Subramania Pillai, and performed the next day in a Thanjavur concert a tricky Natakuranji *pallavi*.[47] These were occasions out of the ordinary.

Subbulakshmi's raga renderings were, beyond doubt, exceptional. If she sought to titillate the audience with adventurous phrases in the higher octave, her raga *alapana*, when sung as part of a *pallavi* suite invariably include slow and thoughtful explorations of the lower octave. She would usually devote a full half of the time she spent on the entire exercise on the development of the raga. The *pallavis* themselves were well conceived and often complicated. There were traditional texts used for the *pallavi*, similar to the *bandish* in *khayal* singing, though it is always open to the artiste to compose her own. Even where the *tala* structure was relatively straightforward, and often they were not, the manner of the execution, and especially the *neraval*, was always of a high quality.

Subbulakshmi is known to have learnt to play the mrdangam in her youth, a skill designed to teach the art of rhythm. The *ragam-tanam-pallavi* presented at the Music Academy in December 1971, for instance, is a traditional *pallavi* text, 'Dasarathe karunapayonidhe inakulatilaka', in Sankarabharanam, in the relatively more common *adi tala*, a beat of eight. The catch, however, is that each beat of the eight has four sub-beats, or *kalai*, making a total of thirty-two, with the text itself starting at the third of the thirty-two beats. In the correct terminology, this would be an *adi tala*, four-*kalai pallavi*.[48] This is sung at four speeds, all within the strict rubric of the *tala*, using the principles of *anuloma* and *pratiloma*. It is an exceedingly tidy demonstration of *laya gnana*, or the sense of beat.

Family matters were a preoccupation in Subbulakshmi's life through the 1950s. Early in 1954, K.R. Athmanathan joined the Kalki Gardens establishment, having been introduced to the family by Semmangudi Srinivasa Iyer as a younger brother of the musicians K.R. Kumaraswami (1913–2005) and K.R. Kedaranathan (1925–2007). 'Athma' was a close friend, companion and intimate of Sadasivam and remained a devoted aide to Subbulakshmi till the very end.

Radha's marriage to G. Viswanathan and Vijaya's to K. Rajendran were conducted in June 1957 with great style. Old-timers still recall the festivities of the 'double' wedding. Through this time, a young grand-nephew of Sadasivam, R. Kannakutti, the son of his niece Mangalam, was a more or less permanent resident of Kalki Gardens. The boy was formally adopted, through Vedic ritual, in June 1961 and given the name S. Tyagarajan.[49]

There is evidence in the shape of a few letters which survive from Subbulakshmi to those in her immediate family circle that she was preoccupied with mundane, domestic events. The letters are replete with references to religious observances, festivals, childbirth, ill-health and social engagements. There is nothing in any of them to suggest that the author sang, leave alone that she was the shining star of her generation.

9

Maestra: The Great Concert Years

भज रे रे चित्त बालाम्बिकाम् भक्त कल्प लतिकाम्[1]

('Chant, besotted mind, chant
Her name nubile
And let her twine
You, entwine you
As to the yonder branch
Does the vine'
from Muthusvami Dikshitar's composition *'Bhaja re re.'*
in the raga Kalyani)

THE core of Subbulakshmi's repertoire was the compositions of the trinity; 'These three great men were born in the same place and were contemporaries of one another. They should be remembered for ever'.[2] Subbulakshmi's contribution towards preserving the heritage of the three composers is to be recognized.[3] Of course, it was what she brought to her renderings of their songs but she was also instrumental in purchasing Syama Sastri's house for ₹8,000 in 1962 and Tyagaraja's house for a larger sum in 1975 and transferring both to the Tiruvarur Music Trinity Commemoration Sabha. She also contributed to the construction of a memorial to Muthusvami Dikshitar as there was no trace of the original house in Tiruvarur.[4]

However, her repertoire itself, as that of other concert performers, included many other more contemporary composers, the most prominent being Papanasam Sivan, to whom we will return. Specific songs of Mysore Sadasiva Rao (1805?–85), Mysore Vasudevacharya and Jayachamaraja Wodeyar were so prominent in Subbulakshmi's repertoire that their reputation lasts along with hers, as also select songs of Patnam Subramania Iyer.

Mysore Sadasiva Rao's 'Sri Kamakoti'/Saveri is one of these songs, not that it is sung very much any more.[5] Subbulakshmi raised the song to cult status, with high-voltage *neraval* at the line, 'Kadamba vana nilaye...' There are less than fifty songs of this composer of which Subbulakshmi sang 'Saketa nagara natha'/Harikambhoji and, late in life, 'Sri Shanmukha janaka'/Sankarabharanam.

Jayachamaraja Wodeyar, the last ruler of Mysore, was an interesting and cultivated man with academic attainments in Indian philosophy and training in Western music on the piano in addition to his abilities as a composer of songs in the Carnatic tradition. Of the many pieces attributed to him, Subbulakshmi famously sang 'Ksheerasagarasayana'/Mayamalavagaula. The UN Concert of 1966 included 'Siva Siva Siva bho'/Nadanamakriya and she also sang 'Chintayami jagadamba'/Hindolam and 'Sri Jalandhara'/Gambhiranata. It is surprising that Subbulakshmi did not favour his compositions any more than she did. He was by way of being a friend and patron and his songs are in the expressive Sanskrit she sang so well. Jayachamaraja Wodeyar composed 108 songs, with ninety-four published, with very few ragas, if any, which have been repeated.[6]

It is possible that Wodeyar was assisted in his musical composition (and the possibility of assistance cannot be ruled out even in the case of that other royal composer, Svati Tirunal of Travancore) by the celebrated Mysore Vasudevacharya, himself from the direct musical line of Tyagaraja and a composer of renown.[7] His 'Brochevarevarura'/

Maestra: The Great Concert Years 157

Khamas must be regarded as the ranking composition in that raga. The song is widely sung but Subbulakshmi's rendering conveys both radiance and clarity.

Vasudevacharya wrote about 200 songs, including *varnams* and *javalis*. Subbulakshmi actually sang very few of them.[8] In a special radio programme, she sang the Khamas piece and '*Sri Chamundeshwari*'/Bilahari, another favourite, but also '*Palukavademira*'/Devamanohari, '*Mamavatu Sri Saraswati*'/Hindolam, '*Ninne Nammiti*'/Simhendramadhyamam, '*Pranatarthiharam*'/Jenjuti and a Surati *tillana*. There is a solitary reference in the available material to '*Ra ra yani pilacite*'/Kharaharapriya, sung in Secunderabad in March 1987.

Patnam Subramania Iyer's reputation rests almost totally on the strength of his belonging to the direct line of discipleship from Tyagaraja, his teacher Manambuchavadi Venkatasubbier being one of Tyagaraja's disciples. His Telugu compositions derive entirely from Tyagaraja in their construction and language. However, even at their best, they do not carry the intensity or dexterity with language found in Tyagaraja. Several devadasi singers learnt from him, notably Lakshminarayani and Rangamma, known as the Enadi Sisters, Pappa and Radha, the daughters of Salem Meenakshi; and Dhanammal's eldest daughter T. Rajalakshmi, later to have herself been a teacher of D.K. Pattammal.[9]

Many compositions of 'Patnam' are published with notation but comparatively few are in currency.[10] Subbulakshmi sang '*Raghuvamsasudha*'/Kadanakutuhalam with éclat, steeping in melody what could easily have become a marching song. '*Sankalpame*'/Kharaharapriya was another favourite in her middle years as were '*Maravakave*'/Sama and '*Marivere*'/Shanmukhapriya. She also sang '*Aparadhamula*'/Latangi in her later years. Patnam Subramania Iyer's presence in her repertoire was, however, most famously established by the *varnam* in Todi, '*Era napai*', which Subbulakshmi sang extremely often, and the Abhogi *varnam*, '*Evari bodhana*'. It is, of course, true, that these *varnams* are sung very often by many musicians.[11]

There are a host of other composers, whose output is less well known on the concert circuit. Tarangambadi Panchanatha Iyer who wrote '*Birana brova idey*'/Kalyani, lives only on the strength of Subbulakshmi's rendering of that one particular song. Of the compositions of Ramanathapuram 'Poochi' Srinivasa Iyengar (1860–1919), Subbulakshmi famously sang '*Saragunapalimpa*'/Kedaragaula and also '*Rama ninne nammitini*'/Saranga, '*Anudinamu*'/Begada, and the *varnam* in Kanada, '*Nera nammitini*'. Subbarama Dikshitar (1839–1906) was primarily a musicologist but of his many compositions Subbulakshmi sang '*Sankaracharyam*'/Sankarabharanam very often. Late in her career, she presented his Telugu song '*Parthasarathi ni sevimpani*' in Yadukulakambhoji. Alone among his compositions, Tirupati Narayanaswami Naidu's '*Ikanaina*' in Pushpalatika has had any sort of popularity and was sung by many women singers and famously by Subbulakshmi. Puliyur Doraswami Iyer's '*Sarasiruhasana*'/Nata was another favourite.

In later years, Subbulakshmi sang selectively of contemporary composers: '*Nidayaledani*'/Dhanyasi of 'Spencer' Venugopal (born 1930); '*Mangalavinayakane*'/Ramapriya and '*Muruga muruga*'/Saveri both of Periasami Thooran (1908–87); '*Karunaipuriya nalla tharunam*'/Sriranjani, '*Kannan idam*'/ragamalika and '*Ambigaye*'/Anandabhairavi, all of Ambujam Krishna (1917–89); and '*Vinayaka Vighnavinasaka*'/Hamsadhwani of Ra. Ganapathi (1935–2012). It is entirely likely that she learnt the songs of other composers as well, even if they were not often aired from the concert stage, such as Andavan Pichai's '*Sharade*' and V. Raghavan's '*Kerala dharani*', both in Mohana. It is believed, for instance, that she studied the songs of T. Lakshmana Pillai (1864–1950) but these are not known from the available concert lists.[12]

Possibly the most significant of contemporary composers, not just as represented in Subbulakshmi's repertoire but in the wider world of the form itself, is *Sangitha Kalanidhi* Papanasam Sivan. She sang his songs through her performing career, starting with those he wrote for her in *Sevasadanam, Sakuntalai* and *Savitri*.[13] It is likely that she learnt these directly from him, as well as other songs not meant for the screen but for the concert stage, so much so that an unpleasant rumour has persisted that Papanasam Sivan was prevented from teaching anyone else the songs he taught Subbulakshmi.

Over the years, Subbulakshmi frequently sang *'Paratpara'*/ Vachaspati, *'Gajavadana'*/Sriranjani, *'Kartikeya'*/Todi, *'Saravanabhava'*/ Shanmukhapriya, *'Narayana divya namam'*/Mohana, *'Devi neeye thunai'*/ Kiravani and *'Saravanabhava'*/Madhyamavati. Concerts in her early career featured *'Paramukham'*/Kharaharapriya, *'Tamadamen'*/Todi, *'Kana kann kodi'*/Kambhoji, *'Ma dayai'*/Vasanta, *'Ikaparam'* and *'Guha saravanabhava'* both in Simhendramadhyamam, *'Ninnarul'* and *'Deviyai pujai'* both in Kamavardhini, *'Saranam Ayyappa'*/Mukhari and *'Kapali'*/Mohana. *'Sankara dayakara'*/Harikambhoji and *'Vijaya dvaraka'*/Gaulipantu appeared later as did *'Srinivasa'*/Hamsanandi; but if one composition of Sivan must be permanently identified with Subbulakshmi it must be *'Ka Va Va'*/Varali, a song she sang beautifully, with all the restraint for which it calls.[14]

Papanasam Sivan did much to shore up the stock of Tamil songs available for performance and is fully entitled to be called a *vaggeyakara*. It is not just that his language was simple, often Sanskrit-inflected, but that he had a fine sense of what made a composition concert-worthy. It is said that he was not, indeed, a great scholar of Tamil, but he knew how to communicate with the ordinary speaker of the language. Of his 2,000-odd songs, about 800 are for the films, and another fifty in Sanskrit, again of a very simple type. Whatever his use of language may have been, Papanasam Sivan was a gifted musician with a sense of *ragabhava* and his songs can stand detailed extemporizing onstage.

Abiding faith appears to have sustained him through success and adversity. Speaking at the Music Academy in 1971, very late in his life, he said,

The Lord then led me to the cinema. He made me see several arts. He gave me wealth and also took it away and made me suffer in penury. He made me suffer in illness and through all this He made me sing of Him again and again. He gave me position and importance. Whatever fortune I enjoyed is all His blessing ... My blooming into a composer is entirely His great compassion.[15]

We need to take note of three great composers in Sanskrit, from a time well before concert pattern and practice, as we now know it, was established, but whose works continue to be performed: Jayadeva of the latter part of the twelfth century, Narayana Tirtha (1650/1675–1745) and Sadasiva Brahmendra of the eighteenth century.

Jayadeva is at once a mystic and a romantic, who in the twenty-four songs of the *Gita Govinda* saw in his love of his beloved Padmavati the love of Krishna for Radha. In his conception, a sensuous, earthly love grows with increased realization into a divine union, a tale of the human soul's relations 'alternately with earthly and celestial beauty'.[16] The verses of the *Gita Govinda*, the *ashtapadi*, are widely known in eastern and southern India and scholars have identified the ragas in which the twenty-four verses may have originally been set. The verses are ideal for dance and are so performed by masters of the Odissi style and in Kathakali, where the rendering is entirely different from the style adopted by the bhajana tradition; but they were considered eminently suitable for rendering in concert and Semmangudi Srinivasa Iyer published a musically notated text in 1963.[17]

Subbulakshmi is believed to have learnt all twenty-four songs from one P.S. Srinivasa Rao[18] but the only one which can be found in the concert lists is the nineteenth song, '*Vadasi yadi kinchidapi*' set in the raga Mukhari, and still so sung by musicians of the Semmangudi school. There is, of course, the first song, on the theme of the *dasavatara*, the ten incarnations of Vishnu, which Subbulakshmi included as part of the Annamacharya series of records in the late 1970s. Alone among the twenty-four songs, this piece may be said to be non-erotic in style and orientation, a fact which may have weighed much with Subbulakshmi's mentors.

Narayana Tirtha hailed from the Telugu regions and his *Krishna lila tarangini* is inspired in style and content by the *Gita Govinda*. It is believed that Tyagaraja was familiar with the songs of the *tarangini*.[19] Subbulakshmi sang 'Madhava mamava'/Nilambari and 'Govindam iha'/ Bagesri often and there was a commemorative concert in 1986,[20] exclusively of songs from the *Krishna lila tarangini*, as was one of her very last concerts, in 1997.

Sadasiva Brahmendra, a near contemporary of Narayana Tirtha, was from the Kaveri region. Semmangudi Srinivasa Iyer set twenty-three of his songs to notation;[21] some of these such as 'Bruhi Mukundeti'/Kuranji, 'Bhajare yadunatham'/Pilu and 'Manasa sancharare'/Sama were prominent in Subbulakshmi's repertoire.

The contemporary reputation of Svati Tirunal Rama Varma, Maharaja of Travancore, owes a great deal to Semmangudi Srinivasa Iyer, and Subbulakshmi as Semmangudi's leading student did much to popularize the maharaja's songs. In 1939, Muthiah Bhagavathar and he were commissioned by the royal house of Travancore to locate authentic notation for songs where such were available, and to actually set a large number of them to raga, a task assigned to them by the formidable Maharani Sethu Parvati Bayi herself.[22] Semmangudi referred to this task as 'restoration and revivification'.[23] It is now accepted that, for the large part, only the texts of Svati Tirunal's songs survive him, assuming that these texts were his own work and not that of palace courtiers.[24] Even as assiduous a supporter of the house of Travancore as *Sachivottama* Sir C.P. Ramaswami Aiyar conceded that the classical musical traditions of the south were shaped by the trinity 'along with the artistic group that surrounded and was dominated by the Royal musician Sri Svati Tirunal'.[25]

Svati Tirunal composed, or encouraged the composition of, pieces in a very wide range of forms including *kirtana, padam, javali* and *tillana*, and in several languages. One source attributes to him texts for opera and seventy-five *padams* meant for dance.[26] Svati Tirunal's Sanskrit is cumbersome and lacks the familiarity of Muthusvami Dikshitar's language, even given that Dikshitar's Sanskrit is classically pure and his songs much the more difficult. As a critic bitingly observed, '...the Maharaja's *kritis*, unlike Dikshitar's, are more a triumph of scholarship than of self-effacing devotion'.[27] He does not stop there. 'In [the songs of Svati Tirunal] one seems to move in a narrow circle of decorum, propriety and courtesy. Not in them the soaring reach of the soul that knocks at the gates of the nine fortresses of Sri Lalitha and demands to be admitted. Not in them the fervid yearning of love that one finds in '*Minakshi me mudam dehi*' or the exultant joy of meeting as in '*Rangapura vihara*'. Against the vast monolithic structures of Dikshitar, Svati Tirunal's compositions look like neatly built villas in a decorous suburb'.

Subbulakshmi, who sang both of these compositions of Muthusvami Dikshitar with all the discipline they call for, did not concern herself with issues of language or, later on, with the debate which raged over the authenticity of Svati Tirunal's songs.[28] She sang the songs taught to her and if Srinivasa Iyer's diligent setting to raga of Svati Tirunal's *sahitya*, and their publication in book form, has ensured that the songs have lived, so have her renderings of the more popular among them.

'*Bhavayami Raghuramam*'/ragamalika was made famous by Subbulakshmi but she sang several other compositions of Svati Tirunal such as '*Sarasaksha*'/Pantuvarali, '*Devadeva kalayami*'/Mayamalavagaula, '*Kripaya palaya*'/Charukesi, '*Gopalaka*'/Revagupti, '*Jaya Jaya Padmanabhanujesha*'/Manirangu, '*Gopanandana*'/Bhushavali, '*Aliveni*'/Kuranji and '*Anjaneya*'/Saveri. Infrequently sung were '*Pahi Sripate*'/Hamsadhwani, '*Devi jagajjanani*'/Sankarabharanam, '*Mamava sada'*/Kanada, *'Paripahimam'*/Mohana, *'Kala kanthi'*/Nilambari, *'Pankajalochana'*/Kalyani, *'Sri Kumara'*/Athana, *'Smara haripada'*/Sama, the ragamalika *'Pannagendrasayana'* and *'Vande sada'*/Navarasakannada.

But, oddly, some of the Svati Tirunal songs with which she is most closely associated did not come from the Semmangudi Srinivasa Iyer tradition. *'Rama Rama gunaseema'*/Simhendramadhyamam was taught to her by Musiri Subramania Iyer and the *tillana* in Dhanasri was set to music by Lalgudi Jayaraman.[29] *'Bhogindra sayinam'*/Kuntalavarali, a Subbulakshmi staple over many decades, is a song she probably learnt from Musiri Subramania Iyer and sang to great effect, a torrent of words set to an ungainly beat of five.[30]

There was also a Svati Tirunal memorial concert, probably of the early 1960s, which includes songs which Subbulakshmi did not commonly sing: *'Sarasijanabha murare'*/Todi, *'Kanakamaya'*/Huseni, *'Nadasudhatava'*/Kuranji and *'Bhujagasayanam'*/Yadukulakambhoji. Interestingly, though she sang Hindi bhajans from her earliest concert days, she did not attempt Svati Tirunal's Hindi pieces, some of which are indeed concert-worthy.

By about the mid 1950s, Subbulakshmi had put together a core stock of bhajans which never left her repertoire. There were, of course, the songs of Mira, mainly from the film. There was a small set of songs of Surdas, including *'He Govinda Hey Gopala'* and *'Akhiyan Hari darasan ki pyaasi'*. Many years later, in 1986, a commercial release included *'Nis din barasat nain hamare'*, *'Madhubana tuma'*, *'Kunja nikunja'* and a few other songs.[31] Subbulakshmi sang Tulsidas's *'Tu dayalu deen haun, tu daani han bhikari'* and *'Bhaja mana Rama charana'* and *'Sri Ramachandra kripalu'*, the latter two songs often prefaced by a Sanskrit sloka. A song attributed to Kabir, *'Bhajore Bhaiyya'*, was hugely popular in her song list, as were songs of Nanak, including *'Thakur tum sharanayi'*, *'Kahe re bana khojana jaaye'*, *'Rama bhaja'* and *'Rama simira'*.

There were many more bhajans Subbulakshmi learnt but did not present often, if at all, in concerts, such as *Gave guni ganika* of Raskhan. Of Nanak, other than the four bhajans mentioned above, she certainly also sang '*Naam japan kyon chhod diya*' and the beautiful '*Sumiran kar le*', a plaintive admission of the fruitlessnes of a life without a realization of God's presence[32] and which Gandhi translated.

> O my soul, remember thy God, thy years are rolling by without His sacred name – man without Harinama is even like a well without water or a cow without milk or a temple without light or a fruit tree without fruit or body without eyes or night without the moon, or the earth without rain or a pundit without a knowledge of the Vedas. O good man watch thy desire, anger, pride and ambition and give them up. Nanakshah says: O God there is no one to befriend save Thee.[33]

The names of two contemporary women mystics will always remain linked to that of Subbulakshmi. Rehana, or Raihana, Tyabji (1900–75) who wrote '*Yaad ave*', for the Hindi film *Meera*, was a follower of Gandhi and devoted to the worship of Krishna, and also the daughter of Badruddin Tyabji, a prominent Congressman of his time. Indira Devi (1920–88) was a disciple of Dilip Kumar Roy of the Sri Aurobindo Ashram in Pondicherry. Almost certainly it was he who introduced Subbulakshmi to the verses composed by his disciple who wrote bhajans in the form and voice of Mira; '*Hari main to, Ghunguru baandh*', '*Hey Govinda Hey Gopala*', '*Kitne dosh ginaaoon*', '*Ghadi ek nahin*' and '*Phir sakhi ritu saavan aayi*' were aired often in concerts of the later years. These songs, unsurprisingly, have disappeared from the repertoires of present-day musicians.

The 1960s were for Subbulakshmi great concert years with frequent *sabha* appearances, wedding concerts and radio programmes. The partial list of benefit concerts has sixty-three such recitals in this decade. There was much travel within the country. Subbulakshmi's well-wishers were plentifully in high office. T.T. Krishnamachari was finance minister, Jawaharlal Nehru was still prime minister, and Sarvepalli Radhakrishnan was the president. Padmaja Naidu was governor in Calcutta, Sucheta Kripalani was chief minister in Lucknow, both friends.

Shanmukhavadivu lived to see her daughter's rise to national fame but her passing on 5 August 1962 was before Subbulakshmi's greatest successes.[34] The papers noted the end respectfully and it appears that Subbulakshmi and her brother and husband were present in Madurai at the time.

It is hard not to think of Shanmukhavadivu's life without sadness. She was Subbulakshmi's first teacher, but she would have lived with the knowledge that her daughter had left her. It is not that there was no contact between them. There were visits to Madurai, but it was no longer a world with which Subbulakshmi had a connection.[35] An intimate writes of Subbulakshmi that she was aware that 'the road to fame could also be the road to infamy', a road she was resolutely unwilling to take.[36] But if Subbulakshmi had rejected her past, her devotion to Shanmukhavadivu's memory was absolute. In her living room, amidst a very large number of photographs of saints and holy men, of dignitaries and statesmen, and of musicians and dancers, the pride of place was always given to a studio photograph of Shanmukhavadivu holding a small black vina, the vina itself in repose beneath the photograph.

Sabha concerts were thick on the ground. Decisions regarding which invitations to accept and which not, which causes to support and which platforms to grace, were all taken by Sadasivam, then as always. A letter of the time from Sadasivam carries the extraordinary line: 'There is a possibility of my accepting one or two engagements in

Calcutta and Delhi during October', and we can be sure that this was his standard practice.[37]

There is another account of the authorities at the great shrine at Tirupati wishing to have Subbulakshmi sing during the visit of Prime Minister Lal Bahadur Shastri and of some Madras notables having to 'visit ... Kalki Gardens and persuade Sadasivam to make it convenient to be at Tirumala during the visit of the Prime Minister'.[38] It does not appear that fees or professional charges were in any way the determining factor in what met his approval but more his sense of how respectfully the invitations were made or how such an engagement would reflect on his wife's image.

Subbulakshmi did not perform in the late 1950s and early 1960s at the annual festival of the Tamil Isai Sangam but made regular Music Academy appearances. Her concert on 30 December 1962 is still remembered for its *ragam-tanam-pallavi* in Begada, preceded by four songs of Tyagaraja, the *'Vachamago'*/Kaikavasi, *'Entaveduko'*/Saraswatimanohari, *'Swararagasudha'*/Sankarabharanam and *'Vara Narada'*/Vijayasri; Muthusvami Dikshitar's *navavarana dhyana kriti* in Todi, *'Kamalambike'*; and two songs of Papanasam Sivan, the *'Ninarul iyamba'*/Pantuvarali and *'Saranam Ayyapa'*/Mukhari. There was also an unusual learning from Musiri Subramania Iyer, Svati Tirunal's *'Sri Kumara nagaralaye'* in Athana. Many of these were to appear frequently on stage in later years, and the concert itself is a model of structure and design.[39]

Appearances in Bombay were frequent, often at the Shanmukhananda Fine Arts & Sangeetha Sabha, a vast theatre seating 3,000 people where musicians from the south were expected to perform twice over a weekend, so that all members of the *sabha* could have access to a live performance. In those days, the only option to live concerts was the radio and the highly knowledgeable and music-starved Bombay audience was always a test even for the most senior performers. A 1963 concert is available on the net; this may have been one of the first where Subbulakshmi was accompanied by V.V. Subramanyam on the violin along with T.K. Murthy, who had been playing with her a while by then, on the mrdangam.[40] It is a concert structured tightly enough, with a *varnam*, 'Era napai', and a *ragam-tanam-pallavi*, 'Sivohamsachhidananda purna bodoham', both in the same raga, Todi, and with familiar pieces in between, 'Vatapi'/Hamsadhwani, 'Rama nannu brovaravemako'/ Harikambhoji, an early appearance of a never-to-be-given-up favourite, 'Ksheerasagarasayana'/Mayamalavagaula, an unusual pairing of two songs in very similar ragas, 'Sri Kantimatim'/Desisimharava and 'Rama Rama gunaseema'/Simhendramadhyamam and an inevitable Sankarabharanam with 'Sankaracharyam'.

A very well-organized 'programme of homage' was organized on radio on the occasion of the Kshetrayya tercentenary in August 1963.[41] Subbulakshmi, Pattammal and Vasanthakumari all sang, as did Musiri Subramania Iyer, Semmangudi Srinivasa Iyer, Balamuralikrishna, Brinda and Muktha, and Jayammal and Balasaraswati.[42] The secrets of this grand celebration are presumably locked in the vaults of All India Radio. We know of a benefit concert for the Rasika Ranjani Sabha Building Fund, Calcutta, at Sri Thyagaraja Hall, Calcutta, on 10 November 1963 and of a Madras concert in December of that year, including the unusual Tyagaraja *kriti*, 'Munnu Ravana' in Todi, a song otherwise not seen in the concert lists available. The Music Academy concert on 29 December 1963 repeated the *varnam/pallavi* pairing in Todi along with another Sankarabharanam. Likewise, in a concert at the Sri Krishna Gana Sabha in June 1965, a recital which included the 'Era napai' *varnam*, and a *ragam-tanam-pallavi*, both in Todi, and a modern Sankarabharanam composition, N.S. Ramachandran's 'Sri Chandrasekhara yatindram'.[43]

A close study of these concert lists lends itself to the view that Subbulakshmi actually applied herself seriously to issues of song selection, structure and design only for her annual appearances at the Music Academy during the season. The recitals on 27 December 1964 and 25 December 1965 are masterpieces. In 1964, the *varnam-pallavi* pairing was in Sankarabharanam, with a cumbersome *jhampa tala varnam* in Malayalam, 'Indumukhi', and a *rupaka tala pallavi*, 'Saravanabhava guru guha sanmukha svaminathena'. There were other strong concert pieces: 'Saketanagaranatha'/Harikambhoji, Syama Sastri's Yadukulakambhoji *svarajati* 'Kamakshi', 'Gopalaka'/Revagupti and Muthusvami Dikshitar's 'Sri Krishnam'/Todi.

There is a poignant account of G.N. Balasubramaniam, at this stage close to the end of his life, hearing this concert of Subbulakshmi on the radio and requesting Semmangudi Srinivasa Iyer to teach him the Todi composition.[44] The printed list includes, unusually, 'Tsakkani raja margamu', Tyagaraja's great song in Kharaharapriya, but it is possible that the *alapana* was followed by some other song.[45] Through this period, her standard post-*pallavi* fare included the Tamil ragamalika 'Vadavaraiyai', verses from the 'Annapurnashtakam' followed by Purandaradasa's 'Dasana madiko enna' in Nadanamakriya and 'Sambho Mahadeva'/Bauli.

Subbulakshmi's Music Academy concert during the 1965 season began with an unusual *varnam*, 'Sarasijamukhiro' in Arabhi, immediately followed by four Tyagaraja *kritis*, 'Endaro'/Sri, 'Sitamma'/Vasanta, 'Nidhi tsala sukhama'/Kalyani and 'Manavyala'/Nalinakanti. 'Sri Subramanyaya namaste'/Kambhoji and 'Kanakasaila'/Punnagavarali ensured that the great composers were all represented after which came a *ragam-tanam-pallavi* in Kiravani, 'Maa madura minakshi maam paahi' set to a Khanda *jati* triputa tala.

As if to prove the counter to this, there was a New Delhi recital on 30 November 1965, at the Fourth Conference of Asian & Pacific Accountants. Fifteen songs were presented, of which eight were bhajans. Sadasivam was obviously of the view that audiences outside Madras wanted to hear only light pieces in many languages. The fact that Subbulakshmi sang in many languages, not that she was the only musician to do so, always weighed very heavily with her manager husband. Here was an artiste in her prime, steeped in tradition and learning, fluent in the grammar of her style and capable of great imagination – and she was being made to perform to a hybrid format of no specific attraction. It must always be regarded as an extraordinary shame.

The year 1963 took Subbulakshmi abroad for her first major concert, to Edinburgh. There had been earlier tours abroad, notably to Jaffna in both 1943 and 1957, but this was a new experience, to be performing before a cosmopolitan, foreign audience. The Madras representative of the British Council, thrilled by this early exposure on a global platform of Indian music at its finest, noted, 'Subbulakshmi sang in the evening as Ravi Shankar played in the morning. She was a delight to hear, a beautifully melodious style of singing and her preliminary improvisations were models of economy, saying all that needed to be said as an introduction to each song. This was an excellent initiation into the delights and intricacies of Carnatic vocal music'.[46] This was a friend writing, and one who had possibly some exposure to the music of India.

A music critic with no exposure to Indian music, while respectful to 'the renowned Mme. Subbulakshmi' observed that 'it took time to get used to the idea of the human voice (and a voice of very appealing timbre at that) being treated more or less as an instrument within the accompanying instrumental consort, and rarely emerging as top dog in the Western way'.[47] To an Indian audience, Subbulakshmi would never have appeared as anything other than the lead performer on stage and nor indeed would her accompanists have thought so. It is interesting that a practised Western ear should have got a contrary impression. In any case, the critic seems to have responded more readily to Ravi Shankar, playing the sitar with Alla Rakha (1919–2000) on the tabla, and again with Ali Akbar Khan (1922–2009) on the sarod, a reaction true of many Indian *rasikas*.[48] The Indian press was more responsive to Subbulakshmi with the *Hindu* making special mention of the *ragam-tanam-pallavi* suite in Simhendramadhyamam.[49]

Subbulakshmi's peer Balasaraswati made an enormous impact in Edinburgh in 1963, building on the attention she had drawn over a major tour of the United States in late 1962. According to her biographer, additional shows had to be arranged over and above the eight scheduled appearances.[50] It is possible that the visual impact of the dance made it easier for foreign audiences to relate to and she had, in performance after performance, a rapturous response. An American critic wrote that it was as if the dancer were saying 'I have seen what it is to be a woman and a great artiste, and there is nothing else I need to know.'[51]

Balasaraswati and Subbulakshmi were both extremely well known at this time; but another star had risen, a dancer, possibly about the only other performer whose name spelt magic – Yamini Krishnamurti. Balasaraswati herself described Yamini as 'the finest of the younger dancers dancing within the classical tradition' and it was agreed that this splendid tribute was entirely deserved.[52] Writing in 1966, a critic raved, 'She has in five years radiated more lustre and joy than do most dancers in a lifetime.'[53]

These three stars were among the favourites of the editor of the *Illustrated Weekly of India*, who lavished attention on them with photographs commissioned by the leading photographers of the day. Between 1959 and 1966, Balasaraswati had as many as seven photo features and interviews, with four in 1963 alone, including the well-known photographs taken by Marilyn Silverstone.[54] Over the same period, Yamini Krishnamurti appeared six times with photographs and text.[55] And even if Subbulakshmi did not speak at all to the press, the paper ran two interviews with her, cautious, even anodyne conversation, in 1955 and 1965, as well a detailed photo feature in 1963.[56]

The release of the '*Sri Venkatesa Suprabhatam*' in 1963, the long-playing record including Svati Tirunal's '*Bhavayami Raghuramam*' and Muthusvami Dikshitar's '*Rangapura vihara*', catapulted Subbulakshmi into becoming a household name and presence.[57] It is possibly still one of the bestselling releases from HMV, the gramophone company.

At the release on 2 November 1963, President Radhakrishnan remarked on Subbulakshmi having 'just returned from a triumphal tour of the West' and went on to say, 'her magnificent voice is one of the richest treasures of our generation'.[58] The 'Sri Venkatesa Suprabhatam' is a fifteenth-century hymn dedicated to the deity at Tirupati, possibly among the best known, of great antiquity and certainly the richest of India's temples.[59] Scholars have noted that the great temple to Vishnu at Srirangam had a tradition of songs to awaken the deity, eighth-century verses in Tamil called 'Thirupalliyezhichi', but with the decline in fame and influence of Srirangam, in addition to marauding outsiders, and the rise of Tirupati, a newer Sanskrit composition of Prativadibhayankara Sri Anantacharya became popular.[60] Years later, Subbulakshmi was to record the 'Thirupalliyezhichi'.[61]

The 'Venkatesa Suprabhatam' is still very widely heard in India and the diaspora.[62] Interestingly, it was first broadcast by Subbulakshmi on the radio.[63] 'The popularity of this invocation soared after HMV recorded the 'Suprabhatam' in MS's voice and, today, dawn breaks over many temple towns, especially in the Tirumala hills in Tirupati, the abode of Venkateswara, as her recorded voice soars to the heavens'[64]. Many temple towns, certainly, but not in all and not even in all Vaishnavite shrines. In a recent matter which went all the way up to the Supreme Court the authorities at the Padmanabhaswami temple at Thiruvananthapuram held, and their claim appears to have been upheld, that their deity is meant always to be in deep sleep and should not under any circumstances be roused, a knotty matter of liturgical practice which, as a leading daily observed, 'even M.S. Subbulakshmi's magic cannot set to rest'.[65]

'Bhavayami Raghuramam' is another piece that has been permanently associated with Subbulakshmi though the credit for making this piece concert-worthy must be given to Semmangudi Srinivasa Iyer who converted Svati Tirunal's text, set entirely in the raga Saveri, into a dazzling ragamalika, with each of six verses describing events in the six *kandas* of the Valmiki Ramayanam, each set to a different raga. As he himself very modestly put it, he did this so that musicians would not render just one or two of the verses.[66] The piece, in its original form, appears to have been part of his repertoire and his senior student *Sangitha Kalanidhi* Tanjore M. Thyagarajan (1923–2007) had sung it years earlier on radio.[67]

Semmangudi himself first presented this newly fashioned piece in his recital at the Navaratri Mandapam in Trivandrum in 1956 and then at the Music Academy during the 1958 season as Subbulakshmi did in her 1959 concert at the same venue, and several times thereafter, always so movingly that 'the story of the Ramayana seemed to come alive in a series of vivid images. A consummate dancer could not have done better.'[68] The song has been presented by several musicians, with its structure and theme making it suitable for dance. Interestingly, even if Subbulakshmi's 1963 rendering has held its ground, Vasanthakumari had released her version of the piece in 1962.[69] Indeed, even Pattammal had sung it in 1959.[70]

Subbulakshmi had sung '*Rangapura vihara*' as early as 1954,[71] but even up until 1952 it was regarded as a 'rare composition' of Muthusvami Dikshitar.[72] The credit for making it widely known must, indeed, go to Subbulakshmi.[73] Beautifully structured, with resounding *sahitya*, it is a grand song, designed to exalt any concert. In this recorded version, Subbulakshmi prefaces the song with a stirring Sanskrit verse, which she did not usually present in concerts.[74]

Old friends were passing on. Jawaharlal Nehru died on 27 May 1964 and a year later on the observance of the first anniversary in New Delhi Subbulakshmi sang Tyagaraja's sombre masterpiece '*Mokshamu galada*' in Saramati. 'On this earth can there be liberation for those who have not found realization?'[75]

Possibly even more significantly, G.N. Balasubramaniam died suddenly on 1 May 1965.[76] A near-exact contemporary of Semmangudi Srinivasa Iyer and Madurai Mani Iyer, he held his own from the time he appeared on stage for the first time and, for all that he was a modest man, grew to acquire a frenzied fan following. G.N. Balasubramaniam was a puzzlement. He was at once a man of distinction and style, urbane and modern-minded and also a deeply religious *upasaka* of the Mother Goddess. A gifted composer, he did not sing his own songs in his concerts, a trait that was regarded as quaintly eccentric by other singer-composers. His disciples were many, the foremost among them being the legendary M.L. Vasanthakumari. Though himself the son of a senior *vidvan*, none of his ten children followed in his steps and, indeed, if village rumour is to be believed, his wife did not in all her life attend a single concert of his. Above all, he was a deeply honourable man; never in his lifetime was a word said of any possible involvement with Subbulakshmi or that any of her letters had been preserved.

It is unlikely that Subbulakshmi and he had anything more than a passing acquaintance in the twenty-five years since *Sakuntalai*. There was certainly some social contact between the families and there is a photograph, taken around 1960, of Subbulakshmi, Pattammal and Radha in a group which includes G.N. Balasubramaniam's sister.[77] Indeed, in Balasubramaniam's family it has always been said that he referred to Subbulakshmi as *tulasi brindavanam*, the holy basil.

Subbulakshmi's United Nations (UN) concert on 23 October 1966 has entered the world of Carnatic lore. Today, more than fifty years later, Carnatic musicians sing everywhere but in 1966 it was still unusual.[78] Preparations for the concert saw Sadasivam at his managerial best. Everything was carefully rehearsed, not least the pieces presented at the UN, for all that they were tried and true. Details of the selection of 'carefully chosen austere and classical pieces'[79] were written up and annotated for the benefit of the foreign audience.[80] Concerts in Europe were scheduled before the visit to the United States, and in London after. The party's departure from Madras was duly reported in the press.[81]

Writing for the *Hindu* after all the hurly-burly was done, Subbulakshmi's friend C.V. Narasimhan raved over the success of the tour.[82] In fifteen concerts and eight private recitals over seven weeks, Subbulakshmi captivated her largely Indian audiences.[83] By the mid 1960s, Hindustani music was reasonably well-known in the United States, with Ravi Shankar, Ali Akbar Khan, Vilayat Khan (1928–2004) and Alla Rakha being primarily responsible for introducing the form, in all its intricacies, to non-Indian audiences.[84] Carnatic music was still relatively unknown.

The foreign critics were impressed by Subbulakshmi. The anonymous reviewer of the *Boston Herald* found the experience 'strange but beautiful. For ears conditioned to meter, harmony and cadence, Indian music, with its basis of pure melody set in tonal formulae and marked by rhythmic cycles, usually represents an enigma ... but for a time ... the enigma began to unravel'.[85] Another critic enthused, 'Kipling was wrong ... The music of Mrs. Subbulakshmi and her obvious artistry did touch the audience.'[86] Another observed '... a series of miracles. Elaborate vocal filigree, sometimes strung in unison or octaves with her daughter Radha Viswanathan, were unbelievable in their poised ease and constancy of flow ... the ability to sustain interest by inflection and improvised variation. Mrs. Subbulakshmi proved a master among masters at this. She sings with a ready yet dark voice and the most extraordinary flexibility'.[87] The revered *New York Times* opined, 'Her vocal communication transcends words. The cliche of "the voice used as an instrument" never seemed more appropriate.'[88] Every recital of the tour was taped by James Rubin and is now available in the public domain.[89]

The UN concert itself was a masterpiece. Every song presented had featured often in Subbulakshmi's recitals in earlier years but shone as part of a tightly put-together bill of fare. The trinity were probably never better represented, in compositions which highlighted their trademark features, with *Sarojadalanetri* in Sankarabharanam, *Rama nannu brovaravemako* in Harikambhoji and *Rangapura vihara* in Brindavanasaranga. Svati Tirunal's *Sarasaksha* in Pantuvarali, Purandaradasa's *Jagadodhharana* in Hindustani Kapi, the Tamil ragamalika *Vadavaraiyai*, Jayachamaraja Wodeyar's *Siva Siva Siva bho* in Nadanamakriya and Mira's *Hari tuma haro* were other highlights.

The one jarring note in the concert was an English verse composed by C. Rajagopalachari, friend, patron and mentor to both Sadasivam and Subbulakshmi. The verse begins, *May the Lord forgive*, words deeply Christian in their evocation but, on the whole, the words and tune are banal and not improved by the singing. The song is best forgotten, though Subbulakshmi was subsequently heard to say to the press, dutifully, that the verse was greatly appreciated everywhere.[90] She must have liked the verse for she sang it later in the year in her concert at the Tamil Isai Sangam.

That UN concert included, for the first time, the verse *Maitreem bhaja*, a piece Subbulakshmi made her invariable concluding item in every concert for the next thirty years. Attributed to the senior Sankaracharya of Kanchi, the piece is said to have been written by the scholar V. Raghavan, probably with the pontiff's blessing. Dr Raghavan's family believes this to be the case and a rendering of the verse is included in *Kavi Kokila Manjari*, a selection of his compositions. It is also possible that it was written by the Sankaracharya with Dr Raghavan's advice.[91] There is also the view that the Sankaracharya, a deeply venerated figure, would not have allowed the piece to be wrongly attributed to him. The entire controversy is somewhat misplaced. Had the verse not been sung by Subbulakshmi, it would have sunk without a trace.[92]

The UN concert is still, after all these years, a memorable listening experience. All India Radio relayed the concert both at the time and later.[93] The UN itself respectfully noted the event.

> Madame M.S. Subbulakshmi, one of India's most eminent musicians, gave a recital of Indian songs today in the General Assembly Hall, as part of a 1966 United Nations Day [24 October] celebrations. Accompanying Madame Subbulakshmi during the recital was a group of five other noted musicians. The proclamation of 24 October as United Nations Day is an acknowledgment of the global efforts and achievements of the Organisation since its founding in 1945. The observance serves as an occasion for renowned musicians from around the world to highlight, celebrate and reflect on the work of the United Nations and its family of offices and agencies through the universal language of music.[94]

From her own perspective, it is possible that the 1966 UN Concert was the crucial determining factor which propelled her mentor to project Subbulakshmi, for ever after, on the world stage, as not only the leading practitioner of the Carnatic tradition but as a great devotional singer. This was to have a major impact on her concert style.

The party returned in triumph to a packed public reception in Bombay and a rousing reception at Madras airport where Subbulakshmi said that her aim to carry the message of India through music to the world had been fulfilled. An endearing story of the visit to the United States is still recalled within the family. The festival of Dipavali fell during the time Subbulakshmi was in the States and she was known to have given small cash presents to younger relatives and friends; however, these gifts were in rupees, the kindly Subbulakshmi having no idea that there was any other kind of currency.[95]

Purandaradasa's *'Jagadodhharana'* in Hindustani Kapi, a great favourite with Subbulakshmi, taught to her by *Sangitha Kalanidhi* K.V. Narayanaswamy, is a brilliant composition, with rich and evocative text.[96] Like everything else attributed to Purandaradasa, the text is all we have now, but *'Jagadodhharana'* has long been sung in the Hindustani Kapi in which it is popular. The otherwise uncelebrated B.S. Raja Iyengar of Mysore made the song famous but it may not have been he who set the words to music.

The Kannada songs of Srinivasa Nayak, known always as Purandaradasa (1485–1565), have long held their place in the Carnatic repertory. Belonging as he did to the northern region of present-day Karnataka, his verses have been sung by musicians of the Kirana gharana of the Hindustani tradition, most notably by Bhimsen Joshi, and more recently by Venkatesh Kumar.[97] There is much to learn from the manner in which Hindustani musicians render devotional verses; it is not that the songs are not structured but just that within their structures they are open to extemporization of the most imaginative kind.

The story of the sinner reformed has a hallowed place in devotional literature around the world. Srinivasa Nayak was a man of the world, and at least in fable, a man dedicated to the making of money[98] but, following his epiphanic realization, devoted himself to singing the praises of his god.[99] His texts, entirely in an easy, spoken Kannada, have been set to the *kriti* format of *pallavi, anupallavi* and *charanam*, and further set to music. Some of his verses, *ugabogas*, continue to be sung similar to the way in which a Tamil *viruttam* or Sanskrit *stotram* is sung.

A good part of the credit for placing Purandaradasa fairly within the Carnatic performing tradition must go to Lalithangi and her daughter Vasanthakumari, who published a book of songs of Purandaradasa in 1941.[100] A 1931 collection, published from Udupi, includes 1,048 ugabogas and songs, many of which have details of raga and tala.[101] It is unlikely that these stated ragas and talas have a provenance which dates to the composer and they probably reflect what was in vogue at the time of publication. 'Jagadodhharana' is indeed even in the 1931 version shown as composed in Hindustani Kapi, as is 'Dasana madiko' in Nadanamakriya and 'Sharanu Siddhivinayaka' in Saurashtra but 'Naneke badavanu', which is nowadays commonly sung in Behag, is stated to be in Mukhari.

Vasanthakumari sang the songs of Purandaradasa all the time and on occasion gave entire concerts just of his compositions.[102] Subbulakshmi gave one such concert at Hampi, which can still be heard on the Internet and includes pieces such as 'Guru vina ghulama'/Pantuvarali and 'Hogadiro Ranga'/Sankarabharanam, not otherwise on her standard concert lists. She actually sang very little of Purandaradasa: 'Dasana madiko enna'/Nadanamakriya, 'Kaliyugadalli'/Jenjuti and 'Naneke badavanu'/Behag were probably sung the most often and over the longest time as was 'Narayana'/Suddhadhanyasi in later years.

Other songs of Purandaradasa in her repertoire included 'Hari Narayana'/Kedara, 'Bhagyada Lakshmi baramma'/Sri, 'Sakalagrahabala neene'/Athana, 'Artana paduve'/Hamsanandi, 'Pillangoviya cheluva Krishna'/Kapi, 'Odi barayya'/Bhairavi and 'Palisemma muddu Sharade'/Mukhari. A rare rendering of 'Srikanta yenagishtu'/Kanada is available on the Internet and of 'Dharanige dorayendu'/Dhanyasi and 'Innudaya baarade'/Kalyanavasantam. A close associate of Subbulakshmi recalls Vasanthakumari visiting to teach her 'Sharanu Siddhivinayaka'/Saurashtra.[103] Most of these pieces can be sourced on YouTube.

Purandaradasa enjoys a *pitamaha* status in the Carnatic pantheon. This is strange especially given that his compositions are recognizably not that of a *vaggeyakara*. Some of the early exercises taught to very young learners are attributed, it is not known with what degree of authenticity, to Purandaradasa but even this could not account for his position. A possibility is that the devotional content of his verses gave them easy acceptability and even popularity. A scholar has commented that the songs 'have a vivid quality; they clicked in the folk mind and lodged in people's memories';[104] in this process he became an important part of the chain of bhakti singing in the region.

Legend has it that Purandaradasa met with Annamacharya, and that Tyagaraja's mother learnt 800 songs of Purandaradasa; all such stories need greater substantiation.[105] Today, there are about 1,300 attributed to him. Certainly, there is a similarity between Tyagaraja and Purandaradasa in their approach, in their colloquial language and in the manner in which they conversed with their chosen deities.

Purandaradasa came from a larger Vaishnava tradition of bhajan and worship, a tradition dating to the philosopher Madhva. The haridasas, or the 'servants of the Lord' – a community which includes such names as Vysaraya (1447–1548) and Kanakadasa (sixteenth century) – lived in the region now identified as northern Karnataka. Vysaraya is credited with what is probably one of the best-known *padas* in the southern music and dance tradition, '*Krishna nee begane baro*', sung in Yamunakalyani. Subbulakshmi has sung this but the piece is more closely associated with the dance tradition and with Balasaraswati; Satyajit Ray's short film *Bala* has her perform this classic piece on the sands of the beach at Madras. Vasanthakumari sang the song to great effect, often for her daughter Srividya's dance.[106] It is a song that appears in the most unlikely places, in film and fusion versions. The verses of Kanakadasa are also well known but in the popular imagination his immortality, and hers, rests on Vasanthakumari's ragamalika rendering of '*Baro Krishnayya*', prefaced by an *ugaboga* of Purandaradasa.

Subbulakshmi's UN concert firmly established her celebrity status. She was still only fifty but had been singing for most of her life with at least twenty-five years of carefully curated appearances and assiduous performance. Her rich voice was at its ripest. Building on her recent appearances on American platforms, World Pacific Records released in 1967 a long-playing record of extracts from a concert at 'Vasanta Vihar', Madras, possibly in the presence of J. Krishnamurti, on 30 December 1965. The pieces are familiar but the singer is in magnificent form. Aeolus of *Shankar's Weekly* wrote at length of Subbulakshmi and her style in 1963. It is ponderous writing, which loses something in credibility in that the artiste's name is consistently spelt wrongly, but it is worth reflection.

> M.S. Subhalakshmi [sic] has become more than a synonym of delightful music. She has become a status-symbol. To attend a performance of hers and praise her soulful singing is distinctly U. Not to attend a performance of hers, and to dismiss her music as unworthy of critical appreciation is, by a singular twist of logic, equally U. There are those who praise her for the ecstatic rapture that she invests her music with; others, who find in her music only such rapture and are, therefore, dissatisfied [sic]. There are some who find her music gaining in richness and a mellow inwardness with the passage of time; others, who never fail to point out how she was singing much better fifteen or twenty years ago. But whatever one's reaction, there is hardly anyone who could be unaware of M.S. or unmindful of her music.

One of the reasons why the music of Subhalakshmi [sic] evokes a definite reaction in the minds of her admirers and detractors is that her music is co-extensive with her personality.[107]

This complete identification of Subbulakshmi's music with her personality is a subject to which we will return.

10

Sangitha Kalanidhi

माणिक्य वल्लकी पाणि मधुर वाणि वराळि वेणि[1]

('She who bears a ruby-studded lute, of beautiful voice, whose dark tresses are as a swarm of bees...',
from Muthusvami Dikshitar's 'Mamava Minakshi' in the raga Varali)

THE success of the UN concert spilled over into the Madras music season of December 1966. Subbulakshmi's Music Academy concert followed the old style, of a *varnam* and a *ragam-tanam-pallavi* in the same raga, Todi in this case, with '*Pakkala*'/Kharaharapriya and '*Sri Chandrasekhara yatindram*'/Sankarabharanam among other pieces. This latter song by the modern composer N.S. Ramachandran, combining as it does a favourite raga and words in praise of a revered guru, featured often in later concerts.

In this concert, Subbulakshmi sang '*Ksheerasagarasayana*'/ Mayamalavagaula, a somewhat awkward composition to which she always performed *neraval* at a wordy line, '*Kumbha sambhava Lopamudra jana toshineem, Kanchi pura vasineem, kanjadalayataksheem, Kamaksheem*'. This was a song learnt from K.V. Narayanaswamy, who did not sing it publicly once it had become a concert staple of Subbulakshmi. It appears that she first showcased it in 1963, sang it frequently in later years, released a commercial recording in 1987,[2] and finally sang it again at her last major recital in 1997. Always musical, the *neraval* in this song has suffered from being offered too often. This being said, it must be noted that Subbulakshmi was not always a creature of habit. The *neraval* for this same line, at a 12 September 1967 recital in Mysore, a recording of which is readily available, is extraordinary. In fact, the entire recital bristles with unexpected and brilliant extemporization.[3]

The 1966 concert at the Tamil Isai Sangam was another resounding success. The *Hindu*'s critic was eloquent in his praise for the Kambhoji, 'slow, subtle and soaring into the empyrean'; for the Saveri, 'both of the earth, earthy and of the sublime'; but he was not just poetic for he cannily observed, 'The reigning mood was one of devotion without any of the unseemly shrieks at the top notes which often pass for bhakti.'[4]

Early in 1967, Subbulakshmi received her first honorary doctorate, a Doctor of Literature (honoris causa) from the Rabindra Bharati University at Santiniketan. She was unable to be present at the ceremony but the chancellor, Padmaja Naidu, daughter of Subbulakshmi's old patroness Sarojini, was warm in her appreciation. 'Smt. Subbulakshmi's golden voice has charmed the hearts of millions all over the world and who [sic] through the brilliance of her artistry, has raised the devotional and folk aspects of Indian music to the level of classical music and has forged new bonds of culture with other countries by the magic of her voice'.[5] Interestingly, even if Subbulakshmi generally received recognition outside the south of India before many of her contemporaries, Balasaraswati had received this honour earlier.[6]

Over the years, other universities felicitated Subbulakshmi: the D.Litt. from the University of Madras in 1987[7] and the Doctor of Letters from the Madurai Kamaraj University in 1994.[8] Degrees are taken very seriously in India, even those received honoris causa, and Subbulakshmi was often addressed in later years with the appropriate honorific that went with her degrees. All these honours recognized what President Radhakrishnan observed in connection with a Calcutta recital of 15 March 1967 in aid of the Prime Minister's Drought Relief Fund, 'The cause is noble and her gifts are unparallelled.'[9]

A sterling recital in Coimbatore on 11 January 1967 needs to be noted if only because a fine recording is available in the James Rubin collection. The items were all familiar, *'Tera tiyaga rada'*/Gaulipantu, Kavikumjara Bharati's *'Taye Idu taranum'*/Kamavardhini, *'Ninnu vina'*/Navarasakannada, *'Tiruvadicharanam'*/Kambhoji, *'Teliyaleru'*/Dhenuka, *'Narayana divya namam'*/Mohana and *'Ka Va Va'*/Varali among others, but the artiste is in fine voice and in full control.

Younger women artistes were singing widely. Radha and Jayalakshmi were the mainstay of *sabhas* in Madras and elsewhere, their racy and engaging style endearing them to their audiences.[10] A critic observed cannily that their music had 'a perpetual unrest' but this was what the listeners liked.[11] They were frequent performers on the radio with regular broadcasts in the Radio Sangeet Sammelan.[12] It was said of them that 'their well-practised rendering of kritis at a brisk pace, with one "sangati" coming tumbling on the heels of the other, is more readily appreciated by the ordinary listener than the more esoteric music of greater singers'.[13] Srirangam Gopalaratnam, a popular Andhra singer, was also performing widely, her voice being commended for its sweetness.[14]

Subbulakshmi's old friend of the pre-Sadasivam years, and erstwhile accompanist, T. Chowdiah, died early in 1967. A 'colourful character who dominated the concert stage for nearly forty years', Chowdiah was well regarded for his encouragement of younger artistes.[15] Subbulakshmi appears to have kept up with him and she travelled to Mysore with Sadasivam to offer her condolences to the family.[16]

This passing was followed soon after by that of Ariyakudi Ramanuja Iyengar and, as was very acutely noted, 'if Chowdiah's death marked the end of a colourful career, that of Ariakkudi [sic] (marks the end) of a colourful epoch ... But probably it is only his epoch that has come to an end. He would live on in the music he loved and taught us to love.'[17] Very unusually, Subbulakshmi gave a public statement:

> Even as the eyes are still wet with tears because of the passing away of Sangeetha Ratnakara Chowdiah, we get another shock in the sad demise of the greatest and tallest of our musicians, Sri Ariyakudi Ramanuja Iyengar. It is a void that just cannot be filled. Sri Ariyakudi was the brightest gem in the galaxy of musicians shedding lustre on the musical firmament of South India for well over five decades. The world of Carnatic music is much poorer today with the passing away of the great Sri Ramanuja Iyengar.[18]

This is an interesting statement. Ariyakudi Ramanuja Iyengar and Subbulakshmi often found themselves on different sides as, for instance, in the *Tamil Isai* movement. Later, in 1955, Ramanuja Iyengar was upset on account of the position accorded to the much-younger Subbulakshmi when Prime Minister Nehru laid the foundation stone for the new building of the Music Academy, and he boycotted the institution for several years.[19] But Subbulakshmi was essentially non-political and naturally deferential to senior musicians and her tribute was heartfelt. Years later, at the Ariyakudi centenary, Subbulakshmi was called upon to give the ceremonial recital.[20]

The *Hindu*'s obituarist called Ramanuja Iyengar 'one of the greatest stylists of our time' and the creator of the *cutcheri*, the modern concert. 'Gifted with a rich voice of uniform timbre in all the octaves, Sri Ariyakudi never overdid a thing. *Raga alapanas* just right, *kirtana* renderings in the right *bani*, *swara* singing in two tempos to impeccable *kalapramana*, all these flowed with effortless ease and the middle of the road listener joined the connoisseur in identifying and enjoying the music.'[21] The eloquent 'Aarabhi' noted pithily, 'At no time did he ever bore his listeners; that would be the highest praise we can bestow on him.'[22] And further, very acutely, something that could easily be said of Subbulakshmi as well, 'They said his music was like recordings, but they forgot the difficulty of endowing the familiar with the aura of the brilliant unusual.'

Ariyakudi privileged his audience. He did not necessarily play to their fancies as much as compelled them to stay engaged. 'He has an infallible knack of judging his audience, not in the manner of a showman or trickster but as one who knows how to conserve his genius. He is willing to please but not at the risk of offending his vocation. His capacity for adjustment has nothing to do with the level of performance but only with the stresses and emphases.'[23]

Ramanuja Iyengar's influence has long outlived him. The form and manner of performance, the hallmarks of superior composition, the appreciation of the cultivated listener, all of these have in one way or the other continued to be shaped by his practice.[24] It is only in the very recent past that some of these norms have begun to be questioned. But Ariyakudi remains the musician's musician. The neuroscientist V.S. Ramachandran fondly recalls that Semmangudi Srinivasa Iyer had on his wall a single photograph, that of Ariyakudi, an unspoken statement that 'this is the only other person whose existence I acknowledge'.[25]

Concert followed upon concert and Subbulakshmi continued to charm. After a Krishna Gana Sabha recital on 3 September 1967, a critic wrote happily:

> The spirit was willing. The rich experience and melodious voice were there too. But the flesh was weak; and an irritating cough kept MS slightly handicapped during the performance last Sunday

at the KGS. But the rare and delectable Dikshitar kriti in Nayaki, *'Ranganayakam'*, and a Mayamalavagaula full of melodic grandeur were enough to keep us bound to her genius. The Sankarabharanam was ample in scope and excellence and she gave us a song on His Holiness of Kanchi. The main raga was Kiravani in which the pallavi was short and sensible. The kriti *'Mokshamu galada'* had thrilled us earlier as also a glowing Purvikalyani. Starting with *'Endaro'*, the artiste soon realized the limitations of the day and the programme was as much a tribute to her common sense as to her innate ability to please us with skilful variations in raga and mood. The Vachaspati, for instance was soaringly beautiful.[26]

A month later, after a recital on 14 October in aid of Kalakshetra, the critic, tiring of his job and the demands it made on him, wrote of his relief at 'the tried and truly soothing beauty of Srimathi MSS', going on to say, 'Only a combination of genius, natural gifts, character and superb training based on orthodox practices can result in music of that rare kind. MS gives us just that.'[27]

The bicentennial of the birth of Tyagaraja was observed in 1967 and the Music Academy, Madras, in a special gesture, chose not to select a president for the year's annual conference and concerts but to dedicate the entire season to the memory of the 'saint composer'.[28] The proceedings began on 21 December with a unique event, a rendering of Tyagaraja's *pancharatna kritis*, not, as is customary, as a mass rendition, as at the annual *aradhana* celebrations, but by individual singers. Semmangudi Srinivasa Iyer sang *'Jagadanandakaraka'* in Nata; Subbulakshmi sang *'Dudukugala'* in Gaula; Vasanthakumari sang *'Sadhincene'* in Arabhi; Brinda and Muktha sang *'Kanakana ruchira'* in Varali; and Pattammal sang *'Endaro Mahanaubhavulu'* in Sri.

An AIR recording survives and can be found on the Internet. It was a great coming together of the finest exponents of the tradition paying homage to the most formative influence on its practice. Ariyakudi Ramanuja Iyengar and G.N. Balasubramaniam had only recently passed on and the musicians who sang that evening were the reigning stars. It may be noted that the 250th anniversary in 2017 passed almost unnoticed.

The *pancharatna kritis* are a set of five songs, brilliant as the name suggests in their conception, design and form. They are important both in and of themselves and in the part they have played in the development of Tyagaraja lore, and are set in the so-called *ghana ragas*. The scholar-musician T.M. Krishna holds that the ragas identified as *ghana* are those which are suited for *tanam* and for the composition of *tana varnams*, though he calls attention to the fact that Varali is not necessarily one such raga. This is not to say that there are no other ragas which meet this definition. The musicologist Ludwig Pesch identifies a *ghana raga* as one with ample scope for *alapana*, *tanam* and ragamalika; or a raga which retains its charm in faster tempo, hence with less ornamentation or *gamaka*.[29]

Some confusion arises from the word *ghana* itself which could be defined as 'weighty'. While every listener would have her own sense of what makes a raga rendition weighty, there would be general agreement that the major concert ragas, Todi, Kambhoji, Sankarabharanam, Kalyani and Bhairavi are all weighty, though not categorized as *ghana*. There is also a classification of *ghana* (weighty), *naya* (delicate) and *desiya* (using foreign techniques) ragas.[30]

The five compositions themselves follow a unique structure, the distinctive feature being *charanas* with many verses, each with a separate tune,[31] and where both *svara* and *sahitya* are sung during performance. Here too, the verses of the *charanas* of the Varali song have only one provenance unlike the other four, for all that there are minor differences even in those songs.[32] It is not at all clear that Tyagaraja intended the five songs to be sung together, but they have been grouped together from the time of Singaracharyulu, and the term *pancharatna* has been in use since the early twentieth century.[33]

Tyagaraja has had a major impact on the form of music and on its public practice. Around 700 of his songs have come down through the various schools established by Tyagaraja's disciples.[34] These songs defined the notion of a *kriti* as a complete musical piece set to a specific raga and specific *tala*; the body of *kritis* established the idea that a raga could have a definitive musical shape, and that the *kritis* themselves, the composed pieces, were demonstrable examples of phrases permitted in that raga. There are many ragas in which but a sole *kriti* of Tyagaraja exists: from Subbulakshmi's repertoire, '*Vachamago*'/Kaikavasi, '*Nadatanum anisam*'/Chittaranjani, '*Vara Narada*'/Vijayasri and '*Teliyaleru*'/Dhenuka.[35] There are ragas in which he has several *kritis* as, for instance, in Saurashtra, Kambhoji, Todi, Kalyani, Bhairavi, Sankarabharanam, Saveri, Arabhi and Madhyamavati. Particularly noteworthy are Kharaharapriya and Harikambhoji, with eleven and ten songs respectively, for they are ragas which he alone among the trinity used and in each of them he has laid down his understanding of *ragabhava* or the essence of the raga.[36] It is also important that there are ragas such as Balahamsa and Ghanta, in each of which Tyagaraja has eight compositions, which have not become part of the collective musical memory. There are many factors at work here.

Many of his compositions fall within the south Indian tradition of bhajana, or group singing, and are relatively easy to comprehend and even perform. Though he lived his life in a Tamil country, he composed in an easy and colloquial Telugu, which was his own tongue. Tyagaraja's use of language is unusual in that for him the language of music was the language of prayer and of dialogue. His everyday Telugu is markedly different from the refined Sanskrit of Muthusvami Dikshitar; it is different from the Telugu of Syama Sastri which is unidimensional, either praising the mother goddess or pleading with her. It is true that, at least according to some students of the language, Tyagaraja's poetry was nowhere near the quality of his music, and 'far below the best in Telugu' even if, 'at his worst, he still does better than Patnam Subramania Iyer'.[37]

This particular critic makes the important point that Tyagaraja, for all his originality, drew substantially from the rich musical heritage of the Kaveri region. Another learned critic makes the point that Tyagaraja's work was primarily *sangita pradhana*, or music driven unlike the *sahitya pradhana*, or text driven, compositions of Annamacharya.[38] Other scholars of Telugu have found in Tyagaraja's texts the influence of earlier composers such as Pothana (1450–1510), who wrote a Telugu version of the Sanskrit Bhagavata Purana, and Bhadracala Ramadas (1620–80), whose songs are still sung.[39]

Tyagaraja's *kritis* have questions and answers, analogies, metaphors and observations on society. Above all, Tyagaraja is always in conversation with his god, and the emotions which drive him are not always, or only, devotion or surrender, but also annoyance, amusement, bewilderment and surprise. Writing of Tyagaraja's songs, a perceptive listener noted, 'There's a wonderful irascibility in Tyagaraja: he's frequently impatient with his listeners, his fellow musicians, himself and at times his God.'[40]

One consequence of these conversations has, however, been that Tyagaraja fails several contemporary benchmarks of political correctness. He is, as we would expect people of his age and caste to be, socially conservative, caste conscious, possibly gender insensitive and comfortable with the ritual observances of his community.[41] Since all we have to assess their lives is the body of compositions which survives them, we do not know if Syama Sastri and Muthusvami Dikshitar were likewise creatures of their age. It is likely that they were. But that is what they were. As the poet William Logan has reminded us, 'We cannot blame the past for being the past.'[42]

Within the *kriti*, Tyagaraja's signal contribution was the use of *sangati* or melodic variations of any one line of the *kriti*, most usually, though not necessarily, the first line. Indeed, the *kriti* itself, for all that it was a known form, and handled by his contemporaries, is seen as having reached perfection in Tyagaraja's hands.[43] Tyagaraja's songs are rich in *sangati*, and while some of these may have originated with him, some may well have been developed by later musicians.[44] From Subbulakshmi's repertoire we have 'O Rangasayee'/Kambhoji, 'Rama nee samanam evaru' / Kharaharapriya, 'Vara Narada'/Vijayasri and 'Tsalakalla'/Arabhi, to name only a few, which fully demonstrate the power of *sangati* to enhance one's appreciation of the song.

Tyagaraja, Syama Sastri and Muthusvami Dikshitar were, all three of them, *vaggeyakaras*. What we have today, for the most part, is as they composed – in word, metre and mode.[45] Relatively little survives from before them in the form in which it was composed. Jayadeva, Purandaradasa and Annamacharya are all represented on the concert platform today, with Subbulakshmi being responsible in no small part for promoting the songs of Annamacharya, but what we have are only their words. This is true of some later composers such as Svati Tirunal, whose apparently original texts have been set to music by twentieth-century musicians, many by Subbulakshmi's teacher Semmangudi Srinivasa Iyer. The fact remains that the songs of the *vaggeyakara* musicians are necessarily more pristine than those where many talents have been at work.

The role of Tyagaraja's many disciples in the propagation of his songs cannot be underestimated. Four schools are always highlighted: Walajapet, Tillaisthanam, Umayalpuram and Manambuchavadi. Walajapet Venkataramana Bhagavathar (1781–1874) was one of the earliest disciples, '...a laudable musician, poet, composer, chronicler and above all an ideal *sishya*, one for whom the guru was god and for whom the propagation of the master's songs became the mission of his life'.[46] His son Krishnaswami Bhagavathar (1824–late 1890s) and grandson Ramaswami Bhagavathar, and Tiruvotriyur S.A. Ramaswami Iyer, who may have later been the first to publish a collection of Tyagaraja *kritis*, played a major role in popularizing, and publishing, the songs of Tyagaraja. Tillaisthanam Rama Iyengar (dates unclear), whose disciple Narasimha T. Bhagavathar published one collection of songs of Tyagaraja in 1908, was another direct disciple of Tyagaraja, and mainly a performer but not a composer. Umayalpuram Krishna Bhagavathar (1828–1908) and Umayalpuram Sundara Bhagavathar (1830–1910), both direct disciples of Tyagaraja, even if very young at the time, were performers, and today there are songs of the master which have only one source, which is Umayalpuram.[47] Another disciple who established a tradition of teaching was Manambuchavadi Venkatasubbayyar (1844–93?).

There were other disciples who did not leave schools behind them. One of these, a direct disciple of Tyagaraja, was Veena Kuppier (1798–1860), who wrote '*Koniyada*'/Kambhoji, a song well-known in Subbulakshmi's repertoire. Others identified by the scholar Sriram V. were Neykarapatti Subbayyar in the Salem/Coimbatore area, Lalgudi Ramayyar in Mysore, Susarla Dakshinamurthy Sastri in Andhra and Kannayya Bhagavathar in Travancore.[48]

Of Tyagaraja's disciples, the Umayalpuram school produced Maharajapuram Viswanatha Iyer, the violinist K.S. 'Papa' Venkatarama Iyer and Semmangudi Srinivasa Iyer. The Manambuchavadi school claims Maha Vaidyanatha Iyer, Patnam Subramania Iyer, Ramanathapuram Srinivasa Iyengar, Ariyakudi Ramanuja Iyengar and Musiri Subramania Iyer.

Alathur Sivasubramania Iyer and Alathur Srinivasa Iyer came from the Tillaisthanam school as does the clarinettist A.K.C. Natarajan with *Vina* Doreswamy Iyengar, T. Chowdiah and Rallapalli Anantakrishna Sarma from the Walajapet school. Tyagaraja's influence can thus be seen to be deeply embedded in the performing tradition, and not necessarily only in the vocal tradition.

Tyagaraja's life, again alone among his peers, is relatively well written up. As early as 1931, he was recognized by Western students of music as a master composer whose 'songs, most of which are dedicated to Rama, have been likened to the Psalms of David, for they "reveal the wonderful evolution of the soul of a neophyte right onwards until he reaches the goal"'.[49]

Some part of Tyagaraja's continued presence in a Tamil country may have to do with the fact that the story of Rama, Tyagaraja's chosen deity, is well and widely known. Prior to the linguistic reorganization of the states in 1956, Telugu, as a spoken and literary form, was an important element in the Tamil heritage.[50] Tyagaraja is revered as one of the trinity but he alone among them is considered a saint, an appellation which can be argued. Devotion and piety mark the compositions of all three but Tyagaraja alone is singled out for the appealing nature of his bhakti. Most accounts of his life dwell on his absolute faith and miraculous happenings. In his study of Tyagaraja's sainthood, William Jackson identifies twelve motifs in the stories that have grown around Tyagaraja's life, motifs which recur in the lives of saints elsewhere in the world, and in the tales about Purandaradasa, Syama Sastri and Muthusvami Dikshitar.[51] The enthusiastic annual observance of Tyagaraja's death anniversary at the *aradhana* in Tiruvaiyaru, where the *pancharatna kritis* are sung in chorus, has sustained the belief in Tyagaraja's sainthood. This tribute is not accorded to his two distinguished contemporaries.

It is also a mistake to believe that Tyagaraja was only an indigent saint, to be revered only for his unquestioned devotion, a popular image reinforced by pictorial and film representations. He was much more than that, and much greater, a consummate musician and lyricist with a superior understanding of poetry, form and metre. It would be a mistake to attribute his substantial gifts, or those of his *confreres*, as only 'god given' and so underplaying their enormous, and entirely human, skills.[52] More creatively though, even if bhakti is the bedrock on which Tyagaraja stands, and scholars have identified various songs which conform to one or the other of the nine forms of bhakti recognized in the scriptures,[53] his songs live not because they are words of prayer but on account of their enormous musical content. Tyagaraja can convey emotion on the vina, the violin, the flute or the mandolin. It is unlikely that all singers understand every nuance of Tyagaraja's Telugu; they are yet able to perform.

At the very time of the bicentenary, an exasperated critic wrote, 'During the course of this year we are likely to hear well-sounding platitudes about bhakti and sangita ... It would be a great mercy if our commentators and lecturers apply themselves the examination of Thyagaraja's art as an expression of human freedom and therefore of man's sense of history.'[54] Tyagaraja has been notoriously the subject of unquestioning adoration and an objective assessment of his work is still awaited.

Subbulakshmi's own concert at the Music Academy in the Tyagaraja bicentenary year, on 25 December 1967, was well received. A grudging critic began by observing merely that '(t)he full house concert by MSS was one of her better efforts' but was sufficiently moved to say later that 'grace, melody, feeling for the music and *sahitya* and tidy *vidwat* were all to the fore in an excellently presented concert'.[55] The recital included pieces she sang only rarely such as '*Santamu leka*'/Sama or '*Mitri Bhagyame*'/Kharaharapriya and old chestnuts such as '*O Rangasayee*'/ Kambhoji (sung 'beautifully with a remarkable sense of its loveliness'[56]), '*Sitamma mayamma*'/Vasanta, '*Naradamuni*'/Pantuvarali[57] and '*Tsallare*'/ Ahiri, all still popular.

Throughout her career, Subbulakshmi sang, and celebrated, Tyagaraja. A quick survey of the concerts for which information is available reveals over ninety songs, of which about twenty-five were very frequently aired. It is entirely possible that she had learnt very many more which she did not sing in concerts.

The Tamil Isai Sangam was celebrating its annual season and Subbulakshmi sang on 31 December 1967, a recital of only Tamil songs, with less familiar pieces jostling with old favourites such as '*Varanamukha*'/Hamsadhwani, '*Sambho Mahadeva*'/Bauli, '*Sabhapati*'/ Abhogi, '*Arta piravi*'/Sankarabharanam and '*Vadavarayai*'/ragamalika. She did not generally sing verses from Andal's Tiruppavai, which Ariyakudi Ramanuja Iyengar had set to music and which Vasanthakumari had recorded, but *'Male manivanna'*/Kuntalavarali featured in this concert and Papanasam Sivan's lively *'Idatthu padam tookki'*/Khamas. A *ragam-tanam-pallavi* in Kalyani was the highlight of this concert.

For Subbulakshmi, 1968 began with a concert of Tamil songs including the vintage *'Tiruvadicharanam'*/Kambhoji at the World Tamil Conference and soon thereafter with a recital at 'Vasanta Vihar' in Madras, the winter home of the seer J. Krishnamurti. The recital which began with *'Endaro'*/Sri included Tyagaraja's *'Ksheerasagarasayana'*/Devagandhari, known to be a favourite of Krishnamurti, who was originally a native speaker of Telugu, and a song she sang for him again in 'Vasanta Vihar' in January 1985.[58] The recital included *'Dhava vibho'*, a Marathi bhajan from her Madurai days and which Sadasivam recalled having heard her sing before he had met her. [59]

Over the course of the year, two stalwarts passed on. Madurai Mani Iyer, Subbulakshmi's friend and possible kinsman, died on 8 June 1968.[60] A very popular, well-respected and well-liked musician, Mani Iyer thrilled his audiences with his *kriti* renderings, exciting *svaraprasthara* and time-tested *pallavis*. It has been said of him, as could easily be said for Subbulakshmi, that his fans 'got accustomed to a set of songs that he repeatedly sang and which, strangely enough, they loved to hear again and again'.[61] The *Hindu* in its obituary recalled Mani Iyer's distinguished uncle Madurai Pushpavanam Iyer, 'the meteor who flashed across the musical horizon five decades ago'.[62]

The other crossing, on 22 July, was of Muthulakshmi Reddy, doctor and activist, and the one person who almost single-handedly brought about the Madras Devadasi (Prevention of Dedication) Act of 1947. There is only a grudging respect for her memory, especially in circles where the devadasi's right to her own agency is prized, but it cannot be denied that the 1947 Act must figure in any listing of legislation in independent India which has promoted human rights.[63]

Other recitals continued at *sabhas*, weddings and on the radio. Of one truly exceptional recital which included '*Dudukugala*'/Gaula, '*Sri Subramanyaya namaste*'/Kambhoji and the luminous '*Cheta Sri Balakrishnam*'/Jujavanti, the critic 'Aarabhi' rhapsodized, 'Much of the music was of the kind to which we listen with unshed tears in eyes and throat, barely able to realize why the tears are there. If there was no applause after *Dudukugala* or *Sri Subramanyaya*, [it is because it is] blasphemous thus to mark approval of music which rivalled in its luminousness the best of mellow organ music in a resounding cathedral'.[64] The critic really was quite overcome by the recital.

> In moments of my most private and darkest depression, like Christian in *Pilgrim's Progress*, I instinctively find myself saying God's name. Why do you look elsewhere? Here is what you seek. I realized this when [she] sang *Cheta Sri*, rendered with a glowing realization of the *sahitya* and free of meretricious embellishments. It came out with a greater emotional impact as a consequence.

The other pieces in this remarkable recital were '*Sri Chamundeswari*'/Bilahari, '*Devi neeye tunai*'/Kiravani, '*Sitamma mayamma*'/Vasanta and '*Ikanaina*'/Pushpalatika. Clearly, there were occasions when attention was given to variety and Subbulakshmi did not simply fall back on the usual stock.

A recital on the National Programme of All India Radio in November 1968 did not receive such a rapturous response. 'For once a concert of Smt. M.S. Subbulakshmi failed to appeal as much as it usually does' fussed the *Hindu's* critic 'Atri'[65] but this recital is significant for it is the one where Subbulakshmi first presented '*Akhilandeshwari*' in Jujavanti, later to become closely identified with her. This did not find favour with the critic: '(a) new Dikshitar song in Dwijavanti, *Sri Akhilandeswari* [sic], did not have the charm of *Cheta Sri* and sounded too flat', and finally 'From MS we seek music which soars aloft, not the kind of pieces carefully chosen by those who have lost the voices of their youth.'

Subbulakshmi always treasured the honour bestowed on her by the Music Academy, Madras, in 1968 of the title of *Sangitha Kalanidhi*. Other honours at home and abroad followed but to Subbulakshmi, recognition by her peers was important. The annual award of the Academy has frequently been controversial but there is no denying that in 1968, the flag still flew high.

There is a needless argument on whether the first presidency by a woman of the Music Academy's annual festival, and the award of the title, should not have gone to Pattammal.[66] The issue did figure in some circles, with comments on Subbulakshmi's alleged lack of *vidvat* and a tendency to play to the gallery. It is unlikely that Pattammal herself was of this persuasion; she was the younger of the two and for all her eminence, or because of her own stature, would have recognized as the citation said that Subbulakshmi was truly 'the most beloved idol of the public in recent annals of Indian music' with a 'voice of unique sweetness and richness and ... ability to harmonize strict standards and popular appeal'. Certainly no one else was complaining. Pattammal's own richly deserved presidency came two years later in 1970, followed over the next few years by Balasaraswati, Brinda and Vasanthakumari.

The proceedings on 20 December 1968 were star-studded, and much was made of the fact that for the first time in its hoary history, the Academy had elected a woman musician to preside over the annual conference and concerts. Vasanthakumari sang the invocation and the great and the good sent their felicitations. Royalty was much in evidence with Sethu Parvati Bayi of Travancore inaugurating the conference, Karan Singh of Jammu and Kashmir slated to preside over the *sadas* which followed on 1 January 1969, and Jayachamaraja Wodeyar of Mysore conveying his greetings to both. C.N. Annadurai, chief minister of Madras, observed gracefully, yet pointedly, 'I am more particularly glad that the traditional patrons of our music have been given important functions in this Conference.'[67]

Subbulakshmi's speech on the occasion is important, if only because it is one of the very few original statements we have from her on her life's work and what it meant to her. Her husband's influence is everywhere, and he may well have written the whole thing, but many of the sentiments expressed can only be hers.[68] Speaking forcefully and with the confidence born of years on the stage, she paid obeisance to her mother and her husband, surely the two most decisive influences on her life.

The scholar Sriram V. has called attention to the Sanskrit verse which Subbulakshmi sang, in the raga Purvikalyani, at the conclusion of her address, the second of the nine verses of the *'Syamala Navaratnamalika'* of Sri Adi Sankara, and finds in it a deeply felt tribute, even prostration, to the memory of the singer's mother, the vina-bearing Shanmukhavadivu.[69] Loosely translated, the verse reads:

She of the deep and compassionate gaze,
Who as our preceptor, elevates us,
And who rests the vina gently on her left breast, Mother,
Who art music itself, I bow to you.[70]

All things considered, it is a particularly felicitous text and while we may suppose that Subbulakshmi knew of it and chose to include it, she would still have needed her husband's permission. That he recognized the significance of the verse is to his credit.

The concert on 22 December 1968 was spectacular. Flanked by her standard accompanists of that decade, V.V. Subramanyam on the violin, T.H. Vinayakram on the ghatam and T.K. Murthy on the mrdangam, and of course with Radha beside her, Subbulakshmi fully vindicated the honour accorded to her. None of the songs presented that evening was from the limited stock to which she was otherwise confining herself. The trinity was handsomely represented with Tyagaraja's *'Enta rani'*/Harikambhoji and *'Gnanamosagarada'*/Purvikalyani,

Dikshitar's *'Sadasivam upasmahe'*/Sankarabharanam and Syama Sastri's *'Neelayatakshi'*/Pharaz. Svati Tirunal's luminous *'Gopalaka'*/Revagupti found a place as did Purandaradasa's *'Jagadodhharana'*/Kapi. Subbulakshmi also presented, importantly, the first two, of twelve, stanzas of the *'Melakarta Ragamalika'* before an elaborate *ragam-tanam-pallavi* in Bhairavi.

The Music Academy requires the president of each year's conference to make a special presentation. On 24 December, Subbulakshmi chose to play the vina, led by her senior contemporary K.S. Narayanaswamy.[71] Unusual pieces were presented, the impact highlighted by her singing both of Syama Sastri's *'O Jagadamba'*/Anandabhairavi and *'Valayunniha nyaan'*, a *padam* in Varali of Svati Tirunal in Malayalam.[72] Many years later, Vijaya Rajendran recalled that Subbulakshmi practised on her vina every day, at least one song, another indication of her discipline and tenacity.[73]

The revelries continued. On 25 December, Kalki Gardens hosted a dinner in honour of the maharaja of Travancore and the maharaja of Kashmir. The hostess performed for the distinguished guests, mainly familiar pieces presented faultlessly, with Semmangudi joining her for the Kambhoji piece.[74] Savita Devi, daughter of Siddheswari Devi, may have sung that evening with Siddheshwari Devi herself performing at the Academy on 31 December.[75]

Despite her commitments at the Music Academy, Subbulakshmi sang at the Tamil Isai Sangam.[76] The old quarrels had long been forgotten and the recital included songs in both Telugu and Sanskrit: *'Vinayakuni'*/Madhyamavati, *'Bhogindra sayinam'*/Kuntalavarali and *'Akhilandeshwari'*/Jujavanti. This was not in itself unusual. The demand for *Tamil Isai* was never that *only* Tamil songs be sung but that many more be sung. A perusal of the souvenirs of the annual festival of the Tamil Isai Sangam indicates that Vasanthakumari, for instance, who regularly sang at that venue from 1954 onwards, always included songs of Tyagaraja and, indeed, on her very first appearance there, in 1944, when the controversies were still raging, sang Tyagaraja's *'Nenaruncinanu'* in Malavi. Ariyakudi Ramanuja

Iyengar even sang a *pancharatna kriti* from that stage while Madurai Mani Iyer sang *navagraha kritis*.

The Committee of Womens' Institutions organized a felicitation for Subbulakshmi.[77] Speaking on the occasion, Rukmini Devi commended her qualities of simplicity, humility, devotion and creative ability. Significantly, of the sum of ₹8,000 collected for the artiste, ₹6,000 was earmarked for an annual award for women *vainikas* in the name of Veena Shanmukhavadivu and ₹2,000 for an endowment to the Thyagaraja Sangeeta Vidvat Samajam towards daily offerings to Tyagaraja.

After the excitement of the 1968 season, the regular concert routine set in again. Eulogies in the press were common. Decades of practice and deft presentation made every one of Subbulakshmi's concerts an event. 'Her melodies now have a matured polish, a sublime finish, the product of years of dedicated effort,' so gushed a critic after a *sabha* concert in Bombay.[78] And it was certainly a well-structured concert, including the Gaula *pancharatna* 'Dudukugala', 'Saketanagaranatha'/Harikambhoji, 'Kamalambike'/Todi – already a very regular offering – two more delightful *kritis* of Muthusvami Dikshitar, 'Sri Lakshmivaraham'/Abhogi and 'Ranganayakam'/Nayaki, and a *ragam-tanam-pallavi* in Kalyani.

Later in the year, a Madras critic was similarly affected by her 'autumnal eloquence' and moved to incoherence. '(W)e listened like nuns at prayer, with uplifted hearts'[79]. A fine selection of songs, all from the core of Subbulakshmi's repertoire, was presented at the Shanmadam Conference in Kanchipuram on 19 June 1969. Subbulakshmi was always quite resourceful in prefacing some songs with a Sanskrit *stotram* or Tamil *viruttam*. In this particular recital, every piece was so prefaced: verses from the '*Ganesa pancaratnam*' before '*Vatapi*'/Hamsadhwani; from the '*Subramanya bhujangam*' before '*Saravanabhava*'/Shanmukhapriya; from the '*Kanakadhara stotra*' before '*Hiranmayim*'/Lalita; and likewise before '*Hari Narayana*'/Kedaram, '*O Rangasayee*'/Kambhoji,

'*Suryamurte*'/Saurashtra, '*Talli ninnu nera*'/Kalyani, '*Sri Dakshinamurte*'/Sankarabharanam, '*Ksheerasagarasayana*'/Mayamalavagaula, '*Sri Kamakoti*'/Saveri, '*Sabhapati*'/Abhogi, '*Sambho Mahadeva*'/Bauli, and even before some bhajans.

A recital at the Poona Sangeetha Sabha in 1969, which included '*O Rangasayee*'/Kambhoji and the first two verses from the '*Melakarta Ragamalika*', is worth noting if only because it was recorded on film and subsequently used extensively in a three-part Films Division documentary on Subbulakshmi. Another important event this year was the benefit recital for the Kesarbai Kerkar Scholarship Fund on 26 July 1969 at Bombay, in the presence of the great lady herself. There is some anecdotal evidence that a young Subbulakshmi had heard Kesarbai sing in Madras.[80] There is a more substantial recollection of Kesarbai's student Dhondutai Kulkarni that Subbulakshmi and Kesarbai were very fond of each other and each had regard for the other's music.[81] This can be believed. For all their very different temperaments, they were both artistes of spectacular presence, both artistes beyond compare.

Subbulakshmi's Music Academy performance on 25 December 1969 must be regarded, over a very long history of memorable concerts, as one of her finest and is fortunately available on the Internet. With her usual accompanists of the time and in addition V. Nagarajan on the kanjira, she commenced her recital with Muthiah Bhagavathar's craftily constructed '*Mathe malayadhwaja pahi sanjate*', a *daru* with a bewitching intertwining of *svara*, *sollukattu* and *sahitya*. It may have been the first occasion the song was presented publicly by her though she sang it often in the years after. It has passed into the repertoire of other musicians but Subbulakshmi's skilful rendering reveals just how totally she was in control.

Subbulakshmi was master of the short *alapana*, which came next, Latangi before Patnam Subramania Iyer's '*Aparadhamula*' and Begada before Poochi Srinivasa Iyengar's '*Anudinamu*'. The verse from the *Kanakadhara stotram* before '*Hiranmayim*' in Lalita can only be described as exquisite. The best though was still to come, and it came in an extensive and brilliant Kharaharapriya, both the *alapana* and the *neraval* for the line '*Tanuvuche...*' in '*Pakkala nilabadi*'. Many renderings by Subbulakshmi of this raga, and of *neraval* for this particular line, are available on the Internet, but the Christmas Day recital of 1969 has to be acknowledged as truly sublime. The third and fourth verses from the '*Melakarta Ragamalika*' and a *ragam-tanam-pallavi* in Todi formed the crown of the recital.

Subbulakshmi sang the next day, at Kalakshetra, another fine recital, where '*Mathe*' in Khamas was sung again, a recital wanting only in comparison to what had passed the day before.

So the decade came to an end, for Subbulakshmi a period of intense practice and performance, of fame and acclaim and of standing and respect. These were the celebrated concert years, when she succeeded in making what she offered uniquely hers. She may have been driven by bhakti or devotion but what she presented was excellence. 'Whatever she sings is transformed by the alchemy of her imagination into a direct avowal of faith. Subbulakshmi does not intellectualize, she does not scrutinize the values of her art; but she gives to it the total energy of her belief.'[82] At this distance there can be some impatience at the fact that there were occasions when she was not trying hard enough but that is really only on account of the knowledge of what she was capable of when she thought it was worth it. It is true that fatigue was beginning to set in after nearly thirty years of unrelenting public appearances. But for all this, and for all that purists were beginning to cavil at her changing concert style, she was truly, at that point in India's cultural history, at the end of the glorious decade of the sixties, in the words used on the American long-playing record release in 1967, 'Subbulakshmi, India's Greatest Singer'.

11

The Singer of Chants

गोपी मधुरा लीला मधुरं युक्तं मधुरं मुक्तं मधुरम् ।
दृष्टं मधुरं शिष्टं मधुरं मधुराधिपतेरखिलं मधुरम्[1]

('*Sweet are the cowherd maidens, and your play with them; Sweet is union, as is liberation,*
Your glance is sweet, and your manner, Lord of Mathura, you are sweetness itself!'
Loosely translated from the '*Madhurashtakam*' of Sri Vallabhacharya)

THE next fifteen years of Subbulakshmi's life, from the early 1970s on, starting from the time she was about fifty-five, saw many changes. She began to age, but she aged gracefully and frailty suited her. The slight plumpness of earlier years, very evident in the UN Concert for instance, disappeared; she began to wear spectacles when not on stage, and usually very unflattering ones. There was an end to the grand living at Kalki Gardens and a move to a first, and then a second modest dwelling. The end of this period marked the commencement of a long retirement.

There were three major developments over this period, all reflecting significantly on Subbulakshmi's performing career: a changed concert pattern; the release of commercial recordings of hymns and chants; and the promotion of the songs of Annamacharya, an early Telugu poet whose songs had long been sung by stalwart Andhra singers, but whose work is now as closely associated with Subbulakshmi in the popular imagination as is that of Mira.

It is not that there was any immediate decrease in the number of concerts, but there were fewer *sabha* appearances and even fewer wedding concerts. 'Benefit recitals'[2] and appearances at miscellaneous venues continued, and the reviews were generally fulsome. 'M.S. Subbulakshmi is good to hear even if she is below her best form.'[3] It was not only the Madras reviewers who were adoring. 'It was a supremely satisfying musical treat', gushed a Bombay reviewer. 'MS's tone and verve are still so youthful they belie her age.'[4]

An important landmark in 1970 was the release by HMV of Subbulakshmi's three-record Concert Album.[5] This was an attempt to present an abridged concert, and had not been tried before. With vocal support from Radha Viswanathan and with V.V. Subramanyam on the violin, T.K. Murthy on the mrdangam and T.H. Vinayakram on the ghatam, it is a tight collection of songs plentifully sung by her in the previous decade: a *varnam*, seven *kritis* of Tyagaraja, three of Muthusvami Dikshitar and one each of Syama Sastri, Purandaradasa, Svati Tirunal and Papanasam Sivan. Interestingly, though Subbulakshmi had completely integrated the bhajan into her concert pattern, this concert does not include one.

As was customary by this time, Subbulakshmi donated the royalties on this recording to charity, in this case the Ramakrishna Mission. This act was hailed as 'entirely consonant with her devotional use of the art of music' and it was noted that the formal release in Delhi was at 'the very hall whose construction had been enabled by a benefit recital given earlier by MS'.[6]

Most critics saw only a spiritual element in Subbulakshmi's performances, a problematic conclusion but one that caught the imagination of the concert-going public. 'To MSS, music is religion, it is not music for an audience alone but music for the soul, ... a charming blend of the highest artistry, perfect aesthetic sensibility, an organic fusion of rhythm and emotion.'[7] This debatable assessment seemed to be serving the artiste well and contributed to a new concert pattern, which was basically an uneven mixture of songs and bhajans and often recklessly repetitive. And indeed, this new concert practice was welcomed as 'reflecting the true spirit of *nadopasana* unhindered by any rigid or hidebound *kaccheri pantha*'.[8]

D.K. Pattammal was selected in 1970 to preside over the annual conference of the Music Academy and receive the title of *Sangitha Kalanidhi*. Damal Krishnaswami Pattammal (1919–2009) was born into Brahmin orthodoxy but under the influence of a broad-minded father learnt music from an early age and broke the convention that prevented women of her background from becoming professional musicians. A singularly thoughtful musician of great style and distinction, Pattammal understood the importance of structure, both of compositions and of a concert. Even after her voice had lost the ringing clarity of her earlier years, she could captivate her audience. Like Subbulakshmi, she had a fantastic repertoire with pride of place given to the brilliantly structured songs of Muthusvami Dikshitar.

Pattammal was largely self-taught.[9] Ambi Dikshitar, T.L. Venkatarama Iyer, Vidyala Narasimhalu Naidu and P. Sambamoorthy are referred to as her teachers but she states in her statement to the Sangeet Natak Akademi made on 1 March 1990 that she is 'self-made' with 'individual training'.[10] Pattammal also learnt *padams* from T. Rajalakshmi Ammal, the eldest daughter of Dhanammal.[11]

Austerity, dignity and a complete lack of fuss marked Pattammal's music. 'Pattammal has chosen the "*chakkani raja marga*", the right royal road in music. She never strays into "*sandula*", bylanes. The result is gratifying; her music is pure, classical to the core and orthodox. She has no use for the antic.'[12] Thirty years later, another critic, using the same analogy, wrote that 'her style is basically one safely anchored in a royal path sans adventure and risks'.[13] An interesting take on Pattammal's performance style is that she refused to include her personal vision in her music. 'It is perhaps possible to relate every phrase in her raga elaboration to some usage in a composition of Dikshitar or Syama Sastri or Thyagaraja. But by a deliberate suppression of her instinctive genius for the telling phrase and the clinching finish, Pattammal has steamrollered her music into a plain and unrhetorical statement of spiritual authorities'[14].

There is comparatively little available of Pattammal's music of the early years but what there is reveals a high, strident voice, clear enunciation and clean phrases. Her gifts were recognized early, and late in life she reminisced of her childhood and of being taken by an adoring father, as a babe of three months, to receive the blessing of Sri Ramana Maharshi of Tiruvannamalai. The sage placed a drop of honey on the tongue of the infant.[15]

Whatever Pattammal sang radiated wholesomeness, an attribute perhaps linked to her rigorous early training in the recitation of Sanskrit devotional verses. Her recording in the early 1960s of the *Syamala dandakam*, a string of verses addressed to the Mother Goddess, attributed to Kalidasa of the fifth century, is a fine example. Pattammal's early initiation into Sanskrit pronunciation can only have helped her subsequent mastery of the *sahitya* of Muthusvami Dikshitar though, in fairness, it has to be admitted that Subbulakshmi's Sanskrit pronunciation, even without early initiation, was of an extremely high order.

Most accounts of Pattammal's life and work recall the fact that she was the first Brahmin woman to have been publicly accepted as a performing musician and to have mastered the complications presented by *ragam-tanam-pallavi*, not generally regarded as suitable for performance by women. While she certainly appeared to revel in *pallavi* intricacies, to say she was the first Brahmin woman to perform publicly may not be entirely correct. Other Brahmin women were appearing on the stage,[16] or singing *pallavis*, but perhaps not with the same regularity. Pattammal herself was, however, proud to state that she was 'the first housewife to give public concerts in *sabhas* ... and the first lady to sing Ragam Thanam Pallavi in public concerts'.[17]

After successfully warding off possible criticism from within the closed circle of the community, essentially because of her father's support, Pattammal appeared early on the platform scene. Her first public concert may have been at the Egmore Mahila Samajam, Madras, in 1933 when she was fourteen. There is a reference to concerts in Bombay when she was sixteen.[18] She appeared in the Music Academy, Madras, during the 1935 season, and barring a few years, sang at that venue for the next sixty years. There was an association of over ten years with playback singing in such sensationally popular films as K. Subrahmanyam's *Thyaga Bhoomi*.

Pattammal's singing is always referred to as traditional. Late in her life, three dominant aspects of her singing were identified: dignity, discipline and depth.[19] Throughout her long career, these were her hallmarks. 'She has a deeply ingrained habit of mind that is not sure that novelty is a good thing in itself. For her the bottom line in all innovative endeavor is "tradition".'[20] The same critic noted that 'even when Pattammal's inventive instincts are in full play, there is never any frenzied display'. Pattammal's ability to convey musicality without histrionics was always commended. 'Her rendering of the *kirtanas* may often seem to be too rigid and rarely flexible, too fastidious about convention and hence not fascinating, but she has a style of her own. There was no semblance of unreality or artifice in her *cutcheri*.'[21]

A somewhat difficult critic wrote of Pattammal in 1962 that she was 'well past her prime'; unfair considering that Pattammal had at least another thirty years of deeply thoughtful music ahead of her.[22]

More to the point was the critic who said, 'Pattammal's music had a singular rectitude about it. She did not want to titillate or intoxicate, but exalt singer and listener.'[23] At her passing, a young listener wrote, 'The complete lack of pretension, or extraneous intent, in Pattammal's music makes it surprisingly captivating.'[24]

Interestingly, Pattammal was close to several people whose association with Subbulakshmi is much better publicized. Papanasam Sivan taught her many songs. Kalki Krishnamurthi was an early patron and close friend as were Rukmini Devi and all the doughty women of the Dhanammal clan. Rajaji was a personal friend. She even appears to have known Lady Mountbatten.[25] As a singer of Tamil songs, especially those of Subramania Bharati, she is entitled to be recognized as a promoter of *Tamil Isai*. Pattammal's story has always been very simply told; an admiring appreciation has her say, and it is entirely credible given what is known of Pattammal's life and work, 'If we surrender ourselves unconditionally to art, Saraswati will reward us beyond measure.'

Subbulakshmi's recital at the Music Academy in the 1970 season is a good example of tight planning and execution.[26] Beginning with a hardy familiar, '*Tera tiyaga rada*'/Gaulipantu, the concert took in the major ragas, Kalyani for '*Bhaja re re*', Kambhoji for '*O Rangasayee*', Ritigaula for '*Janani*' and Bhairavi for the *ragam-tanam-pallavi*. '*Guruleka*'/Gaurimanohari and '*Govardhana girisam*'/Hindolam were surprise additions, not being on her standard list of songs.

There were other engagements that season. The Tamil Isai Sangam, for so long the recipient of her support, awarded her the title of *Isai Perarignar*, the second woman to be so honoured, after K.B. Sundarambal. The title translates as Great Scholar of Music; Rajaji is believed to have said that she would have been more appropriately honoured as *Isai Perarasi*, or Great Queen of Music.[27] This quip actually comes off better in Tamil. Her singing of *tevaram* and *tiruppugazh* at the Tamil Isai

Sangam in that season is remembered from a concert which included a predictable '*Arta piravi*' Sankarabharanam and a *ragam-tanam-pallavi* in Kiravani.[28]

The season saw a stunningly imaginative recital at the Krishna Gana Sabha.[29] This recital began predictably enough with '*Entoprema*'/Surati *varnam* famed in the school of Semmangudi Srinivasa Iyer, '*Vatapi*'/Hamsadhwani and '*Naradamuni*'/Pantuvarali but went on to include Svati Tirunal's '*Jaya Jaya Padmanabhanujesha*'/Manirangu, '*Cheta Sri Balakrishnam*'/Jujavanti, an extremely surprising '*Devi jagajjanani*'/Sankarabharanam, one of Svati Tirunal's Navaratri *kirtanas*, a lively '*Nenaruncinanu*'/Malavi and a *ragam-tanam-pallavi* in Mayamalavagaula. The concert sent out a message. Subbulakshmi was still capable of the imagination, the exactitude and the style to perform in high Ariyakudi *margam*, but sadly, only when she was permitted to do so.

Subbulakshmi's recital in February 1971 at the Mylapore Fine Arts Society displays the virtuosity she always possessed even if it were not often displayed.[30] '*Mathe*'/Khamas and '*Naradamuni*'/Pantuvarali were performed again, and '*Vallabha nayakasya*'/Begada, '*Kannatandri*'/Devamanohari, '*Sri Chandrasekhara yatindram*'/Sankarabharanam, Syama Sastri's Todi *svarajati* '*Rave Himagiri Kumari*' and a *ragam-tanam-pallavi* in Kharaharapriya. The critics were delighted.

> MS is the Sirius among the stars of the Semmangudi school... Not even Semmangudi could have handled Kannatandri with greater elan and verve. The Todi's brilliance is difficult to describe in words. It was mellifluous, it was full of range and depth, its delineation was highly imaginative and the vocalist's voice obeyed every wish of her tremendous genius. We heard the swarajati in adoring silence.[31]

The post-*pallavi* crop of smaller pieces included a little heard Marathi abhang '*Sundarathe dhyana*'.

The Singer of Chants

A later recital in August 1971, again at the Krishna Gana Sabha, has '*Mathe*'/Khamas and '*Tera tiyaga rada*'/Gaulipantu and '*Enati nomu*'/Bhairavi, both from the Concert Album, and, interestingly, Tyagaraja's '*Dhyaname*'/Dhanyasi, Dikshitar's '*Ranganayakam*'/Nayaki and a *ragam-tanam-pallavi* in Sankarabharanam. This concert may have been one of the first airings of the Dakshinamurti *stotram* with which she henceforth began all her recitals.[32] The devoted critic of the *Hindu* was again in attendance and marvelled at

> her unrivalled beauty of expression, marked by an emphasis on sense, clarity and emotional content ... The mellowness of the performance left listeners moved and pleased. She never strains after effect by merely showing off her technical skill (which, of course, is immense) and never forgets that our music, first and last, must touch the heart of the listener ... Her music has grown gracefully with the years and its beauty today, though different from that of its youth, is still Orphean.[33]

The Music Academy concert on 25 December 1971, another old-style concert, included in addition to the familiar '*Vanajakshi, ata tala varnam*' in Kalyani, and an even more familiar Sankarabharanam, at least five songs not common at all in Subbulakshmi's concert history.[34] These are Tyagaraja's '*Merusamana*'/Mayamalavagaula, Papanasam Sivan's '*Sankara dayakara*'/Harikambhoji, a tribute to the composer who was presiding over the year's proceedings, Syama Sastri's '*Ninnu vina*'/Ritigaula, Ramanathapuram Srinivasa Iyengar's '*Rama ninne*'/Saranga and a very unusual Tyagaraja song on Siva, '*Deva Sri Tapastirthapuranivasa*'/Madhyamavati. The Sankarabharanam itself was the finely structured *pallavi* we have noted earlier. It is indeed a sterling recital and the *Hindu* grudgingly opined that '...though MSS failed to touch her best form, yet there was so much to enthuse in her felt rendering of *Dasarathe*'.

Subbulakshmi's later recitals that season at the Tamil Isai Sangam and the Indian Fine Arts Society, for all that they included a *ragam-tanam-pallavi* in Saveri and Todi respectively, were full of standard, often presented items. The *Hindu* was in a better mood. 'MSS's concert was soulful, each song saturated with pure melody and rendered in a worshipful mood.'[35] Subbulakshmi was still, at least in Madras *sabha* concerts, conscious of the fact that her audience required her to sing a *ragam-tanam-pallavi*; one such recital in January 1972, at the Mylapore Fine Arts Club had her presenting a *varnam*, 'Viriboni'/Bhairavi, a *pancharatna kriti*, 'Endaro'/Sri, selected Tyagaraja *kritis*, a grand Muthusvami Dikshitar composition, 'Sri Subramanyaya'/Kambhoji and a *ragam-tanam-pallavi* in Kiravani. The lighter, post-*pallavi* pieces, by this stage, were almost always bhajans.

One more concert of this period, and the details of a concert that was not given, will serve to highlight the attention to style and detail that Subbulakshmi could on occasion give. An early December 1972 recital at Mulund, Bombay, was skilfully presented, with an opening *varnam* in Kanada, the popular 'Nera nammiti', but not common in Subbulakshmi's stock, a grand 'Koniyada' in Kambhoji and a tight *ragam-tanam-pallavi* in Dhanyasi.[36] For those who have never heard Subbulakshmi in concert, it is well worth the effort of finding it on the net. Both the Kambhoji and the Dhanyasi were slated to be presented at the Christmas Day concert at the Music Academy, along with Tyagaraja's 'Evarani'/Devamritavarshini, Muthusvami Dikshitar's 'Seshachalanayakam'/Varali and Syama Sastri's 'Durusuga'/Saveri but the recital was cancelled on account of the illness of C. Rajagopalachari, who died that same evening.

There is record of an outstanding concert in Bombay in 1973. Subbulakshmi began with the by now well-worn 'Mathe'/Khamas and took care to include compositions of the major composers: Tyagaraja's 'Tsalakalla'/Arabhi with its exacting *sangatis*, 'Manasuloni marmamu'/Suddha Hindolam (Varamu) and 'Dasarathe'/Todi, Muthusvami Dikshitar's 'Seshachalanayakam'/Varali and 'Ranganayakam'/Nayaki,

Syama Sastri's *'O Jagadamba'*/Anandabhairavi and Svati Tirunal's *'Paripaahimam'*/Mohana and *'Aliveni'*/Kuranji. The recital was crowned by a *ragam-tanam-pallavi* in Hemavati.

Another *sabha* recital of November 1973, of which a recording is available on the net, is less interestingly put together, but is still a fine example of Subbulakshmi's mid-career concert style. Several often-sung pieces including *'Tera tiyaga'*/Gaulipantu, *'Manasuloni marmamu'*/Suddha Hindolam (Varamu), *'Ksheerasagarasayana'*/Mayamalavagaula, *'Sarasaksha'*/Pantuvarali, *'Enati nomu'*/Bhairavi came between a *varnam* in Vasanta, two segments of the *'Melakarta Ragamalika'* and a *ragam-tanam-pallavi* in Sankarabharanam. The lighter pieces are again entirely expected.

The concert at the Music Academy at the 1973 season was well crafted, one of the last of its type in Subbulakshmi's career. Tyagaraja's *'Mosaboku'*/Gaulipantu was an unusual choice, a welcome variation from *'Tera tiyaga rada'* in the same raga and sung repeatedly by her. *'Ksheerasagarasayana'*/Devagandhari and *'Sitamma'*/Vasanta were followed by Svati Tirunal's *'Jaya Jaya Padmanabhanujesha'* in Manirangu, Syama Sastri's *'Durusuga'*/Saveri, Muthusvami Dikshitar's seldom-heard *'Maha Ganapatim'* in Todi and, in due course, a *ragam-tanam-pallavi* in Kambhoji.

The 1973 season was important for the reason that T. Balasaraswati was awarded the *Sangitha Kalanidhi* that year, still the only dancer to have been so honoured for her peerless contribution to the art of music. As a distinguished student of hers observed,

> The *Natya Sastra* stipulates that a dancer should herself sing the music to which she performs *abhinaya*, yet Balasaraswati is practically alone today in her ability to do so with style and confidence. She owes this distinction in part to the extraordinary household in which she

was raised, one held in high esteem by the greatest musicians of her time. Her famous grandmother, Vina Dhanammal, and her mother Jayammal bequeathed to her the very essence of Karnatak music, a prodigious repertoire of *Kshetragna* (also *Kshetrayya*) *padams* and Dikshitar *kritis*, and the profoundly expressive style of singing for which the family is justly renowned.[37]

Years earlier, the impresario G. Venkatachalam had observed, 'Srimati Balasarasvati's knowledge of music is no less profound than her mastery over the difficult techniques of laya and bhava inherent in this ancient art, and of which she is unquestionably the ablest and most gifted interpreter today'.[38]

Balasaraswati was the last of the devadasi dancers, a traditionalist to the core and proud of the integral quality of the performing tradition practised by her family. Her arrival and continued presence on the dance scene coincided with the disputes which raged around the 1947 legislation outlawing the dedication of girls and women to temple service, and the trend within society of girls from caste Hindu households, especially Brahmin households, to learn and publicly perform dance.[39]

All her life, Balasaraswati resisted, and possibly resented, this appropriation of what was to her a customary and family tradition, a way of life which to its practitioners was the way to spiritual upliftment, and its transformation to a stylized form of entertainment. Hidden in this process was the shift in the ethos of dance; at the risk of simplification it can be said that the transformation of *sadir* to Bharatanatyam glossed over the element of *sringara*, or romantic love, as a means of expression of love for the divine.

It would be incorrect to hold that *sringara* was replaced by bhakti, for the whole point of the traditionalists' argument was that *sringara* was indeed a way of expression of love for the divine. What is probably more accurate is to say that with the opening up of the practice of the dance form to women who did not come from a background of ritual worship or have an understanding of the redemptive power of intoxicating love, the dance repertory changed to accommodate what these women did understand, which was primarily devotional worship and prayer.

Balasaraswati would not have any of this. In 1975, at the Tamil Isai Sangam, she spoke her mind, '*Sringara* stands supreme in [the] range of emotions. No other emotion is capable of better reflecting the mystic union of the human with the divine. I say this with deep personal experience of dancing to many great devotional songs which have had an element of *sringara* in them.'[40] 'To Bala, that last great descendant of the devadasi clan, "all dance is sringara". She speaks of bhakti in Bharatanatyam with the utmost disdain. "Bhakti," she says, "is only towards the art".'[41]

It is, of course, true that Balasaraswati held her own.[42] Her recital at the Music Academy in the 1970 season on the day the award was conferred on Pattammal is remembered for the reason pointed out by an observant *rasika* that 'the *rangasthalam* was her domain'.[43] The stage of the Music Academy, Madras, was indeed always available to her and starting with the 1935 season, which was also Pattammal's first, she performed in twenty-three seasons till 1973, her year as president of the conference. For most of the time till the early 1970s, the only other dancers who commanded the attention of the Madras audience were Kamala, who performed at the Academy's season in twenty of the thirty years between 1948 and 1978 and Vyjayantimala, who performed at ten of the twenty years between 1958 and 1978. The real explosion in dance happened after the 1970s but by that time Balasaraswati was largely retired.

What Balasaraswati did enjoy, in addition, was a formidable reputation abroad. With Subbulakshmi, she was a performer at the Edinburgh festival in 1963 and had earlier visited Japan in 1961.[44] It is possible that while Subbulakshmi drew rapturous, if uninformed, audiences, Balasaraswati caught the attention of the greatest dancers. It is believed that Ted Shawn (1891–1972), a pioneer of innovative dancing in the United States, said of her Jacob's Pillow appearance, 'You are in the presence of greatness.'[45] An unnamed critic wrote, 'I shall thank God every day that I have been born in the same age as Bala and that I have seen her dance.'[46] A dancer and dance critic, a good forty years older than Balasaraswati, called her 'one of the greatest dancers of all time'.[47] Another critic simply wrote, 'Words cannot begin to capture her spell. Go and see her yourself.'[48]

Subbulakshmi was indeed giving some vintage *sabha* concerts still, occasionally reaching deep into her armoury, but these were, sadly, being phased out. There are many examples from 1974 onwards of a slackening in the structure and tempo of Subbulakshmi's concerts. The new, especially for recitals outside Madras,[49] was a random collection of very familiar and often-presented pieces, interspersed with bhajans, followed by a raga elaboration, another familiar song and more bhajans. Recitals in Madras may have included a few more traditional pieces, but the *ragam-tanam-pallavi* was generally given up.

An August 1974 recital at the Brahma Gana Sabha includes such major Tyagaraja songs as '*Endaro*'/Sri, '*Darini*'/Suddhasaveri, '*Naradamuni*'/Pantuvarali, '*Meevalla*'/Kapi and '*Vinayakuni*'/Madhyamavati, Dikshitar's '*Kamalambike*'/Todi and Syama Sastri's '*Mayamma*'/Ahiri, but the recital does not have the central stability which a *pallavi* would have provided. The concert list of a recital at Bala Mandir in October 1974 reveals the same trend. These are indications that if Subbulakshmi was still prepared to sing, she would now do so only for causes Sadasivam wished to support. But more significantly, at this stage of her career, she no longer needed to prove anything.

A crucial development in Subbulakshmi's life, in 1974, was the award of the Ramon Magsaysay Award in the category of public service. The awards, given annually since 1958, were instituted to honour 'greatness of spirit and transformative leadership in Asia'[50] and from India only the charismatic Jayaprakash Narayan had won an award till that time in the category of public service.[51] All of Subbulakshmi's honours up to this point were specifically, and justifiably, linked to her musicianship. The Magsaysay was the first recognition of her role as a public figure and benefactor, and though the award was linked to the regime of Ferdinand Marcos, it was received in India with great pride.[52] In fairness, it must be conceded that the Magsaysay Award over the years has recognized the work mostly, if not always, of extraordinary Indians.

The biography circulated at this time was neatly done; a detailed account of the official version of Subbulakshmi's life, and for the first time mention was made of the unknown Madurai Subramania Iyer as her father. The singer herself in her speech at the award ceremony unambiguously took the position that 'Indian music is orientated solely to the end of divine communion' while paying her tributes to Gandhi, Rajaji, Nehru, the Paramacharya of Kanchi and to T. Sadasivam. 'My all I owe to my husband, Sri T. Sadasivam. By his loving care he is my parent; by his unerring guidance he is my preceptor.'[53] It is beyond irony that he both wrote the speech and heard it delivered.

Possibly more significantly, Subbulakshmi's brother M.S. Sakthivel passed away in hospital in Vellore on 18 October 1974.[54] Subbulakshmi and Sadasivam accompanied the body to Madurai for the last rites. Very little is known of his life and career after the late 1940s when he accompanied his sister on the mrdangam; other than that he had some association with the radio, but those familiar with the Kalki Gardens establishment recall his occasional visits, when he was usually to be found lurking around in the kitchen and stores.[55] The Coimbatore-based family of his sister Vadivambal's patron likewise recall him and his cousin K. Raju Pillai travelling from Madurai to seek money or other assistance.[56] Unusually for his time, he was a graduate, but this does not seem to have helped much.[57] On his death, his widow Angulakshmi left for her native Coimbatore, where she lived on till 2016. The house on West Hanumantharayan Koil Street passed on Sakthivel's death to the family of Raju Pillai, the son of Shanmukhavadivu's brother, or cousin, Kandaswamy, whose daughter R. Subbulakshmi and grandson Kumaran still live there.

Sakthivel's death was the snapping of the last links to Madurai and Subbulakshmi in her bereavement cancelled several concert engagements, including possibly her appearances in the December season that year. On one of these occasions, Radha performed without her. As with Shanmukhavadivu and Vadivambal, it is hard not to think of Sakthivel's life without regret.

In 1975, Subbulakshmi was awarded the Padma Vibhushan, the second-highest national recognition of distinction, followed shortly thereafter by the fellowship of the Sangeet Natak Akademi. Before her, only Allauddin Khan and Uday Shankar among performing artistes had won the award, in 1971, and as in the case of the Padma Bhushan, Subbulakshmi was recognized well before many of her peers. Balasaraswati, Bismillah Khan and Ravi Shankar were recognized in 1977, 1980 and 1981 respectively, with Semmangudi Srinivasa Iyer receiving a shamefully belated recognition in 1990 and Pattammal and Lata Mangeshkar only in 1999. The system of selection for national honours has always been criticized on grounds of opacity and whimsy and, as in the case of the *Sangitha Kalanidhi*, it is never very clear what the deciding qualifications are. But happily in Subbulakshmi's case, both for the Padma Vibhushan and years later at the time of the Bharat Ratna, there was no doubt at all, and only celebration, at so appropriate an honour.

A short recital on 29 September 1975 to commemorate International Music Week was well received. '*Bhajare re chitta Balambikam*'/Kalyani was the main piece, with extensive *neraval*, along with '*Jagadanandakaraka*'/

Nata, *'Mayamma'*/Ahiri, *'Jaya Jaya Padmanabhanujesha'*/Manirangu, *'Narayana'*/Suddhadhanyasi, possibly the first airing of what became a favourite, and a soaring *'Srinivasa'*/Hamsanandi. Along with bhajans and other songs, it was a very brisk ninety minutes, but one can agree with the *Hindu's* opinion that 'Music is well served when it sways the listener into a state of self-forgetfulness and M.S. Subbulakshmi's enduring popularity rests principally on this gift.'[58] In this ponderous statement is a core of truth.

A concert at the Krishna Gana Sabha on 5 October followed, as did a New Delhi recital for the ITC Sangeet Sammelan on 7 October and a benefit recital for the Don Bosco Matric School Kindergarten Benefit Fund on 26 October. The concert grind was maintained through the December 1975 season and there is a record of a recital at the Indian Fine Arts Society with a fine Kharaharapriya and an unusual, for her, rendering of Tyagaraja's *'Tsakkani raja margamu'*, followed by a *ragam-tanam-pallavi* in Mohana. Early in 1976 was a brief appearance singing an invocation at the 6th Afro-Asian Congress of Ophthalmology, the event itself living in the record on account of the piece which she sang, a hymn in Sanskrit, Arabic, Japanese, English and Tamil, the verses themselves taken from various religious texts. The underlying message was powerful even if the piece was of no great musical value.

Subbulakshmi was always inclined to associate herself with saints and spiritual mentors. The list of benefit concerts shows innumerable concerts in aid of the Sri Ramakrishna Mission, quite possibly the result of her association, and Sadasivam's, with Swami Ranganathananda, who ran the Mission for most of this period. There were several private recitals for J. Krishnamurti during his winter sojourns at 'Vasanta Vihar', Madras, occasions which were marked for their quiet repose.[59] Short excerpts are available of a 1973 concert which Subbulakshmi gave in Tiruvannamalai in aid of the Arunachaleswara temple. In addition to '*Vatapi*'/Hamsadhwani, '*Vachamago*'/Kaikavasi and '*Paratpara*'/Vachaspati, there is a set of verses in praise of Sri Ramana Maharshi. In February, she sang in aid of the Sri Ramana Kendra in New Delhi and some years later Subbulakshmi sang on the radio for the centenary of Sri Ramana, a recording of which is available,[60] and also at the Sri Ramanasrama.[61]

The senior Sankaracharya of Kanchi, a continuous presence in her life, enjoyed her absolute devotion.[62] In her statement in 1974 to the Sangeet Natak Akademi she states, or was encouraged to state, that she 'cherishes most her singing before His Holiness, the Sage of Kanchi, now in His 81st year'. She sang for Swami Chinmayananda and the Chinmaya Mission founded by him, Swami Sivananda in Rishikesh, Sri Ma Anandamayi, and the Pejavar Mutt in Udupi. In her later years, Subbulakshmi turned to Sathya Sai Baba and even recorded a set of songs on and by him.[63]

It seems obvious that as a devout Hindu she was well versed in the rules of conventional ritual worship, was demonstratively religious and always ready to pay obeisance to a spiritual leader; we do not know much of what, if any, specific realization she had reached. But it is as a reciter of chants and hymns that she is probably best known to modern-day listeners. The '*Venkatesa Suprabhatam*' in 1960 and the '*Vishnu Sahasranamam*' in 1970 had established her mastery over Sanskrit *uchharam*, or enunciation, and she now developed this genre with the '*Kamakshi Suprabhatam*' in 1974, the '*Kasi-Rameshwaram Suprabhatams*' in 1977, and the '*Meenakshi Suprabhatam*' in the late 1980s. In 1983, she recorded the '*Radhamadhavam*', a long hymn in Malayalam by Sri Atmananda to be followed in 1996 with a set of his compositions.[64] Subbulakshmi developed some kind of attachment to Sri Atmananda's ashram in Malakkara in Kerala, and made it a point over nearly twenty years to visit each year and sing for the gathering there.

The '*Vishnu Sahasranamam*' and '*Bhaja Govindam*' record was released at many locations to much praise.[65] At the Hyderabad release, President

V.V. Giri observed that 'Srimathi M.S. Subbulakshmi is an outstanding example of how gifted individuals can use their talent in the service of humanity.'[66] The '*Vishnu Sahasranamam*' is an ancient chant stringing together the thousand names of Vishnu and frequently recited both in more conventional homes and in temples. Where the '*Venkatesa Suprabhatam*' has been a part of temple ritual for centuries, the '*Vishnu Sahasranamam*' has always been a prayer which householders can recite.[67] Subbulakshmi's 1970 recording continues, even in these more modern times, to hold attention. It is a grand composition, an ancient text from the earliest versions of the Mahabharata, and the story is told often of the diligence with which she and Radha learnt the text.[68] It is a masterly rendering, the Sanskrit pronunciation pure and ringing, the result of much dedicated learning from experts.[69]

The '*Bhaja Govindam*' of Adi Sankara is a major, didactic text, not particularly meant for musical setting, but the verses, set to tune by Trivandrum R.S. Mani and taught by him to Subbulakshmi, became another favourite.[70] '*Sri Kamakshi Suprabhatam*' was released in 1974.[71] Subbulakshmi's 1960 recording of the '*Sri Venkatesa Suprabhatam*' has long remained one of the most successful releases of HMV[72] and this appears to have encouraged her to popularize similar chants for other shrines; however, where the '*Sri Venkatesa Suprabhatam*' is a fifteenth-century text, the '*Sri Kamakshi Suprabhatam*' and others recorded by Subbulakshmi are all written by contemporary scholars. Authorship of the '*Sri Kamakshi Suprabhatam*', which was set to tune by Kadayanallur S. Venkataraman,[73] is credited to one Lakshmikantha Sharma. It has an interesting structure in that it is set to raga, and while every verse ends with beseeching the goddess' awakening, or *suprabhatam*, the last lines themselves are all different.

A distinguished scholar of Hindi recalls even after many decades the '*Kamakshi Suprabhatam*' being played every morning in the temples of Mathura.[74] The whole package was very competently put together with the record including compositions of the trinity, '*Kanjadalayataksi*'/

Kamalamanohari, *'Vinayakuni'*/Madhyamavati, *'Kanakasaila'*/ Punnagavarali, and the frequently heard *'Sri Kamakoti'*/Saveri, each song prefaced by an appropriate hymn chosen from various texts.[75]

Two more chants of this type were released in 1977, the *'Sri Kasi Viswanatha Suprabhatam'* and the *'Sri Rameswara Ramanatha Suprabhatam'*, harking back to the ancient Saivite practice of a pilgrimage to Kasi (Varanasi) being followed by one to Rameswaram.[76] Again, both were set to tune by Subbulakshmi's long-term associate Kadayanallur S. Venkataraman. The *'Sri Kasi Viswanatha Suprabhatam'* is believed to have been composed by a team of scholar priests in Varanasi.[77] Subbulakshmi's ringing voice still awakens that ancient city every morning as the *Suprabhatam* is played over the public address system. The *'Sri Rameswara Ramanatha Suprabhatam'*, a more cumbersome piece, the text of which is not particularly suited to recitation, is the work of the distinguished Sanskritist V. Raghavan.

12

Subbulakshmi

वीणा गान दश गमक क्रिये[1]

('*Who, on the vina, plays gamakas*',
loosely translated from Muthusvami Dikshitar's '*Minakshi memudam*'
in the raga Gamakakriya)

THE year 1975 was observed as the bicentenary of Muthusvami Dikshitar, revered always as one of the trinity, and to some, the greatest of them. A composer of extraordinary stature and style, it would be inappropriate to regard him only as a man of devotion, which he undoubtedly was. He was a superlative poet with an exquisite sense of rhythm, of the placement of words and of the use of literary embellishments. Sanskrit is a language rich in synonyms and Muthusvami Dikshitar was a master in the creation and use of words. He was also a tantric, with a deep knowledge of text and practice.

A useful way of appreciating the quality of the musical output of Muthusvami Dikshitar is to study his group compositions.[2] There are several types of these. Firstly and most famously, there are the *vaara kritis* in praise of the seven principal planets; these are set in the seven principal *talas*.³ There are some doubts regarding the authenticity of two subsidiary *kritis* in praise of Rahu and Ketu, which are, however, included as *navagraha kritis*.⁴ Subbulakshmi sang these often, at home in her personal devotions and in concert, with '*Angarakam*'/Surati (on Mars) and '*Divakara tanujam*'/Yadukulakambhoji (on Saturn) being particular favourites. Some years after Subbulakshmi's passing, Radha Viswanathan released a recording of the *navagraha kritis*, establishing their place in Subbulakshmi's repertoire.

Another category of group compositions are the *vibhakti* (or 'declension') *kritis*, sets of eight songs where each song is cast in each of the eight declensions of Sanskrit nouns. These are songs in praise of Muttukumara at Tiruttani (the 'guruguha' *vibhakti kritis*),⁵ in praise of Abhayamba at Mayuram, in praise of Tyagaraja at Tiruvarur and separately on his consorts Kamalamba⁶ and Nilotpalamba.⁷ There are other embellishments to these songs.⁸ Of these sets of *vibhakti* compositions, Subbulakshmi actually sang very few.

There are eleven Kamalamba *navavarana kritis*, including the eight set in different declensions of the principal noun of the song, and of these Subbulakshmi repeatedly sang '*Kamalambike*' in Todi. On occasion, she also sang '*Kamalamba samrakshatu mam*' in Anandabhairavi and '*Kamalambam*' in Kalyani and there is a reference to '*Sri Kamalambikaya*' in Sankarabharanam being in her repertoire.⁹ It is likely that she also knew the Ahiri and Punnagavarali *navavarana kritis*.¹⁰ The *vibhakti kritis* relate in all cases to particular shrines. From among the large number of songs composed by Muthusvami Dikshitar on Rama in his various forms, scholars have identified eight which can be grouped as a set, following the *vibhakti* principle.¹¹ Of these, Subbulakshmi sang '*Ramachandrena*' in Manji.

There are two other sets of songs on Siva; the lesser known are a set of five on five Sivalinga shrines within the great temple complex at Tiruvarur, but the much better-known set consists of five songs on the manifestations of Siva as the five elements of creation: earth, fire, water, wind and space.[12] Of these stunning and majestic songs, we have an early record of Subbulakshmi singing '*Chintaya makanda*'/Bhairavi on the *prithvi lingam* at Kanchipuram, but she does not appear to have handled any of the others, in itself a puzzlement, as they are the kind of songs she sang with involvement and full understanding.[13]

It would be doing Muthusvami Dikshitar a disservice if the group compositions alone, for all that they are masterpieces of structure, were seen as an example of his virtuosity. There are a large number of *kritis* composed in praise of the deities at various shrines in the south, which stand as testament to the fine technique of the composer, poetry rendered in raga, full of iconographic and scriptural detail, and always concert-worthy. It would be another mistake to assume that the great composers wrote only for themselves or for their chosen objects of worship; there is enough in the clever detailing of many of the great pieces to suggest that intriguing the attention of the audience was also a motivating factor during composition. An example from the works of Tyagaraja could be the use of *sangatis*; in Dikshitar it could be the use of rhyming texts and alliteration, the use of the *madhyama kala*, or a second speed, the use of allusions to stories from the classical texts and of word play such as introducing the name of the raga into the text.

It is of interest that Muthusvami Dikshitar, for his time, was a widely travelled man. He had not only visited shrines across the south but had also, with his two wives, spent several years in Benares.[14] The exact dates are unclear and the time he spent in north India is given variously as five to eight years. Many interesting questions arise, for which at this distance of time there are no answers. Almost certainly he would have learnt some Hindi, and heard the verses of Tulsidas recited in their customary manner and accent. Again, equally certainly, he would have come across Muslims whose daily and ritual practices were quite different from those of Muslims nearer home.

It is entirely possible that he visited the Buddhist shrine at Sarnath, only a few miles from the ghats at Benares, and for all that we know, even the shrines at Kushinagar and Gaya, all in the general region. Perhaps he witnessed the Kumbh Mela at Prayag (Allahabad) in 1798? Some of his later compositions demonstrate a familiarity with Hindustani musical styles, but we will never know whether the composer who wrote of the deity as *bhasamana badari sthitam*, 'he who is at the radiant Badri', in 'Sri Satyanarayanam'/Sivapantuvarali actually visited Badrinath in the inner Himalaya.

Muthusvami Dikshitar's musical legacy was carried forward by his students and family and, if they were not as large in number as the Tyagaraja following, were as influential. A permanent place has been secured for the legacy of Muthusvami Dikshitar through the *Sangita Sampradaya Pradarsini* compiled by his descendant Subbarama Dikshitar (1839–1906).

A more difficult question to answer is how and why, in the perception of the listening public, Tyagaraja moved so quickly to sainthood, an attribute not commonly given to Muthusvami Dikshitar or Syama Sastri. Tyagaraja's first biographer in English, writing in the 1920s, dismisses both of his contemporaries as 'varnam composers', an unfair and completely inaccurate assessment.[15] Whatever the reason for this prejudice, it is still recognized that among the many reasons for the great influence and continuing presence of the trinity was their individual styles of defining the *kriti*, the song, which is at the heart of the Carnatic repertory, and their individual ways of combining text (*sahitya*) with metre (*tala*) and melody (*raga*). A scholar has observed that Muthusvami Dikshitar drew both on the *kirtana* tradition, used in bhajan and group singing, and *stotra*, or devotional lyrics. It is relevant that he chose Sanskrit as his medium, at a time when Telugu was still the language of literature and culture in the region.[16]

Muthusvami Dikshitar was widely celebrated through the bicentenary year. At a recital in March 1975 on the occasion of the award to Subbulakshmi of the Fellowship of the Sangeet Natak Akademi, she sang several of his compositions, the *vaara kriti* 'Sri Sukra'/Pharaz,

'Sri Lakshmivaraham'/Abhogi, 'Cheta Sri Balakrishnam'/Jujavanti and 'Tyagaraja yoga vaibhavam'/Anandabhairavi in a programme otherwise heavy with bhajans.[17]

More significantly, two great recitals, entirely of the compositions of Muthusvami Dikshitar, were given by Subbulakshmi in the course of 1975. The foremost representatives of the performing form appeared at carefully curated events in Bombay and Madras. Subbulakshmi's Bombay concert at the grand Shanmukhananda Hall in March 1975 was sponsored by the National Centre for the Performing Arts with the December concert being at the Music Academy, Madras. The Bombay concert list makes impressive reading with familiar and unusual songs alike, including 'Vatapi'/Hamsadhwani, the luminous 'Veena pustaka dharini'/Vegavahini, a learning from T. Brinda sung as it is in the traditional style of that school, 'Minakshi' in Gamakakriya, both the Anandabhairavi and Todi navavarana kritis, 'Sadasivam upasmahe'/Sankarabharanam, 'Hariharaputram'/Vasanta, the appropriate vaara kriti for the day, 'Divakara tanujam'/Yadukulakambhoji, 'Ranganayakam'/Nayaki, 'Sri Parvati'/Bauli, the evergreen 'Rangapura vihara'/Brindavanasaranga, 'Maye'/Tarangini, 'Gange mam pahi'/Jenjuti and 'Mamava Pattabhirama'/Manirangu.

The December recital in Madras was, if anything, even more beautifully structured. Several items were repeated from Bombay, but the recital's commencement with the radiant Telugu daru in Sriranjani, 'Nee sati daivamu' and 'Sri Muladhara chakra vinayaka'/Sri, an uncommon song, indicated that this was a concert out of the ordinary. The fare included 'Sri Kantimatim'/Desisimharava and 'Tyagaraja yoga vaibhavam'/Anandabhairavi and the vaara kriti for the day, 'Angarakam asrayamyaham'/Surati. The Hindu observed with concern that she had burdened herself with a very heavy programme, which is true, but that she built on 'the combined strength of faithful renditions and an auditorium filling tone'.[18]

Subbulakshmi always sang the songs of Muthusvami Dikshitar extremely well and in addition to the songs which she rendered at the thematic concerts held over 1975, her repertoire included '*Bhaja re re chitta balambikam*'/Kalyani, '*Akshayalingavibho*'/Sankarabharanam, '*Sri Subramanyaya namaste*'/Kambhoji, '*Kanjadalayatakshi*'/Kamalamanohari, '*Mahalakshmi*'/Madhavamanohari, '*Sri Krishnam*'/Todi, '*Anandamritakarshini*'/Amritavarshini, '*Hiranmayim Lakshmim*'/Lalita and less frequently, '*Seshachalanayakam*' and '*Mamava Minakshi*', both in Varali, '*Vinabheri*'/Abheri, '*Ramanatham*'/Kasiramakriya and '*Sri Maha Ganapati*'/Gaula. There are concerts where she sang '*Maha Ganapatim*'/Todi, '*Kamakshi*'/Sumadyuti and '*Ehi Annapurne*'/Punnagavarali.

Subbulakshmi turned sixty in 1976, a significant milestone for Hindus of a certain age and disposition. There is no record of any elaborate celebration but her admirers rejoiced. 'She has traversed the years with grace and dignity. Likewise, her music has grown in width and depth. Time has not staled her charm. It has only added to her wisdom and the bonds of affection between her and her countless admirers'.[19] In the December of that year, her friend and senior contemporary T. Brinda was awarded the title of *Sangitha Kalanidhi* by the Music Academy. She had always been a highly respected performer and, indeed, the Music Academy had long recognized the powerful impact of the Dhanammal *bani*, or school.

Brinda and her sister Muktha, with their sister Abhiramasundari on the violin, had appeared on the Academy's stage as early as 1936 and had made another ten appearances over the next twenty-odd years. The sisters sang at the Music Academy almost continuously through the decade of the 1960s, when they parted ways, at least on stage. Brinda appeared alone a few more times, including in 1973, when her cousin Balasaraswati was presiding over the event and then in 1976, her own presidential year. The honour was richly deserved with the only unresolved issue being why Muktha who sang for so long as Brinda's partner was not selected for the award as well. The rumour that Brinda had refused to countenance such a possibility did nothing to improve her reputation.[20]

Brinda and her sisters were the daughters of Dhanammal's youngest daughter T. Kamakshi Ammal (1893–1953)[21] and her patron S. Soundararaja Iyengar.[22] There were also three sons from this union which appears to have been quite publicly recognized.[23] The sisters were born in a home where music was sung, played and taught continuously, but in a quite remarkable move Brinda and Muktha were sent out of Madras by their mother to Kanchipuram to learn from the distinguished Kanchipuram Naina Pillai, with Brinda always recognized as the student and Muktha as the companion who learnt what she could by absorption.

The songs of the trinity, and of their disciples, constituted the bulk of the sisters' repertoire, but it is for their store of *padams* and *javalis* that they are most renowned. *Padams*, at their most simple, are poems of love; the beloved one is, however, divine. The *ashtapadis* of Jayadeva, who wrote in Sanskrit in the twelfth century, are the precursors to the great Telugu love poems, primarily of Kshetrayya, sometimes Sanskritized to Kshetragna, of the mid seventeenth-century. About 400 of these songs survive and though addressed to Krishna as Muvvagopala, they belong 'less to the temple than to the courtesans' quarters of the Nayaka royal towns'.[24] The genre of *padams* also includes songs of fourteenth-century Annamacharya, or Annamayya.

Padams are slow and stately in structure, with limited words, the emphasis being on prolonged repetition of each line, the performer's skill being tested by her ability to stretch the contours of the raga over the framework of the song. Kshetrayya is famed as a *vaggeyakara* who used a limited range of ragas capable of being rendered with depth and emotion, and particularly meant for *abhinaya*.[25] There is no doubt they were meant for performance, set as they were to music, but it is an open question whether the ragas in which the *padams* of Kshetrayya are presented today are his original conception. In a 1952 compilation of 429 *padams* of Kshetrayya, of which twenty-five are believed to be the work of others, scholars of the order of P. Sambamoorthy and E. Krishna Iyer accept that the ragas are as laid down by Kshetrayya, and used by him to convey a very wide range of emotions.[26]

Given that very little is now understood of composition and the use of raga until immediately before the trinity, it is possible that the ragas in which Kshetrayya's poems are performed today date only to Dhanammal's time. The original raga settings of Annamayya are likewise now lost. Brinda was believed to have learnt about thirty of these Telugu *padams*.[27] A listing of her cousin Balasaraswati's repertoire includes a staggering ninety-seven *padams*, of which over fifty are in Telugu, the others being in Tamil and Kannada.[28]

There is another interesting debate here. The musicologist Matthew Harp Allen has called attention to the divergent views held by different sets of admirers of the *padam* form; there are those who see it — in that it is an accompaniment for dance — as essentially a 'lighter' or semi-classical form and those who see it as the very essence of classicism.[29] This latter view is linked to the huge resurgence of adoration, this side idolatry, of Dhanammal and her style, in the past thirty years.

Dhanammal's family, 'this great and gifted family which has fostered Karnatak [sic] music with such devotion and understanding',[30] was famed for their stock of *javalis*, faster, lighter pieces meant primarily for dance and more overtly erotic in content than *padams*. Davesh Soneji characterizes *javalis* as 'unabashedly erotic, sometimes sarcastic and always upbeat, javalis are also signs of the volatile, sexually charged space of the salon, one that was diametrically opposed to the contained, private sexuality of the conjugal home'.[31] In 1960, Brinda published a volume of thirty *javalis*[32] composed by Dharmapuri Subbarayar, Patnam Subramania Iyer and others while Balasaraswati is credited with having performed to fifty-one *javalis*.[33]

Brinda and Muktha between them established a solid tradition of performance. They were a regular presence at the Music Academy and other *sabhas*, even if they did not draw large crowds.[34] They were wedded to the performing tradition of their clan; as a critic noted, 'They are custodians rather than creators. They transmit definitive versions of songs and even definitive forms of raga. To a mind which is bewildered by the freakishness of originality and caprice of creative genius, Brinda and Muktha offer the infallible solace of fixed frames of reference.'[35] Their rendering of *padams*, with the text of the song being at times indistinguishable from the raga elaboration was particularly well suited for dance performance.

Subbulakshmi did not particularly sing either *padams* or *javalis*, these having effectively been left behind in Madurai, but there are recordings of '*Paiyyada*' in Nadanamakriya, '*Moratopu*' in Sahana and '*Kuvalayakshiro*' in Gaulipantu,[36] all learnt from Brinda.[37] And many years later, at a recital to commemorate Brinda's eightieth birthday, Subbulakshmi sang the *padam* '*Valapu tala*' in Athana.[38]

Brinda was a much-respected teacher. For many years, she was on the staff of the College of Carnatic Music in Madras, an odd choice for a musician who came from a strong tradition of *kulaparampara*; she taught several students, many of whom remember her as kindly and caring, but very strict and demanding during classes.[39] She taught in the old style, without notebooks and tape recorders, and students recall her endless patience in teaching a song till every line had been learnt well.[40]

Brinda was highly regarded by fellow musicians, admired by the cognoscenti and commended for her sensitivity, taste and authority.[41] But the reaction she most often inspired was respectful distance. Late in life she appeared on a documentary;[42] towards the end she chuckles with a low, and self-satisfied, growl, '*Brindamma aana yellarkum bhayam daan*,' Everyone is a little afraid of Brinda. That was her.

Muktha, who always deferred to her strong-willed sister, on and off stage, continued to sing and teach.[43] At the very time of Brinda's public honour, she was singing on her own and commanding respect as a representative of 'the uncompromising values of traditional Carnatic music'[44] and for her style and emotion-laden singing, 'the rare type of artiste who can so gloriously fulfil herself in song interpretation'.[45] Older *rasikas* rejoiced when the sisters sang together in October 1988 to commemorate the fiftieth anniversary of Dhanammal's passing.[46] Subbulakshmi was in the audience as old favourites from their repertoire were presented.[47] There was also, and this was entirely par for the course, some onstage bickering between the sisters.[48]

The Music Academy eventually recognized Muktha's art in 1995 with the title of *Sangitha Kala Acharya*. She continued to sing for the truly appreciative in chamber concerts.[49] Very late in life, at the age of eighty-nine she even performed at a music festival in Cleveland, and observed, acutely, that she had a bigger audience than anyone in her family, including Dhanammal herself, had ever had.[50] Shortly thereafter, in the last year of Subbulakshmi's life, an even older Muktha sang for her at her house.[51] When she passed on in 2007, the last of Dhanammal's grandchildren, the great devadasi matriarchies can be said to have come to an end.[52]

Subbulakshmi rose handsomely to the occasion of Brinda's presidency of the Music Academy's conference and concerts. Her concert on 19 December 1976 began with Dikshitar's *'Gananayakam bhajeham'*/Rudrapriya followed by Tyagaraja's *'Ra ra mayinti daka'*/Asaveri, both well-known songs but not in her regular stock of songs and included *Koniyada*, Veena Kuppier's grand Kambhoji piece, *'Ramanatham bhajeham'*/Kasiramakriya, *'Sri Kumara nagaralaye'*/Athana, *'Devi brova samayamide'*/Chintamani, possibly aired for the first time, and a *ragam-tanam-pallavi* in Bhairavi.

Significantly, the recital included the last two, of twelve, segments of Maha Vaidyanatha Iyer's *'Melakarta Ragamalika'*. With this the entire composition had been presented by her in six concerts at the Music Academy starting 1968. This should always be recognized as one of Subbulakshmi's most enduring achievements and one which will at all times ensure her a place on the commanding heights.

The season included an appearance at the Tamil Isai Sangam. Following her early and enthusiastic support to the Sangam in the 1940s, her appearances on that stage through the 1950s and 1960s were erratic and it was only in the 1970s that she was again regularly featured at the Sangam during the season. But now even this was coming to an end and the 1976 performance was one of her last Sangam performances. There were, as is only to be expected, many Tamil songs, of ancient and modern composers: Kotiswara Iyer, Nilakanta Sivan, Manikkavachagar, Subramania Bharati, Periasami Thooran, Arunachalakavi, Thaayumanavar, Sundarar and Kalki. There was a Tyagaraja song, 'Ksheenamai'/Mukhari, a great favourite of the Semmangudi school, and a *ragam-tanam-pallavi* in Kiravani.

The 1976 season recital at the Indian Fine Arts Society was another highlight with several of her signature songs: 'Needucharana'/Kalyani, 'O Jagadamba'/Anandabhairavi, 'Darini'/Suddhasaveri and, very unusually, Muthusvami Dikshitar's 'Kamakshi kamakotipithavasini'/Sumadyuti. This was Subbulakshmi at her finest, when she was capable of evoking the mood of surrender not through obviously devotional pieces, bhajans, hymns and the like but through disciplined and note-perfect classical renderings.

> The quality of M.S. Subbulakshmi's music is that it strives to speak to the soul. She has well understood what is the most enduring of classical Carnatic music, namely devotion, and the truth forces iself upon the listeners at every moment of her concert. On hearing her ... there descends on the listeners a feeling of the supreme reality of God and one's nearness to Him. In the articulation of the sahitya there is pensive, sublime, solemn sweetness.[53]

The pace of benefit concerts had not flagged with over seventy such in the years 1970–76, in the metropolitan cities and in Quilon, Varanasi, Eluru, Erode, Hassan, Hubli, Karnal, Gwalior, Rajamundhry, Gudivada and Bhopal. Subbulakshmi and her party were still travelling mainly by train for their engagements and this pace could not have been easy. Several people have commented on the fact that whenever the party travelled, Subbulakshmi and Sadasivam always insisted that the accompanying artistes be given the same facilities as themselves in the matter of transport and lodgings.[54] That this should be remembered and commented on from this distance of time suggests, regrettably, that this was not the usual practice.

By this stage in her performing career, Subbulakshmi had, with the exception of *sabha* concerts, changed the format of her concerts entirely. The *ragam-tanam-pallavi* was not offered except in very exceptional cases. Most concerts had a preponderance of bhajans, interspersed with often-repeated songs of the trinity.[55] An extreme example is of a concert in Bangkok in 1975 where Tyagaraja's 'Ma Janaki' in Kambhoji came after three bhajans and before another four. There are many others of this type, as for instance a concert at Houston in 1977 with *twenty four* separate songs, of which nine were bhajans and eight were oft-presented *tukkadas*. Another concert at Toronto in the same series had seventeen songs, including five bhajans and seven *tukkadas*. A London concert in September 1977 likewise has a *ragam-tanam-pallavi* in Dharmavati thrown into a medley of bhajans, light verses and endlessly repeated songs. Her audiences were not always pleased. 'The justifications of her articulate husband' fussed one adoring critic, 'for her mixing her fare with non-classical and light pieces to cater to mixed audiences do not amuse me'.[56]

Subbulakshmi's recital at Carnegie Hall in New York was on the contrary a shining example of tight planning and execution.[57] Her friend and patron C.V. Narasimhan helped arrange this, partly in order to divert her from personal difficulties in India, and it was only appropriate that India's greatest artiste should appear on one of the world's greatest platforms.

The pattern adopted was the one that had by now become her standard; there was no *varnam* and no *ragam-tanam-pallavi* but instead a mixture of pieces from the classical repertoire and bhajans. 'O Rangasayee'/Kambhoji was, as on so many earlier occasions, the centrepiece, but there was also a glowing *'Rama Rama gunaseema'*/ Simhendramadhyamam and a relatively new addition to her stock, Syama Sastri's *'Devi brova samayamide'*/Chintamani. The recital commenced with *'Sri Maha Ganapati'*/Gaula.[58]

On the bill of fare was *'Ikanainana'*/Pushpalatika, famed for Subbulakshmi's *neraval* at the *anupallavi*. This particular piece of *neraval* had indeed been a special feature of Musiri Subramania Iyer's concerts but Subbulakshmi took it to an altogether new level.[59] In a recital given years earlier when this piece was presented, the critic wrote, 'In the *neraval* her *vidwat* was as much in evidence as her instinctive sense of appropriateness in picking up the proper phrase for embellishment always emphasizing the emotional content.'[60] It starts innocuously enough but very soon reaches dramatic heights; even those listeners who find it somewhat frenzied must admire the admirable control, and for all its clamour it is never unmusical.[61] Interestingly, Subbulakshmi appears to have recorded this song years earlier though this version is not traceable;[62] given the short duration of recorded piece it is unlikely to have included the famed *neraval*.

'O Rangasayee' from the Carnegie Hall recital has had a life of its own and has become the vocal track for a modern dance performed by Mark Morris in 1984 and recreated in 2016 by Dallas McMurray. Tyagaraja's text and Subbulakshmi's voice form the score to energetic modern dance.

> The solo goes on for twenty minutes, accompanied by a recording of the great Carnatic vocalist M.S. Subbulakshmi. She is singing a raga by the late-eighteenth-century composer Sri Tyagaraja. 'O Rangasayee', Subbulakshmi calls out again and again in a clear, warbling voice, invoking the reclining incarnation of Vishnu. 'When

I call you earnestly, can't you respond by uttering 'O' and appearing?'
Like many Carnatic lyrics, it is a song of longing. Structurally, it is a massive edifice built out of variations on a theme.[63]

The Carnegie Hall recital was the centrepiece of a longer visit to the United States, with many concert appearances in university campuses and other locations. The concerts themselves were now comfortably of the new concert pattern Subbulakshmi had adopted, with songs from the Carnatic repertory interspersed with miscellaneous bhajans, and only one raga rendering.[64] That Subbulakshmi by this stage of her career was somewhat mechanical in her approach to concerts is evidenced by the fact that exactly the same set of songs as in Carnegie Hall, with possibly one exception, was presented by her in Geneva on her return journey to India. We can be sure that the *neraval* at 'Ikanainana' was identical.

But that she could not be written off is evident from a recital at the Wesleyan University on 11 October 1977 which included a *varnam* ('*Indumukhi*' in Sankarabharanam), a *navavarana kriti* ('*Kamalambike*'/ Todi), the trinity suitably represented, the first two segments of the '*Melakarta Ragamalika*' and *ragam-tanam-pallavi* in Dharmavati, '*Sundara sakhi sumangali madura mīnākshi mām pāhi*'. The lighter pieces finely complemented the fare which had gone before. This is also true of the Boston recital. A sprightly '*Mathe*'/Khamas, followed by '*Ramanatham*'/ Kasiramakriya, an unusual *alapana* in Kapi followed by the old favourite '*Meevalla*', many bhajans and an excellent *ragam-tanam-pallavi* in Shanmukhapriya.[65]

Twenty years later, in the late 1990s, the James A. Rubin Collection of South Indian Classical Music was commissioned at Harvard University's Eda Kuhn Loeb Music Library. Subbulakshmi and Sadasivam knew Rubin well and he was closely associated with the 1966 tour of the United States and with the 1977 tour. The heart of the collection is a set of almost 400 reels of tape recorded by Rubin on eighteen trips to India between 1964 and 1987. The recordings are not only of Subbulakshmi but cover many winter seasons, many radio recitals and several private concerts. It is an invaluable resource and Subbulakshmi readily gave her consent for these tapes to be placed in the public domain subject to the condition that they would not be used for any commercial gain.[66]

The success of the foreign visit notwithstanding, it was a poignant return to India for Subbulakshmi because it was in her absence abroad that Kalki Gardens, her home for over thirty-five years, a stately residence that had seen the most exclusive gatherings and been host to the most lavish entertainments, had been sold, essentially in order to meet the growing debts being incurred by *Kalki*, debts which appear to have arisen out of gross mismanagement.[67]

This, indeed, was not a new development. Decades earlier, friends of the family had deplored the wanton expenditure of the establishment. 'Their habits of mind and imprudent living have brought the "Kalki" people to this pass.'[68] The magazine itself was revived after a brief gap, under a new management, and went on to recover its position among Tamil periodicals, but Sadasivam was no longer associated with it.

It was the end of a spectacle, a long-running play. A friend of the family noted that everything in Kalki Gardens was *natakam*, or drama.[69] A leading lady, gatherings of the elite, song and dance, grand meals, garden parties and, like in all plays, acting and make-believe. Intimates and friends of those years recollect that for all that Kalki Gardens existed because of Subbulakshmi and sustained itself on her munificence, it was never a home over which she had the least control or where she was, strange as it may seem, taken seriously. Her complete lack of worldly wisdom and her unfamiliarity with politics or current affairs were generally taken to indicate simple-mindednesss, surely an unbearable situation for a woman as intelligent as she, but this was where she had chosen to cast her lot.

Disciplined as always, Subbulakshmi took the loss of her stately home in her stride.[70] While in the United States, she had spoken to friends of her anxieties, but she returned, seemingly composed, to a very modest home near Valluvar Kottam in Madras. The cheque for whatever amount was due to her after the tour of the United States was endorsed in favour of Radha Viswanathan and friends marvelled that she was as gracious and gentle as ever, with no apparent recrimination and no stated regrets.[71] Given that everything being earned, and spent, and lost, either by the household or by *Kalki*, was hers, this restraint can only be regarded as admirable.

Subbulakshmi did not sing at all in any *sabha* in the season of 1977, but the selection that year by the Music Academy of M. L. Vasanthakumari to preside over the conference and concerts and receive the title of *Sangitha Kalanidhi* was widely appreciated. She had, of course, received many titles earlier, rich and evocative titles such as *Sangeethavani, Sangeetharatnakaram, Thiruppavaimani, Amruthaganavarshini, Saptagiri Asthana Vidushimani*,[72] and every one of these was no less deserved than the *Sangitha Kalanidhi* in 1977.

Madras Lalithangi Vasanthakumari was possibly the most imaginatively gifted of Carnatic musicians in the twentieth century.[73] Her voice was silken smooth, her vision inspired and her gifts awesome. Her music reflected precision and absolute control combined with courage, adventure and daring. A student initially of her parents Lalithangi and Koothanur Ayyaswami Iyer, Vasanthakumari came to be G.N. Balasubramaniam's star student, and one for whom even her guru had unstinted praise.

Vasanthakumari's repertoire was vast and she could never be faulted for repeating a song, any song, to the point of tedium, a criticism that can unfortunately be made of Subbulakshmi. Raga rendering and *svaraprasthara* was child's play to her and critics noted this appreciatively.

Shanmukhavadivu
[1889–1962]
[Courtesy: V. Shrinivasan]

Subbulakshmi
[1916–2004]
[Courtesy: N. Ram]

Shanmukhavadivu with her daughters Subbulakshmi and Vadivambal, the child Radha and other friends at Harikesanallur Muthiah Bhagavathar's residence in Trivandrum, 1940
[Courtesy: V. Shrinivasan]

Subbulakshmi, early 1940s
[Courtesy: V. Shrinivasan]

Balasaraswati bidding farewell to Subbulakshmi at Central Station, Madras, 1956. Subbulakshmi was travelling to Delhi to receive the Sangeet Natak Akademi award.
[Courtesy: V. Shrinivasan]

T. Balasaraswati and M.S. Subbulakshmi, 1937 or earlier, The Taj Mahal Hotel, Bombay
[Courtesy: Shanta Guhan]

T. Brinda, T. Muktha and T. Abhiramasundari, the daughters of T. Kamakshi, 1940s
[Courtesy: V. Navaneeth Krishnan]

D.K. Pattammal with T.S. Ranganayaki on the mrdangam, possibly mid-1930s.

[Courtesy: post of Pon Dhanasekaran dated 2 November 2018 on blog site inmathi.com]

T. Dhanammal with her daughters and grandchildren, 1936

[Courtesy: V. Shrinivasan]

M.S. Subbulakshmi and T. Sadasivam on their wedding day, 10 July 1940. Photograph taken by Ellis Dungan.

[Courtesy: Seetha Ravi]

In and as 'Sakuntalai', with G.N. Balasubramaniam as Dushyanta, 1940
[Courtesy: V. Shrinivasan]

'Meera', 1945
[Courtesy: Ellis Dungan Collection, West Virginia State Archive]

With Jawaharlal Nehru at the December 1947 release of 'Meera'
[Courtesy: V. Shrinivasan]

At a radio recording, around 1947
[Courtesy: Lakshmi Natarajan, Kalki]

In concert, with Kalpathi Ramanathan on the mrdangam and T. Chowdiah on the violin, 1941
[Courtesy: V. Shrinivasan]

In concert with R.K. Venkatarama Sastri on the violin, Tanjavur Upendran on the mrdangam, Umayalpuram Kothandarama Iyer on the ghatam, and Radha Viswanathan as accompanying singer, Fort High School, Bangalore, 1953
[Courtesy: N. Ram]

In concert, with Chalakudi Narayanaswami Iyer on the violin and Mavelikkara Krishnankutti Nair on the mrdangam, 1950s
[Courtesy: V. Shrinivasan]

Subbulakshmi felicitating C. Saraswathi Bai, 1953
[Courtesy: Lakshmi Natarajan, Kalki]

Subbulakshmi receiving the Padma Bhushan from Sri Prakasa, Governor of Madras, 1954
[Courtesy: N. Ram]

In concert, with Umayalpuram Kothandarama Iyer on the ghatam, 1950s
[Courtesy: V. Shrinivasan]

Balasaraswati in performance, 1960, photograph by Marilyn Silverstone
[Courtesy: Shanta Guhan]

In concert with T.K. Murthy on the mrdangam, Tiruvalangadu Sundaresa Iyer on the violin and Radha Viswanathan as accompanying singer, possibly 1963

[Courtesy: V. Shrinivasan]

In concert with T.K. Murthy on the mrdangam, 1960s

[Courtesy: V. Shrinivasan]

Wedding concert with Tiruvalangadu Sundaresa Iyer on the violin, T.K. Murthy on the mrdangam and Umayalpuram Kothandarama Iyer on the ghatam, early 1960s
[Courtesy: Lakshmi Natarajan, Kalki]

In concert with T.K. Murthy on the mrdangam, V.V. Subramanyam on the violin, T.H. Vinayakaram on the ghatam, Vijaya Rajendran on the tambura and Radha Viswanathan as accompanying singer, United Nations, 1966
[Courtesy: V. Shrinivasan]

Subbulakshmi receiving the Sangitha Kalanidhi from Karan Singh, The Music Academy, Madras, January 1969

[Courtesy: N. Ram]

In concert with Kandadevi Alagiriswami on the violin, V. Nagarajan on the kanjira, and Radha Viswanathan as accompanying singer, possibly 1970

[Courtesy: V. Shrinivasan]

Lalithangi and her daughter Vasanthakumari, late 1940s
[Courtesy: Sriram V.]

M.L. Vasanthakumari in concert with Tanjavur Krishnamurthy Rao on the mrdangam, K.M. Vaidyanathan on the ghatam, R.S. Gopalakrishnan on the violin and T.M. Prabhavathi and K.V. Charumathi as vocal support, June 1968
[Courtesy: Sucharita and S. Ranganathan]

D.K. Pattammal, T. Balasaraswati, M.S. Subbulakshmi and M.L. Vasanthakumari, 1973
[Courtesy: Lakshmi Natarajan, Kalki]

Rukmini Devi Arundale, 1940s

In concert with Karaikudi R. Mani on the mrdangam, V.V. Subramanyam on the violin, V. Nagarajan on the kanjira, and Radha Viswanathan as accompanying singer, Kozhikode, 1973

[Courtesy: V. Shrinivasan]

In concert with Kandadevi Alagiriswami on the violin, Palghat Kunjumani on the mrdangam, V. Nagarajan on the kanjira and Radha Viswanathan as accompanying singer, Malakkara, 1978

[Courtesy: V. Shrinivasan]

In concert with Dwaram Mangathayaru on the violin, K.V. Praṣad on the mrdangam, and Radha Viswanathan as accompanying singer, Tiruvaiyaru, 1986

[Courtesy: N. Ram]

Subbulakshmi, early 1990s

[Courtesy: N. Ram]

Rajam Pushpavanam, daughter of Madurai Pushpavanam Iyer, around 1990

[Courtesy: V. Swaminathan]

Subbulakshmi receiving the Padma Vibhushan from
President Fakhruddin Ali Ahmed, 1975
[Courtesy: N. Ram]

Subbulakshmi receiving the Bharat Ratna from President K.R. Narayanan, 1998
[Courtesy: N. Ram]

Subbulakshmi, August 1991

[Courtesy: Kalaimamani Yogi]

'The GNB clan has got a bias for rendering rare ragas in extenso' said one.[74] 'Here is a mind that rejoices in the difficult scale. Her great merit lies in perceiving change within the accepted parameters. Her art is inevitably modern, presented in terms that are strictly classical and artistic,' said another.[75] She was also a consummate master of *laya* intricacies. An early admirer wrote,

> She seems to take anything in music that is considered as beyond the pale of women as a challenge. This propensity is very pronounced in her elaboration of *pallavis*. She has built up a large repertoire of rare and intricate *pallavis*. Clear in statement and crisp in form, they are born of methodical and assiduous practice. Myriads of sparkling rhythmic figures flow with a metronomic precision, leaving her audience breathless.[76]

Thirty years later, in a tribute after her passing, it was again observed that 'mastery over *laya* made her one of the finest singers of *pallavi*. *Pallavis* in complex tala structures was an easy thing for her. She would pull off one with aplomb having created it just a few hours before the concert.'[77]

Vasanthakumari was blessed with a delightful voice, cool and limpid, and ever mobile. It was a voice which would not rest. 'M.L.V.'s voice at its clearest has the heady tang of the cold morning breeze or of fresh spring water. It is more intoxicating, at times, than the honey-sweet, spice-laden voice of Subbulakshmi.'[78] For a while, Vasanthakumari enjoyed a parallel career as a classical and a playback singer for films, but she opted out of films, recognizing that her fame was linked to that of the film actors on whom her songs were picturized.[79]

Starting from 1954 from when she began to appear regularly on the stage of the Music Academy, she remained till the end a major presence during the season: 'At both places, she says, a singer must give of her very best.'[80] She was widely in demand for *sabha* and wedding concerts with a 1960 report citing over 1,500 performances till that time.[81] Around the same time, another critic observed that her 'voice is perhaps the most attractive among all the women singers of Carnatic music today'.[82]

Vasanthakumari's repertoire was extremely large, and she displayed its riches all the time. She never toyed with the basic *cutcheri* format, though in later years she reduced the number of *alapanas* in her concerts. She sang bhajans, of Tukaram, Jnanadev, Tulsidas and Kabir, but selectively. Vasanthakumari had a fantastic musical imagination, and spontaneity was the hallmark of her recitals. There was probably no raga, howsoever obscure, that she would not sing. Her recitals were almost completely unrehearsed, as compared to the highly finished style of Subbulakshmi, and were sometimes truly magical.[83]

Two aspects of Vasanthakumari's performance need special mention. Following the efforts of her parents, she promoted the songs of Purandaradasa extensively and was capable of giving entire concerts only of these songs.[84] One such concert was presented at the Academy during the 1977 season. The other aspect was her vast collection of lighter pieces, or *tukkadas*, presented in the last portion of a concert. For an artiste who was capable of the most exacting classicism, her light pieces were a joy to hear and if only one is to be identified as forever linked to her it must be, as noted earlier, 'Baro Krishnayya', a ragamalika suite of verses from Purandaradasa and Vysaraya. Subbulakshmi's lighter pieces were effectively limited to her stock of bhajans, and occasional Tamil verses. Vasanthakumari's stock included bhajans, film-based songs, *javalis*, Tamil songs, Purandaradasa songs and *tillanas*.

A large number of Vasanthakumari's recitals have been recorded and are easily accessible on the Internet. What is remarkable about these is her adherence to form, irrespective of where the concert was, or who the audience included. Every recital includes a *ragam-tanam-pallavi*, in common and unusual ragas, with the selection of a staggering 122 currently available on the non-profit website, sangeethapriya. org. These include nineteen in Todi, sixteen in Shanmukhapriya and fifteen in Bhairavi but also Devamanohari, Gaurimanohari, Andolika, Hamsanandi, Kamavardhini, Kambhoji, Kalyani, Kiravani, Natabhairavi, Latangi, Manirangu, Madhyamavati, Amritavarshini, Suddhadhanyasi, Subhapantuvarali and Hindolam. Significantly, in this list of 122, Sankarabharanam appears but once. Vasanthakumari was at once at ease in the great concert ragas as in the less known, if no less complicated, modes. Her peers were nowhere near as adventurous, and for those fortunate enough to have heard Vasanthakumari, her concerts were unforgettable.

Vasanthakumari, unlike Subbulakshmi, taught extensively and was reputed to be a caring and generous teacher.[85] If she was an adornment to the G.N. Balasubramaniam school, several of her students became successful concert performers. Her long-term violinist, the hugely gifted *Sangitha Kalanidhi* A. Kanyakumari, was easily her best disciple and Vasanthakumari was warm in her praise of her. 'She is truly talented and totally devoted to the cause of music.'[86]

Above all, Vasanthakumari was 'truly a thinking musician in the real sense of the term'.[87] Her creativity was spontaneous, an attribute 'which MS could never match',[88] and her mind always questioning. In an interview given in 1964, when she was thirty-five with at least twenty years of serious performance behind her, she was asked about the future. Her surprising answer was, 'I am seriously contemplating to practice classical Hindustani music, to attain the same proficiency as in Karnatak [sic] music. Learning both the systems, I can not only enrich my art but also show the basic unity of Indian music.'[89]

The year 1977 marked the 150th death anniversary of Syama Sastri but the occasion was largely uncommemorated. Vasanthakumari, presiding over the Music Academy's annual conference, included in her recital a composition of V. Raghavan specifically composed for the occasion, '*Syama sastrin namostute*'/Sama, but that was about it. There was nothing comparable to the elaborate observance of the Tyagaraja bicentenary in 1967 and the Muthusvami Dikshitar bicentenary in 1975.

Some of this indifference may be due to the relative paucity of compositions by Syama Sastri. The sheer number of compositions by his peers ensures that entire concerts can be devoted to them, a feature further enabled by the great variety of raga, structure and detailing provided by those compositions. A conservative estimate credits Syama Sastri with three *svarajatis*, two *varnams* and thirty-six *kritis*.[90] A later record credits him with three *gitams*, three *svarajatis*, three *varnams* and sixty-two *kritis*.[91] That on the basis of this slender output he is revered as one of the progenitors of the Carnatic tradition and that his compositions continue to be sung is a mark of their melodic excellence.

The Syama Sastri legacy has been preserved largely through his son Subbaraya Sastri's descendants and disciples. Of these, Annaswami Sastri was the teacher of T. Kamakshi Ammal, grandmother of 'Vina' Dhanammal; Rangacharlu was the teacher of the Tachhur Singaracharyulu brothers who were biographers of Tyagaraja; and Kanchi Kachi Sastri taught Kanchipuram Dhanakoti Ammal, whose line later included Naina Pillai, T. Brinda, T. Muktha and Chittoor Subramania Pillai.

In several of his *kritis*, Tyagaraja reasons, even argues, with his chosen deity. Syama Sastri adopts only the voice of pleading surrender. Neither was more devout or more evolved than the other; their modes of expression were different. It is as if Tyagaraja had the confidence in his faith to enter into conversation with Rama. Syama Sastri's confidence was that Kamakshi would guard him. The operative verb in many of Syama Sastri's *kritis* is the Telugu '*brovu*' or 'protect'.[92] That was really all he was seeking.

Syama Sastri's use of ragas is necessarily limited but as his songs '*Devi brova samayamide*'/Chintamani and '*Parvati ninnu ne nera nammiti*'/Kalgada reveal, he was not unaware of raga intricacies. These two songs continue to remain the only songs in those ragas. His hallmark was the ability to structure simple, appealing words within intricate *tala* arrangements. In Syama Sastri's compositions, the raga is developed and stretched tightly across the frame of the *tala*. These are not songs that can be sung fast; there is nothing racy or sprightly about them. The Telugu he uses is on the whole more Sanskrit-inflected and less colloquial than Tyagaraja's, and very easy to understand.

Syama Sastri is famed, justly, for his three *svarajatis*, 'Kamakshi'/Bhairavi, '*Rave Himagiri kumari*'/Todi and '*Kamakshi*'/Yadukulakambhoji. These stand on a par with Tyagaraja's *ghana raga pancharatna kritis* and Muthusvami Dikshitar's Kamalamba *navavarana kritis*. All three *svarajatis* were staple items in Subbulakshmi's repertoire and sung often, the Bhairavi piece in particular being a great hit,[93] with its *neraval* at 'Syama Krishna sahodari Sivasankari Parameswari'. The composer's genius lies in his ability to use a very simple song structure to create great concert pieces.

Subbulakshmi sang Syama Sastri well, with a well-articulated Telugu and a good sense of the pace of the songs. '*Saroja dala netri*'/Sankarabharanam, '*Durusuga*'/Saveri and '*Talli ninnu nera*'/Kalyani were very frequently presented, as were '*Devi brova samayamide*'/Chintamani, '*Mayamma*'/Ahiri, '*O Jagadamba*'/Anandabhairavi, '*Kanakasaila viharini*'/Punnagavarali and '*Palintsu kamakshi*'/Madhyamavati. Some pieces such as '*Neelayatakshi*'/Pharaz, '*Ninnu vina marigalada*'/Ritigaula, '*Brovavamma*'/Manji and '*Marivere*'/Anandabhairavi made very rare appearances. A radio recital of Syama Sastri compositions presented around 1960 included '*Ninne namminanu*'/Todi and the Tamil '*Tarunam idamma*'/Gaulipantu,[94] not otherwise heard from her on the concert rounds.[95]

The world of Syama Sastri saw sudden excitement in 1989 with the recording by Semmangudi Srinivasa Iyer's disciples of a set of songs attributed to Syama Sastri, in a variety of ragas not otherwise used by him; these included some very sprightly numbers.[96] These were taken from a 1947 compilation, reissued in 1979, and their provenance had been attested by senior scholars, but had hitherto not attracted any attention. There was a mild burst of outrage, but with the waning of interest even on the part of the senior scholars, the songs have disappeared. Subbulakshmi did not involve herself with the controversy and did not sing any of these songs. It is, of course, true that there are compositions of Syama Sastri in manuscript and these have been examined by scholars, but there have not been any undisputed additions to the available stock of songs.[97]

No reference to Syama Sastri is complete without recognizing the continued importance to the repertory of the works of his son Subbaraya Sastri (1803–62) on an even more slender output of twelve songs.[98] His songs, while fully built on the pattern of a *kriti*, have something of the *padam* in their construction and gait, with attention to both raga and *bhava*.[99] Unequalled among these is '*Janani ninu vina*'/Ritigaula, sung often and to great creative effect by Subbulakshmi and, indeed, by most other musicians. To many this must remain the ranking *kriti* in the raga.[100] Of Subbaraya Sastri's songs, Subbulakshmi also sang '*Sankari neeve*'/Begada and '*Ninnu vina*'/Kalyani.

The late 1970s were crowded with events, both rewarding and otherwise. Subbulakshmi did not sing at the music season in 1977 but she made a mesmerizing appearance at the Tyagaraja *aradhana* on 28 January 1978. The recital, which was broadcast live on All India Radio in its National Programme, had the critics enthralled.

> A touch of glamour and then a wave of excitement. For it was going to be 9.30 at night and it was time for MSS to sing ... As 'MS' entered the pandal, looking the very picture of Mira or a latter day Andal, accompanied by her husband and her step-daughter Radha Viswanathan, there was a stampede. The audience surged forward to have a better glimpse of her ... the audience of ten thousand sat

spellbound. She gave a deeply satisfying performance, shorn of all frills and the only rasa she inspired was bhakti.[101]

It was indeed a fine recital beginning with a taut *'Ela ni daya radu'*/ Athana, and including *'Rama nee samanam evaru'*/Kharaharapriya, *'Evari mata'*/Kambhoji and *'Sobhillu'*/Jaganmohini. There was one unfamiliar song, *'Muripemu galige'*/Mukhari, and three old favourites, *'Tsallare'*/ Ahiri, *'Tava dasoham'*/Punnagavarali and *'Ennaga manasu'*/Nilambari. The recording, which is available on the net is a clean example of what Subbulakshmi was capable of when she stuck to the Carnatic form.

No recital could be more different from what was presented at Tiruvaiyaru than a recital the very next month at the Asia Plateau, Panchgani, a hurried mixture of well-known pieces, *'Mathe'*/Khamas, *'Ennaganu'*/Pantuvarali, *"Meevalla gunadosham'*/Kapi, *'Sri Kamakoti'*/ Saveri, *'Sitamma'*/Vasanta, *'Narayana divya namam'*/Mohana, at least ten bhajans and Rajaji's English hymn resurrected from the UN Concert. The only reason we need to take note of this offering is that the notes accompanying the recording on the Internet state confidently that Subbulakshmi was accompanied by *Sangitha Kalanidhi* Palghat Mani Iyer on the mrdangam.[102]

An August 1978 recital which is worth noting is the one Subbulakshmi gave at the National Centre for the Performing Arts in Bombay. *'Vatapi'*/Hamsanadam, *'Cheta Sri Balakrishnam'*/Jujavanti, *'Banturiti'*/Hamsanadam, *'Marakatamanivarna'*/Varali, *'Nidhi tsala sukhama'*/Kalyani and *'Kamakshi'*/Bhairavi formed the core of the recital. For regular listeners, there was nothing new but it was flawlessly performed.[103]

It was on 24 December 1978 that Subbulakshmi performed at the Music Academy, Madras, for the last time during its annual season. Indeed, it does not appear that she performed at any venue during the season over the next twenty years that she still made public appearances. With Radha accompanying her and Kandadevi Alagiriswami on the violin, T.K. Murthy on the mrdangam, T.H. Vinayakram on the ghatam and V. Nagarajan on the kanjira, it was a grand conclusion to forty years of Academy appearances.

As always in her concert planning, the trinity was appropriately represented: Muthusvami Dikshitar with *'Sri Maha Ganapati'*/Gaula, Tyagaraja, unusually, with *'Nenendu'*/Karnataka Behag and Syama Sastri with *'Devi brova samayamide'* in Chintamani. There were Subbarama Dikshitar's *'Parthasarathi'*/Yadukulakambhoji, a long and laboured piece, *'Chandrasekharam'*/Kiravani by her old friend and patron V. Raghavan, the often heard *'Gopanandana'*/Bhushavali of Svati Tirunal, an inevitable Sankarabharanam and *'Emineramu'* leading on to a *ragam-tanam-pallavi* in Todi. It was a recital 'of balanced beauty' that revealed the strengths of her art; a fabled repertoire, her awareness of structure, her prowess at *alapana*, *neraval* and *tanam* and her ability to, at all times, hold her audience.[104]

Another recital the same season, at the Indian Fine Arts Society, with Pattammal in the presidency of that *sabha's* events and honoured as *Sangitha Kala Sikhamani*,[105] saw Subbulakshmi presenting *'Rama ni samanam evaru'*/Kharaharapriya, *'Parthasarathi'*/Yadukulakambhoji, *'Anjaneyam'*/Saveri and a *ragam-tanam-pallavi* in Kambhoji. And for all that it was her last season, Subbulakshmi sang also at the Tamil Isai Sangam, where Vasanthakumari was presiding, and was being honoured as *Isai Perarignar*.[106]

The period which followed saw Subbulakshmi working on the Annamacharya songs. In all, she was to record thirty-one *samkirtanas*, *'Vandeham'*/Hamsadhwani sung at Carnegie Hall, twenty released over 1980 and 1981 and a further ten in 1994.[107] She also sang *'Narayanate namo namo'* in ragamalika, though this was not recorded.

Most accounts of the life and work of Tallappakka Annamacharya, the fifteenth-century bhakti poet and singer, agree that he spent most of his life in the worship of Sri Venkateswara at Tirupati, which still houses, on copper plate, the text of approximately 13,000 *samkirtanas*, out of the 32,000 he is believed to have composed.[108] Annamacharya's translators have pointed out that his poems are editorially divided into two major categories, *sringara*, erotic, and *adhyatma*, metaphysical. The former which comprise nearly three quarters of the entire surviving corpus, or 12,027 out of 14,218 available songs according to another scholar,[109] '... deal with the infinite varieties and nuances of the god's love life, which the poet knows intimately. Usually these poems are couched in the female voice. So-called *adhyatma* poems are, by way of contrast, sung in the poet's own voice and deal with his sense of himself as an agonized, turbulent human being in relation to the god he worships'.[110]

The *sringara* poems are songs of desire where the male worshipper uses, in the persona of a woman, the language and idiom of carnal love to express his/her longing for Venkateswara, the God on the Hill.[111] The *adhyatma* poems are more conventionally worshipful, with references to the heroes of mythology such as Vishnu, Rama and Krishna, and where the poet is continuously aware of his own puny existence in the presence of Venkateswara.

The songs of Annamacharya were sung in the Telugu areas and even recorded but Subbulakshmi brought them into common knowledge.[112] Most of the *samkirtanas* recorded by Subbulakshmi are in the *adhyatma* category: '*Vandeham jagatvallabham*'/Hamsadhwani, '*Sriman Narayana*'/Bauli, '*Devadevam*'/Hindolam, '*Nanati bratuku*'/Revati and many others. A possible exception is '*Okapari*'/Kharaharapriya, which could be interpreted as in the *sringara* tradition, but according to an expert this is a composition of Annamacharya's son.[113] Indeed, it was left to the remarkable M.L. Vasanthakumari to sing, with great delicacy and feeling, a poem in the *sringara* tradition, '*Emako ciguruta*'/Tilang.

The popularity of the songs was due in no small part to the tuneful setting to raga by experts such as *Sangitha Kalanidhi* Nedunuri Krishnamurthi[114] and a few have survived into the repertoire of current-day singers.[115] Two amongst them, '*Sriman Narayana*'/Bauli and

'Bhavayami Gopalabalam'/Yamunakalyani, were tuned by Kadayanallur S. Venkataraman.[116]

There is circulating on the Internet, and consequently in the public imagination, a long and elaborate explanation of how and why Subbulakshmi came to sing Annamacharya in the first instance. It has been suggested that it was mostly the result of an attempt by the senior Sankaracharya of Kanchi, a personage of great importance in Subbulakshmi's life, to provide for her an opportunity to earn royalties at a time when she was in some financial distress. Whether or not this is an accurate version, it does explain the selection of the songs.[117] And whatever her financial situation at the time, the sale of the records have brought in goodly sums for the Tirupati establishment, a sum of ₹15 crore being mentioned in 2006.[118]

The opportunity to record Annamacharya was used by Subbulakshmi to include in the recordings a variety of hymns and chants. She had, of course, chanted the verses rendered as *suprabhatam* in Tirupati, Varanasi and Rameshwaram and the *'Sri Vishnu Sahasranamam'*, but she was always partial to Sanskrit verses set to raga. Adi Sankara's *'Bhaja Govindam'*, *'Annapurnashtakam'* and *'Siva Pancakshara stotram'* were all very popular with her audiences. The Annamacharya recordings included, with no particular relevance, more pieces of Adi Sankara such as the *'Ganesa pancaratnam'*, *'Kanakadharastavam'* and *'Govindashtakam'* and Vallabhacharya's *'Madhurashtakam'*, Madhvacharya's *'Dvadasa stotram'*, Chaitanya Mahaprabhu's *'Sikshashtakam'* and Ramanuja's *'Sri Ranganatha gadyam'*.[119]

The scholar who worked with her in the selection of these pieces and in explaining their meaning to her recalls her diligence and striving for perfection.[120] Interestingly, she recorded, from outside high tradition, such pieces as the *'Nama Ramayana'*, a Sanskrit telling for children of the ancient story, attributed to Lakshmanachar, Jayadeva's *dasavatara* composition and Tulsidas' '*Hanuman Chalisa*', a spirited Bhojpuri prayer, still very much a part of daily household worship in north India.[121]

With hindsight it appears that this focus on simple devotional verses was part of the image Subbulakshmi had assumed, of a great bhakta, of a woman of piety and devotion rather than of phenomenal talent. It is a strange choice to have made but it may have ensured a longer presence in the collective memory of the people, and an even longer afterlife.

13

The Years of Retirement

মা ভাগিরথী, জাহ্নবী, সুরধুনি, কল-কল্লোলিনী গঙ্গে [1]
(Ganga, who is Bhagirathi, who is Jahnavi, divine being, sonorous in her beauty, Mother!,
Loosely translated from Dilip Kumar Roy's Bengali hymn
Patitodhharini Gange)

SUBBULAKSHMI'S retirement was both long and long-drawn-out. From about the mid 1970s, when she was sixty, the pace of concerts began to slow down. A fine National Programme was broadcast in July 1979 and survives in a mutilated form in a commercial release by the AIR. What was originally presented as a tight ninety minutes built around *'Dasarathe'*/Todi has been reduced to thirty minutes of the original recital followed by miscellaneous bhajans, a consequence of the notion that this is what people wanted to hear.[2]

Another radio recital was broadcast as part of the Radio Sangeet Sammelan in November 1979; a well-crafted ninety minutes which AIR has fortunately not yet released.[3] Subbulakshmi was still making the annual pilgrimage to Tiruvaiyaru for the annual Tyagaraja *aradhana*. She sang at that event in 1980[4] and again in 1984, of which recital excerpts are available on the net; the Kharaharapriya *alapana* and *neraval* for

'Pakkala' is well scripted, and captivating. She sang again at the *aradhana* in 1986[5] with her last appearance there probably being in 1990.[6]

Another annual event like the December season at the Music Academy, Madras, and the Tyagaraja *aradhana* at Tiruvaiyaru, at least for musicians of Subbulakshmi's generation, was the Rama Navami concert at Rama Seva Mandali, Bangalore. Subbulakshmi appeared there through the 1980s, always giving her best, but the 1980 concert is worth searching for. A throwback to the old type, it has the Bhairavi *varnam* and a *ragam-tanam-pallavi* in Bhairavi and in between them, Tyagaraja's '*Enta rani*'/Harikambhoji and '*Marugelara*'/Jayantasri, Dikshitar's '*Bhaja re*'/Kalyani, Syama Sastri's '*Palintsu Kamakshi*'/Madhyamavati, Subbaraya Sastri's '*Janani*'/Ritigaula, Annamacharya's '*Cheri Yasodaku*'/ Mohana, Periasami Thooran's '*Muruga*'/Saveri and Purandaradasa's '*Hari Narayana*'/Kedara.

Visva-Bharati, which was the first institution to give Subbulakshmi an honorary degree in 1969, awarded her the Desikottama in 1980.[7] In an ingenious tribute to Tagore she recalled that if Sadasivam was her guru, Rajaji was his, and if Rajaji's guru was Gandhi, it was the Mahatma who hailed Tagore as Gurudev. It was a heartfelt speech in which she shied away from the praise implied in the title and asked instead for blessings that she attain the status of *sisyottama*, the best of students. 'All my life I have been a student...'.[8]

Subbulakshmi, 'perhaps the most venerated classical singer in India', sang at the closing of the celebrations of the Fifth International Conference-Seminar of Tamil Studies in Madurai in early January 1981:[9] a celebration not only of the language and its history but of the mass appeal of her old friend from the sets of *Meera*, Chief Minister M.G. Ramachandran.

Financial difficulties seem to have continued, even after the sale of Kalki Gardens. There is a particularly unfortunate letter from Subbulakshmi dated 22 January 1981 addressed to B.K. Birla, the well-known industrialist of Calcutta, seeking a loan of ₹30,000 to be repaid in quarterly instalments of ₹5,000. That this letter should have been made public by B.K. Birla speaks more of his bad taste than of her situation.[10] It does, however, remain a matter of speculation why she should have been so badly off; the pettiness of the amount makes it especially distressing.

Whatever their personal situation, Sadasivam ensured that Subbulakshmi's image continued to remain that of a selfless performer for public causes. The fee received by her of ₹34,873 for her concert in London in March 1982 for the Festival of India was returned to the government with the remark that it would be inappropriate to receive payment for her promotion of the national cause.[11] That this should have been done at the exact time when Birla's quarterly payments were presumably being made is truly odd.

An honour which Subbulakshmi received in late 1981 and which is not generally known is her election as Member of Honour, one of sixteen worldwide, to the International Music Council of UNESCO.[12] Shortly thereafter, the London concert was warmly covered in the Indian press. The inaugural event for the Festival of India, the evening of 22 March 1982, in the presence of royalty and prime ministers, had Subbulakshmi, Ravi Shankar and Zubin Mehta on the stage. Subbulakshmi's recital was a neat, brief affair with *'Banturiti'*/Hamsanadam, *'Akshayalingavibho'*/Sankarabharanam and *'Hari tuma haro'*.

The reviewer in the *Times* was at once bewildered, respectful and impressed: '… there were rises and falls of intensity within this group that were quite unpredictable to the Western ear. At the same time, one soon got a sense of this music being an intricate commentary on the vocal line. The violin playing, at once so intriguingly similar and dissimilar to European practice, is what one most easily relates to, although there was also a marvelous percussion interlude towards the end. His was full of invention and subtlety'.[13] Ravi Shankar performed 'Raga-Mala' with Lalit, Bairagi, Yamankalyan and Mian Ki Malhar, but what made this event exceptional was that it was performed with Zubin Mehta conducting the London Philharmonic Orchestra.

Subbulakshmi had other recitals in the United Kingdom and on the radio and the *Hindu* appreciatively quoted the music critic of the *Guardian* who said of H.D. Yoganarasimham's luminous '*Sada saranga nayane*'/Ranjani that 'the words were set with precision and love as a jeweler would set precious gems'.[14] However, in the period immediately following these events of March 1982, Radha Viswanathan's sudden and serious illness caught both Subbulakshmi and Sadasivam unawares. It was to be a while before Subbulakshmi sang publicly again, at a recital in March 1983 in aid of the Sri Minakshi temple at Houston, where a weakened, but still spirited, Radha appeared on the platform.

In February 1985, Subbulakshmi sang in Bangalore at an event to commemorate the fiftieth anniversary of the establishment of the Indian Academy of Sciences by C.V. Raman, whose nephew and fellow Nobel Laureate S. Chandrasekhar gave the inaugural lecture. A scientist present recalled the occasion as 'a remarkable glimpse of creativity, genius and accomplishment in science and music'. At this glittering event a very distinguished scientist commented that he was not about to address the artiste by the degree which she had been awarded for in that gathering there were very many doctors but only one Subbulakshmi.[15] This was a reference to the many doctorates she was awarded by Indian universities as a consequence of which she was often referred to as Dr M.S. Subbulakshmi.[16] It does not seem to have occurred to anyone else that this was unnecessary.

Through these years, starting with the Subramania Bharati centenary celebrations in 1982, Subbulakshmi was a frequent visitor to Gandhigram,[17] and consequently Madurai, a constant reaffirmation of her origin. Miscellaneous recordings continued to issue. A set of songs of Subramania Bharati was issued in 1983;[18] it appears that this was to have been the first of a series of records, but the comparative failure of the record to sell put these plans to rest.[19] Then there is a long Malayalam hymn, 'Radhamadhavam',[20] followed by Surdas bhajans in 1987.[21] In 1988, Subbulakshmi released a recording of the songs of the contemporary composer H.D. Yoganarasimham.[22] The story has often been told of Subbulakshmi's long recording career with HMV, the relevant fact being her complete concentration on the task at hand and her willingness to repeat an item as many times as it took to get a perfect recording. This dedication shows in the final products.[23]

She was not singing often but Subbulakshmi was constantly in the news. Even when there was no particularly newsworthy event where she was present, warm, gushing tributes continued to appear in the press.[24] 'Age has not withered her mellifluous voice.'[25] 'She remains still, undisputably [sic], the songstress nonpareil.'[26] 'Her name today is synonymous with devotional music.'[27] '(I)t was music which evoked in the listeners a feeling of self-forgetting absorption and relishable [sic] peace and pleasure.'[28] 'Subbulakshmi has achieved what few musicians did – a spiritual bond with her listeners.'[29] 'She can refract melody into music in the same marvellous way that a prism refracts light into dazzling colours.'[30] 'When she sings, she sings for the Divine Presence...'.[31] The popular magazine *Sruti* invited its readers to comment on Subbulakshmi's music; the tributes poured in.[32]

There was the other kind of writing as well, such as the 1982 publication of R.K. Narayan's short story 'Selvi'.[33] There has been critical writing on this work, in the context of Narayan's treatment of women characters, but these do not mention the fact that much in the life of Selvi and her manager husband Mohan could have been taken from the story of Subbulakshmi and Sadasivam, and specifically Mohan's complete control over Selvi's musical presentation, her appearance, her friends and her image.[34] In Narayan's story, Selvi finally breaks away from her overbearing husband and returns to her lower-class roots, and the home where her neglected mother has died. No such option was available to Subbulakshmi in real life, and we do not also know if this is something she would have wished for.

Subbulakshmi, well into retirement, was called upon to participate in the Festival of India at Moscow. Her performance on the occasion has been commercially released and includes familiar pieces of the trinity, *'Vatapi'*/Hamsadhwani, *'Pakkala'*/Kharaharapriya and *'Durusuga'*/Saveri, in addition to *'Sankaracharyam'*/Sankarabharanam.[35] 'The raga Sankarabharanam is the exclusive territory of Subbulakshmi' noted a critic.[36] A second recital in Moscow had *'Nidhi tsala, sukhama'*/Kalyani as the high point of the main recital.[37]

Age was beginning to catch up with her, to the genuine regret of *rasikas* of old. 'The ageing of that distinguished female trio D.K. Pattammal, M.S. Subbulakshmi and M.L. Vasantakumari [sic] is a sad but undeniable fact which we have to accept; the establishment of Mani Krishnaswamy's position as a mature singer of classicism and musicality cannot quite make up for this.'[38]

A sign of the times was the passing of friends. Balasaraswati's death on 9 February 1984 came first. For decades she had been close to Subbulakshmi, even if their personal ideologies were as far removed as the circumstances of their lives. To the end, she held her own and if Subbulakshmi never spoke of her own sense of who she was or what she had achieved, Balasaraswati, who could not suffer fools, was in no doubt that she was, if we may borrow a term used in ballet for the greatest performers in any generation, *prima ballerina assoluta*.

Her elder contemporary and jousting partner Rukmini Devi, also a friend and patron of Subbulakshmi, died on 24 February 1986. Kalakshetra mourned her passing: 'She is now dancing with the moon and the stars.'[39] Rukmini Devi was a strong and determined character, gentle and sensitive at all times but still the builder of an institution that has stood the test of time. Much has been made of the perceived differences between these two remarkable women, the younger Balasaraswati portrayed as the inheritor and protector of an ancient tradition, yet excluded by the norms of caste society from her rightful position, a woman always reminded of her subaltern status, and the elder Rukmini as the ambitious amateur, drawn from high Vedic tradition and European intellectualism, fastidious in her upper-caste ways and supremely successful in her stated objective of 'rescuing' the art form both women claimed as their own. In a bizarre mistake, a UNESCO publication of 1963 identified a photograph of Rukmini Devi as that of Balasaraswati,[40] and even if the latter never knew of this, she knew very well that times had changed.

The truth, as always, lies somewhere in between. It cannot simply be reduced to a debate between *sringara*, which is more than erotic love, and bhakti, which is more than ritualized devotion. Both women agreed that Bharatanatyam was primarily a religious art.[41] Both endorsed what they saw as worthy of worship; both fought for what they saw as the lifeblood of the art; and both served the muse with unwavering devotion.

Subbulakshmi was not singing publicly as frequently as in earlier years but the available record indicates a string of concerts and ceremonial events. There were still some *sabha* appearances, as in Hyderabad in October 1984[42] or in Trivandrum in October 1988[43] and again in April 1990.[44] She no longer sang during the December season at the Music Academy or anywhere else but she did perform at the Music Academy both on 14 December 1986[45] and 14 November 1987, this latter recital being described as 'splendid and blemishless' and including a *ragam-tanam-pallavi* suite.[46]

There were still benefit recitals as in Bombay in May 1986 for the Sri Rajagopuram Fund for the temple in Srirangam.[47] Then there were events for Tyagaraja as in Tiruvarur in May 1986,[48] in March 1987[49] and in Tirupati in August 1992.[50] And lastly, there were events celebrating or commemorating fellow artistes, as for instance for Balasaraswati in January 1986,[51] Maharajapuram Viswanatha Iyer in April 1986,[52] the Ariyakudi centenary in 1990 or Brinda's eightieth birthday in 1992.

A recital given in Coimbatore which can be dated to the late 1980s is available on the Internet and is a good example of Subbulakshmi's concert style in the fading years of her career; there are twenty-one songs of which at least twelve are lighter, ever-popular songs, but there is also a well-grounded *ragam* and *tanam* in Todi followed by Dikshitar's 'Sri Krishnam'.[53]

In addition to all this, there were several recordings issued during this period, most significantly the '*Melakarta Ragamalika*' of Maha Vaidyanatha Iyer.[54] It is fair to say that while this exacting composition would have been familiar to most of Subbulakshmi's senior male contemporaries, it was given to her to bring out onto the concert platform the beauty embedded in those verses. No verses could have been more alien to Subbulakshmi's highly emotive style; no singer could have sung them better. Musicologists have long debated the differences between *laksya*, aesthetics or emotion, and *laksana*, grammar or order, but Subbulakshmi's rendering of the '*Melakarta Ragamalika*' shows that neither can exist without the other.[55]

The other recordings of this period include several sets of Tamil verses and chants[56] and two records devoted to the Sankaracharya of Kanchi.[57] These are, on the whole, of limited interest.

The University of Madras gave Subbulakshmi yet another honorary D. Litt in 1987[58] and in 1989 she was appointed a 'National Professor' under a scheme of the government to honour distinguished academics and research scholars for their valuable contribution to the advancement of knowledge.[59] The more substantial part of this five-year appointment was that it came with a monthly cheque, more needed now than before when singing engagements were fewer but donations to charitable causes remained unabated. The same year saw the award of the Kalidas Samman by the Government of Madhya Pradesh.[60] Late in 1989, she received the Hafiz Ali Khan award for 1988, which she shared with Bismillah Khan of the shehnai and John Williams of the classical guitar.[61]

Vasanthakumari died on 31 October 1990. She was only sixty-two but illness finally got the better of her. Friends recall that for all her gifts and warm generosity she was a troubled soul, plagued with financial and personal difficulties. Her last public appearance was at a wedding concert in May of the same year where, though already ailing, she kept her word to an old friend to perform at his daughter's wedding. Subbulakshmi, who was present, listened attentively, and with obvious enjoyment, to the entire concert.[62]

M.L. Vasanthakumari would in any age have been regarded as a classical musician of the first rank but it is instructive to recollect that she acquired this reputation at a time when many formidable performers were at their peak. A perceptive, if verbose, critic had this to say when Vasanthakumari was still in her thirties:

> It was all too easy to compare her music with Pattammal's and say that she lacked the latter's ample majesty of movement, and to compare her with 'M.S.' and say she lacked the latter's intensity of expression. But even these critics could not deny her that tonal clarity, that celerity of phrasing, that boldness of imagination which have become the distinguishing features of her music ... Vasanthakumari's music sports an Ariel-like freedom which is absent in the others ... [and] belongs to the wide expanses of the world, not to the cloistered academies of Pattammal's music nor to the incense laden bowers of M.S.'s music ... And yet, surprisingly, Vasanthakumari is probably the most learned of the women singers in Karnatak music.[63]

Vasanthakumari was a woman both entirely confident of herself and utterly free of any sense of competition. Only one such would have sung, with complete aplomb, hardy perennials from the MS stock as '*Sriman Narayana*'/Bauli and '*Kurai onrum illai*'/ragamalika.[64] These are exquisitely sung and it is worth the effort to seek them out on the net. A long-term student of hers, later a student of the Semmangudi school, asked many years later, 'When shall we see the like of you again?'[65]

The news of the passing was kept from Subbulakshmi, who was in Delhi to receive the Indira Gandhi Award for National Integration, but a persistent journalist sought her comment even as she was entering the hall where the award function was to be held. Shaken, she continued with the event, sang '*Mein hari charanana*' and received the award.[66] There is reason to believe that she was inclined to cancel the singing of *shabads* at a Guru Nanak-related event the next day in Rashtrapati Bhavan but was, inappropriately and unfortunately, persuaded to continue with it.[67]

In a characteristic gesture however, the ₹5 lakh received with the Award for National Integration was given to the Cancer Research Institute, Madras, a 'revered institution where people from all walks of life and religion came to receive treatment'. And Vasanthakumari's family still recalls with gratitude Subbulakshmi's kindness to them in their loss.[68]

There were still the occasional concerts but these were now elaborately staged, high-profile events such as the one in Bombay in April 1992.[69] Her last Delhi concert was in January 1993, in aid of those affected by riots in north India, following the destruction of the Babri Masjid in Ayodhya in December 1992, and included the inevitable Sankarabharanam.[70] A member of the audience wrote to a friend, 'MS was frail and her voice tired. The concert never really took off and she had clearly not thought too much about it. But it is awe inspiring to be in her presence.'[71] For all this, even if she were semi-retired, Subbulakshmi still dominated both the stage and the audience. 'At 76, MS can still hold audiences spellbound. Her detractors point out that it is not music but her devotion that attracts them. Critics come down heavily on imaginary shortcomings. Younger musicians seethe that she still holds centre stage.'[72]

A significant event of these years was Subbulakshmi's concert at Kalakshetra on 14 November 1992 for Brinda's eightieth birthday.[73] The concert included a *padam* and a *javali* specifically chosen for the occasion. She had spoken earlier, in 1990, at an event curated by Dhanammal's grandson *Sangitha Kalanidhi* T. Viswanathan, where young performers demonstrated aspects of the Dhanammal *bani*, of her close links with the family and the style.[74]

Awards continued to pour in. The Dinanath Pratishthan Award, 1994, was presented to Subbulakshmi by Lata Mangeshkar on 16 April 1995.[75] As was customary by now, she gave away the award money of ₹50,000 to the Sankara Nethralaya, an eye hospital for which she had much regard. A similar amount received with the Konark Samman was donated to the Public Health Centre, West Mambalam.[76] There is likewise a reference to a concert sponsored by 'Mardi Gras' in early 1993 for which she was paid the then large sum of ₹50,000, which she gave to charity.[77]

It is possible that Subbulakshmi's advisers were not always very discreet in their choice of platforms on which she was made to appear. Certainly, tongues wagged when, in October 1992, she inaugurated a music festival sponsored by a leading manufacturer of alcoholic beverages and, indeed, she had appeared before in events sponsored by India's biggest cigarette manufacturer.[78]

Ellis Dungan visited Chennai after many decades in 1994 and met with Subbulakshmi and Sadasivam.[79] At a public felicitation where Subbulakshmi appeared unexpectedly and sang, an observer noted, 'there was not a dry eye in the house'.[80] His death some years later was noted with sadness in Chennai; whether he knew it or not, he had become a part of south Indian cultural history.[81]

Her eightieth birthday was observed in 1996 and Subbulakshmi was hailed as 'the embodiment of music, the most charismatic artiste of our times', but the perceptive critic went on to note that it was not the voice alone which defined Subbulakshmi, for all that it was an exceptional voice. 'It is more her mind that has helped her produce such unqualified artistry.'[82]

Tanjavur Brinda's passing in August 1996 was mourned widely, and it was recalled that '[w]ith fostering care and utter dedication she strove to preserve the prestigious stamp of the Dhanammal tradition.'[83] Their roots and background were identical; their natural gifts were abundant and she was Subbulakshmi's exact contemporary, but the course of their lives could not have been more different. It was said of Brinda that she was destined to be a musician;[84] so was Subbulakshmi, but their paths diverted. In her professional and personal life, Brinda followed the calling of her mother and grandmother, an option which Subbulakshmi rejected. Brinda settled into a long career of teaching, conscious at all times that she was the repository of a tradition that needed to be passed on.[85] Subbulakshmi, quite simply, *was* the tradition she chose for herself. Interestingly, as Brinda's obituarist noted, while both singers came from families dedicated to performance for an audience, it was Brinda who did not concede to audience tastes and dilute her style to what she thought the audience would like. Subbulakshmi, notoriously, pandered to popular demands.

A distinguished public speaker said of Brinda that '... [she] took the position that strict adherence to what the masters have taught is paramount, that the *margam* is a given sequence like the preliminary set of symmetrically arranged dots for a *kolam*. A pair of skilful hands must join them, loop around them, curl and turn about them, embracing one here, sidelining one there, gliding past this one here, coalescing with that one there. The flowing line plays with the pre-existing pattern, line and dots engaging in conversation'.[86]

Over the course of a very long performing career, Subbulakshmi had several very able accompanying artistes. It is popular today for accompanying artistes to be referred to as co-performers but in Subbulakshmi's case, as for several of the performers of her generation, the musicians on the violin, mrdangam and ghatam were quite emphatically meant to accompany the main artiste.

The earliest records have one Sankaranarayana Iyer on the violin and T.S. Ranganayaki of Pudukottah (1910–98) on the mrdangam at a December 1934 recital.[87] Mayavaram Govindaraja Pillai (1912–79) accompanied her on the violin at the Music Academy season concerts in 1939 and 1941 but a Master T.D. Sankara Iyer (1912–88) played at the Music Academy recital in December 1942, and at a Nagpur recital in February 1946. The celebrated T. Chowdiah played for Subbulakshmi, as did Kumbakonam Rajamanickam Pillai (1898–1970), Varahur Muthuswami Iyer (1902–70)[88] and Chalakudi N.S. Narayanaswami, (1925–2003)[89] but a longer innings was that of Tiruvalangadu N. Sundaresa Iyer (1900–66), who played with her over the period 1951–64. R.K. Venkatarama Sastri (1907–93), famed for his emerald ear studs,[90] began playing regularly for Subbulakshmi from about 1956.

In the early 1960s, the violinist *Sangitha Kalanidhi* M.S. Gopalakrishnan (1931–2013) played for her. Several decades later when his brother, the violinist M.S. Anantharaman (1924–2018), passed away, one of the few things noted of his musical career was that he accompanied Subbulakshmi in the film version of *Katrinilae*.[91] Such was her compelling presence in the history of the art. R.S. Gopalakrishnan (1918–96) played for her, both at the Edinburgh appearances and for the 1963 recording of the '*Sri Venkatesa Suprabhatam*'. V.K. Venkataramanujam (1931–2005) played for her briefly, as also V. Thyagarajan (1928–2005), but by

1963, V.V. Subramanyam (born 1944) was her regular accompanist on the stage,[92] and remained with her through the high-profile years and certainly till about September 1975, when Kandadevi Alagiriswami (1925–2000), who has been recorded as playing for Subbulakshmi even in 1967, took over as the regular violin partner. S. Seshagiri Rao (born 1944) was an occasional accompanist in the 1980s but it was Venkatarama Sastri's grandson R.K. Shriram Kumar (born 1966) who became Subbulakshmi's last regular accompanist. Even in the last stages of her career, Shriram Kumar recalls playing in at least a hundred concerts over the period 1989 to 1997.[93]

There has always been an issue on the Carnatic stage relating to men accompanying women vocalists. M.S. Gopalakrishnan was an exception and played extensively for M.L. Vasanthakumari,[94] but stopped, much to her vexation, as his own career was progressing.[95] R.S. Gopalakrishnan certainly played for Pattammal, Vasanthakumari, Radha and Jayalakshmi but again, that was unusual.[96] Sundaresa Iyer, who had years earlier accompanied Madurai Pushpavanam Iyer, was not only a performer on stage with Subbulakshmi; he taught and guided her.[97] Subbulakshmi does not appear to have favoured women violinists on the stage with her, though Savitri Satyamurthy (1934–2014),[98] T. Rukmini (1936–2020),[99] Dwaram Mangathayaru (born 1937),[100] and N. Rajam (born 1938)[101] all played for her.

Subbulakshmi had likewise solid support from her mrdangam partners. The 1939 Music Academy concert has Kalpathi Ramanathan (1916–86), Palghat Mani Iyer's first disciple, accompanying her, as he was to do through the 1940s. The available record also shows Nagercoil Ganesa Aiyar (1905–78) listed for the 1940 concert (which was not given) and Tanjavur Krishnamurthi Rao (1926?–84), later to be Vasanthakumari's long-term partner, in 1941. Subbulakshmi's 1942 Music Academy concert has Master Murthy accompanying her. This is *Sangitha Kalanidhi* T.K. Murthy (born 1924), who went on to be her accompanying artiste for the longest time.[102]

Her brother M.S. Sakthivel (1912–74) played for her, it is not known how consistently, in the late 1940s. Mavelikara Krishnankutti Nair (1920–88)[103] and Tanjavur Upendran (1934–91) played for her in the early 1950s, when T.K. Murthy took over in about 1953 and continued for about the next thirty years. *Sangitha Kalanidhi* Palghat Raghu (1928–2009) and Guruvayur Dorai (born 1935) were also regular accompanists as were Palghat Kunjumani (1932?–84), T.A.S. Mani (1936–2020), Mannargudi Easwaran (born 1947), Yella Venkateswara Rao (born 1947) and Thiruvaarur Bakthavathsalam (born 1952). K.V. Prasad (born 1958) was Subbulakshmi's last regular mrdangam accompanist.

In a rare statement, Subbulakshmi acknowledged that Palghat Mani Iyer had played for her at a private concert and this may have been the February 1978 recital at Panchgani noted earlier.[104] If the celebrated mrdangam *vidvan* never played publicly for her, he was still generous in his praise. In a 1978 interview, Mani Iyer listed Ariyakudi Ramanuja Iyengar, Chembai Vaidyanatha Bhagavathar and M.S. Subbulakshmi, three artistes with outstanding voices, as musicians who 'had sung straight to the audience for years and knew the art of relating themselves to their listeners and establishing a rapport with them'.[105]

The music historian Sriram V. credits Subbulakshmi with restoring to a place of honour on the stage the artistes who played the 'secondary' instruments, the *upa-pakavadyam*, such as the ghatam, kanjira and morsing.[106] Alangudi Ramachandran (1912–75) was her first recorded ghatam accompanist at the famous comeback recital at the Music Academy in 1947 and is found to be playing for her even as late as 1972.[107] Starting from the late 1940s, Umayalpuram Kothandarama Iyer (1899–1966) played for Subbulakshmi for nearly twenty years, though starting from 1965 it was the gifted T.H. Vinayakram (born 1942) who was the regular ghatam accompaniment, all the way till the late 1980s.[108] Vinayakram's brother T.H. Subhash Chandran (1946–2020) also played ghatam for Subbulakshmi[109] as did K.S. Manjunath (1928–89) and Bangalore K. Venkataram (1934–2003).

An early kanjira accompanist was Venu Naicker (1917–87);[110] later for several years it was V. Nagarajan (1939?–2002) and later still G. Harishankar (1958–2002), H.P. Ramachar (1924–2006) and Latha Ramachar (born 1964). Pudukkottai Mahadevan and Mannargudi Natesa Pillai (1902–73) are listed as occasional morsing accompanists. As Mike Marqusee, Marxist and *rasika*, has noted, '[One] of the special charms of Carnatic music is that, for all its urbanity and sophistication, it finds room for the humble morsing and ghatam. In other musical cultures, the likes of the Jew's harp and the clay pot are relegated to the nether regions of folk primitivism. In Carnatic music, they're vehicles for the exquisite.'[111] Subbulakshmi may not have recognized the idiom but she certainly understood the sentiment. And in any case, she always encouraged a large supporting cast on the stage. A critic once fussed, 'The dais seemed to groan under the party,' but it was very much her style.[112] Even Rajaji, on seeing Subbulakshmi and party leave for a concert, once observed that she seemed to be taking her audience with her![113]

At the earliest concert for which there is a full record, on 30 December 1939 at the Music Academy, Subbulakshmi was accompanied by Mayavaram Govindaraja Pillai on the violin and Kalpathi Ramanathan on the mrdangam. Nearly sixty years later, at her last public recital on 27 June 1997, again under the auspices of the Music Academy, she was accompanied by Gowri Ramnarayan in the singing, R.K. Shriram Kumar on the violin, K.V. Prasad on the mrdangam, Lata Ramachar on the kanjira and Umayalpuram K. Narayanaswami on the ghatam.

It is necessary to record the enormous significance of these years of sustained performance. Several generations of musicians joined Subbulakshmi on the stage and even in those instances where the professional relationship ceased, she was always held in the highest esteem by her colleague musicians, a difficult achievement in a career as long as hers.[114] Long-term listeners aver that the V.V. Subramanyam, T.H. Vinayakram, T.K. Murthy and V. Nagarajan combination was perhaps the most successful team Subbulakshmi mounted – the team that played with and for her at the UN concert.[115]

Of course, the most significant relationship on stage was with Radha Viswanathan.

Radha was born in 1934 before her father had met Subbulakshmi but appears to have taken to her from the time the singer entered her parents' home. She has admitted as much in her account of her childhood that she did not remember her mother at all, her life having been, from the very earliest years, linked to that of Subbulakshmi.[116] From being a lively and talented child who played small parts in two of Subbulakshmi's films, *Sakuntalai* and *Meera*, she enjoyed a few years of fame as a dancer, a disciple of Vazhuvoor Ramiah Pillai, the teacher of Kamala, but gave up performance to grow into being Subbulakshmi's constant companion and accompanying singer, even after she married and left her father's home. 'Marriage and motherhood could not slacken Radha's musical and moral support to her mother.'[117]

Strangely, both Radha and her younger sister Vijaya were denied any form of conventional education, at the persuasion, it is believed, of *Rasikamani* T.K. Chidambaranatha Mudaliar, a friend and patron of both Subbulakshmi and Sadasivam,[118] but Radha, at least, had formal training in music. She was taught at various times by T.R. Balasubramaniam, a disciple of G.N. Balasubramaniam, by Ramnad Krishnan, by Mayavaram V.V. Krishna Iyer, by T. Brinda, and by T. Balasaraswati.[119] There is no doubt that she learnt either on her own or with Subbulakshmi from Musiri Subramania Iyer. Her sister Vijaya learnt music for a while from B. Rajam Iyer, a disciple of Ariyakudi Ramanuja Iyengar and over the years was occasionally seen to be accompanying Subbulakshmi on stage, but it was mainly Radha who shared the honours.

For all her training and experience, Radha Viswanathan settled into the role of accompanying singer and even expressed the very modest view that having sung with Subbulakshmi without incurring blame was all the honour she sought.[120] As an accompanying singer, she perfected the style of singing in the higher octave while the lead singer sang in the lower octave, a traditional practice followed by Brinda and Muktha, and which actually serves to highlight the lead singer.[121] Recordings of live concerts provide many such examples, as in 'Ka Va Va'/Varali, 'Tera tiyaga rada'/Gaulipantu, the *svarajatis* and selected verses in the '*Melakarta Ragamalika*'.

Despite a major illness in 1982,[122] Radha continued to be seen on the stage with Subbulakshmi and following Subbulakshmi's passing, on Radha's seventieth birthday, she became teacher and mentor and even occasional performer. In a November 2007 concert, she made the effort to repeat many of the 'MS hits'[123] and again in December 2008, after the release of a book, *MS and Radha*.[124] Radha Viswanathan lived on in quiet retirement, teaching a few students, and was remembered at her passing in January 2018 as the keeper of the MS flame, 'an amalgam of the Musiri–Semmangudi–T. Brinda traditions'.[125]

Subbulakshmi, at the age of eighty, was still recording. Some of these, such as the bhajans in praise of Sri Sathya Sai Baba or the compositions of Sri Atmananda whose '*Radhamadhavam*' she had recorded earlier, are forgettable.[126] Possibly the last recording Subbulakshmi made for HMV was the '*Meenakshi Suprabhatam*' in 1996.[127] This long and tricky text was composed for Subbulakshmi by V. Raghavan but it was recorded by her many years after his passing.[128] Of the five *suprabhatam* compositions sung by Subbulakshmi, only the '*Venkatesa Suprabhatam*' has had an afterlife, essentially because it has been part of temple practice for centuries.[129] It was her contribution to have made it accessible to believers around the world. The other four exist now as museum pieces, a tribute to Subbulakshmi's dexterity in singing hymns. Even so, the '*Meenakshi*' shows signs of fatigue and strain.

Other events marked the passage of time. She sang again, in early 1993, at the Tamil Isai Sangam, to mark the golden jubilee of that remarkable movement;[130] a few years later, that organization gave her an award in the name of Rajah Sir Annamalai Chettiar.[131] Subbulakshmi and Pattammal were both honoured during the golden jubilee celebrations of India's independence.[132] A Chembai Centenary Award came her way in 1996[133] and even new titles, such as a somewhat meaningless Kala Ratna in 1997.[134]

Surprisingly, she was still singing at weddings. There are several excerpts on YouTube of one such 1993 concert with *'Minakshi'*/Gamakakriya, *'Meevalla'*/Kapi, *'O Rangasayee'*/Kambhoji, *'Ksheerasagarasayana'*/Mayamalavagaula, *'Katrinilae, Naneke'*/Behag, *tiruppugazh, viruttam*, and *'Govindashtakam'*.[135] It is necessary to list these only to recall Subbulakshmi's diligence, even at her age. And for all that, *'Meevalla'* had been sung by her for over sixty years; the *alapana* of Kapi in this 1993 concert is exquisite.

There were other wedding concerts, as in the family of her old friend Chinnani in February 1995 and December 1996. A recital at Nanganallur, a Chennai suburb, drew 'an astonishingly large gathering' where in addition to several familiar pieces a new Todi piece, *'Thanjam unai'* was featured.[136] Her accompanying singer respectfully noted her 'individual style, grand, resonant, prayerful, hiding marathon training behind spontaneity'.[137] In keeping with the tradition of a lifetime, Subbulakshmi gave away to charity the large sum she was paid for this concert.[138]

Subbulakshmi's last major public concert, when she received the Swaralaya Puraskaram, was on 29 June 1997, some months before Sadasivam's death; the recording is commercially available.[139] The cash award that went with the award was donated to the Sri Mahalakshmi Matrubhuteshwar Trust. At nearly eighty-one, she gamely went through the motions, falling back as always on the known and familiar.[140] The critics were kind and commended her absolute devotion.[141] *'Vatapi'*/Hamsadhwani, *'Banturiti'*/Hamsanadam, *'Ksheerasagarasayana'*/Mayamalavagaula and the inevitable Sankarabharanam were all presented but listeners will recognize that the voice is tired and her concert days are behind her. Even so, it has been a very, very long innings of over sixty years.[142]

Despite her age, Subbulakshmi continued to pay her dues. She had sung in July 1996 to commemorate Annamacharya; a concert on the same theme in July 1997 was described as 'grace and peace all the time'.[143] There is a record of a concert of compositions of Narayana Tirtha, also in July 1997.[144] In the event the last actual concert may have been on 17 August 1997, for the Tirumala Tirupati Devasthanams. *"Tera tiyaga rada'/* Gaulipantu led on to several Annamacharya *samkirtanas*, a recital steeped in devotion and surrender.[145] The theme of the concert was *sravanam*, or listening to the name of God, as one of the nine modes of devotion.

14

Bharat Ratna

నీ పదాంబుజములే సదా నమ్మిన నమ్మ శుభమిమ్మ
శ్రీ మీనాక్షమ్మ [1]

('I have rested my faith always at the lotus feet of Minakshi',
translated loosely from the Telugu of
Syama Sastri's *Sarojadalanetri* in the raga Sankarabharanam)

AT ninety-five, Sadasivam's death, when it occurred on 21 November 1997, could be said to have been expected.[2] His long life ensured that he was remembered in many ways, as a freedom fighter, a votary of khadi, a journalist, a philanthropist, an impresario, a devoted follower of Rajaji from at least 1920, and a devotee of the Sankaracharya of Kanchi.[3] A friend remembered him as an old-style patriot, wearing and promoting khadi, and singing the songs of Subramania Bharati.[4] Another old friend recognized that he could be 'intolerant and domineering' but also that he 'protected and sustained Subbulakshmi's musical genius and moulded her personality'.[5]

An even older friend commented, 'True, Sadasivam controlled her in every way and control is not easy on creativity. But he was a very intelligent man. He ensured that M.S. reached the peak and stayed there, not in popularity or social status alone, but in dignity, elegance and bhakti.'[6] It was recalled that for all his high-handed ways, Subbulakshmi was never ever known to have complained. 'To Amma, Mama's words were gospel, his wish was her command.'[7]

Sadasivam's career as a journalist, editor and publisher was recalled, with *Ananda Vikatan*, *Kalki* and latterly, *Swarajya*.[8] In addition, his defining traits were remembered: his determination, ambition and resolve, his famed loyalty to his friends, his devotion to his protégés, his witty repartees,[9] his sweeping generosity and his fierce protection of his wife's image; he was hailed, not entirely correctly, as a Dharmatma.[10] But if all this is true, it is still also true that he can only be remembered as someone who for close to sixty years had walked in the shadows of greatness.[11]

Subbulakshmi was prostrate with grief at his passing.[12] It was not a marriage without its rocky moments.[13] There has always been speculation on the nature of the marriage and whether it rested on any emotional basis. An intimate of the family, who knew the couple for decades, has only this to say, 'They were both products of tumultuous times and difficult circumstances.'[14] Even so, Subbulakshmi, for whom the ideal of a *nityasumangali* could not have been forgotten, dreaded the idea of widowhood. She spoke of this often to her friends and in interviews and those close to her grieved that her oft-stated wish was not to be.[15] She was past eighty and was well into retirement, but with Sadasivam's death she seemed to lose her grip on life and over the few years left to her drifted into reclusive solitude. 'Like a withered flower shedding its petals she too wilted in grief.'[16]

Subbulakshmi allowed Sadasivam to take over and manage her life.[17] A compilation of tributes to him was produced in 1996 and dedicated to Subbulakshmi, 'The pride of Indian womanhood and the dazzling diamond which Mama discovered, polished and preserved for humanity.'[18] This was precisely what Sadasivam wanted; to be known always as the creator of Subbulakshmi. As a discerning admirer has observed '... the voice so unparalleled had no speech of its own, the mind so intersticed no thoughts to call its own, the eyes so bewitching no vision of their own. She sang what she was trained to sing, thought was she was told to think and saw what she was permitted to see'.[19] But this was her choice and whatever the secrets of their marriage, it was a relationship of over six decades and whatever be the perception of any third person he was close to her even if it was 'in the sort of way that water is close to a stone that it has worn down over the decades'.[20]

Life after Sadasivam did, however, have to go on. Subbulakshmi was sheltered in the affection and care of her immediate family. It is recalled that even her brother Sakthivel's widow travelled from Coimbatore to offer her condolences. A great moment, Subbulakshmi's last great moment, came in early 1998, when she was awarded the Bharat Ratna, the second artiste, after Satyajit Ray, and the first performing artiste to be so honoured, to be followed in subsequent years by Ravi Shankar, Lata Mangeshkar, Bismillah Khan, Bhimsen Joshi and Bhupen Hazarika.[21] There was widespread rejoicing at the award; the redoubtable D.K. Pattammal spoke for the world of music when she said she was 'overwhelmed with joy'.[22]

The Bharat Ratna had been long anticipated. A leading politician of the south publicly appealed to the Government of India in 1986 to confer the award on her.[23] In 1996, the distinguished historian of contemporary India, Ramachandra Guha, in a widely read column, argued for a Bharat Ratna to be given to Subbulakshmi and Lata Mangeshkar.[24] In a longer version of this article published after both singers had been awarded the title, he made the telling point, 'We know them as "MS" and "Lata" not out of easy familiarity but because we love, cherish and honour them, because we cannot imagine life or India without them.'[25]

The Bharat Ratna was, and is, highly political. The selection of individuals for national awards in India is expected to be non-partisan.

'A Bharat Ratna, for example, should invite no reservation or doubts or questions in any part of the country or with any section of society.'[26] However, the same writer admits that the recommendations of the committee set up for the purpose of national awards 'represent a mix of subjectivity and objectivity as well as of noble ignorance and low cunning'.

Happily, in the case of Subbulakshmi, there was only rejoicing. An old friend and cultural sophisticate who had asked 'Who better than Subbulakshmi, whose music has given so many a glimpse of the celestial and made their hearts purer?' rejoiced when the award was announced. 'M.S. Subbulakshmi has long been a Bharat Ratna in the people's reckoning and has now been designated as one. A daughter of Madurai she has soared like a *gopuram* of the Madurai temple amidst other southern musicians of our time.'[27] Chief Minister M. Karunanidhi observed that the Bharat Ratna to MS was as if the Kohinoor was embedded in her crown.[28] Another old friend wrote, 'Her glorious voice, called the voice of the century, is God's gift to her, and to us, her listeners. Perfect alignment of *sruthi*, complete command of *laya*, clarity of diction, faultless pronunciation, immaculate execution, are the hallmarks of her musicianship.'[29] One critic, known for his bite and general bad temper, grudgingly agreed, 'better late than never'.[30]

The national dailies editorialized in admiration. '[I]n an epoch that has been notably lacking in heroic figures who might provide a model for people to follow, M.S. Subbulakshmi stands out as a radiant example'.[31] Another opined that the award '... symbolizes a hope, however slender, that music can help to save the nation's soul, even in these trying times when moral bankruptcy stares it in the face. That M.S. Subbulakshmi can achieve this is an everlasting tribute to the magic of her music.'[32] 'If ever there was one person who symbolized all that is glorious and enchanting in Indian music that is M.S. Subbulakshmi.'[33] 'In honouring her the government has honoured itself.'[34] 'This is a moment of glory not only for the gifted singer but for all who cherish India's rich musical heritage.'[35] 'We cannot think of more than a small number of Indians about whom it can be said in honesty: his or her achievement is likely to endure a hundred years from now ... We can certainly say it about *Sangitha Kalanidhi* M.S. Subbulakshmi.'[36] One very enthusiastic *rasika* even called for the Nobel Peace Prize.[37]

The Hindi press, significantly, was warm in its appreciation. One paper hailed the award as belonging not just to the world of music but to the world of the mind itself, to the *vita contemplative*.[38] Another recalled the confluence of Mira and Tyagaraja in her singing and further that there was probably no household in the south unfamiliar with her voice, *jo unke svaron se aparichit ho*.[39]

Subbulakshmi's characteristic response was quiet and understated. It is not just that she was still in mourning; that was simply the way she had been trained. 'I am grateful to the President for conferring upon me the highest honour of our land, which I accept in all humility.'[40] The award function itself was glittering. The scroll states in elegant and well-considered Hindi that the award is in recognition of personal qualities, *vyaktigat gunon ke liye*. Over forty years earlier, when the Padma Bhushan was awarded to her, she made it a point to write to her mother in Madurai that her name was announced as Madurai Shanmukhavadivu Subbulakshmi.[41] The same name, redolent with tradition and ancestry, was again called out in the high domed Durbar Hall of the Rashtrapati Bhavan.

In a brief statement distributed on her behalf, Subbulakshmi said, 'Every citizen of this great land is a *ratna*.'[42] The statement included the sentiment, 'Let us be honest to our own lapses, sink all our differences, unilaterally shed mutual hatred and disbelief, rise up as one nation, march forward in absolute harmony and take the glory of the nation to greater and nobler heights.' The language is not hers, but the sentiments are. This was, after all, a woman who revered Gandhi.

Subbulakshmi was particular about attending the rehearsal for the actual event and learning her steps, as it were, and later held court at a lunch in her honour.[43] Throughout the proceedings she was gracious, modest, self-contained and entirely aware of who she was. There may well have been regret that Sadasivam was not there to share her special moment but there was satisfaction that the moment was hers.[44] If ever she had doubts, this was the time to dispel them. She was MS!

Late in the same evening, her old friend Ravi Shankar came to greet her, and touched her feet in respect. Placing her hand on his shoulder she said, in her halting English, 'Next, you,' a happily soon to-be-fulfilled prediction. The conversation drifted to musical matters and to Subbulakshmi's peeve at musicians who did not reveal the raga they were singing but would tend to linger on ambiguous phrases which could belong to one of many ragas. As, for instance, in Kalyani and Latangi. The sitarist agreed, '*Dhaivat ka antar hai*' he said in Hindi, There is a difference in the *dhaivata*, note. '*Adey daan*,' the singer replied in Tamil, precisely. For those who were watching this exchange, it was a magical moment.

Earlier that evening, *Meera* was screened at a small function.[45] After the event the then prime minister turned to Subbulakshmi and said, 'India is in your debt.'

More awards came Subbulakshmi's way, the Sri Chandrasekharendra Saraswati National Eminence Award for Community Service[46] and the S.V. Narayanaswamy Rao Memorial National Award, which recognized her large donations to varied causes and specifically to the Sri Rama Seva Mandali, Bangalore, where she had sung for over forty years.[47] Other titles included the Special Platinum Jubilee Award of the Music Academy,[48] the award of the title of National Artiste by the Government of India,[49] the Lifetime Achievement Award of the Government of Delhi,[50] which occasion saw the release of an audio-visual presentation, *A Gift of the Gods*, directed by Avinash Pasricha and the Sangeetha Saraswathi Award of the Manava Seva Kendra, Bangalore.[51] There was also an award from CMANA, the Carnatic Music Association of North America.[52]

The cash which came with some of these awards was given to the construction of the Mahaswami Manimandapam Project, a memorial to the Paramacharya of Kanchi. Prasar Bharati, the Central broadcasting agency released a set of recordings from the collections of All India Radio and Doordarshan in the 'Bharat Ratna Series' though these are thoughtlessly annotated and edited.[53] Prasar Bharati, indeed, went on to honour Subbulakshmi and several other veteran performers with a National Artist Award, much to the annoyance of at least one veteran who was not so honoured.[54] The Subbulakshmi–Sadasivam Music and Dance Resources Institute, SAMUDRI, which had been set up in 1999[55] had Ravi Shankar playing at a fund-raising concert.[56] The Films Division produced a two-hour documentary on Subbulakshmi and her music, a tribute soaked in devotion.[57]

Subbulakshmi had stopped active performance for at least fifteen years and had not even been seen much since Sadasivam's passing, but she continued to attract attention and a steady stream of warm tributes in the papers.[58] None of these tributes add significantly to all that was already known about her, but they do establish the adoration in which she was held.

The popular weekly magazine *Outlook* in a special Independence Day feature identified three great musicians: Allauddin Khan, Bismillah Khan and Subbulakshmi. 'M.S. ... links her art with a spiritual quest and beyond her music, it's her image of a *sadhika* that will endure the test of time'.[59] A popular paper, *Tehelka*, in an Independence Day round-up of iconic Indians shied away from labelling Subbulakshmi as a Carnatic singer or a bhajan singer 'because that would be yoking the infinite'.[60] *The Week* included Subbulakshmi in its popular poll of Ten Most Admired Women, an odd, and revealing, inclusion in a clutch of high-profile women from politics and films.

Many of these appreciations include a reference to a Tamil piece sung very often by Subbulakshmi since 1980, '*Kurai onrum illai*' ('No regrets have I'), by Rajaji.[61] It is composed in the spirit of surrender, which marks many older pieces in the bhakti tradition and drew much of its concert effect from the stirring music in Sivaranjani, Kapi and Sindhubhairavi set by Kadayanallur Venkataraman.[62]

A sensitive listener has called attention to the possible connection between Rajaji's text and his experience in 1925 of having to appear in court, breaking the rules of non-cooperation that was the call of the day, on behalf of a person who by the codes of the time was not allowed to enter a temple and who, seized by devotion, made so bold as to enter the portals of the temple to Lakshmi at Tiruchanur. Rajaji secured the man's acquittal and it has been suggested that he could not quite comprehend that the man's devotion was unshaken by the fact that he was prevented even from seeing the idol of the god he worshipped.[63] It is an ingenious interpretation even if perhaps reading somewhat too much into what is in the end a simple poem.

There were other writings as well. Indira Menon's *The Madras Quartet* in 2000; V. Gangadhar's little book, *M S Subbulakshmi, The Voice Divine*, in 2002; and Lakshmi Viswanathan's *Kunjamma, Ode to a Nightingale* in 2004 all told the story well, based on existing sources.[64] *MS: A Life in Music* by T.J.S. George, a senior journalist with the *Indian Express* who was known as the biographer of the politician V.K. Krishna Menon and film actor Nargis, was published in early 2004.[65] This broadly followed the received version of the Subbulakshmi story but for two significant exceptions. For the first time, some details were made public of the shadowy goings-on over the period 1938 to 1940 when Subbulakshmi fled the protection of her mother's home for Madras and Sadasivam.[66] Much of this history has disappeared from public memory, not least due to Sadasivam's strenuous efforts.

Possibly what caused more, if momentary, comment was the publication, in English translation, as an appendix to the biography, of what are Subbulakshmi's personal letters to G.N. Balasubramaniam, written at the exact time of *Sakuntalai*, when she was presumably living with Sadasivam and his elder daughter, the wife and younger daughter somewhere in the country.

The letters are intensely personal and are somewhat inappropriately appended to the text of the *Life*. The provenance of the letters has never been made clear and their publication in Subbulakshmi's lifetime, possibly without her permission or even her knowledge, caused disquiet to many. Her health was already failing and it is entirely likely that she did not know of their publication. Certainly, there was no response from her. In a letter written at the time to an admirer, and in a slightly different context, Subbulakshmi's aide Athmanathan wrote, 'For ... Amma, honours or abuses do not mean anything. Even factual errors in their biographies can be ignored as even factually correct events have no meaning in such people's lives'.[67]

Semmangudi Srinivasa Iyer died on 31 October 2003, at the age of ninety-five. He would have always been remembered as a musician of the most superior classicism, but his longevity has ensured a lasting influence.[68] Srinivasa Iyer learnt from Tirukkodikaval Krishna Iyer, who was born in 1857 and could conceivably have known people who knew Tyagaraja; he was also teacher to T.M. Krishna, born in 1976 and in every sense a twenty-first-century musician.[69] Over the decades, he taught students of four generations, and was said never to have accepted payment in return for tuition, in addition to the students at the Sree Swathi Thirunal College of Music at Thiruvananthapuram where he served as principal for over twenty years.[70]

Semmangudi Srinivasa Iyer was not only a teacher; he was a master performer who understood the importance of concert structure. His concert career was incredibly long with his first appearance on stage being in 1926 in Kumbakonam and his last public concert at the Music Academy in 2000. He was a staunch votary of the Ariyakudi pattern but the whole concert experience was heightened, despite a recalcitrant voice, by his vivacious *kriti* rendering. If the songs of the master composers were the centrepiece of his concerts, his rendering of Sanskrit slokas was famed. His students and intimates have written of his lengthy, off-stage raga *alapanas*.

Semmangudi's concerts were marked by a composite liveliness and even if not planned in the way Subbulakshmi's recitals were, still planned to enhance overall impact. His version usually became the recognized version of many songs. He was a singer who delighted in *ragam-tanam-pallavi* suites.[71] Above all, his concerts were experiences to be relished, not least by the performer. 'His joy in his performance is physical as well as spiritual, and the wide gestures of the arms, the wagging of the head, the throwing around of the body, all fit the music so that you feel that without them it would be more difficult to sing like this.'[72]

He outlived all his contemporaries and for the last twenty years or so of his life enjoyed *pitamaha* status, a role which by all accounts he enjoyed enormously.[73] Sadasivam was among the last of his set to pass on. Srinivasa Iyer writes that he met both Kalki R. Krishnamurthi and T. Sadasivam at the Congress exhibition in Kumbakonam in 1933, where Sadasivam was running the *khadi* stall.[74] This may have been the occasion when Srinivasa Iyer first heard Subbulakshmi sing, though that may have actually been earlier, in 1928 or 1929, and of which he has spoken elsewhere.[75] It was a lifelong relationship, with Sadasivam always playing the patron to Srinivasa Iyer's performer.[76]

It is clear that even if Subbulakshmi always regarded Musiri Subramania Iyer as her principal teacher, Semmangudi Srinivasa Iyer was still very much a mentor.[77] A contemporary musician recalls how very late in both their lives, after Sadasivam's passing, Subbulakshmi still paid Semmangudi Srinivasa Iyer the tribute due to a teacher by calling on him on *Vijaya Dasami*, the day devoted to blessing new beginnings, and learning a new song.[78]

Subbulakshmi lived very reclusively after Sadasivam's passing but was still, in the initial years at least, singing at home.[79] She made a rare appearance at an event driven by many young musicians where a host of young children were to sing '*Maitreem bhaja*', the hymn she had sung countless times. Her careful attention to detail on that occasion is still remembered.[80] But the end was near and starting from early 2002, Subbulakshmi, famed for her razor-sharp memory and demonic attention to detail, drifted into illness, forgetfulness and confusion.

For a while, she continued to show interest in musical events and her family recalls affectionately that any mention of a concert by any artiste would elicit the two questions most relevant to a seasoned concert artiste such as herself, 'Who were the accompanists?', and, 'Was there a crowd?'[81] But it was a sad time and more than one close associate recalled that she spoke, in her anxiety, of being orphaned, with no mother, sister or brother.[82] Another recalls that she received the news of the passing of intimate friends with dignified regret but without the grief that may have been expected.[83] There were lucid intervals, but these were becoming infrequent and it was only her natural grace and courtesy that concealed her condition.[84] She was hospitalized once in May 2004 and seemed to recover, but a second hospitalization in December marked the end.[85]

M.S. Subbulakshmi was called to her ancestresses in the quiet of the early night of 11 December 2004. The nation mourned her passing. The *Hindu*, for so long a friend, ran banner headlines on the 12th and the 13th.[86] The paper editorialized, 'The *Hindu* joins millions of Indians in saluting one who brought beauty, grace, bhakti and humanity to everything she touched, a musical genius of the kind encountered only once in an epoch.'[87]

Politicians, musicians, dancers and film actors paid their tributes, as did the national press. The Hindi press was warmly respectful.[88] In an otherwise anodyne obituary, the *Guardian* of London called out 'Subbulakshmi's technical mastery and capacity for self-criticism [which] enabled her to bring a strong sense of spontaneity to her art'.[89] Madurai grieved, and called for a memorial in the city.[90] Parliament observed silence in her memory. President A.P.J. Abdul Kalam, who had shared honours with her in March 1998 when the Bharat Ratna was conferred on both of them, broke protocol and flew to Chennai for the funeral. His tribute to Subbulakshmi in verse was spoken from the heart.[91]

In the days that followed, friends, family and admirers alike wrote of Subbulakshmi's art, and of their loss.[92] Her great contemporary D.K. Pattammal spoke feelingly, 'MS was like an elder sister to me. We both started out together and there has never been any quarrel or difference of opinion between us. Just unbounded affection.'[93] This loss was shared by very many people who had never known or met her. A large number wrote to the papers simply to express their sorrow. One *rasika* wrote, 'Never before have I seen so many letters of praise for a departed soul in the *Hindu* or any other newspaper. Praising Kalidasa's *Shakuntalam*, Max Müller had said, "Say Shakunthala and all is said." One can say that of M.S. too.'[94] The artist M.F. Husain, in exile in Dubai, painted a portrait of Subbulakshmi as soon as he heard the news.[95]

Subbulakshmi's passing was mourned through the Chennai music season later in December 2004 with at least one irritated critic commenting on the innumerable, and often poor, renderings heard of '*Maitreem bhaja*' and '*Kurai onrum illai*'.

Subbulakshmi has had a long afterlife, and adoring appreciations have continued to appear in the press.[96] She very quickly became, if she had not already been, identified with Tamil heritage. 'Not only is Rajnikant [sic] India's biggest star but from S. Ramanujan to Viswanathan Anand to T.N. Seshan to C. Rajagopalachari to R.K. Narayan to M.S. Subbulakshmi, Tamil Nadu rules on culture, brain power and political acumen.'[97] The arrival lounge at the Chennai international airport has, for no particular reason at all, portraits of people seen as having brought distinction to the Tamil people; there are five men, all born in the nineteenth century: V.O. Chidambaram Pillai, Subramania Bharati,

Srinivasa Ramanujan, Sarvepalli Radhakrishnan and C.V. Raman; a twentieth-century man, A.P.J. Abdul Kalam; and one twentieth-century woman, M.S. Subbulakshmi.

A postage stamp was released with Subbulakshmi's image in December 2005.[98] A second stamp was issued in 2016. There is reason to believe that Subbulakshmi had asked in her will that no monument to her be erected. Despite this, a statue of Subbulakshmi was unveiled in Tirupati in 2006, created in bronze by a sculptor from Kakinada;[99] years later, the general neglect of the statue was bemoaned, and attention called to the fact that the tambura carried by Subbulakshmi was being used as a prop for electricity cables.[100]

The Shanmukhananda Sabha in Mumbai set up the Bharat Ratna Dr M.S. Subbulakshmi Auditorium,[101] instituted an award in her name and installed a statue at its entrance.[102] The T.N. Rajarathinam Muthamizh Peravai Hall in Chennai, which seeks to commemorate the isai vellalar heritage, prominently displays Subbulakshmi's image. Starting from 2005, the Music Academy, for so long graced by Subbulakshmi's presence, instituted an award to be given to each year's president in her name.

Subbulakshmi featured in a 2007 listing of sixty successful men and women without whom the country would not be where it is today.[103] The Hindu Saregama M.S. Subbulakshmi Award was set up in 2010 to be given annually to a promising Carnatic vocalist. Speaking on the occasion, the representative of HMV recalled gratefully that '[h]er albums are always among our top five best-sellers all over the country'.[104]

Two young singers edited and produced a coffee-table tribute to seven extraordinary musicians: Ariyakudi Ramanuja Iyengar, T.N. Rajarathinam Pillai, Semmangudi Srinivasa Iyer, G.N. Balasubramaniam, Palghat Mani Iyer, M.S. Subbulakshmi and T.R. Mahalingam.[105] There can be no quarrel with this list. A quite different production in 2012 was by Amar Chitra Katha, the well-known publisher of cartoon books for children, which told Subbulakshmi's story in the form of a graphic novel.

Tributes were paid in strange ways. In August 2009, a popular artiste actually sang Subbulakshmi's Music Academy concert of 1968, the year she was given the *Sangitha Kalanidhi*, surely denying all chances of any sort of *manodharma*.[106] Some years later, another promising young artiste sang the United Nations concert.[107] In truth, it must be admitted that Subbulakshmi's highly rehearsed concert structure and song selection does lend itself to easy imitation, though what the actual impact is on the listener is another matter.

The Subbulakshmi promotion went into fevered overdrive during 2016, the centenary year. From within the family, Swati Thiyagarajan, daughter of Sadasivam and Subbulakshmi's adopted son S. Tyagarajan, produced a short film for TV, 'MS Amma, a shy girl from Madurai'.[108] The Hindu Group organized public competition 'in any art form' [Pay Tribute to MS AND WIN BIG!].[109] The Hindu Saregama MS Subbulakshmi Award 2016 was conducted with éclat.[110]

A well-known vina player made a detailed presentation on Subbulakshmi's *ragam-tanam-pallavi* suites, with her long-term mrdangam accompanist T.K. Murthy in attendance.[111] Violinist Kanyakumari led a programme of mass violin playing by over a hundred players of Subbulakshmi's popular hits.[112] Several *sabhas* in Chennai organized events with renderings of her film songs, dance recitals, whistle concerts, debates and the like.[113] Subbulakshmi's old patron Karan Singh, at whose hands she received the *Sangitha Kalanidhi* all those years ago, unveiled a portrait and dutifully observed that she 'infused divinity' in her singing.[114] Her ageing accompanists spoke at a seminar in Delhi.[115] The M.S. Swaminathan Research Foundation sponsored a recital by the singer T.M. Krishna.[116] An organization dedicated to the memory of Ariyakudi Ramanuja Iyengar, no less, organized a concert dedicated to Subbulakshmi's memory.[117]

Two books were released during this time. *MS Revisited: Tracing the Nightingale's Golden Journey*, was a collection of articles from the *Hindu* over the decades, containing respectful, adoring and extremely familiar accounts of Subbulakshmi's life and work.[118] *Song of Surrender* published by the Sruti Foundation carries slightly more unusual pieces by lesser-known associates of Subbulakshmi. The Music Academy provided a platform during the annual season in December 2016 to Revathy Sankaran for a *katha kalakshepam* on Subbulakshmi's life, a presentation originally performed in Subbulakshmi's lifetime and which has as its theme the notion that she was an incarnation of a divine vina and that Sadasivam was an incarnation of Siva. This has apparently always been received very well.[119]

Many of the centenary tributes concentrated on the devotional aspects of Subbulakshmi's style and delivery, with occasional references to the Annamacharya verses.[120] It is true that Subbulakshmi had a long performing life and there are comparatively few people who would have any recollection of the magnificent concert years but at least one of them, a veteran who first heard Subbulakshmi in 1940, had noted with regret some time earlier, 'It would be a pity if her popularity in devotional music, *suprabhatam*, and bhajans were to mask the excellence of her classical music output.'[121] Another critic mourned, 'MS's music is more than her bhakti singing and it deserves to be highlighted. She was a brilliant musician – one of the most versatile. The classical musician in her was very prominent until the seventies, and it is an aspect of her music that not many people have been exposed to.'[122]

Vasanthakumari's disciple *Sangitha Kalanidhi* Sudha Ragunathan sang at the United Nations on 2 October 2016,[123] an occasion jointly, and somewhat bizarrely, commemorating Gandhi, Subbulakshmi's centenary, the fiftieth anniversary of her United Nations concert, the International Day of Non-violence and the Sankara Nethralaya, which had sponsored the event, an organization to which she was always close.[124] The UN released a special stamp of Subbulakshmi. The Government of India released a set of commemorative coins. And even as the centenary revelries ceased, the Ministry of Culture sponsored a major exhibition in September 2017, somewhat unimaginatively called *Kurai Onrum Illai*.

Subbulakshmi's long years made for a life of purpose and dedication, a life of extraordinary diligence and unequalled magic, a life lived in the shadows and under the chandeliers. We still know very little of what made her who she was or of what it took to make the transition from the tumult of her turmeric-drenched youth to the sedate camphor and jasmine of her adult life, but we do know that it was a lifetime of unquestioning service and pursuit of excellence.

The film historian Nasreen Munni Kabir cites a remark of the sarod player Ali Akbar Khan quoted in his obituary. 'If you practice for ten years, you may begin to please yourself, after twenty years you may become a performer and please your audience, after thirty years you may please even your guru, but you must practice many more years before you finally become a true artist — then you may please even God.'[125] Whichever force Subbulakshmi believed in, and there is no denying she believed in a higher agency, would surely have been pleased.

15

A Life

मीनालोचनि पाशमोचनि[1]

(She of the shapely eyes, She who releases from bondage...
from Muthusvami Dikshitar's 'Minakshi memudam' in the
raga Gamakakriya)

M.S. Subbulakshmi's musicianship and personality were closely intertwined. Any discussion of her music eventually becomes a study of her manner, her beliefs and her image. This is a great pity for she was, first and foremost, a consummate artiste. And it is for that reason that we must separate her music from what there is that is known of her as a person.

Subbulakshmi's style was based on an appreciation of what was most beautiful in the vina, nagasvaram and vocal performances she heard around her.[2] It is known that she played the pieces she sang on the vina to enable a deeper understanding of the pace and meaning. Her song rendering was always superb and marked by purity and considered restraint.

Every Carnatic performer has to build a recital around composed pieces, and in her concerts familiar and unknown pieces alike were cleanly presented, the most difficult sung with deceptive simplicity.

A character in a short story has this to say on Bach. 'I think there has to be an authority of expression; a sense of control that is combined with effortlessness – what the Italians call *sprezzatura*. It never shows how hard it is. It seems easy, right, natural, even if it is hard to play.'[3] That was Subbulakshmi. Her song renditions had the glow and polish of ceaseless repetition. 'With constant practice and more practice her rendition of *sangatis* would shimmer like burnished gold.'[4] But if she was a master of technique, she had the gift to transcend it.[5] Technique is what ensured her the platform but after that it was what she brought to the words she sang, the way she used her voice, her understanding of the emotional basis of the song and her acute sense of what was appropriate.[6]

The songs of the trinity were always the core of her concerts, but those of newer composers were carefully introduced. There is a charming account of Subbulakshmi singing Annamacharya's '*Bhavayami Gopala balam*'/Yamunakalyani, at her home for a visiting Vasanthakumari with the younger woman commenting when the song was rendered, 'This is perfection.'[7] Several songs are permanently associated with her: '*Rangapura vihara*'/Brindavanasaranga, '*Naradamuni*' and '*Ennaganu*' in Pantuvarali, the ragamalika '*Bhavayami Raghuramam*', '*Bhogindra sayinam*'/Kuntalavarali, '*Pakkala nilabadi*'/Kharaharapriya, '*Sarojadalanetri*'/Sankarabharanam, '*Narayana divya namam*'/Mohana, '*Vara Narada*'/Vijayasri, '*Rama nannu brovaravemako*'/Harikambhoji, '*Nee irangayenil*'/Athana, the list is endless.

She had a gift for languages, and sang Telugu, Sanskrit and Kannada as naturally as in her native Tamil. While singing Telugu, she committed none of the barbarisms that Tamil speakers are wont to make, but equally she did not make a caricature of it, as is notorious among Telugu-speaking musicians. Her Sanskrit enunciation was a joy to hear, and she sang both songs and hymns, without making one sound like the other.

There is, of course, a caveat to this. For all the richness of her repertoire, possibly well over 2,500 songs,[8] Subbulakshmi showed very little of it at a time. Certain pieces, tried and tested, were presented time and time again. Songs such as 'Sri Kamakoti'/Saveri, 'Ksheerasagarasayana'/Mayamalavagaula, or 'O Rangasayee'/Kambhoji, beautiful as they are in themselves, were done to death. Very many songs were learnt for an occasion, presented in concert and never sung again.[9]

All performers will tend to fall back on a basic stock, but in Subbulakshmi's case, the stock, even if it kept changing after every so many years, was always provokingly small. Sadasivam's insistence on deciding the concert list for every performance, and his strong views on what was concert-worthy and what was likely to appeal was, of course, responsible for this. She acquiesced, but at the cost of her musician's sense of control. Madurai Mani Iyer also endlessly repeated his favourite songs, and as in her case, seemed to have the approbation of his public. 'It is the pursuit of the perfect song that lays him open to the charge of choosing the all-too-familiar fare. His audience appears to appreciate his point. The familiar does not stale.'[10]

More positively, we can say of Subbulakshmi what was said of 'Vina' Dhanammal, that her music was of the essence. From her vast treasure she selected and presented little gems; a dab of *attar* on the wrist as compared to a garden of fragrant flowers.

Raga *alapana* was a highlight of Subbulakshmi's concerts, and in her prime she would present at least four ragas in addition to the one chosen for *tanam* and *pallavi*. The major concert ragas, Bhairavi, Kalyani, Todi, Kambhoji, Kharaharapriya, and the ubiquitous Sankarabharanam were second nature to her. Other favourites included Pantuvarali, Purvikalyani, Abhogi, Ritigaula, Punnagavarali, Dhanyasi, Yadukulakambhoji, Kiravani and Saveri. Even her short *alapanas* were complete in themselves.

Alapana as a form cannot be taught and what a performing artiste actually sings effectively depends on how she has internalized all that she has heard, the compositions in that raga, her understanding of structure and her sense of what is appropriate.[11] Different musicians singing the same raga will sing it differently.[12] Her teacher Semmangudi

Srinivasa Iyer commended Subbulakshmi's long raga phrases, *karvais*, as 'resplendent'.[13] There was never any gimmickry, and she often said that it was the duty of a musician during *alapana* to immediately reveal the identity of the raga and not to tease the audience by lingering on ambiguous phrases that could be used in different ragas. Subbulakshmi's *neraval*, or improvisation, was always of a high class even when excessively familiar as in *Kadanba vana nilaye...* in '*Sri Kamakoti*'/Saveri or *Narayana namamulanu* in '*Naradamuni*'/Pantuvarali or for the *pallavi* line in '*Sogasuga*'/Sriranjani.

The allegation of sameness cannot be dismissed lightly; sameness is linked to the place of the composed piece in a concert. Subbulakshmi's approach to the composed piece was similar to that of a Western classical musician: the emphasis was on an intuitive understanding of the piece and on finely honed rendition, rather than on spontaneous and ever-changing presentation. This single-minded pursuit of perfection can be understood in the context of pre-composed pieces, but in Subbulakshmi's case it extended even to those elements of musicianship where virtuosity is looked for, as in *alapana*, *neraval* and *svaraprasthara*. Subbulakshmi's *alapanas* and *neraval*, while perfect, were really always the same. Even when people caught on, they were mesmerized into acceptance. It has been said of her that she 'cleverly put through all that was available in her armoury and made the audience sing along with her'.[14] A lesser artiste could not have managed this.

On rare occasions, she would offer an *alapana* in Vijayanagari or Ravichandrika or a similarly unfamiliar raga, or a detailed *pallavi* in Hemavati, but mostly it was the familiar and well-worn. In all that she attempted, she was famously risk-averse. There was never a false step, and only very seldom an adventurous one. What she offered was uniquely hers, no one else had the voice or the training or the magic to do it, but she offered it within self-imposed limits. She never offered an explanation either, and may not have been permitted to do so, but it caused distress, especially among her admirers who knew exactly of what she was capable.[15]

If a rich repertoire and strength in raga *alapana* were two distinctive features of Subbulakshmi's art, a third was the fabulous voice. The accusation is sometimes made that, somehow, she lacked in *vidvat*. Implicit in this is the assumption that her style was based on voice alone, an inherent ability, and not on scholarship, an acquired ability. There is also a suspicion, occasionally aired, that musicality is antithetical to classicism or scholarship.[16] This is fallacious.

Subbulakshmi's style was obviously built around her voice, but all artistes seek to build on their strengths. Further, voice alone is inadequate. There are very many artistes today whose voices are sweet enough but whose music has nothing else to commend it. 'Good music need not be a triumph of the vocal cords, though where such a triumph is reinforced by a personal statement of artistic faith as in M.S. Subbulakshmi, there is music of a kind that is spoken of only in superlatives.'[17] Or, as an admirer put it more bluntly in a centenary tribute, 'It is one thing to have a great voice, but it all depends on what you do with it; or really, what you do not [do] with it.'[18]

Subbulakshmi combined the impact of her voice with the meaning of the *sahitya* she was singing. It has been said very often that she was a perfectionist when it came to understanding and memorizing the words she was singing, in whichever language. 'She made vocal perfection and lyrical elegance the cornerstones of her style.'[19] Another perceptive critic wrote, 'MS's music is characterized by an element of ecstasy at all times ... She loads every rift with ore, and does it with such obvious relish that one would have to be a clod of earth not to feel moved by the revelation of such. Yet in one less gifted than MS such display of wealth would appear wanton.'[20]

Almost alone amongst her peers, she cultivated and trained her voice, and believed in the importance of voice culture, speaking appreciatively of Hindustani vocalists in this connection. She understood voice modulation[21] and her music had powerful impact in the lower octave.[22] She sang full-throatedly and when she sang her voice filled the space in which she was singing. Her control over *sruti*, or pitch, was absolute and over a very long performing career it fell only slightly towards the end of her performing career. A 'votary of Hindustani music' is credited with the view that her voice reminded him of the shehnai; 'it has the same richness of tone, its smoothness, vibrancy and above all its hypnotic quality'.[23] All said and done, as anyone who heard Subbulakshmi in her prime will attest, it was a voice beyond compare.

Subbulakshmi was always aware that if she was adored and worshipped by large numbers of lay listeners, she was judged critically by purists, who found her wanting in classicism especially when compared to Pattammal and Vasanthakumari.[24] There were also the trite observations of pandits that she and Pattammal and Vasanthakumari represented bhakti, *aacharam* and *buddhi*, or devotion, tradition and knowledge, a categorization that pays mean tribute to all three.[25] This, for a woman as intelligent as she, must have been hard to bear, that 'her own Herculean labours, play of intelligence and self-reflexivity remained unrecognized'.[26] It was the unusual critic who recognized that while '[t]here is, perhaps, a binding factor in her feeling of devotion but far more important is her devotion to sincerity in her art'.[27] She must indeed have been aware that this was the price that she was paying for the compromises she had made.

The allegation of lack of *vidvat* persists, with Subbulakshmi often being held as not belonging to the 'inner circle'.[28] Some part of this stems from her identification as a devotional singer, and the easy availability of records and cassettes only from the later years of her performing career. There is also a mistaken linkage between scholarship and aggressive sense of rhythm, or *laya gnanam*. True, *pallavi* singing, where this is put to the test, was not central to Subbulakshmi's concerts, but even here, this is truer of the later years. In the middle years, as we have seen earlier, she sang *pallavis* as much as anyone else, even if *pallavi* singing was not considered important or even desirable in the musical tradition where her roots lay. More importantly several associates and accompanying musicians have spoken of Subbulakshmi's superlative sense of beat and rhythm, her easy familiarity with *tala* complexities and the obvious enhancement of her vocal style by her early training in mrdangam from her brother Sakthivel.[29]

Vidvat can be understood as scholarship, or reflected in dexterity or knowledge. It could even be simply the joy of being totally in control. The point need not be laboured. Deryck Cooke, the musicologist, writing of classical Western music observes that music can be related to each of the three arts of 'architecture, in its quasi-mathematical construction; to painting, in its representation of physical objects, and to literature, in its use of language to express emotion'.[30] It does not take much imagination to read into this the principles of *laya*, *bhava* and *sahitya*, the three principles on which the Carnatic tradition is built, principles which were wholly assimilated into Subbulakshmi's performing style.

M.S. Subbulakshmi established a grand tradition of performance. Over the central forty years of her career, when she performed on possibly a few thousand occasions, she was always on test and always in control. Her stage presence, and the manner in which she conducted herself, 'the matchless M.S. Subbulakshmi who is grace and dignity personified on stage', were much commended.[31]

The fans who thronged her recitals were often demanding *rasikas* who would not be satisfied with anything but the best. She came to cultivate a wider fan base, of people who may not have been familiar with the minutiae of Carnatic technique but were, nonetheless, thrilled by her overtly devotional songs. She was a skilled performer, who knew how to hold the attention of the audience. But despite these crowds, Subbulakshmi was hailed over the years, oddly enough, as a musician who sang not for the public but in response to an inner calling.

A Life

The performances themselves were rigorously planned and thought out. There were seldom any last-minute changes. It is a pity that today we have access only to studio recordings or to selectively released tapes, which do not indicate the style and format in which she usually performed. The *sabha* concerts of the 1950s and 1960s reveal diligence, virtuosity and an ever-growing repertoire.

It is possible to distinguish, over Subbulakshmi's very long performing career, several stages, each with a dominant aspect. Ramaswami R. Iyer, civil servant and *rasika*, has identified seven stages and we can select, from among the available recordings of Subbulakshmi, presentations that best depict those stages, and approximate time periods.[32] In her *very early career*, essentially over the 1930s, Subbulakshmi's bell-like voice was the marker, best represented by, from among the few recordings we still have, the song 'Syama sundara' from *Sevasadanam* or the ragamalika *viruttam* from *Sakuntalai*. The 1940s reveal a voice which is still bell-like and crystal clear but *more classically oriented* as in the 1942 recording of Suddhananda Bharati's 'Arul purivai'/Hamsadhwani or the 1950 'Narayana divya namam'/Mohana.

Our *rasika* identifies the third stage in Subbulakshmi's performing career as one where she was *maturing as a great artiste*; the 1956 concert at Bhavani is a fine exemplar of this time with its tight structure, fast renderings and a full display of musical virtuosity. The *full flowering* of Subbulakshmi's musical prowess came with the early 1960s. The ragamalika 'Bhavayami Raghuramam', or the 1966 United Nations concert in its entirety represent this stage, a time when her voice was at its most rounded, most mature and capable of the most extraordinary feeling and had not yet begun to show signs of fatigue.

The late 1960s to the mid 1970s had Subbulakshmi shining as a *great classical musician* but one whose voice had lost its bell-like quality of the previous decades. To many, this was Subbulakshmi at her best. The recordings of the Music Academy concerts of 1968, 1969, 1970 and 1971 show her in complete, joyous control. The pace is slower and more measured, the *alapanas* more thoughtful, the concert structure more complete. The sixth stage is Subbulakshmi's *late mature* phase; '*Vande Vasudevam*'/Sri from the Annamacharya selections is a good example of this period.

The last stage in her performing career relates actually to a time when she had effectively retired but was still singing; a period when she was *ageing*. This was beginning to be obvious as in the 1989 recording of '*Sada saranga nayane*'/Ranjani. We could even add an eighth, and last, stage of Subbulakshmi *well into retirement*, as in the June 1997 Swaralaya concert.

Subbulakshmi's all-India image and appeal was the result of several conscious decisions and carefully planned moves. *Meera* was the beginning. Frequent *sabha* appearances outside the south certainly helped, as did association with national leaders. Ravi Shankar, Bismillah Khan and Subbulakshmi held a monopoly on all major national and international functions, the Gandhi centenary, the Festivals of India, and such like. But most significant was her decision to expand her repertoire to include bhajans and verses in languages other than the south Indian.

The incorporation of bhajans, mainly in Hindi, into the Carnatic concert was a significant element of Subbulakshmi's performing style. Hindi is not traditionally spoken in south India, but that does not mean that compositions in Hindi cannot be part of the Carnatic music system. Ariyakudi Ramanuja Iyengar composed the music for Andal's Tiruppavai and musicians at all times have set Tamil texts to tune, even texts which may not have been composed for musical performance. Subbulakshmi did the same with bhajans in variants of Hindi.

The evolution of the bhajan tradition and its links to the bhakti movement are subjects which call for detailed study. Subbulakshmi adapted a defined musical form from the north and gave it an unmistakably southern impress. Bhajans are cast in simple language and a loose structure; they spring from deep religious experience, and are widely appealing. In the north Indian tradition, bhajans would be considered popular devotional items, which some Hindustani *vidvans* sing in their concerts, usually as concluding pieces.

Such pieces exist in the Carnatic tradition as well, as for instance the *viruttam, padam, javali, kavadichindu, tillana* and sloka. There are other light pieces of no specific definition, but recognized as *tukkadas*. Subbulakshmi sang all of these with aplomb, but she also sang bhajans of Mira, Surdas, Tulsidas, Narsi Mehta, Kabir, Tukaram and Nanak, most taken from the *Ashrama Bhajanavali* used in Gandhi's ashrams.

A few Bengali songs found their way into her stock and it is possible that she first sang Tagore at the time of the centenary in 1961, when she may have learnt them from Pankaj Mullick.[33] 'He Nutan' and 'Mallika boney' were never to leave her active repertoire, and also 'Jakhan porbe' and 'Tabu mone rekho'. 'He Nutan' has an interesting backstory in that it was possibly one of the last pieces Tagore set to music, a few months before his death in August 1941.[34]

Subbulakshmi acknowledged Dilip Kumar Roy of Pondicherry as her guru in the matter of bhajan singing, but she consciously adapted the style of D.V. Paluskar. She sang Tulsidas's 'Kahan ke pathik kahan' and Surdas's 'Suneri main ne nirbal ke balram' to the basic tune set by Paluskar, but with much more rigour. In general, she disregarded the convention by which singers used the loose structure of bhajans to allow for spontaneity, and instead fitted them into the *pallavi-anupallavi-charanam* format of the *kriti*, and set them to music.

Subbulakshmi's bhajans became an integral part of her musical persona, and hence familiar, and beloved. She had the capacity to render as weighty and concert-worthy the lightest of pieces 'and transform them into powerful musical statements'.[35] Her involvement with the devotional mood helped, and over the years, every honour or citation she received acclaimed her as a devotional singer.

Where the stock of Carnatic songs on display was small, but slowly changing, Subbulakshmi's stock of bhajans never changed.

Four generations of *rasikas* would have heard 'Baso more nayanana mein, Nandalala!', sung in exactly the same way, with the same impassioned '*Mor mukut makarakriti kundala aruna tilaka!*' To large numbers in the south of India, the notion of a bhajan is invariably '*Mein Hari charanana ki dasi*' or '*More to giridhara gopala*', sung exactly as Subbulakshmi sang them. Songs such as '*Giridhara Gopala*', '*Brindavan ki kunj galin mein*', '*Hey harey!*' or '*Ghanashyam aaya re*', which were written for the film *Meera*, became the norm for light classical, filmy numbers.

One particular song, not a bhajan, needs attention, not necessarily because it is well presented but for the sheer unlikeliness of it. The 1974 record of ten songs in ten languages, another of Sadasivam's efforts to project his wife as only a devotional singer, includes a ghazal of Ghalib, a 'brave and bhakti-filled rendition', a piece at once both obscure and erotic, and said to have been taught by Begum Akhtar. It would indeed be charming to believe that the Malika-e-ghazal had herself taught Subbulakshmi this piece but in actual fact it was some now-forgotten musician in Calcutta.[36] A sympathetic critic writes, 'But we must suspend all judgement awhile when MS sings Ghalib; we must try and not judge even ourselves. We must not forget that we are in the presence of a woman capable of charging words in any language with the current of music. Barriers like pronunciation and incomprehension do not come in the way once MS sets her mind on something'.[37]

Purists winced; a tired critic wrote in 1964 that Subbulakshmi's bhajan singing was as unenchanting as *Sangitha Kalanidhi* M. Balamuralikrishna's *ashtapadis* or *Sangitha Kalanidhi* Madurai Mani Iyer's 'western note' but was gracious enough to concede that these items were always presented 'to the delight of the great public'.[38] Many women singers continue to sing bhajans in the same patterned style set by Subbulakshmi. However, we must still ask whether these innovations were for the good.

We can agree that the larger Carnatic music space can accommodate many languages. We can also agree that such an assimilation would be simpler where the texts were religious in nature, as that is the received Carnatic tradition. The point is that a bhajan is a lighter type of composition, if no less lacking in spiritual import, and aimed at attracting the attention of the less knowledgeable listener. The puzzle is why a classical musician of the highest rank should have sought to be identified as a popular singer. This is particularly strange when contrasted with, for instance, Lata Mangeshkar's strenuous claim to belong to the Bhendi Bazar gharana on the strength of her brief training with Ustad Aman Ali Khan.[39]

An assumption, possibly mistaken, made for Subbulakshmi was that there were no takers outside south India for the traditional Carnatic form. It is worth noting that no Hindustani musician of repute would pander to the supposed lack of familiarity of any audience. Bade Ghulam Ali Khan and Ravi Shankar have performed to packed halls in the south. The fabulous Kesarbai Kerkar has sung in Madras as has Siddheshwari Devi, who sang at the Music Academy in 1968, as the guest of Subbulakshmi, who presided over the season's concerts. The vocalist Parveen Sultana has always had very appreciative audiences in Madras. None of these performers made any exception to their customary styles; all of them received a rapturous response.

It is clearly unacceptable, and even simple-minded, to believe that the devotional mood can be evoked only, or mainly, through popular devotional verses. The musicologist Deepak Raja is emphatic on this score. 'To regard devotional lyrics as the exclusive flag-bearers of bhakti in music is a misrepresentation of the character of music as an art, as well as bhakti as a human aspiration.'[40] The strength of the Carnatic tradition is the powerful synthesis of devotion with intellectual and musical rigour. No one who has heard Syama Sastri's *Kamakshi* in Bhairavi, or Muthusvami Dikshitar's *Bhaja re re chitta Balambikam* in Kalyani or Tyagaraja's *Mokshamu galada* in Saramati, to name only three songs drawn by way of examples from Subbulakshmi's repertoire, could be in any doubt of this. The point was made rather more plainly by M.L.Vasanthakumari in her speech at the Music Academy on 21 December 1977: 'The compositions of the Trinity are an amalgam of laya, raga, sahitya and bhava and will instill bhakti even in atheists if they sing them with a full understanding of their meaning.'[41] Or even by the philosopher Simone Weil, as quoted by Pico Iyer as an epigraph at the beginning of a recent book, 'Attention, taken to its highest degree, is the same thing as prayer.'[42]

These questions continue to engage us. An artiste of Subbulakshmi's calibre would have drawn crowds anywhere, and did not need to create a genre of performance that was distinctly lowbrow.

Subbulakshmi's personality and manner became an essential part of her image, and no discussion of the musician can avoid the public perception of the woman. To some admirers, there was '... perfect harmony between her musical personality and her actual persona. Both had the same ephemeral, luminous quality.'[43] A family member noted that '[b]eing kind and sensitive towards others were woven into her music, her fame, her very being'.[44] Years earlier, Rukmini Devi had said of her, 'Not only her voice but the fact that she is a lady of highest refinement and character has won her a special place in India.'[45] In a 2019 birthday tribute to Subbulakshmi on social media, Lata Mangeshkar used the Hindustani word '*shaleen*' to describe her. *Shaleen* is not easy to translate and could mean any or all of graceful, elegant, cultivated, refined or courteous, all of which can be used to describe Subbulakshmi.

Goodness, humility and devotion can be said to be the three attributes most often spoken of in relation to Subbulakshmi, most often recalled and most often identified as the qualities which shaped her music. Along with a few, a very few, of her contemporaries, Subbulakshmi is remembered as 'a noble soul'.[46] Her very publicized singing for charity – not that she was the only musician who performed for worthy causes – strengthened this image. It is not her talent, or her diligence or discipline, or her extraordinary musicality which identifies her in the public imagination but her image as a pious and charitable bhakta. Even accepting that this image was chosen for her, one cannot help reflecting that an injustice has been done. By all accounts Subbulakshmi was an extraordinarily good woman, gentle, gracious and seemingly without any airs but, as we have seen, she was primarily a musician of enormous significance for the tradition she represented.

When the musician *Sangitha Kalanidhi* M. Balamuralikrishna (1930–2016) passed on, a music critic was reported as having said that Balamuralikrishna himself ascribed his many eccentricities to *vidyagarvam*, or pride in one's scholarship.[47] Certainly an artiste cannot be unaware of her stature, howsoever modest her demeanour, and it is entirely possible that Subbulakshmi knew exactly where she stood. But she did not, in all her public interactions, allow this knowledge of who she was to take away from her natural kindliness and grace of manner.

However, there is also the extraordinary suggestion that for all her gifts, Subbulakshmi, at the time when it came to making decisions for herself, was really only looking for security and safety, for respectability even, all possibilities represented by the ambitious, if married, Sadasivam. Radha Viswanathan believed this to be true, believing that Subbulakshmi was '...first and foremost a family woman and only then a musician'.[48] If this were truly the case, it speaks of considerable modesty and humility, attributes of which Radha was well aware.[49] This further implies that even if she were subordinate to Sadasivam's directions in all matters personal and musical, it was still only 'because she willed it'.[50] And it is possible that she had willed it because for all that she was a performing artiste capable of the most sublime creativity, she would still rather not carry what in her mind was the slur of courtesan.

Is it that she 'longed for freedom, for release from the social stigma of being a devadasi?'[51] And towards this end was she prepared to 'submit completely to the demands made of her in terms of content and perfection of delivery and never entertain the thought of indulging in her own artistic urges?'[52] We still do not have a picture of her own musical imagination, though she is on record as saying that Sadasivam was responsible for guiding and directing her musical expression which was otherwise running wild.[53] We will never know what more wildness would have produced.

Subbulakshmi's religious devotion was publicly worn. 'M.S. wears her faith as a flaming livery of devotion. That is perhaps why one does not find in her music that indrawn quality which is the mark of personal identity.'[54] She was seen always as singing not for the joy of performance, or the thrill of creativity or the quiet satisfaction of being in control, but for the love of the divine. Often she was herself regarded as divine.

The story has been frequently told of *Sangitha Kalanidhi* Chembai Vaidyanatha Bhagavathar, as beloved amongst his peers as amongst his audiences, weeping with joy and devotion at hearing Subbulakshmi sing.[55] The dancer Rhadha recalls that to her mother, 'MS was a goddess.'[56] A *rasika* observed of her that her smile 'had a unique divinity, a holiness, which compelled the most conceited to surrender voluntarily with reverence and respect' – a somewhat overblown expression but spoken from the heart.[57] Another commented, 'MS Amma was the spark of Divine Splendour.'[58] The contemporary music historian Sriram V. calls her an 'angel in human shape'.[59] *Sangitha Kalanidhi* R. Vedavalli observed that 'MS Amma was born to sing chaste and beautiful music.'[60] *Sangitha Kalanidhi* Aruna Sairam says, 'MS Amma to me is divinity personified.'[61] To *Sangitha Kalanidhi* S. Sowmya she is 'an embodiment of love'.[62] Musician and teacher Premeela Gurumurthy, who grew up in Colombo in the 1950s, recalls that for her parents 'M.S.Subbulakshmi was like a goddess.'[63] This perception, and this was true even among people whom Subbulakshmi did not know personally, was widespread.

Subbulakshmi's few available public statements reinforce this conviction. 'Music itself has only one purpose – that of divine communication.'[64] Addressing the Music Academy in December 1968, she expressed the view that music had 'the higher purpose of directing the minds of the listeners towards God and His manifestations'.[65] Two decades later, at the same venue, she again urged, 'It is Bhakti alone that constitutes the root and fruit of our music.'[66] In an interview given even later in life she said, 'It is not enough to be able to sing; one must feel deeply. Otherwise one is merely singing a collection of words and clever musical phrases.'[67]

There is a larger question here. The art music of south India, to use a phrase which is slightly more accurate than classical music, is built fundamentally on a foundation of composed pieces almost exclusively religious in content and orientation. Some pieces sung in concerts today will live forever in the canons of devotional literature. Subbulakshmi was a believer, and regarded herself as blessed that she was able, through her art, to communicate her faith, and possibly enable her listeners to believe likewise. This leaves the difficult question of what the non-believing musician is expected to do, and if she could build a career of performance based on received texts which to her are, simply, texts.

To regard music as a means to attain the divine is not necessarily a conventional, or uniquely Indian, notion. As the contemporary modern musician A.R. Rahman has said, 'Music is a penance. You cannot have anything impure in it.'[68] Art music of the western European tradition has both secular and religious pieces, including set works composed for the organ to be played in church during worship. However, the suggestion is not often made that the classical western European musician necessarily be a man or a woman of faith. This suggestion is not made in the Hindustani tradition, where there are routinely both secular and religious themes. The Carnatic tradition, however, has consistently laboured with the notion that a successful or gifted musician is *necessarily* one who responds to the religious impulse as much as the famous composers did. Subbulakshmi certainly regarded this as an essential truth of her art, as did most of her contemporaries. It is only in more recent times that the question is being asked of whether this is so, and it is not easy to answer.

Subbulakshmi was a master performer with a voice, repertoire, training and opportunities to propel her stardom. Her all-India appeal was linked to her fame as a singer of devotional verses, so much so that she was seen as to be imbued with divinity herself. She firmly represented the widely accepted view that religious belief was an integral part of musical understanding. There is one last aspect to which we must return, which is caste.

Caste is subtly incorporated into the representation of music. The scholar Amanda Weidman, who has studied the linkages between the growth of nationalism and its manifestation through the female voice, suggests that Subbulakshmi became The Voice. As a country or society looked towards regeneration, or in the case of India, independence, it became necessary to establish and document the older cultural and artistic traditions, with a singing voice of a 'respectable' woman, in itself combining notions of purity, chastity, domesticity, 'classicism', tradition, each of these nebulous concepts defined, of course, by the ruling elite, becoming the 'voice of the nation'. 'The new discourse on classical music combined ideas of art and the artist with a notion of Indianness formed in opposition to the West, and a sense of the central role of music in defining what it meant to be modern while retaining a safely delineated realm called "tradition".'[69]

If Subbulakshmi had to be seen as representing 'tradition' and 'respectability' a change of image was necessary. If she was to be the 'voice of the nation', could she have been depicted as anything other than a conservative, chaste, old-fashioned, respectable, Brahmin woman?[70] This matter has recently been asked again and for all the liveliness of the debate the relevant issues have been confused by an excited social media and it is necessary to parse out the points made.

Subbulakshmi cast aside her past, and the way of life that went with the courtesan tradition of south India, willingly and seemingly without regret. Only this can explain her extraordinary action in seeking the protection, if not the affection, of a married man outside of her circle. The process of Sanskritization, for that is precisely what it was, is well studied and Subbulakshmi was by no means the only person looking at this avenue for upward social mobility. From the world of the arts itself we have, at the same time, both Kanan Devi and Begum Akhtar who made similar marriages, for similar purposes.

Then there is the question of whether Subbulakshmi's repertoire, singing style and musicality changed, and for the worse, by the transformation in her social situation. There is comparatively little of her music now available from the early years and even from the later years, the public imagination has been swamped by the frequent reissue of the Annamacharya and subsequent recordings, primarily of the simple bhakti variety. It is certainly possible to say that in the first part of her career, the first three stages of the eight stages we have seen earlier, there was a much wider display of what she had to offer. In the later years, even when she stayed within the boundaries of the established *margam*, it is possible to see an excessive regimentation and repetition. The difficulty, of course, is that she was so very skilled at communicating – ironically, the hallmark of a devadasi's art – to a receptive audience.[71]

Given that Subbulakshmi went along with the changes that were demanded of her, in her associations and lifestyle, in her musical understanding and choices and dutifully accepted, even sought, the image of Brahmin respectability – the ideal aesthetic of the Tamil Brahmin woman – is it then the case that this is what won her the adoration of her public?[72] There is also the larger charge against Subbulakshmi that if she were prominent in the public representation of art music as an upper-caste, Brahmin preoccupation, it was only taking the form itself further away from its subaltern roots.[73]

On reflection, these charges do not hold.

This may well have been true of a lesser artiste, one who needed the acceptance of the concert-going public, but not of one with a talent such as she possessed. In positing that Subbulakshmi sought the image she acquired because she saw this as the way to public esteem does her little credit, and denies the potential of great artistry to display itself. If the argument is that the listening public saw in her the embodiment of what it admired as upper-caste purity, then that is really more to do with the public than with her. And even if Subbulakshmi chose to cast away what she saw as her lower-caste origins, it did not at any stage mean that she also cast away her sense of tradition or of her musical ancestry.

None of this can deny the dominance, often highly exclusionary, of the upper castes today over the intricate network of teachers, students, cultural administrators, *sabha* organizers, audiences, music and dance critics which constitutes the ecosystem of contemporary Carnatic music. The implications of this situation will continue to be debated. A historian of south India has recently offered the conservative, and undoubtedly contentious, view that '[f]or all the privileges they awarded themselves and for all the discrimination that this engendered, the Brahmins were and still are a quite extraordinary phenomenon, not just as keepers of the Vedic flame over millennia but as a small cadre of largely unsung intellectuals, scientists and healers whose learning brought great lustre to their culture'.[74] Even if we admit the lustre, the shadow cast is of significant concern.

Subbulakshmi's voice, style and *kriti* rendering made her an obvious role model for both aspiring and established women musicians. Even today, women who could possibly have never heard Subbulakshmi in concert adopt what they see as the 'MS style'. In her own lifetime, of course, Subbulakshmi inspired younger musicians.[75] Mani Krishnaswami is quoted as saying, 'The richness of her voice, the melody of her music and the impeccable diction of the lyrics made me follow her style.'[76] C. Saroja and C. Lalitha were said to 'have succeeded in emulating M.S. Subbulakshmi'.[77] Aruna Sairam has observed that Subbulakshmi's voice besides being powerful and melodious also 'gives you an experience of being in the presence of something permanent *and* ethereal'.[78] And no less than D.K. Pattammal said of Subbulakshmi that 'there is restraint in everything that she attempts, be it the delineation of a raga, or the rendering of *kriti* or *swara*. Her golden voice is of course a gift from the gods: it can capture and enrapture everyone.'[79]

Subbulakshmi appealed even to individuals who had no exposure to her art form. A young American cellist of Indian ancestry describes going through 'a period of listening to Subbulakshmi's Carnegie Hall concert frequently. I still don't understand the intricacies but now I can appreciate that it stems from the same universal language that also produced Western classical music. And I find it very beautiful.'[80] The Tyagaraja scholar William J. Jackson has recalled his enchantment at hearing 'the incomparable MS' in 1977 at Cambridge, Massachusetts, long before his own deep understanding of the Carnatic form had developed.[81] And Paula Richman, the scholar of the Ramayana, has spoken of being 'mesmerized' when she first heard Subbulakshmi in 1976.[82]

Kanan Devi and Begum Akhtar are important in understanding that Subbulakshmi was not alone in the circumstances she faced or in making the decisions she did; but they were all very different women in their world view, their imagination and their style. Kanan Bala, 'born on the flip side of society' made the transformation into Kanan Devi, the daughter-in-law of Brahmo orthodoxy, but always lived life on her own terms. She never really assimilated upper-caste and upper-class mores and when one marriage failed she made another. Like Subbulakshmi 'she spelled charm, glamour, dazzle, grace to India's fledgling middle class' but when her glamour began to fade, she disappeared into anonymity.[83]

Akhtari Bai Faizabadi, later Begum Akhtar, like Kanan Devi and Subbulakshmi, conjured wonder.

The impact of Begum Akhtar's music and personality on our generation is in many ways an inexplicable phenomenon. Many of her contemporaries were as gifted, as well-trained, and as much in command of their audiences as she was. Some were decidedly more hard-working and unlike her did not spare themselves in the matter of discipline and practice. Many had larger repertoires and more extensive vocal ranges. Their singing styles were more elaborate and complicated than hers, and their musical material far more sophisticated. Yet her voice had a magic nothing can explain and this special something had very little to do with musical skill or training.[84]

There is much here that can apply to Subbulakshmi, including one crucial feature, her voice had a magic nothing can explain.

Begum Akhtar left behind her *tawa'if* mother's life but never forgot it. She is on record as saying, 'You don't have a choice of your birth. You are born here. You must accept your birth,'[85] and the difference between her past and later lives caused her distress.[86] Subbulakshmi left Madurai but it is impossible that she forgot Madurai or Shanmukhavadivu and, for all that Subbulakshmi's personal life was a closed book, several of her associates have hinted at unspoken sorrows. 'She could, and did, often shed tears. She experienced grief, disillusionment, tragedy.'[87]

If Subbulakshmi was seen to be giving utterance to the voice of the nation, there were women of her age in many cultures and musical traditions, in many countries of the world, who were recognized as The Voice. As was said of one of them, 'These are voices that transcend generations, and will sound down the ages.'[88] Umm Kulthum (1904–75), Edith Piaf (1915–63), Ella Fitzgerald (1917–96), Maria Callas (1923–77) and Joan Sutherland (1926–2010) were five such divas, women of phenomenal gifts and distinction, women who raised performance to a new level altogether, women who were national icons.

Born in a simple village home and growing up singing religious songs, Umm Kulthum became a cultural symbol of her country, Egypt, and the face and voice of Arab music around the world.[89] Her career coincided with the growth of radio in Egypt and it was said that Egypt came to a halt at the time of her weekly radio broadcasts. She sang a range of traditional Arab songs, always investing pre-composed songs with her own, often entirely spontaneous, improvisations. Much was always made of her knowledge of the Qur'an, her piety, the nobility of her character and her deep connections with the peasantry and villages of Egypt. She was a successful professional and was widely regarded as having raised the status of musicians in society. When she died, millions thronged the streets of Cairo. Forty years after her passing, she is remembered as an iconic Arab woman even if musical tastes in the Arab world have changed. Umm Kulthum's biographer said of her, 'Imagine a singer with the virtuosity of Joan Sutherland or Ella Fitzgerald, the public persona of Eleanor Roosevelt and the audience of Elvis and you have Om Kalthoum.'[90]

Subbulakshmi paid a much-publicized visit to Umm Kulthum in Cairo in 1966. This was possibly the idea of V.K. Narayana Menon, the reigning cultural czar, and it was an inspired suggestion. In her time, Subbulakshmi came to enjoy the same national status, and for similar reasons.

The plaque over the doorway of a house in the 20th arrondissement in Paris states, 'On the steps to this house there was born on 19 December 1915, in utter destitution, Edith Piaf, whose voice was later to shatter the world.'[91] As it happens, Edith Gassion, the daughter of Louis-Alphonse Gassion and Anetta Maillard, was not actually born in that house but the sentiment is true. Piaf's upbringing was distinctly unorthodox. Her part-Algerian mother's people were circus performers; at a time she, having been effectively abandoned by her mother, lodged in a brothel with her father's mother. Her early years were spent mainly in singing in cheap clubs and bars, or while accompanying her father's street acrobatics. A sudden break when she was twenty catapulted her into one of the better clubs of Paris, and then there was no looking back.

A series of mentors, for want of a better word, helped put together a repertoire which suited Piaf's voice and style and her fame spread. After the war, she travelled to the United States and farther afield, but she was really always the quintessential singer from the streets of Paris, raw, hurting and magnificent. Piaf died young, when she was only forty-seven. Parisians in their thousands paid their respects at the Pere Lachaise cemetery, where she rests along with Oscar Wilde, Chopin, Proust, Modigliani and Jim Morrison. Piaf is still a national treasure in France and around the world the name Edith Piaf still evokes the name of her most celebrated song, *Non, je ne regrette rien*, I regret nothing.

Ella Fitzgerald was, quite simply, the Queen of Jazz. As an adoring tribute says, 'She performed at top venues all over the world, and packed them to the hilt. Her audiences were as diverse as her vocal range. They were rich and poor, made up of all races, all religions and all nationalities. In fact, many of them had just one binding factor in common – they all loved her.'[92] The child of a broken home, Fitzgerald had no training of any sort but her natural talent attracted attention and by the time she was twenty-one, her record sales were soaring. Her first recording was in 1935 and for the next twenty years faced no competition. It was said of her that 'she could always make any song better than it was, but it is also true that, the better the song, the better Ella sings'.[93] Over her career, she sang at New York's Carnegie Hall a record twenty-six times and lives on in the collective musical memory of America and the world.

The flamboyant Maria Callas was born in America, to unhappily married parents, and began her musical education in New York, but it was in her native Greece where, still in her teens, she made her sensational debut in 1940. Callas achieved spectacular fame, but aroused bitter resentment among opera lovers, and her dramatic private life kept her always in the news.[94] Her voice was not considered suitable for classical opera but she established a technique of her own, and made every role she sang her own.

'No singer of her time, and very few in history, could so dominate an audience,' wrote an obituarist in the *New York Times,* who went on to commend her 'unique combination of electricity and brains'. And there is an observation that could apply absolutely to Subbulakshmi. 'She immersed herself in her roles, studying every word and every phrase for maximum musical and dramatic effect. Her singing was full of subtle inflections, accentuations, shadings, that were foreign territory to most other sopranos.'[95]

Joan Sutherland was born in Australia, in marginally better circumstances, and made her first London appearance at around the same time as Callas. Sutherland, for all her raging talent, was a much more modest woman who applied herself to what she knew was her strength, a voice she believed to God-given. Early in the 1950s, she caught the attention of the impresario and music administrator Lord Harewood (who later invited Subbulakshmi to Edinburgh in 1963), but her entry on to the world stage was at Covent Garden in 1959, in *Lucia di Lammermoor*. She was in her late thirties, but if she had made a late entrance, she never, after that, left centre stage. She was praised for her technique, her discipline, her vocal stamina and her strong work ethic. And it was said of her that if she was modest and even humble off stage, 'on stage she radiated glamour and star quality'. Joan Sutherland received the Order of Merit[96] and when she passed on was hailed as 'without a doubt one of the greatest singers of her time'.[97]

Subbulakshmi and her sisters, in their vastly different spaces, had their commonalities. All came from very modest backgrounds and had distinctly unstable upbringings. In one way or another, their mothers were a formative influence, and not always happily so. Each one of them had to work very hard for all that they achieved. And all of them embodied the maxim attributed to the 'divine Melba', 'When you are climbing up, you just do your best. When you are the diva, you have to be the best always.'[98]

With all the limitations she imposed on herself, Subbulakshmi was without doubt amongst the greatest performing artistes of her century. The musician and raconteuse Sheila Dhar has distinguished between 'musicians', 'those who forged the language of music' and the 'performers', virtuoso artistes 'whose accomplishment, no less considerable on a different stage, is mistakenly demeaned by comparison'. In the category of 'musicians' were Zohrabai, Kesarbai Kerkar, Gangubai Hangal, Mallikarjun Mansur, Bade Ghulam Ali Khan and Amir Khan. The 'performers' included Bhimsen Joshi, Begum Akhtar and Rashid Khan. Dhar notes, somewhat acidly, that Kishori Amonkar could belong to either category 'depending on her mood on a particular day'.[99]

Subbulakshmi drew from a family heritage of performance, but it cannot be denied that she added to the language and practice of music. Subbulakshmi, Pattammal and Vasanthakumari all broke away from the convention that women musicians merely purveyed what they were taught. They transformed their inheritance into something uniquely their own, exposing listeners over the years to different aspects of their art.

It was given to these three remarkable musicians to establish the fact of women singing publicly, as professional performing artistes. The flautist and scholar Ludwig Pesch has observed that a fundamental change in the conditions under which women sang in public was 'not achieved until the family of Vina Dhanammal and her descendants began to assert its proper place in Carnatic music'.[100] There is an ongoing, lively debate on the nature and importance of the Dhanammal *bani*, with very aggressive proponents of the belief that a hereditary tradition of musical learning is the only true tradition. Dhanammal has had enormous influence, more since her death than in her lifetime, and is remembered for her insistence on preserving the sanctity of tradition, but she and her family did not really pave the way for women artistes. That distinction belongs to Subbulakshmi, Pattammal and Vasanthakumari, singers each of overwhelming presence and immense ability.

For over fifty years, M.S. Subbulakshmi was the voice and face of Carnatic music. What remains are fragments of songs, heard and never forgotten: 'Sritajana paripalam Gopalam balam' from *Sri Krishnam*, or 'Shatodari Shankari Chamundeswari Chandrakaladhari Gauri' from *Mathe malayadhwaja*, or 'Ek tum hi ab dhani hamare, Krishna nata nagara!' from the song in *Meera*, 'Kannulaku ni sogasento' from 'Ninnu vina', 'Vinave na manavini, vini nannu brovumu' from *Janani*, 'Brahmakaina telusuno, teliyado?' from *Sankalpame*, 'Kamaksi ninnu vina bhoomilo premato kapadevarevarunnaru?' from *Devi brova samayamide*, 'Valli Deivayanai manavala va' from 'Ka Va Va', or the staccato 'Kripanidhi!' from *Sabhapati*. Thanks to technology, her long, soaring phrases from brilliantly constructed *alapanas*, the Sankarabharanam, the Simhendramadhyamam, the Kharaharapriya and the Pantuvarali, all still engage new listeners. 'Every day MS's music stops someone somewhere in the world. As for her life, those who observed it can recall an unbroken harmony of goodness and beauty.'[101] Such was the life and art of Subbulakshmi of Madurai, the daughter of Shanmukhavadivu.

Notes

PREFACE

1. Maud Mann begins her *Some Indian Conceptions of Music* (London: Theosophical Publishing Company, 1913) with the line 'There is a beautiful custom in some parts of India, of invoking the goddess of poetry, eloquence and music before commencing any study, public or private' after which she quotes, and appears to have sung when the text of her paper was presented in London on 16 January 1912, Muthusvami Dikshitar's *'Kalavati'* in the raga Kalavati. The translation is that of Mrs Mann.
2. Chitra Banerjee Divakaruni, Jaipur Literary Festival, 20 January 2017.
3. Vishnu Vasudev, 'Happy 95th: the sublime comfort of M.S. Subbulakshmi', blog of 16 September 2011.
4. Gowri Ramnarayan, 'Mukti – Voicing Freedom', in Gowri Ramnarayan, Savita Narasimhan and V. Ramnarayan (eds), *Song of Surrender, A Centenary Tribute to M.S. Subbulakshmi*, Chennai: The Sruti Foundation, 2016.
5. Aeolus, 'In Memorium', *Shankar's Weekly*, 29 January 1967.
6. Conversation between M.S. Subbulakshmi and Bandana Mukhopadhyay, a member of the Indian Information Service and senior official of All India Radio, New Delhi, 29 February 1998.

7. Gopalkrishna Gandhi, speech on 15 September 2010 at Chennai, reported in *The Hindu*, Chennai, 16 September 2010.
8. Hoshang Merchant, M.S. *Subbulakshmi Sings Meera*, 1973/2016, Purdue/Hyderabad; http://scroll.in/article/816578/how-ms-subbulakshmi-inspired-hoshang-merchant-to-write-his-first-ever-poem.
9. Shama Futehally, *Songs of Meera: In the Dark of the Heart*, New Delhi: HarperCollins *Publishers* India, 1994.

1: SANGITA VADYA VINODINI

1. '*Bhakti* is derived from the root, *bhaj*, to serve, and means service of the Lord', S. Radhakrishnan, *The Bhagavadgita*, New Delhi: HarperCollins *Publishers* India, 1993, originally published 1948.
2. Tony Joseph, 'How genetics is settling the Aryan migration debate', *The Hindu*, Chennai, 16 June 2017. This fascinating discussion has been further developed by the author in *Early Indians*, New Delhi: Juggernaut, 2018. The argument based on archaeological and other evidence that the population of the subcontinent today is descended from succeeding waves of migrants from elsewhere is disputed by a more 'nationalistic' school of thought which believes that there were no migrations and the subcontinent has had at all times an entirely indigenous population. The matter continues to rage in the national press. See Tony Joseph, 'Who were the Harappans? Who were the Arya?', *The Hindu*, Chennai, 15 September 2019.
3. S. Radhakrishnan, *Indian Philosophy: The Vedas and the Six Systems*, Madras: Madras Christian College, Vol. XXVI, July 1908–June 1909.
4. Emmie te Nijenhuis, *A History of Indian Literature, Musicological Literature*, Wiesbaden: Otto Harrassowitz, 1977.
5. Kalidasa's dates are contested but fifth century AD is a good approximation. Interestingly, scholars have, on the basis of internal and textual evidence, estimated the chronological order of Kalidasa's works, while there is considerable contestation on what his actual dates are.
6. Clarence Maloney, 'The Beginnings of Civilization in South India', *The Journal of Asian Studies*, Vol. 29, No. 3 (May 1970).

7. Emmie te Nujenhuis and Sanjukta Gupta, *Sacred Songs of India: Dikshitar's Cycle of Hymns to the Goddess Kamala*, Part I, Winterthur, Switzerland: Forum Ethnomusicologicum 3, Amadeus 1987.
8. V. Raghavan, *The Great Integrators*, Patel Memorial Lectures, 1964. This discussion is elaborated in John Stratton Hawley, *A Storm of Songs, India and the Idea of the Bhakti Movement*, Cambridge, Massachusetts: Harvard University Press, 2015. Map 2 on page 22 is particularly suggestive.
9. Emmie te Nujenhuis and Sanjukta Gupta, *Sacred Songs of India*...
10. Kabir's dates are alternately given as 1398–1448 or as 1440–1518; see also Ranjit Hoskote, 'Kabir: The Paradoxical Saint', *Open*, 5 July 2019.
11. Davesh Soneji, 'The Powers of Polyglossia: Marathi Kīrtan, Multilingualism, and the Making of a South Indian Devotional Tradition', *International Journal of Hindu Studies*, Vol. 17, No. 3 (December 2013).
12. Emmie te Nujenhuis and Sanjukta Gupta, *Sacred Songs of India*...
13. Aeolus, 'The Utopian and the Absolute', *Shankar's Weekly*, 2 October 1966.
14. Mrinal Pande, 'While Hindi chauvinists abandon the language and opt for "English" medium, its isolation from Urdu weakens it', *National Herald*, New Delhi, 20 September 2020.
15. Chapter 1, 'Religion, Culture and Art: Man's Spiritual Universe', in Pradip Kumar Sengupta, *Foundations of Indian Musicology*, New Delhi: Abhinav Publications, 1991.
16. Aneesh Pradhan, 'Listen: Decoding the shruti, the smallest detectable note in Indian classical music', Scroll, 3 January 2017. This article also has Vidyadhar Oke demonstrating each of the twenty-two *srutis* on the harmonium, a very neat introduction to what is otherwise a complicated notion.
17. Lakshmi Subramanian, *From the Tanjore Court to the Madras Music Academy, A Social History of Music in South India*, Oxford and New Delhi: Oxford University Press, 2006.
18. Robert E. Brown, sleeve notes to long playing record, *Ten Graces*, Nonesuch Explorer Series LP (H-72027).

19. Such as the *Svaramela Kalanidhi* of Ramamatya (1550) and the *Raga-Vibodha* of Somanatha (1614). See also Emmie te Nijenhuis, *A History of Indian Literature, Musicological Literature*.
20. Lakshmi Subramanian, *From the Tanjore Court to the Madras Music Academy...*
21. Robert Brown, 'Introduction to the Music of South India', from Festival of Oriental Music and the Related Arts, University of California at Los Angeles, 1960. 'The essence of Indian melody is summed up in the word raga. If one has some grasp of what a raga is, he is well on the way to an elementary understanding of the Indian musical aesthetic. Because it is modal music, the raga is first of all a scale. The exclusive use of a certain fixed group of tones gives each raga an individual character which is one of the essential unities of the music. No foreign tones can be added, therefore the music can never modulate or change key.'
22. G.H. Ranade, *Hindustani Music, Its Physics and Aesthetics*, Bombay: Popular Prakashan, 1971 (3rd edition). Reviewed by Chetan Karnani in *Quest* 73, November-December 1971.
23. All, as it happens, ragas which would be regarded as more appropriate for light numbers. It is hard to think of a major concert raga, capable of creative interpretation by a Carnatic musician, which is identified as a borrowing from Hindustani music.
24. R.R. Diwakar, Minister of State for Information and Broadcasting, Government of India, reported in *The Hindu*, Madras, 14 March 1951; G. N. Balasubramanian, 20 December 1958, Speech at the Music Academy, Madras.
25. Aeolus, 'The function of the song', *Shankar's Weekly*, 18 September 1966.
26. Ibid.
27. Peggy Holroyde, *The Music of India*, Westport, Connecticut: Praeger Publishers, 1972.
28. Narayana Menon, 'The Music of India', in S. Radhakrishnan (ed.), *A Centenary Volume, Rabindranath Tagore 1861-1961*, New Delhi: Sahitya Akademi, 1992.
29. John M. Rosenfield, 'India, Rasa and Raga', from Festival of Oriental Music and the Related Arts, University of California at Los Angeles, 1960.

30. 'Performance proceeds from a religious sensibility, however diffuse the term "religion" may be', Susan L. Schwartz, *Rasa, Performing the Divine in India*, New Jersey: Columbia University Press, 2004.
31. Formerly Tanjore. Members of the family of T. Dhanammal always spelt the word as Tanjavur.
32. For a detailed study of these texts, see T.M. Krishna, *A Southern Music, The Karnatik Story*, Noida: HarperCollins Publishers India, 2013.
33. Muddu Venkatamakhin's work inspired in later years the *Sangita Sampradaya Pradarsini* (1904) of Subbarama Dikshitar and the *Hindustani Sangeet Paddhati* (1909 onwards in four volumes) of Vishnu Narayan Bhatkhande.
34. V. Raghavan, Introduction to *Music Program of M.S. Subbulakshmi*, 1966, privately printed and circulated.
35. B. Chaitanya Deva, *An Introduction to Indian Music*, New Delhi: Publications Division, 1973.
36. Quoted in S. Anand, 'Cauvery in a Puddle', *Outlook*, 21 January 2002.
37. Yoshitaka Terada, 'T.N. Rajarattinam Pillai and Caste Rivalry in South Indian Classical Music', *Ethnomusicology*, Vol. 44, No. 3, Fall 2000.
38. *Hindu Music and the Gayan Samaj*, Published in Aid of the Funds of the Madras Jubilee Gayan Samaj, Bombay: The Bombay Gazette Steam Press, 1887.
39. Tacchhuru Singaracharyulu and Tacchhuru Chinna Singaracharyulu, *Gayakasiddhanjanam*, Part II, Madras: Ganallosini Office, 1905.
40. This may also be the person referred to as Tiruvarur Peria Kamala Muthammal in a lecture by B.M. Sundaram, 25 December 2000, at the Music Academy, Chennai, 'Pioneer among divine composers', *The Hindu*, Chennai, 5 January 2001.
41. These details are taken from the wall charts at the TAG Digital Centre, Music Academy, Chennai.
42. Aeolus, 'Cymbals and Seven Strings', *Shankar's Weekly*, 11 August 1963.
43. Aeolus, 'Story and Song', *Shankar's Weekly*, 19 March 1967; also M. Premeela, 'Harikatha – A Composite Art Form', *Kalakshetra Quarterly*, Vol. IX, No. 4, 1988.
44. Lakshmi Subramanian, 'Negotiating Orientalism: The Kaccheri and the Critic in Colonial South India', in Martin Clayton and Bennett Zon (eds.), *Music and Orientalism in the British Empire, 1780s-1940s, Portrayal of the East*, Abingdone, Oxfordshire and New Delhi: Routledge, 2016.

45. Ananda Coomaraswamy, article in *The Musical Quarterly*, Vol. III, No. 2, April 1917.
46. T. Viswanathan and Matthew Harp Allen, *Music in South India*, Oxford and New Delhi: Oxford University Press, 2004; see also *Hindu Music and the Gayan Samaj*, 1887. The Madras branch was supported by Maharaja Sahib Pusapati Sir Ananda III Gajapathi Raju Manea Sultan Bahadur, (1850–97), 12th Zamindar of Vizianagaram, and an early patron of T. Dhanammal.
47. David Shulman, 'A sublime experience', *The Hindu*, Chennai, 21 March 2010.
48. Tacchhuru Singaracharyulu and Tacchhuru Chinna Singaracharyulu, *Gayakasiddhanjanam*, Part II. Tanjore is, of course, Thanjavur and Pudukkottai, Tirunelveli, Mysuru and Vizianagaram are referred to by earlier names.
49. V. Raghavan, in his study of the *Sarva Deva Vilasa*, a text written around 1800, notes that even before the establishment of the *sabhas*, the temples and merchant families of Madras were known as patrons of the arts, and of courtesan musicians and dancers. V. Raghavan, 'Music, artists and patrons of yore', *Sruti*, Vol. 27, No. 8, August 2020.
50. The phenomenon referred to as 'the invention of tradition'. See Eric Hobsbawm, 'Inventing Traditions', in Eric Hobsbawm and Terence Ranger (eds), *The Invention of Tradition*, Cambridge: Cambridge University Press, 1983.
51. Kathleen L'Armand and Adrian L'Armand, 'Music in Madras', in Bruno Nettl (ed.), *Eight Urban Musical Cultures, Tradition and Change*, Urbana: University of Illinois Press, 1978.
52. Kanakalatha Mukund, 'New Social Elites and the Early Colonial State: Construction of Identity and Patronage in Madras', *Economic and Political Weekly*, Vol. 38, No. 27, 5–11 July 2003.
53. The Madras Mahajana Sabha Golden Jubilee souvenir, 8 October 1936.
54. *The Madras Mail*, 20 August 1883.
55. Sriram V., 'The December Season', Talk in Chennai, 15 December 2016.
56. Jon B. Higgins, 'From Prince to Populace: Patronage as a Determinant of Change in South Indian (Karnatak) Music', *Asian Music*, Vol. 7, No. 2, 1976.

57. Achhuru Singaracharyulu and Achhuru Chinna Singaracharyulu, *Ganendusekharam*, Madras, 1912. (These persons are referred to in the literature as the Tachhur Brothers, see Note 48 above, though their names, written in the Telugu script, are given as Achhuru.)
58. *The Garland Encyclopedia of World Music, Volume 5, South Asia: The Indian Subcontinent*, New York: Garland Publishing Inc., 2005.
59. The nagasvaram is a double-reed wind instrument, held to be auspicious, and played in temples and on festive occasions such as weddings. It is often called nadasvaram though the Sanskritist V. Raghavan has held definitively that the word 'nagasvaram' is correct. V. Raghavan, 'Nagaswara or Nadasvara?' in *Collected Works on Indian Music*, Vol. III, Chennai: Dr. Raghavan Centre for Performing Arts, 2007.
60. Janaki Nair, 'The Devadasi, Dharma and the State', *Economic and Political Weekly*, 10 December 1994.
61. Vasudha Narayanan, 'Brimming with Bhakti, Embodiments of Shakti: Devotees, Deities, Performers, Reformers, and Other Women of Power in the Hindu Tradition', in Arvind Sharma and Katherine K. Young (eds.), *Feminism and World Religions*, New York: SUNY Press, 1999.
62. The scholar Leslie Orr has noted that the term devadasi was itself rarely encountered before the twentieth century though the institution to which the term referred was known for over a thousand years. See Leslie C. Orr, *Donors, Devotees and Daughters of God, Temple Women in Medieval Tamilnadu*, Oxford: Oxford University Press, 2000.
63. Vasudha Narayanan, 'Performing Arts, Reforming Rituals: Women and Social Change in India', in Tracy Pintchman (ed.), *Women's Lives, Women's Rituals in the Hindu Traditions*, New York: Oxford University Press, 2007.
64. Speech by T. Balasaraswati at Indian Fine Arts Society, December 1981, reproduced in *Sruti*, Vol. 25, Issue 2, February 2018, p.22.
65. Amrit Srinivasan, 'Gurukulam', *Kalakshetra Journal*, Issue 2, 2014.
66. Mrinal Pande, 'Lage raho, Naresh bhai', *The Indian Express*, New Delhi, 15 March 2018.
67. Amrit Srinivasan, 'Reform and Revival: The Devadasi and her Dance', *Economic and Political Weekly*, Vol. XX, No. 44, 2 November 1985.

68. Review by Lakshmi Subramanian of K.K. Jordan, *From Sacred Servant to Profane Prostitute: A History of Changing Legal Status of the Devadasis in India 1857-1947*, Delhi: Manohar, 2003, in *South Asia*, Vol. XXVII, No. 3, December 2004.
69. Judith Lynne Hanna, 'Music and the Art of Seduction', *Dance Research Journal*, Vol. 37, No. 1, University of Amsterdam, 19–22 May, 2005.
70. Davesh Soneji, 'Siva's Courtesans: Religion, Rhetoric and Self-Representation in Early Twentieth Century Writings of Devadasis', *International Journal of Hindu Studies*, Vol. 14, No. 1, April 2010.
71. Joep Bor, 'Mamia, Ammani and other Bayaderes, Europe's Portrayal of India's Temple Dancers', in Martin Clayton and Bennet Zon (eds.), *Music and Orientalism in the British Empire, 1780s-1940s*, Farnham, UK: Ashgate Publishing Ltd., 2007.
72. Amrit Srinivasan, Personal communication, 6 December 2016.
73. Amrit Srinivasan, 'The Apsara in the Text: Some notes from the field', in Amrit Srinivasan (ed.), *Approaches to Bharata's Natyasastra*, New Delhi: Sangeet Natak Akademi, Hope India Publications, 2007.
74. C.J. Fuller, *Servants of the Goddess, The Priests of a south Indian temple*, Cambridge: Cambridge University Press, 1984.
75. S. Radhakrishnan, *Religion and Society*, London: George Allen & Unwin, 1948.
76. Davesh Soneji, quoted in Gokul M. Nair, 'Courtesans and their forgotten art form', *The New Indian Express*, Chennai, 19 December 2016.
77. Sita Anantha Raman, *Getting Girls to School – Social Reform in the Tamil Districts, 1870-1930*, Kolkata: Stree, 1996; also Vasudha Narayanan, *Brimming with Bhakti*.
78. David Shulman, *Tamil: A Biography*, Cambridge, Massachusetts: Harvard University Press, 2016.
79. Yoshitaka Terada, 'Temple Music Traditions in Hindu South India: "Periya Mēlam" and Its Performance Practice', *Asian Music*, Vol. 39, No. 2 (Summer–Fall, 2008).
80. Ananya Vajpeyi, 'An equal music, a beautiful society', *The Hindu*, Chennai, 24 December 2016.
81. Arun Janardhanan, 'A young dancer takes a hard look at Bharatanatyam's burden of caste', *The Indian Express*, New Delhi, 16 February 2020.

82. The singer T.M. Krishna, for instance, has spoken of the appropriation by the upper castes, mainly Brahmins, of the devadasi community. Talk in Hyderabad, 24 November 2017.
83. S. Anand, 'Cauvery in a Puddle'...
84. Ally Adnan, 'The history, art and performance of ghazal in Hindustani sangeet', *Daily Times*, Lahore, 22 December 2017.
85. Veena Oldenburg, 'Lifestyle as Resistance: The case of the courtesans of Lucknow', *Feminist Studies*, Vol. 16, No. 2, 1990.
86. Kombai S. Anwar, 'A Hindustani tradition, right in the heart of Madras', *The Hindu*, Chennai, 5 January 2018.
87. Aneesh Pradhan, 'Perspectives on Performance Practice: Hindustani Music in Nineteenth and Twentieth Century Bombay (Mumbai)', *South Asia: Journal of South Asian Studies*, Vol. XXVII, No.3, December 2004.
88. Janaki Bakhle, *Two Men and Music*, Ranikhet: Permanent Black, 2005. The reference is to the Marathi honorific, *tai*, for a married woman, and the appellation *bai* used for a woman from the entertainer community. In contemporary usage, when no person is identified as being from the community of hereditary musicians and dancers, both terms *bai* and *tai* can be used as a polite form of address though, interestingly, *tai* is used only with the first or personal name and *bai* only with the surname, thus Prabha *tai* but Atre *bai*. I am grateful to Seemantini Apte for this insight.
89. Charlie Gillett in a blog entry of 23 June 2011 writes, '...a rich, visually impaired Frenchman called Maurice Delage heard one of Coimbatore Thayi's records. Delage was a pianist and a music connoisseur and he was so astonished by Thayi's singing that he set out on a trip to Madras to meet her and later composed a series of poems called "Les quatres poemes hindous" inspired by the experience.'
90. 'Unswerving loyalty to tradition', *The Hindu*, Chennai, 22 June 2001.
91. Lakshmi Vishwanathan, 'Rani Jayalakshmi Nachiyar, The dancer Pandanallur Jayalakshmi (1930-2017)', www.narthaki.com, 18 March 2017.
92. Nandini Ramani, 'Torchbearer of Bharatanatyam tradition', *The Hindu*, Chennai, 15 August 2003.
93. Disciple of Ponnayya (1804–64), of the Thanjavur quartet, all four of whom were disciples of Muthusvami Dikshitar. B.M. Sundaram,

'The Tanjavur Quartet Margadarsis of Bharatanatyam', *Sruti*, October 2017.
94. Vikram Sampath, 'The voice of Salem Godavari', *The Hindu*, Chennai, 14 August 2014; also Vikram Sampath, 'Salem Godavari, Carnatic vocalist who fought superstitions to record erotic compositions', blog of 12 May 2019, The Print.
95. As for instance, Baroda Gauri and Baroda Kantimathi who came to the Thanjavur court in 1881, from, naturally, Baroda, now Vadodara.
96. Cited in Suanshu Khurana, 'The Lost Song of Naina Devi: Revisiting the life of the musician, 100 years on', *The Indian Express*, New Delhi, 7 January 2018.
97. Cover of Lakshmi Subramanian, *Veena Dhanammal, The Making of a Legend*, New Delhi: Routledge, 2009.
98. *Dhanam*, Chennai Fine Arts, November 2017.
99. A Doordarshan programme confidently states her father to have been one Subbaraya Sastri, but this person, whoever he was, should not be confused with the composer Subbaraya Sastri (1802–62), son of Syama Sastri.
100. C.R. Srinivasa Iyengar, writing in 1925, described her as 'old, poor, infirm and breaking up' though still capable of the most exalted music. *The Hindu*, Madras, 26 April 1925.

2: SHANMUKHAVADIVU

1. '*Emani ne nee mahima delupudun(u) amma?*', from Subbaraya Sastri's masterpiece in Mukhari.
2. Alain Danielou (trans.), *Shilappadikaram* (The Ankle Bracelet) by Prince Ilango Adigal, Penguin Books, 1965. Danielou places the composition of this text, rather exactly, at AD 171. The references to the temples to Vishnu, Balarama and Muruga could be, respectively, to the shrine of Sri Koodal Azhagar, one of the 108 *divyadesa* sites, the shrine at Thirumaliruncholai, another of the 108 *divyadesa* sites, where a temple to both Krishna and Balarama has been known and the shrine at Thiruparankundram, one of the six sites in the Tamil country sacred to Muruga or Subramanya.

3. Shastry V. Mallady, 'I am overwhelmed by this great city', *The Hindu*, Chennai, 29 March 2012.
4. Animesh Chandra Ray Choudhury, 'Madurai's Minakshi Temple', *The Illustrated Weekly of India*, 1 January 1961.
5. Ross E. Dunn, *The Adventures of Ibn Battuta, A Muslim Traveler of the Fourteenth Century*, Berkeley: University of California Press, 2012; Manu S. Pillai, *Rebel Sultans*, New Delhi: Juggernaut, 2018.
6. K.A. Nilakanta Sastri in *The Illustrated Weekly of India*, Bombay, 1 September 1963.
7. Animesh Chandra Ray Choudhury, 'Madurai's Minakshi Temple'...
8. Chapter 9, 'Madurai: Groom for the Goddess', in Devdutt Pattanaik, *Pilgrim Nation, The Making of Bharatvarsh*, New Delhi: Aleph, 2020.
9. Or more likely jadeite, of which large deposits are in nearby Myanmar. Hence *'mechakangi'* or 'the one with green-hued limbs' as in *Minaksi memudam*/Gamakakriya.
10. Reigning presence in the popular imagination. In a very detailed examination of temple practice and festivals, C.J. Fuller suggests that the relationship between Minakshi and Sundaresvara tends quite often to be similar to that of any other conventionally wedded couple. 'The Divine Couple's Relationship in a South Indian Temple: Mīnākṣī and Sundareśvara at Madurai', *History of Religions*, Vol. 19, No. 4, May 1980.
11. Charles Allen, *Coromandel: A Personal History of South India*, New York: Little, Brown and Company, 2017.
12. C.J. Fuller, *Servants of the Goddess, The Priests of a south Indian Temple*, Cambridge: Cambridge University Press, 1984.
13. The scholar Amrit Srinivasan has noted an interesting ideological dilemma faced by the community. Would it not be more appropriate for women of their attainments to work towards 'being mothers, perpetuating a professional class and not someone's wife, perpetuating a private lineage?' But these questions were possibly ones that only very few devadasis could actually afford to ask. Amrit Srinivasan, 'The Apsara in the Text: Some notes from the field', in Amrit Srinivasan (ed.), *Approaches to Bharata's Natyasastra*, New Delhi: Sangeet Natak Akademi, Hope India Publications, 2007.

14. Jo-Ann Wallace, 'Lotus Buds: Amy Wilson Carmichael and the Nautch-Girls of South India', *Victorian Review*, Vol. 24, No. 2 (Winter 1998).
15. *The Madura Country. A Manual*, Compiled by Order of the Madras Government by J.H. Nelson, MA, of the Madras Civil Service and late fellow of King's College, Cambridge, 1868.
16. A region covering the present-day districts of Madurai, Theni, Dindigul, Ramanathapuram, Sivaganga and Virudhunagar.
17. T. Sankaran, 'Women Singers', *Kalakshetra Quarterly*, Vol. VIII, Nos 1-2.
18. Kalki, 'Veenai Shanmukhavadivu', *Kalki*, 28 February 1954.
19. A life of Subbulakshmi in Telugu, published in 2016, has such fine details such as that the zamindar of Ramnad arranged for her great-great-great grandmother to be fetched on an elephant, that the nawab of Arcot likewise provided a palanquin for her great-great-grandmother and that the ruler of Sivaganga sent a horse for her great-grandmother. All this told in the context of Subbulakshmi's mother walking to a concert engagement, vina in hand. (Clearly, things weren't what they used to be). There is no substantiation for any of this and the fairly extensive conversations recorded in that book reflect only the author's creative imagination. Pallavi, *Susvaarala Lakshmi Subbulakshmi*, privately published, 2016.
20. Conversation with R.K. Shriram Kumar, 9 September 2017.
21. From Ramachandra Guha's winning phrase on page 461 of *Gandhi: the years that changed the world*, Gurgaon: Allen Lane, Penguin Random House, 2018.
22. Monica Felton, *A Child Widow's Story*, London: Victor Gollancz, 1966.
23. As of January 2018. This was a tailoring establishment till recently.
24. As for instance, Indira Menon, *The Madras Quartet*, New Delhi: Roli Books, 1999; Lakshmi Vishwanathan, *Kunjamma...Ode to a Nightingale: M.S. Subbulakshmi*, New Delhi: Roli Books, 2003; T.J.S. George, *MS: A Life in Music*, New Delhi: HarperCollins Publishers India, 2004; Gowri Ramnarayan, *MS and Radha*, Delhi: Wordcraft, 2012; Gowri Ramnarayan, Savita Narasimhan and V. Ramnarayan (eds), *Song of Surrender, A Centenary Tribute to M S Subbulakshmi*, Chennai: The Sruti Foundation, 2016.

25. *Sruti* 256, January 2006, p. 16.
26. R. Rangaramanuja Ayyangar, *History of South Indian (Carnatic) Music*, Madras: R. RangaramanujaAyyangar, 1972, p. 119.
27. 'Those Were the Days', *Kalakshetra Quarterly*, Vol. VIII, Nos. 1-2, 1986; see also *Sruti* 57 & 58, June-July 1989, p. 38. Similar descriptions are found in the chapter on Madurai Mani Iyer in Indira Menon, *Great Masters of Carnatic Music 1930-1985*, New Delhi: Indialog Publications Pvt. Ltd., 2004.
28. All, incidentally, prominent in Subbulakshmi's repertoire. Her singing of *'kavadichindu'* in particular was always commended. 'The "*kavadichindu*" left us spellbound. Why can no one else sing it with equal beauty and imagination?' *The Hindu*, Madras, 18 July 1969. The reference to *'Ksheerasagarasayana'* is also endorsed by an earlier musician who had heard Pushpavanam Iyer sing. Soolamangalam Vaidyanatha Bhagavathar (1866-1943), *Cameos*, Chennai: Sunadham, 2005.
29. Unattributed blog, https://upclosed.com/people/madurai-pushpavanam/
30. Extracts from Sivan's memoirs, in translation, in blog of V.N. Muthukumar and M.V. Ramana, 29 October 2001, http://www.parrikar.org/carnatic/sivan/
31. T.J.S. George, *MS: A Life in Music*, pp. 92-93.
32. A. Mahalinga Sastri, MA, BL, *Madurai Pushpavanam Iyer*, Madras: Bharatamani, 1938 (in Tamil).
33. R. Rangaramanuja Ayyangar, *Musings of a Musician, Appendix to History of South Indian (Carnatic) Music*. Vinayaka Chaturthi falls on the fourth day in the month of Bhadrapada, when the god Vinayaka is worshipped. Muthusvami Dikshitar's *'Siddhivinayakam'*/Chamaram, which Subbulakshmi sang often, has the phrase *'Bhaadrapada maasa chaturthyaam...'*
34. P. Srinivasa Iyer (violinist), *Articles on Carnatic Music*, Tirupapuliyur: The Kamala Press, 1937.
    Extract from article in 1921 in *The Daily Express*, Madras: 'A couple of years ago, if a question was addressed to any individual in any part of South India with a taste for music as to who the leading exponents of the art were, he would have readily and unhesitatingly

replied:-"Pushpavanam Iyer of Madura, Srinivasa Iyengar of Ramnad, Vydianatha Iyer of Konerirajapuram, Anantharama Bagavathar of Palghat".'

35. I owe this recollection, 10 November 2016, to V. Swaminathan, son of Rajam Pushpavanam who heard it from his grandmother Sundarathammal.
36. Conversation with Namagiri Ammal (1907-95), daughter of C. Rajagopalachari, New Delhi, 1988.
37. V. Navaneeth Krishnan, in Gowri Ramnarayan, Savita Narasimhan and V. Ramnarayan (eds), *Song of Surrender*...
38. Also noted by S. Rajam, *Sruti* 256, January 2006, p. 22; Letter from S.V. Narayanan, *Sruti* 259, April 2006, p. 5.
39. *Cinema Thoothu*, 7 January 1944. This magazine was edited at the time, and till January 1944, by one Lakshmikanthan, 'a person of bad character' who was known 'for the writing of the most scurrilous articles attacking the characters of prominent persons, especially persons well known in the cinema world'. He set up another paper *Hindu Nesan* in July 1944 and was murdered in November 1944. (In re: M.K. Thiagaraja Bhagavathar vs. Unknown, (1946) 1 MLJ 42, dated 29 October 1945). The same article in *Cinema Thoothu* talks of Shanmukhavadivu and Subbulakshmi's association with one Lakshmana Chettiar, who was also subsequently murdered.
40. Kalki, 'Veenai Shanmukhavadivu', *Kalki*, 28 February 1954.
41. HMV Record No. 3620 'Veena Shanmuga Vadivoo (Madura)' in two parts, 80-3714 and 80-3715. Available on YouTube as part of the collection of Rantideb Maitra, who dates the recording to about 1925.
42. Lakshmi Vishwanathan, *Kunjamma...Ode to a Nightingale*, p. 20.
43. Lakshmi Subramanian, *From the Tanjore Court to the Madras Music Academy, A Social History of Music in South India*, New Delhi: Oxford University Press, 2006, p. 131.
44. T.S. Parthasarathy, 'An Interview with M.S. Subbulakshmi', *Indian Horizons*, Vol. XXI, Nos. 2-3, April–June 1972.
45. Gowri Ramnarayan, 'When MS Danced', in Gowri Ramnarayan, Savita Narasimhan and V. Ramnarayan (eds), *Song of Surrender*...
46. Gowri Ramnarayan, *Past Forward, Six Artists in Search of Their Childhood*, Delhi: Oxford University Press, 1997.

47. R.K. Shriram Kumar, 'Travel with Lakshmi and Sarasvati: A Tribute to Smt. M.S. Subbulakshmi', blog on Indian Fine Arts Academy, San Diego, https://www.indianfineartsacademy.org/travel_with_lakshmi_sarasvati/
48. Aradhana Mudambi, 'Kunjamma of the beautiful voice', *Deccan Herald*, Bangalore, 16 September 2005. This article refers to Subbulakshmi as a child of a broken home, an entirely inappropriate description for what should more accurately have been called a female-headed household.
49. It is difficult to date events and people accurately. Madurai Srinivasa Iyengar had a more distinguished younger brother *Sangitha Kalanidhi* Madurai Srirangam Iyengar (1904–70) who is believed to have moved to Mannargudi by 1941 after his brother's death. The citation given to Srirangam Iyengar by the Music Academy in 1969 states that the brothers sang together for thirty years. These dates do not tally with Subbulakshmi's recollection that Srinivasa Iyengar died early.
50. *Sruti* 19, October 1985, p. 23.
51. Performances on the radio on February 1942 and 2 May 1945. *The Indian Listener*, All India Radio, New Delhi, 7 February 1942 and 22 April 1945.
52. S. Murugaboopathy (ed.), *Madhurakavi Baskradossin Naatkurippugal*, Chennai: Bharathi Puthakalayam, 2009. I am grateful to Sriram V. for this reference.
53. The diary entries refer also to someone called Buffoon Shanmukham. Clearly this was a recognized professional category.
54. B.V.K. Sastry, 'M.S. Subbulakshmi', *The Illustrated Weekly of India*, 9 July 1965.
55. Conversation with Arvind Shankar, Madurai, 9 January 2018.
56. Padma Swaminathan, 'A man of many parts', *Sruti* 330, March 2012.
57. Gowri Ramnarayan, *MS and Radha*...
58. Randor Guy, blog of 23 November 2003.
59. 'S.V. Venkataraman: Composer, Actor & Singer', *Sruti* 166, July 1998.
60. G. Venkatachalam, *My Contemporaries*, Bangalore: Hosali Press, 1966.
61. C.R. Srinivasa Iyengar (1860s–1930s) was known as 'Kirtanacharya' which translates loosely as 'scholar of songs'. *The Hindu*, Madras, 20 December 1970.
62. 'From 50 years ago', *The Hindu*, Chennai, 14–20 December 1920.

63. This view was prevalent for many decades. The critic Aarabhi in *The Hindu*, Madras, 14 April 1967, notes, 'When our ladies sing, whether they are masters of music like MS, or the tyros whom Akashvani sometimes inflicts on us, we want the song element to predominate, not neraval, swaram, raga alapana.'
64. *The Hindu*, Madras, 'Notes' from 30 November to 6 December 1920.
65. I am grateful to Sriram V. for calling my attention to the 1925 articles. *The Hindu*, Madras, 12 April 1925 and 19 April 1925.
66. Vidya Shah, *Jalsa, Indian Women and their Journeys from the Salon to the Studio*, New Delhi: Ministry of External Affairs, Government of India/Tulika Books, 2016.
67. F.W. Gaisberg, *Music on Record*, London: Robert Hale Limited, 1946.
68. In the collection of the Raja Muthiah Library, Chennai.
69. Michael Kinnear, *The Gramophone Company's First Indian Recordings 1899-1908*, Bombay: Popular Prakashan, 1994; Michael Kinnear, *The Gramophone Company's Indian Recordings 1908-1910*, Bajakhana, https://bajakhana.com.au/2000.
70. For a very fanciful, fictionalized version of the story of Janki Bai Ilahabadi, see Neelum Saran Gour, *Requiem in Raga Janki*, Gurugram: Penguin Viking, 2018.
71. *The Hindu*, Madras, 9 February 1933.
72. Whatever this last phrase may mean; also *The Hindu*, Madras, 9 February 1933.
73. *The Hindu*, Madras, 21 February 1933.
74. Subbudu, in *The Statesman*, Kolkata, of 28 May 2004, states that the disc sold at Re 1, 4 annas. However since he also states that the song was *Marakatavallim* in Kambhoji and that Subbulakshmi was six, this may or may not be accurate.
75. http://www.msstribute.org/pdf/MSS-Discography.pdf, Commercial recordings of M.S. Subbulakshmi released during her lifetime. Compiled by Navaneet Venkatesan, also V. Navaneeth Krishnan. Other versions state that *Marakatavadivu* was recorded when Subbulakshmi was ten.
76. T.M. Krishna, *The Caravan*, 1 October 2015.
77. These last two songs are identified by Gowri Ramnarayan in *The Hindu*, Chennai, 19 June 2006.

78. 'Golden songs so long gone', *The Hindu*, Chennai, 11 August 2001.
79. *The Hindu*, Madras, 28 February 1933. There is, however, in the same review a bizarre and meaningless comment on Sundarambal that her music 'like charity, covers a multitude of sins'.
80. *The Hindu*, Madras, 9 February 1933.
81. Report on Gandhi Heritage Sites. Committee chaired by Gopalkrishna Gandhi, Governor of West Bengal, 2008, unpublished.
82. It was only on 8 July 1939 that the temple was opened to persons of Dalit origin, then referred to as Harijan. The historian Ramachandra Guha, a biographer of Gandhi, believes that Gandhi, in his adult life, only visited a shrine twice, the first to the Minakshi Temple in Madurai (in 1934 he went up to the doorway, and in 1946 to mark the temple entry of Dalits), and the next to the Bakhtiyar Kaki shrine in Mehrauli, on 27 January 1948, three days before the assassination. Quoted in Sowmiya Ashok, 'The Mahatma's Footprints: From Mehrauli Dargah to Birla House', *The Indian Express*, New Delhi, 28 January 2018.
83. *Speeches and Writings of Sarojini Naidu*, Madras: G.A. Natesan & Co., 1925.
84. *Sruti* 244, January 2005, pp. 5–6.
85. 'Concerts for a cause', *The Hindu*, Madras, 15 November 1987.
86. *Engum nirai nadabrahmam*, Chennai: Sarigamapadani Foundation, 2006, p. 145.
87. Recollections of a long time rasika, Annalakshmi Chellam in conversation with the author, 17 January 2017.
88. Vikram Sampath, 'Bangalore Nagarathnamma, the singer who took to Sanskrit and feminism in 19th century India', The Print, 26 May 2019.
89. *The Hindu*, Madras, 2 January 1951.
90. Ibid., 3 October 1955.
91. Randor Guy's seventeen-part blog series on K.B. Sundarambal, sangeetham.com, November 2003–September 2004; also 'Avvaiyar Day', *The Hindu*, Madras, 4 February 1954. This site may have vanished.
92. Randor Guy, K.B. Sundrambal, blog dated 28 September 2004 on sangeetham.org.
93. Rajeev Nair, *A Rasika's Journey Through Hindustani Music*, New Delhi: Indialog Publications Pvt. Ltd., 2007; see also Namita Devidayal, *The Music Room*, New Delhi: Random House India, 2007.

94. *The Illustrated Weekly of India*, Bombay, 15 July 1984; also Mohan Nadkarni, *The Great Masters, Profiles in Hindustani Classical Vocal Music*, New Delhi: HarperCollins Publishers India, 1999.
95. Deepak S. Raja, blog of 9 March 2011.
96. Priya Chaturvedi, 'Philomena Thumboochetty: Portrait of an Artiste', *Serenade*, 11 June 2019.
97. Rajeev Nair, *A Rasika's Journey Through Hindustani Music*...
98. Gowri Ramnarayan, 'Her Master's Voice', *The Hindu*, Chennai, 2 April 2006.
99. Jyotirmaya Sharma, 'The music of love and loss', *The Hindu*, Chennai, 27 December 2005; also Nisha Sahai, 'Queen of Ghazals', *Shankar's Weekly*, 22 December 1974.
100. *Shankar's Weekly*, 27 April 1958.
101. Randor Guy, *Vasundhara Devi... The 'Glamor Gal' of 1940s!*, eight-part series in 1983 on sangeetham.com. This site may have vanished.
102. G. Swaminathan, 'Remembered for their melody and style', *The Hindu*, Chennai, 1 December 2018.
103. Rajeswari, 'Peppy Vocalist', *Shankar's Weekly*, 25 August 1974; also, Volga, 'Vasanth Kannabiran and Kalpana Kannabiran', *Womanscape*, Amrita Resource Centre for Women, Secunderabad, 2001.
104. *Sangitha Kalanidhi* Nedunuri Krishnamurthi (1927–2014), Voleti Venkateswarulu (1928–89) and Nookala Ch. Satyanarayana (1923–2013).
105. B.M. Sundaram, 'Madurai Ponnutayi, Equal to male vidwans', *Sruti* 332, May 2012, p. 25.
106. Manjari Sinha, 'Thumri loses its star', *The Hindu*, Chennai, 27 October 2017.
107. Rajeev Nair, *A Rasika's Journey Through Hindustani Music*...; see also Nikhil Inamdar, 'What made Kishori Amonkar's music sublime, complex and radical? Her foremost disciple explains', Scroll, 1 March 2019.
108. Smarth Bali, 'All She had was Music to give', *The Hindu*, Chennai, 26 October 2018.
109. *Lata Mangeshkar ...in her own voice, Conversations with Nasreen Munni Kabir*, New Delhi: Niyogi Books, 2009.
110. Girija Rajendran, *The Hindu*, Madras, 1990; http://giitaayan.com/satish/art-127.htm

111. 'Kumari Kamala', *The Illustrated Weekly of India*, 8 December 1963; also 'She danced her way to stardom', *The Hindu*, Chennai, 7 January 2002.
112. '7 women get M.S. Subbulakshmi Awards', *The Hindu*, Chennai, 14 September 2016. The others were Teejan Bai, Aruna Sairam, Visakha Hari and Yamini Krishnamurti.

3: A CHILD OF HER TIMES

1. '*Parameswari Sundaresu rani balamba madhuravani...*'
2. Lakshmi Subramanian, 'The Reinvention of a Tradition: Nationalism, Carnatic music and the Madras Music Academy, 1900-1947', *The Indian Economic and Social History Review*, Vol. 36, Issue 2, 1999.
3. S. Radhakrishnan, *Manjari*, 10 April 1954, *Occasional Speeches and Writings*, First Series, October 1952–January 1956, New Delhi: Publications Division.
4. Rabindranath Tagore, 'Personality', quoted in S. Radhakrishnan, *The Philosophy of Rabindranath Tagore*, Baroda: Good Companions Publishers, 1961.
5. Quoted in Mahendra Kulshreshtha (ed.), *Tagore Centenary Volume*, Hoshiarpur: Vishweshwarananad V.R. Institute, 1961.
6. Madhu Kishwar, 'Gandhi on Women', *Economic and Political Weekly*, Vol. 20, No. 41, 1985, pp. 1753–58. JSTOR, www.jstor.org/stable/4374920.
7. Tanika Sarkar, 'Gandhi and Social Relations', in Judith M. Brown and Anthony Parel (eds), *The Cambridge Companion to Gandhi*, Cambridge: Cambridge University Press, 2011.
8. Radha Kumar, *The History of Doing, An Illustrated Account of Movements for Women's Rights and Feminism in India 1800-1990*, New Delhi: Kali for Women, 1993.
9. Speech at Pudupalayam on 21 March 1925, reported in *The Hindu*, Madras, 23 March 1925, reprinted in Pushpa Joshi (ed.), *Gandhi on Women*, Ahmedabad: Navajivan Publishing House/Centre for Women's Development Studies, 1988.
10. Ashwini Tambe, 'Gandhi's "Fallen" Sisters: Difference and the National Body Politic', *Social Scientist*, Vol. 37, No. 1/2, 2009, pp. 21–38. JSTOR, www.jstor.org/stable/27644308.
11. *Young India*, 16 April 1925, cited in Pushpa Joshi, *Gandhi on Women*.

12. *The Hindu*, 10 September 1927, cited in Pushpa Joshi, *Gandhi on Women*.
13. S. Radhakrishnan, *Religion and Society*, London: George Allen & Unwin, 1948.
14. Suguna Iyer, *The Evening Gone*, New Delhi: Penguin, 2001. This tale of unhappy, and much abused, Brahmin women from the 1920s and 1930s has many widows in its cast.
15. Sita Anantha Raman, *Getting Girls to School: Social Reform in the Tamil Districts, 1870-1930*, Calcutta: Stree, 1996.
16. S. Radhakrishnan, 'Great Women of India', Sri Sarada Devi Commemoration Volume, 1953, *Occasional Speeches and Writings*, First Series, October 1952-January 1956, New Delhi: Publications Division.
17. Mythili Sivaraman, *Fragments of a Life, a family archive*, New Delhi: Zubaan, an imprint of Kali for Women, 2006, a memoir of the unfulfilled life of the author's grandmother S. Subbalakshmi (1897–1978)
18. *The Hindu*, Madras, 27 March 1917.
19. *Report on Public Instruction in the Madras Presidency*, Vol. I, 1901–02, p. 47.
20. Partha Chatterjee, *The Nation and its Fragments*, New Jersey: Princeton University Press, 1993.
21. Mrinalini Sinha, 'Gender in the Critiques of Colonialism and Nationalism: Locating the Indian Woman', in Joan Wallach Smith (ed.), *Feminism and History*, Oxford and New Delhi: Oxford University Press, 1996.
22. S. Radhakrishnan, 'Shrimati Sarojini Naidu Lectures', 9 April 1962, *Occasional Speeches and Writings*, Third Series, July 1959–May 1962, New Delhi: Publications Division.
23. From a lecture on Equality of Sexes, 1 September 1918, reproduced in Verinder Grover and Ranjana Arora (eds), *Great Women of Modern India 3*, Delhi: Deep and Deep Publications, 1993.
24. Usha Rajagopalan, *Selected Poems, Subramania Bharati*, Everyman, 2012.
25. S. Theodore Baskaran, *The Message Bearers, The Nationalist Politics and the Entertainment Media in South India, 1880-1945*, Madras: Cre-A, 1981. 'Bande Mataram', or Hail to the Mother, is a poem by the Bengali writer Bankim Chandra Chatterjee (1838–94), included in his novel *Anandamath* (1872), and still widely known across India.

26. S. Anandhi, 'Women's Question in the Dravidian Movement, c. 1925-1948', in Sumit Sarkar and Tanika Sarkar (eds), *Women and Social Reform in Modern India, A Reader*, Bloomington: Indiana University Press, 2008.
27. *The Hindu*, Madras, 29 September 1927; Mrinalini Sinha, 'Gender in the Critiques of Colonialism and Nationalism: Locating the Indian Woman.'
28. Rajalakshmi Nadadur Kannan, 'Gendered violence and displacement of devadasis in the early twentieth-century south India', *Sikh Formations*, Vol. 12, Nos. 2-3, 2016, pp. 243-65.
29. Kamil V. Zvelebil, 'A Devadasi as the Author of a Tamil Novel', *Journal of the Institute of Asian Studies*, September 1987.
30. Kalpana Kannabiran, 'Judiciary, Social Reform and Debate on "Religious Prostitution" in Colonial India', *Economic and Political Weekly*, 28 October 1995.
31. Mytheili Sreenivas, 'Creating Conjugal Subjects: Devadasis and the Politics of Marriage in Colonial Madras Presidency', *Feminist Studies*, Vol. 37, No. 1; *Conjugality and Sexual Economies in India*, Spring 2011.
32. Hanne M. de Bruin, 'The Devadasi Debate and the Public Sphere', in M.D. Muthukumaraswamy and Molly Kaushal (eds), *Folklore, Public Sphere and Civil Society*, New Delhi: Indira Gandhi National Centre for the Arts, and Chennai: National Folklore Support Centre, 2004.
33. T.M. Krishna, 'Parayan, poramboku and devadasi: The dark casteist history of these common words', The Print, 27 January 2018.
34. Bob van der Lenden, *Music and empire in Britain and India: Identity, Internationalism and Cross-Cultural Communication*, London, New York, New Delhi and Chennai: Palgrave Macmillan, 2013.
35. *The Hindu*, Madras, 9 March 1920.
36. Now Kanchipuram.
37. *The Hindu*, Madras, 7 March 1920; ibid., Weekly Edition, March 1920.
38. Ibid., 5 March 1920.
39. Ibid., 6 and 18 March 1920.
40. Ibid., 23 February 1951.
41. Ibid., 1 December 1978.

4: THE MOVE TO MADRAS

1. *Emandune muddu balamani-ki, nen(u)*..., from Dharmapuri Subbarayar's *javali* recorded by Subbulakshmi in 1932. Some versions have the song in Mukhari or Saindhavi ragas.
2. An endearing feature of these diary entries is that they often begin with a note on the amount spent on beedis on that day.
3. S. Muthiah, 'MS and the 2 centenarians', *The Hindu*, Chennai, 5 April 2004.
4. Foreword to Lakshmi Vishwanathan, *Kunjamma... Ode to a Nightingale*, New Delhi: Roli Books, 2003.
5. Lakshmi Vishwanathan, *Kunjamma...*, p. 24. Lakshmi Vishwanathan also dates the Kumbakonam concert to 1933, which is unlikely.
6. Gopalkrishna Gandhi, 'M.S. Subbulakshmi; The Song Celestial', *The Indian Express*, Madras, 12 March 1988.
7. Kalki, 'Veenai Shanmukhavadivu', *Kalki*, 28 February 1954.
8. *Journal of the Music Academy*, Madras, Vol. XL, 1969. In the original Tamil as spoken by Subbulakshmi, Dhanammal's words are 'நன்றாய் மன்னுக்க வருவாள்', NaNrai muNNakku varuvaal.
9. Sriram Venkatkrishnan, 'Rhythm king from Pudukottai', *The Hindu*, Chennai, 23 December 2011.
10. Interview by Mani Krishnaswami, *Sruti* 144, September 1996.
11. Lakshmi Vishwanathan, *Kunjamma...*, p. 29.
12. *Cinema Thootu*, 7 January 1944. This very lowbrow paper was published by one C.N. Lakshmikanthan, who was later murdered, described by the diarist N.D. Varadachariar as 'a coarse and elemental force, stirring up the cesspools of society'. (Entry for 10 November 1944). In an earlier entry of 26 January 1944, Varadachariar describes the paper as 'replete with scandals' but in a very lawyerly fashion goes on to add, 'Of course, every sentence is a libel according to the law, but also, I am told, substantially true.' N.V. Sampath, Malathi Rangaswami and N.V. Kasturi (eds), *The Kasi Diaries, Excerpts from the Diaries of N.D. Varadachariar, 1903–1945*, Chennai: EastWest Books (Madras) Pvt. Ltd.

13. The murder of O. Rm. Om. S.P. Lakshmanan Chettiar, a prominent banker of 'Devakottah', was reported in *Indian Express*, Madras, 10 March 1943. I am grateful to R. Venketesh for this reference.
14. Rajeev Nair, *A Rasika's Journey Through Hindustani Music*, New Delhi: Indialog Publications Pvt. Ltd., 2007.
15. Sriram V., 'The season, 75 years ago', *Sruti* 291, December 2008, p. 52.
16. 'The Musical Chettys of Chennai', Sruti 278, November 2007.
17. I am grateful to Sriram V. for this reference, 25 August 2019.
18. Sriram V., 'A tale of two Advertisements', 1 December 2008, https://sriramv.wordpress.com/2008/12/01/a-tale-of-two-advertisements/
19. Sriram V., 'Leaves from past music seasons', *The New Sunday Express*, Chennai, 9 December 2007.
20. As for instance both in Douglas M. Knight Jr., *Balasaraswati, Her Art & Life*, Middletown, Connecticut: Wesleyan University Press, 2010 and in Sunil Khilnani, *Incarnations, India in 50 Lives*, London: Allen Lane, 2016.
21. I am grateful to Shanta Guhan for this reference.
22. Lakshmi Vishwanathan, *Kunjamma*...
23. @RadhakrishnanMW on 7 February 2017.
24. Douglas M. Knight Jr., *Balasaraswati, Her Art & Life*.
25. Kalki R. Krishnamurthi, 'Abhinaya-kachheri', *Ananda Vikatan*, 23 December 1934.
26. Website of the Music Academy, Madras, http://musicacademymadras.in/book-month-oldest-bharatanatyam-brochure; Janet O'Shea, *At Home in the World: Bharata Natyam on the Global Stage*, Middletown, Connecticut: Wesleyan University Press, 2007.
27. Girish Karnad, 'The arts and social change in India', in Karel Werdler, Girish Karnad, Felix van Lamsweerde and Urvashi Butalia (eds), *India's culture in motion: Tradition and change in the arts*, Amsterdam: Royal Tropical Institute, the Netherlands, 1998.
28. Sunil Kothari, 'Revolutionising Sadir', *Seminar* 540, August 2004. Rukmini Devi's biographer places this event in the 1932 season of the Music Academy; Leela Samson, *Rukmini Devi*, New Delhi: Penguin Viking, 2010; see also Rukmini Devi, 'Mylapore Gowri Amma', *The Hindu*, Madras, 22 January 1971.

29. *The Kasi Diaries*, entry for 28 December 1933.
30. Collection of The Madras Music Academy, Chennai.
31. Oliver Craske, *Indian Sun: The Life and Music of Ravi Shankar*, London: Faber & Faber, 2020, p. 53.
32. Kalki R. Krishnamurthy, *Ananda Vikatan*, 16 August 1936.
33. *Journal of The Madras Music Academy*, Vols. VI–VIII, 1935–37.
34. Rukmini Devi, 'Music and Dance', in *Contribution of the South to the Heritage of India*, New Delhi: Publications Division, Government of India, May 1961.
35. Rukmini Devi gave four addresses at the Rasika Ranjani Sabha which were reported in *The Hindu*, Madras, of 26 February; 3 March; 10 March; and 12 March 1948.
36. K. Sankara Menon, 'A Brief Report on Kalakshetra 1936-1961', from *Kalakshetra News*, Vol. II, Nos. 3 & 4, December 1961.
37. Matthew Harp Allen, 'Rewriting the Script for South Indian Dance', in Davesh Soneji (ed.), *Bharatanatyam, A Reader*, New Delhi: Oxford University Press, 2010.
38. Lakshmi Viswanathan, 'Rukmini Devi Arundale: A catalyst to change', *The Hindu*, Chennai, 16 March 2003. Anne-Marie Gaston makes the point that Leila Sokhey (1899–1946), who performed under the name of Madame Menaka, did for Kathak what Rukmini Devi did for Bharatanatyam. See 'Two Early Visions for Classical Indian Dance: Rukmini Devi Bharata Natyam and Madam Menaka (Leila Sokhey) Kathak', *Kalakshetra Journal*, Issue 7, 2018.
39. Kalki R. Krishnamurthi uses this term in *Ananda Vikatan*, 23 December 1934, reviewing Balasaraswati. The term may have been known earlier, and there is no claim that the upper-caste 'reformers' of the 1930s invented it. Kannalmozhi Kabilan states in 'An Unequal Art', *The New Indian Express*, Chennai, 9 July 2020, that Pudukkottai Ammalu, born in 1835 to Tiruvaiyyaru Angu Ammal signed her letters with the prefix 'Bharatanatyamu'.
40. A character Kalyani in Srividya Natarajan's *The Undoing Dance*, a novel of devadasi lives and mores, notes bitterly of her dance class, 'There were Brahmin girls in the class now, smug and thin lipped.' This is a common trope. A character Subbu in Gitanjali Kolanad's *Girl Made*

of Gold, a novel of a devadasi family in decline, mourns the fact that 'women in the Brahmin houses know nothing except how to make a proper rasam'. (Not in itself a skill to be scorned.)

41. Girish Karnad, 'The arts and social change in India'...
42. Years later, in Subbulakshmi's last residence in Kotturpuram, Chennai, four photographs hung in three rows on a wall. In the top row, Dhanammal. In the second row, Rukmini Devi and Balasaraswati. In the third row, Vasanthakumari, Subbulakshmi and Pattammal all laughing happily at the camera. There is a pattern here, and a lesson. Personal observation, 31 December 2001.
43. Uttara Asha Coorlawala, 'The Sanskritized Body', *Dance Research Journal*, Vol. 36, No. 2 (Winter, 2004).
44. http://guruguha.org/wp/?p=1271, blog dated 25 December 2013 by Ravi and Sridhar.
45. Talk at TAG Centre, Chennai, 25 December 2016; also 'Titan from Kanchipuram', *The Hindu*, Chennai, 15 May 2009.
46. With the possible exception of 1942, 1943, 1950 and 1967.
47. Gowri Ramnarayan, 'Matriarch of Music', *Frontline*, 1–14 August 2009.
48. Nitya Menon, 'Witnessing the making of a music legend', *The Hindu*, Chennai, 10 December 2014: *The Hindu*, Madras, published on on 1 January 1935, a four-line listing of the concert in the 'Engagements for tomorrow' column on page 12 of the paper. It read, '5.30 p.m.–7.30 p.m. Sri Subbalakshmi [sic] of Madura – Vocal, Mr. Sankaranarayana Aiyer – Violin, Hamsa Damayanti – Mridangam...'
49. 'Bhakti is the root of Music: MS', *The Hindu*, Madras, 19 December 1987.
50. G.K. Vale continued to use Subbulakshmi's photographs, without naming her, in their advertisements. Presumably her distinctive looks would have spoken for her, and for G.K. Vale. See *Kalki*, 16 February 1942.
51. G. Sundari, *Sruti* 244, January 2005, pp. 18–19.
52. Letter from N. Hariharan, *Sruti* 245, February 2005, p. 4.
53. Parassala Ponnammal, *Sruti* 282, April 2008, p. 31.
54. *The Kasi Diaries*, entry for 30 October 1938.

55. V. Swaminathan, 13 October 2017; also 'They set the trend...', *The Hindu*, Chennai, 21 July 2011. There is reason to believe Rajam was born in February 1917.
56. Indira Menon, 'Rajam Pushpavanam (1916–91), A Victim of Orthodoxy', *Sruti* 256, January 2006. Another woman who had a driving licence was Subbulakshmi's friend the actor S.D. Subbulakshmi.
57. P.N. Venkatraman, 'She Came, She Sang, She Conquered', *Sruti* 25, October 1986.
58. Nitya Menon, blog of 22 January 2014.
59. *Madras Musings*, Vol. XXII, No. 6, July 2012.
60. Iqbal Singh, 'All India Radio, From Within and Without' (A Symposium), Part 1, *The Illustrated Weekly of India*, 15 August 1965.
61. Lionel Fielden, 'All India Radio, From Within and Without' (A Symposium), Part 1, *The Illustrated Weekly of India*, 15 August 1965.
62. Narayana Menon, *The Communications Revolution*, New Delhi: National Book Trust, 1976.
63. *The Indian Listener*, 7 May 1939.
64. Ibid., 7 January 1942.
65. Neutron, 'VUM-A Retrospect', *Indian Radio Review*, August 1939.
66. Broadcast on 30 June 1942, *The Indian Listener*, 7 June 1942.
67. *The Indian Listener*, 22 March 1942, 14 April 1942.
68. Broadcast on 12 January 1942 (*The Indian Listener*, 22 December 1941), Broadcast on 25 February 1942 (*The Indian Listener*, 7 February 1942), Broadcast on 25 March 1939 (*The Indian Listener*, 7 March 1939).
69. '*Gopala (varnam)*'/Kiravani, '*Durjata*'/Gauri, '*Sri Rukmini*'/Adana, '*Meenalochana*'/Dhanyasi, '*Sri matrubhutam*'/Kannada, '*Tyagaraja*'/Nilambari, '*Neyyamuna*'/Ganta, '*Modi jesu*'/Khamaj, '*Varugalamo*'/Manji, '*Sami ninne*'/ragamalika, '*Mariyada*'/Surati, '*Saranu saranu*'/Jhinjhoti, '*Tillana*'/Edukala Kambodi.
70. Aneesh Pradhan, *Chasing the Raag Dream: A Look into the World of Hindustani Music*, Noida: HarperCollins Publishers India, 2019.
71. Gregory D. Booth, 'The Madras Corporation Band: A Story of Social Change and Indigenization', *Asian Music*, Vol. 28, No. 1 (Autumn, 1996–Winter, 1997).

5: SADASIVAM

1. 'Puranapurusham puraantakam Sankarabharana bhaasamaana deham...'
2. T. Sadasivam, in documentary *Nauka Caritram*, directed by Saroj Satyanarayan, 1997. An otherwise pointless effort, the documentary must be remembered only for Pattammal's fond reminiscences of her childhood in Kanchipuram.
3. *Deccan Herald*, Bangalore, 23 November 1997.
4. Personal communication, Gopalkrishna Gandhi.
5. Sadanand Menon, *The Hindu*, Chennai, 1 April 2017.
6. Gowri Ramnarayan, *MS and Radha*, Chennai: Wordcraft, 2012.
7. Karan Mahajan, Review of *Thus Bad Begins* by Javier Marias, *The New York Times* International Edition, 22 November 2016.
8. One example will suffice. J.S. Raghavan, 'Divine music, humble singer', *The Hindu*, Chennai, 30 September 2018.
9. Whoever they may have been.
10. *The Kasi Diaries, Excerpts from the Diaries of N.D. Varadachariar, 1903-1945*, Chennai: EastWest Books (Madras) Pvt. Ltd., entry for 26 December 1937.
11. *The Hindu*, Madras, 27 December 1937. The quaint references are to *Tyagaraja palayasumam* in Gaula, *Suryamurte* in Saurashtram and *Brova smayamide* in Gaurimanohari by Karur Dakshinamurthi, also known as Garbhapurivasa. It is now not known exactly what kind of Hindustani music was presented by the sisters.
12. *The Kasi Diaries*, entry for 28 December 1937.
13. T.J.S. George, *MS: A Life in Music*, New Delhi: HarperCollins Publishers India, 2004; p. 113.
14. Neepa Majumdar, *Wanted Cultured Ladies only!: Female Stardom and Cinema in India 1930s-1950s*, Champaign, Illinois: University of Illinois Press, 2009.
15. Stephen Putnam Hughes, 'Music in the Age of Mechanical Reproduction: Drama, Gramophone and the beginnings of Tamil Cinema', *The Journal of Asian Studies*, Vol. 66, No. 1, February 2007.
16. S. Theodore Baskaran, 'Music for the people', *The Hindu*, Chennai, 6 January 2002.

17. S. Viswanathan, 'A progressive film-maker', *Frontline*, Vol. 21, No. 14, 3–16 July 2004.
18. 'A reel revolution from 85 years ago', *The Hindu*, Chennai, 1 November 2016.
19. Volga, 'Vasanth Kannabiran and Kalpana Kannabiran', *Womanscape*, Amrita Resource Centre for Women, Secunderabad, 2001.
20. Randor Guy, 'Seva Sadanam 1938', *The Hindu*, Chennai, 1 February 2008.
21. Padma Subrahmanyam, 'She Sang for God and Guru', in Gowri Ramnarayan, Savita Narasimhan and V. Ramnarayan (eds), *Song of Surrender*, Chennai: The Sruti Foundation 2016.
22. *The Hindu*, Madras, 9 April 1971.
23. Randor Guy, 'Melody-filled screen presence', *The Hindu*, Chennai, 23 October 2009.
24. From the introduction by Vasudha Dalmia to *Sevasadan*, by Premchand, translated by Snehal Shangavi, Delhi: Oxford University Press, 2005.
25. Blog by Veejay Sai, 16 September 2016, http://www.thenewsminute.com/article/when-ms-subbulakshmi-acted-movie-based-story-munshi-premchand-49958.
26. G. Dhananjayan, *Pride of Tamil Cinema 1931-2013*, Chennai: Blue Ocean Publishers, 2014.
27. *Filmindia*, April 1938.
28. G. Dhananjayan, *Pride of Tamil Cinema...*
29. https://blog.msstribute.org/ms-repertoire-songs-from-sevasadanam/ has 'Guha saravanabhava', 'Needu charane', 'Enna seiven', 'Unuruvam' and 'Adaravartavarkkellam'. 'Enna seiven' in Sriranjani is sung to the same tune as Tyagaraja's *Marubalka*.
30. *Filmindia*, May 1938.
31. Kalki R. Krishnamurthi, 'Sevasadanam', *Ananda Vikatan*, 22 May 1938.
32. *The Kasi Diaries*, entries for 2 May 1938 and 4 January 1940.
33. http://www.msstribute.org/pdf/MSS-Discography.pdf, Commercial recordings of Smt. M.S. Subbulakshmi released during her lifetime. Compiled by Navaneet Venkatesan, p. 3.
34. *Sruti* 263, August 2006, p. 21.
35. Gowri Ramnarayan, Talk at M.S. Swaminathan Research Foundation, 28 September 2016.

36. Conversation with Seetha Ravi, 9 July 2017.
37. Sriram Venkatkrishnan, 'The passing of Veena Dhanam', *The Hindu*, Chennai, 14 October 2005.
38. *The Hindu*, Madras, 15 December 1967; Dhanammal's singing occasioned this remark from N.D. Varadachariar, 'They say her vocal music is unendurable, but it is that which I so greatly like. It seems to be the marrow, the pith, the quintessence of melody and purity of style', *The Kasi Diaries*, entry for 17 September 1933.
39. *The Kasi Diaries*, entry for 15 October 1938.
40. '*Inta chalamu*' (Begada varnam), '*Nenaruncinanu*' (Malavi), '*Brovabharama*' (Bahudari) are some of the recordings available on YouTube.
41. Original in Tamil. *Journal of the Music Academy*, Madras, Vol. XLVII, 1974.
42. *Sangitha Kalanidhi S. Pinakapani* (1913–2013), Interview conducted in February 1993, *Sangeet Natak*, No. 107: January–March 1993.
43. D.P. Mukerji, *The Great Masters I have heard*, Radio Sangeet Sammelan 10-15 November 1955, New Delhi: Publications Division, Ministry of Information and Broadcasting, Government of India, November 1955.
44. Kalki R. Krishnamurthi, 'Veenae Dhanammal-um vidvan-gal koottam', *Ananda Vikatan*, 19 July 1936; also Kalki R. Krishnamurthi, 'Dhanam pochhu', *Ananda Vikatan*, 23 October 1938.
45. Lakshmi Subramanian, *Veena Dhanammal, The Making of a Legend*, New Delhi and Chennai: Routledge, 2009.
46. R. Rangaramanuja Iyengar, 'Veena Dhanam, A Great Artiste', *The Hindu*, Madras, 26 September 1935. The author identifies brevity, freshness, beauty and comprehensiveness as the defining qualities of Dhanam's *alapana* and also estimates that she knew over a thousand songs.
47. *Dhanam*, Chennai Fine Arts, November 2017, privately published booklet.
48. *The Kasi Diaries*, entry for 7 May 1939.
49. T.V. Subba Rao, 'Veena Dhanam', *Souvenir of the Madras Music Academy*, 1948, spoken at a public meeting on 27 October 1948. The musicologist Harold Powers noted of Subba Rao's writings that if one 'knows where to read between the lines, where to sprinkle the pinch of salt, and where to make allowances for both over-enthusiasms and defensiveness – in short, if one knows something of both the musical

and the linguistic tradition behind such writings – one can find many stimulating and perceptive insights in Sri Subba Rao's essays'. 'Indian Music and the English Language: A Review Essay,' *Ethnomusicology*, Vol. 9, No. 1 (January 1965).

50. T.J.S. George, *MS: A Life in Music*, New Delhi: HarperCollins Publishers India, 2004.
51. Gopalkrishna Gandhi, The Wire, 16 September 2016.
52. One of Subbulakshmi's biographers states that Sadasivam's wife was away at her parents' home for her second delivery at the time of Subbulakshmi's arrival at the marital home (T.J.S. George, *MS: A Life in Music*). Another believes that Parvati had not yet left (Gowri Ramnarayan, *MS and Radha*.)
53. T.J.S. George, *MS: A Life in Music*, pp. 115–16.
54. This is the understanding of Seetha Ravi, Vijaya's daughter, even if the facts are very unclear.
55. Interview by Vaasanthi, *India Today*, 30 September 1996.
56. Personal Communication, V. Ranganayaki, December 1978.
57. Geeta Sahai, 'She loved talking music', *The Times of India*, New Delhi, 26 July 2009.
58. Speech by T.T. Vasu, Music Academy, reported in 'Bhakti is the root of music', *The Hindu*, Madras, 19 December 1987.
59. '*Evarunnaru*' in Malavasri, '*Vaddanevaru*' in Shanmukhapriya, '*Sangita Gnanamu*' in Dhanyasi and '*Mariyada gadayya*' in Bhairavam.
60. *Ananda Vikatan*, 8 January 1939.
61. Neutron, 'VUM-A Retrospect', *Indian Radio Review*, August 1939.
62. *Ananda Vikatan*, 15 January 1939.
63. 'D.K. Pattammal', blog by Randor Guy, 1 July 2000, sangeetham.com
64. Sriram V., 'The long association as Sivan's disciple', *The Hindu*, Chennai, 18 March 2018.
65. *The Kasi Diaries*, entry for 8 August 1943.
66. *Ananda Vikatan*, 8 January 1939.
67. Sriram V., *The Hindu*, Chennai, 28 November 2008.
68. Lecture by Sriram V., 24 December 2017, at TAG Centre, Chennai.
69. From *Ananda Vikatan*, 8 January 1939.
70. *The Hindu*, Madras, 23 June 1944; ibid., 28 December 1949.
71. Randor Guy, 'Vasanthakokilam', blog, 1 May 2000, sangeetham.com
72. *Sruti* 30, March 1987, p. 22.

73. *Sruti* 190, July 2000, p. 2.
74. Randor Guy, *The Hindu*, Chennai, 30 January 2010.
75. The list of songs included one sung by happy fishermen, set to the tune of Rabindranath Tagore's *Ekla chalo re*. This may well have been Subbulakshmi's introduction to Tagore, at least two of whose songs, *He nutan* and *Mollika Bone*, she was to sing in later years. This was not the only tune to have been borrowed. 'Engum nirai nadabrahmam' is set to a variation on D.V. Paluskar's famous '*Thumak chalata Ramachandrai*', not a song sung by Subbulakshmi in later years though she did sing other of his bhajans.
76. Ellis R. Dungan, 'Reminiscences on Directing M.S., the Musician–Movie Star', http://www.sangam.org/articles/view2/?uid=691
77. G. Sundari, *Sruti* 244, January 2005, p. 18.
78. Mani Rao, *Kalidasa for the 20th century reader*, New Delhi: Aleph, 2014.
79. Wendy Doniger, *The Ring of Truth, Myths of Sex and Jewelry*, Speaking Tiger, 2017.
80. Arundhathi Subramaniam, From Poem 4, from *Eight Poems for Shakuntala*, in *When God is a Traveller*, Noida: HarperCollins Publishers India, 2014.
81. S. Rajam, *Sruti* 244, January 2005, p. 36.
82. T.S. Parthasarathy, 'An Interview with M.S. Subbulakshmi', *Indian Horizons*, Vol. XXI, Nos. 2-3, April–June 1972.
83. *Sruti*, 121, October 1994, p. 36.
84. Sakunthala Ramanathan, 'Anna', in Lalitha Ram and V. Ramnarayan (eds), *Gandharva Ganam*, Chennai: Privately published by GNB Family, 2009. It is pleasing to speculate that G.N. Balasubramaniam named his daughter, born around the time, after his leading lady.
85. *Filmindia*, March 1941.
86. T.S. Vedagiri, K.S. Muthuraman and K.S. Mahadevan, *G.N.B.: A Biography*, published by G.B. Duraiswamy, 1985.
87. *Filmindia*, July 1941.
88. *The Kasi Diaries*, entry for 23 February 1941.
89. Performed on radio, 23 June 1942, *The Indian Listener*, 7 June 1942.
90. *Filmindia*, March 1940.
91. VS on 3 May 1939, (*The Indian Listener*, 22 April 1939), 28 January 1942, (*The Indian Listener*, 7 January 1942), PLS on 30 June 1939, (*The

Indian Listener, 7 June 1939), JS on 22 January 1945, (*The Indian Listener*, 22 January 1945), KS on 19 April 1942, (*The Indian Listener*, 7 April 1942), and on 28 May 1945, (*The Indian Listener*, 7 May 1945). TSS on 9 April 1942, (The Indian Listener, 22 March 1942), S of T sang on 21 June 1939, (*The Indian Listener*, 7 June 1939).

92. 16 May 1939, (*The Indian Listener*, 7 May 1939). The initials refer to the singers named in the text.
93. Kalki R. Krishnamurthi, *Ananda Vikatan*, 7 January 1940; also Sriram V., 'The season, 75 years ago', *Sruti* 363, December 2014.
94. Kalki R. Krishnamurthi, *Ananda Vikatan*, 8 January 1939.
95. Ibid., 7 January 1940.
96. Conversation, Alamelu Rajagopalan, 18 September 2017.
97. 'Indian Film Star weds', *The Madras Mail*, 13 July 1940.
98. G. Pallavi, *Susvaraala Lakshmi Subbulakshmi*, privately published, 2016 (in Telugu).
99. Personal communication, K.R. Athmanathan.
100. *The Illustrated Weekly of India*, 4 August 1940.
101. Conversation with Seetha Ravi, 9 July 2017.
102. Sriram V., 'Semmangudi Srinivasa Iyer', public lecture, Chennai, 25 December 2016.
103. Gowri Ramnarayan, 'She Loved Instrumental Music', in Gowri Ramnarayan, Savita Narasimhan and V. Ramnarayan (eds), *Song of Surrender...*
104. *Sruti* 257, February 2007, p. 20.
105. This is pure speculation but Subbulakshmi seems to have liked Muthiah Bhagavathar. It is not only that she and her mother and sister were welcome guests in his house, but Shanmukhavadivu would have met him while shooting for her film in Bombay in 1934, the film for which Bhagavathar composed all sixty-six songs! Several of his songs, '*Jalandhara*' in Valaji, '*Vijayambike*' in Vijayanagari and '*Mate malayadhaja*' in Khamas recur in her concert history and there are other songs she would have certainly known.
106. Gowri Ramnarayan, *MS and Radha...*, p. 42; also *Sruti* 300, September 2009, p. 45.
107. Maya Jasanoff, *The Dawn Watch Joseph Conrad in a Global World*, London and New York: William Collins, HarperCollins, 2017.

108. 'Nee patta mahishi aahapore', 'நீ பட்ட மஹிஷி ஆகப்போரே', from *Sakuntalai*.

6: THE POLITICS OF LANGUAGE

1. *Alaimagal Kalaimagal pani girvani!*
2. The diarist N.D. Varadachariar notes on 3 June 1941 that the contract for 'Kalki' is being drafted. *The Kasi Diaries, Excerpts from the Diaries of N.D. Varadachariar, 1903-1945*, Chennai: EastWest Books (Madras) Pvt. Ltd.
3. Sunda, *Ponniyin pudalvar*, Chennai: Vanathi Padippakam, 1976.
4. *Sruti* 364, January 2015, p. 59; An abiding friendship, *The Hindu*, Chennai, 17 September 2004. Also K.S. Mahadevan, *Musings on Music and Musicians*, Chennai: K.S. Mahadevan, 2003. Also conversation with Nirmala and M.K. Ramasubramanian, 31 January 2018. See also Bala Shankar, 'Love-without-marriage relationship', *The Hindu*, Chennai, 24 January 2020, where he describes his grandmother Chinnani Mahadevan as 'the classic combo of deep but amateur interest and stoic detachment'.
5. Conversation with the author, 31 December 2001. The charmingly affectionate term used by Subbulakshmi for Chinnani was *snehiti*.
6. Malathi Rangarajan, 'Vintage culture is here to stay', *The Hindu*, Chennai, 17 July 2000.
7. *Sruti* 62, p. 39, article by Randor Guy. Also see Venkatesh Ramakrishnan, 'Those Were The Days: Prodigy, singer, freedom struggle icon, and actor – the many lives of Suryakumari', *DT Next*, 15 September 2019.
8. Shanta Apte, *Jaaun Mee Cinemaat?*, Bombay: Govind, Khatauwadi, 1940.
9. Neepa Majumdar, 'Gossip, Labor and Female Stardom in Pre-Independence Indian Cinema, The case of Shanta Apte', in Christine Gedhill and Julia Knight (eds), *Doing Women's Film History, Reframing Cinemas, Past and Future*, Champaign, Illinois: University of Illinois Press, 2015.
10. Sunda, *Ponniyin pudalvar*...

11. Blog of M.K. Ramasubramanian, son of Subbulakshmi's friend Chinnani Mahadevan, 9 August 2009, rasikas.org
12. Conversation with Gowri Ramnarayan, 1 August 2017.
13. T. Sadasivam, *My Wife M.S. Subbulakshmi, Bharat ke sangeet ratn*. Also, T. Sadasivam, *Random jottings on the musical career of M.S. Subbulakshmi*, privately published, September 1966.
14. Conversation with the author, 31 December 2001.
15. 'Brother of the more famous Jack', or in this case the Tamil film actor Ranjan. Conversation with V. Shrinivasan, 25 July 2017. Also, Gowri Ramnarayan, 'But history will remain', *The Hindu*, Chennai, 11 June 2003.
16. https://mymazaa.com/Tamil/devotionalsongs/album/DK+Pattammal.html
17. http://gaana.com/artist/ariyakudi-ramanuja-iyengar; *Swadesamitran* of 15 February 1948 also carried Ariyakudi Ramanuja Iyengar's notation for this song.
18. *The Hindu*, Chennai, 1 December 2002.
19. As for instance *Sangtha Kalanidhi* Sudha Ragunathan and Bombay Jayashri. T.M. Krishna also has a creative interpretation of this basic tune.
20. Gandhi translated the songs in the *Ashrama Bhajanavali* into English, while in Yeravada Jail in 1930, for his disciple Mirabehn. (Ramachandra Guha, *Gandhi-the years that changed the world*, Gurgaon: Penguin Random House, 2018).
21. *The Collected Works of Mahatma Gandhi*, Vol. L, p. 376.
22. N.14408 OME 4254.
23. Collection of Roja Muthiah Library, Chennai; https://www.youtube.com/watch?v=KtjVM3yJWIk, https://www.youtube.com/watch?v=6mS6_ziAVmk
24. *The Hindu*, Madras, 19 September 1941.
25. Ibid., 19 May 1941.
26. Ibid., 13 January 1942.
27. Srinath Raghavan, *India's War, The Making of Modern South Asia 1939-1945*, New Delhi: Allen Lane, 2016. For a more fictional account, Introduction to C.S. Lakshmi (ed.), *The Unhurried City, writings on Chennai*, New Delhi: Penguin Books, 2001.

28. V. Sriram, 'When the music was suspended', *The Hindu*, Chennai, 1 May 2020; *Sruti* 381, p. 22.
29. Kalki R. Krishnamurthi, *Ananda Vikatan*, 27 Sptember 1942.
30. David Shulman, *Tamil, A Biography*, Cambridge, Massachusetts: Harvard University Press, p. 308.
31. An upper middle-class locality of Madras, where many Brahmin lawyers and professionals built their homes.
32. I am grateful to Venkatesh Ramakrishnan for this reference. I have a copy of the notice cut out of a newspaper without any date.
33. Lakshmi Subramanian, *Veena Dhanammal: The Making of a Legend*, New Delhi and Chennai: Routledge, 2009.
34. T.M. Krishna, *A Southern Music*, Noida: HarperCollins Publishers India, 2013.
35. Felicitation on the Occasion of the Shastyabdapurthi of Raja Sir Annamalai Chettiar, Kt. L.L.D. by *Gayanapatu, Kirthanapatu, Abhinava Saraswathi, Kirthana Saraswathi, Sangitha Samskritha Vidyaratna* C. Saraswathi Bai, in B.V. Narayanaswamy Naidu (ed.), *Rajah Sir Annamalai Chettiar Commemoration Volume*, Chidambaram: Annamalai University, 1941.
36. Sriram Venkatkrishnan, 'The great Enchanter', *The Hindu*, Chennai, 23 November 2007.
37. 'The Tamil Isai Movement', blog by Sriram V., 17 November 2010. The name was given by C. Rajagopalachari.
38. The title *Rasikamani* translates somewhat weakly as 'Connoisseur'. Chidambaranatha Mudaliar was a wealthy patron of Tamil writing, poetry and the arts generally. The title, affectionately bestowed if somewhat pretentious, is always used.
39. Sunda, *Ponniyin pudalvar*...
40. Sriram Venkatkrishnan, 'The charm of Ariyakudi', *The Hindu*, Chennai, 29 August 2008.
41. Address by *Sangitha Kalanidhi* Umayalpuram Swaminatha Iyer, 23 December 1936, The Music Academy. Also Address by Sir M. Venkatasubba Rao to the 16th Annual Conference of the Music Academy, 24 December 1942.
42. Indira Parthasarathy, 'Bhaskaradas, the people's bard', *The Hindu*, Chennai, 27 October 2009. I am grateful to Sriram V. for pointing

out that Bhaskara Das notes in his diary in 1944 that he had, at Shanmukhavadivu's request, mailed the text and notation of some songs to 'Sangeetam Subbulakshmi'.
43. Sriram V., Lecture, Chennai, 24 December 2017.
44. Sriram V., Talk on 'The December Season', Chennai, 15 December 2016. The Mylai Sangeetha Sabha, incidentally, was a flourishing organization. In the 1947 season, the year Subbulakshmi returned to the Music Academy, the Sabha featured Ariyakudi Ramanuja Iyengar, G.N. Balasubramaniam, Vasanthakokilam, Maharajapuram Viswanatha Iyer and Madurai Mani Iyer.
45. *The Liturgy of the Church of South India (in Carnatic music)*, Church of South India, 1970, includes verses set to Mohana, Hamsadhwani, Mayamalavagaula, Madhyamavati, Behag and Kambhoji, and published with staff notation.
46. These letterheads are on letters written by Subbulakshmi to Chinnani Mahadevan, and were shown to me by her son K.S. Ramasubramanian on 31 January 2018.
47. Gowri Ramnarayan, 'But history will remain....', *The Hindu*, Chennai, 11 June 2003.
48. Letter from K. Srinivasan to Devadas Gandhi, 8 August 1950.
49. Gopalkrishna Gandhi, 'The Pedestrian', speech on the occasion of Kalki Sadasivam Ninaivu Sorpozhivu, 20 March 2010.
50. Very close to the end of his life, Rajaji inscribed for Sadasivam a copy of a volume of tributes, *Rajaji 93*, with the words, 'How can I repay you for what you have every minute of your life been doing for me? God bless you and your wife. C. Rajagopalachari, 5.12.71.'
51. Gowri Ramnarayan, 'Remembering MS-Part 1', *Sruti* 38, November 2012.
52. Mrinalini Sarabhai and Geeta Chandran, 'A conversation with Mrinalini Sarabhai', *India International Centre Quarterly*, Vol. 34, No. 2 (Autumn 2007).
53. Kalki went to jail three times, in 1922, 1930 and 1941.
54. Gopalkrishna Gandhi, 'The Pedestrian'.
55. Personal communication, Gowri Ramnarayan, 1 August 2017.
56. *The Indian Listener*, 22 April 1939.
57. Personal communication, Seetha Ravi, 9 July 2017.

58. Personal communication, Gopalkrishna Gandhi.
59. Set to the tune of K.L. Saigal's *'Balam Aye Baso More Man Mein'* from *Devdas* (1935), from Sriram V., https://sriramv.wordpress.com/2018/02/23/musing-on-some-film-songs-1/; 'Poonguyil Pattammal', by Seetha Ravi, *The Hindu*, Chennai, 16 March 2018.
60. *The Hindu*, Madras, 3 September 1954.
61. Sunda, *Ponniyin pudalvar...*
62. *Sruti* 183, November 1999, p. 52.
63. Amanda Weidman, 'Gender and the Politics of Voice: Colonial Modernity and Classical Music in South India', *Cultural Anthropology*, Vol. 18, No. 2, 2003.
64. 'Kasturba's outstanding qualities were not of greatness, but of goodness. The world is full of clever, intelligent, brilliant men, each great in his own way, but it lacks its fair share of the goodness that should accompany these qualities. Hence our plight'. M.R. Masani in 'Foreword' of 11 March 1944 to R.K. Prabhu (ed.), *Sati Kasturba*, Bombay: Hind Kitabs, 1944.
65. *The Hindu*, Madras, 11 May 1944, 29 April 1944.
66. Ibid., 30 April 1944.
67. Ibid., 12 May 1944, 6 June 1944.
68. Ibid., 1 August, 4 September, 3 September 1954.
69. M.C. Chagla, Chief Justice of Bombay High Court quoted in *The Hindu*, Madras, 11 April 1955.
70. *MS The Queen of Song*, The Music Academy, Madras, 1987. The list of 244 benefit recitals over 1944–87 provided here is quite possibly incomplete.
71. Sunda, *Ponniyin pudalvar...*
72. News items from *The Hindu*, Madras, 28 November 1944, 10 January 1946, 9 November 1949 referred to in Shantha Thiagarajan, *D.K. Pattammal: A Maestro and Her Timeless Music*, Chennai: Notion Press, 2019.
73. *The Hindu*, Madras, 27 May 1944, 2 June 1944, 23 June 1944, 25 June 1944, 1 July 1944, 20 January 1945, 19 January 1945, 17 June 1945, 19 October 1946, 9 November 1946, 7 December 1946, 12 December 1946, 20 October 1947, 11 January 1948, 11 February 1948, etc.
74. *Sruti* 65, February 1989, p. 5.

75. Randor Guy, 'N.C. Vasanthakokilam: The singing star who faded away', *Sruti* 275, August 2007.
76. *The Hindu*, Madras, 21 April 1944.
77. Ibid., 4 June 1944, 16 January 1945, 11 October 1946, 18 October 1946. She sang in aid of the Rising Star Football Club Fund in June 1944, at another benefit concert in Karaikudi in January 1945, under the auspices of the Sir Ashley Biggs Institute in October 1946, in aid of the Karnataka Provincial Tamilar Kazhagam in Bangalore and again in October 1947.
78. Personal communication. V. Swaminathan, 11 November 2016.
79. Conversation with Rajalakshmi Bhaskaran and K. Lalitha, sisters who were students of Rajam Pushpavanam, 4 November 2017.
80. *The Kasi Diaries*, entry for 28 January 1932.
81. *The Hindu*, Madras, 5 May 1944.
82. Ibid., 30 June 1944.
83. Mudicondan Venkatarama Iyer, 'Late Srimathi Lalithangi', *The Hindu*, Madras, 3 October 1955.
84. *The Indian Listener*, 7 January 1939 and 22 December 1941 and 20 January 1939 and 15 January 1941.
85. *The Indian Listener*, 7 June 1939 and 18 June 1939.
86. 'The Voice of Tradition-MLV Interview', *Femina* 1978, reproduced in *Writings & Reminiscences K.S. Mahadevan Birth Centenary 2013*, Chennai: K S Mahadevan (Regd.) Trust, 2013.
87. *The Hindu*, Madras, 12 December 1938.
88. 18 January 1942, *The Indian Listener*, 7 January 1942. The issue also includes a photograph of 'Rahitangi [sic] and Kumari Vasanta'.
89. *The Hindu*, Madras, 10 June 1944, *The Indian Listener*, 22 December 1944, 22 February 1945 and 7 May 1945.
90. *The Indian Listener*, 22 December 1941 and 7 January 1945.
91. 'The Voice of Tradition-MLV Interview', *Femina* 1978.
92. *The Madras Music Academy Journal*, Volume XV, 1944. Mother and daughter sang a Svati Tirunal composition, *Padmanabha pahi* in Hindolam.
93. *The Hindu*, Madras, 10 June 1944.
94. Sriram V., 'The Season, 75 years ago', *Sruti*, Vol. 26, Issue 12, December 2019.

95. *The Hindu*, Madras, 9 November 1946.
96. Randor Guy, 'M.L. Vasanthakumari', *Movies and Musicians*, 30 October 2001.
97. *The Hindu*, Madras, 7 November 1947, 8 November 1947.
98. Ibid., 6 November 1946, 16 February 1948.
99. Ibid., 6 January 1945, 14 December 1946, 1 March 1948.
100. Ibid., 2 June 1944; also The Music Academy, 1946 season.
101. Ibid.,1 January 1945.
102. Ibid., 2 January 1945. Hemamalini Arni (1934–2019) was a student of Vazhuvoor Ramaiah Pillai (1910–79) and also of Balasaraswati, Mylapore Gowri Amma, and the flamboyant Ram Gopal (1912–2003). Her music teachers were Maharajapuram Viswanatha Iyer, Musiri Subramania Iyer and Myavaram V.V. Krishna Iyer. See also *Sruti* 26, November 1986, p.32 and *Sruti*, Vol. 26, Issue 9, September 2019, p. 48.
103. The Music Academy, 1945 and 1947 seasons.
104. The Music Academy, 1942, 1945 and 1948 seasons.
105. The Music Academy, 1943, 1944 and 1945 seasons.
106. *The Indian Listener*, 7 February 1945 and 22 April 1945.
107. *The Hindu*, Madras, 12 January 1948, 20 February 1948.
108. 'Understanding the greatness of Balasaraswati', Douglas Knight in conversation with Veejay Sai, *The Hindu*, Chennai, 21 December 2011. See also Beryl de Zoete, *The Other Mind, A Study of Dance in South India*, New York: Theatre Arts Books, 1960.
109. Letter to the editor from 'Music Lover', *The Hindu*, Madras, 11 November 1948.
110. *Sruti* 141, June 1996, Back Cover.
111. Letter from E.N. Purushothaman, *Sruti* 164, May 1998.
112. *The Kasi Diaries*, entry for 1 January 1944. Varadachariar consistently writes the name as Subbulaxmi.
113. *The Hindu*, Madras, 10 November 1946.
114. Ibid., 14 January 1948.
115. Ibid., 24 January 1948; the recital scheduled for early February was postponed following Gandhi's assassination.
116. Ibid., 26 January 1948; the recital scheduled for 20 February was postponed following Gandhi's assassination.

117. Ibid., 16 October 1946.
118. Letter of 22 November 1946 of T.K. Chidambaranatha Mudaliar, from *Eppo Varuvaaro..., Selected letters from T.K. Chidambaranatha Mudaliar to MS. Subbulakshmi and T. Sadasivam*, (in Tamil), privately published by Valli Muthiah, 2016.
119. *The Hindu*, Madras, 5 March 1948.
120. Ibid., 13 October 1947. Kalki sought subscriptions towards the ₹50,000 required for the construction.
121. Ibid., 10 October 1947.
122. Ibid., 11 October 1947.
123. Letter of Kamala Vasudevan, *Sruti* 146, November 1996.
124. Madhu Ramaswamy, 'Ramaswamy R. Iyer: a son's tribute', *Sruti* 373, October 2015.
125. V.K. Narayana Menon, Introduction to *Music Program of M.S. Subbulakshmi*, at the UN, 1966.
126. *The Times of India*, Bombay, 5 May 1945.
127. Ibid., 27 April 1946.
128. 'Thalaimai sthanam, Bombay!', *Kalki*, 12 May 1946.
129. *Sruti* 33/34, June-July 1987, p. 45.
130. *The Times of India*, Bombay, 29 April 1946.
131. *The Bombay Chronicle Weekly*, 8 June 1947.
132. *Sruti*, 39 & 40, December 1987–January 1988, p. 79.

7: MEERA

1. *Ek tu hi ab dhani hamare, Krishna nat nagara!*, from the song in *Meera*, composed by Narendra Sharma and set to tune by S.V. Venkataraman. I owe this translation to Gopalkrishna Gandhi.
2. Madhu Kishwar and Ruth Vanita, 'Poison to Nectar: The Life of Mirabai', *India International Centre Quarterly*, Vol. 19, No. 4, 1992, pp. 65–75. JSTOR, www.jstor.org/stable/23004009
3. H. Goetz, 'Mira Bai: Her Life and Times: A Tentative Critical Biography', *Journal of the Gujarat Research Society*, Vol. XVIII, No. 2, April 1956.
4. M. S. Subbulakshmi vs Commissioner of Income-Tax, etc., on 21 March 1955, *AIR* 1956 Mad 529, 1955 28 ITR 561 Mad.

5. And who provided M.G. Ramachandran (1917–1987) with his first role in cinema in *Sathi Leelavathi* in 1936 (*The Hindu*, Chennai, 18 December 2016). MGR, as the charismatic actor-politician was known had a bit role in *Meera*, as a commander, the only role that could be found for an actor with a 'wooden face', R. Kannan, *MGR: A Life*, Gurgaon: Penguin Books, 2017.
6. Gowri Ramnarayan, 'Brindavan to Dwaraka – Meera's pilgrimage', *The Hindu*, Chennai, 19 September 2004.
7. Kanniks Kannikeswaran, 'The MS Soundscape,' in Gowri Ramnarayan, Savita Narasimhan and V. Ramnarayan (eds.), *Song of Surrender*, Chennai: The Sruti Foundation, 2016.
8. S. Theodore Baskaran, 'Reeling under nostalgia', *The Hindu*, Chennai, 7 April 2002; Kanniks Kannikeswaran, 'The MS Soundscape; Sriram V., 'The Tune behind Katrinilae Varum Gitam', 30 May 2018 blog.
9. As in 4 above.
10. John Stratton Hawley, *A Storm of Songs, India and the Idea of the Bhakti movement*, Cambridge, Massachusetts: Harvard University Press, 2015.
11. Karan Bali, 'The Making of M.S. Subbulakshmi's "Meera", her final and finest film', Scroll, 16 September 2016, http://scroll.in/reel/816654/the-making-of-ms-subbulakshmis-meera-her-final-and-finest-film.
12. Randor Guy, *The Hindu*, Chennai, 17 December 2004.
13. Oliver Craske, *Indian Sun, The Life and Music of Ravi Shankar*, London: Faber & Faber, 2020, p. 421.
14. There was a preview in mid May in Delhi,*The Bombay Chronicle Weekly*, 8 June 1947. It is believed that the lukewarm response to this preview led to a more high-intensity publicity campaign including the addition of the introduction by Sarojini Naidu.
15. *The Times of India*, Bombay, 8 November 1947.
16. Ibid., 15 November 1947.
17. Ibid., 22 November 1947.
18. Ibid., 29 November 1947.
19. Ibid., 6 December 1947.
20. *The Hindu*, Madras, 27 September 1947, advertisement for an HMV record of *Meera*.
21. Nayantara Sahgal, email of 17 October 2019.

22. Randor Guy, 'Nagaiah – noble, humble and kind-hearted', *The Hindu*, Chennai, 8 April 2005.
23. *Filmindia*, January 1948.
24. *The Times of India*, Bombay, 29 November 1947.
25. *Jiya jale, The Stories of Songs, Gulzar in conversation with Nasreen Munni Kabir*, New Delhi: Speaking Tiger, 2018.
26. *Meera Bhajans*, HMV ECSD 2371, 1968.
27. Juthika Roy (1920–2014), *Songs of Devotion*, HMV ECLP2278, 1962.
28. *Mharo Pranam*, HMV ECSD 2971, 1984.
29. Foreword by M.S. Subbulakshmi to Shama Futehally, *Songs of Meera, In the Dark of the Heart*, New Delhi: HarperCollins Publishers India, 1994.
30. News18.com, http://www.news18.com/photogallery/movies/100-years-of-indian-cinema-the-100-greatest-indian-films-of-all-time-903065-101.html, 10 June 2015, included *Meera* in its list of 100 greatest Indian films. This is a respectable list which includes *Charulata, Nayak, Pather Panchali, Malleswari, Maya Bazaar, Nartanashala, Shankarabharanam, Anand, Awara, Dewaar, Do Bigha Zameen, Garam Hawa, Mera Naam Joker, Mother India, Mughal-e-Azam, Naya Daur, Pakeezah, Saaransh, Sholay, Ghatashraddha, Samskara* and *Chemmeen*.
31. Rajiv Menon, 'Her Stage Presence', in Gowri Ramnarayan, Savita Narasimhan and V. Ramnarayan (eds), *Song of Surrender*...
32. Letters dated 30 April 1950 and 11 August 1950, *Eppo Varuvaaro*...
33. Letter from K. Srinivasan to Devadas Gandhi, 8 August 1950, courtesy of Gopalkrishna Gandhi.
34. Balaji Vital and Anirudha Bhattacharjee, *Gaate Rahe Mera Dil: 50 Classic Hindi Film Songs*, Noida: HarperCollins Publishers India, 2015; https://www.youtube.com/watch?v=7Sd3j3zAjlc
35. Rokus de Groot, 'The Reception in the Netherlands of an Indian Singing Saint: Meerabai in Film, in Translation and in Concert', Tijdschrift van de Koninklijke Vereniging voor Nederlandse Muziekgeschiedenis, Deel 56, No. 1 (2006).
36. The musician T.M. Krishna sang 'Pagh ghunghuru bandh', using the basic structure set by Subbulakshmi, but with considerable extemporization, at a public gathering at Shaheen Bagh, New Delhi, on 7 February 2020.

37. https://www.youtube.com/watch?v=7Sd3j3zAjlc
38. Samanth Subramanian, 'Her Hymn', Livemint, 29 January 2009.
39. *The Collected Works of Mahatma Gandhi*, Vol. L, p. 367.
40. Sadasivam Thiagarajan, 'A person of Integrity', in Gowri Ramnarayan, Savita Narasimhan and V. Ramnarayan (eds), *Song of Surrender*...
41. All notices reprinted in *The Indian Express*, Madras, 12 August 1947.
42. Gopalkrishna Gandhi, *The Telegraph*, Kolkata, 2 October 2016.
43. Lakshmi Subramanian, *Singing Gandhi's India, Music and Sonic Nationalism*, New Delhi: Roli Books, 2020.
44. Gopalkrishna Gandhi, 'Gopalkrishna Gandhi on Hinduism vs. Hindutva: My first religious memory is shrouded in death', *India Today*, 19 January 2018.
45. *The Hindu*, Madras, 6 February 1948.
46. Hemalatha Murli, personal communication, 22 December 2016.
47. *The Hindu*, Madras, 12 February 1948; Gandhi's ashes were immersed at various spots across the broad expanse of what was still the Presidency; in the sea at Madras, Rameswaram, Malabar and Cape Comorin, in the Krishna at Bezwada and in the Kaveri at Srirangam and Mysore.
48. T.M. Krishnaswami Iyer (1884–1967), lawyer, Judge of the Travancore High Court, famed for his singing of verses from the Tiruppugazh.
49. This song recurs in the repertory, as in a Bombay concert on 4 April 1992, but there is some doubt of whether it is undisputedly Muthusvami Dikshitar's creation. It is, however, a very lively piece.
50. Letter of 5 April 1949 from T.K. Chidambaranatha Mudaliar to Velammal, A.R. Venkatachalapathy (ed.), *Annai Itta di*, Nagercoil: Kalachuvadu Publishers, 1998.
51. Speaking in parliament years later, on 14 November 1966, Nehru's long-term friend J.B. Kripalani noted that with all his strengths Nehru 'lacked one quality and that was that he was not a great connoisseur of music'. *Tributes to the Memory of Jawaharlal Nehru from Members of Parliament*, published by Lok Sabha Secretariat, March 1967.
52. So much so that very many years later all that a Chennai post-graduate student 'knew', in her woeful ignorance, about Nehru was that 'he slept with Edwina Mountbatten and M.S. Subbulakshmi'. (Pramila N. Phatarphekar, 'Ungreatfuls', *Outlook*, 19 August 2002).

53. 'Royjee' in *Shankar's Weekly*, 10 April 1949.
54. *The Hindu*, Madras, 7 November 1949.
55. Ibid., 17 December 1949, 25 December 1949, 1 January 1950, 11 November 1950, 18 November 1950, 23 November 1950, 5 December 1950, 11 February 1951, 31 May 1951.
56. Ibid., 17 November 1950, 23 November 1950.
57. Randor Guy, 'Memorable voice, evergreen songs', *The Hindu*, Chennai, 31 July 2009.
58. *The Hindu*, Madras, 8 March 1951.
59. Ibid.,1 January 1950, 9 November 1950.
60. *Sruti* 26, November 1986, p. 18. See also Sunda, *Ponniyin pudalvar*, Vanathi Padippakam, 1976.
61. *Sruti* 393, June 2017.
62. Veejay Sai, 'A pity that Chennai forgot Radha', *The New Indian Express*, Chennai, 4 January 2018.
63. *The Hindu*, Madras, 26 September 1947.
64. Gowri Ramnarayan, 'Remembering MS Part-2', *Sruti* 339, December 2012.
65. *The Hindu*, Madras, 1 January 1950, 5 November 1950, 11 November 1950, 5 December 1950, 4 January 1951, 3 April 1951, 4 May 1951, 31 May 1951. The reference is to Vyjayanthimala's hit film (1949) in Tamil, *Vaazhkai*, which translates as 'Life'.
66. *The Hindu*, Madras, 21 September 1947, 27 September 1947, 29 December 1949, 9 November 1950, 11 November 1950, 16 November 1950, 17 November 1950, 5 December 1950, 24 March 1951, 27 March 1951, 31 May 1951. On the dancers Lalitha, Padmini and Ragini, 'Though the dancing of the Travancore Sisters was not classical in the strict sense of the term, it was very attractive and held the audience spellbound.' G. Sundari, letter to *Sruti* 267, December 2006.
67. *The Hindu*, Madras, 26 September 1947, 1 November 1947, 2 January 1950, 14 January 1951, 24 March 1951.
68. 'Meet the danseuse (Kumari Chandralekha)', *Freedom*, Vol. 1, No. 3, September 1952.
69. *The Hindu*, Madras, 1 November 1947.

70. Ibid., 30 October 1947.
71. Letter of 15 December 1947 from T.K. Chidambaranatha Mudaliar to Pattabhi, from *Rasanayin Oli*, Peacock Publications, 1984; and of 18 April 1948 to Justice Maharajan, from *Annai Itta di*.
72. *The Hitavada*, Nagpur, 17 February 1946.
73. Ibid., 21 February 1949.
74. Ibid., 22 February 1949.
75. Letter of 6 December 1948 from *Rasikamani* T.K. Chidambaranatha Mudaliar, from *Annai Itta di*.
76. *The Hindu*, Madras, 24 December 1949 and for the Congress Exhibition at Exhibition Grounds in Madras on 3 January 1950.
77. Ibid., 29 January 1950.
78. Ibid., 19 December 1949.
79. Ibid., 23 December 1949.
80. Personal communication, Usha Krishnan, 30 March 2017.
81. Personal communication, C.B. Srinivasan, 1 February 2017.
82. T.J.S. George, *MS: A Life in Music*, New Delhi: HarperCollins *Publishers* India, 2004.
83. Letter of 14 November 1947 from Subbulakshmi to Chinnani Mahadevan, courtesy of her son.
84. Front page advertisement in *The Hindu*, Madras, 4 October 1947.
85. 'The MS Connection', *Sruti* 266, November 2006, p. 42.
86. Thangam Ananthanarayanan, 'When a peacock danced to her song', *Sruti* 378, March 2016.
87. Conversation with M.K. Ramasubramaniam, 31 January 2018.
88. https://www.sangeethamshare.org/asokan/CARNATIC/043-Vadivambal-Oct-28/. Uploaded by Raju Asokan.
89. This second song was a hit from Ellis Dungan's 1936 film *Sathi Leelavathi* where it was sung by M.R. Gnanambal.
90. Chenjaiah, 'Sacrament of the dawn', *The Guardian*, London, June 1947.
91. *The Illustrated Weekly of India*, Bombay, 17 August 1975.
92. S.V.V., *The Illustrated Weekly of India*, Bombay, 25 April 1965.
93. *The Bombay Chronicle Weekly*, 8 June 1947.

8: MS: THE GROWTH OF THE NAME

1. The first line of Tyagaraja's great Kharaharapriya composition, '*cakkani rāja mārgamulundaga sandula dūranēla ō manasā*'.
2. Other than Subbulakshmi, four other students of the 'Musiri school' went on to be decorated as *Sangitha Kalanidhi*: Mani Krishnaswami (1993), T.K. Govinda Rao (1999), and C. Saroja and C. Lalitha (2010).
3. Sriram Venkatkrishnan, 'More a Teacher', *The Hindu*, Chennai, 26 August 2010.
4. Extracts from Musiri Subramania Iyer's concert at the Music Academy in 1958 have recently become available on YouTube and include the first (Kanakangi to Tanarupi) of the twelve segments of the *Melakarta Ragamalika*. It is an enchanting rendering with *neraval* in each of the six ragas, and also *kalpana svaras* for one.
5. Subbulakshmi did not sing at the Academy in 1972 and 1974, and the 1975 concert was devoted to the songs of Muthusvami Dikshitar.
6. The Music Academy, *MS: The Queen of Song*, 1987...
7. Blog by Shoba Narayan, 1 March 2013.
8. Sikkil Mala Chandrasekhar, *A Grand Daughter-in-law remembers*, and V. Chandrasekhar, *Nostalgic memories*, Sruti 244, January 2005.
9. A story is told in a recent life of J.Krishnamurti. 'For one of her concerts at the Rishi Valley School, M.S. Subbulakshmi wore strings of large diamonds, rubies and emeralds around her neck. Several people commented that it was insensitive of her to be dressed that way in the presence of Krishnamurti who, they assumed, advocated simplicity and no ostentatious display of wealth. On greeting the fabled artist, he graciously complimented her on her jewels, much to the chagrin of a few unappreciative onlookers.' Lee, R.E. Mark, *World Teacher: The Life and Teachings of J.Krishnamurti*, New Delhi: Hay House Publishers India, 2020.
10. Vikram Doctor, 'MS Blue', *The Economic Times*, Mumbai, 16 December 2004.
11. She did not appear at the Music Academy in 1954.
12. Alepey Venkatesan, Pathfinder of Carnatic music, *Sruti* 369, June 2015.

13. V.K. Narayana Menon, 'The Music of Ariyakudi', 1963, reprinted in *Sri Ariyakudi Ramanuja Iyengar Commemoration Volume*, 19 May 1990, Madras: privately published.
14. V.V. Sadagopan in *Indian Music Journal*, No. 8, 1967, p. 97, quoted in article on Sadagopan by N. Ramanathan, *Sruti* 367, April 2015, p. 30.
15. Lakshmi Subramanian, 'Negotiating Orientalism: The Kaccheri and the Critic in Colonial South India', in Martin Clayton and Bennet Zon (eds), *Music and Orientalism in the British Empire, 1780s-1940s*, Farnham, Surrey: Ashgate Publishing Ltd., 2007.
16. Aeolus, 'Wit in Music', *Shankar's Weekly*, 7 April 1963.
17. Mallika, 'As Others see Us, *Shankar's Weekly*', 15 October 1950.
18. *The Hindu*, Madras, 3 September 1954. There is some confusion on account of the fact that the award originally made to Subbulakshmi was Padma Vibhushan (Dusra Varg). In a subsequent notification of 11 October 1954, it was clarified that this category would be called Padma Bhushan.
19. Radio Sangeet Sammelan, 10–15 November 1955, New Delhi: The Publications Division, Ministry of Information and Broadcasting, November 1955. Price As (annas) 8.
20. 'Musicians of the Year,' *The Hindu*, Madras, 27 March 1956.
21. *The Hindu*, Madras, 12 April 1956.
22. I am grateful to V. Navneeth Krishnan for this information, 25 March 2019.
23. T. Sadasivam, *Random jottings on the musical career of M.S. Subbulakshmi*, privately published, September 1966.
24. *The Hindu*, Madras, 1 December 1953.
25. Inder Malhotra, *The Indian Express*, New Delhi, 13 November 2014.
26. *The Hindu*, Madras, 6 October 1955; also Sriram Venkatkrishnan, 'Nehru and the Music Academy', *The Hindu*, Chennai, 13 January 2006.
27. *Shankar's Weekly*, 22 August 1954, p. 8; the popular dancers Lalitha (1930–82), Padmini (1932–2006) and Ragini (1937–76), known as the Travancore Sisters were given the latter title as well, but only in Third Class.
28. *Sruti* 313, October 2010, p. 37.
29. 'Sweet singer passes away young', *The Hindu*, Madras, 9 November 1951.

30. *The Hindu*, Madras, 19 May 1951, notice of a Bangalore concert on 27 May. Very little, sadly, is still known about Vasanthakokilam. We learn from Jothirlata Girija in *Eppadi marakkalam?*, published in *Dinamani* on 20 November 2019 that Vasanthakokilam, in her will, left a sum of ₹1 lakh for the cause of women's education.
31. *The Hindu*, Madras, 22 May 1951, notice of MLV's concert at wedding of Valli and G. Narayanan. 'Smt. M.L. Vasanthakumari rendered excellent music'.
32. *Shankar's Weekly*, 3 April 1955, p. 22.
33. https://www.youtube.com/watch?v=IK2Ogpd3BH8&feature=youtube
34. Maya Rao, 'Venkatalakshamma—Teacher of Abhinaya', *The Illustrated Weekly of India*, 5 August 1962.
35. *Journal of the Music Academy*, 1958.
36. *The Hindu*, Madras, 3 January 1958.
37. https://blog.msstribute.org/ms-singing-jana-gana-mana/
38. *The Indian Express*, New Delhi, 24 August 1959.
39. *The Indian Express*, Madras, 16 September 1961.
40. *Shankar's Weekly*, New Delhi, 11 November 1962. In aid of the National Defence Fund, New Delhi, 8 November 1962. The recital which began with '*Evaribodha*' varnam in Abhogi included '*Talli ninnu*' in Kalyani and '*Sankaracharyam*' in Sankarabharanam.
41. Most likely the Kalakshetra Benefit Fund recital on 17 September 1961. The recital which began with '*Era napai*' varnam in Todi also included '*Birana brova*' in Kalyani, '*Kanjadalayatakshi*' in Kamalamanohari and '*Sarasksha*' in Pantuvarali. These are all songs which were sung for the next thirty years.
42. *The Indian Express*, Madras, 16 September 1961.
43. R. Vedavalli, 'The pole star of Carnatic music', *Sruti* 374, November 2015.
44. See Glossary.
45. Presentation by Kiranavali Vidyasankar, 18 December 2016, Ragasudha Hall, Chennai, https://www.youtube.com/watch?v=ujbj_Yf9SxE
46. https://www.youtube.com/watch?v=ns_hJ7qhQ80&feature=youtu.be

47. V. Navaneeth Krishnan, 'An Eternal Student', in Gowri Ramnarayan, Savita Narasimhan and V. Ramnarayan (eds), *Song of Surrender, A Centenary Tribute to M S Subbulakshmi*, Chennai: The Sruti Foundation, 2016.
48. https://blog.msstribute.org/ms-repertoire-ragam-tanam-pallavi/
49. Sadasivam Thiagarajan, 'A Person of Integrity', in Gowri Ramnarayan, Savita Narasimhan and V. Ramnarayan (eds), *Song of Surrender*...

9: MAESTRA: THE GREAT CONCERT YEARS

1. *Bhaja re re chitta Balambikam, bhakta kalpa latikam.* I owe this enchanting translation to Gopalkrishna Gandhi.
2. M.S. Subbulakshmi, speech on 20 December 1968, Music Academy, Madras.
3. V. Raghavan, 'Syama Sastri's Genius: A Bicentenary Homage', *The Hindu*, Madras, 5 May 1962.
4. *Sruti* 243, December 2004 pp. 64–65; see also *Sruti* 359, August 2014, pp. 12–13.
5. T. Chennakeshaviah, 'Mysore Sadasiva Rao', *The Hindu*, Madras, 25 January 1970.
6. It is claimed that the maharaja wrote *all* his compositions over the period 18 August 1946 to 28 December 47. Sowmya Rajaram, 'Jayachamarajendra Wadiyar's Carnatic music *kritis* to be revived; here's how', *Bangalore Mirror*, 11 February 2019.
7. S. Krishnamurthy (ed.), *Vasudeva Kirtana Manjari*, Darpan, 2015, describes him as the maharaja's 'chief mentor'; also B.V.K. Sastry, 'Mysore Vasudevacharya: Some Memories', *The Illustrated Weekly of India*, 24 June 1962.
8. *Vasudeva Kirtana Manjari* includes fifteen *varnams*, 151 songs, ten *tillanas* and six *javalis*; see also H. Yoganarasimham, 'Mysore Vasudevacharya', *The Hindu*, Madras, 1 March 1970.
9. Sriram V., 'The Madhava Perumal Temple, Mylapore', *Sruti* 253, October 2005.
10. N.C. Parthasarathy and N.C. Dwaraka Parthasarathy (eds), *Compositions of Sri Patnam Subramanya Iyer*, Madras: Madras Sangitha

Kalasala Publications, 1972, includes eighteen *varnams*, forty songs, three *tillanas* and three *javalis*.

11. *Era napai* is sometimes attributed to Patnam Subramania Iyer's contemporary Kothavasal Venkatarama Iyer, as are also *Sarasuda*, the *varnam* in Saveri, which Subbulakshmi sang often and *Valachi*, the *navaraga varnam*.
12. *Sruti* 84, September 1991, p.31.
13. *Sruti* 62, November 1989, p.39.
14. Sulochana Pattabhiraman, 'They shared a special bond', *The Hindu*, Chennai, 15 September 2006.
15. *The Music Academy Journal*, 1972.
16. Edwin Arnold, *The Light of Asia and The Indian Song of Songs*, Bombay: Jaico Publishing House, 1949.
17. Barbara Stoler Miller, *Jayadeva's Gitagovinda, Love Song of the Dark Lord*, New Delhi: Oxford University Press, 1978.
18. *Sruti* 340, January 2013, p. 5.
19. V. Raghavan, 'Tirtha Narayana', *The Hindu*, Madras, 4 January 1970; also 'Narayana Teertha', blog post by Sriram V, 30 June 2010, https://sriramv.wordpress.com/2010/06/30/narayana-teertha-2/
20. 'Homage to Narayana Tirtha', *The Hindu*, Chennai, 7 March 2003.
21. *Sruti* 32, May 1987, p. 37.
22. 'Genius shining in regal style', *The Hindu*, Chennai, 6 July 2001; also Sriram V., 'The discovery of Swati Tirunal', *The Hindu*, Chennai, 29 December 2011.
23. Semmangudi Srinivasa Iyer, 'Maharaja Swati Tirunal-II', *The Hindu*, Madras, 20 November 1970.
24. K.V. Ramanathan, 'The Swati Tirunal Compositions', *Sruti* 142, July 1996; also Dr Achuthsankar S. Nair, 'Travancore's composer king', by *Sruti* 345, June 2013.
25. C.P. Ramaswami Aiyar, 'Sri Tyagaraja Brahmam and his times', Address on the occasion of the inauguration of the Ninety-eighth Aradhana Celebrations at Tiruvadi on 1 January 1945.
26. V. Madhavan Nair, 'Maharaja Swati Tirunal: Influence on Music in Kerala', *The Hindu*, Madras, 22 November 1953.
27. Aeolus, 'Le Roi Et Les Trois', *Shankar's Weekly*, 24 February 1963.

28. Saeed Naqvi, 'That voice of silk and flame', *The Indian Express*, New Delhi, 17 December 2004.
29. As stated on the Svati Tirunal related website http://www.swathithirunal.in. In the course of discussion on a musical blog it has also been held that the *tillana* was composed in the now-extinct raga Mulunji Dhanyasi.
30. Musiri Subramania Iyer's 1959 Music Academy concert, recently available on YouTube, includes *Bhogindra sayinam*, and it is clear Subbulakshmi learnt this from him.
31. 'Surdas Bhajans (Hindi Devotional) – Sangeeta Kalanidhi M.S. Subbulakshmi', p. 1986 (STHVS65009).
32. This song can be heard in the Krishna Gana Sabha concert of August 1970, to which we will refer later.
33. *The Collected Works of Mahatma Gandhi*, Vol. L, p. 364.
34. *The Hindu*, Madras, 6 August 1962.
35. T. Sadasivam's letter of 12 April 1958 to N. Ramachandran, 'We too left the same night for Madura to look up Kunjakkal's mother who is not well for many months now. The old lady was happy that we spent a couple of days in Madura and Kunjakkal too naturally was quite pleased.' From the collection of V. Shrinivasan.
36. Gowri Ramnarayan, 'End Note', in Gowri Ramnarayan, Savita Narasimhan and V. Ramnarayan (eds), *Song of Surrender, A Centenary Tribute to M S Subbulakshmi*, Chennai: The Sruti Foundation, 2016.
37. T. Sadasivam, letter of 28 July 1958 to N. Ramachandran. From the collection of V. Shrinivasan.
38. Letter from M. Krishnaswami to *The Hindu*, Chennai, 17 December 2004.
39. And is fortunately available on YouTube, mistakenly identified as a 1955 concert. Also in TAG Digital Listening Archives, The Music Academy, Chennai.
40. This concert is available at www.sangeethapriya.org This may even be the concert in July 1963 where Subbulakshmi sang, along with Ariyakudi Ramanuja Iyengar, at the inauguration of the grand hall of the sabha, *Sruti* 50, November 1988, p. 28. The violinist's name is spelt variously as Subramaniam, Subramanyam and Subrahmanyam. I have

used Subramanyam as that is the way it is used in the official guide book to the 1966 UN concert tour.
41. A long review of these performances by Aeolus in *Shankar's Weekly* of 25 August 1963 turns out to be a clumsy, if admiring, essay on Kshetrayya/Kshetragna without a mention of any of the artistes who performed, leave alone an assessment of their performances.
42. Akashvani, 17 August 1963. Programmes broadcast over 11–17 August 1963.
43. The other pieces presented were all too familiar save the Sahana *padam*, '*Moratopu*'.
44. Lakshmi Sreeram, 'The days with my guru', *The Hindu*, Chennai, 29 July 2016.
45. James Rubin's notes. The James A. Rubin Collection of South Indian Classical Music, Archive of World Music, Eda Kuhn Loeb Music Library, Harvard College Library.
46. Dr. R.T. Taylor, reproduced in the Music Academy, Madras souvenir, 1963, courtesy All India Radio.
47. *The Times*, London, 31 August 1963.
48. Ibid., 3 September 1963.
49. 'MS in Edinburgh', *The Hindu*, Madras, 4 September 1963.
50. Douglas M. Knight Jr, *Balasaraswati Her Art & Life*, Middletown, Connecticut: Wesleyan University Press, 2010.
51. Robert E. Brown, 'Balasaraswati in America', *The Illustrated Weekly of India*, Bombay, 3 March 1963.
52. Srota, 'Absurd Virtuosity', *Shankar's Weekly*, New Delhi, 8 March 1954.
53. *The Illustrated Weekly of India*, Bombay, 9 October 1966.
54. Ibid., 1 November 1959, 13 August 1961, 3 June 1962, 3 March 1963, 24 November 1963, 15 December 1963, and 29 December 1963.
55. Ibid., 13 September 1959, 2 July 1961, 9 December 1962, 8 December 1963, and 9 October 1966.
56. Ibid., 13 November 1955, 7 July 1963, 25 April 1965, and 19 September 1965.
57. 'Sri Venkatesa Suprabhatam – M.S. Subbulakshmi', 1963 (SFHV847032 & CDNF153190)

58. *President Radhakrishnan's Speeches and Writings*, May 1962–May 1964, New Delhi: Publications Division, 1965.
59. S. Krishnaswamy Aiyangar, *A History of Tirupati, Volumes I and II*, Tirupati: Tirupati-Tirumala Devasthanams, 1952.
60. Personal communication, Vasudha Narayanan, 4 January 2017.
61. 'Tiruvenkatamudaiyaan Tiruppalliyezhuchi (Sri Venkatesa Suprabhatam in Tamil) – M.S. Subbulakshmi', 1991 (TPHVS32718 & CDNF147027)
62. 'For me the first Carnatic connection was perhaps M.S. Subbulakshmi's *Suprabhatam* played softly during opening time in Mumbai's Handloom House and a few other establishments.' Gouri Dange, 'Will the twain meet?', *The Hindu*, Chennai, 29 September 2019.
63. *Frontline*, Madras, 31 December 1993.
64. *The Indian Express*, New Delhi, 14 October 2015.
65. Ibid.
66. Semmangudi Srinivasa Iyer, 'Maharaja Svati Tirunal-II', *The Hindu*, Madras, 20 December 1970.
67. 8 April 1942, *The Indian Listener*, 22 March 1942; It is quite likely though that it was sung in some mutilated form, as Semmangudi Srinivasa Iyer feared, for six songs including '*Bhavayami*' were presented in half an hour. Also *Sruti* 231, December 2003, p. 34.
68. *The Indian Express*, New Delhi, 24 August 1959.
69. Michael Kinnear, *A Discography of Hindustani and Karnatic Music*, (Discographies: Association for Recorded Sound Collections Discographic Reference), California: Greenwood Press, 1985.
70. A recording is available of a concert which also included the Kalyani Ata tala varnam, '*Tsakkani raja margamu*'/Kharaharapriya, '*Rangapura vihara*'/Brindavanasaranga and '*Ehi Annapurne*'/Punnagavarali. A fine recital of Pattammal at her best.
71. Award of Padma Bhushan at Raj Bhavan, Madras.
72. Proceedings of the Music Academy, Madras, 24 December 1952, *Music Academy Journal* 1953.
73. And the credit for bringing another of Muthusvami Dikshitar's Brindavanasaranga songs, '*Soundararajam*', into currency must go to Pattammal. It is probable that this borrowing from the Hindustani

tradition derives from Muthusvami Dikshitar's years of apprenticeship in Benares; the raga is used differently in the songs, but both carry the raga-mudra, with *'Rangapura vihara'* set in a mode more akin to the Hindustani Brindavani and *'Soundararajam'*, with its use of the *sadharana gandharam*, a more robustly Carnatic melody. If Subbulakshmi claimed ownership of the one song, *'Soundararajam'*, a majestic creation with exquisite *sahitya*, was always Pattammal's to perform.

74. The verse, which is simply described as a *mangala stotram*, and which hails the dieties at Srirangam, Tirumala and Kanchipuram, is: *Srirangamandala jalanidhim karunaanivaasam, Sri Venkataadri shikharaalaya kaalamegham, Srihastishaila shikharojvala paaarijaatam, Srisham namaami shirasaa, yadushaila deepam!*
75. William J. Jackson, *Tyagaraja Life and Lyrics*, Oxford: Oxford University Press, 1991.
76. *The Hindu*, Madras, 2 May 1965.
77. Personal communication from Annalakshmi Chellam.
78. Sriram Venkatkrishnan, 'A moment of pride for India', *The Hindu*, Chennai, 16 September 2005.
79. *The Hindu*, Madras, 16 September 1966.
80. *Music programme of M.S. Subbulakshmi*, 1966 contains the details of sixty songs, of which thirty only are identified as 'austere and classical' and thirty as songs 'in which devotion is more pronounced'. Needless to say this is a misleading classification. In the sixty are eleven songs of Tyagraja, six of Muthusvami Dikshitar and one of Syama Sastri, one *padam* and one *javali*. There are also three *pallavis* in Sankarabharanam, Todi and Sanmukhapriya.
81. *The Hindu*, Madras, 20 September 1966.
82. Ibid., 11 December 1966.
83. 'Carnatic Music Breakthrough in the U.S.', *Sruti* 20 & 20-S, December 1985.
84. Peter Lavezzoli, *The Dawn of Indian Music in the West*, London and New York: Continuum, 2006.
85. *The Boston Herald*, 14 October 1966.
86. *The Washington Daily News*, 22 October 1966.
87. *San Francisco Chronicle*, 7 November 1966.
88. *The New York Times*, 13 November 1966.

89. The James A. Rubin Collection of South Indian Classical Music, Harvard College Library.
90. *The Hindu*, Madras, 6 December 1966.
91. The matter was discussed, inconclusively, in *Sruti* 214, July 2002, p. 34; *Sruti* 217, October 2002, pp. 3–4 and *Sruti* 221, February 2003, pp. 4–5.
92. An interesting sidelight linking literary traditions across the world is that the verse in itself invokes the *upanisadic* injunctions of *damyata*, self-control, *datta*, giving, and *dayadhvam*, compassion. These concepts are known outside the arcane world of *upanisadic* philosophy in T.S. Eliot's *The Waste Land*, an exhortation to man in an increasingly violent world. Eliot himself was a student of Sanskrit at Harvard.
93. *The Hindu*, Madras, 25 November 1966.
94. UN website; a certain Gopal Krishnan mailed me the details from the website on 20 August 2016.
95. Conversation, Seetha Ravi, Chennai, 29 January 2018.
96. Taught to her by K.V. Narayanaswamy.
97. https://www.youtube.com/watch?v=4oOn2qUEGIE&feature=youtu.be
98. V. Sitaramiah, *Purandaradasa*, New Delhi: National Book Trust, India, 1971.
99. T.V. Subba Rao, 'Karnataka Composers', *The Journal of the Music Academy*, Vol. XIII, Parts I–IV, 1942.
100. *The Hindu*, Chennai, 20 October 2006.
101. *Purandaradasara keertaane*, Parts 1 to 5, Udupi: Srimannadhvasiddhanta granthalaya, 1931.
102. The author recalls attending one such recital in Bombay on 4 March 1973, as also the special recital at the Music Academy in 1977, the year Vasanthakumari was elected president.
103. Conversation with Gowri Ramnarayan, 28 June 2017.
104. William J. Jackson, *Songs of Three Great South Indian Saints*, Oxford and New Delhi: Oxford University Press, 1998.
105. Prof. P. Sambamoorthy, *Tyagaraja*, New Delhi: National Book Trust, India, 1967.
106. The Music Academy, 27 December 1972.

107. Aeolus, 'Gnosis in Three Octaves', *Shankar's Weekly*, 10 November 1963. The three octaves, the *mandara sthayi*, *madhya sthayi* and the *tara sthayi*, or the lower, middle and upper octaves, translate in the author's imagination to the octaves of self-exploration, self-comprehension and self-transcendence. All leading to gnosis, knowledge.

10: SANGITHA KALANIDHI

1. '*Manikya vallaki-paaNi, Madhura-vaaNi, varaaliveNi....*'
2. HMV, Sri Sankara Stuti – M.S. Subbulakshmi (TPHVS32449).
3. I am grateful to V. Navneeth Krishnan for calling my attention to this, 12 August 2017.
4. *The Hindu*, Madras, 6 January 1967.
5. Ibid., 11 January 1967.
6. Ibid., 6 December 1964.
7. *Mid-Day*, Bombay, 1 October 1987.
8. *The Hindu*, Madras, 8 November 1994.
9. S. Radhakrishnan to Padmaja Naidu, 26 February 1967, Sarvepalli Radhakrishnan Archive. The archive has recently been gifted to Ashoka University.
10. G. Swaminathan, 'A tribute to Radha–Jayalakshmi', *The Hindu*, Chennai, 30 November 2018.
11. Aeolus, 'Festival Music II', *Shankar's Weekly*, 8 January 1967.
12. As in 1972, 1973 and 1980.
13. Srota, 'Current Trends', *Shankar's Weekly*, 16 August 1964.
14. Aeolus, 'Sangeet Sammelan', *Shankar's Weekly*, 13 November 1966.
15. Aeolus, 'In Memorium', *Shankar's Weekly*, 29 January 1967.
16. Letter of 29 July 1967 from T. Sadasivam to K. Srikantiah, a grandee of Mysore, who organized music concerts at his home.
17. Aeolus, 'In Memorium', *Shankar's Weekly*, New Delhi, 29 January 1967.
18. *The Hindu*, Madras, 25 January 1967.
19. V. Sriram, 'Leaves from past music seasons', *The New Sunday Express*, Chennai, 9 December 2007.
20. The recital in May 1990 included pieces that were old and overdone ('*O Rangasayee*'/Kambhoji), unusual (Svati Tirunal's '*Smarahari pada*'/

Sama), from the films ('*Bruhi Mukundeti*'/Kuranji) and from her later period (*Kurai onrum illai*/ragamalika).
21. *The Hindu*, Madras, 24 January 1967.
22. Ibid., 28 January 1967.
23. Bala, 'Music', *Shankar's Weekly*, New Delhi, 11 October 1964.
24. Barbara Benary, 'Composers and Tradition in Karnatic Music', *Asian Music*, Vol. 3, No. 2, Indian Music Issue (1972); see also Raymond E. Ries, 'The Cultural Setting of South Indian Music', *Asian Music*, Vol. 1, No. 2 (Autumn, 1969).
25. Meera Srinivasan, 'Semmangudi's music allows you to transcend', *The Hindu*, Chennai, 27 July 2008; an account of a conversation between V.S. Ramachandran and Semmangudi Srinivasa Iyer in 2001.
26. *The Hindu*, Madras, 9 September 1967.
27. Ibid., 20 October 1967.
28. Scholars have placed Tyagaraja's birth variously. M.S. Ramaswami Aiyer, Tyagaraja's first biographer in English, and who had actually met several people who had seen and known Tyagaraja, states that he was born in 1759. *Thiagaraja*, London: Everyman's Library, 1927. However, V. Raghavan in *Tyagaraja*, New Delhi: Sahitya Akademi, 1983, and P. Sambamoorthy in *Tyagaraja*, New Delhi: National Book Trust, 1967, both assert that he was born on 4 May 1767.
29. Ludwig Pesch, *The Illustrated Companion to South Indian Music*, London: Oxford University Press, 1999.
30. T.M. Krishna, *A Southern Music*, Noida: HarperCollins *Publishers* India, 2013.
31. Unlike many Tyagaraja songs with several *charanas*, all set to the same tune. There are other songs such as '*Brochevarevare*' in Sriranjani or '*Enduku nirdaya*' in Harikambhoji, where the many *charanas* are sung to different tunes, but the *svaras* for the *sahitya* of the *charanas* are not sung. Both *svara* and *sahitya* are sung for the many *charanas* of '*Sri Raghukula*'; this is set in the weighty Kambhoji, a raga which lends itself admirably to *tanam* but the song is very slight when compared to the five *pancharatnas*.
32. The Umayalpuram school, and primarily from *Sangitha Kalanidhi* Maharajapuram Viswanatha Iyer.

33. 'Tyagaraja's Ghanaraga Pancharatna', *Sruti* 188, May 2000. See also Sriram V., 'How did the Pancharatna kritis originate?', *The Hindu*, Chennai, 16 January 2020.
34. K. Veerabhadra Sastri, *Tyagaraja Keertanulu, Visesha Vivaranamu*, Vol. I (1975) and Vol. II (1978) have 657 compositions. An earlier compilation, *Tyagaraja keertanalu*, with an introductory essay by Kalluri Veerabhadra Sastri, edited by Vissa Appa Rao, Rajamahendravaram: Andhra Gana Kala Parishat, 1948, lists 633 compositions with twenty-seven *utsava sampradaya kirtanas*. *Rare and Unpublished Kirtanams of Thyagaraja*, edited by T.V. Subba Rao, Andhra Gana Kala Parishat, 1951, lists another seventy-odd songs.
35. A popular website (https://shodhganga.inflibnet.ac.in/bitstream/10603/83938/8/08.chapter%202.pdf) has the information that there are 119 ragas in which Tyagaraja has just a single composition. It is possible though that some of these ragas were used at his time by other composers.
36. 'Some of his creations/finds have become popular on the concert platform today – Malayamarutam, Chittaranjani, Jayantasri, Saramati, Kalyanavasantam, Abhogi, Devamritavarshini, Nalinakanti, Kapi Narayani, Kuntalavarali, Chenchu Khambodi, Navarasakannada, Bahudari, Nagasvaravali, Janaranjani, Ranjani, Hamsanadam and Saraswati are a few examples. It is only when you peruse the list that you realise how incomplete our concert experience would have been had these ragas not been given form and structure by Tyagaraja.' Sriram V., 'A liking for rare ragas', *The Hindu*, Chennai, 2 February 2017. There is also considerable speculation on Tyagaraja's choice and use of ragas, and the possibility that his biographers and disciples played around with his texts.
37. V. Subramaniam, 'Tyagaraja – Time for Re-assessment', *Shankar's Weekly*, New Delhi, 30 July 1967.
38. V.A.K. Ranga Rao, 'Annamacharya – a lecture', 12 August 2003, sangeetham.com
39. Pappu Venugopala Rao, 'Tyagaraja's art and craft', *Sruti* 393, June 2017.
40. Mike Marqusee, 'The alchemy of art', *The Hindu*, Chennai, 14 May 2006.

41. V. Sriram, 'A product of his times', *The Hindu*, Chennai, 12 January 2018; also T.M. Krishna, 'A case of aesthetic extravagance', *The Hindu*, 4 May 2017. For instance, in *'Samayamu telisi'*/Asaveri, Tyagaraja asks, *'Turaka veedhi-lo vipruniki paanaka-pooja, neraya-cheseyemi, cheyakunte yemi?'*, Does it matter if one offers, or does not offer, prayers in the Muslim areas?'. Likewise in *'Dudukugala'*/Gaula, he sings of how, in his ignorance, he has consorted with and taught *'sudrulu vanitalu'*, which William J. Jackson in *Tyagaraja: Life and Lyrics*, Oxford and New Delhi: Oxford University Press, 1991, translates as 'dancers and womanizers, low life types as well as the weaker sex'. C. Ramanujachari (ed.), *The Spiritual Heritage of Tyagaraja*, with an Introductory Thesis by V. Raghavan, Madras: Sri Ramakrishna Math, 1966, translates the phrase as 'women and ignorant and low folk'.
42. William Logan, 'Notes towards an Introduction', *The New Criterion*, Vol. 36, No. 9, May 2018. A longer extract deserves reading. 'We cannot blame the past for being the past, for having attitudes that strike us as unfortunate or even horrifying. None has much influence on the poetry—it has effect only when critics decide that all authors should be taken to the pillory, if not the gallows. Such uses of the past condescend to the poet for failing to anticipate, within the roil of his life, what our advanced age would think, not of his poetry, but of his prejudices. We're allowed to shake our heads a little at what previous ages thought (or more usually failed to think), but we cannot escape the knowledge that the future may look askance at moral failings to which we are blind.'
43. William J. Jackson, 'Features of the Kriti: A Song Form Developed by Tyāgarāja', *Asian Music*, Vol. 24, No. 1 (Autumn, 1992 – Winter, 1993).
44. V.K. Narayana Menon, *The Tyagaraja legacy*, *AIR Miscellany 1959*, New Delhi: The Publications Division, 1959.
45. Or *sahitya, tala* and raga.
46. *The Hindu*, Chennai, 1 December 2006.
47. The musicologist T.S. Parthasarathy (1913–2006) was of the opinion [Interview with Lakshmi Devnath in *Sruti* 217, October 2002; Conversation with R. Vedavalli in *Sruti* 377, February 2016] that as the Umayalpuram brothers were only ten and twelve years old when

they came to Tyagaraja, most of what they learnt were from other disciples of Tyagaraja. The Tillaisthanam and Walajapet students learnt from Tyagaraja over a much longer period and the versions of songs sung in those traditions may be closer to what Tyagaraja actually sang, though the bulk of what is accepted as Tyagaraja on the concert platform today is from Umayalpuram.

48. Sriram V., 'The "secret" behind Tyagaraja's fame', *The Hindu*, Chennai, 5 May 2017.

49. Ethel Rosenthal, 'Tyagaraja: A Great South Indian Composer', *The Musical Quarterly*, Vol. 17, No. 1 (January 1931).

50. Gopalkrishna Gandhi, 'The Literary Styles of M.K. Gandhi and C. Rajagopalachari', Alladi Memorial Lecture 2017, Hyderabad, 5 October 2017. When Rajaji was asked in 1953 to contribute to a proposed volume on Tyagaraja being published out of Hyderabad he had it conveyed to the authorities 'that Sri Tyagaraja was a good Tamilian of Tanjore district and that only Tamilians know how to sing his compositions properly and that Rajaji is unable to contribute any article that will hand over Tyagaraja to the Andhras'.

51. William J. Jackson, 'A Life Becomes a Legend: Srī Tyāgarāja as Exemplar', *Journal of the American Academy of Religion*, Vol. 60, No. 4 (Winter, 1992).

52. Walter Isaacson in his *Leonardo da Vinci: The Biography* (Simon & Schuster, 2017) says of his subject, 'Slapping the "genius" label on Leonardo oddly minimizes him by making it seem as if he were touched by lightning ... In fact, Leonardo's genius was a human one, wrought by his own will and ambition.' Interestingly, Isaacson sees Newton and Einstein as each being a 'divine recipient ... of a mind with so much processing power that we mere mortals cannot fathom it'. Clearly, it is all a question of perception, and of faith.

53. C. Ramanujachari (ed.), *The Spiritual Heritage of Tyagaraja*, with an Introductory Thesis by V. Raghavan.

54. Aeolus, Bicentenary of Thyagaraja, *Shankar's Weekly*, 14 May 1967.

55. *The Hindu*, Madras, 29 December 1967.

56. Ibid.

57. From a limited selection of concert details available, it appears that in 1967 alone Subbulakshmi sang '*Naradamuni*' twice in concerts at

Mysore, once in Bombay, once in Madras and once on the National Programme of Music on All India Radio. All this in addition to the Christmas Day recital.

58. The song which has earlier been mentioned as a hit of Madurai Pushpavanam Iyer was one of Dhanammal's favourites. 'Though any *krti* she handled was indeed of a very high order, special mention should be made of '*Kshira sagara sayana* in *raga* Devagandhari, in which she would take up the line, "*Narimaniki*" in the *charana* and come up with such exquisite *sangatis* that I can vouchsafe it has never been handled so expertly by any other musician.' Soolamangalam Vaidyanaha Bhagavathar (1866–1943), *Cameos*, SUNADHAM, 2005.

59. Gowri Ramnarayan, 'Born To Sing', in Gowri Ramnarayan, Savita Narasimhan and V. Ramnarayan (eds), *Song of Surrender, A Centenary Tribute to M S Subbulakshmi*, Chennai: The Sruti Foundation, 2016. Happily, the song survives in the repertoire of T.M. Krishna.

60. Chitravina N. Ravikiran, 'As pitch-perfect in life as in music', *The Hindu*, Chennai, 27 December 2011.

61. Indira Menon, *Great Masters of Carnatic Music 1930-1965*, New Delhi: Indialog Publications Pvt. Ltd., 2004.

62. *The Hindu*, Madras, 9 June 1968.

63. V.R. Devika, 'Many firsts to her credit', *The Hindu*, Chennai, 9 September 2007.

64. *The Hindu*, Madras, 16 August 1968.

65. Ibid., 6 November 1968.

66. N. Pattabhi Raman, 'A trailblazing traditionalist', *The Hindu*, Madras, 27 March 1994; also *Sruti* 113, February 1994.

67. *Journal of the Music Academy*, 1969.

68. S. Thyagarajan recalls Sadasivam reading the speech, or parts of it, on the phone for Musiri Subramania Iyer's approval. Personal communication, 14 November 2016.

69. Lecture, TAG Centre, Chennai, December 2015.
दयमानदीर्घनयनां देशकरूपेण दर्शिताभ्युदयाम् । वामकुचनिहितवीणां वरदां संगीतमातृकां वन्दे ॥ २ ॥
dayamAnadIrghanayanAM deshakarUpeNa darshitAbhyudayAm |
vAmakuchanihitavINAM varadAM saMgItamAtRRikAM vande || 2||

70. A danger in attempting to translate from the Sanskrit is that what is richly evocative in the original ends up sounding corny in English.

71. It appears that they performed together often, if only privately. The Rubin Collection has a recording of 29 December 1966. James Rubin Collection, Harvard University. Most of the pieces are unidentified by the cataloguers. This probably requires a closer listening.
72. This unusual piece can be heard at https://youtu.be/vMwLr4NLdVk
73. Vijaya Rajendran, 'Amma', in R. Venkatesh (ed.), *Engal MS*, Chennai: Kalki Publications, 2010.
74. James Rubin Collection, Harvard University. The concert included '*Vatapi*', "*Tera tiyaga rada*', '*Kanjadalayatakshi*', '*O Rangasayee*', all tried and true.
75. The fare included a *khayal* in Puria Kalyan, a *dhrut* in Jaita Kalyana and a *thumri* in Misra-Khamaj.
76. Extracts can be heard on https://www.msstribute.org/music.php
77. *The Hindu*, Madras, 6 January 1969.
78. *The Times of India*, Bombay, 27 April 1969.
79. *The Hindu*, Madras, 18 July 1969, review of Krishna Gana Sabha recital on 12 July.
80. Rajeev Nair, *A Rasika's Journey Through Hindustani Music*, New Delhi: Indialog Publications Pvt. Ltd., 2007.
81. Namita Devidayal, email, 8 October 2017.
82. Aeolus, 'Festival Music II', *Shankar's Weekly*, 8 January 1967.

11: THE SINGER OF CHANTS

1. The *Madhurashtakam* of Sri Vallabhacharya (1479–1531), a Vaishnavite mystic, was recorded by Subbulakshmi in 1980; eight couplets extolling the 'madhuram' or 'sweetness' of Krishna of Mathura.
2. The available list indicates at least ninety-five benefit concerts in the decade of the 1970s, significantly more than in the previous decade.
3. Aarabhi, *The Hindu*, Madras, 27 March 1970. See also ibid., 17 April 1970.
4. *The Times of India*, Bombay, 9 September 1971.
5. *The Hindu*, Madras, 21 December 1970.
6. *Shankar's Weekly*, New Delhi, 27 December 1970.
7. *The Times of India*, Bombay, 27 April 1969.

8. Ibid., 12 October 1969. *Nadopasana* is, most simply, '*worship through music*'. *Kachheri pantha* is '*concert practice*'.
9. Gowri Ramnarayan, 'Trailblazing Traditionalist, Part 1', *Sruti* 1, October 1983, and 'Trailblazing Traditionalist, Part 2', *Sruti* 2, November 1983.
10. D.K. Pattammal, 'Proforma for Fellows/Awardees', Sangeet Natak Akademi, 1 March 1990.
11. Anonymous, *Gana Saraswathi D.K. Pattammal: Dimensions of a Divine Songster*, Coimbatore: Bharatiya Vidya Bhavan, 2007.
12. Anonymous, 'Pattammal in fine form', *The Times of India*, New Delhi, 20 August 1960. The reference is to Tyagaraja's composition, see Note 1, Chapter 8.
13. *The Hindustan Times*, New Delhi, 4 July 1993.
14. Aeolus, 'Sabres and Steamrollers', *Shankar's Weekly*, New Delhi, 29 September 1963.
15. *Gana Saraswathi D.K. Pattammal: Dimensions of a Divine Songster*.
16. A Mrs Nagaswamy Iyer also performed at the Music Academy's 1935 season.
17. D.K. Pattammal, 'Proforma for Fellows/Awardees', Sangeet Natak Akademi, 1 March 1990.
18. K.S. Mahadevan, 'The sound of classical purity', *The Indian Express*, Madras, 16 April 1989; Charumati Supraja, Musical moments, *The Deccan Herald*, Bangalore, 8 June 2003.
19. S. Kalidas, 'Matriarch of Music', *India Today*, 15 February 1999.
20. K.S. Mahadevan, *The Indian Express*, Madras, 16 April 1989.
21. *The Hindu*, Madras, 22 December 1978.
22. *Shankar's Weekly*, 21 October 1962.
23. Gowri Ramnarayan, 'Elegance, not flamboyance, was her forte', *The Hindu*, Chennai, 17 July 2009.
24. Vishnu Vasudev, 'Who was Pattammal?', blog, 17 July 2009.
25. *Gana Saraswathi D.K. Pattammal: Dimensions of a Divine Songster*.
26. This is available on YouTube.
27. Conversation with Gopalkrishna Gandhi, Coonoor, 30 December 2017.
28. *Sruti*, 27 & 28, December 1986, p. 3.

29. This is fortuitously available on the excellent, non-profit website, sangeethapriya.
30. Again, on sangeethapriya.
31. Aarabhi, *The Hindu*, Madras, 5 March 1971.
32. Commentaries on the *Sri Daksinamurti Stotra* of Adi Sankara suggest that the particular verse sung by Subbulakshmi is one of six additional verses 'purported to be part of the original hymn'. ॐ नमः प्रणवार्थाय शुद्धज्ञानैकमूर्तये । निर्मलाय प्रशान्ताय दक्षिणामूर्तये नमः, '*Obeisance to Him who is the inner meaning of the (sacred) syllable Om, and whose nature is pure consciousness. Obeisance to Sri Daksinamurti, the stainless and serene beyond measure*'. Translation from *Sri Sankaracarya's Daksinamurti Stotra with the Varttika Manassolasa of Suresvararya* by Swami Harshananda, Ramakrishna Math, Bangalore, 1992
33. Aarabhi, *The Hindu*, Madras, 13 August 1971. See also ibid., 23 October 1971.
34. A mutilated version of this fine concert has been commercially released, with no annotation.
35. *The Hindu*, Madras, 31 December 1971.
36. This can be heard at sangeethapriya.
37. Jon Higgins, 'Padams and Balasaraswati', reproduced in Programme Book of 11th Dance Festival, January 2017, The Music Academy, Madras.
38. G. Venkatachalam, review of *Bharata Natyam* (in Tamil) by T. Balasarasvati and V. Raghavan, Avvai Noolagam, Madras, published in *The Journal of the Madras Music Academy*, Vol. XXX, 1959.
39. Kimiko Ohtani, 'Bharata Nāṭyam, Rebirth of Dance in India', *Studia Musicologica Academiae Scientiarum Hungaricae*, T. 33, Fasc. 1/4 (1991).
40. *Sruti* 4 & 5, February-March 1984. See full text at Balasaraswati, 'On Bharata Natyam', *Dance Chronicle*, Vol. 2, No. 2 (1978).
41. Shanta Serbjeet Singh, 'Sringara – The Erotic in Dance', *The Illustrated Weekly of India*, 12 June 1977.
42. 'In the history of dance, we find every now and then a supreme artist who dominates the field for a generation, enriching the existing tradition, providing a corrective to current practices and setting standards for generations to follow. Anna Pavlova was one such artist and so was Vaslav Nijnsky. And today in India Balasaraswati

is one.' Narayana Menon, *Balasaraswati*, with photographs by Marilyn Silverstone, New Delhi: Inter-National Cultural Centre, n.d., [Silverstone's photos are from 1960].
43. Letter from E.N. Purushothaman, *Sruti* 164, May 1998.
44. Leela Venkataraman, 'The Incomparable Bala', *Link*, 16 June 1985.
45. K.N. Raghavendra Rao, 'Curtain Call', *India Today*, 29 February 1984.
46. V. Patanjali, *The Illustrated Weekly of India*, 25 May 1969.
47. Beryl de Zoete, *The Other Mind, A Study of Dance in South India*, New York: Theatre Arts Books, 1960.
48. *The Washington Post*, 6 November 1962.
49. As for instance, Bombay, 24 January 1974; Varanasi, 28 January 1974.
50. Ramon Magsaysay Award, http://rmaward.asia/
51. Winners in this category in subsequent years have included the Gandhian social worker Baba Amte and the physicians Banoo Coyaji and V. Shanta. Of Jayaprakash Narayan, older readers will recall the striking slogan of early 1977 when India went to the polls, '*Andhere mein ek prakash, Jayaprakash, Jayaprakash!*, In the darkness, one light!'
52. Githa Hariharan, 'The Sari and the Fan', *The Telegraph*, Kolkata, 4 December 2005.
53. The 1974 Ramon Magsaysay Award for Public Service, Biography, M.S. Subbulakshmi, Presented on 31 August 1974.
54. Conversation with K.R. Athmanathan, 13 January 2018.
55. Conversation with Gowri Ramnarayan, 28 June 2017.
56. Conversation with C.B. Srinivasan, 1 February 2017.
57. T.J.S. George, *MS: A Life in Music*, New Delhi: HarperCollins Publishers India, 2004.
58. *The Hindu*, Madras, 3 October 1975.
59. Ravi and Sridhar, 'The nightingale has flown', blog on sangeetham. com, 14 December 2004.
60. "Radio Recitals (Excerpts) – M.S. Subbulakshmi", 1994 (CDNF147767).
61. Personal communication from David Godman.
62. Including two sets of songs, "Sri Sankara Stuti – M.S.Subbulakshmi", 1987 (TPHVS32449) and "SatAbdi samarpaN by M.S. Subbulakshmi", 1993 (CDNF147719).

63. 'Satya Sai Sangeetanjali – An offering at His Lotus Feet by M.S.Subbulakshmi', 1996 (SFHVS849343).
64. For more on this particular householder mystic, see also David McIver, 'Guru Sri Atmananda', *The Illustrated Weekly of India*, 19 September 1965.
65. And even at New York. *The Hindu*, Madras, 12 December 1970.
66. Ibid., 25 August 1970.
67. Vasudha Narayanan, *Singing the Glory of the Divine Name: Parasara Bhattar's commentary on the Visnu Sahasranama. Festschrift on the 60th Birthday of Dr. S.S. Janaki*. Madras: Kuppuswami Sastri Research Institute, 1991, pp. 306–19.
68. Not all listeners were enthralled. Mariamma Chacko, the unhappy protagonist of Manu Joseph's novel, *The Illicit Happiness of Other People*, was woken daily to 'Subbulakshmi's morning chant from a thousand bad radios, which sounds like a medieval woman's list of complaints in Sanskrit about the men of her time'.
69. Yadav Murti Sankaran, 'Kunjamma and Sankaranna', in Gowri Ramnarayan (ed), *Song of Surrender*, Chennai: Sruti Publications, 2016. See also T. Sankaran, *Sruti* 25, October 1986, p. 25. There is still in the collection of Subbulakshmi's family a six-stringed Miraj tambura, crafted by Prof. Haji Abdul Karim of Miraj, gifted to her by Balasaraswati and other members of the Dhanammal family around the time of the *Sahasranamam* recording and possibly used during that recording. The companion tambura to this one, also from Miraj (and with the family) (Collection of S. Aishwarya, Bangalore, 25 July 2017) is the famous instrument which belonged to Semmangudi Srinivasa Iyer and which has in place of the small knobs used to tighten the strings, as a gift from Musiri Subramania Iyer, small golden horses which once belonged to Kanchipuram Naina Pillai.
70. *Sruti* 60 & 61, September-October 1989, p. 59.
71. 'Sri Kamakshi Suprabhatam & other songs in praise of Sri Kamakshi – M.S. Subbulakshmi (Devotional)', 1974 (SFHVS847114).
72. So much so that Prof. Vasudha Narayanan, Distinguished Professor, Department of Religion, at the University of Florida has been known to say, and only partly in jest, that Subbulakshmi did more for the spread of Vaisnavism than Ramanuja himself.

73. *Sruti* 235, April 234, p. 41.
74. Rupert Snell, email of 16 January 2018.
75. 'Sri Kamakshi Suprabhatam & other songs in praise of Sri Kamakshi – M.S. Subbulakshmi (Devotional)', 1974 (SFHVS847114).
76. 'Kashi-Rameswaram Suprabhatam – M.S. Subbulakshmi (Sanskrit Devotional)', 1977 (TPHVS32303).
77. As stated at a public function in Varanasi on 17 March 1977, Rama Navami by the Hindu calendar. I have a vivid memory of the day's beginning, a pre-dawn recitation of the hymn by Subbulakshmi and Radha at the Viswanath temple.

12: SUBBULAKSHMI

1. *veena-vaadana-dasa-gamakakriye*. A *gamaka* refers to an embellishment or ornamentation which a performer may bring to the exposition of a raga.
2. For more details on the discussion which follows, see Emmie te Nijenhuis and Sanjukta Gupta, *Sacred Songs of India, Dikshitar's Cycle of Hymns to the Goddess Kamala*, Winterthur, Switzerland: Amadeus, 1987.
3. *Vaara* means day, hence a *vaara kriti* is the song for the day. The scholar-musician T.M. Krishna has studied in great detail the *vaara kritis*, the *guruguha vibhakti kritis* and the *Tyagaraja vibhakti kritis*, as they are presented in Subbarama Dikshitar's *Sangita Sampradaya Pradarsini* (SSP) (1905). He states that all of these songs as presented today differ in subtle ways from the notation in the SSP, suggesting that difficult and unusual phrases visualized by Muthusvami Dikshitar have been replaced in concert practice by phrases which are easier to render. The fact that the songs as presented today have great musical merit complicates the issue. All this suggests that there were many ideas on what phrases were and were not permissible in a raga, a feature rather similar to different renderings of a raga by different gharanas in the Hindustani style [Muddusvami Dikshitar's Vaara Kritis from the Sangeetha Sampradaya Pradarshini, Presented by T.M. Krishna, Raga Sudha, Chennai, 5 May 2019].
4. *Navagraha*, or nine planets; the seven principal planets, other than the earth, and Rahu, the Dragon's Head, and Ketu, the Dragon's Tail,

making nine. Rahu and Ketu are not identified, astronomically, with any known planet but with points in space where the trajectories of the sun and moon intersect.

5. Commercial recording, S. Sowmya.
6. Commercial recording, D.K. Jayaraman.
7. Commercial recording, S. Sowmya.
8. There are fragments, of what may have originally been sets of eight songs, consisting presently only of a limited number, on Balamba at Vaidyesvarakoil, Govindaraja at Chidambaram, Mangalamba at Kumbakonam and Ekamranatha at Kanchipuram.
9. Gowri Ramnarayan, Savita Narasimhan and V. Ramnarayan (eds), *Song of Surrender*, Chennai: Sruti Foundation, 2016.
10. Conversation with Gowri Ramnarayan, 28 June 2017, Chennai. *Navavarana*, or nine appearances, in this case of the mother goddess. The *navavarana kritis* are steeped in tantric text.
11. Commercial recording, T.M. Krishna.
12. Commercial recording, D.K. Jayaraman. The *kriti* 'Sri Kalahastisa'/Huseni, which Subbulakshmi was not known to sing, on the manifestation as the wind, includes the imaginative phrase 'anila-akasa-bhumi-salila-agni prakasa', or 'the one who manifests as wind, sky, earth, water and fire'.
13. In a very detailed study of the Abhayamba *kritis*, David Shulman has argued that Muthusvami Dikshitar moved the locus of south Indian classical music from the temples to more secular settings but without in any way taking away from devotional and ritual content. His compositions, rich in iconographic detail and in layers of more and more intense levels of worship, shine in a concert setting. They are not necessarily either part of temple practice or of private devotions. David Shulman, *Muthusvami Dikshitar and The Invention of Modern Carnatic Music, The Abhayamba Vibhakti-kritis*, Amsterdam: J. Gonda Fund Foundation of the KNAW, 2014.
14. Chandra S. Balachandran and Surinder M. Bhardwaj, 'Geography as Melody in Muthusvami Dikshitar's Indian Musical Works', *Geographical Review*, Vol. 91, No. 4 (October 2001); also Nandini Ramani, 'Dikshitar's Varanasi connection', *The Hindu*, Chennai, 22 June 2017.

15. M.S. Ramaswami Aiyar, *Thiagaraja, A Great Musician Saint*, Madras: Everyman's Press, 1927.
16. Indira V. Petersen, 'Sanskrit in Carnatic Music: The songs of Muthusvami Dikshitar', *Indo-Iran J* (1986) 29: 183. https://doi.org/10.1007/BF00959107
17. Rajeswari, 'Festivals full of pep', *Shankar's Weekly*, 16 March 1975.
18. *The Hindu*, Madras, 26 December 1975.
19. K. Swaminathan, 'Golden voice of India', *The Indian Express*, Madras, 3 October 1976.
20. *Sruti* 302, November 2009, p. 47.
21. *Sruti* 273, June 2007, p. 28.
22. S. Soundararaja Iyengar was the elder brother of S. Kasturiranga Iyengar (1859–1923), Managing Director of *The Hindu* from 1905 onwards. S. Kasturiranga Iyengar's son K. Srinivasan (1887–1959), Managing Director/Chief Editor of *The Hindu* from 1923 onwards, was one of the witnesses at Subbulakshmi's marriage in 1940, an admirer and promoter of the theatre and film actor and singer K.B. Sundarambal, and a witness at M.L. Vasanthakumari's marriage. Dewan Bahadur N. Gopalaswami Ayyangar (1882–1953), defence minister in Prime Minister Nehru's cabinet was a son of a sister of S. Soundararaja Iyengar and S. Kasturiranga Iyengar, and consequently cousin to both T. Brinda and K. Srinivasan. His elder son-in-law C. Bhashyam Iyengar (1902?–59) was the patron of Subbulakshmi's sister M.S. Vadivambal. His younger son-in-law V.K. Thiruvenkatachari (1904–84) was T. Balasaraswati's lawyer in the property dispute which arose after the death of her patron R.K. Shanmukham Chetty. In these various ways were the personal and professional lives of these well-placed Iyengar families linked with the devadasi clans.
23. *Sruti*, 273, June 2007, p. 26.
24. A.K. Ramanujan, Velcheru Narayana Rao and David Shulman (edited and translated by), *Where God Is a Customer, Telugu Courtesan Songs by Kshetrayya and Others*, Berkeley, California: University of California Press, 1994. There is also some recent speculation that Kshetrayya the poet did not exist and that even if he did the poems attributed to him were actually the work of erudite courtesans, presumably the only persons with any understanding of carnal desire. Swarnamalya

Ganesh, 'Kshetrayya and the legacy of erasing women's voices from erotic poetry', *The News Minute*, 14 February 2020, citing the work of Harshita Mruthinti Kamath of Emory University.

25. Aeolus, 'Allegory of Love', *Shankar's Weekly*, New Delhi, 25 August 1963.
26. Gidugu Venkata Sitapati (compiled by), *Kshetrayya Padamulu* (in Telugu), Pithapuram, 1952.
27. Blog by Ram of 19 January 2009 with details of lecture by Dr Nirmala Sundararajan and Dr Subhashini Parthasarathy, 23 December 2008.[https://ramsabode.wordpress.com/2009/01/19/padams-javalis-as-handled-in-brinda-mukta-bani/]
28. Narayana Menon, *Balasaraswati*, New Delhi: Inter-National Cultural Centre, year of publication not specified, probably 1960.
29. Matthew Harp Allen, 'Tales Tunes Tell: Deepening the Dialogue between "Classical" and "Non-Classical" in the Music of India', *Yearbook for Traditional Music*, Vol. 30 (1998).
30. Aeolus, *Shankar's Weekly*, 5 March 1967.
31. Davesh Soneji, *Unfinished Gestures*, Ranikhet: Permanent Black, 2012.
32. T. Brinda, *Javalis*, The Music Academy, 1960.
33. Shanta Serbjeet Singh, 'Sringara – The Erotic in Dance', *The Illustrated Weekly of India*, 12 June 1977.
34. Nirmala Sundararajan, Personal communication, 13 August 2017.
35. Aeolus, 'Music In Opera And Dance', *Shankar's Weekly*, 5 May 1963.
36. HMV, Radio Recitals (Excerpts) – M.S. Subbulakshmi, 1994 (CDNF147764/147766).
37. Conversation with Gowri Ramnarayan, 28 June 2017.
38. Gowri Ramnarayan, 'Mukti, Voicing Freedom', in Gowri Ramnarayan, Savita Narasimhan and V. Ramnarayan (eds), *Song of Surrender...*
39. Conversation with K. Sujatha Rao, 7 September 2017.
40. Kiranavali Vidyasankar, 'A musician's musician', *The Hindu*, Chennai, 18 April 2004.
41. Rajeswari, 'Music', *Shankar's Weekly*, 14 July 1974.
42. *Nauka Charitram*, directed by Saroj Satyanarayana, 1996. See also Saroj Satyanarayana, 'Lingering impressions', *The Hindu*, Chennai, 22 March

1998. Also 'Nauka Charitramu: A Pretentious Film, Off-Target too', *Sruti* 150, March 1997, p. 17.
43. Conversation with Nirmala Sundararajan, 13 August 2017.
44. *The Hindu*, Madras, 1 October 1976.
45. Ibid., 26 November 1976.
46. Ravi & Sridhar, 'Brinda-Muktha: Bastions of a Glorious Tradition', *Sruti* 273, June 2007, p. 23.
47. 'Trip down memory lane',*The Hindu*, Madras, 28 October 1988.
48. Email from R.K. Shriram Kumar, 24 February 2018.
49. Kripa Subrahmaniam, 'Majestic like the Ganga', *The Hindu*, Chennai, 14 February 2003.
50. Conversation, M. Ravindra Narayanan (Ravi), Tiruvannamalai, 26 January 2018.
51. *The Hindu*, Chennai, 12 March 2007.
52. 'Musician T. Muktha passes away', *The Hindu*, Chennai, 12 March 2007; Ritha Rajan, 'She enriched the Dhanammal legacy', ibid., 16 March 2007; Gowri Ramnarayan, 'Different schools, own style', ibid., 9 February 2007.
53. *The Hindu*, Madras, 24 December 1976.
54. Conversation with Janaki Nathen, 15 January 2017.
55. As for instance, a random selection from a larger list, on 22 January 1974 in Bombay, at the Brahma Gana Sabha on 18 August 74, for the Satabhishekam of Kanchi Acharya at Kasi Viswanatha Temple, Mambalam in June 1975, at Venus Colony in May 1975, at Connemara Hotel for International Music Week on 29 Sep 1975 and in March 1977 at Varanasi.
56. Thirumalai, 'Subbulakshmi', *The Times of India*, Bombay, 11 October 1976.
57. M.S. Subbulakshmi – Live at Carnegie Hall, New York, 1981, (CDNF147808/809).
58. A song she had performed forty years earlier at her first Academy appearance in 1938, and which she was to perform again in the Academy in December 1978, her last season appearance on that stage.
59. Vidya Shankar, *Musiri's Concept of Music*, Madras: The Music Academy, 1999.
60. *The Hindu*, Madras, 16 August 1968.

61. Other recordings of this piece, with the *neraval*, are available, as for instance, in a Music Club recital of March 1970 and a Krishna Gana Sabha recital of February 1976, both in the archives of the TAG Digital Listening Centre, The Music Academy, Chennai.
62. Record played on AIR Madras, 22 January 1942.
63. *The New Yorker*, 1 November 2016.
64. A record can be found of such recitals at Boston (with the *ragam-tanam-pallavi* in Shanmukhapriya) and at Amherst, Washington, Seattle, Houston, Chicago and Detroit at the website msstribute.org
65. This can be heard at the website msstribute.org
66. Letter of 18 April 2000 from M.S. Subbulakshmi to the Library Director, Eda Kuhn Loeb Music Library.
67. Gowri Ramnarayan, 'But history will remain...', *The Hindu*, Chennai, 11 June 2003. Another old friend referred to the Kalki Gardens establishment as *nityakalyanam*, or continuous wedding festivities. Janaki Nathen, 15 January 2017. See also T.J.S. George, *MS: A Life in Music*, pp. 230–33.
68. Letter from C.R. Krishnaswami to Devadas Gandhi, 11 August 1950.
69. Gopalkrishna Gandhi, at Amethyst, Chennai, 14 October 2017.
70. Sriram Venkatkrishnan, 'A trip to remember', *The Hindu*, Chennai, 18 September 2009.
71. Personal communication from Hemalatha Murli, 23 December 2016. Also, from Usha Krishnan and R. Ganesh, 30 March 2017. Also, Dr C. V. Krishnaswami, 'Being Her Physician', in Gowri Ramnarayan, Savita Narasimhan and V. Ramnarayan (eds), *Song of Surrender*...
72. That these meant something to her is evident from the fact that she has listed these carefully in the 'Life Sketch and Bio-data proforma' demanded by the Sangeet Natak Akademi of its Fellows. No Fellow, howsoever grand, Subbulakshmi, Balasaraswati, Pattammal, was exempted from filling out this form.
73. *Sruti* 39 & 40, December 1987–January 1988, p.17, *Sruti* 75 & 76 December 1990-January 1991, p.14.
74. *The Statesman*, Calcutta, 11 December 1989.
75. *Free Press Journal*, Bombay, 7 November 1990.
76. B.V.K. Sastry, *The Illustrated Weekly of India*, Bombay, 1963.
77. R. Sarada, 'The complete musician', *The Economic Times*, New Delhi, 31 October 1992.

78. Aeolus, 'Festival Music', *Shankar's Weekly*, 15 January 1967.
79. Randor Guy, *The Hindu*, Madras, 9 November 1990; Rupa Gopal, 'Voice with an enchanting lilt', *The Hindu*, Chennai, 8 November 2002.
80. Subbudu, 'A Singer from the South', *The Statesman*, Calcutta, 5 March 1960.
81. Ibid.
82. *The Hindu*, Madras, 21 April 1960.
83. Sudha Ragunathan, 'A Friend of My Guru', in Gowri Ramnarayan, Savita Narasimhan and V. Ramnarayan (eds), *Song of Surrender...*
84. *The Hindu*, Madras, 14 January 1951.
85. *Sampradaya*, Newsletter, 5 October 1991, has a detailed account of Vasanthakumari's views on music teaching. See also Gowri Ramnarayan, 'Perfect foil for her guru', *The Hindu*, Chennai, 2 November 2007; *Sruti* 74, November 1990, p. 46, where 21 students paid tribute to their teacher, and *Sruti* 4 & 5, February-March 1984, p. 8.
86. Letter from M.L. Vasanthakumari to the Chairman, Sangeet Natak Akademi, New Delhi, 10 February 1989.
87. R. Sarada, 'The complete musician', *The Economic Times*, New Delhi, 31 October 1992.
88. Ibid.
89. B.V.K. Sastry, M.L. Vasanthakumari, *The Illustrated Weekly of India*, 23 February 1964.
90. N.C. Parthasarathy and N.C. Dwaraka Parthasarathy, *Compositions of Sri Syama Sastri*, Madras: Madras Sangita Kala Sala Publications, 1970.
91. T.K. Govinda Rao (compiled and edited by), *Compositions of Syama Sastri, Subbaraya Sastri and Annaswami Sastri*, Chennai: Ganamandir Publications India, 1997.
92. See Glossary.
93. So much so that one critic fussed, 'Are there no other *swarajatis*?', *The Hindu*, Madras, 6 November 1968.
94. https://blog.msstribute.org/ms-repertoire-tarunam-idhamma-composer-shyama-sastri/
95. I owe this information to V. Navaneeth Krishnan.
96. *Sruti* 57 & 58, June-July 1989, p. 7.

97. V. Raghavan, 'Syama Sastri's Genius: A Bicentenary Homage', *The Hindu*, Madras, 5 May 1962.
98. M.S. Ramaswami, *The Art of Subbaraya Sastri*, Souvenir of the Music Academy, Madras, 56th Conference, 1982.
99. Aeolus, 'A Gifted Family', *Shankar's Weekly*, New Delhi, 5 March 1967.
100. V. Raghavan, 'Syama Sastri's Genius: A Bicentenary Homage', *The Hindu*, Madras, 5 May 1962. 'It will be no exaggeration to say that the art of Karnatic-Kriti composition reached its acme in the author of *Janani ninuvina* and *Emanine*.' See also *Subbaraya Sastri left us almost nothing, and left us everything*, blog post by Vishnu Vasudev, 4 November 2019.
101. RGK, 'Homage to Tyagaraja', *The Illustrated Weekly of India*, Bombay, 26 March 1978.
102. Recording at TAG Digital Listening Centre, The Music Academy, Chennai.
103. Masterworks from the NCPA Archives, Sony Music, 2015.
104. *The Hindu*, Madras, 29 December 1978.
105. Ibid., 19 December 1978.
106. Ibid., 22 December 1978.
107. HMV 'Sri Venkateswara (Balaji) Pancharatnamala – Sri Annammacharya Samkirtanas – M.S. Subbulakshmi', 1980 Vol. 1 and 2 (CDNF147080/147082) with eight and six Annamacharya songs each, Vol. 2 also including two *Tamil* verses from the Vaishnava tradition, one of which is Rajaji's *Kurai onrum illai*; 'Sri Venkateswara (Balaji) Pancharatnamala – Sri Annammacharya Samkirtanas – M.S.Subbulakshmi', 1981 Vol. 5 (CNF147082) with six Annamacharya songs; HMV 'Sri Annammacharya Samkirtanas – M.S.Subbulakshmi', 1994 (CDNF147058) with ten Annamacharya songs.
108. Velcheru Narayana Rao and David Shulman (trans.), *God on the Hill, Temple Poems from Tirupati, Annamayya*, New Delhi: Oxford University Press, 2005; William J. Jackson, *Songs of Three Great South Indian Saints*, New Delhi: Oxford University Press, 1998.
109. Pappu Venugopala Rao, *Flowers at His Feet, an insight into Annamacharya's compositions*, Hyderabad: Saptaparni, 2nd edition, 2014.

110. Velcheru Narayana Rao and David Shulman (trans.), *God on the Hill*...
111. A fine selection of these may be found in A.K. Ramanujan, Velcheru Narayana Rao and David Shulman, (eds), *Where God Is a Customer*...
112. Review by V.A.K. Ranga Rao of Indira Menon, *The Madras Quartet*, *Sruti* 194, November 2000, p.49.
113. V.A.K. Ranga Rao, *Sruti* 238, July 2004, p. 3.
114. *Sruti* 202, July 2001, p. 32 and *Sruti* 268, January 2007, p. 12.
115. *Sruti* 29, February 1987, p. 20.
116. Gowri Ramnarayan, 'Songs shone with his quiet genius', *The Hindu*, Chennai, 20 February 2004.
117. Anviksha, 'An Indian Perspective', 5 October 2013, http://anviksha.vakmumbai.org/balaji-pancharatnamala-story-behind-it/
118. *Sruti* 265, October 2006, p. 46.
119. HMV, 'Sri Venkateswara (Balaji) Pancharatnamala – M.S.Subbulakshmi', 1981 Vol. 3 and 4 (CDNF147079/147081) both consisting only of chants, eight in *Sanskrit* and one in *Hindi*.
120. Conversation with R. Veezhinathan, 8 September 2017.
121. Parvez Dewan (ed.), *The Hanuman Chalisa of Goswami Tulasi Das*, New Delhi: Viking, 2001.

13: THE YEARS OF RETIREMENT

1. The last, plaintive lines of Dilip Kumar Roy's song to the Ganga in Bengali, '*Maa, Bhagirathi, Jahnavi, suradhuni, kala kallolini Gange!*', in a fuller translation, *Ganga, who is Bhagirathi, who came to the earth being moved by Bhagiratha's penance, who is Jahnavi, who was swallowed by the mighty Jahnu and then, in his compassion, released by him, divine being, sonorous in her beauty, Mother!*
2. The recital consisted of '*Vandeham*'/Hamsadhwani, '*Vachamago*'/Kaikavasi, '*Anandanatamaduvar*'/Purvikalyani, '*Hariharaputram*'/Vasanta, '*Dasarathe*'/Todi, '*Aliveni*'/Kurinji, '*Narayana*'/Suddhadhanyasi and '*Nanati bratuku*'/Revati. Akashvani Sangeet, 2005 includes only four of the pieces and several bhajans, suggesting misleadingly that that was the concert.
3. '*Nee sati daivamu (daru)*'/Sriranjini, '*Banturiti*'/Hamsanadam, '*Natanala bhramayaku*'/Lalita, '*Mayamm'a*/Ahiri, '*Kerala dharini*'/Mohana,

'*Pakkala*'/Kharaharapriya, '*Kailasa saila bhuvane*' (sloka)/Dhanyasi, Valaji, Sindhubhairavi, '*Patitodhharini gange*'. Recorded in Calcutta on 28 October 1979 and broadcast on 17 November 1979.

4. '*Nenendu*'/Karnataka Behag, '*Tulasidala*'/Mayamalavagaula, '*Nidhi tsala*'/Kalyani, '*Ksheerasagarasayana*'/Devagandhari, '*Sitamma*'/Vasanta and '*Vinayakuni*'/Madhyamavati.

5. '*Vidulaku*'/Mayamalavagaula, '*Rama nannu brovaravemako*'/ Harikambhoji and '*Nidhi tsala*'/Kalyani.

6. '*Tsalakalla*'/Arabhi, '*Apparamabhakti*'/Pantuvarali, '*Giripai*'/Sahana, '*Tsallare*'/Ahiri, '*Sobhillu*'/Jaganmohini, '*Emineramu*'/Sankarabharanam and '*Karunajaladhe*'/Nadanamakriya.

7. 'A saint when she sings', *The Hindu*, Madras, 20 December 1981.

8. Sakuntala Narasimhan, 'Striking a note of perfection', *The Indian Express*, Madras, 12 February 1989; Lakshmi Viswanathan, *Kunjamma*, New Delhi: Roli Books, 2003, p. 124.

9. Norman Cutler, 'The Fish-eyed Goddess Meets the Movie Star: An Eyewitness Account of the Fifth International Tamil Conference', *Pacific Affairs*, Vol. 56, No. 2 (Summer, 1983).

10. Kesoram Year Book 2008, with extracts from *A Rare Legacy Echoes from within* by B.K. Birla.

11. *The Hindu*, Madras, 15 April 1982.

12. André Jurres, Egon Kraus, John Evarts, Hadelin Donnet and H.H. Stuckenschmidt, 'Bulletin of the International Music Council' (UNESCO) 1/1982, *The World of Music*, Vol. 24, No. 1 (1982).

13. Max Harrison, 'Eastern approach', *The Times*, London, 23 March 1982.

14. 'MS delights London audience', *The Hindu* 2 April 1982.

15. 'Science and Music: Truth and Beauty', Editorial by P. Balaram, *Current Science*, Vol. 87, No. 12, 25 December 2004.

16. 'D. Litt for M.S.', *Mid-Day*, Bombay, 1 October 1987 (from the University of Madras); 'M.K. Varsity to honour M.S. Subbulakshmi', *The Hindu*, Madras, 8 November 1994 (from the Madurai Kamaraj University).

17. Conversation with Kezevino Aram, 28 November 2017. Gandhigram is a rural university near Madurai.

18. 'Bharati Songs (Tamil) – M.S. Subbulakshmi', 1983 (CDNF158603); also *The Hindu*, Madras, 12 September 1983.

19. *Sruti* 245, February 2005, p. 5.
20. 'Radhamadhavam – Sangeeta Kalanidhi M.S.Subbulakshmi', 1983 (TPHVS32423); also *The Hindu*, Madras, 6 December 1983.
21. 'Surdas Bhajans (Hindi Devotional) – Sangeeta Kalanidhi M.S. Subbulakshmi', 1986 (STHVS65009). The bhajans were tuned for Subbulakshmi by P.S. Srinivasa Rao, *Sruti* 340, January 2013, p. 5.
22. 'New Classicals – M.S. Subbulakshmi', 1988 (CDNF147881).
23. Gowri Ramnarayan, 'Recording a Legend', *The Hindu*, Chennai, 16 September 2010; also H.M.V. Raghu, '*Totally Cooperative*', in in Gowri Ramnarayan, Savita Narasimhan and V. Ramnarayan (eds), *Song of Surrender*...
24. '50 Indians who matter', *The Illustrated Weekly of India*, Bombay, 27 January-2 February 1985; S. Shankar Menon, 'Greatness', *The Economic Times*, Bombay, 4 May 1986; T. Sadasivam, 'My Wife M.S. Subbulakshmi', *The Illustrated Weekly of India*, Bombay, 18 May 1986; 'The Genius of M.S. Subbulakshmi', *The Times of India*, 7 February 1987; Visalam R. Krishnan, 'An evening with M.S.', *Hindustan Times*, New Delhi, 27 April 1987; Gowri Ramnarayan, 'The musical genius of MS', *The Hindu*, Madras, 29 July 1987; Madan S. Pathania, 'MS: Above all musical prejudices', *Patriot*, New Delhi, 4 November 1987; 'Concerts for a cause', ibid., 15 November 1987; 'Six decades of divine music', *The Sunday Statesman*, Calcutta, 14 March 1993; K.S. Mahadevan, 'Spiritual beauty, humility', *The Indian Express*, Madras, 13 September 1991; Vatsala Vedantam, 'The magic of Subbulakshmi', *Deccan Herald*, Bangalore, 9 May 1993; H.Y. Sharada Prasad, 'When Music is both penance and liberation', *Deccan Chronicle*, Hyderabad, 1996; Subbudu, 'The woman who ennobles', *The Statesman*, Calcutta, 11 November 1996; R. Varadarajan, 'Transporting rasikas into spiritual realm', *The Hindu*, Chennai, 3 April 1998.
25. *The Sunday Statesman*, Calcutta, 14 March 1993.
26. Vasumathi Badrinathan, *Business & Political Observer*, 10 April 1992.
27. Subbudu, *The Statesman*, Calcutta, 11 November 1996.
28. M.G. Swaminath, *The Evening News*, New Delhi, 29 January 1993.
29. Vatsala Vedantam, *Deccan Herald*, Bangalore, 9 May 1993.
30. K.S. Mahadevan, *The Indian Express*, Madras, 13 September 1991.
31. P. Murari, *The Times of India*, New Delhi, 7 February 1987.

32. *Sruti* 33&34, June/July 1987, pp. 39–47.
33. S. Krishnan (ed.), *Malgudi Landscapes, The Best of R.K. Narayan*, New Delhi: Penguin, 1982.
34. Alessandro Vescovi, 'R.K. Narayan's 'Selvi' as a reflection upon the feminine self', *Annali della Facolta di Lettere e Filosofia dell'Universita degli Studi di Milano (ACME)*, Vol. LXIV, Fascicolo 1, Gennaio-Aprile 2011. In an earlier 2008 piece, 'R.K. Narayan's '*Selvi*' as a rewriting of *The Guide*', Vescovi makes the case that the plot of *Selvi* was also used by Narayan in his much more famous novel published in 1958, *The Guide*.
35. M.S. Subbulakshmi, Live at Russia, Saregama CDNF 157100/157101.
36. 'Steeped in divinity', *The Hindu*, Chennai, 3 February 2006.
37. *Sruti* 36, September 1987, p. 8.
38. Ramaswamy R. Iyer, *Karnatak Music: The Recent Years*, South Delhi Music Circle Souvenir, December 1988. In fairness, it must be recognized that when it was Mani Krishnaswami's turn to be honoured by the Music Academy, she was handsome in her tribute: 'Women artistes of today and tomorrow owe a debt of gratitude to the illustrious stalwarts Smt. M.S. Subbulakshmi, Smt. D.K. Pattammal, Smt. M.L. Vasanthakumari, Smt. Brinda and Smt. Balasaraswati,' *Journal of the Music Academy*, 1994, speech on 17 December 1993.
39. *Kalakshetra Quarterly*, Vol. VII, No. 4.
40. Ayana D. Angadi and Franz Walter, manifestations de la saison, The World of Music, Vol. 5, No. 4 (July-August 1963).
41. Vasudha Narayanan, 'Performing Arts, Reforming Rituals: Women and Social Change in India', in Tracy Pintchman (ed.), *Women's Lives, Women's Rituals in the Hindu Traditions*, Albany: State University of New York Press, 2007.
42. *Sruti* 15, March 1985, p. 6.
43. *Sruti* 50, November 1988, p. 13.
44. *Sruti* 69&70, June-July 1990, p. 15.
45. *Sruti* 26, November 1986, p. 47.
46. *Sruti* 41, February 1988, p. 26.
47. *Sruti* 25, September 1986, p. 26.
48. *Sruti* 23, June-July 1986, p. 13.
49. *Sruti* 30, March 1987, p. 5.
50. *Sruti* 97, October 1992, p. 8.

51. *Sruti* 21-S, March 1986, p. 5.
52. *Sruti* 22-S, May 1986, p. 7.
53. https://www.youtube.com/watch?v=W5aFn5l_CyM
54. 'Melaragamalikachakra (Classical Vocal) – M.S.Subbulakshmi' p. 1989 (HTC8159).
55. Sulochana Pattabhiraman, 'Two sides of a coin', *The Hindu*, Chennai, 2 December 2000.
56. 'Agaval & other songs (Tamil Devotional) – M.S. Subbulakshmi', 1990 (TPHV847229), 'Tiruvenkatamudaiyaan Tiruppalliyezhuchi (Sri Venkatesa Suprabhatam in Tamil) – M.S. Subbulakshmi', 1991 (TPHVS32718 & CDNF147027) and 'Kamban Kaviyamudam (Tamil) – M.S. Subbulakshmi', 1992 (TPHVS32800).
57. 'Sri Sankara Stuti – M.S. Subbulakshmi', 1987 (TPHVS32449) and 'SatAbdi samarpaN by M.S. Subbulakshmi', 1993 (TPHVS32991 & CDNF147719). See also 'Musical homage to Sankara', *The Indian Express*, Madras, 19 June 1987.
58. *Sruti* 39 & 40, September 1987, p. 15.
59. 'M.S. Subbhalakshmi [sic] honoured', *The Statesman*, Calcutta, 13 May 1989; also *Sruti* 57 & 58, June-July 1989, p. 15.
60. *Sruti* 51 & 52, December 1988-January 1989, p. 12.
61. *Sruti* 62, November 1989, p. 17. See also *Confer 'Sangeeta Kalanidhi' on Northern artistes: Semmangudi, Indian Express*, Madras, 29 December 1989.
62. C.V. Krishnaswami, *The Final Mangalam*, privately circulated.
63. Aeolus, 'Of "Abhangs" and Ariels, *Shankar's Weekly*, New Delhi, 1 September 1963.
64. Pittsburgh, early 1980s; Tamil Isai Sangam, 1983.
65. Sulochana Pattabhiraman, 'Colossus of Carnatic Music', *The Hindu*, Chennai, 1 November 2002.
66. *The Hindu*, Madras, 1 November 1990.
67. Personal communication, Gopalkrishna Gandhi. Subbulakshmi's words to her husband on that occasion, *Unga ishtam*, or 'As you wish'.
68. Personal communication, S. Vijayalakshmi, 2 November 2017.
69. Including *'Namo namo'*/Nata, *'Tsalakalla'*/Arabhi, *'Rama Rama gunaseema'*/Simhendramadhyamam, *'Vinabheri'*/Abheri and

'*Sarojadalanetri*'/Sankarabharanam. See also 'Still reigning', Vasumathi Badrinathan, *Business & Political Observer*, New Delhi, 10 April 1992.
70. Including '*Ganesa pancaratnam*'/ragamalika, '*Namo namo*/Nata, '*Naradamuni*'/Pantuvarali and '*Sri Chandrasekhara*'/Sankarabharanam. M.G.Swaminath, 'Melody par excellence', *The Evening News*, New Delhi, 29 January 1993.
71. Letter of 31 January 1993 from Keshav Desiraju to Gopalkrishna Gandhi.
72. Vatsala Vedantam, *Deccan Herald*, Bangalore, 9 May 1993.
73. *Sruti* 273, June 2007, p. 32; also *Sruti* 99&100, December 1992-January 1993, p. 22.
74. *Sruti* 71, August 1990, p. 8.
75. *The Hindu*, Madras, 17 April 1995; also Sruti 117, June 1994, p. 7 and *Sruti* 128, May 1995, p. 18.
76. *Sruti* 80, May 1991, p. 15.
77. *Sruti* 99 & 100, Winter 1992, p. 79.
78. *Sruti* 98, November 1992, p. 7; *Sruti* 127, April 1995, p. 30.
79. *The Pioneer*, New Delhi, 22 January 1994.
80. *An American in Madras*, film by Karan Bali.
81. S. Muthiah, 'He made MS a film star', *The Hindu*, Chennai, 21 January 2002; Randor Guy, 'He transcended barriers with aplomb', *The Hindu*, Chennai, 25 January 2002.
82. Sulochana Pattabhiraman, 'The Nightingale nonpareil', *The Hindu*, Chennai, 13 September 2003.
83. SVK, 'Uncompromising adherence to tradition', *The Hindu*, Chennai, 9 August 1996.
84. Lakshmi Ramakrishnan, 'A musician's musician: T. Brinda 1912–1996', *Frontline*, Chennai, 13 December 1996. Also, Savita Narasimhan, 'A sum total of the Carnatic aesthetic tradition', *The Hindu*, Chennai, 24 December 2011.
85. Ravi & Sridhar, 'Brinda and Mukta—repositories of a great tradition', 3-part blog on sangeetham.com
86. Gopalkrishna Gandhi, Speech at the Sivakami Pethachi Auditorium, Chennai, 2 July 2012. This remarkable speech needs to be read in its entirety.

87. Sriram V, 'The December Music Season of 1934', *Sruti* 303, December 2009, p. 45. Thirugokarnam S. Ranganayaki Ammal was the daughter of Sivarama Nattuvanar and Nallammal, both attached to the Pudukkottai durbar. She was a student of Pudukkottai Dakshinamurthi Pillai, and is said to have first accompanied Subbulakshmi when she was standing in for Shanmukhavadivu at a recital in the Mysore durbar. I have been unable to find any other reference to this Mysore concert. [Blog of Pon Dhanasekaran of 2 November 2018].
88. *Hitavada*, Nagpur, 21 March 1949, also *Sruti* 216, September 2002, p. 39.
89. *Sruti* 224, May 2003, p. 6.
90. Recollection of S. Tyagarajan, 13 February 2018.
91. 'Renowned violinist M.S. Anantharaman passes away', *The Hindu*, Chennai, 20 February 2018.
92. Lakshmi Sreeram, V.V. Subramanyam, 'A yogi at the altar of music', *Sruti* 334, July 2012, p.13.
93. Conversation with R.K. Shriram Kumar, 9 September 2017; also *Sruti* 265, June 2008, p. 22.
94. *The Hindu*, Chennai, 30 June 2011.
95. 'The Voice of Tradition', MLV Interview, *Femina*, 1978, reproduced in *Writings & Reminiscences K.S. Mahadevan Birth Centenary 2013*, Chennai: K.S. Mahadevan (Regd.) Trust, 2013.
96. *Sruti* 142, July 1996, p. 13.
97. Gowri Ramnarayan, 'Uncanny sense of timing', *The Hindu*, Chennai, 14 April 2000.
98. Gowri Ramnarayan, 'She Loved Instrumental Music', in Gowri Ramnarayan, Savita Narasimhan and V. Ramnarayan (eds), *Song of Surrender...*
99. *Sruti* 182, November 1999, p. 38.
100. Volga, 'Vasanth Kannabiran and Kalpana Kannabiran', *Womanscape*, Amrita Resource Centre for Women, Secunderabad, 2001.
101. *Sruti* 224, May 2003, p 6.
102. *Sruti* 44, May 1988, p. 20, interview with T.K. Murthy.
103. *Sruti* 224, May 2003, p. 6.
104. Lakshmi Viswanathan, *Kunjamma...*, 2003, p. 124; also *Sruti* 144, September 1996, interview by Mani Krishnaswami, p.24.

105. 'Musings of a mrdangam maestro', *The Hindu*, Madras, 22 January 1978.
106. Blog of 20 July 2012, https://sriramv.wordpress.com/2012/07/20/remembering-alangudi-ramachandran/
107. Remembering Alangudi Ramachandran, blog by Sriram V., 20 July 2012, https://sriramv.wordpress.com/2012/07/20/remembering-alangudi-ramachandran/
108. 'Ghatam' Vinayakram, 'Maikkuvatthi kachheri', in R. Venkatesh (ed.), *Engal MS*, Chennai: Kalki Publications, 2010.
109. *Sruti* 385, October 2016, p. 19.
110. *The Hindu*, Chennai, 17 November 2017.
111. Mike Marqusee, 'A rasika's tribute', *The Hindu*, Chennai, 17 December 2006.
112. *The Hindu*, Madras, 17 April 1970.
113. Speech by Gopalkrishna Gandhi reported in V. Balasubramanian, 'The living legend', *The Hindu*, Chennai, 14 March 2008.
114. V.V. Subramanyam, 'A yogi at the altar of music', *Sruti* 334, July 2012, p. 19.
115. Gowri Ramnarayan, 'She Loved Instrumental Music', in Gowri Ramnarayan, Savita Narasimhan and V. Ramnarayan (eds), *Song of Surrender*...
116. Gowri Ramnarayan, *MS and Radha*...
117. Gowri Ramnarayan, 'Matchless accompanist', *The Hindu*, Chennai, 12 January 2018.
118. Blog of M.K. Ramasubramanian, son of Subbulakshmi's friend Chinnani Mahadevan, 8 August 2009, rasikas.org
119. Veejay Sai, 'A pity that Chennai forgot Radha', *New Indian Express*, Chennai, 4 January 2018.
120. Gowri Ramnarayan, 'The Radha Story: Lights & Shadows', *Sruti* 7, May 1984, p. 17.
121. Ranjini Govind, 'In her mother's footsteps', *The Hindu*, Chennai, 21 September 2012.
122. *Sruti* 312, September 2010, p. 56.
123. Sulochana Pattabhiraman, 'M.S. revisited', *The Hindu*, Chennai, 23 November 2007.
124. *Sruti* 293, February 2009, p. 45.

125. V. Shrinivasan quoted in Ranjini Govind, 'A voice that accompanied M.S. falls silent', *The Hindu*, Chennai, 4 January 2018.
126. 'Satya Sai Sangeetanjali – An offering at His Lotus Feet by M.S.Subbulakshmi', 1996 (SFHVS849343); 'Keertanams from Atmanandam (Malayalam) M.S. Subbulakshmi', 1996 (CDNF148747).
127. 'Meenakshi Suprabhatam and Other Songs (Sanskrit/Tamil) M.S. Subbulakshmi', 1996 (CDNF 147183).
128. Nandini Ramani, 11 October 2017.
129. Vasudha Narayanan, 'Venkateswara' in Knut Jacobsen, Vasudha Narayanan, Angelika Malinar, and Helene Basu (eds.), *Brill's Encyclopedia of Hinduism*, volume 1. *Regions, Pilgrimage, Deities*. Brill, 2009.
130. *Sruti* 101, February 1993, p. 34.
131. *Sruti* 170, November 1998, p. 7.
132. *Sruti* 144, September 1996, p. 67.
133. *Sruti* 145, October 1996, p. 11.
134. *Sruti* 152, May 1997, p. 5.
135. Email from V. Navaneeth Krishnan, 12 October 2017.
136. 'Versatile and verdant', *The Hindu*, Chennai, 5 April 1997. A video recording of this particular song, a composition of K.R. Athmanathan, as sung at this event, has very recently been released on YouTube. Interestingly, Subbulakshmi includes a *tanam* after her raga rendering; it is worth searching for this fine example of the artiste at the very end of her long performing career.
137. 'An enchanting note', *Frontline*, 24 January 1997, p. 126.
138. *Sruti* 149, February 1997, p. 46.
139. 'M.S. Subbulakshmi honoured', *The Hindu*, Chennai, 30 June 1997; 'Sangeeta Kalanidhi M.S. Subbulakshmi in her Swaralaya Puraskaram Kanchi Mahaswami Manimandapam Concert (STHVS847993/994).
140. Gowri Ramnarayan, 'Diva of sublimity', *Frontline*, 25 July 1997; 'Self and the Supreme', *The Hindu*, Chennai, 4 July 1997.
141. Ibid., 4 July 1997.
142. http://www.msstribute.org/pdf/MSS-Discography.pdf, p. 18.
143. 'Ananda of Annamacharya', *The Hindu*, Chennai, 26 July 1996. The recital included '*Vande Vasudevam*'/Sri, '*Idiye sadhana*'/Ritigaula, '*Sarvopantamula*'/Kalyani, '*Ra ra chinnanna*'/Jenjuti and '*Ni namam*'/

Madhyamavati; 'Ananda of Annamacharya', *The Hindu*, Chennai, 11 July 1997. The recital included '*Namo namo*'/Nata, '*Koluvudi bhakti*'/Kedaragaula, '*Deenude nenu*'/Saveri, '*Enta matramuna*'/ragamalika and '*Ksheerabdhi kanya*'/Kuranji.

144. *The Hindu*, Chennai, 18 July 1997, '*Govindam*'/Bagesri, '*Pooraya*'/Bilahari, '*Madhava mamava*'/Nilambari, '*Mamakaparadha*'/Todi and '*Pari pahimam*'/Bauli.

145. 'Sublime music in divine atmosphere', *The Hindu*, Chennai, 22 August 1997. The recital included '*Tera tiyaga rada*'/Gaulipantu, '*Vande vasudevam*'./Sri, '*Natanala*'/Lalita, '*Enta matramuna*'/ragamalika, '*Meevalla*'/Kapi, '*Ksheerabdhi kanya*'/Kuranji and '*Kurai onrum illai*'/ragamalika.

14: BHARAT RATNA

1. *Nee padaambujamule sada nammina, namma shubhamimma, Sri Minakshamma*, from Syama Sastri's '*Sarojadalanetri*'/Sankarabharanam.
2. *The Hindu*, Chennai, 22 November 1997.
3. Ibid. and ibid., 8 December 1997.
4. K. Vedamurthy, 'A true Gandhian', *The Hindu*, Chennai, 26 November 1999.
5. H.Y. Sharada Prasad, 'All in All', *Deccan Herald*, Bangalore, 30 November 1997.
6. 'The guru on his sishya', excerpts from a 1986 interview of Semmangudi Srinivasa Iyer by Gowri Ramnarayan, *The Hindu*, Chennai, 13 December 2004.
7. K.R. Athmanathan, 'Couple Extraordinary', *The Hindu*, Chennai, 15 September 2006.
8. *Deccan Herald*, Bangalore, 23 November 1997.
9. K. Vedamurthy, 'Dedicated freedom fighter', *The Hindu*, Chennai, 28 November 1997.
10. Athma and Murali, 'Homage to a patriot', *The Hindu*, Chennai, 30 August 2002. 'Dharmatma' translates in Hindi as 'saint' or possibly 'sage'. In Tamil, where 'dharmam' could also mean charity, it could mean philanthropist.

11. *The Hindu*, Chennai, 7 December 1997.
12. 'T. Sadasivam passes away', *Sruti* 159, December 1997,
13. Amanda J. Weidman, *Singing the Classical, Voicing the Modern*, The postcolonial politics of Music in South India, Calcutta: Seagull, 2007, p. 116.
14. Shankar Ramachandran, 'Can we emulate her in generosity?', *Sruti* 376, January 2016, p. 42.
15. H.Y. Sharada Prasad, *Deccan Herald*, Bangalore, 30 November 1997. Also conversation with M.S. Subbulakshmi, Raj Bhavan, Bombay, 4 April 1992; Interview by Vaasanthi, *India Today*, 30 September 1996.
16. Lakshmi Devnath, 'M.S. – the woman and her music', *The Hindu*, Chennai, 9 December 2005.
17. J.S. Raghavan, 'Divine music, humble singer', *The Hindu*, Chennai, 30 September 2018.
18. *Kurai Onrum Illai, A Life of Fulfilment*, Chennai: privately published, 1996.
19. Gopalkrishna Gandhi, email to the author.
20. I owe this marvellous imagery to Jessie Burton, *The Muse*, London: Picador, 2016.
21. 'For nobody could match the extraordinary ability of Bhimsen – always Bhimsen to his listeners – to capture the essential character of a raga, whether playful or grave, and send audiences out into the night humming, with the music under their skin, almost stunned with the force of something they could not quite comprehend.' *The Economist*, London, 3 February 2011, reproduced in The Indian Express, 9 February.
22. *The Indian Express*, Chennai, agency release, 14 January 1998.
23. Ramakrishna Hegde, then chief minister of Karnataka, quoted in *The Indian Express*, 20 September 1986. Also, *Sruti* 25, October 1986, p.25.
24. *India Today*, 15 September 1996. The roots of this essay lie in a bus journey to Tiruvannamalai in June 1996 with Gopalkrishna Gandhi and Keshav Desiraju.
25. Ramachandra Guha, 'Redeeming the Bharat Ratna: M.S.Subbulakshmi and Others', from *An Anthropologist Among the Marxists and other essays*, Ranikhet: Permanent Black, 2001.

26. Harish Khare, *The Hindu*, Chennai, 19 January 2003.
27. H.Y. Sharada Prasad, *Deccan Chronicle*, Hyderabad, 1996; H.Y. Sharada Prasad, 'Bharat Ratna: No prizes for guessing it right', *Deccan Chronicle*, Hyderabad, 25 January 1998.
28. 'Bharat Ratna to M.S. Subbulakshmi', *Sruti* 161, February 1998. Chief Minister Karunanidhi himself belonged to the isai vellalar community. A.R. Venkatachalapathy, *Tamil Characters, Personalities, Politics, Culture*, New Delhi: Pan Macmillan, 2018.
29. C.V. Narasimhan, *The Hindu*, Chennai, 17 January 1998.
30. Subbudu, 'Bharat Ratna for MS or vice-versa?', *The Statesman*, Calcutta, 26 January 1998.
31. 'Spirit of Music', *The Times of India*, New Delhi, 15 January 1998.
32. 'The golden melody', *The Indian Express*, New Delhi, 16 January 1998.
33. 'Queen of music', *Hindustan Times*, New Delhi, 16 January 1998.
34. 'Honour well deserved', *The Deccan Chronicle*, Hyderabad, 16 January 1998.
35. 'Glitter restored', *The Pioneer*, New Delhi, 16 January 1998.
36. Editorial, *Frontline*, Chennai, 6 February 1998.
37. Letter from A. Seshan, *Sruti* 163, April 1998, p.4.
38. 'Subbulakshmi ki svar sugandh se suvaasit "Bhart Ratn"', *Dainik Bhaskar*, Jabalpur, 16 January 1998. The exact phrase is *samuche chintan ke abhamandal...*
39. *Jansatta*, New Delhi, 16 January 1998.
40. *The Hindu*, Chennai, 16 January 1998.
41. Gowri Ramnarayan, *MS and Radha...*, p. 69.
42. *The Hindu*, Chennai, 2 March 1998.
43. Hosted by Tara and Gopalkrishna Gandhi.
44. Gowri Ramnarayan, 'First lady of Indian music', *The Hindu*, Chennai, 25 January 1998.
45. Rashtrapati Bhavan, New Delhi, 1 March 1998.
46. *The Hindu*, Chennai, 29 December 2000.
47. 'Award presented to MS', *The Hindu*, Chennai, 18 January 2001; also Choodie Sivaram, 'Living up the past', *Deccan Herald*, Bangalore, 30 June 2001; *The Hindu*, Chennai, 25 April 2002; also 'Sree Ramaseva Mandali Celebrated Diamond Jubilee'; *Sruti* 163, April 1998, p. 13.

48. *The Hindu*, Chennai, 8 October 2002.
49. Ibid., 4 April 2004.
50. Ibid., 22 June 2004; also *Sruti* 239, August 2004, p. 7.
51. Ibid., 6 July 2004.
52. *Sruti* 185, February 2000, p. 41.
53. *The Hindu*, Chennai, 6 March 2004.
54. *Sruti*, 236, May 2004, pp. 4–5.
55. *Sruti* 173, February 1999, p. 15.
56. 'Time to pay tribute', *The Hindu*, Chennai, 9 February 2001.
57. 'Forever a legend', *The Hindu*, Chennai, 23 September 2001; 'Magic of MS music', ibid., 12 October 2001.
58. Aruna Srinivasan, 'The Queen of Song Sang Again', *The Pioneer*, New Delhi, 21 February 1993; Alka Raghuvanshi, 'When Meera came to life...', ibid., 25 February 1995; V. Gangadhar, 'Melody is her middle name', *The Hindu*, Chennai, 1 January 1998; Gowri Ramnarayan, 'First lady of Indian music', ibid., 25 January 1998; Vatsala Vedantam, 'A woman called Kunjamma', ibid., 1 March 1998; Saroj Satyanarayana, 'Lingering impressions', ibid., 22 March 1998; SVK, 'Music at its divine best', ibid., 5 October 2001; Subbudu, 'Serene highness', *The Statesman*, Kolkata, 28 May 2004; T.S. Nagarajan, 'Portraits of a diva', *The Hindu*, Chennai, 20 June 2004; Sulochana Pattabhiraman, 'A life of Shreyas', *The Hindu*, Chennai, 10 September 2004; Gowri Ramnarayan, 'An abiding friendship', ibid., 17 September 2004.
59. *Outlook*, New Delhi, 19 August 2002.
60. *Tehelka*, New Delhi, 21 August 2004.
61. The song was first published in *Kalki*, 15 January 1967, where Rajaji acknowledges the assistance of M.P. Somu, editor of *Kalki*. I am grateful to Seetha Ravi for this reference.
62. Gowri Ramnarayan, 'Songs shone with his quiet genius', *The Hindu*, Chennai, 20 February 2004.
63. Gopalkrishna Gandhi, 'Rajaji's unknown collaborator', *The Hindu*, Chennai, 22 December 2002.
64. Indira Menon, *The Madras Quartet*, New Delhi: Roli Books, 2000. See also H.Y. Sharada Prasad, 'The quartet of south Indian music', *Deccan Chronicle*, Hyderabad, 6 August 2000; V. Gangadhar, M S Subbulakshmi, *The Voice Divine*, New Delhi: Rupa, 2002; Lakshmi

Viswanathan, *Kunjamma, Ode to a Nightingale*, New Delhi: Roli Books, 2004. See also 'Twilight zone', *The Hindu*, Chennai, 30 November 2003.
65. T.J.S. George, *MS: A Life in Music*, New Delhi: HarperCollins Publishers India, 2004. Reviewed by Sulochana Pattabhiraman, *The Hindu*, Chennai, 9 March 2004.
66. At least one insensitive review of the *Life* was entitled 'The nightingale who eloped', Ananda Majumdar in *Hindustan Times*, New Delhi, 22 February 2004. The review is helpfully, if tastelessly, subtitled, 'Subbulakshmi made her mum miserable, for the sake of art'.
67. Letter of K.R. Athmanathan dated 13 September 2004 addressed to Amitabha Bhattacharya.
68. Gowri Ramnarayan, 'Semmangudi—a link with the past', *The Hindu*, Madras, 18 December 1986; Gowri Ramnarayan, 'End of an era', *The Hindu*, Chennai, 9 November 2003; SVK, 'Traditionalist of Trinity culture', Ibid., 7 November 2003.
69. T.M. Krishna, '*Chakkani Raja margamu*', blog of November 2003.
70. V. Subrahmaniam & Sriram V., *Semmangudi Srinivasa Iyer, Life and Music*, Chennai: EastWest, 2008.
71. V. Subrahmaniam, *The Hindu*, Chennai, 22 June 2001, 29 June 2001, 6 July 2001, 13 July 2001, 20 July 2001.
72. George Harewood, The Critic's Column• Tribune du Critique • Forum des Kritikers, *The World of Music*, Vol. 12, No. 2 (1970).
73. *Sruti* 231, December 2003, p.32.
74. Semmangudi R. Srinivasa Iyer, 'Naan arinda Sadasivam', in *Kurai onrum illai, A Life of Fulfilment*, a volume of tributes to T. Sadasivam, privately published, 1996.
75. 'The guru on his sishya, 'excerpts from a 1986 interview of Semmangudi Srinivasa Iyer by Gowri Ramnarayan', *The Hindu*, Chennai, 13 December 2004.
76. *Sruti* 60 & 61, September-October 1989, p. 51.
77. Gowri Ramnarayan, 'Teacher to Generations', *Sruti* 231, December 2003, p. 32.
78. *Sruti* 231, December 2003, p. 36.

79. R.K. Shriram Kumar, 'A year without the Nightingale', blog of 12 December 2005, sangeetha.com
80. Sriram V., 'Her melody touched millions', *Hindustan Times*, New Delhi, 13 December 2004; also Sanjay Subrahmanyan blog, 14 December 2004, sangeetham.com; see also N. Vijay Siva, 'Her Selfless Art', in Gowri Ramnarayan, Savita Narasimhan and V. Ramnarayan (eds), *Song of Surrender...*
81. Conversation with Seetha Ravi, Chennai, 29 January 2018. '*Pakkavadyam yaaru?*' and '*Kootam irunddu-da?*'
82. Conversation with Gopalkrishna Gandhi, 22 June 2002; also Gowri Ramnarayan, 'An elegant simplicity', *The Hindu*, Chennai, 19 December 2004; also Gowri Ramnarayan, 'Remembering MS Part-3', *Sruti* 340, January 2013, p.34.
83. K.R. Athmanathan, 13 January 2018.
84. Sriram V., 'M S Subbulakshmi', blog on sangeetham.org, 21 September 2004.
85. *The Hindu*, Chennai, 21 May 2004, ibid., 3 December 2004.
86. Ibid., 12 December 2004, 13 December 2004.
87. Ibid., 13 December 2004.
88. 'Truly the nightingale of India', *The Hindu*, Chennai, 13 December 2004; R. Venkataraman, 'Singer of the ages', *The Indian Express*, New Delhi, 15 December 2004; R. Sujatha, 'We are orphaned, say artistes', *The Hindu*, Chennai, 13 December 2004; 'Voice of Temple India MS dies, leaving resonant legacy', *The Indian Express*, New Delhi, 12 December 2004; 'Queen of Carnatic music dead', *The Telegraph*, Kolkata, 12 December 2004; 'Nation bids adieu to the Queen of Music', *The Times of India*, New Delhi, 13 December 2004; 'Temple singer who became a legend', *The Statesman*, Kolkata 12 December 2004; 'MS merges into music of eternity', *Deccan Herald*, Bangalore, 13 December 2004; Mrinal Pande, 'M.S. *Subbulakshmi hone ka arth*', *Hindustan*, New Delhi, 19 December 2004; Radha Viswanathan, '*Gayaki ke tirath ko hamara naman*', *Hindustan*, New Delhi, 20 December 2004; *Dainik Jagaran*, Kanpur, 12 and 13 December 2004; *Jansatta*, New Delhi, 13 December 2004; *Dainik Bhaskar*, Jabalpur, 13 December 2004.

89. Jai Kumar, 'MS Subbulakshmi, Singer of Carnatic music respected in India and around the world', *The Guardian*, London, 17 December 2004.
90. S. Vijay Kumar and M.R. Aravindan, 'A colossal loss to music', *The Hindu*, Chennai, 13 December 2004; Padmini Sivarajah, 'Madurai home has no memories of MS', *The Indian Express*, New Delhi, 13 December 2004.
91. Sriram V., 'Her melody touched millions', *Hindustan Times*, New Delhi, 13 December 2004.
92. Gowri Ramnarayan, 'A voice that enchanted', *The Hindu*, Chennai, 12 December 2004; Gowri Ramnarayan, 'You sing like an angel', *The Hindu*, Chennai, 12 December 2004; Sulochana Pattabhiraman, 'Epitome of bhakti', *The Hindu*, Chennai, 13 December 2004; H.Y. Sharada Prasad, 'The singer is still', *The Asian Age*, New Delhi, 14 December 2004; Sudhamahi Regunathan, 'Meera Lives On in Voice of Bhakti', *The Times of India*, New Delhi, 16 December 2004; SVK, *The Hindu*, Chennai, 17 December 2004; Renuka Narayanan, 'Chakar Rakho Ji', *The Indian Express*, New Delhi, 19 December 2004; Sadanand Menon, 'Song on the Breeze', *Outlook*, 27 December 2004.
93. 'Humility was her hallmark: stalwarts', *The Indian Express*, New Delhi, 12 December 2004.
94. V.S. Venkatavaradan, *The Hindu*, Chennai, 22 December 2004.
95. 'M.S. recreated', *The Hindu*, Chennai, 16 December 2004.
96. K.G. Vijayakrishnan, 'MS Magic', *The Hindu*, Chennai, 2 January 2005; K.R. Athmanathan, 'Couple Extraordinary', *The Hindu*, Chennai, 15 September 2006; Sulochana Pattabhiraman, 'They shared a special bond', *The Hindu*, Chennai, 15 September 2006; 'Echoes and memories of MS', ibid., 11 May 2007.
97. Sagarika Ghose, *The Times of India*, New Delhi, 13 February 2017.
98. Stamps on T.R. Rajarathinam Pillai, T. Balasaraswati and T. Dhanammal were issued in December 2010. D.K. Pattammal and Gangubai Hangal were featured on stamps issued in September 2014.
99. 'Statue of MS unveiled at Tirupati', *The Hindu*, Chennai, 29 May 2006; also ibid., 31 May 2006. See also *Sruti* 265, October 2006, p. 46.

100. B. Venkat Sandeep, 'SPB takes up neglect of MS statue', *The Hindu*, Chennai, 1 September 2016. 'The matter of the electric wires seems to have been attended to', ibid., Tirupati, 30 November 2018.
101. *Sruti* 261, June 2006, p. 33.
102. *Sruti* 351, December 2013, p. 66.
103. *Hindustan Times*, New Delhi, 10 August 2007.
104. *The Hindu*, Chennai, 10 September 2010.
105. Bombay Jayashri and T.M. Krishna, with Mythili Chandrasekar, 'Voices Within, Carnatic Music: passing on an inheritance', MATRKA, Chennai, 2006.
106. *Sruti* 308, May 2010, p. 49. The artiste was Gayathri Venkataraghavan.
107. Sujatha Vijayaraghavan, 'Cleveland Festival: The future has arrived', *Sruti* 382, July 2016.
108. 'Amma once more!', *The Hindu*, Chennai, 20 December 2007.
109. Ibid., 22 September 2016.
110. Ibid., 16 September 2016; 6 November 2016.
111. Ibid., 18 December 2016.
112. 'Melody marathon', *The Hindu*, Chennai, 30 September 2016.
113. 'Tribute to M.S.', *The Hindu*, Chennai, 9 September 2016.
114. Ibid.
115. 'M.S. Subbulakshmi: The Rainbow Voice of Indian Music', *Outlook*, New Delhi, 30 December 2016.
116. 'Remembering MS once again', *The Hindu*, Chennai, 27 September 2016.
117. *The Hindu*, Chennai, 28 October 2016.
118. Ibid., 17 September 2016; 'Tracing MS' musical journey through the pages of a daily', ibid., 18 September 2016.
119. *Sruti* 186, March 2000, p. 8; also *Sruti* 194, November 2000, p. 8.
120. Gowri Ramnarayan, 'Mukti, Voicing Freedom', in Gowri Ramnarayan, Savita Narasimhan and V. Ramnarayan (eds), *Song of Surrender*...
121. K.V. Ramanathan, 'A Holistic Package', in Gowri Ramnarayan, Savita Narasimhan and V. Ramnarayan (eds), *Song of Surrender*...
122. Letter from A.R.S. Mani to *Sruti*, Issue 374, November 2015, p. 5.

123. 'UN to host Sudha's musical tribute to MS on 2 October', *The Hindu*, Chennai, 30 August 2016.
124. *The Hindu*, Chennai, 28 October 2016; Vatsala Vedantam, 'Her voice, their vision', *Deccan Herald*, Bangalore, 11 December 1999; also *Sruti* 181, October 1999, p. 11; also *Sruti* 270, March 2007, p. 14.
125. Nasreen Munni Kabir, *Zakir Husain: A Life in Music*, Noida: HarperCollins *Publisher* India, 2018.

15: A LIFE

1. *Minalochani pasamochani...*
2. Gowri Ramnarayan, 'She Loved Instrumental Music' and V. Navaneeth Krishnan, 'The Eternal Student', Gowri Ramnarayan, Savita Narasimhan and V. Ramnarayan (eds), *Song of Surrender*, Chennai: The Sruti Foundation, 2016.
3. The character Hildegard in *Authenticity*, in James Runcie, *The Grantchester Mysteries, Sidney Chambers and the Persistence of Love*, London: Bloomsbury, 2017.
4. Sulochana Pattabhiraman, 'The Music of MS', *Sruti* 244, January 2005, p. 13.
5. Savita Narasimhan, 'The Technique She Forgot', and Mythili Prakash, 'A Model of Auchithyam', in Gowri Ramnarayan, Savita Narasimhan and V. Ramnarayan (eds), *Song of Surrender...*
6. Contemporary Carnatic musicians could learn from this. There are a large number of skilled performers with enviable repertoires of songs and considerable dexterity in raga and *tala* complications, each of them an exemplar of where technique can take one. Very few among them have the understanding, the intelligence or the humility to grow beyond technique.
7. Conversation with V. Shrinivasan, 25 July 2017.
8. V. Gangadhar, *M.S. Subbulakshmi The Voice Divine*, New Delhi: Rupa & Co., 2002.
9. Conversation with Seetha Ravi, 21 April 2018.
10. Bala, 'Music', *Shankar's Weekly*, 18 October 1964.

11. T. Viswanathan, 'The Analysis of Rāga Ālāpana in South Indian Music', *Asian Music*, Vol. 9, No. 1, Second India Issue (1977).
12. M.L. Vasanthakumari's Music Academy concert in 1975, the year of the Muthusvami Dikshitar bicentenary, and available on YouTube, has raga *alapana* in Sriranjini and Mohana, sung respectively for 'Sri Ramachandro' and 'Pahimam Parvati'. Both ragas are commonly sung, by Subbulakshmi and every other singer, but Vasanthakumari's raga renderings are like no other. The recital also includes a lengthy Todi *alapana* for 'Sri Krishnam'.
13. *Sruti* 231, December 2003, p. 39.
14. Letter from B.R. Kumar, *Sruti* 258, March 2006, p. 5.
15. Letter from V. Sivaswamy, *Sruti* 27 & 28, December 1986-January 1987, p. 3.
16. P.K. Doraiswamy, 'Classicality and Musicality, Do the Twain Always Meet?', *Sruti* 255, December 2005, p.41.
17. Aeolus, 'Sangeet Sammelan', *Shankar's Weekly*, 13 November 1966.
18. Ramesh Vinayakam, 'She pledged her soul to song', *Sruti* 382, July 2016, p. 34.
19. Sriram Parasuram, 'Intelligent and Resourceful', in Gowri Ramnarayan, Savita Narasimhan and V. Ramnarayan (eds), *Song of Surrender...*
20. Aeolus, *Shankar's Weekly*, New Delhi, 18 August 1963.
21. *Sruti* 340, January 2013, p. 34.
22. R. Vedavalli, '*The Polestar*', in Gowri Ramnarayan, Savita Narasimhan and V. Ramnarayan (eds), *Song of Surrender...*
23. B.V.K. Sastry, 'M.S. Subbulakshmi', *The Illustrated Weekly of India*, 9 July 1965.
24. Nisha Rajagopalan, 'The Perfect Sankarabharanam', in Gowri Ramnarayan, Savita Narasimhan and V. Ramnarayan (eds), *Song of Surrender...* T.M. Krishna, 'Unequal Music', *Economic and Political Weekly*, Vol. 53, No.12, 24 March 2018.
25. Manirangu in *Sruti* 41, February 1988, p. 26.
26. Gowri Ramnarayan, 'Born to Sing', in Gowri Ramnarayan, Savita Narasimhan and V. Ramnarayan (eds), *Song of Surrender...*

27. Aeolus, *Shankar's Weekly*, 8 January 1967, p. 22.
28. T.M. Krishna, 'Unequal Music...'
29. Gowri Ramnarayan, 'She Loved Instrumental Music'; K.V. Prasad, 'An Honour to Accompany Her'; Chitravina N. Ravikiran, 'The Handicap She Overcame', all in Gowri Ramnarayan, Savita Narasimhan and V. Ramnarayan (eds), *Song of Surrender*...
30. Deryck Cooke, 'The Language of Music', Oxford: Oxford University Press, 1959.
31. Madhavi Ramkumar, 'Stage Presence', *Sruti* 236, May 2004, p.27.
32. Ramaswamy R. Iyer in *Sruti* 350, November 2013, p. 6.
33. Recollections of Bandana Mukhopadhyay, email of 14 November 2017.
34. Sanghamitra Mazumdar, 'Pochishe Boishakh: The story behind "He Nutan", Rabindranath Tagore's birthday song', *The Statesman*, Kolkata, 8 May 2018.
35. Ramaswamy R. Iyer, *Sruti* 212, May 2002, p. 42.
36. Conversation with Gowri Ramnarayan, 26 April 2018.
37. S. Anand, 'Be one with what you see', *Hindustan Times*, New Delhi, 9 September 2016.
38. *Shankar's Weekly*, New Delhi, 14 June 1964.
39. Jyoti Nair, 'A style as intriguing as the name', *The Hindu*, Chennai, 5 January 2018.
40. Deepak Raja, 'Bhakti in Hindustani music', *Sruti*, Vol. 25, Issue 1, January 2018.
41. Translated from the original Tamil, *The Journal of the Music Academy*, Madras, Vol. XLIX, 1978.
42. Pico Iyer, *A Beginner's Guide to Japan, Observations and Provocations*, Gurgaon: Penguin/Viking, 2019.
43. Alarmel Valli, 'Perfect Harmony', in in Gowri Ramnarayan, Savita Narasimhan and V. Ramnarayan (eds), *Song of Surrender*...
44. Swati Thiagarajan, 'Was She Lonely?', in Gowri Ramnarayan, Savita Narasimhan and V. Ramnarayan (eds), *Song of Surrender*...
45. Rukmini Devi, 'The President's Letter', *Kalakshetra News*, Vol. II, No. 2, June 1961.
46. *Sruti* 273, June 2007, p. 35.
47. Mayavarathaan Chandrasekaran, cited by Express News Service, 22 November 2016.

48. Radha Viswanathan, 'Amma Poured Her Love in Us', *The Dance India*, Vol. 1, No. 3, September 2016.
49. S. Aishwarya, 'Remembering Radha', *The Times of India*, New Delhi, 6 January 2018.
50. Seetha Ravi, 'Her Life was Her Art', in Gowri Ramnarayan, Savita Narasimhan and V. Ramnarayan (eds), *Song of Surrender...*
51. Gowri Ramnarayan, 'Born To Sing', in ibid.
52. Bombay Jayashri, 'She Surrendered to Her Own Cause', in ibid.
53. B.V.K. Sastry, 'M.S. Subbulakshmi', *The Illustrated Weekly of India*, Bombay, 9 July 1965.
54. Aeolus, 'Form and Feeling', *Shankar's Weekly*, 18 August 1963.
55. Letter from S. Venkataraman, *Sruti* 101, February 1993, p. 6; also letter from V.K. Viswanathan, *Sruti* 247, April 2005, p. 5.
56. *Sruti* 280, January 2008, p. 21.
57. Letter from B.R.C. Iyengar, *Sruti* 244, January 2005, p. 3.
58. Letter from K. Sivaraman, *Sruti* 249, June 2005, p. 6.
59. Blog, 16 September 2013.
60. R. Vedavalli, 'The pole star of Carnatic music', *Sruti* 374, November 2015, p.28.
61. Interview, *Sruti*, Vol. 26, Issue 1, January 2019, p.25.
62. Address to the Madras Music Academy, Chennai, at the inauguration of the 93rd Annual Conference, 15 December 2019.
63. Prof. Premeela Gurumurthy, 'Destiny's child with a mind of her own', *Sruti*, Vol. 25, Issue 12, December 2018, p. 54.
64. Acceptance Speech following Magsaysay Award for Public Service, August 1974, quoted in *Sruti* 303, December 2009, p. 49.
65. *Journal of The Music Academy*, Madras, 1969.
66. 'Bhakti is the root of music: MS', *The Hindu*, Madras, 19 December 1987.
67. Maithily Jagannathan, *HT Weekly*, New Delhi, 22 November 1970.
68. A.R. Rahman in conversation with Bharat Bala, Chennai International Centre, 8 September 2017.
69. Amanda Weidman, 'Stage goddesses and studio divas in South India: On agency and the politics of voice' in Bonnie S. McElhinny (ed.), *Words, worlds, and material girls: Language, gender, globalization*, Berlin; New York: Mouton de Gruyter, c.2007.

70. T.M. Krishna, speech at Hyderabad, 24 November 2017.
71. Priyadarsini Govind, 'Demure yet Powerful', in Gowri Ramnarayan, Savita Narasimhan and V. Ramnarayan (eds), *Song of Surrender*...
72. Rajiv Menon, 'Her Stage Presence', in ibid.
73. T.M. Krishna, *Reshaping Art*, New Delhi: Aleph, 2018.
74. Charles Allen, *Coromandel: A Personal History of South India*, New York: Little, Brown and Company, 2017.
75. Amritha Murali, 'Exemplary Voice Exercises', in Gowri Ramnarayan, Savita Narasimhan and V. Ramnarayan (eds), *Song of Surrender*...
76. Mani Krishnaswami, 'Expression of gratitude', *The Hindu*, Chennai, 22 February 1998.
77. *Sruti* 85, October 1991, Note by K. S. Krishnamurti, p. 22.
78. *Sruti* 333, June 2012, p. 37.
79. *Sruti* 299, August 2009, p. 15.
80. Raman Ramakrishnan, interview in *The Times of India*, New Delhi, 7 November 2009.
81. *Sruti* 284, June 2008.
82. Suganthy Krishnamachari, 'Making the epic contemporary', *The Hindu*, Chennai, 7 December 2007.
83. AM, 'Calcutta Diary', *Economic and Political Weekly*, 1–8 August 1972.
84. Sheila Dhar, *The Cooking of Music and Other Essays*, New Delhi: Permanent Black, 2001.
85. Shanti Hiranand, *Begum Akhtar: The story of my ammi*, New Delhi: Viva Books Private Limited, 2005.
86. Ashok Mitra, *Calcutta Diary*, London: Frank Cass & Co. Ltd., 1976.
87. Gowri Ramnarayan, 'End Note'; also R.K. Shriram Kumar, 'An Excellent Teacher', and Alarmel Valli, 'Perfect Harmony', all in Gowri Ramnarayan, Savita Narasimhan and V. Ramnarayan (eds), *Song of Surrender*...
88. Editorial on the 100th birthday of Dame Vera Lynn, *The Daily Telegraph*, London, 20 March 2017.
89. Virginia Danielson, *The Voice of Egypt, Umm Kulthum, Arabic Song, and Egyptian society in the Twentieth Century*, Chicago: Chicago Studies in Ethnomusicology, 1997.

90. Virginia Danielson in *The Harvard Magazine*, quoted in 'Remembering Om Kalthoum, Egyptian legend and The star of the East', blog post *Middle East Revised*, dated 27 April 2014.
91. Margaret Crosland, *A Cry from the Heart, a biography of Edith Piaf*, London: Arcadia Books Ltd., 1985.
92. 'Ella 100, A Centennial Celebration, April 25th, 2017 – April 25th, 2018', www.ellafitzgerald.com
93. Sleeve Notes by Bill Simon, Ella Fitzgerald sings the Rodgers and Hart Song Book, Vol. 1, MG V-4022, 1957.
94. Arianna Huffington, *Maria Callas: The woman behind the legend*, Maryland: Cooper Square Press, 1981.
95. Harold C. Schonberg, *The New York Times*, 17 September 1977.
96. Stanley Martin, *The Order of Merit, One Hundred Years of Matchless Honour*, London: L.B. Tauris, 2007.
97. Norma Major, *Joan Sutherland: The Authorized Biography*, New York: Little, Brown and Company, 1994.
98. Norma Major, *Joan Sutherland: The Authorized Biography*...
99. Notes to LP Record, *The Great Tradition: Masters of Indian Music*, quoted in Rukun Advani, 'Pungent Melody: The Life of Sheila Dhar', *The Hindu*, Chennai, 26 August 2001.
100. Ludwig Pesch, *The Oxford Illustrated Companion to South Indian Classical Music*, Oxford University Press, 2009.
101. Rajmohan Gandhi, *Modern South India*, New Delhi: Aleph, 2018.

Appendix I
DRAMATIS PERSONAE

A. Kanyakumari (born 1952), student of Ivaturi Vijayeshwara Rao, of the school of Dwaram Venkataswami Naidu (1893–1964), and *Sangitha Kalanidhi* M. Chandrasekharan (born 1937), long-term accompanist of M.L. Vasanthakumari, solo violinist, teacher, composer. Awarded the *Sangitha Kalanidhi* in 2016.

Vina A. Shanmukhavadivu (1889–1962), daughter of Akkammal and M.S. Swaminathan, *vainika*, mother of M.S. Sakthivel, M.S. Subbulakshmi and M.S. Vadivambal.

A.K.C. Natarajan (born 1931), *Sangitha Kalanidhi*, clarinettist, also learnt vocal music from Alathur Venkatesa Iyer (1895–1958).

A.P.J. Abdul Kalam (1931–2015), Bharat Ratna, scientist, closely associated with India's space programme, President of India (2002–07), amateur vina player.

Ambujam Krishna (1917–89), composer of songs in Tamil for which tunes were set by others. Of her songs, Subbulakshmi often sang '*Kannan idam*'/ ragamalika.

Anandhi Ramachandran (1933–2005), daughter of Rukmini and Kalki R. Krishnamurthi, wife of T. Sadasivam's nephew N. Ramachandran, dancer, teacher, author, intimate of Subbulakshmi.

Rajah Sir Annamalai Chettiar (1881–1948), industrialist, educationist, philanthropist, leading supporter of the movement for *Tamil Isai*.

Annapurna Devi (1927–2018), also Roshanara, Padma Bhushan, daughter of Madina Begum and Ustad Allauddin Khan (1881–1972), disciple of her father, first wife of Ravi Shankar, famously reclusive performer on the surbahar, teacher, recipient of the title *Desikottama* and Fellow of the Sangeet Natak Akademi.

Annie Besant (1847–1933), writer, theosophist, socialist, Indian nationalist, president of the Indian National Congress in 1917.

Ariyakudi Ramanuja Iyengar (1890–1967), *Sangitha Kalanidhi*, Padma Bhushan, among the foremost singers of his time, teacher of several distinguished musicians.

Asha Bhosle (born 1933), Padma Vibhushan, daughter of Shevanti 'Mai' and Dinanath Mangeshkar, playback singer for film, known for her versatile style.

Vidyasundari **Bangalore Nagaratnamu** (1878–1952), daughter of Putta Lakshmiammal Vaishnavi and M. Subba Rao, scholar, musician, widely known in Mysore and Madras, prime mover behind the Tyagaraja *aradhana* events.

Banni Bai (1912–99), born Alamelumanga Thayar, the daughter of Doraisani, and possibly from a family of traditional performers, *Harikatha* exponent, film actor and teacher.

Begum Akhtar (1914–74), Padma Bhushan, daughter of Mushtri Begum, sang for the films and even appeared in Satyajit Ray's *Jalsaghar* (1958), famed as the queen of ghazal.

Bhadracala Ramadas (1620–80), composer of Telugu devotional verses, believed to have also set them to music though these settings are currently unavailable. A small stock of *kritis* of Ramadas are available of which Subbulakshmi famously sang '*Ennaganu Rama bhajana*' in Pantuvarali.

Bhimsen Joshi (1923–2011), Bharat Ratna, Hindustani vocalist of the Kirana gharana, student of many teachers and famously of Sawai Gandharva (1886–1952).

Appendix I

Bismillah Khan (1916–2006), Bharat Ratna, famed shehnai player, of Dumraon, Bihar, and student of his uncle at Benares. Played from the Red Fort in Delhi on the occasion of India's Independence, also appeared in Satyajit Ray's *Jalsaghar* (1958).

C. Rajagopalachari (1878–1972) (Rajaji), Bharat Ratna, Chief Minister of Madras (1937–39), Governor of West Bengal (1947–48), Governor-General of India (1948–50), Union Minister (1950–51), Chief Minister of Madras (1952–54), founder of the conservative Swatantra Party, patron and mentor to Sadasivam and Subbulakshmi.

C. Saraswathi Bai (1892–1974), daughter of Rangammal and Gooty Rama Rao, student of Pandit Krishnachar, *Harikatha* exponent, singer, from a young age a very successful performer.

C. Saroja (born 1936), *Sangitha Kalanidhi*, Padma Shri, and **C. Lalitha** (born 1938), *Sangitha Kalanidhi*, Padma Shri, popularly known as the Bombay Sisters, disciples of T.K. Govinda Rao.

C.N. Annadurai (1909–69), known as *Araignar*, 'Learned One', orator and charismatic leader, led the Dravida Munnetra Kazhagam to electoral victory in 1967, Chief Minister of Tamil Nadu 1967–69.

C.P. Radha (born 1935), daughter of Kalpakammal and C.P. Doraiswami Iyengar; and **R. Jayalakshmi** (1934–2014), daughter of Pattammal and R. Rangachary, known always as **Radha-Jayalakshmi**, popular and widely recorded singers over 1950–80, students of T.R. Balasubramaniam, himself the student of G.N. Balasubramaniam.

C.P. Ramaswami Aiyar (1879–1966), lawyer, educationist, Dewan of Travancore.

C.V. Narasimhan (1915–2003), ICS, MBE, Padma Vibhushan, student of *Sangitha Kalanidhi* Musiri Subramania Iyer, international civil servant.

C.V. Raman (1888–1970), Bharat Ratna, physicist and teacher, winner of the Nobel Prize for Physics in 1930.

Chembai Vaidyanatha Bhagavathar (1896–1975), *Sangitha Kalanidhi*, Padma Bhushan, vocalist famed for his grand presence, composer, teacher of K.J. Yesudas and the Subbulakshmi's violinist V.V. Subramanyam.

Chittoor Subramania Pillai (1898–1975), *Sangitha Kalanidhi*, vocalist, student of Kanchipuram Naina Pillai, also composer and teacher.

Coimbatore Thayi (1872–1917), born Coimbatore Palanikunjaram, one of the earliest musicians to record for a gramophone company.

D.K. Pattammal (1919–2009), *Sangitha Kalanidhi*, Padma Vibhushan, daughter of Rajammal and Damal Krishnaswami Dikshitar, major presence in the twentieth-century music scene, teacher of her brother *Sangitha Kalanidhi* D.K. Jayaraman (1928–90), renowned for her grasp of tradition.

D.V. Paluskar (1921–55), son of V.D. Paluskar (1872–1931), the founder of the Gandharva Mahavidyalaya, himself a leading singer of the Gwalior gharana, well known for his bhajan singing.

Dharmapuri Subbarayar (1864–1927), composer of *padams* and *javalis*, close associate of 'Vina' Dhanammal.

Dilip Kumar Roy (1897–1980), son of the poet and composer Dwijendralal Roy (1863–1913), also a poet, singer and mystic, long-term associate of the Sri Aurobindo Ashram, Pondicherry, taught Subbulakshmi bhajans and recorded two along with her, 'Vande Mataram' and 'Dhano dhanyo pushpa bhora'. Subbulakshmi also sang the verses of his disciple Indira Devi (1920–88).

Dwaram Venkataswami Naidu (1893–1964), *Sangitha Kalanidhi*, Padma Shri, violinist, well-known performer and teacher.

E. Krishna Iyer (1897–1968), Padma Shri, lawyer, nationalist, dancer, student of Madhurantakam Jagadambal (1873–1943), did much to promote Bharatanatyam, ally of Rukmini Devi.

Edith Piaf (1915–63), widely celebrated French singer and performer.

Ella Fitzgerald (1917–96), hailed as the Queen of Jazz, widely recorded and much-loved artiste.

G. Venkatachalam (1894–1968), aesthete and impresario, met Subbulakshmi in 1929, promoter of Balasaraswati and Shanta Rao.

G.N. Balasubramaniam (1910–65), *Sangitha Kalanidhi*, son of Visalakshi and G. Narayanaswami Iyer, singer, composer, actor, teacher of M.L. Vasanthakumari, extremely popular concert artiste, hugely influential for the tradition.

Appendix I

Gangubai Hangal (1912–2009), Padma Vibhushan, daughter of Ambabai, disciple of Sawai Gandharva, leading singer of the Kirana gharana.

George Lascelles, 7th Earl of Harewood (1923–2011), minor royal, opera enthusiast, friend of Maria Callas, among the earliest to recognize Joan Sutherland, and responsible for Subbulakshmi's appearance at the Edinburgh Festival in 1963.

Girija Devi (1929–2017), Padma Vibhushan, classical singer of the Benares gharana, most associated with the *thumri*, teacher.

Gopalakrishna Bharati (1811–96), Tamil composer, most famously of the '*Nandanar Charitram*', and also of '*Sabhapati*'/Abhogi, '*Adum Chidambaramo*'/Behag and '*Eppo varuvaro*'/Jaunpuri, all prominent in Subbulakshmi's repertoire.

Gowri Ramnarayan (born 1950), daughter of Anandhi and N. Ramachandran, musician, journalist, playwright, theatre director, accompanying singer to Subbulakshmi in the last part of her career, author of several works related to her life.

H. Yoganarasimham (1897–1971), a contemporary composer from Karnataka. Subbulakshmi recorded a set of his compositions, including '*Sada saranga nayane*'/Ranjani.

H.Y. Sharada Prasad (1924–2008), Padma Bhushan, son of H. Yoganarasimham, journalist and civil servant, close associate of Prime Minister Indira Gandhi, friend of Subbulakshmi and Sadasivam.

Harikesanallur Muthiah Bhagavathar (1877–1945), *Sangitha Kalanidhi*, singer, composer in Sanskrit, Telugu, Kannada and Tamil, *Harikatha* exponent.

Hirabai Barodekar (1905–89), Padma Bhushan, also Champakali, daughter of Tarabai Mane and Ustad Abdul Karim Khan, distinguished and highly regarded singer.

Indira Gandhi (1917–84), Bharat Ratna, daughter of Kamala and Jawaharlal Nehru, Prime Minister (1966–77, 1980–84).

Indrani Rahman (1930–99), Padma Shri, daughter of Ragini Devi and Ramlal Bajpai, a dancer with striking looks and stage presence, and widely popular.

J. Krishnamurti (1895–1986), philosopher, writer and teacher, raised out of obscurity by the Theosophists, whom he later rejected, his work is now widely known through the Krishnamurti Foundation.

James Rubin (1927–91), well-known promoter of Indian music in the USA, founder of Pan Orient Arts Foundation, facilitated Subbulakshmi's 1966 tour of the US, made extensive recordings over thirty years of live concerts and radio performances, and which now constitutes the James A. Rubin Collection of South Indian Classical Music, Eda Kuhn Loeb Music Library, Harvard University.

Jawaharlal Nehru (1889–1964), Bharat Ratna, Prime Minister (1947–64).

Jayachamaraja Wodeyar (1919–74), son of Yuvaraja Kanteerava Narasimharaja Wadiyar and Yuvarani Kempu Cheluvarajamanni, Maharaja of Mysore (1940–50), musician and composer, connoisseur of Western music, philosopher.

Jayadeva (12th century), composer of the *Gita Govinda*, devotional verses in Sanskrit, verses still presented in concert and in performances of Odissi dance.

Jayaprakash Narayan (1902–79), Bharat Ratna, socialist, political leader and activist, friend of Jawaharlal Nehru and also of Indira Gandhi, whose policies he opposed, closely associated with the creation of the Janata Party which defeated Indira Gandhi in the general elections of 1977, winner of the Magsaysay Award for Public Service (1965).

Joan Sutherland (1926–2010), OM, DBE, soprano, greatly beloved singer to many devotees of opera.

Jon Higgins (1939–84), American musicologist and trained singer of Western classical music, student of vocal Carnatic music from *Sangitha Kalanidhi* T. Viswanathan, friend of several members of the Dhanammal family, a scholar of dance lyric and texts, who performed widely in concerts and on radio, affectionately called *bhagavathar*.

Juthika Roy (1920–2014), Padma Shri, very popular singer of devotional songs in Bengali and Hindi.

K. Subrahmanyam (1904–71), film-maker, impresario, early patron of Subbulakshmi, producer of *Sevasadanam*, his films provided opportunities for Papanasam Sivan, D.K. Pattammal and Kalki R. Krishnamurthi.

Appendix I

K.B. Sundarambal (1908–80), Padma Shri, stage and film artiste, singer of popular devotional songs, member of the Madras Legislative Assembly.

K.R. Athmanathan (born 1934), friend, associate and intimate of Sadasivam and aide to Subbulakshmi since 1954.

K.S. Narayanaswamy (1914–99), *Sangitha Kalanidhi*, Padma Bhushan, son of Narayani Ammal and Sivarama Iyer, *vainika*, teacher, traditionalist, played with Subbulakshmi.

K.V. Narayanaswamy (1923–2002), *Sangitha Kalanidhi, Padma Shri*, son of Muthulakshmi Ammal and Kollengode Viswanatha Iyer, disciple of Ariyakudi Ramanuja Iyengar, a popular and well-regarded vocalist, teacher who taught Subbulakshmi a few songs.

K.V. Prasad (born 1958), student of T.K. Murthy, mrdangam accompanist for Subbulakshmi for about fifteen years in the last stage of her career.

Kadayanallur S. Venkataraman (1929–2004), musician who provided the tune for many of Subbulakshmi's lighter pieces, including some of the Annamacharya compositions.

R. Krishnamurthi (1899–1954), journalist, author, nationalist, intimate of T. Sadasivam, known always as 'Kalki', composer of many of Subbulakshmi's film songs, a figure of considerable influence on her life through the 1940s and beyond.

Kamala (born 1934), Padma Bhushan, daughter of Rajalakshmi and Ramamurthy, dancer, student of Vazhuvoor Ramaiah Pillai, film actor who played the part of Krishna in Subbulakshmi's *Meera*, dance teacher in New York for many years.

Kanchipuram Dhanakoti Ammal and her sisters **Kanchipuram Palani Ammal** and **Kanchipuram Kamakshi Ammal** (19th–20th century) aunts and mother respectively, of the famous Kanchipuram Naina Pillai.

Kanchipuram Naina Pillai (1888/1889?–1934), singer of some importance to the tradition, teacher of T Brinda and T. Muktha, revered as an inspiration by D.K. Pattammal.

Kandadevi Alagiriswamy (1925–2000), student of T. Chowdiah, provided violin accompaniment for Subbulakshmi for most of the 1970s and 1980s.

Karan Singh (born 1931), Padma Vibhushan, successively Regent, Sadr-i-Riyasat and Governor of Jammu & Kashmir (1949–67), Union minister, Ambassador, Member of Parliament, author, poet and musician.

Surasri **Kesarbai Kerkar** (1892–1977), Padma Bhushan, legendary singer, disciple of Ustad Alladiya Khan, famed for her grand style and manner.

Ganasaraswati **Kishori Amonkar** (1931–2017), Padma Vibhushan, daughter of Mogubai Kurdikar, singer of legendary virtuosity of the Jaipur gharana, disciple of her mother and also of Anjanibai Malpekar (1883–1974).

Konerirajapuram Vaidyanatha Iyer (1878–1921), famous vocalist, roughly contemporary with Madurai Pushpavanam Iyer.

Kumbakonam Balamani (1870?–1935?), singer, manager of a drama troupe.

Lakshmi Shankar (1926–2013), daughter of Visalakshi and R.V. Shastri, the first editor of Gandhi's *Harijan* and a member of Subbulakshmi's circle of friends in the 1940s, student at Uday Shankar's school at Almora, Hindustani vocalist, disciple of Abdul Rehman Khan and also of Ravi Shankar, had early training in Bharatanatyam and Carnatic music, and also sang for films.

Lalgudi Jayaraman (1930–2013), Padma Bhushan, violinist and composer, student of his father Lalgudi Gopala Iyer, teacher of his son G.J.R. Krishnan and daughter Vijayalakshmi, as also of several vocalists.

Lata Mangeshkar (born 1929), Bharat Ratna, daughter of Shevanti 'Mai' and Dinanath Mangeshkar, playback singer who has sung for over a thousand films.

M. Balamuralikrishna (1930–2016), *Sangitha Kalanidhi*, Padma Vibhushan, vocalist, composer, playback singer and teacher, partnered often with Hindustani performers in *jugalbandi* recitals.

M. Karunanidhi (1924–2018), known as *Kalaignar*, or 'Artist', journalist, film scriptwriter, politician, five-time chief minister of Tamil Nadu.

M. Lalithangi (1907–55), adopted daughter of Perumalkoil Narayanamma, singer, student of Coimbatore Thayi, mother of M.L. Vasanthakumari, published the songs of Purandaradasa.

M.G. Ramachandran (1917–87), *Bharat Ratna*, film actor, politician, played a small part in *Meera*, chief minister of Tamil Nadu 1977–87.

M.K. Gandhi (1869–1948), *Mahatma*, a barrister from Gujarat who trained Indians in South Africa to resist injustice by non-violent passive resistance; on return to India in 1915 adopted same methods to resist British rule; assassinated by a Hindu fanatic; knew and recognized Subbulakshmi and her music; and **Kasturba Gandhi** (1869–1944).

M.L. Vasanthakumari (1927–90), *Sangitha Kalanidhi*, Padma Bhushan, daughter of Lalithangi and Koothanur Ayyaswami Iyer, disciple of G.N. Balasubramaniam, leading vocalist of her generation, famed alike for her creative imagination and her understanding of tradition, mother of the dancer and film actor Srividya (1953–2006).

M.S. Gopalakrishnan (1931–2013), *Sangitha Kalanidhi*, Padma Bhushan, violinist, disciple of his father Parur Sundaram Iyer, student also of the Hindustani style.

M.S. Sakthivel (1912–74), son of Vina Shanmukhavadivu, mrdangist, accompanied Subbulakshmi in the late 1940s.

M.S. Vadivambal (1925–47), younger daughter of Vina Shanmukhavadivu.

Madurai Pushpavanam Iyer (late 1880s?–1917/1920?), greatest star of his generation of Carnatic musicians.

Madurai Mani Iyer (1912–67), *Sangitha Kalanidhi*, son of Subbulakshmi and Madurai Ramaswami Iyer, disciple of Harikesanallur Muthiah Bhagavathar, popular and much-admired singer.

Madurai Srinivasa Iyengar (dates unclear), and his younger brother *Sangitha Kalanidhi* **Madurai Srirangam Iyengar** (1904–70),were the disciples of Namakkal Narasimha Iyengar (1836–1924?).

Maha Vaidyanatha Iyer (1844–93), musician and composer of the *Melakarta Ragamalika*, student of Manambuchavadi Venkatasubbier (1803–62), himself a direct disciple of Tyagaraja.

Maharajapuram Viswanatha Iyer (1896–1970), *Sangitha Kalanidhi*, vocalist of the school of Maha Vaidyanatha Iyer, teacher of Semmangudi Srinivasa Iyer.

Malaikottai Govindaswami Pillai (1879–1931), violinist, teacher of K.S. 'Papa' Venkatarama Iyer.

Malka (also **Malika**) **Pukhraj** (1912–2004), ghazal and folk singer, for many years attached to the Jammu & Kashmir darbar, migrated to Pakistan.

Mani Krishnaswami (1930–2002), *Sangitha Kalanidhi*, disciple of Musiri Subramania Iyer, student of Kalakshetra.

Maria Callas (1923–77), soprano, hugely influential in the world of opera.

Mazhavarayanendal Subbarama Bhagavathar (1888–1951), *Sangitha Kalanidhi*, singer and early teacher of Subbulakshmi.

Ganatapasvini **Mogubai Kurdikar** (1904–2001), Padma Bhushan, student of Ustad Alladiya Khan, widely revered singer, teacher of many prominent singers, most notably her daughter Kishori Amonkar.

Louis Mountbatten, 1st Earl Mountbatten of Burma, 1st Earl (1900–79), Viceroy of India, March–August 1947, Governor-General of India, August 1947–June 1948; and **Edwina, Countess Mountbatten** (1901–60).

Mrinalini Sarabhai (1918–2016), Padma Bhushan, daughter of Subbaram and Ammu Swaminadhan, dancer, teacher, choreographer, student of Pandanallur Meenakshisundaram Pillai, also studied for varying lengths of time at Kalakshetra, Madras, Kerala Kalamandalam and Santiniketan, Bengal.

Musiri Subramania Iyer (1899–1975), *Sangitha Kalanidhi*, vocalist, teacher, Principal of College of Carnatic Music, Madras, recognized by Subbulakshmi as her guru, widely respected figure in the world of Carnatic music.

Muthulakshmi Reddy (1886–1967), Padma Bhushan, daughter of S. Narayanaswami Aiyer and Pudukkottai Chandrammal, first woman medical graduate in Madras, first woman to enter a house of legislature in India, founder of the Avvai Home for destitute women and orphaned children, prime mover behind the devadasi abolition legislation of 1947.

Mysore Sadasiva Rao (1805?–85), disciple of Walajapet Venkataramana Bhagavathar, a direct disciple of Tyagaraja, *asthana vidvan* in the Mysore court, composer of '*Sri Kamakoti*' in the raga Saveri, a staple in Subbulakshmi's repertoire.

Appendix I 419

Mysore Vasudevacharya (1865–1961), *Sangitha Kalanidhi*, Padma Bhushan, composer of about 200 songs, most famously of '*Brochevarevarura*' in the raga Khamas, and singer, for many years a teacher at Kalakshetra.

Mylapore Gowri Ammal (1892–1971), daughter of Doraikannu, in the 1930s was teacher of Rukmini Devi Arundale, Esther Sherman aka Ragini Devi (1896–1982), the American mother of Indrani Rahman, and of Vyjayantimala and Yamini Krishnamurti.

N.C. Vasanthakokilam (1919–51), formerly Kamakshi, daughter of N. Chandrasekhara Iyer, charismatic and popular singer and film actor.

Narayana Tirtha (1650/1675–1745/1750), composer of Telugu songs known as *tarangam*, also the *Krishna lila tarangini* in Sanskrit, lived in the Thanjavur region.

Nargis, also Nargis Dutt (1929–81), Padma Shri, daughter of Jaddan Bai (1897?–1950), daughter of Dilipa Devi (1867?–?), actor, politician, whose best-known films are *Mother India*, *Shree 420* and *Awara*.

Nedunuri Krishnamurthi (1927–2014), *Sangitha Kalanidhi*, vocalist, well known for his work with the compositions of Annamacharya.

Dame **Nellie Melba** (1861–1931), born Helen Mitchell, Australian soprano, hugely popular in Europe and the USA, hailed as 'the divine Melba'.

Nilakantha Sivan (1839–1900), composer of '*Sambho Mahadeva*' in the raga Bauli, and of '*Ananda natamaduvar*' in Purvikalyani, both prominent in Subbulakshmi's repertoire.

P. Sambamoorthy (1901–73), *Sangitha Kalanidhi*, musicologist and author.

P.V. Subramaniam 'Subbudu' (1917–2007), music critic, for many years with the *Statesman*.

Padmaja Naidu (1900–74), daughter of Sarojini and Govindarajulu Naidu, Governor of West Bengal (1957–67).

Palani Subramania Pillai (1908–62), *Sangitha Kalanidhi*, provided mrdangam accompaniment to many senior *vidvans* of his time, teacher of *Sangitha Kalanidhi* Trichy Sankaran (born 1942).

Palghat Mani Iyer (1912–81), *Sangitha Kalanidhi*, legendary player of the mrdangam, who accompanied many of the leading vocalists of his time; also played for both D.K. Pattammal and M.L. Vasanthakumari at a time when many men did not accompany women singers.

Pankaj Mullick (1905–78), Padma Shri, composer and playback singer, known also for his Rabindra sangeet. Recipient in 1972 of the Dadasaheb Phalke Award for lifetime contribution to Indian cinema.

Pandanallur Jayalakshmi (1930–2017), daughter of Rajayi, famed dancer, married the Raja of Ramnad.

Papanasam Sivan (1890–1972) *Sangitha Kalanidhi*, composer in Tamil, many of whose songs, both for the film and for the concert stage, were sung to great effect by Subbulakshmi.

Parveen Sultana (born 1950), Padma Bhushan, Hindustani vocalist from the Patiala gharana, also famous for her film songs, ghazals and bhajans.

Patnam Subramania Iyer (1845–1902), musician and composer, student of Manambuchavadi Venkatasubbier (1803–62), himself a direct disciple of Tyagaraja, and teacher of Mysore Vasudevachar.

Periasami Tooran (1908–87), composer of Tamil songs, of which Subbulakshmi sang '*Muruga muruga*'/Saveri, '*Gananathane*'/Saranga and '*Taye Tripurasundari*'/Suddhasaveri.

Philomena Thumboochetty (1913–2000), violinist, from a Telugu-speaking family of Mysore, trained at the Paris Conservatoire where she was a student of George Enescu, also the teacher of Yehudi Menuhin, played to rave audiences in London in the 1930s, with the popular magazine *Punch*, in its Silver Jubilee Number of May 1935, carrying a poem with the memorable line, '*Compared to her, Yehudi, Young Menuhin, must yield*'.

Pudukkottai Dakshinamurthi Pillai (1875–1936/37), mrdangam *vidvan*, provided encouragement to Subbulakshmi in her early years, teacher of Palani Subramania Pillai.

Puliyur Doraswami Iyer (19th century?), very little known of this composer. His sole composition appears to be '*Sarasiruhasanapriye*' in Nata, a song prominent in Subbulakshmi's repertoire as in those of many others.

Purandaradasa (1485–1565), hailed as *pitamaha*, composer of devotional verses in Kannada, a steady presence on the concert platform. Other members of the *dasakuta*, or community of Vaishnavite *dasas* are Vysaraya (1447–1548) and Kanakadasa (16th century).

R. Vedavalli (born 1935), *Sangitha Kalanidhi*, student of Madurai Srirangam Iyengar, brother of Subbulakshmi's very early teacher Madurai Srinivasa Iyengar, and also of *Sangitha Kalanidhi* Mudicondan Venkatarama Iyer (1897–1975).

R. Rangaramanuja Ayyangar (1901–80), musicologist and writer, believed to be a disciple of Dhanammal.

R.K. Narayan (1906–2001), Padma Vibhushan, writer of short stories and novels, member of the Rajya Sabha (1980–86).

R.K. Shanmukham Chetty (1892–1953), economist, India's first finance minister, member of the Madras legislative assembly, supporter of the *Tamil isai* movement, partner of T. Balasaraswati.

R.K. Shriram Kumar (born 1966), violin accompanist for Subbulakshmi for about the last ten years of her career, student of his grandfather R.K. Venkatarama Sastri, also Subbulakshmi's violinist.

R.K. Venkatarama Sastri (1907–93), student of T. Chowdiah, violinist, long-term accompanist of Subbulakshmi.

K.S. 'Papa' Venkataramiah (1901–72), *Sangitha Kalanidhi*, violinist.

R.S. Gopalakrishnan (1918–96), violinist, accompanied many women singers, including Subbulakshmi on her 1963 Edinburgh visit.

R.L. Subbalakshmi (1886–1969), Padma Shri, daughter of Visalakshi and R.V. Subramania Iyer, possibly the first Hindu woman graduate of the University of Madras, in 1911, child widow who became the founder of the Sarada Ladies Union, the Sarada Vidyalaya and the Sarada Ashram, social reformer and activist, always known as 'Sister Subbalakshmi'.

Rabindranath Tagore (1861–1941), poet, playwright, musician, artist, philosopher, founder of Santiniketan, winner of the Nobel Prize for Literature in 1913 for *Gitanjali*. The Bengali songs composed and set to music by him constitute Rabindra sangeet.

Radha Viswanathan (1934–2018), elder daughter of Apitakuchamba/Parvati and T. Sadasivam, dancer and later teacher, possibly Subbulakshmi's closest companion and long-term accompanying singer.

Raja Ram Mohan Roy (1772–1833), founder, in 1828, of the Brahmo Samaj, aimed at ridding orthodox Hinduism of its ritualistic elements and drawing on the common features of Upanisadic Hinduism, Islam and Christianity; many upper-class, anglicized Bengalis were drawn to the Brahmo Samaj.

Rajam Pushpavanam (1917–91), daughter of Sundarathammal (also Sundarambal) and Madurai Pushpavanam Iyer, vocalist, teacher, and for a brief while a possible competitor to Subbulakshmi.

Rallapalli Anantakrishna Sarma (1893–1979), *Sangitha Kalanidhi*, composer and musician.

Ramanathapuram 'Poochi' Srinivasa Iyengar (1860–1919), vocalist and composer, disciple of Patnam Subramania Iyer.

Ravi Shankar (1920–2012), Bharat Ratna, son of Hemangini Devi and Shyam Shankar Chowdhury, disciple of Ustad Allauddin Khan, sitarist and composer, recipient in 1992 of the Ramon Magsaysay Award for Journalism, Literature and the Creative Communication Arts, the best-known amongst Indian musicians in the West.

Rukmini Devi Arundale (1904–86), Padma Bhushan, daughter of Seshammal and Nilakanta Sastri, theosophist, dancer, parliamentarian, founder of Kalakshetra, 'a renaissance woman one who enriched the nation with highest artistic traditions and values of life' (Sunil Kothari, *Seminar* 540, August 2004).

S. Pinakapani (1913–2013), *Sangitha Kalanidhi*, vocalist, teacher, medical doctor, teacher of many popular Andhra musicians, including Nedunuri Krishnamurthi, Voleti Venkateswarulu (1928–1989) and Srirangam Gopalaratnam.

S. Radhakrishnan (1888–1975), OM, Bharat Ratna, philosopher, author, educationist, statesman, Spalding Professor of Eastern Religions and Ethics, University of Oxford (1936–52), Vice President of India (1952–62), President of India (1962–67).

S. Tyagarajan (born 1947), born R. Kannakutti, son of Mangalam, the son of Sadasivam's sister Rajalakshmi, and Ramamurthi, adopted June 1961 by Subbulakshmi and Sadasivam.

Appendix I

Sadasiva Brahmendra (xxxx–1714), mystic, composer in Sanskrit, from the Kaveri region, his dates are disputed but he is said to have been a contemporary of Shahuji (1672–xxxx) and Sarabhoji I (1675–1728) of Thanjavur.

Sarojini Naidu (1879–1949), daughter of Varadasundari and Aghorenath Chattopadhyaya, student at King's College, London and Girton College, Cambridge, poet, nationalist and politician. President of the Indian National Congress in 1925, Governor of Uttar Pradesh (1947–49).

Satyajit Ray (1921–92), Bharat Ratna, son of Suprabha and Sukumar Ray, film-maker, musician, artist, recognized as one of the greatest film-makers of the twentieth century, recipient in 1967 of the Ramon Magsaysay Award for Journalism, Literature and the Creative Communication Arts, director of *Charulata, Devi, Kanchenjunga, Pather Panchali, Aparajito, Apur Sansar, Shatranj ke Khiladi, Ghare Baire*, among many other films.

Salem Godavari (xxxx–1911), one of the earliest musicians recorded in south India, who gave substantial money to the Pachaiyappa's Trust for the promotion of education.

Semmangudi Srinivasa Iyer (1908–2002), *Sangitha Kalanidhi*, Padma Vibhushan, vocalist, patriarch and *eminence grise* of the Carnatic world, one of the two teachers always acknowledged by Subbulakshmi, well known for his contribution to popularizing the songs of Svati Tirunal (1813–46), Maharaja of Travancore.

'Vina' Seshanna (1852–1926), vina player at the Mysore court.

Moolam Thirunal Sethu Parvati Bayi (1896–1983), Junior Maharani of Travancore, granddaughter of the celebrated artist Raja Ravi Varma, musician and patroness of Subbulakshmi's guru Semmangudi Srinivasa Iyer; also a somewhat sinister intriguer famed alike for 'her individual accomplishments and fascinating social unorthodoxy' (Manu Pillai, *The Ivory Throne*).

Shanta Rao (1930–2007), student of Pandanallur Meenakshisundaram Pillai; also studied Kathakali, Mohini Attam, now largely forgotten but at one time recognized as an exceptional dancer, photographed by Sunil Janah, admired by Yehudi Menuhin and promoted by G. Venkatachalam.

Siddheshwari Devi (1903–77), Padma Shri, daughter of Shyama Devi and Shyamu Mishra, famed singer of *thumri* and *khayal*, hailed along with Begum Akhtar, Rasoolan Bai (1902–74) and Badi Moti Bai as one of 'the four great pillars of Hindustani light classical music' (Susheela Misra, *Great Masters of Hindustani Music*).

Sikkil Kunjumani (1927–2010), *Sangitha Kalanidhi*, and **Sikkil Neela** (born 1940), *Sangitha Kalanidhi*, popularly known as the Sikkil Sisters, flautists, later related to Radha Viswanathan by marriage, awarded the title in 2002.

Sri Atmananda (1883–1959), *vedantist* and teacher; composer of *Radhamadhavam*, a hymn in Malayalam recorded by Subbulakshmi.

Sri Chandrasekhara Saraswati (1894–1994), sixty-eighth Sankaracharya or pontiff of the Sri Kanchi Kamakoti peetham, greatly revered by Saivite Brahmins in south India, known as Paramacharya.

Sri Ma Anandamayi (1896–1982), born Nirmala Sundari in a Bengali family and married as a child but very early on developed mystic powers and gathered around her a large following who revered her as a saint.

Sri Ramana Maharshi (1879–1950), sage and thinker, held in great veneration. The Sri Ramanasrama at Tiruvannamalai remains to this date a place of quiet introspection.

Sri Sathya Sai Baba (1926–2011), god-man, educationist, with an extensive following across India and abroad, songs in whose praise were recorded by Subbulakshmi.

Srirangam Gopalaratnam (1939–93), Padma Shri, student of S. Pinakapani, popular singer from Andhra Pradesh.

Subbarama Dikshitar (1839–1906), musicologist and composer, from the lineage of Muthusvami Dikshitar, author of *Sangita Sampradaya Pradarsini*.

Subbaraya Sastri (1803–62), son of Syama Sastri, student of Tyagaraja, composer of very few songs, in particular 'Janani' in the raga Ritigaula, most of which survive in the repertoire of contemporary musicians, father of the composer Annaswami Sastri (1827–1900).

Mahakavi **Subramania Bharati** (1882–1921), nationalist, poet, journalist, musician, inspiring leader of the Tamil people.

Appendix I 425

Suddhananda (Shuddhananda) Bharati (1897–1990), mystic, disciple both of Sri Ramana Maharshi and Sri Aurobindo, musician and poet who composed in Tamil, English and French; his most popular songs include *'Eppadi padinaro'*/Jaunpuri, *'Arul purivai'*/Hamsadhwani and *'Jhankarastuti'*/Purvikalyani.

Svati Tirunal Rama Varma, Maharaja of Travancore (1813–46), ruler and composer of songs, operas and other texts.

Swami Chinmayananda (1916–93), spiritual leader, writer and teacher, founder of the Chinmaya Mission.

Swami Ranganathananda (1908–2005), major figure within the Ramakrishna Mission and president from 1998 onwards.

Swami Sivananda (1887–1963), spiritual leader and teacher, author, in early life a trained physician, founder of the Divine Life Society.

T. Abhiramasundari (1919–73), violinist, daughter of T. Kamakshi and S. Soundararaja Iyengar, student of K.S. 'Papa' Venkatarama Iyer.

T. Balasaraswati (1918–86), *Sangitha Kalanidhi*, Padma Vibhushan, daughter of T. Jayammal and 'Dare House' Moddevarupu Govindarajulu Naidu, dancer, musician, and great representative of the performing tradition.

T. Brinda (1914–96), *Sangitha Kalanidhi*, daughter of T. Kamakshi and S. Soundararaja Iyengar, singer and *vainika*.

T. Chowdiah (1895–1967), *Sangitha Kalanidhi*, son of Sundaramma of Hassan and Agastya Gowda, student of Bidaram Krishnappa (1866–1931), violin accompanist to Subbulakshmi in the late 1940s.

'Vina' T. Dhanammal (1866–1938), daughter of Sundarammal, *vainika*, famed for her sensitive and refined interpretations of songs of the great composers, and particularly of *padams*.

T. Jayalakshmi, also **Jayammal** (1890–1967), third daughter of T. Dhanammal, sang to her daughter T. Balasaraswati's dance. An obituary notice had this to say: 'Like Bindusara between Chandragupta and Asoka, or Humayun between Babar and Akbar, Jayammal has been handicapped by having come between Dhanammal and Balasaraswati'. (Aeolus, *Shankar's Weekly*, 5 March 1967.)

T. Kamakshi (1892/3–1953), fourth daughter of T. Dhanammal.

T. Lakshmiratnam (1888–1940), second daughter of T. Dhanammal, musician, teacher.

T. Muktha (1914–2008), daughter of T. Kamakshi and S. Soundararaja Iyengar, musician, teacher.

T. Rajalakshmi (1885–1957), eldest daughter of T. Dhanammal, student of Patnam Subramania Iyer, known to have taught *padams* to D.K. Pattammal.

T. Sadasivam (1902–97), journalist, freedom fighter, film producer, impresario, husband first of Apitakuchamba/Parvati and then of M.S. Subbulakshmi, whom he promoted assiduously.

T. Sankaran (1906–2001), son of T. Lakshmiratnam, singer, administrator with All India Radio, friend of Subbulakshmi.

T. Suryakumari (1925–2005), popular singer in the Andhra area, dancer, film actor, beauty queen, theatre actor in New York and London.

T.H. Vinayakram (born 1942), Padma Bhushan, ghatam *vidvan*, long-term accompanist to Subbulakshmi, member of the fusion music group Shakti.

T.K. Chidambaranatha Mudaliar (1882–1954), known as *Rasikamani*, author and leading figure in the Tamil renaissance of the 1930s and 1940s, Member of the 1937 Legislative Council, an intimate friend of Sadasivam and Subbulakshmi.

T.K. Govinda Rao (1929–2011), *Sangitha Kalanidhi*, vocalist, student of Musiri Subramania Iyer, musicologist, teacher, editor of several volumes of compositions of the trinity.

T.K. Murthy (born 1922), *Sangitha Kalanidhi*, disciple of Tanjavur Vaidyanatha Iyer (1895–1947), accompanied Subbulakshmi on the mrdangam for forty years.

T.L. Venkatarama Iyer (1892–1971), *Sangitha Kalanidhi*, authority on the compositions of Muthusvami Dikshitar, Judge of the Supreme Court of India, teacher of D.K. Pattammal, also believed to have taught a few songs to Subbulakshmi.

T.M. Krishna (born 1976), vocalist, student of B. Seetarama Sarma and of Semmangudi Srinivasa Iyer, also writer, public speaker and social activist, recipient of Magsaysay Award for Emergent Leadership 2016 and the Indira Gandhi Award for National Integration 2017.

T.M. Tyagarajan (1923–2007), *Sangitha Kalanidhi*, vocalist, senior disciple of Semmangudi Srinivasa Iyer.

T.R. Rajarathinam Pillai (1898–1956), nadasvaram *vidvan*, flamboyant and widely regarded artiste.

T.T. Krishnamachari (1899–1973), businessman and politician, Union minister (1952–65), patron of Subbulakshmi and Sadasivam.

Talapakkam Annamacharya (1424–1503), composed over 14,000 devotional verses in Telugu, many of which are of an erotic nature. Subbulakshmi did much to popularize a set of these (non-erotic) compositions, set to music by Nedunuri Krishnamurthi and Kadayanallur S. Venkataraman.

Tarangambadi Panchanatha Iyer (dates unclear), alternately described as a disciple of Subbaraya Sastri (1803–62) and a twentieth-century composer, author of '*Birana brova*' in the raga Kalyani.

Tiruppamburam Swaminatha Pillai (1898–1961), *Sangitha Kalanidhi*, flautist, scholar of Muthusvami Dikshitar.

Tirupati Narayanaswami Naidu (1873–1912), composer, most famously of '*Ikanainana*' in the raga Pushpalatika, well known in Subbulakshmi's repertoire.

Tiruvarur Rajayi (1896–1926), daughter of Kuttiyammal, popular singer known to have performed at the courts of Ramnad and Mysore, student of Jalatarangam Subbayyar and Ramanathapuram Srinivasa Iyengar.

Travancore Sisters, **Lalitha** (1930–82), **Padmini** (1932–2006) and **Ragini** (1937–76), popular and widely acclaimed dancers since the 1940s.

The **Trinity**, **Syama Sastri** (1762–1827), **Tyagaraja** (1767–1837) and **Muthusvami Dikshitar** (1775–1835), all three born in Tiruvarur, formerly Tanjavur, now Tiruvarur district, Tamil Nadu, who have had a lasting impact on the form, style and practice of Carnatic music.

Umayalpuram Kothandarama Iyer (1889/1899–1966), accompanist to Subbulakshmi on the ghatam through the 1950s.

Umm Kulthum (sometimes **Kalthoum**) (1904–75), hailed as one of the greatest Arab musicians, singer, film actor. In a handwritten note to Subbulakshmi, she writes her name as Um Kulsum.

V. Nagarajan (1919–2004), son of the violinist K.S. 'Papa' Venkatarama Iyer, for many years accompanied Subbulakshmi on the kanjira, and occasionally on the mrdangam.

V. Raghavan (1908–79), Padma Bhushan, Sanskritist, musicologist, composer, long-term secretary of the Music Academy, Madras.

V. Ranganayaki (1927–2017), vocalist, musicologist, disciple of Namakkal Sesha Iyengar, singer for T. Balasaraswati through the 1950s.

V.O. Chidambaram Pillai (1872–1936), freedom fighter, shipping merchant. For a quick account of his strange and sad life, see 'The Champion of Tuticorin', in *The Courtesan, the Mahatma and the Italian Brahmin*, by Manu S. Pillai, New Delhi: Context, 2019.

V.V. Subramanyam (born 1944), violinist, student of Chembai Vaidyanatha Bhagavathar and Semmangudi Srinivasa Iyer, accompanist to Subbulakshmi through the 1960s.

Vasundhara Devi (1917–88), daughter of M.N. Srinivasan and Yadugiri Devi, talented actor–musician, and disciple of Pandit Narayan Rao Vyas, who performed Hindustani music at the Music Academy. Her film *Mangamma Sapatham* (1943) was a great hit. She recorded widely and was often presented on radio.

Vazhuvoor Ramaiah Pillai (1910–79), teacher of dance, of Radha Viswanathan, and more famously of Kamala, and also of the Travancore Sisters, Vyjayantimala, Padma Subrahmanyam and many other successful dancers.

Vijaya Rajendran (1938–2011), younger daughter of Apitakuchamba/Parvati and T. Sadasivam, occasional accompanying singer to Subbulakshmi.

Vyjayantimala (born 1933), Padma Shri, daughter of M.D. Raman and Vasundhara Devi, student of Vazhuvoor Ramaiah Pillai and also of K.N. Dhandayudhapani Pillai, dancer with regular appearances at the Music

Academy, Madras, choreographer, film actor whose best-known films include *Naya daur*, *Madhumati*, *Amrapali*, *Gunga Jumna*, *Devdas* and *Sangam*, politician and member of both houses of parliament.

Yamini Krishnamurti (born 1940), Padma Vibhushan, dancer, teacher, student originally of Kalakshetra, also learnt from Mylapore Gowri Amma; Bharatanatyam, Kuchipudi and Odissi performer.

Appendix II
SOME NOTES ON SONGS

This is a list, with details, and suggestions on where one might hear them, of some of the songs Subbulakshmi sang more often than others. These are not by any means the only songs of these composers that she knew, but she tended to stick to a small set of songs within her repertoire. I have not looked at the bhajans or the hymns. A great deal more is available on the net, on YouTube, where new songs, and some full concerts, are being selectively, and continuously released, and on sites such as www.sangeethapriya.org, which also has full concerts, including *ragam-tanam-pallavi* suites.

Subbulakshmi was a seasoned concert artiste, and this attempt at identifying songs which were well known in her repertoire should not be taken to mean that she was merely a singer of songs. The commercially released CDs are often a random intermixing of songs from more than one concert, and do not suggest that the original concerts had any internal integrity, which they often did.

Those interested should find *Meera*, in either Tamil or Hindi, on YouTube. It is always watchable. *Sakuntalai*, likewise, is on YouTube, as is the four-part Films Division documentary. The *Melakarta Ragamalika* in its entirety is also recommended listening.

MUTHUSVAMI DIKSHITAR

Most of the great compositions of Muthusvami Dikshitar have the most extraordinary, luminous text. A simple understanding of Sanskrit vocabulary would help in getting the drift, even if comprehending the songs in all their intricacies would call for more scholarship.

'Akhilandeshwari'/Jujavanti/Adi. 1969 Concert Album. Also Charsur CD of Detroit 1977 concert. Doordarshan Bharat Ratna Series Part II.

T.L. Venkatarama Iyer, a leading scholar of Muthusvami Dikshitar, was of the view that *'Akhilandeshwari'* is not an authentic composition of Muthusvami Dikshitar. (Lecture Demonstration by R.K. Shriram Kumar, the Music Academy, 18 December 2017). It does, however, remain a wondrous composition; whoever was masquerading as the master was doing quite a good job. The *madhyama kala* ending to the *charanam* is a thrilling piece of composition, describing the goddess as *'jujavanti raga nute, jalli maddala jharjhara vadya nada mudite'*, 'she who is praised in the raga jujavanti, to the accompaniment of the jalli, maddala and jharjhara', all ancient instruments.

The composition is on the deity at Tiruvanaikaval. Also at this temple is Siva in His manifestation as water, the *appu lingam*, and where Muthusvami Dikshitar composed *'Jambupate'* in Yamunakalyani. This song was not sung by Subbulakshmi but there are several very superior renderings available online as for instance by M.L. Vasanthakumari and T.M. Krishna.

'Angarakam'/Surati/Rupaka. Charsur CD of 25 December 1956 concert. CD Guru Guha Vani.

Every one of the *navagraha kritis* is a listening experience and Subbulakshmi's renderings of *'Suryamurte'*/Saurashtra, *'Chandram'*/Asaveri and *'Divakara tanujam'*/Yadukulakambhoji are relatively easy to access online. *Angarakam*, in praise of Mars, was a favourite with her, taut, sprightly, rich with *gamaka*. For a breezy introduction to this masterpiece see 'Mars' bars', by Renuka Narayanan, *The Indian Express*, New Delhi, 1 September 2003.

'*Bhaja re re chitta Balambikam*'/Kalyani/Triputa. Legend has it that Muthusvami Dikshitar was born after his parents had worshipped at the shrine of Balambika at Vaidyeswarankoil, *bhava-raga-tala modinim*, She who is the embodiment of music. There is a reference to this in the last line of this beautiful song, '*Guru guha rupa muttukumara janani*', 'mother of Muttukumara who is guruguha'. Subbulakshmi's rendering is available on YouTube and is worth looking for. Among the greatest of the compositions of Muthusvami Dikshitar. See endnote 1 to Chapter 9.

'*Cheta Sri Balakrishnam*'/Jujavanti/Rupaka. Sony/NCPA Record of August 1978 recital.

This is Jujavanti presented in a more Carnatic form. A stunning composition, a staple of the Semmangudi school, as of the Dhanammal tradition, which Subbulakshmi presented only selectively. Listen carefully to the *sahityam*.

'*Hariharaputram*'/Vasanta/Jhampa. 1969 Concert Album. Charsur CD of 25 December 1956 concert. Also Charsur CD of 25 December 1966 concert.

In praise of the deity at Sabarimala, '*shaurigiri viharam*', and overlooking the Pandya and Kerala countries, '*pandya keral(a)di desa prabhakaram*'.

'*Hiranmayim*'/Lalita/Rupaka. Sung at the Music Academy recital in December 1969, available on YouTube. Also Carnatica CD Sangamam, along with Semmangudi Srinivasa Iyer.

In this song the composer, secure in the protection of *hiranmayi*, the one decked in gold, vows to shun the protection, *asraya*, of low men, *hina-manava*. '*Hiranmayim Lakshmim sada bhajami, hina-manav(a)srayam tyajami*'.

'*Kamalambike*'/Todi/Rupaka. CD Guru Guha Vani. Also on YouTube, in a clip from a 1986 Tiruvarur recital.

Of the eleven songs which constitute the full Kamalamba Navavarana, Subbulakshmi sang '*Kamalambike*' in Todi to the virtual exclusion of all the others ('*Kamalamba samrakshatu mam*' in Anandabhairavi and '*Kamalambam bhaja re'* in Kalyani are known). As in many other compositions of Muthusvami Dikshitar, the text is bewitching. One descriptive phrase for the Goddess is *'a-ka-cha-ta-tha-pa adi varne'*, or 'the one who is the personification of words, or language'.

'*Kanjadalayatakshi*'/Kamalamanohari/Adi. 1974 Sri Kamakshi Suprabhatam record.

The *sahitya* for this song includes the mesmerising phrase *'ekanekakshari'* or 'she who is the one syllable and the many'. Subbulakshmi sings this song with verve, highlighting the composer's great ability to use the *madhyama kala* but many listeners prefer Pattammal's stately rendering, one of her learnings from Ambi Dikshitar, of the composer's family.

'*Mamava Minakshi*'/Varali/Misrachapu. CD Meenakshi Suprabhatam and Other Songs.

Subbulakshmi sang this sparingly in concerts, if at all, but included it in her very last recording, sung in her great age, a tribute to Minakshi who is *'manikya vallaki pani'*, the one who bears the ruby studded lute, and *'madhuravani'*, sweet voiced, *'varaliveni'*, whose dark tresses are as a swarm of bees', this last phrase introducing the name of the raga.

'*Minakshi*'/Gamakakriya/Adi. 1969 Concert Album.

'*Madhura puri nilaye!*', or 'She who dwells in Madhura (Madurai), '*Minalochani pasamochani*', or 'She of shapely eyes like a fish, She who releases from bondage...' and '*veeNa-vaadana-dasa-gamakakriye*', 'Who, on the vina, plays (or plays with) (the ten) gamakas', these are just some of the expressive phrases in this song which Subbulakshmi sang often. The raga is more popularly known as Purvikalyani. For a deeply emotional and evocative understanding of this great composition, see Justin McCarthy's 'Navtej Johar, Meenakshi', in Anita E. Cherian (ed.), *Dance Ecologies in India*, New Delhi: Tulika Books, 2016.

'*Ranganayakam*'/Nayaki/Adi. This masterpiece is in praise of Vishnu as Ranganatha in Srirangam, the partner of Ranganayaki,

'*Ranganayaki sametam...*' Subbulakshmi's version, from the 1988 recital at the *Kumbhabhishekham* at Srirangam, can be found on YouTube. D.K. Pattammal's version is worth looking for.

'*Rangapura vihara*'/**Brindavanasaranga**/**Rupaka**. 1966 UN Concert. Also Charsur CD of 25 December 1960 concert.

A grand composition at any time, and again in praise of Vishnu as Ranganatha in Srirangam it is one to which Subbulakshmi brought great lustre. My personal affection for this song is linked in my mind to listening to the UN Concert, on AIR Delhi, with Subbulakshmi on the day the Bharat Ratna was conferred on her; and of her suddenly looking up at the words '*Enanka ravi nayana...*', 'He whose eyes are as the moon and the sun', and saying 'do you know difficult that is ?'

'*Sadasivam upasmahe*'/**Sankarabharanam**. CD Guru Guha Vani. Also on YouTube.

In praise of Siva but does not appear to be specific to any one shrine. Subbulakshmi chose this song to represent the composer in her presidential concert at the Music Academy, Madras, in 1968.

'*Sri Kantimatim*'/**Desisimharava**/**Adi**. CD Divine Unison, along with Semmangudi Srinivasa Iyer. CD Guru Guha Vani.

Composed on the deity at Tirunelveli, on the river Tamraparni, hence '*suddha Tamraparni tata-sthitaa*'. The raga is more popularly known as Hemavati.

'*Sri Krishnam*'/**Todi**/**Adi**. The scholar musician T.M. Krishna, who has himself sung this piece to effect, believes that, beautiful as it is, it may not actually be by Muthusvami Dikshitar. The song is in praise of the deity at Guruvayur, in Kerala, hence *Guru-pavana-pur(a)dhisam*.

'*Sri Subramanyaya namaste*'/**Kambhoji**/**Rupaka**. In praise of Subramanya or Kumara or Kartikeya but does not appear to be specific to any one shrine.

A rendering with *alapana* and *neraval* at the line '*vasavadi sakala...*' is available on YouTube. There are, fortunately, many Kambhojis of Subbulakshmi accessible online: Tyagaraja's '*O Rangasayee*', '*Evari mata*' and '*Ma Janaki*' and Gopalakrishna Bharati's '*Tiruvadicharanam*'.

'***Vatapi Ganapatim***'/**Hamsadhwani/Adi.** Saregama CD Live At Russia 1987. CD Swaralaya Puraskaram 1997.

This ubiquitous composition remains a sprightly beginning to any concert, as, for instance, Subbulakshmi's last public concert, in 1997. Muthusvami Dikshitar's father Ramasvami Dikshitar is said to have identified the raga Hamsadhwani, now often heard sung by Hindustani musicians, famously by Amir Khan, Kankana Banerjee, Bade Ghulam Ali Khan and Kishori Amonkar. For a scholarly introduction to the composition, see Amy Caitlin, '*Vatapi Ganapatim*: Sculptural, Poetic, and Musical Texts in a Hymn to Ganesa', in Robert L. Brown (ed.), *Ganesh: Studies of an Asian God*, Albany, NY: State University of New York Press, 1991.

'***Vinapustakadharini***'/**Vegavahini/Jhampa.** CD Guru Guha Vani.

Subbulakshmi learnt this from T. Brinda and presented it at both the memorial concerts held in 1975 for Muthusvami Dikshitar. Vishnu Vasudev, in an interesting blog on Chakravakam/Vegavahini, observes that Muthusvami Dikshitar's compositions in that raga, when compared to Tyagaraja's, are 'worshipful and tributary and without much pathos'. He is looking here at Dikshitar's '*Gajanana yutam*' and '*Vinayaka Vighnanasaka*', both in a mode of Vegavahini more akin to Tyagaraja's Chakravakam, and not at the magisterial '*Vinapustakadharini*', which is more authentically Vegavahini. But the point about pathos in Tyagaraja is well taken; very many of his songs are personal expressions of grief, wonder, doubt and pathos. And '*Vinapustakadharini*' remains one of the greatest of Muthusvami Dikshitar's compositions. '*Nirantaram bhakta-jihva(a)gravaasaa*', She who lives forever on the lips of her devotees.

PURANDARADASA

As we have noted in the text, Subbulakshmi had a small, if respectable, selection of Purandaradasa which were always on display. These served her very well.

'Dasana madiko enna'/Nadanamakriya/Adi. CD Swaralaya Puraskaram 1997. Subbulakshmi recorded this song early on and also sang it often in concerts.

'Hari Narayana'/Kedara/Adi. On YouTube.

'Jagadodhharana'/Hindustani Kapi/Adi. 1966 UN Concert. Charsur CD of Detroit 1977 concert. Also Charsur CD of 25 December 1966 concert. Also Saregama CD Nada Sudha Rasa.

This wonderful song, which has been performed in dance, talks of Yashoda's love for the child Krishna, whom she adored and played with, not knowing (and at the same time knowing?) that her child was *'Jagadodhharana'*, 'the uplifter of the world'. It also includes the remarkable phrase *'anoraneeyana mahato maheeyana'*, the one who is 'smaller than the smallest and bigger than the biggest'.

'Kaliyugadalli'/Jenjuti/Adi. A rendering by a very young Subbulakshmi can be heard on YouTube.

'Narayana'/Suddhadhanyasi/Khanda Chapu.* 1977 Carnegie Hall. Saregama CD Live At Russia 1987.

This song may actually have been introduced into the concert circuit by Radha and Jayalakshmi but Subbulakshmi made it her own. The poet dwells on the magic of the name of Narayana, *Kashtadall(i)rali, utkrishtadall(i)rali*, may the name stay with me in bad times and good, and prays that even if the thousand names of Vishnu are in his heart, all he asks at the last moments of his life, *'antakaladalli'*, are that the *'ashtakshara'*, or the eight syllables of Narayana, come to his mind. Subbulakshmi always sang this with great pathos and feeling.

'Naneke badavanu'/Behag/Rupaka. 1969 Concert Album.

SVATI TIRUNAL

A crucial question, which may just about have been put to rest, relates to the authenticity of Svati Tirunal's compositions, and whether both lyric and tune can be accurately ascribed to him. The consensus appears to be that the lyrics in most cases can be more reasonably attributed to him than the raga setting. Harikesanallur Muthiah Bhagavathar and Semmangudi Srinivasa Iyer were largely responsible for setting many of the texts attributed to Svati Tirunal to raga, and making them concert-worthy. Svati Tirunal wrote in Sanskrit, but compositions in Malayalam, Hindi, Telegu and Kannada are known.

'Bhogindra sayinam'/Kuntalavarali/Jhampa. 1969 Concert Album.

Subbulakshmi sang this very often; however, Semmangudi Srinivasa Iyer has a gentler, slower and altogether much finer version. This can be sourced on the net.

'Gopalaka'/Revagupti/Misrachapu. That Subbulakshmi chose to include this luminous song, as representative of Svati Tirunal, in her presidential concert at the Music Academy, Madras, in 1968 suggests something. When Subbulakshmi sang Svati Tirunal, years of constant practice brought a glow to what could otherwise have been clumsy text. This song has very long phrases in complicated Sanskrit, and *sollukattu* in addition, but is truly beautiful.

'Gopanandana'/Bhushavali/Adi. Charsur CD of 25 December 1956 concert. Wordy, and yet sprightly.

'Jaya Jaya Padmanabhanujesha'/Manirangu/Rupaka. Sung at the Music Academy recital in December 1969, available on YouTube. Sony/NCPA Record of August 1978 recital. The song is in praise of Siva, the

husband (*isha*) of the younger sister (*anuja*) of Vishnu (Padmanabha). Such constructions are very common in Sanskrit.

'*Rama Rama*'/Simhendramadhyamam/Adi. 1977 Carnegie Hall.

Subbulakshmi sang this magnificent song often, always preceded by *alapana* and with *neraval* and *svara* for the line, *Muni maanasa dhaama mriga mada sulalaama*.

'*Sarasaksha*'/Pantuvarali/Rupaka. 1966 UN Concert. Charsur CD of 25 December 1956 concert. Also Charsur CD of 25 December 1960 concert. Also Akashvani Sangeet CD (1965).

The *neraval* and *svara* for the line *Bhamini samudaya*... is electrifying.

SYAMA SASTRI

Syama Sastri's compositions are tightly structured, highly constructed pieces, but his lyrics are simple and direct. There are no complicated conversations as in Tyagaraja, or choice and expressive phrases as in Muthusvami Dikshitar. In most of his songs he only asks for protection, using the Telegu word *brovu*. As for instance *Brovavamma, Biranavaralichi brovumu, Nannu brovu lalita, Triloka mata nannu brovu, Devi brova samayamide, na vinnapamu vini brovumu Ninne namminanu, Devi Meenanetri brova, brocutaku Mari vere gati evaramma?, Meenalochana brova, Nannu brova rada?, nanu neevu javamuna brovu O Jagadamba!*, etc.

'*Devi brova*'/Chintamani/Adi. 1977 Carnegie Hall. Doordarshan Bharat Ratna Series Part II.

Syama Sastri used a limited set of ragas, usually those known as *rakti* ragas, or ragas which are identified not by their scales but by characteristic phrases; however, as his use of the raga Chintamani shows, he was a master even of the obscure.

Appendix II

'Durusuga'/**Saveri/Adi.** Saregama CD Live At Russia 1987. The song prays for the wellness of body (*drda sarira*) and good health (*a-roga*).

'Kamakshi'/**Bhairavi/svarajati.** Sony/NCPA Record of August 1978 recital. Carnatica CD Sangamam, along with Semmangudi Srinivasa Iyer. In principle, a *svarajati* is an elementary type of composition, meant for beginners, and not at all for the concert platform. Syama Sastri's *svarajatis* stand entirely on another footing, and greatly enhance the classicism and rigour of any concert. Subbulakshmi's distinctive addition to this song was *neraval* at the ringing line *syamakrishna sahodari sivasankari parameswari*!

'Kamakshi'/**Yadukulakambhoji/Adi/svarajati.** Charsur CD of 25 December 1960 concert.

A long, and even cumbersome piece, this song is less often heard than the other two *svarajatis*, but Subbulakshmi always gave it prominence.

'Kanakasaila viharini'/**Punnagavarali/Adi.** 1974 Sri Kamakshi Suprabhatam record.

'Mayamma'/**Ahiri/Adi.** A beautiful composition in the plaintive raga Ahiri, and sung often. *Maatlada-raada-naato? Nyayama? Minakshi, neekidi...?* 'Can You not speak with me? Is this fair, Minakshi, for You?' A fine version, preceded by a verse from the *Minakshi pancharatnam*, is available on Youtube.

'O Jagadamba'/**Anandabhairavi/Adi.** One of the many songs of Syama Sastri in Anandabhairavi, a fine rendition with *alapana* is available on YouTube, said to be from a 1978 Bombay recital.

'Rave Himagirikumari'/**Todi/Adi/svarajati.** Charsur CD of 25 December 1956 concert. Also CD Divine Unison, along with Semmangudi Srinivasa Iyer.

Another staple, regularly sung.

'*Sarojadalanetri*'/Sankarabharanam/Adi. 1966 UN Concert. Charsur CD of 25 December 1956 concert.

A great favourite with Subbulakshmi, this was even recorded in the early 1960s and presented at the UN concert. The characteristic *neraval* at '*samagana vinodini gunadhama syamakrishna nute...*' is a high point.

'*Talli ninnu nera*'/Kalyani/Misrachapu. On YouTube, an extract from a 1974 Bangkok recital.

A favourite with Subbulakshmi, this was presented often.

TYAGARAJA

Translations marked WJJ are from William J. Jackson, *Tyagaraja Life and Lyrics*, Oxford University Press, 1991. This work has interesting notes on all the songs translated. In many of his songs, Tyagaraja has embellishments in the form of *sangatis*, pre-composed variations on a line, usually the *pallavi* line.

'*Banturiti*'/Hamsanadam/Adi. Sony/NCPA Record of August 1978 recital. Also Charsur CD of 25 December 1966 concert. CD Swaralaya Puraskaram 1997.

Sung often, notably at Tiruvaiyaru in 1978, where it follows a beautiful *alapana* (www.sangeethapriya.org). 'Master Rama, have you a position for me in your court, as a guardsman?... I shall wield the finest sword, the Rama nama.' (WJJ)

'*Darini*'/Suddhasaveri/Adi. A song in praise of the Goddess. '*Darini telusukonti, Tripurasundari, ninne sharananti...*', 'Having discovered the path, I have, Tripurasundari, sought refuge in you...'. Can be found on YouTube.

'*Dasarathi*'/Todi/Adi. CD Nadamrutham.

'O son of Dasaratha, how could I ever pay off my debt to you? O Lord whose name is supremely pure ... Crest-jewel of connoisseurs, you made me illustrious in distant regions to my great satisfaction! O Dasarathi how could I ever settle my account with you?' (WJJ)

'Devadideva'/Sindhuramakriya/Sanskrit. In praise of Siva, 'whose eyes of fire as are as the sun and the moon', *'dina-natha sudhakara dahana nayana'*. Subbulakshmi began a 1986 recital in Tiruvarur with this song, and the clip is available on YouTube. Clad in 'MS blue', she is accompanied by Radha Viswanathan, Dwaram Mangathayaru on the violin and K.V. Prasad on the mrdangam.

'Dudukugala'/Gaula/Adi/*pancharatna*. 'I'm so full of folly, what prince would protect me?' (WJJ). Subbulakshmi was chosen to sing this at the Tyagaraja bicentenary celebrations at the Music Academy in December 1967, and it is possibly this particular rendering which is on YouTube. The *pancharatna kritis* bear careful listening, both sung by individual singers and in mass rendition as at the annual *aradhana* in Tiruvaiyaru.

'Enati nomu'/Bhairavi/Adi. 1969 Concert Album. Also CD Divine Unison, along with Semmangudi Srinivasa Iyer.
A simple song, which Subbulakshmi sang often, with *neraval* at the line *'sundaresha suguna brinda Dasharatha nandana aravinda nayana pavana'*.

'Endaro'/Sri/Adi/*pancharatna*. Akashvani Sangeet CD (1965).
'To as many great souls as there be I bow respectfully'. (WJJ). This is possibly the most popular of the *pancharatna kritis*.

'Enta rani, tana(k)enta poni, ni chinta viduvajaala'/Harikambhoji/Adi.
'Whatever I win, whatever I lose, How could I ever stop thinking of you, Sri Rama?' (WJJ). Sung at the 1968 *Sangitha Kalanidhi* concert.

'Evarimata'/Kambhoji/Adi. Sung at Tiruvaiyaru 1978 (available at www.sangeethapriya.org. Also CD Divine Unison, along with Semmangudi Srinivasa Iyer.

'To whose advice have you turned your ear? Won't you come to me here?' (WJJ).

***'Jagadanandakaraka'*/Nata/Adi/*pancharatna*/sanskrit.** Saregama CD Nada Sudha Rasa.
'O Cause of the cosmos' rejoicing, we cheer your victory-*Jai*! O Lifebreath of Sita!' (WJJ). This *pancharatna kriti* is in Sanskrit and consists only of epithets – a grand and dramatic composition.

***'Kaligiyunte'*/Kiravani/Adi.** Saregama CD Nada Sudha Rasa. Also on YouTube, an extract from a 1974 Bangkok recital.
'Is it not that your grace will come to me only if I have earned it?, O One who fulfils desires!'

***'Ksheenamai'*/Mukhari/Adi.** Charsur CD of 25 December 1956 concert. A favourite of Semmangudi Srinivasa Iyer and of his school.

***'Ksheerasagarasayana'*/Devagandhari/Adi.** 'O Lord in repose on your milky sea, Why should you bring worries to me, O Rama.' (WJJ)
This great composition recounts incidents from myth and legend where Vishnu came to the succour of his devotees. *Narimani-ki cheeral (i)chhinadi nade ne vinnanura,* 'I've heard that long ago you gave a sari to Draupadi, that jewel amongst women, and *Nirajakshi-kai niradhi daatina ni kirtini vinnanura,* 'I've heard you celebrated for crossing the ocean for Sita, whose eyes are so lovely'. In Subbulakshmi's rendering (Tyagaraja *aradhana* in January 1980 is available on YouTube), both languor and tautness come to the fore.

***'Manasuloni'*/Varamu/Adi.** Akashvani Sangeet CD (1958). CD Swaralaya Puraskaram 1997.
'*Manasuloni marmamulu delusuko, manarakshaka marakatanga.*', 'Discover the secrets in my mind, O emerald hued protector!' This song is usually sung in raga Hindolam but in some schools, as in Subbulakshmi's, in a raga called Varamu, where the *suddha dhaivata* in Hindolam is replaced by the *chatusruti*

dhaivata, giving the raga an entirely different aspect. Vasanthakumari's version in Hindolam is also available.

'*Manavyala*'/Nalinakanti/Adi. Another very popular song, with vocalists and instrumentalists alike.

'*Meevalla*'/Kapi/Jhampa. '*Meevalla guna-dosham-emi, Sri Rama, Naa vallane-gani...*' 'Virtues and faults are not of your making, but only of mine...' Subbulakshmi sang this song over sixty years, and a fine version form the early 1990s is available on the net.

'*Mokshamu galada*'/Saramati/Adi. 'On this earth can there be liberation for those who have not found realization?' (WJJ).

'*Nagumomu*'/Abheri/Adi. Saregama CD Nada Sudha Rasa.
'Knowing my grief at not seeing your smiling face can't you come save me O Sri Raghuvara!'(WJJ). Subbulakshmi probably learnt this from her teacher Musiri Subramania Iyer who was famous for his version.

'*Naradamuni*'/Pantuvarali/Rupaka. A song in praise of Narada, and a favourite with Subbulakshmi, with *neraval* at *Narayana namamulanu*...

'*Nenaruncinanu*'/Malavi/Adi. A charming song which Subbulakshmi sang often. Faddists will be interested in 'Raga Malavi leaving as is A Misnomer', a blog post by Ravi Rajagopalan, dated 31 July 2018, http://guruguha.org/wp/?p=2455

'*Nidhi tsala sukhama*'/Kalyani/Triputa. Sony/NCPA Record of August 1978 recital.
'Is the joy of *presents* more gratifying than the bliss of Rama's *presence* so satisfying, Tell me truly, O mind of mine...' (WJJ). A famous composition of Tyagaraja, with its contrasting of *nidhi* (wealth) with *sannidhi* (presence).

'*Ninnu vina*'/Navarasakannada/Adi. Charsur CD of Detroit 1977 concert. Saregama CD Nada Sudha Rasa.

This very lively composition, with its thrilling *sangatis* in the *anupallavi* is, or used to be, a concert staple of many vocalists and instrumentalists.

'*O Rangasayee*'/Kambhoji/Adi. 1977 Carnegie Hall.

'When I call on you as "Ranga Sayi" can't you answer, "I'm coming!" and then come?' (WJJ). A concert favourite, with tried and tested *neraval* at '*Bhooloka vaikuntam....*'

'*Pakkala nilabadi*'/Kharaharapriya/Triputa. Sung at the Music Academy recital in December 1969, available on YouTube. Charsur CD of 25 December 1966 concert. Saregama CD Live At Russia 1987. Akashvani Sangeet CD (1958). Doordarshan Bharat Ratna Series Part II.

Subbulakshmi sang this song very often, and always with *neraval* at the line '*tanuvuche vandana...*' In the ecstasy of bhakti, Tyagaraja is actually addressing Sita and Lakshmana, the son of Sumitra, 'Can I also not see the way you, standing beside the Lord, serve Him?' Tyagaraja alone among his peers composed in Kharaharapriya and through his many songs defined and gave body to what were, till his time, mere scales. Of his songs, Subbulakshmi sang '*Pakkala*' but also '*Rama ni samanam*', '*Chakkani rajamargamu*' and '*Mitri bhagyame*'.

'*Rama nannu brovaravemako*'/Harikambhoji/Rupaka. 1966 UN Concert. Also Charsur CD of 25 December 1956 concert. Doordarshan Bharat Ratna Series Part II.

A hardy favourite with Subbulakshmi, it is yet another affirmation by Tyagaraja of his abiding faith. '*Rama, nannu brovaravemako?*', 'Rama, can you not protect me...?' Harikambhoji, like Kharaharapriya (above) is Tyagaraja's creation. Subbulakshmi also sang '*Enta rani*' and '*Dinamani-vamsa-tilaka*' in this raga.

'*Rama ni samanam*'/Kharaharapriya/Rupaka. Sung at Tiruvaiyaru 1978 (available at www.sangeethapriya.org), CD Divine Unison, along with Semmangudi Srinivasa Iyer.

'*Rama, nee samanam evaru? Raghuvamsodhharaka!*' 'Who is your equal, O Rama, greatest of the Raghus!'. The *neraval* at the line '*paluku paluku laku tene...*' is always very lively.

'*Sadhincene*'/Arabhi/Adi/*pancharatna*. 'He got the better of me, O my heart and soul! Making a mockery of His own persuasive words of righteousness, he made His will prevail, Getting the better of me, O my mind, He spoke nice words to fit each occasion' (WJJ). One of the *pancharatna kritis*, a rendering by Subbulakshmi is available on YouTube, clearly the opening piece of a concert, a neat, tight version.

'*Sitamma*'/Vasanta/Adi. 'Sita is my mother, and Sri Rama is my father! Hanuman (*vatatmaja*, or the son of Vayu, the wind), Lakshmana (*soumitri*, the son of Sumitra), Garuda (*vainateya*, the son of Vinata), Shatrughna (*ripumardana*, the slayer of his enemies) and Bharata are all my brothers!' Subbulakshmi's rendering at the Tyagaraja *aradhana* in January 1980 is available on YouTube.

'*Sobhillu*'/Jaganmohini/Rupaka. 1977 Carnegie Hall. 'O mind serve and worship the beautiful shapes of the seven tones which are shining' (WJJ).

'*Sogasuga*'/Sriranjani/Adi. 1969 Concert Album.
'Where is that hero who delights you with his songs? Could it be Tyagaraja?' Subbulakshmi's *neraval* for the *pallavi* line, though often repeated, is very appealing.

'*Tera tiyaga rada*'/Gaulipantu. 1969 Concert Album.
'Won't You draw back the curtain within me O Lord Venkateswara of Tirupati, open up this screen of envy!' In the Tyagaraja legend, he composed this piece at the temple at Tirupati when he was unable see the deity behind a curtain. And again in the legend, the curtain is said to have fallen away when he sang the song.

'Tsalakalla'/**Arabhi**/**Adi.** A lovely song with delightful *sangatis*, Subbulakshmi's rendering can be heard on YouTube. One of many compositions in which Tyagaraja reaffirms his faith.

'Tsallare'/**Ahiri**/**Triputa.** 1969 Concert Album. Also on YouTube.

A song of ritual devotion in the plaintive Ahiri, it seeks offerings to Rama of many flowers, *champaka, tamara, parijata, jaji* and of '*hrit-kumuda-sumamulu*', 'the lilies of my heart'.

'Vachamago'/**Kaikavasi**/**Adi.** This song which Subbulakshmi sang often is possibly the only known composition in this raga. It tells the story of a deer, not the *mayamriga* which led to much grief, but another deer which Rama, in the Ramayana, tried to shoot and then, in his infinite compassion, saved. '*Banambunatu chedara seyaleda?*', 'Did he not recall the sped arrow?'.

'Vara Narada'/**Vijayasri**/**Adi.** 1969 Concert Album.

This beautiful song, with its many *sangatis*, is in praise of Narada, the famously mischievous and wandering minstrel of the heavens.

'Venuganalolu'/**Kedaragaula**/**Rupaka.** 1969 Concert Album. Also Charsur CD of 25 December 1960 concert.

'*Venuganaloluni-gana-veyyi kannulu kaavalane*', 'To see your beauty, O Lord of the Flute, one needs a thousand eyes!' This is a song in praise of Krishna.

'Vidulaku'/**Mayamalavagaula**/**Adi.** 1969 Concert Album. Also Charsur CD of 25 December 1960 concert.

'I bow with respect to those who know music.' (WJJ)

'Vinayakuni'/**Madhyamavati**/**Adi.** 1974 Sri Kamakshi Suprabhatam record.

A song in praise of Kamakshi at Kanchipuram. '*Vinayakuni valenu brovave*', 'Protect me as you would your son Vinayaka!'

OTHERS

'Arta piravi'/Sankarabharanam/Adi/Manikkavacagar/*tiruvembavai*/ Tamil. Charsur CD Bhavani 1956 concert.

This was sung many times during the 1966 US tour and can be sourced in the James Rubin Collection, once with *tanam* preceding the song.

'Bhavayami Gopala balam'/Yamunakalyani/Jhampa/Annamacharya/ *samkirtana*/Sanskrit. Saregama CD Live At Russia 1987.

An exquisite composition which Subbulakshmi always sang, strange as it may sound, with a mixture of passion and restraint. It is worth searching for a concert rendering of this song if only for the sensational *sangati* for the last line, *'paramapurusham gopala balam'*, which Subbulakshmi always added in live concert.

'Birana brova ide'/Kalyani/Adi(tisram)/Tarangambadi Panchanada Iyer/Telugu. Saregama CD Nada Sudha Rasa. A sprightly song which Subbulakshmi alone sang, with predictable, but still musical, *neraval* at the line 'Ni *paada pankajamu*...'.

'Brochevarevarura'/Khamas/Adi/Mysore Vasudevacharya/Telugu. Charsur CD of Detroit 1977 concert. Saregama CD Nada Sudha Rasa.

This must surely be considered the ranking composition in the extremely popular raga Khamas often enhanced by Subbulakshmi's *neraval* at *'Sitapate, na pai neek(a)bhimanamu leda?'*, 'Do you not care for me at all, O Lord of Sita?'

'Era napai'/Todi/Adi/Patnam Subramania Iyer/varnam/Telugu. Charsur CD of 25 December 1966 concert. Saregama CD Nada Sudha Rasa.

'Janani'/Ritigaula/Misrachapu/Subbaraya Sastri/kriti/Telugu. Saregama CD Nada Sudha Rasa.

As in the case of *Brochevarevarura*, *Janani* is the truly defining composition in the evergreen Ritigaula, a raga with a very large number of songs.

'*Ka Va Va*'/Varali/Adi/Papanasam Sivan/Tamil. Of Papanasam Sivan's many songs which Subbulakshmi sang with feeling, '*Ka Va Va*' must shine. Several renditions by her are available on YouTube.

'*Ksheerasagarasayana*'/Mayamalavagaula/Ata/Jayachamaraja Wodeyar/Sanskrit. Charsur CD of 25 December 1966 concert. CD Swaralaya Puraskaram 1997.

It is worth searching for the video recording of this, Subbulakshmi's last major recital which is on YouTube. Most of the recital can indeed be so found. It is Subbulakshmi in her great age, serene and in control.

'*Kurai Onrum Illai*'/Ragamalika/Adi/Rajaji/hymn/Tamil. Doordarshan Bharat Ratna Series Part II.

'No regrets have I...' In the last stages of her career, Subbulakshmi sang this very often.

'*Manju nihar*'/Jenjuti/Misrachapu/Annamalai Reddiar/*kavadichindu*/Tamil. CD Nada Sudha Rasa.

'*Mathe malayadhwaja*'/Khamas/Adi/Muthiah Bhagavathar/*daru*/Sanskrit. Sung at the Music Academy recital in December 1969, available on YouTube.

A brilliantly structured song, which Subbulakshmi sang with aplomb, reflecting total control, and the capacity to make the most wordy, complicated text utterly musical.

'*Mudi ondri*'/Ragamalika/Periyalwar/*pasuram*/Tamil. CD Nada Sudha Rasa. Charsur CD of 25 December 1960 concert. Charsur CD Bhavani 1956 concert. Charsur CD of 25 December 1956 concert.

'*Nanati bratuku*'/Revati/Adi/Annamacharya/*samkirtana*/Telugu.

Despite the general lamentation in this song on the futility of life's drama, this song was always very popular with Subbulakshmi's audiences. The song's message is quite grim. '*Puttutayu nijamu povutayu nijamu nattanadimipani natakamu*', 'Birth and death are realities, all that passes in between is make-believe' and '*tegadu paapamu teeradu punyamu, nagi nagi kalamu natakamu*', 'there is no end to sinfulness, no completion to goodness, everything in-between is make-believe'.

'*Narayana divya namam*'/Mohana/Papanasam Sivan/Tamil. Also Charsur CD of 25 December 1960 concert. A great hit in its time.

'*Needu charana*'/Kalyani/Adi/Pallavi Gopal Iyer/Telugu. Charsur CD of Detroit 1977 concert.

This song is not heard any more but Subbulakshmi sang it often, and always with *neraval* at '*O Jagajjanani manonmani omkara rupini kalyani...*'

'*Paratpara*'/Vachaspati/Adi/Papanasam Sivan/Tamil. 1969 Concert Album.

A lively and expressive song.

'*Sabhapati*'/Abhogi/Rupaka/Gopalakrishna Bharati/Tamil. Saregama CD Subham-Sivam 2002.

A popular song, with *neraval* often performed for the wordy line, '*Orutharam Shiva Chidambaram Endru Sonnal Podhume, Paragathi Pera Veru Puniyam Panna Vendumaa*', 'If one says the name of Sivachidambaram once, one attains salvation, what need is there of other acts of piety?'

'*Sada saranga nayane*'/Ranjani/Adi/H.Yoganarasimham/kriti/ Sanskrit. CD New Classicals 1988.

A modern piece in Sanskrit, patterned on the compositional style of Muthusvami Dikshitar, with rich and evocative text, and sparkling *chittaswaram*.

'*Sambho Mahadeva*'/Bauli/Rupaka/Nilakantha Sivan. Charsur CD of 25 December 1960 concert. Charsur CD Bhavani 1956 concert. Akashvani Sangeet CD (1958).

A great favourite, sung most often prefaced by a Sanskrit verse.

'*Saravanabhava*'/Shanmukhapriya/Adi/Papanasam Sivan/Tamil. More than one version available on YouTube, including with *alapana*.

'*Sri Kamakoti*'/Saveri/Adi/Mysore Sadasiva Rao/Sanskrit. 1974 Sri Kamakshi Suprabhatam record. Also Charsur CD of Detroit 1977 concert. Charsur CD Bhavani 1956 concert.

Sung on every possible occasion with *neraval* for the line 'Kadamba vana nilaye...', the song is not heard anymore. It remains, however, a perfect example of *neraval*.

'*Sriman Narayana*'/Bauli/Adi/Annamacharya/*samkirtana*/Telugu.

Recorded as part of the Annamacharya series released in the late 1970s.

'*Tiruvadicharanam*'/Kambhoji/Adi/Gopalakrishna Bharati/Tamil.

A favourite from the stock of Musiri Subramania Iyer, Subbulakshmi's rendering, can be found on YouTube.

'*Viriboni*'/Bhairavi/Ata/Pachhimiriyam Adiseshiah/*varnam*/Telugu. 1969 Concert Album, Charsur CD of 25 December 1960 concert. Charsur CD Bhavani 1956 concert.

Glossary

These notes are only by way of an introduction. More detailed explanations are provided in such texts as Ludwig Pesch, *The Illustrated Companion to South Indian Classical Music*, Oxford University Press (OUP), 1999; Ludwig Pesch, *The Oxford Illustrated Companion to South Indian Music*, 2nd edition, OUP, 2019; T. Viswanathan and Matthew Harp Allen, *Music in South India*, OUP, 2004; and L. Subramaniam and Viji Subramaniam, *Classical Music of India A Practical Guide*, Tranquebar Press, 2018.

Abhang is the name given to devotional verses in Marathi addressed to Vitthala at Pandharpur, an output of the wave of Vaishnavite bhakti which spread in the region, following Jnanadev of the thirteenth century. *Abhang* is often differentiated from bhajan in allowing for greater spontaneity in rendering. *Abhang* is popular on the concert platform and it is possible that the tradition came to the south along with the Maratha rulers of Tanjore. Subbulakshmi famously sang '*Sundarathe dhyana*' and '*Baare Panduranga*' of Tukaram (16th century), both easily found on the net. Also available are M.L Vasanthakumari's stunning versions of Jnanadev's '*Saguna nirguna donhi*', and of '*Maaze manoratha*' and '*Amrutahuni goda*', both by Namdev (13th century).

Alapana refers to the extempore development of a raga in a concert, most often as a prelude to a song. The Ariyakudi *margam* (see below) encouraged a series of short *alapanas*, of possibly five to eight minutes or so, leading up to a *ragam-tanam-pallavi* (see below) where the raga *alapana* may have gone beyond ten minutes. Vasanthakumari was known for her long, exploratory *alapana*, but it is also true that in Subbulakshmi's relatively shorter *alapanas* she said all that there was to be said. Audiences familiar with *khayal* renderings in the Hindustani tradition, where the *alap* could last for fifty minutes, have often found the Carnatic *alapana* frustratingly brief.

Anupallavi, or the second movement of a *kriti* or *kirtana*.

Aradhana, which in the original Sanskrit would only mean a worship, or glorification (of God), refers in the Carnatic context, to the annual observance in Tiruvaiyaru of the passing of Tyagaraja, and the mass rendering of the *pancharatna kritis*. There are also individual performances.

Arohana is the term for the notes in ascending sequence of a raga. Hence, *sa ri ga pa da sa* in the raga Mohana. Not necessarily always symmetrical.

Avarohana is the term for the notes in descending sequence of a raga. Hence, *sa da pa ga ri sa* in the raga Mohana. Not necessarily always symmetrical.

Bhajan is a simple devotional verse, derivative of the bhakti movement, and usually refers to verses in Hindi. Bhajans arise from deep religious and spiritual impulses and were always only meant to be devotional offerings, and not as concert items. Subbulakshmi was substantially responsible for incorporating the bhajan into the Carnatic repertoire, even if similar pieces from the south Indian tradition were already being sung. *Bhajana*, as used in the south, refers to a more general tradition of group singing or chanting of devotional verses.

Bhakti, quite simply, translates as devotion but is used to refer to the upsurge of popular devotion from the ninth century onwards, leading to the composition of a vast amount of religious verse, some of which has found its way into musical performance.

Bhava, or *ragabhava*, is, simply put, emotion. If a raga is to transcend the mere recitation of the notes of which it is defined, it is *ragabhava* that does this. The term *bhava sangitam* is also used. *Bhava*, raga and *tala* are traditionally regarded as the core elements of wholesome music.

Glossary

Briga is an ornamentation to song or *alapana*, a sudden, rapid burst of melody, heard often in the music of G.N. Balasubramaniam, M.L. Vasanthakumari and Radha and Jayalakshmi. Pesch derives the word from the sanskrit *bhrig*, 'crackling sound of fire'.

Charanam or the third, and often successive, movements of a *kriti* or *kirtana*.

Chittasvaram is the pre-composed *svara* passage after the *anupallavi* and *charanam* of a *kriti*. Songs such as 'Sitamma'/Vasanta, 'Brochevarevarura'/ Khamas, 'Sobhillu'/Jaganmohini, and 'Sri Kantimatim'/Desisimharava all have *chittasvaram*.

Gamaka, or embellishment refers to the accenting of a note or phrase in the course of a raga elaboration. The use of *gamaka* helps differentiate one raga from another even if both use the same note. Some traditions of music, as for instance, that of Brinda and Muktha, are laden with *gamaka*. The use of *gamaka* is not as prominent in the tradition of G.N. Balasubramaniam and Vasanthakumari. Of course, all of this is within the folds of the classical. Film music based on traditional ragas, charming as can be, is usually quite free of *gamaka*.

Ghana ragas are traditionally Nata, Gaula, Arabhi, Varali and Sri, in which the five *pancharatna kritis* of Tyagaraja are composed.

Ghatam is the clay pot, with brass, iron or copper filings, used as a percussion accompaniment to a vocal, or violin or vina, recital.

Harikatha, a form of entertainment popular in the Telugu- and Kannada-speaking areas, involves storytelling on devotional themes, often laced with humour, using song, verse, chants and even philosophical explanations. The exponents of *Harikatha* were usually very learned with a range of talents.

Javali, like *padam* (see below) is a love song, usually in Telugu, meant primarily for dance but also heard often in music concerts. A *javali* is almost always quicker and livelier than a *padam*. Subbulakshmi did not sing *javali* often, but a recording of Dharmapuri Subbarayar's 'Sakhi prana' in Jenjuti is known (CD Divine Unison, along with Semmangudi Srinivasa Iyer). Very early in her career, she had also recorded Subbarayar's 'Nenendu ne muddu balamani' in Khamas. Her version of Pattabhiramiah's 'Cheli nenetlu'/Paras is available on YouTube.

Kachheri, or *cutcheri*, is quite simply, a concert. The word derives from the Urdu for court.

Kanjira is in the category of *upa-pakka vadyam*, or secondary accompaniment and is similar to a tambourine, with metallic jingles attached to a round frame.

Kavadichindu refers to a type of Tamil, devotional verses, set to light classical, folk tunes. Annamalai Reddiar (1865–91) is primarily associated with these. Subbulakshmi often sang *kavadichindu*. One example is 'Manju nihar in Jenjuti (CD Nada Sudha Rasa).

Kirtana refers to devotional verses, as in Marathi kirtan singing, and is often used interchangeably with *kriti* (see below). It is suggested that the term *kirtana* is more applicable to a verse which is primarily devotional and where the music is merely a means of conveying a prayer whereas a *kriti* is a composition with musical values at least as important as the lyrical.

Kriti, literally creation, is the term given to the composed piece which forms the core of Carnatic repertory. A *kriti* usually consists of an introductory *pallavi*, an *anupallavi* to follow, and a *charanam*, or foot, to conclude. The *charanam*, of which there can be more than one, even if not all are performed in concert, is usually longer than the *pallavi* or *anupallavi*. Tyagaraja was the unquestioned master of the *kriti* in its present form, and his oeuvre include songs with one *charanam* ('Nenaruncinanu', 'Pakkala nilabadi' and 'Vachamago' from Subbulakshmi's stock), many *charanams* set to the same *svara* pattern ('Darini', 'Ela ni daya radu', 'Enta rani' and 'Muripemu' likewise) and many *charanams* set to different *svara* patterns (the *pancharatna kritis*). Many songs of Syama Sastri have several *charanams* set to the same tune ('Sarojadalanetri', 'Palinchu Kamakshi'). Muthusvami Dikshitar wrote many songs without an *anupallavi* ('Vinabheri', 'Anandamritakarshini').

Madhyama kala is the term given to that portion of the *charanam* of a song, and occasionally even in the *anupallavi* or *pallavi*, which is sung at a faster speed. Almost every song of Muthusvami Dikshitar has a *madhyama kala* passage, as does Tyagaraja's 'Darini'/Suddhasaveri.

Glossary

Manodharma or *manodharma sangita* is creative improvisation, but within the rules and grammar of the style. *Alapana, svaraprasthara, tanam* and *pallavi* are all demonstrations of a performer's *manodharma*, but so is a refined rendering of a composed piece.

Margam, or laid-down pattern, used most often in the context of Bharatanatyam, where a traditional *margam* is a set of pieces learnt by the dancer and performed in a set order. The concert pattern laid down and popularized by Ariyakudi Ramanuja Iyengar is called the Ariyakudi *margam*.

Melakarta ragas are ragas which take all seven notes in ascent and descent. At one level they are simply a set of scales, but between them they define every raga. The seventy-two *melakarta* ragas are the *janaka* ragas from which a vast number of derivative, or *janya* ragas, can be identified. *Melakarta* ragas are not necessarily the more important, or the better suited for either composition or *alapana*, though some such as Todi (Hanumatodi), Kalyani (Mechakalyani), Sankarabharanam (Dhirasankarabharanam), Kharaharapriya, Harikambhoji do indeed fall in the category of 'great concert ragas'. But there are many, many *janya* ragas, such as Saveri, Dhanyasi, Madhyamavati and Begada also in this category.

Morsing is in the category of *upa-pakka vadyam*, or secondary accompaniment. An ancient instrument similar to the Jew's Harp.

Mrdangam is the principal drum used in south Indian musical performance.

Mudra, or sign, in the Carnatic world, usually means the composer's signature in the song. Tyagaraja used his name while Syama Sastri used *Syamakrishna* and Muthusvami Dikshitar used *Guruguha*. Subbaraya Sastri used *Kumara*, Swati Tirunal used *Padmanabha* (*Sarasaksha*) or variants thereon, *Varijanabha* (*Rama rama guna seema*), *Sarojanabha* (*Gopalaka*), etc. Papanasam Sivan's *mudra*, *Ramadasa*, is not found invariably in all his songs. Muthusvami Dikshitar was also known to introduce the name of the raga into his text, or *raga mudra*. Examples are *Vinabheri* in *Vinabheri*/Abheri, **Hamsadhwani** bhushita in *Vatapi*/Hamsadhwani, *Mangalalay(a)bhogi nuta padam* in *Sri Lakshmi Varaham*/Abhogi.

Neraval, sometimes *niraval*, refers to the improvisation on a line of a composed piece during a concert. Many songs have lines which are regarded as suitable for *neraval*, though it is up to the performer. Subbulakshmi's *neraval*, if unchanging, was also very beautifully structured, as for instance for *Kadamba vana nilaye*... in 'Sri Kamakoti'/Saveri, *Rama namamani* in 'Banturiti'/Hamsanadam, *Meppulakai*... in 'Rama nannu brova'/Harikambhoji or *Samaganavinodini*... in 'Sarojadalanetri'/Sankarabharanam. In principle, though, *neraval* is to be improvised on the spot and should not be always the same.

Padam is a love song, verses usually in Telugu, addressed to a divine lover, and meant for dance. The *padam* and the *javali* (see above) constituted the core of a devadasi's repertoire. Kshetrayya is the name most closely associated with the *padam* though there are also pieces by Annamacharya which fit this description. Tamil *padams* are also known. A Malayalam composition prominent in Subbulakshmi's repertoire, Svati Tirunal's '*Aliveni*' in the raga Kuranji, is described as a *padam*. Also known are Swati Tirunal's '*Itu sahasamulu*' in Saindhavi (CD Divine Unison, along with Semmangudi Srinivasa Iyer) and Kshetrayya's '*Paiyyada*' in Nadanamakriya (Charsur CD 25 December 1956 recital, AIR Excerpts from Radio Concerts Vol. 3) and Kshetrayya's '*Kuvalayakshiro*' in Gaulipantu (AIR Excerpts from Radio Concerts Vol. 1).

Pallavi is the introductory stanza of a *kriti* or *kirtana*. It can also refer to the composed phrase taken up for elaboration as part of a *ragam-tanam-pallavi*.

Raga, in its simplest sense, is a mode; but it is a mode defined by an ordered set of notes. It is, of course, very much more than notes alone and much depends on how every performing musician understands how those notes can be combined, what phrases are permitted and how emotions can be aroused in the minds of the listeners. *Alapana* (see above) is an elaboration of raga. The same raga based on the same notes and the same usages can sound quite different when rendered by different performers. Some ragas, the great concert ragas, necessarily allow more elaboration than others, though contemporary musicians have experimented successfully with raga elaborations of what would have been considered minor ragas incapable of any particular development. Subbulakshmi stayed with the tried and the true.

Ragam-tanam-pallavi is neatly defined in the Sleeve Notes by Robert E. Brown, Associate Professor of Music, Wesleyan University, Connecticut, to *The Voice of K.V. Narayanaswamy*, Liberty Records, WPS 21450, 1960s:

'An elaborate Ragam, Tanam and Pallavi is the centrepiece of most full-length concerts in South India. Here the free improvisation in free rhythm within the raga structure (ragam, or alapana) and the continuation of that improvisation with the added element of rhythmic pulse (tanam) find their fullest and most complete expression. The performer is judged both on his ability to bring out the individual beauty of the raga through clear statement of its traditional and typical melodic phrases, and for his ability to so arrange and juxtapose these phrases so that he is able to project a fresh musical mood unique to that particular performance. The improvisation of the Pallavi melody, a short but succinct composed piece that follows the Ragam and Tanam, generally makes use of one of two types of improvisation that are done upon the metrical base of the tala. These are known as niraval (newly created melodic variations using the original poetic text) and svara kalpana (insertion of phrases sung in the Indian solfa syllables – SA RI GA MA PA DHA and NI, representing the seven tones of the scale). A special type of rhythmic doubling, quadrupling and tripling in speed of the entire melody over the constant unchanging pattern of the tala, as well as the same technique in reverse, where the melody is, for instance, twice as slow over the constant tala, is almost always applied to the Pallavi. Sometimes the performer includes excursions into other ragas (*ragamalika*). The Pallavi is a musical tour de force and demonstrates the performer's mastery of complex techniques of melodic and rhythmic improvisation.'

Samkirtana is the term usually given to the songs of Tallapakka Annamacharya (1408–1503).

Sangati refers to pre-composed variations on a line of the lyric, not to be confused with *neraval* which is an extemporization on a pre-composed line. Tyagaraja's songs are rich in *sangati* and from Subbulakshmi's active repertoire, only by way of example, one can list *'O Rangasayee'*/Kambhoji, *'Darini telusukonti'*/Suddhasaveri, *'Vara Narada'*/Vijayasri and *'Tsalakalla'*/Arabhi. Muthusvami Dikshitar's songs do not depend on *sangati* for their melodic impact and the well-known *sangatis* for the extremely popular *'Vatapi Ganapatim'*/Hamsadhwani are the work of Maha Vaidyanatha Iyer (1844–93).

Sollukattu is the term for clusters of phrases used for dance in the course of a song. Famous examples, from Subbulakshmi's repertoire, of songs including *sollukattu* are *'Sri Maha Ganapati'*/Gaula (CD 1977 Carnegie Hall), *'Gopalaka'*/Revagupti and *'Mathe Malayadhwaja'*/Khamas. (Sung at the Music Academy recital in December 1969, available on YouTube.) Also the *pallavi* portion of the *Melakarta Ragamalika*.

Sruti is pitch. Every musician is expected to adhere scrupulously to *sruti* through a concert. Subbulakshmi was famous for her *sruti-suddham*, or perfect adherence to pitch.

Stotram refers to free flowing, devotional verse in Sanskrit, quite often meant to be sung. Subbulakshmi was given to prefacing some songs with a *stotram*. Among the most effective of these are *Namostu devyai bhrigunandanayai...* before *'Hiranmayim'* in Lalita, *Karacharana kritam va...*, a *stotram* before a Tamil song *'Sambho Mahadeva'* in Bauli and *Sa chitra sayi...* from the *'Sri Ranganatha Ashtakam'* before a Telugu song *'O Rangasayee'* in Kambhoji. It is also worth searching the net for her 1979 National Programme, where she sang a stunning *stotram*, *'Kailasa saila bhuvane...'*, in Dhanyasi, Valaji and Sindhubhairavi before a Bengali song *'Patitoddharini Gange'*. For the last twenty-five years and more of her performing career, she always commenced her recitals with a verse from the *Dakshinamurti stotram*. Semmangudi Srinivasa Iyer's rendition of *stotram* was legendary.

Stotram could also mean long Sanskrit hymns with many verses such as the *suprabhatam* compositions or the *'Sri Vishnu sahastranama stotram'*, the *'Annapurnashtakam'* and the *'Sri Lakshmi karavalamba stotram'*. Pattammal's rendering of the *'Syamala dandakam'* or Vasanthakumari's of the *'Soundaryalahari'* are worth searching for.

Glossary

Svara is quite simply, note. As in other musical systems, Indian music recognizes seven basic notes (*shadja, rishabha, gandhara, madhyama, panchama, dhaivata* and *nishadha*) over an octave, or the interval between one pitch and the next. The Carnatic and the Hindustani systems have each developed semitones between the notes, making a total of twelve semitones. The Carnatic system further allows for four of these semitones to be used varyingly, i.e., the highest *rishabha* is sometimes used as the lowest *gandhara*, and the highest *dhaivata* as the lowest *nishadha*, so allowing for sixteen semitones. Ragas within the *melakarta* structure (see above) which use these additional semitones are called *vivadi* ragas (see below).

Svaraprasthara or *svarakalpana* is a distinctly Carnatic musical embellishment, where a musician extemporizes using the notes of the raga being presented, at one or more speeds.

Tala refers to a system of rhythmic cycles. Every composition in the Carnatic style is set to a specific *tala*. The principle on which the system of *tala* is built consists of seven *tala* types (*Dhruva, Matya, Rupaka, Jhampa, Triputa, Ata* and *Eka*), each with five possible variations, *jati* (*Tisra* or three, *Chatusra* or four, *Khanda* or five, *Misra* or seven and *Sankirna* or nine), giving a total of thirty-five. These can be further developed giving trickier *tala* structures, often on display in *ragam-tanam-pallavi*. The most commonly used *talas* are *Rupaka* (strictly *Chatusra jati Rupaka*), a beat of six, *Adi* (strictly *Chatusra jati Triputa*), a beat of eight, *Jhampa* (strictly *Misra jati Jhampa*), a beat of ten and *Ata* (strictly *Khanda jati Ata*), a beat of fourteen. *Rupaka* as a beat of three and *Misrachapu* as a beat of seven are commonly used terms. It gets quite a bit more complicated after that.

Tambura, or *tanpura* in Hindustani concert practice, is a drone, which keeps the performer aligned to the correct pitch through the recital.

Tanam refers to the style of vocalization of a raga using short, accelerated phrases, usually *anantam* or variations thereof. *Tanam* usually comes after raga *alapana* and before a *pallavi*, or text set to a fixed *tala* structure, is taken up for elaboration and extemporization. Subbulakshmi's *tanam* was always of an extraordinary quality.

Tani avartanam are the sections of any concert where the percussionists play alone without the lead performer. Most often, a singer would have a mrdangam and ghatam accompaniment, and Subbulakshmi was famous for also having kanjira and, occasionally, morsing accompaniment as well. *Tani avartanam* is usually part of the *ragam-tanam-pallavi* suite or of the central piece of the concert, as for instance after '*Sarojadalanetri*' in the UN Concert or '*O Rangasayee*' in the Carnegie Hall concert. There is nothing, however, to prevent the musicians on stage to introduce a *tani avartanam* at any stage of the concert.

Tevaram are Saivite devotional verses in Tamil, mostly from the seventh to the ninth century. The names of Tirugnana Sambandar and Sundaramurti Nayanar are most frequently associated with this form. Verses from *tevaram* are usually sung to tunes set by the performing musician. Subbulakshmi often sang '*Sirai aarum*' in Suddhasaveri (CD Nada Sudha Rasa).

Tillana is a lively piece meant primarily for dance and includes in addition to lyric and *svarajatis* or phrases used in dance. The dance repertory includes a large number of *tillanas* and contemporary musicians such as Lalgudi G. Jayaraman, Maharajapuram Santhanam and M. Balamuralikrishna have added significantly to the number. Subbulakshmi did not sing *tillana* often but one that she did sing was Svati Tirunal's composition '*Dhanasri*'/Adi (1969 Concert Album) for which the music was composed by Lalgudi Jayaraman.

Tiruppavai are Vaishnavite devotional verses in Tamil attributed to Andal of the ninth century. Verses from Tiruppavai are sung often in concert, often in the raga and format set by Ariyakudi Ramanuja Iyengar. Subbulakshmi is known to have sung '*Maale manivanna*' in Kuntalavarali. Vasanthakumari's recorded version, of the entire *Tiruppavai* series, is worth searching for.

Tiruppugazh are devotional verses in Tamil attributed to the fifteenth-century Arunagirinathar in praise of Murugan, or Kartikeya. '*Naada bindu kaladhi*' set to the raga Jenjuti was a favourite with Subbulakshmi (1969 Concert Album, Charsur CD Music Academy 25 December 1956, Charsur CD Music Academy 25 December 1966).

Glossary

Tiruvembavai are the Saivite devotional verses in Tamil attributed to Manickavasagar of the ninth century. An example of *tiruvembavai* sung by Subbulakshmi is *'Paadaalam'* in Suddhasaveri (Charsur CD of 1956 Bhavani concert).

Tukkada is a colloquial term for the lighter pieces towards the end of a recital, possibly derived from the Hindustani word *tukda*, meaning a bit. Not all pieces at the tail end of a recital are necessarily light. A *padam* is obviously not a *tukkada*. G.N. Balasubramaniam and M.L. Vasanthakumari both substantially raised the standard of the *tukkada* section of a recital.

Vaggeyakara is the term given to the composers who are credited with both the text, *sahitya*, and the tune, both the raga and the setting, of their songs. Syama Sastri, Tyagaraja, Muthusvami Dikshitar, Subbaraya Sastri, Patnam Subramania Iyer and Papanasam Sivan are all recognized as *vaggeyakaras*. Purandaradasa, Bhadracala Ramadas and Annamacharya are believed to be *vaggeyakaras* even if we are not now aware of their original raga settings. Svati Tirunal is a complicated case.

Varnam is an introductory piece, both to the concert and to the raga itself. In structure it is simpler than the *kriti*, and is expected to fully outline the raga, using characteristic or representative phrases. A *varnam* thus serves a didactic purpose and requires the singer to sing both lyrics and *svaras*. Most *varnams* are set to the eight-beat *adi tala* or the fourteen-beat *ata tala*. A *pada varnam* is meant primarily for dance, and far from being introductory, is the central piece of a traditional *margam*. A *varnam* which is sung in a concert is a *tana varnam*. Subbulakshmi's *'Viriboni'*, the *ata tala varnam* in Bhairavi can be heard on many recordings: 1969 Concert Album, Charsur CD of 25 December 1960 concert, Charsur CD Bhavani 1956 concert.

Vina is the leading string instrument in south India, meant always for solo presentation and not as an accompaniment. Subbulakshmi came from a *vainika* tradition, but played publicly only very rarely, as for instance in 1968 at the Music Academy.

Viruttam refers to free-flowing, devotional verse in Tamil, quite often meant to be sung. Subbulakshmi sang *viruttam* all the time. A fine example from the 1977 Carnegie Hall recital is '*Petra thai thanai...*' in Nadanamakriya, composed by Vallalar Chidambaram Ramalingam (1823–74), sung before the Tamil song '*Arar aasai padar*'. In a very late recording, Subbulakshmi has sung the same *viruttam* in Revati as a preface to the Sanskrit '*Siva* panchakshara stotram'.

Viruttam in Tamil is basically the same as a *stotram* in Sanskrit (see above) or *ugaboga* in Kannada, of the type Purandaradasa was famous for. The contemporary musician T.M. Krishna has recently shown that even the Prakrit text of Asoka's edicts can be sung in the style of a *viruttam*, *stotram* or *ugaboga*.

Vivadi ragas are ragas which use the additional semitones referred to above (see *svara*). Contemporary musicians sing *vivadi* ragas frequently but older musicians tended not to do so. Tyagaraja and Muthusvami Dikshitar both used these ragas extensively. Other than the raga Varali, also Jhalavarali, Subbulakshmi did not sing *vivadi* ragas, a situation she may have regretted. She did, however, display her considerable prowess *svara suddham*, or purity in rendering of the notes, in her rendering of the '*Melakarta Ragamalika*.' (CD Mela-Raga-Malika-Chakra).

Bibliography and Suggested Readings

Anonymous. *Gana Saraswathi D.K. Pattammal: Dimensions of a Divine Songster*, Coimbatore: Bharatiya Vidya Bhavan, 2007.

Anonymous. *The Indian Fiddler Queen A Short Sketch of Philomena Thumboochetty*, Dr K.N. Kesari at the Lodhra Press, Madras, 1937.

Acharya, B.T., *Haridasa Sahitya: The Karnatak Mystics and their Songs*, Bangalore: Indian Institute of Culture, 1953.

Allen, Charles. *Coromandel: A Personal History of South India*, New York: Little, Brown, 2017.

Anantha Raman, Sita. *Getting Girls to School – Social Reform in the Tamil Districts, 1870-1930*, Kolkata: Stree, 1996.

Arnold, Edwin. *The Light of Asia and The Indian Song of Songs*, Bombay: Jaico Publishing House, 1949.

Atre, Prabha. *Enlightening the Listener, Contemporary North Indian Classical Vocal Music Performance*, Delhi: Munshiram Manoharlal, 2000.

Bakhle, Janaki. *Two Men and Music*, Ranikhet: Permanent Black, 2005.

Bali, Vyjayantimala with Jyoti Sabharwal. *Bonding... A Memoir*, Delhi: Stellar Publishers Pvt. Ltd., 2007.

Baskaran, S. Theodore. *The Message Bearers, The Nationalist Politics and the Entertainment Media in South India, 1880-1945*, Chennai: Cre-A, 1981.

Bly, Robert and Jane Hirschfield. *Mirabai Ecstatic Poems*, New Delhi: Aleph, 2017.

Bondyopadhyay, Swapan Kumar. *An Unheard Melody: Annapurna Devi*, New Delhi: Roli Books, 2005.

Brinda, T. *Javalis*, Madras: The Music Academy, 1960.

Chatterjee, Ashoke. *Dances of the Golden Hall*, photographs by Sunil Janah, New Delhi: Indian Council for Cultural Relations, 1979.

Chitre, Dilip. *Says Tuka*, Mumbai: Poetrywala, 2013.

Craske, Oliver. *Indian Sun, The Life and Music of Ravi Shankar*, London: Faber & Faber, 2020.

Crosland, Margaret. *A Cry from the Heart, a biography of Edith Piaf*, London: Arcadia, 2002.

Danielson, Virginia. *The Voice of Egypt, Umm Kulthum, Arabic Song and Egyptian Society in the Twentieth Century*, Chicago: The University of Chicago Press, 1997.

Dayananda Rao, B. (ed.), *Carnatic Music Composers*, Hyderabad: The Triveni Foundation, 1995.

de Zoete, Beryl. *The Other Mind, A Study of Dance in South India*, New York: Theatre Arts Books, 1960.

Desai, Kishwar. *Darlingji: The True Life Story of Nargis and Sunil Dutt*, New Delhi: HarperCollins Publishers India, 2007.

Devadoss, Manohar. *Multiple Facets of My Madurai*, Chennai: East West Books Pvt. Ltd., 2007.

Devidayal, Namita. *The Music Room*, New Delhi: Random House India, 2007.

Devidayal, Namita. *The Sixth string of Vilayat Khan*, New Delhi: Context, 2018.

Dewan, Parvez [Translated and with an Introduction by], *The Hanuman Chalisa of Goswami Tulasi Das*, New Delhi: Viking, 2001.

Dewan, Saba. *Tawaifnama*, New Delhi: Context, 2019.

Dhar, Sheila. *The Cooking of Music and Other Essays*, Ranikhet: Permanent Black, 2001.

Doniger, Wendy. *On Hinduism*, New Delhi: Aleph, 2013.

Doniger, Wendy. *The Ring of Truth, Myths of Sex and Jewelry*, New Delhi: Speaking Tiger, 2017.

Felton, Monica. *A Child Widow's Story*, London: Victor Gollancz, 1966.

Fuller, C.J. *Servants of the Goddess, The Priests of a south Indian temple*, Cambridge: Cambridge University Press, 1984.

Futehally, Shama. *Songs of Meera, In the Dark of the Heart*, New Delhi: HarperCollins Publishers India, 1994.

Gandhi, Rajmohan. *Modern South India, A History from the 17th century to our times*, New Delhi: Aleph, 2018.

Ganesh, Deepa. *A Life in Three Octaves: The Musical Journey of Gangubai Hangal*, New Delhi: Three Essays Collective, 2014.

George, T.J.S. *MS: A Life in Music*, New Delhi: HarperCollins Publishers India 2004.

Gopal, Rupa. *GNB Centenary Special*, Chennai: Rupa Gopal, 2009.

Gopal, Rupa. *The one and only MLV*, privately published, 2014.

Guruswamy Sastrigal, V.S.V. *Melaragamalika of Maha Vaidyanatha Sivan*, Madras: The Music Academy, 2018.

Guy, Randor. *Memories of Madras (Its Movies, Musicians & Men of Letters)*, Kolkata: Creative Workshop, 2016.

Hangal, Gangubai. *The Song of My Life*, Hubli: Sahitya Prakashana, 2003.

Hawley, John Stratton. *A Storm of Songs, India and the Idea of the Bhakti Movement*, Cambridge, Massachusetts: Harvard University Press, 2015.

Hess, Linda. *Singing Emptiness, Kumar Gandharva Performs the Poetry of Kabir*, Calcutta: Seagull Books, 2009.

Hiranand, Shanti. *Begum Akhtar: The story of my ammi*, New Delhi: Viva Books Private Limited, 2005.

Holroyde, Peggy. *The Music of India*, New York: Praeger Publishers, 1972.

Holroyde, Peggy. *An ABC of Indian Culture*, Ahmedabad: MapinLit, 2007.

Huffington, Arianna. *Maria Callas: The woman behind the legend*, New York: Cooper Square Press, 2002.

Iyer, Suguna. *The Evening Gone*, New Delhi: Penguin, 2001.

Jackson, William J. *Songs of Three Great South Indian Saints*, New Delhi: Oxford University Press, 1998.

Jackson, William J. *Tyagaraja Life and Lyrics*, New Delhi: Oxford University Press, 1991.

Jackson, William J. *Tyagaraja and the Renewal of Tradition*, Delhi: Motilal Banarsidass Publishers, 1994.

Jayakar, Pupul. *J.Krishnamurti: A Biography*, New Delhi: Penguin Books, 1986.

Jayashri, Bombay and T.M. Krishna, with Mythili Chandrasekar. *Voices Within Carnatic Music: Passing On An Inheritance*, Chennai: MATRKA, 2006.

Joshi, Raghavendra Bhimsen. *Bhimsen Joshi, My Father*, New Delhi: Oxford University Press, 2016.

Kabir, Nasreen Munni. *Zakir Husain: A Life in Music, In Conversation with Nasreen Munni Kabir*, Noida: HarperCollins Publishers India, 2018.

Kalki. *'Kalki' valartha kalaigal*, Chennai: Vanathi Padippakam, 2008.

Kalki. *Kalai Sirakka Konjam Sirakka..!*, Chennai: Vanathi Padippakam, 2016.

Kannan, Rajalakshmi Nadadur. 'Performing "Religious" Music: Interrogating Karnatic Music within a Postcolonial Setting', Ph.D. thesis, University of Stirling, 2013.

Katrak, Ketu H. and Anita Ratnam. *Voyages of Body and Soul: Selected Female Icons of India and Beyond*, Newcastle upon Tyne: Cambridge Scholars Publishing, 2014.

Kersenboom, Saskia C. *Nityasumangali, Devadasi Tradition in South India*, Delhi: Motilal Banarsidass, 2002.

Kinnear, Michael. *The Gramophone Company's First Indian Recordings 1899-1908*, Bombay: Popular Prakashan, 1994.

Kinnear, Michael. *The Gramophone Company's Indian Recordings 1908-1910*, London: Sangam, 2000.

Kumar, Radha. *The History of Doing, An Illustrated account of Movements for Women's Rights and Feminism in India 1800-1990*, New Delhi: Kali for Women, 1993.

Krishna, T.M. *A Southern Music, The Karnatik Story*, Noida: HarperCollins Publishers India, 2013.

Krishna, T.M. *Reshaping Art*, New Delhi: Aleph, 2018.

Krishnamurti, Yamini with Renuka Khandekar. *A Passion for Dance: My Autobiography*, New Delhi: Viking, 1995.

Krishnamurthy, S. (ed.), *Vasudeva Kirtana Manjari*, Bangalore: Darpan, 2015.

Knight Jr., Douglas M. *Balasaraswati: Her Art & Life*, Middletown, Connecticut: Wesleyan University Press, 2010.

Lakshmi, C.S. *The Singer & the Song*, New Delhi: Kali for Women, 2001.

Lalitha, Ram and V. Ramnarayan, *Gandharva Ganam*, Chennai: G. B. Bhuvaneswaran, 2009.

Lavezzoli, Peter. *The Dawn of Indian Music in the West*, New York: Continuum, 2006.

Mahadevan, K.S. *Musings on Music & Musicians*, Chennai: K.S. Mahadevan 2003.

Menon, Indira. *The Madras Quartet*, New Delhi: Roli Books, 1999.

Menon, Indira. *Great Masters of Carnatic Music 1930-1965*, New Delhi: Indialog Publications Pvt. Ltd., 2004.

Menon, Raghava R. *The Musical Journey of Kumar Gandharva*, New Delhi: Vision Books, 2001.

Miller, Barbara Stoler. *Jayadeva's Gitagovinda, Love Song of the Dark Lord*, New Delhi: Oxford University Press, 1977.

Mishra, Amar. *Some Musical Memories*, New Delhi: Rupa & Co., 2004.

Nadkarni, Mohan. *The Great Masters, Profiles in Hindustani Classical Vocal Music*, New Delhi: HarperCollins Publishers India, 1999.

Nair, Rajeev. *A Rasika's Journey Through Hindustani Music*, New Delhi: Indialog Publications Pvt. Ltd., 2007.

Nandakumar, Prema. *Bharati*, New Delhi: Sahitya Akademi, 1981.

Narayana Rao, Velcheru and David Shulman. (trans.), *God on the Hill, Temple Poems from Tirupati, Annamayya*, New Delhi: Oxford University Press, 2005.

National Centre for the Performing Arts, *Muttuswami Dikshitar*, Bombay: NCPA, 1975.

Novetzke, Christian Lee. *History, Bhakti and Public Memory, Namdev in Religious and Secular Traditions*, Ranikhet: Permanent Black, 2017.

Parthasarathy, N.C. and N.C. Dwaraka Parthasarathy. (eds) *Compositions of Sri Patnam Subramanya Iyer*, Madras: Madras Sangitha Kalasala Publications, 1972.

Parthasarathy, N.C. and N.C. Dwaraka Parthasarathy. (eds) *Compositions of Sri Syama Sastri*, Madras: Madras Sangita Kalasala Publications, 1970.

Parthasarathy, T.S. (ed.), *The Musical Heritage of Sri Muthuswami Dikshitar*, Bombay & Baroda: Indian Musicological Society, 1976.

Pesch, Ludwig. *The Illustrated Companion to South Indian Classical Music*, Delhi: Oxford University Press, 1999.

Pesch, Ludwig. *The Oxford Illustrated Companion to South Indian Classical Music, Second Edition*, New Delhi: Oxford University Press, 2009.

Pillai, Manu S. *The Ivory Throne, Chronicles of the House of Travancore*, Noida: HarperCollins Publishers India, 2015.

Pradhan, Aneesh. *Chasing the Raag dream, A Look into the World of Hindustani Music*, Noida: HarperCollins Publishers India, 2019.

Pranesh, Meera Rajaram. *Harikeshanallur Dr L Mutthaih Bhagavatar A Biography*, Bangalore: Vanamala Centre for Art and Culture, 2014.

Pukhraj, Malka. (edited and translated from the Urdu by Saleem Kidwai), *Song Sung True: A Memoir*, New Delhi: Kali for Women, 2003.

Radhakrishnan, S. *The Bhagavadgita*, New Delhi: HarperCollins Publishers India, 1993, originally published 1948.

Radhakrishnan, S. *Religion and Society*, London: George Allen & Unwin, 1948.

Raghavan, V. *The Great Integrators*, New Delhi: Patel Memorial Lectures 1964.

Raghavan, V. *Dikshitar's Shishya Parampara*, in *Muttuswami Dikshitar*, Bombay: National Centre for the Performing Arts, 1975.

Rahman, Sukanya. *Dancing in the Family*, New Delhi: HarperCollins Publishers India, 2001.

Raja, Deepak S. *The Raga-ness of Ragas*, New Delhi: DK Printworld, 2016.

Rajan, Chandra. *The Loom of Time*, New Delhi: Penguin, 2007.

Rajendran, Kalki K. *Adhu oru Porkalam*, Chennai: Vanathi Padippakam, 2012.

Rajagopalan, Usha. *Selected Poems, Subramania Bharati*, Gurgaon: Hachette, 2012.

Ramanujan, A.K., Velcheru Narayana Rao and David Shulman. *When God is a Customer, Telugu Courtesan Songs by Kshetrayya and Others*, Berkeley, California: University of California Press, 1994.

Ramanujachari, C. (ed.), *The Spiritual Heritage of Tyagaraja*, Madras: Sri Ramakrishna Mutt, 1966.

Ramnarayan, Gowri. (trans.), *Kalki: Selected Stories*, New Delhi: Penguin, 1999.

Ramnarayan, Gowri. *Past Forward, Six Artists in Search of Their Childhood*, New Delhi: Oxford University Press, 1997.

Ramnarayan, Gowri. *MS and Radha*, Chennai: Wordcraft, 2012.

Ramnarayan, Gowri , Savita Narasimhan and V. Ramnarayan (eds). *Song of Surrender, A Centenary Tribute to MS Subbulakshmi*, Chennai: The Sruti Foundation, 2016.

Rangaramanuja Ayyangar, R. *History of South Indian (Carnatic) Music*, Madras: R. Rangaramanuja Ayyangar, 1972.

Rao, Mukunda. *Sky-Clad, the extraordinary life and times of Akka Mahadevi*, Chennai: Westland, 2018.

Rao, Vidya. *Heart to Heart Remembering Nainaji*, New Delhi: HarperCollins *Publishers* India, 2011.

Roncken Lynton, H. *Born to Dance*, Hyderabad: Orient Longman, 1995.

Roy, Juthika. *My World of Music*, Mumbai: Bharatiya Vidya Bhavan, 2013.

Sadasivam, T. (ed.), *Rajaji 93*, Madras: Rajaji Ninetythree Souvenir Committee, 1971.

Sadashiva Rao, Mysore. *Compositions of Mysore Sadashiva Rao*, Mysore: Sangeetha Kalabhivardhani Sabha, 1954.

Sai, Veejay. *Drama Queens, Women who created history on stage*, New Delhi: Roli Books, 2017.

Sambamoorthy, P. *Tyagaraja*, New Delhi: National Book Trust, 1967.

Sampath, N.V., Malathi Rangaswami and N.V. Kasturi. (eds), *The Kasi Diaries: Excerpts from the diaries of N.D. Varadachariar (1903-1945)*, Chennai: East West Books Pvt. Ltd., 2004.

Sampath, Vikram. 'My Name is Gauhar Jaan!', New Delhi: Rupa & Co., 2010.

Samson, Leela. *Rukmini Devi: A Life*, New Delhi: Penguin, 2010.

Sarabhai, Mrinalini. *The Voice of the Heart, An Autobiography*, New Delhi: HarperCollins *Publishers* India, 2004.

Saran, Gour Neelum. *Requiem in Raga Janki*, Gurgaon: Penguin Viking, 2018.

Sarukkai Chabria, Priya and Ravi Shankar. *Andal: The Autobiography of a Goddess*, New Delhi: Zubaan, 2015.

Sathyanarayana, R. *Karnataka Music As Aesthetic Form*, New Delhi: Centre for Studies in Civilizations, 2004.

Savita Devi and Vibha S. Chauhan, *Maa... Siddheshwari*, New Delhi: Roli Books, 2000.

Seetha, S. *Tanjore as a Seat of Music During the 17th, 18th and 19th centuries*], Madras: University of Madras Press, 1981.

Sengupta, Mekhala. *Kanan Devi: The First Superstar of Indian Cinema*, Noida: HarperCollins Publishers India, 2015.

Shankar, Ravi. *Raga Mala: An autobiography*, New York: Welcome Rain Publishers, 1999.

Shankar, Vidya. *Shyama Sastry*, New Delhi: National Book Trust, 1970.

Shulman, David. *Tamil: A Biography*, Cambridge, Massachusetts: The Belknap Press of Harvard University Press, 2016.

Sitaramiah, V. *Purandaradasa*, New Delhi: National Book Trust, 1971.

Sivaraman, Mythili. *Fragments of a Life, a family archive*, New Delhi: Zubaan, An Imprint of Kali for Women, 2006.

Soneji, Davesh. (ed.), *Bharatanatyam, A Reader*, New Delhi: Oxford University Press, 2010.

Srinivasier, Semmangudi R. *Maharaja Swathi Thirunal*, New Delhi: National Book Trust, 1986.

Sriram V. *The Devadasi and the Saint*, Chennai: East West Books Pvt. Ltd., 2007.

Sriram V. and Malathi Rangaswami. *Four Score & More, The History of the Music Academy Madras*, Chennai: East West Books Pvt. Ltd., 2010.

Subrahmaniam, V. and Sriram V. *Semmangudi Srinivasa Iyer: Life and Music*, Chennai: East West Books Pvt. Ltd., 2008.

Subramaniam, L. and Viji Subramaniam. *Classical Music of India: A Practical Guide*, Chennai: Tranquebar Press, 2018.

Subramanian, Lakshmi. *From the Tanjore Court to the Madras Music Academy, A Social History of Music in South India*, New Delhi: Oxford University Press, 2006.

Subramanian, Lakshmi. *New Mansions for Old, Performance, Pedagogy and Criticism*, New Delhi: Social Science Press, 2008.

Subramanian, Lakshmi. *Veena Dhanammal, The Making of a Legend*, New Delhi: Routledge 2009.

Subramanian, Lakshmi. *Singing Gandhi's India, Music and Sonic Nationalism*, New Delhi: Roli Books, 2020.

Sunda, (M.R.M. Sundaram), *Kalki: A Life Sketch*, Chennai: Vanathi Pathippakam, 1993.

Sundaram, B.M. *Marabu thantha manikkangal*, Chennai: Dr V. Raghavan Centre for Performing Arts, 2003.

Sundaram, B.M. *Divinity of Music and Dance, Volume 2*, Pudukkottai: Kala Pariseelana, 2018.

te Nujenhuis, Emmie and Sanjukta Gupta, *Sacred Songs of India, Diksitar's Cycle of Hymns to the Goddess Kamala, Part I*, Forum Ethnomusicologicum 3, Winterthur, Switzerland: Amadeus, 1987.

The Music Academy, M.S.: *The Queen of Song*, Madras: The Music Academy 1987.

Thiagarajan, Shantha. *D K Pattammal: A Maestro and Her Timeless Music*, Chennai: Notion Press, 2019.

Vaidyanatha Bhagavathar, Soolamangalam. *Cameos*, Chennai: Sunadham, 2005.

van der Lenden, Bob. *Music and empire in Britain and India, Identity, Internationalism and Cross-Cultural Communication*, London: Palgrave Macmillan, 2013.

Vanita, Ruth. *Dancing with the Nation, Courtesans in Bombay Cinema*, New Delhi: Speaking Tiger, 2017.

Vedagiri, T.S., S. Muthuraman and K.S. Mahadevan, *G N B: A Biography*, Madras: G.B. Duraiswamy, 1985.

Venkatachalapathy, A.R. *Who Owns that Song?*, New Delhi: Juggernaut, 2018.

Venkatachalapathy, A.R. *Tamil Characters, Personalities, Politics, Culture*, New Delhi: Pan Macmillan, 2018.

Venkatarama Aiyar, T.L. *Muthuswami Dikshitar*, New Delhi: National Book Trust, 1968.

Venkataraman, Shankar. *Engum nirai nadabrahmam*, Chennai: SaRiGaMaPaDaNi Foundation, 2006.

Venkatasubramanian, T.K. *Music as History in Tamilnadu*, New Delhi: Primus Books, 2010.

Venkatesan, Archana. *The Secret Garland, Andal*, Noida: Harper Perennial, 2016.

Vishwanathan, Lakshmi. *Kunjamma...Ode to a Nightingale*, New Delhi: Roli Books, 2003.

Vishwanathan, Lakshmi. *Women of Pride: The Devadasi Heritage*, New Delhi: Roli Books, 2008.

Viswanathan, T. and Matthew Harp Allen. *Music in South India*, New Delhi: Oxford University Press, 2004.

Wade, Bonnie C. *Music in India: The Classical Traditions*, New Delhi: Manohar 1987.

Wade, Bonnie C. *Thinking Musically*, New York: Oxford University Press, 2004.

Weidman, Amanda. *Singing the Classical Voicing the Modern, The Postcolonial Politics of Music in South India*, Calcutta: Seagull Books, 2007.

Wodeyar, Jayachamaraja. *Sri Vidya ganavaridhi* (in Kannada), Bangalore: R. Rajachandra, 2010.

ARTICLES

Asian Music, 'In Memory of Jon Borthwick Higgins', Vol. 16, No. 2 (Spring–Summer, 1985).

Allen, Matthew Harp. 'Tales Tunes Tell: Deepening the Dialogue between "Classical" and "Non-Classical" in the Music of India', *Yearbook for Traditional Music*, Vol. 30 (1998).

Anandhi, S. 'Women's Question in the Dravidian Movement, c. 1925-1948', in Sumit Sarkar and Tanika Sarkar (eds), *Women and Social Reform in Modern India, A Reader*, Bloomington: Indiana University Press, 2008.

Balasaraswati, T. 'On Bharata Natyam', *Dance Chronicle*, Vol. 2, No. 2 (1978).

Barnett, Elise B. 'Special Bibliography: Art Music of India', *Ethnomusicology*, Vol. 14, No. 2 (May 1970).

Brown, Robert E. 'T. Ranganathan (March 13, 1925–December 21, 1987)', *Ethnomusicology*, Vol. 32, No. 2 (Spring–Summer, 1988).

Hallstorm, Lisa Lassell. 'Anandamayi Ma, God Came as a Woman', in John Stratton Hawley and Vasudha Narayanan (eds), *The Life of Hinduism*, New Delhi: Aleph, 2017.

Higgins, Jon B. 'From Prince to Populace: Patronage as a Determinant of Change in South Indian (Karnatak) Music', *Asian Music*, Vol.7, No. 2, (1976).

Higgins, Jon B. 'An American in Madras', *Asian Music*, Vol. 1, No. 1 (Winter, 1968–1969).

Karnad, Girish. 'The arts and social change' *in India*, in Karel Werdler, Girish Karnad, Felix van Lamsweerde and Urvashi Butalia (eds), *India's culture in motion: Tradition and change in the arts*, The Netherlands: Royal Tropical Institute, 1998.

Krishna, T.M. 'Classically Yours', *Social Scientist*, Vol. 44, No. 7/8, (2016).

L'Armand, Kathleen and Adrian L'Armand, 'Music in Madras', in Bruno Nettl (ed.), *Eight Urban Musical Cultures, Tradition and Change*, Champaign, Illinois: University of Illinois Press, 1978.

Lath, Mukund. 'When (and how) did Hindustani ragas become ascribed to different times of the day?', Scroll, 30 June 2017.

Majumdar, Neepa. 'Gossip, Labor and Female Stardom in Pre-Independence Indian Cinema, The case of Shanta Apte', in Christine Gedhill and Julia Knight (eds), *Doing Women's Film History, Reframing Cinemas, Past and Future*, Champaign, Illinois: University of Illinois Press, 2015.

Morris, Robert. 'The Survival of Music: Musical Citizenship in South India', *Perspectives of New Music*, Vol. 42, No. 2 (Summer, 2004).

Petersen, Indira V. *Sanskrit in Carnatic Music: The songs of Muttusvami Diksita*, Indo-Iranian Journal, Vol. 29, No. 183 (1986).

Post, Jennifer. 'Professional women in Indian music: the death of the courtesan tradition', in Ellen Koskoff (ed.), *Women and music in cross-cultural perspective*, Champaign, Illinois: University of Illinois, 1989.

Ram, Kalpana. 'Being "Rasikas": the Affective Pleasures of Music and Dance Spectatorship and Nationhood in Indian Middle-Class Modernity', *The Journal of the Royal Anthropological Institute*, Vol. 17, (2011).

Sambamoorthy, P. 'Tyagaraja's sishya parampara', Cocanada: Sri Tyagarajaswami Centenary Souvenir and Programme of Sri Saraswati Gana Sabha, 1947.

Sinha, Mrinhalini. 'Gender in the Critiques of Colonialism and Nationalism: Locating the Indian Woman', in Joan Wallach Scott (ed.), *Feminism and History*, New Delhi: Oxford University Press, 1996.

Srinivasan, 'Manna'. 'D.K. Pattammal (1919–2009)', *India International Centre Quarterly*, Vol. 36, No. 2 (Autumn 2009).

Subramanian, Lakshmi. 'The Reinvention of a Tradition: Nationalism, Carnatic music and the Madras Music Academy, 1900–1947', *The Indian Economic and Social History Review*, Vol. 36, issue 2, (1999).

Subramanian, Lakshmi. 'Negotiating Orientalism: The Kaccheri and the Critic in Colonial South India', in Martin Clayton and Bennet Zon (eds.), *Music and Orientalism in the British Empire, 1780s–1940s*, Farnham, United Kingdom: Ashgate Publishing Ltd., 2007.

Terada, Yoshitaka. 'Tamil Isai as a Challenge to Brahmanical Music Culture in South India', *Senri Ethnological Studies*, Vol. 71, pp. 203–26, (2008).

Wade, Bonnie C. 'Fixity and Flexibility, From Musical Structure to Cultural Structure', *Anthropologica*, New Series, Vol. 18, No. 1.

Weidman, Amanda. 'Gender and the Politics of Voice: Colonial Modernity and Classical Music in South India', *Cultural Anthropology*, Vol. 18, No. 2, (2003).

Weidman, Amanda. 'Stage goddesses and studio divas in South India: On agency and the politics of voice', in Bonnie S. McElhinny (ed.), *Words, worlds, and material girls: language, gender, globalization*, Berlin; New York: Mouton de Gruyter, 2007.

Zvelebil, Kamil V. 'A Devadasi as the Author of a Tamil Novel', *Journal of the Institute of Asian Studies*, Vol. 5, No. 1 (September 1987).

Index

'Aarabhi', 185, 195
abhinaya, 9, 26, 89, 118, 131, 211, 227
Abhiramasundari, T., 69, 77, 80, 116, 117, 118, 226
Adiappier, Pachhimiriyam, 13
Akashvani Sangeet Sammelan, 77
Akhtar, Begum, 50, 294, 301, 303, 308
Akka Mahadevi, 4
Akkammal, 35, 148
Alagiriswami, Kandadevi, 244, 261
Alamelu Mangal 117
alapana, 43, 85, 94–95, 136, 139, 145, 149, 150, 152, 168, 184, 187, 200, 201, 234, 238, 244, 248, 266, 277, 286–88
Ali AkbarKhan, 169, 174, 283

All India Music Conference, 1944, 54, 119
All India Radio (formerly Indian Broadcasting Company), 74, 142, 248
  early performers on 75–76
Alla Rakha, 169, 174
Alladiya Khan, 48–49
Allamaprabhu, 4
Allauddin Khan, 51, 216, 274
Allen, Matthew Harp, 228
Alwars, 3, 5
Aman Ali Khan, Ustad, 295
Amar Chitra Katha, 280–81
Ambi Dikshitar, 204
Ambujammal, S., 82
Ambur Sisters 117
Amir Khan, 308
Amirbai Karnataki, 101
Ammani, Vallalarkoil, 15, 23

INDEX

Amonkar, Kishori, 51, 52, 126, 308
Anand, Viswanathan, 279
Ananda Vikatan, 82
Anandamayi, Sri Ma, 218
Anantacarya, Prativadibhayankara Sri, 171
Anantakrishna Sarma, Rallapalli, 191
Anantharaman, M.S., 260
Anasuya Devi, Vinjamuri, 50
Andal, 3, 4, 5, 242, 193, 292
Andavan Pichai, 158
Anjaneyulu Chetty, C.Y., 66
Annadurai, C.N., 196
Annamacharya, 4, 13, 161, 179, 189–90, 203, 227–28, 244–46, 249, 267, 282, 285, 292, 301
Annamalai Chettiar, Rajah Sir, 106, 266
Annamalai Reddiar, 17
Annapurna Devi, 51
Annaswami Sastri, 30, 240
Apitakuchamba (Parvati), 79, 87
Apte, Shanta, 50, 99
Arni, Hemamalini, 117
Arunachalakavi, 231
Arunagirinathar, 45
Arundale, George, 62–63
Arundale, Rukmini Devi, 26, 48, 62–63, 68, 69–70, 141, 199, 207, 253–54, 296
Ashrama Bhajanavali, 76, 101, 293
Asoka, 85
Athmanathan, K.R., 153, 276
Atre, Prabha, 51

Avvaiyar, 48
Ayyaswami Iyer, Koothanur, 236
AzhaganambiPillai, 37

Bade Ghulam Ali Khan, 295, 308
Baktha Chetha, 93
Bakthavthasalam, T., 262
Bala, 179
Balamani, Kumbakonam, 29
Balamuralikrishna, M., 294, 297
Balasaraswati, T., 22, 31, 49, 67–70, 85, 107, 115, 117–18, 141, 142, 144, 167, 169, 170, 179, 182, 196, 211–14, 216, 226, 228, 253–54, 264
Balasubramaniam, G.N., 40, 50–51, 73, 88, 90–94, 97, 99, 108, 111, 115–16, 133, 142–44, 148, 168, 173, 187, 236–37, 239, 264, 275, 280
Balasubramaniam, T.R., 50–51, 92, 264
Bali, Vyjayantimala, 52, 213
Balusvami Dikshitar, 37
Banni Bai, 16
Barodekar, Hirabai, 49, 50
Basava, 4
Besant, Annie, 62, 66
Bhadrachala, Ramadas, 13
Bhagavad Gita, 2
Bhagavata Purana, 3, 189
bhagavathars (singers of religious music), 19, 21
bhajan tradition, 4, 292–94
Bhakta Prahlada(1931), 81

Index

bhakti movement, 1–5, 14, 124, 292, 294, 299
BhaktimargaPrasanga Sabha, 18
Bhama Vijayam, 91
Bhanumathi, Kumbakonam, 29, 69
Bharata, *Natya Sastra*, 6, 211
Bharatanatyam, 26, 70, 212, 213, 254
Bharathi Gana Sabha, 145, 147
Bharati Memorial, Ettayapuram, 119
Bharati, Gopalakrishna, 17
Bharati, Kavikunjara, 17, 94
Bharati, Subramania, 58, 111, 119, 207, 231, 251, 268, 280
Bharati, Suddhananda, 108, 291
Bhaskara Das, M., 41, 64, 108
Bhatkhande, V.N., 54
Bhavani, Tiruvidaimarudur, 30
Bhosle, Asha, 51–52
Birla, B.K., 249–50
Bismillah Khan, 118, 216, 270, 274, 292
Brihadiswara Temple, 11
Brinda,T., 49, 69, 76, 80, 101, 118, 131, 151, 167, 186, 196, 225, 226–30, 240, 255, 258–59, 264–65. *See also* Muktha, T.
Buddha, 3
Buddhism, 61

Callas, Maria, 304, 306
Carnatic music, 1–10, 13, 26, 50, 71, 75, 77, 114, 141, 142, 169, 174–76, 177–79, 224, 229, 231, 236, 240, 261, 263, 284, 290, 293-94, 299, 302, 309
  and Tamil Isai 103–09,
caste, 21–27, 300
Chaitanya Mahaprabhu, 4, 246
Chandralekha, 132
Chandraprabha Cinetone, Madras, 83, 90
Chandrasekhar, S., 251
Chandrasekhara Iyer, Nagapattina, 89
Chattopadhyaya, Kamaladevi, 141
Chaudhuri, Tara, 132
Chidambaram Pillai, V.O., 279
Chidambaranatha Mudaliar, T.K., 95, 107–8, 110, 126–27, 264
Chinmayananda, Swami, 218
chhina melam, 21
Chinnabhaskar, Buffoon, 41
Chintamani (1933), 82
Cholas, 6, 11, 33
Chopin, 306
Chowdiah, T., 42, 66, 71, 90, 120, 130, 147–48, 183–84, 191, 260
Columbia (recording company), 44, 119
Committee of Women's Institutions, 199
Conrad, Joseph, 97
Cooke, Deryck, 290
Coomaraswamy, Ananda, 17
courtesan, 28–29, 31, 44, 50, 66, 69, 75, 90, 227, 297, 300

Dakshinamurthi Pillai, Pudukkottai, 37, 41, 42, 65
Dakshinamurthy Sastri, Susarla, 191
Devadasis (see also courtesan), 15, 21–22, 23–25, 29, 30, 34, 44, 55, 56, 59–60, 69, 70–71, 111, 157, 212
   baijis, 28, 29, 44
   bayaderes, 23–24
   loss of hereditary rights, 70
   loss of agency, 25–26, 27
   tawa'ifs, 28, 304
   visit to France by, 23–24
   well-known devadasis 29–30
Devakunjari, Ramanathapuram, 76
Devika Rani, 81
Dhanakoti Ammal, Kanchipuram, 15, 29, 45
Dhanam, Tanjavur (also 'Vina' Dhanammal), 19, 22, 29–31, 45, 46, 49, 65, 68–69, 76–77, 80, 84–85, 116, 157, 204, 207, 212, 226–28, 230, 240, 258–59, 286, 308
   family, 30–31
Dhar, Sheila, 308
Divyaprabandham, 3
Dorai, Guruvayur, 262
Doraikannu Ammal, M.P., 29, 114
Doraswami Iyer, Puliyur, 158
Doreswamy Iyengar, 191
Dravidar Kazhagam (DK), 105
Dravidian movement, 58

Dungan, Ellis R., 90, 95, 123, 258
Durairaj, T.S., 93
Duraiswami Iyer, Trivadi, 94

East India Company, 33
Easwaran, Mannargudi, 262
Egmore Dramatic Society, 114

Fitzgerald, Ella, 304, 305, 306

Ganapathi, Ra., 158
Gandharva, Sawai, 50
Gandhi, Kasturba, 113, 121
Gandhi, M.K., 47, 53–55, 57, 59, 62, 76, 87, 100–2, 110–11, 121, 127–29, 132, 150, 164, 215, 249, 272, 282, 292, 293
Ganesa Aiyar, N., 261
Gauhar Jan, 45
Gautier, Theophile, 24
Gayakaparijatam, 20
George, T.J.S., 40, 91
Ghalib, 294
gharanas, 28
Giri, V.V., 219
Girija Devi, 51
Godavari, Salem, 30, 45
Good Shepherd Convent, 84
Gopala Iyer, Pallavi, 83
Gopalakrishnan, M.S., 149, 260
Gopalakrishnan, R.S., 260, 261
Gopalaratnam, Srirangam, 51, 183
Govinda Dikshitar,
   Sangraha Chudamani, 13

Sangita Sudha, 12
Govindaraja Pillai, Mayavaram, 260, 263
Govindaswami Pillai, M., 37
Gowri Ammal, Mylapore., 29, 68
Gowri, Kumbakonam, 68
Gramophone records, 44
    early recordings, 45
Guha, Ramachandra, 270
Gurumurthy, Premeela, 298
Gururajappa, 66

Hamsa Damayanti, 116, 117
Hangal, Gangubai, 50, 87, 308
Harikatha, 15–16, 40, 45, 48, 67
Harishankar, G., 263
Hema Malini, 124
Higgins, Jon, 19
Hindustani music, 6–10, 16, 28, 48–52, 80, 88–89, 120, 141, 174, 177–78, 224, 239, 288–89, 293, 295, 299
HMV, 42, 44, 119, 171, 203, 252, 280
Hum Dono (1960), 127
Husain, M.F., 279

Ibn Battuta, 33
Indian Cultural Bureau, 68
Indian Fine Arts Society, 19, 66, 68, 72, 105, 217
Indian National Congress, 47, 53–54, 87, 105
Indian Penal Code, 1861, 60

Indira Devi, 164
Isai Vellalar Sabha, 96
isai vellalar, 23, 25–26, 71, 280
Iyer, Pico, 296
Iyer, Ramaswami R., 291

Jackson, William J., 192, 303
Jagannatha Bhakta Sabha, 19
Jairam, Vani, 126
Janabai, 4
Janki Bai Ilahabadi, 45
Jayadeva, 4, 13, 116, 160, 190, 227, 247
Jayalakshmi (Jayammal), T., 30, 31, 49, 118, 142, 167, 183, 212, 261
Jayalakshmi, Pandanallur, 29
Jayalakshmi, R. *See* Radha-Jayalakshmi
Jeevaratnam, 29, 30, 68
Jharia, Kamla, 52
Jnanadev, 4, 238
Joseph, Pothan, 141
Joshi, Bhimsen, 177, 270, 308
Justice Party, 47, 105

Kabir, 4, 163, 238, 293
Kalakshetra (International Academy of the Arts), 19, 63, 69–70, 186, 201, 253
Kalam, A.P.J. Abdul, 278, 280
Kalidasa (1931), 81, 82
Kalidasa, 2, 24, 90, 205
    Sakuntalam, 24
Kalki, 90, 98, 127, 235–36
Kalki Gardens 109, 235–36

Kalyani, Tiruvallaputtur, 29, 68
Kamakshi, T., 15, 30, 31, 49, 227, 240
Kamala, 52, 131, 132, 264
Kamalambal, Tiruvarur, 29
Kanakadasa, 4, 179
Kanakamala, Tanjavur, 30
Kanakambujam, 117
Kanan Devi (also Kanan Bala), 50, 52, 128, 301, 303
Kandaswamy, 216
Kannayya Bhagavatar, 191
Kanyakumari, A., 239, 281
Karan Singh, 196, 281
Karunanidhi, M., 271
Kasturba Gandhi Memorial Fund, 113, 122
kavadichindu, 37, 136
Kedaranathan, K.R., 153
Keechaka Vadham (1916), 81
Kerkar, Kesarbai, 48, 52, 66, 200, 295, 308
Kesi, 117
Khote, Durga, 81
kirana gharana, 50, 177
kirtana, 3–5, 16, 162, 184, 206, 208, 224, 244, 245, 267
Knight, Aniruddha, 31
Knight, Dhanalakshmi Shanmukham, 31
Knight, Douglas, 67
Komalavalli, 117
KothandaramaIyer, Umayalpuram, 262
KotiswaraIyer, 231

Kripalani, Sucheta, 165
Krishna, Ambujam, 158
Krishna, T.M., 45, 187, 276, 281
Krishna Bhagavathar, Thanjavur, 16
Krishna Bhagavathar, Umayalpuram, 191
Krishna Gana Sabha, 166, 185–86, 208, 209, 217
Krishna Iyer, E., 68, 228
Krishna Iyer, Ghanam, 17
Krishna Iyer, Mayavaram V.V., 136, 264
Krishna Iyer, T., 39, 276
Krishna Menon, V.K., 274
Krishnamachari, T.T., 65, 66, 107, 165
Krishnamurthi, Kalki R., 68, 70, 72, 83, 85, 88–89, 94, 95, 98, 100, 107–8, 110–12, 119–20, 123, 127, 131, 207, 231, 277
Krishnamurthy Rao, T., 261
Krishnamurthy, Neduuri, 246
Krishnamurti, J., 179, 194, 217
Krishnamurti, Yamini, 170
Krishnan, N.S., 93
Krishnan, R., 264
Krishnankutti Nair, M., 262
Krishnaswami Iyer, Alladi, 113
Krishnaswami, Mani, 144, 253, 302
Krishnaswamy, S.Y., 84
kriti, 5, 9, 15, 20, 77, 139–40, 162, 177, 183, 188–89, 194, 221–25, 240–42, 276, 293, 302–09

Kshetrayya (also Kshetragna), 13, 26, 123, 167, 212, 227–28
Kulkarni, Dhondutai, 200
Kulthum, Umm, 304, 305
Kumaraswami, K.R., 153
Kunjamani, Sikkil, 144
Kunjumani, Palghat., 262
Kunku, 99
Kuppier (also Kuppayar), Vina, 17, 30, 191, 230
Kurai Onrum Illai (exhibition), 283
Kurdikar,Mogubai, 49, 51

Lakshmana Pillai, T., 17, 158
Lakshmanachar, 247
Lakshmanan Chettiar, 66
Lakshmi Sastri (later Shankar), 89
Lakshminarayani, Enadi, 43, 157
Lakshmiratnam, T., 30, 77
Lal Ded, 4
Lalitha, C., 132, 144, 302
Lalitha, Padmini and Ragini, 132
Lalithangi, M., 48, 50, 69, 72, 116, 177, 236
Logan, William, 189
London Philharmonic Orchestra, 251

Madhvacharya, 2, 179, 246
Madras
  musical traditions, 18–19
Madras Corporation Radio, 74
Madras Devadasi (Prevention of Dedication) Act (1947), 25, 194

Madras Mahajana Sabha, 18
Madras Native Association, 18
Madras Radio Club, 74
Madras United Artists Corporation, 83, 93
Madrasi Education Society, 130
Madurai 34, 47
  Minakshi temple, 40
Madurai Diraviyam Thayumanavar Hindu College, Tirunelveli, 48
Madurai Girls Boarding School, 56
Mahabharata, 2, 219
Mahadeva Rao, 38
Mahadevan, Narayani (Chinnani), 98
Mahadevan, Pudukkottai, 149, 263
Mahalingam, T.R., 280
Mahavira, 3
Malpekar, Anjanibai, 48
Mangathayaru, Dwaram, 261
Mangeshkar, Lata, 51–52, 101, 126, 127, 216, 258, 270, 295, 296
Mani Iyer, Madurai, 36–38, 73, 92, 102, 115, 142, 173, 194, 199, 286, 294
Mani Iyer, Palghat, 47, 142, 243, 261, 262, 280
Mani, Tiruppugazh, 129
Mani, T.A.S., 262
Mani, Trivandrum R.S., 219
Manickam, T.N., 45
Manikkavacakar, 3, 231
Manjunath, K.S., 262

Manku Thampuran, Princess of Cochin, 89
Mansur, Mallikarjun, 308
Maratha Nayak rulers, 11, 16, 33, 77
Marcos, Ferdinand, 215
Marimuthu Pillai, 13
Marqusee, Mike, 263
Mathuram, T.A., 93
Mayo, Katherine 57, 59
McMurray, Dallas, 233
Meenakshi, Mannargudi., 30
Meenakshi, Salem, 157
Meenakshisundaram Pillai, P., 132
Meera (1945, Tamil), 36, 42, 113, 120, 122–33, 142, 144, 249, 264, 273, 292, 294, 309
Meera (1947, Hindi), 123–25, 131, 164
Meerabai (1947, Hindi), 126
Megasthenes, 33
Mehta, Zubin, 250–51
Menon, Sadanand, 14
Mira, 4, 5, 42, 122–29, 163–64, 175, 203, 242, 272, 293
Modigilani, 306
Morris, Mark, 233
Morrison, Jim, 306
Mountbatten, Lord and Lady, 125–26, 207
MS Amma, a shy girl from Madurai, 281
Muktha, T., 49, 69, 76, 80, 101, 118, 131, 167, 186, 226–30, 240, 265
Mullick, Pankaj, 293
Murthy, T.K., 149, 167, 197, 203, 244, 261–63, 291

Music Academy, Madras, 19, 20, 54, 64–66, 69, 71–73, 88–89, 92, 94, 96, 99–100, 102, 116–18, 130, 136, 138, 143–47, 149, 153, 159, 166–68, 172, 181, 184, 186, 193, 196, 198, 200, 204, 206–07, 209–11, 213, 225–26, 228, 230, 236–37, 239, 243, 249, 254, 260–63, 273, 276, 280–82, 291, 295–96, 298
    and Tamil Isai 105–09,
Muthiah Bhagavatar, Harikesanallur, 17, 94, 96, 97, 161, 200
Muthulakshmi Reddy, 59, 194
Muthusvami Dikshitar, 12, 13–15, 20, 37, 72, 78, 103, 130, 155, 156, 162, 172, 181, 188–90, 192, 203–05, 221–25, 240, 284, 295
    disciples of, 15, 224
Muthuratnambal, 80
Muthuswami Iyer, Varahur, 260
Mylai Sangeetha Sabha, 19, 105, 109, 114
Mylapore Fine Arts Society, 208

Nagarajan, V., 145, 146, 148, 200, 244, 263
Nagaratnam Panthanallur, 69
Nagaratnamu, (Nagaratnammal), Bangalore, 29, 48, 60
nagasvaram, 21, 22, 25, 51, 77, 142, 284
Naidu, Padmaja, 165, 182

Naidu, Sarojini, 47, 57–58, 125–26, 134
Naina Devi, 30
Naina Pillai, Kanchipuram, 41, 49, 71, 227, 240
Namdev, 4, 5
Nanak, Guru, 4, 163, 164, 257, 293
Narasimha Bhagavathar, T., 190
Narasimhalu Naidu, Vidyala, 204
Narasimhan, C.V., 174, 233
Narayan, R.K., 252, 279
Narayana Iyengar, K.S., 101
Narayana Menon, V.K., 305
Narayana Tirtha, 13, 159, 161, 267
Narayanamma, Perumalkoil, 48
Narayan, Jayaprakash, 215
Narayanan, Kalanidhi, 89
Narayanan, Vasudha, 21
Narayanaswami Chalakudi, N.S., 260
Narayanaswami, Naidu, Tirupati, 17, 258
Narayanaswami, K.S., 142, 198
Narayanaswami, U. K., 263
Narayanaswamy, K.V., 142, 177, 181
Narsi Mehta, 4, 293
Natarajan, A.K.C., 191
Natesa Iyer, F.G., 42
Natesa Pillai, Mannargudi, 263
Nathamuni band, 77
Navaneetham, T.R., 75, 117
Nayanars (or Nayanmars), 3
Neela, Sikkil, 144
Neelakantan, V.I., 95

Nehru, Jawaharlal, 121, 125, 130, 142–43, 165, 172–73, 184
Nelson, J.H., 34

Odeon, 44

Paluskar, D.V., 293
Panchanatha Iyer, Tarangambadi, 158
Panchapakesa Sastrigal, T., 16
Pandarpur shrine, kirtan tradition, 16
Parsi Gayan Uttejak Mandali, 29
Partition, 128–29
Parveen Sultana, 295
Pasricha, Avinash, 273
Patel, Baburao, 83
Patel, Maniben, 127
Pattammal, D. K., 46, 49, 52, 71, 73–74, 76, 88–89, 95, 101, 111–12, 114–16, 119, 129, 131, 142, 144, 151, 157, 167, 172–73, 186, 196, 204–7, 213, 216, 244, 253, 256, 261, 266, 270, 279, 289, 303, 308, 309
Pattammal, M.S., 117
Pavalakkodi (1934), 81–82
periyamelam, 21, 25, 71
Periyanayaki, P.A., 117
Pesch, Ludwig, 187, 308
Piaf, Edith, 304, 305, 306
Pinakapani, S., 50
Ponnammal, Parassala, 76
Ponnusamy Pillai, M., 41
Ponnutayi, M., 51

Poona Gayan Samaj, 19, 29
Pothana, 189
Prasad, K.V., 262
Premchand, Munshi, 82
Pukhraj, Malka, 50
Purandaradasa (Srinivasa Nayak),
    4, 13, 48, 116, 168, 177–79, 190,
    192, 198, 203, 238, 249
Pushpavanam, Rajam, 38–39, 49,
    73, 76, 80, 114–15, 144.
Pushpavanam Iyer, Madurai, 19,
    36–41, 49, 115, 194, 261

Radha, C.P..*See* Radha-
    Jayalakshmi
Radha-Jayalakshmi, 50, 117, 131, 183
Radhakrishnan, Sarvepalli, 54,
    141, 150, 165, 171, 183, 280
Radio Sangeet Sammelan, 142
ragam-tanam-pallavi, 76, 138–39,
    146–49, 151–53, 166–67,
    169, 181, 194, 199, 201, 205,
    207–11, 214, 217, 231–34, 244,
    249, 277, 281
raga, 6–12
Raghavan, V., 3, 4, 158, 175, 220,
    239–40, 244, 265
Raghu, Palghat, 262
Ragunathan, Sudha, 282
Rahman, A.R., 299
Rahman, Indrani, 52
Raja, Deepak, 295
Raja Iyengar, B.S., 177
Rajagopala Sarma, Thuriayur, 90
Rajagopalachari, C. (Rajaji), 107,
    110, 113, 121, 175, 207, 210, 215,
    243, 249, 263, 268, 275
Rajagopalan, Rukmini, 76
Rajalakshmi, T., 29, 30, 68, 157,
    204
Rajalakshmi, T.P., 82
Rajam Iyer, B., 264
Rajam, N., 261
Rajamanickam Pillai,
    Kumbakonam, 96, 260
Rajaraja Chola, 11
Rajarathinam Pillai, T.N., 71, 115,
    142, 280
Rajasekharan (1937), 73
Rajayee, Pandanallur, 75
Rajayi, Tiruvarur, 30
Rajendran, K., 112, 153
Rajendran, Vijaya, 79, 84, 87, 96,
    112, 148, 153, 198, 264
Rajnikant, 279
Raju Pillai, K., 215
Rama Iyengar, T., 190, 191
Ramachandra Ayyar, E., 37
Ramachandra Bhagavathar, E., 41
Ramachandran, Anandhi, 112, 131,
    132
Ramachandran, N., 112, 132
Ramachandran, Alangudi, 120,
    148, 262
Ramachandran, M.G., 249
Ramachandran, N.S., 167, 181
Ramachandran, V.S., 185
Ramachar, H.P., 263
Ramachar, Latha, 263
Ramadas, Bhadracala, 189

Ramaiah Pillai, Vazhuvoor 131, 264
Ramakrishna Mission, 143, 203, 217
Ramamirtham Ammaiyar,
    Moovalur., 59
Ramamurthi, Balam, 117
Raman, C.V, 102, 141, 251, 280
Ramanathan, Kalapathi, 120, 261, 263
Ramanuja Iyengar, Ariyakudi, 19,
    41, 64, 71, 88, 92, 101, 107, 115,
    118, 133, 139–42, 184–85, 187,
    191, 193, 198–99, 208, 262,
    264, 280, 281, 292
    and concert pattern 139, 208
Ramanuja, 2, 246
Ramanujan, Srinivasa, 279, 280
Ramaswami Aiyer, C.P., 161
Ramaswami Iyer, M., 36, 37
Ramaswami Naicker, *Periyar* E.V.,
    58, 59, 105
Ramatilakam, Dasari, 82
Ramayyar, Lalgudi, 191
Ramnarayan, Gowri 84, 263
Rangacharlu, 240
Rangamma, Enadi, 157
Ranganathan, T., 117
Ranganathananda, Swami, 217
Ranganayaki, T.S., 260
Ranganayaki, V., 117, 144
Rangaramanuja Ayyangar, R., 37, 38
Rao, Shanta, 52
Rashid Khan, 308
Rasika Ranjani Sabha, 19, 114, 116,
    145, 149
Raskhan, 4, 164
Ravi Varma, Raja, 48

Ray, Satyajit, 179, 270
Richman, Paula, 303
Roosevelt, Eleanor, 305
Roshanara Begum, 5052, 118
Roy, Dilip Kumar, 164, 293
Roy, Juthika, 126
Roy, Raja Ram Mohan, 55
Rubin, James A., 174, 183, 234
Rukmini, T., 30, 261

Sabaranjitham, 69
Sabhesa Iyer. T.S., 136
Sadagopan, Ananthalakshmi, 133
Sadasiva Brahmendra, 13, 159–61
Sadasiva Rao, Mysore, 17, 156
Sadasivam, T., 47, 67, 78–97, 98,
    105, 107–13, 121, 122–25, 131–
    33, 138, 143, 153, 165–66, 168,
    173, 175, 183–84, 194, 214–15,
    217, 232, 234, 235, 249–52,
    258, 264, 266, 281–82, 286,
    294, 297–98
    meeting with Subbulakshmi,
        78–80, 86
    death, 268–70, 273–77
Sahir Ludhianvi, 127
Saivite poets, 3
Sakthivel, M.S., 39, 215–16, 262,
    270, 290
Sakuntalai (1941), 90–92, 93,
    95–96, 159, 173, 264, 275, 291
Sambamoorthy, P., 204, 228
Sambasiva Iyer, Karaikudi, 39, 142
SankaraIyer, T.D., 260
Sangam era, 2

Sangeetha Lava Kusa (1933), 81
Sangita Sampradaya Pradarsini, 224
Sankara Nethralaya, 258, 282
Sankara, 2, 197
    BhajaGovindam, 219, 246
    Ganesa pancaratnam, 199, 246
    Govindashtakam, 246
    Kanakadharastavam, 246, 199, 200
    Saundaryalahari, 2
Sankaracharya of Kanchi (also Paramacharya), 37, 218, 246, 255
Sankaradeva, 4
Sankaran, Revathy, 282
SankaranarayanaIyer, 260
Sarabhai, Mrinalini, 50
Saranayaki, 68, 75
Sarangadeva, 6
Sarangapani, 13
Saraswat Gayan Samaj, 29
Saraswathi Bai, C., 16, 40, 48, 67, 76, 83–84, 102, 106, 115
Sarkar, Sheela, 123
Saroja, C., 144, 302
Sathya Sai Baba, 218
Sati Anasuya, 91
Satyamurthy, Savitri, 261
Saundarya Mahal, Madras, 65, 66
Saurashtra Sabha, Madurai, 56
Savita Devi, 198
Savitri (1941), 50, 98–100, 159
Savitri Ammal, 117
Seetha Devi, Vinjamuri, 50
Self-Respect Movement (SuyamariathaiIyakkam), 58, 105–06
Sesha Iyengar, Margadarsi, 13

Sesha Iyengar, Namakkal, 144
Seshagiri Rao, S., 261
Seshan, T.N., 279
    Seshayyar, Pallavi, 17
Sethu Parvati Bayi, Maharani of Travancore, 117, 161, 196
Sethupathi High School, 56
Sevasadanam, 81, 82, 84, 88, 95, 99, 159, 291
Shankar, Lakshmi. *See* Lakshmi Sastri,
Shankar, Ravi, 68, 124, 126, 130, 169, 174, 216, 250, 270, 273–74, 292, 295
Shankar, Uday, 216
Shanmukham Chetty, R.K., 67, 107, 144–45
Shanmukhasundari, 36
Shanmukhavadivu, Vina A., 35–42, 47, 64–65, 72, 76, 81, 86, 97, 147, 165, 197, 199, 216, 272, 304, 309
Shanmukhvadivu, Tiruchendur., 30, 45,
Sharan Rani, 51
Sharma, Lakshmikantha, 219
Shastri, Lal Bahadur, 166
Shawn, Ted, 214
Shriram Kumar, R.K., 261
Shulman, David, 25
Siddheswari Devi, 49, 198, 295
Silverstone, Marilyn, 169
Sivan, Nilakantha, 17, 231
Sivan, Papanasam, 37, 81, 83, 89, 90, 93, 94, 96, 98–100, 146, 156, 158–59, 166, 194, 203, 207, 209

Index

Sivananda, Swami, 218
Sivanandam, 15
Sivasubramania Iyer, Alathur, 102, 142, 191
social reform in India, 35, 55–57
Somasundaram Chettiar, C., 47
Soundararaja Iyengar, S., 227
Sri Mahalakshmi Matrubhuteshwar Trust, 266
Sri Parthasarathi Swami Sabha, 19, 114
Sri Rajagopuram Fund, 254
Sri Ramakrishna, 55
Sri Ramana Maharshi, 41, 205, 218
Sri Ranganathaswami Temple, 12
Sri Sarada Gana Sabha, 19
Srinivasa Iyengar, C.R., 43, 131
Srinivasa Iyengar, Madurai., 41
Srinivasa Iyengar, Ramanathapuram (Poochi), 17, 40, 158, 191, 209
SrinivasaIyer, Alathur, 191
Srinivasa Iyer, Semmangudi, 37, 39, 64, 73, 96, 130, 133, 136, 142, 152, 153, 160–61, 163, 167–68, 171–73, 185, 186, 190, 191, 198, 208, 216, 231, 241, 257, 265, 276–77, 280, 286
Srinivasa Rao, P.S., 160
Srinivasan, Kasturi, 95, 112, 131
Sriram V., 71, 84, 197, 262, 302
Sairam, Aruna, 298
Sruti Foundation, 282
Subba Rao, T.V., 85
Subbalakshmi, Sister R.S., 35
Subbarama Bhagavathar, M., 100

Subbarama Dikshitar, 15, 158, 224, 244
Subbaraya Sastri, 15, 142, 249
Subbarayar, Dharmapuri, 17, 31, 64, 65, 228
Subbulakshmi, Madurai Shanmukhavadivu (M.S.), 31
  awards and honours, 141–42, 182, 249, 255–58, 266, 270–74, 279
  and Annamcharya, 245,
  and Balasaraswati, 67, 118, 213, 253
  and Magsaysay Award, 215
  and Muthusvami Dikshitar, 225–26
  and other composers, 158
  and Papanasam Sivan 158–59,
  and Svati Tirunal, 162–63
  and SyamaSastri, 241
  and Tyagaraja, 193
  benefit recitals, 118–20, 132–33, 143, 149–50, 156, 200, 203, 217–19, 254, 257
  birth, 35
  books and films on, 281–82
  charity, 203, 257–58, 266
  childhood, 53–63
  concerts in foreign countries, 108, 146, 169, 232–35, 253,
  contemporaries, 48–52
  death, 230, 278–79
  devotional recitals, 217–20, 221–47
  generosity, 131
  move to Madras, 64–77

marriage, 63, 269
career in films, 36, 42, 48, 50, 64, 76, 80–81, 84, 90–94, 96–97, 98, 103, 110–13, 120, 123–27, 131, 134, 159, 163, 179, 260, 264, 294; renounced films, 134
other artistes of same name 93
restraint, 236–37
retirement, 248–67
United Nations concert, 1966, 156, 173–76, 179, 181, 202, 264, 291
Subbulakshmi, R., 216
Subbulakshmi, S.D., 81, 82, 93
Subbulakshmi–Sadasivam Music and Dance Resources Institute (SAMUDRI), 274
Subhash Chandran, T.H., 262
Subrahmanyam, K., 64, 81–82, 88, 95
Subramania Iyer, Justice, 42
Subramania Iyer, Madurai, 36, 40, 215
Subramania Iyer, Musiri, 73, 93, 102, 135–37, 163, 166, 167, 191, 233, 264–65, 277
Subramania Iyer, Patnam, 17, 145, 156, 157, 188, 191, 200, 228
Subramania Pillai, Chittoor, 71, 73, 240
Subramania Pillai, Palani, 71, 152
Subramaniam, Arundhathi, 91
Subramanian, Lakshmi, 20, 24, 40, 53, 85, 129, 140

Subramanyam, V.V., 166–67, 197, 203, 261, 263
Sundara Bhagavathar, Umayalpuram, 191
Sundaram Iyer, P., 73
Sundaram, A.R., 23, 75
Sundaram, N.A., 114
Sundarambal (Sundarathammal), K. B., 30, 37, 38, 46, 48, 76, 95, 112, 115, 131, 207
Sundarar, 3, 231
Sundaresa Bhattar, Seithur, 41
Sundaresa Iyer, T.N., 260, 261
Sundari and Varalakshmi, 45
Surdas, 4, 163, 252, 293
Suryakumari, T., 76
Sutherland, Joan, 304, 305, 307
Svati Tirunal Rama Varma, 17, 130, 145, 147, 148, 149, 156, 161–63, 166, 170, 175, 190, 198, 203, 208, 211, 244
Swaminatha Iyer, U., 136, 145, 146, 149
Swaminatha Pillai, T., 71
Swaminathan, M.S., 35, 148
Syama Sastri, 13–15, 20, 103, 155, 188–90, 192, 205, 224, 239–42, 244, 249, 295
disciples of 15, 30

Tacchur Singaracharyulu brothers, 20, 188, 240
Tagore, Rabindranath, 54, 249, 293
Tambiappan Pillai, Suddhamandalam, 15, 30

Index

Tamil Isai movement, 103, 129, 184
Tamil Isai Sangam, 19, 106–9, 114, 116, 133, 166, 175, 182, 193, 198, 207, 210, 213, 231, 244, 265
Tamil Christian lyrics, 109
Tampi, Iraiyaman, 17
Thaayumanavar, 231
Thakur, Omkarnath, 120
Thanjavur (also Tanjore, Tanjavur), 11–12, 16
Thanjavur Quartet, 15
Thayi, Coimbatore, 29, 45
Theosophical Society, Madras, 60–61, 72
Theosophy, 61
Thite, Narayan Rao, 99
Thiyagarajan, Swati, 281
Thooran, Periasami, 158, 231, 249
Thumboochetty, Philomena, 49
thumri, 51
Thyaga Bhoomi (1939), 88, 131, 205
Thyagabrahma Gana Sabha, 114
Thyagarajan, T. M., 172
Thyagarajan, V., 260
Tirumala Nayak, 33
Tondaimandalam Sabha, 18
Tukaram, 4, 293
Tulsidas, 4, 163, 223, 247, 293
Tyabji, Badruddin, 164
Tyabji, Rehana, 164
Tyagaraja, 13–14, 20, 29, 46, 77, 85, 89, 103, 107, 135 139, 155–57, 161, 172, 179, 186–94, 223, 233, 241, 272, 276, 295, 303
 aradhana 242, 248–49,
 disciples of 15, 30, 190,
 his faith 192
 pancharatnakritis, 186–87, 188, 192, 241
 use of language 188, 240,
Tyagarajan, S., 78, 128, 153, 281

Upanishads, 2
Upendran,Tanjavur, 262

Vadivambal, M.S., 39, 39, 65, 97, 133–34, 215–16
vaggeyakara, 16, 106, 159, 178, 190, 227
Vaidyanatha Bhagavathar, C., 73, 262, 298
Vaidyanatha Iyer, K., 40
Vaidyanatha Iyer, Maha, 19, 136, 191, 230
Vaidyanathan, 101
Vale, G.K., 72
Vallabhacharya, 246
Valli Thirumanam, 48
Valmiki Ramayanam, 172
Vanajakshi, M., 30
Varadachariar, N.D., 73, 83, 85, 89, 93, 115
Varalakshmi, Saridey, 29, 68, 69, 82
varnams, 20, 139–40, 146, 152, 157,167, 187, 224, 233–34, 240, 249
Vasantha Sena (1936), 73
Vasanthakokilam, N.C., 49, 72–73, 76, 80, 89–90, 99, 108, 114, 129, 131, 144

Vasanthakumari, M.L., 50, 112, 116, 131, 142, 144, 145, 151, 167, 172–73, 178–79, 186, 194, 196, 198, 236–39, 244–45, 256–57, 261, 282, 285, 289, 296, 308–9
Vasudevacharya, Mysore K., 17, 149, 156–57
Vasundhara Devi, 50, 76, 89
Vedas, 1–2, 10, 302
Vedavalli, R., 144, 152, 298
Veeraswami Pillai, 115
Venkatachalam, G., 42, 52, 212
Venkatamakhin, 12
Venkatamakhin, Muddu, 12
Venkataram, B.K., 262
Venkatarama (or Venkataramana) Bhagavathar, K., 39, 41, 148
Venkatarama Iyer, K.S. 'Papa', 191
Venkatarama Iyer, T.L., 115, 204
Venkatarama Sastri, R.K., 145, 146, 148, 260, 261
Venkataraman, K., 274, 275
Venkataraman, K.S., 219, 220, 246
Venkataraman, M.S., 95
Venkataraman, S.V., 42, 123
Venkataramana Bhagavathar, Walajapet, 190, 191
Venkataramanujam, V.K., 260
Venkatasubbayyar, M., 136, 157, 191
Venkataswami Naidu, Dwaram, 71, 106, 142
Venkatesh Kumar, 177
Venkateswara Rao, Y., 262

Venu Naicker, 263
Venugopal, Spencer, 158
Vidyapati, 4
Vidyasagar, Ishwar Chandra, 55
Vijayanagar Empire, 11, 33
Vilayat Khan, 174
Vinayakram, T.H., 203, 244, 262
Viswanatha Iyer, Maharajapuram., 73, 92, 142
Viswanatha Sastri, Mayuram., 17
Viswanathan, G., 147, 153
Viswanathan, Radha, 78, 79, 84, 87, 92, 97, 116, 124, 126, 131, 136, 147, 153, 173, 174, 197, 203, 216, 219, 222, 236, 242, 251, 264–65, 297
Viswanathan, T., 142, 258
Vivekananda, Swami, 55
Vyas, Narayan Rao, 83
Vysaraya, 179, 238

Weil, Simone, 296
Wilde, Oscar, 306
Wodeyar, Jayachamaraja, 147, 156–57, 196
women composers, 16

World Pacific Records, 179

Yoganarasimham, H.D., 251, 252

Zohrabai Agrewali, 45, 308
Zoroastrianism, 61

Index of Songs

Adaravatravar, 76
Aggini Endrariyaro, 99
Akhilandeshwari/Jujavanti, 195, 198
Akhiyan Hari darasan ki pyaasi, 163
Akshayalingavibho/
    Sankarabharanam, 37, 149, 226, 250
Aliveni/Kuranji, 162, 211
Allah tero naam, 127
Ambigaye/Anandabhairavi, 158
Anandamritakarshini/
    Amritavarshini, 226
Andavanae/Shanmukhapriya, 94
Angarakam asrayamyaham/Surati, 146, 222, 225
Anjaneyam/Saveri, 135, 162, 244
Annapurnashtakam, 168
Anudinamu/Begada, 158, 200
Aparadhamula/Latangi, 157, 200
Arta piravi/Sankarabharanam, 145, 193, 208

Artana paduve/Hamsanandi, 178
Arul purivai/Hamsadhwani, 119, 291

Banturiti/Hamsanada, 243, 250, 266
Baro Krishnayya, 179, 238
Baso more nainana mein, Nandalala!, 294
Bhagyada Lakshmi baramma/Sri, 178
Bhaja Govindam, 218, 219, 246
Bhaja mana Rama charana, 163
Bhaja re Gopalam/Hindolam, 99
Bhaja re re chitta Balambikam/
    Kalyani, 216, 226, 249, 295
Bhaja re yadunatham/Pilu, 161
Bhajo re Bhaiyya, 142, 163
Bhavayami Gopala balam/
    Yamunakalyani, 246, 285
Bhavayami Raghuramam, 147, 162, 170, 171, 285, 291
Bhogindra sayinam/Kuntalavarali, 198, 285

INDEX OF SONGS

Bhujagasayanam/
    Yadukulakambhoji, 163
Birana brova idey/Kalyani, 147, 149, 158
Brindavan ki kunj galin mein, 294
Brochevarevarura/Khamas, 156
Brovavamma/Manji, 100, 241
Bruhi Mukundeti/Kuranji, 99, 161

Chandrasekharam/Kiravani, 244
Chelinenetlu, 123
Cheri Yasodaku/Mohana, 249
Cheta Sri Balakrishnam/Jujavanti, 195, 208, 225, 243
Chinnam chiru kiliye, 119
Chintaya makanda/Bhairavi, 94, 223
Chintayami jagadamba/Hindolam, 156

Darini/Suddhasaveri, 80, 147, 214, 231
Dasana madiko enna/
    Nadanamakriya, 168, 178
Dasarathe/Todi, 209, 210, 248
Deivatamizh nattinilae, 119
Deva Sri Tapastirthapuranivasa/
    Madhyamavati, 209
Devadeva kalayami/
    Mayamalavagaula, 149, 162
Devadevam/Hindolam, 245
Devi brova samayamide/Chintamani, 230, 233, 240, 241, 244, 309
Devi jagajjanani/Sankarabharanam, 136, 162, 208
Devi neeye thunai/Kiravani, 159, 195

Deviyai pujai/Kamavardhini, 100, 159
Dhano dhanya pushpa bhora, 102
Dharanige dorayendu/Dhanyasi, 178
Dhava vibho, 194
Dhyaname/Dhanyasi, 146, 209
Dinamanivamsa/Harikambhoji, 145
Divakara tanujam/
    Yadukulakambhoji, 222, 225
Dudukugala/Gaula, 186, 195, 199
Durusuga/Saveri, 135, 138, 147, 210, 241, 253
Dvadasa stotram, 246

Eduta nilacite/Sankarabharanam, 138
Ehi Annapurne/Punnagavarali, 226
Ek sahara tera, 76
Ela ni daya radu/Athana, 100, 130, 243
Elagu daya vachu/Sankarabharanam, 94
Elavatarame/Mukhari, 46, 76
Ella arumaigalum peravendum iraiva, 46
Emako ciguruta/Tilang, 245
Emandune muddu balamani/Kapi, 65
Emineramu, 244
Enakkum irupadam, 76
Enati nomu/Bhairavi, 209, 211
Endan idadu, 76
Endaro Mahanaubhavulu/Sri, 168, 186, 194, 210, 214
Ennadu ullame, 123
Ennaga manasu/Nilambari, 243

Index of Songs

Ennaganu Rama bhajana/
  Pantuvarali, 76, 83, 94, 100,
  147, 243, 285
*Enta rani/*Harikambhoji, 197, 249
*Entaveduko/*Saraswatimanohari,
  166
*Entoprema/*Surati, 208
*Eppadi manam/*Huseni, 146
*Era napai/*Todi, 146, 157, 167
*Evarani/*Devamritavarshini, 210
Evari bodhana, Abhogi, 157
*Evarimata/*Kambhoji, 148, 243

*Gajavadana/*Sriranjini, 159
*Gananayakam bhajeham/*Rudrapriya,
  230
Ganesa pancaratnam, 246
*Gange mam pahi/*Jenjuti, 225
Gave guni ganika, 164
Ghadi ek nahin, 164
Ghanashyam aaya re, 131, 294
Ghunguru baandh, 164
Giridhara Gopala, 123, 294
*Gnanamosagarada/*Purvikalyani,
  148, 197
*Gopalaka/*Revagupti, 162, 168, 198
*Gopanandana/*Bhushavali, 138, 147,
  149, 162, 244
*Govardhana girisam/*Hindolam, 207
*Govindam iha/*Bagesri, 161
Govindashtakam, 246, 266
Guha saravanabhava/
  Simhendramadhyama, 159
*Guru vina ghulama/*Pantuvarali, 178
*Guruleka/*Gaurimanohari, 207

Hanuman Chalisa, 247
Hari main to, 164
*Hari Narayana/*Kedaram, 178, 199,
  249
Hari tum haro, 127–28, 129, 175
*Hariharaputram/*Vasanta, 138, 146,
  225
He Nutan, 293
Hey Govinda Hey Gopala, 163, 164
Hey harey!, 294
*HiranmayimLakshmim/*Lalita, 1,
  199, 201, 226
*Hogadiro Ranga/*Sankarabharanam,
  178

*Idatthu padam tookki/*Khamas, 194
*Ikanaina/*Pushpalatika, 158, 195,
  233, 234
*Ikaparam/*Simhendramadhyama,
  159
*Indumukhi/*Sankarabharanam, 168,
  234
*Innudaya baarade/*Kalyanavasantam,
  178
*Ivanaro/*Kambhoji, 94

*Jagadanandakaraka/*Nata, 149, 186,
  216
*Jagadodhharana/*Kapi, 175, 177, 178,
  198
Jakhan porbe, 293
*Jalandhara/*Valaji, 94
*Janani ninu vina/*Ritigaula, 138,
  207, 242, 249, 309
*Janani pahi/*Suddhasaveri, 136

INDEX OF SONGS

Jaya Jaya Padmanabhanujesha/
  Manirangu, 162, 208, 211, 217

Ka Va Va/Varali, 149, 159, 183,
  265, 309
Kaddanuvariki/Todi, 100
Kadirkamakandan/Kambhoji, 146
Kahan re pathik kahan, 142, 293
Kahe re bana khojana jaaye, 163
Kairatnama/Punnagavarali, 134
Kala kanthi/Nilambari, 138, 148, 163
Kalai thookki/Yadukulakambhoji,
  131
Kaliyugadalli/Jenjuti, 178
Kamakshi/Bhairavi 241, 243, 295
Kamakshi/Yadukulakambhoji, 168,
  241
Kamakshi kamakotipithavasini/
  Sumadyuti, 226, 231
Kamakshi Suprabhatam, 218, 219,
Kamalamba samrakshatu mam/
  Anandabhairavi, 222
Kamalambam/Kalyani, 222
Kamalambikaya/Sankarabharanam,
  222
Kamalambike/Todi, 138, 148, 166,
  199, 214, 222, 234
Kana kann kodi/Kambhoji, 96, 159
Kanakadharastavam, 246
Kanakamaya/Huseni, 163
Kanakana rucira/Varali, 186
Kanakasaila/Punnagavarali, 168,
  220, 241
Kanjadalayatakshi/
  Kamalamanohari, 146, 148,
  220, 226

Kannan idam/ragamalika, 158
Kannatandri/Devamanohari, 208
Kapali/Mohana, 93, 94, 159
Kartikeya/Todi, 159
Karuna/Hemavati, 94
Karunaipuriya nalla tharunam/
  Sriranjani, 158
Sri Kasi Viswanatha Suprabhatam,
  218, 220
Katrinilae varum geetam, 112, 120,
  123, 266
Kerala dharani/Mohana, 158
Kitne dosh ginaaoon, 164
Koniyada/Kambhoji, 191, 210, 230
Korisevimpa/Kharaharapriya, 46
Kripaya palaya/Charukesi, 130, 162
Krishna lila tarangini, 161
Krishna nee begane baro/
  Yamunakalyani, 46, 68, 179
Ksheenamai/Mukhari, 146, 231
Ksheerasagarasayana/Devagandhari,
  37, 194
Ksheerasagarasayana/
  Mayamalavagaula, 156, 167, 181,
  200, 211, 266, 286
Kunja nikunja, 163
Kurai Onrum Illai/ragamalika, 257,
  279
Kuvalayakshiro/Gaulipantu, 228

Ma dayai/Vasanta, 100, 159
Ma Janaki/Kambhoji, 232
Ma ramanan/Hindolam, 93
Madhava mamava/Nilambari, 161
Madhubana tuma, 163
Madhurashtakam, 202, 246

Index of Songs

Maha Ganapatim/Todi, 211, 226
Mahalakshmi/Madhavamanohari, 226
Main nirgunia, 76
Maitreem bhaja, 175, 278, 279
Male manivanna/Kuntalavarali, 194
Mallika boney, 293
Mamava Minakshi/Varali, 181, 226
Mamava Pattabhirama/Manirangu, 96, 225
Mamava sada/Kanada, 138, 162–63
Mamavatu Sri Saraswati/Hindolam, 157
Manamohananga, 92
Manamuleda/Hamirkalyani, 76
Manasa etulo/Malayamarutam, 76
Manasa sancharare/Sama, 161
Manasuloni marmamu/Suddha Hindolam, 210, 211
Manavyala/Nalinakanti, 168
Mangalavinayakane/Ramapriya, 158
Manju nigar, 136
Marakatamanivarna/Varali, 243
Marakatavadivu/Jenjuti, 45
Maravakave/Sama, 157
Maravene, 123
Marivere/Anandabhairavi, 96, 241
Marivere/Shanmukhapriya, 157
Mariyada gadayya/Bhairavam, 94
Marugelara/Jayantasri, 249
Mathe/Khamas, 200, 201, 208, 209, 210, 234, 243, 309
Mayamma/Ahiri, 214, 217, 241
Maye/Tarangini, 225
Meenakshi Suprabhatam, 218

Meevalla/Kapi, 93, 94, 130, 214, 234, 243, 266
Mein hari charanana, 257, 294
Melakarta Ragamalika, 136, 198, 200, 201, 211, 230, 234, 255, 265
Merusamana/Mayamalavagaula, 209
Minakshi me mudam dehi/ Gamakakriya, 162, 221, 225, 266
Mitri Bhagyame/Kharaharapriya, 193
Mokshamu galada/Saramati, 172, 186, 295
Moratopu/Sahana, 228
More aangan mein murali bajao re, 127
More to giridhara gopala, 294
Mosaboku/Gaulipantu, 211
Munnu Ravana/Todi, 167
Murali mohana, 124
Muripemu galige/Mukhari, 243
Muruga Muruga/Saveri, 135, 158, 249

Naam japan kyon chhod diya, 164
Nadasudha/Arabhi, 94
Nadasudhatava/Kurinji, 163
Nadatanum anisam/Chittaranjani, 188
Nagumomu/Abheri, 37, 148
'*Nainan gungat me,*' 76
Nama Ramayana, 247
Nanati bratuku/Revati, 245
Nandabala, 124
Naneke badavanu/Behag, 142, 178, 266
Nannu palimpa/Mohana, 147
Naradamuni/Pantuvarali, 193, 208, 214, 285, 287

Narayana divya nama/Mohana, 159, 183, 243, 285, 291
Narayana/Suddhadhanyasi, 178, 217
Narayanate namo namo/ragamalika, 244
Nee irangayenil/Athana, 285
Nee sati daivamu/Sriranjini, 225
Needu charana/Kalyani, 94, 95, 231
Neelayatakshi/Pharaz, 198, 241
Nenaruncinanu/Malavi, 198, 208
Nenendu/Karnataka Behag, 244
Nera nammitini/Kanada, 158, 210
Nidayaledani/Dhanyasi, 158
Nidhi tsala sukhama/Kalyani, 168, 243, 253
Ninnarul/Kamavardhini, 159, 166
Ninne namminanu/Todi, 241
Ninne Nammiti/Simhendramadhyama, 157
Ninnu vina/Balahamsa, 46
Ninnu vina/Kalyani, 142, 242, 309
Ninnu vina/Navarasakannada, 183
Ninnu vina/Ritigaula, 209, 241
Nis din barasat nain hamare, 163

O Jagadamba/Anandabhairavi, 76, 81, 198, 211, 231, 241
O Rangasayee/Kambhoji, 135, 190, 193, 199, 200, 207, 233-34, 266, 286
Odi barayya/Bhairavi, 178
Okapari/Kharaharapriya, 245

Paadalum/Suddhasaveri, 146

Pahi Sripate/Hamsadhwani, 162
Paiyyada/Nadanamakriya, 228
Pakkala nilabadi/Kharaharapriya, 100, 138, 181, 201, 249, 253, 285
Palintsu Kamakshi/Madhyamavati, 148, 241, 249
Palisemma muddu Sharade/Mukhari, 178
Palukavademira/Devamanohari, 157
Pankajalochana/Kalyani, 163
Pannagendrasayana/ragamalika, 163
Paraloka bhayamu/Mandari, 46
Paramukham/Kharaharapriya, 94, 96, 100, 159
Paratpara/Vachaspati, 159, 218
Paripahimam/Mohana, 163, 211
Parthasarathi ni sevimpani/Yadukulakambhoji, 158, 244
Parvati ninnu ne nera nammiti/Kalgada, 240
Phir sakhi ritu saavan aayi, 164

Pillangoviya cheluva Krishna/Kapi, 178
Poonkuyil koovum, 112
Pranatarthiharam/Jenjuti, 157
Premayil, 92

Ra ra mayinti daka/Asaveri, 230
Ra ra yani pilacite/Kharaharapriya, 157
Radhamadhavam, 218, 252
Raghupati Raghava Rajaram, 102
Raghuvamsasudha/Kadanakutuhalam, 157
Rama bhaja, 163

Index of Songs

Rama nannu brova ravemako/
  Harikambhoji, 130, 138, 146,
  147, 148, 167, 175, 285
Rama nee samanam evaru/
  Kharaharapriya, 39, 190, 244
Rama ninne nammitini/Saranga, 158,
  209
Rama Rama gunaseema/
  Simhendramadhyama, 135, 163,
  167, 233
Rama simira, 163
Ramachandrena/Manji, 222

Ramanatham/Kasiramakriya, 145,
  226, 230, 234
Ranganayakam/Nayaki, 186, 199,
  209, 210, 225
Rangapura vihara/
  Brindavanasaranga, 138, 142,
  147, 149, 162, 170, 172, 175,
  225, 285
Rave Himagiri Kumari/Todi, 208,
  241

Sabhapatikku/Abhogi, 100, 138,
  193, 200, 309
Sada saranga nayane/Ranjani, 251,
  292
Sadasivam upasmahe/
  Sankarabharanam, 138, 198,
  225
Sadhincene/Arabhi, 81, 120, 186
Sakalagrahabala neene/Athana, 178
Saketanagaranatha/Harikambhoji,
  156, 168, 199

Sambho Mahadeva/Bauli, 146, 168,
  193, 200
Sankalpamettido/Kharaharapriya,
  145, 157
Sankara dayakara/Harikambhoji,
  159, 209
Sankaracharyam/Sankarabharanam,
  147, 158 167, 253
Sankari neeve/Begada, 242
Santamu leka/Sama, 193
Santana Rama/Hindolavasanta, 138

Saragunapalimpa/Kedaragaula, 76,
  158
Saranam Ayyappa/Mukhari, 159,
  166
Saranam saranam/Sourashtra, 146
Sarasaksha/Pantuvarali, 138, 146,
  162, 175, 211
Sarasijamukhiro/Arabhi, 168
Sarasijanabha murare/Todi, 163
Sarasiruhasana/Nata, 96, 158

Saravanabhava/Madhyamavati, 159
Saravanabhava/Shanmukhapriya,
  159, 199
Sarojadalanetri/Sankarabharanam,
  130, 138, 146, 147, 148, 175,
  241, 268, 285
Seshachalanayakam/Varali, 210, 226
Sharade/Mohana, 158
Sharanu Siddhivinayaka/Saurashtra,
  178
Sikshashtakam, 246
Sita manohara/Ramapriya, 138

INDEX OF SONGS

Sitamma mayamma/Vasanta, 168, 193, 195, 211, 243
Siva Siva Siva bho/Nadanamakriya, 156, 175
Sivadikshapari/Kuranji, 76
Smara haripada/Sama, 163
Sobhillu/Jaganmohini, 243
Sogasuga/Sriranjini, 144, 287
Sri Chamundeshwari/Bilahari, 157, 195
Sri Chandrasekhara yatindram/Sankarabharanam, 135, 167, 181, 208
Sri Dakshinamurte/Sankarabharanam, 200
Sri Jalandhara/Gambhiranata, 156
Sri Kamakoti/Saveri, 145, 147, 148, 149, 156, 200, 220, 243, 286, 287
Sri Kantimatim/Desisimharava, 147, 149, 167, 225
Sri Kasi Viswanatha Suprabhatam, 218, 220
Sri Krishnam/Todi, 168, 226, 309
Sri Kumara/Athana, 136, 163, 166, 230
Sri Lakshmivaraham/Abhogi, 199, 225
Sri Maha Ganapati/Gaula, 226, 233, 244
Sri Muladhara chakra vinayaka/Sri, 225
Sri Parvati/Bauli, 147, 225
Sri Raghukula/Huseni, 46
Sri Ramachandra kripalu, 163
Sri Rameswara Ramanatha Suprabhatam, 218, 220
Sri Ranganatha gadyam, 246

Sri Satyanarayanam/Sivapantuvarali, 224
Sri Shanmukha janaka/Sankarabharanam, 156
Sri Subramanyaya namaste/Kambhoji, 37, 168, 195, 210, 226
Sri Sukra bhagavantam/Pharaz, 147, 224
Sri Venkatesa Suprabhatam, 170–71, 218, 219
Sri Visnu Sahasranama, 2, 218, 219, 246
Srikanta yenagishtu/Kanada, 178
Sriman Narayana/Bauli, 245, 246, 257
Srinivasa/Hamsanandi, 159, 217
Subramanyena/Suddhadhanyasi, 130
Sumiran kar le, 14

Sundarathe dhyana, 208
Suneri main ne nirbal ke balram, 293
Suryamurte/Saurashtra, 200

Swararagasudha/Sankarabharanam, 166
Syama sastrin namostute/Sama, 240
Syama sundara, 291
Syamala dandakam, 205

Tabu mone rekho, 293
Talli ninnu nera/Kalyani, 200, 241
Tamadamen/Todi, 159
Tappagane/Suddhabangala, 138
Tarunam idamma/Gaulipantu, 241
Tattvamariya/Ritigula, 93

Index of Songs

Tava dasoham/Punnagavarali, 243
Taye Idu taranum/Kamavardhani, 183
Teliyaleru/Dhenuka, 144, 183, 188
Tera tiyaga rada/Gaulipantu, 183, 207, 209, 211, 265, 267
Thakur tum sharanayi, 163
Thamasamen/Todi, 94
Thavavum Palithathamma, 119
Thaye Yashoda/Todi, 131
Theyilai Thothathile/Jenjuti, 134
Thirupalliyezhichi, 171
Thondru nigazhntha, 119
Tiruvadicharanam/Kambhoji, 135, 183, 194
Toot gayi man bina, 123
Tsakkani raja margamu/Kharaharapriya, 135, 147, 168, 217
Tsalakalla/Arabhi, 190, 210
Tsallare/Ahiri, 193, 243
Tu dayalu deen haun, tu daani han bhikari, 163
Tulasi jagajjanani/Saveri, 46
Tyagaraja yoga vaibhavam/Anandabhairavi, 225

Udal Uruga, 123
Unnuruvam, 76
Uttukuliyinile, 45

Vachamago/Kaikavasi, 166, 188, 218
Vadasi yadi kinchidapi/Mukhari, 160
Vadavarayai/ragamalika, 168, 175, 193
Vadera daivamu/Pantuvarali, 76
Vaishnava jana to, 101, 129, 150
Valapu tala/Athana, 228
Valayunniha nyaan/Varali, 198
Vallabha nayakasya/Begada, 208
Vallagada/Sankarabharanam, 93

Vanajakshi/Kalyani, 209
Vandadum Solai, 119
Vande Mataram, 102
Vande sada Padmanabham/Navarasakannada, 145, 163
Vande Vasudevam/Sri, 292
Vandeham jagatvallabham/Hamsadhwani, 244, 245
Vandinam/Todi, 93–94
Vara Narada/Vijayasri, 166, 188, 190, 285
Varanamukha/Hamsadhwani, 193
Vatapi Ganapatim/Hamsadhwani, 37, 99–100, 138, 144, 167, 199, 208, 218, 225, 243, 253, 266
Veena pustaka dharini/Vegavahini, 225
Vidajaladura/Janaranjani, 46
Vidulaku/Mayamalavagaula, 138
Vijaya dvaraka/Gaulipantu, 159
Vijayambike/Vijayanagari, 96
Vinabheri/Abheri, 226
Vinayaka Vighnavinasaka/Hamsadhwani, 158
Vinayakuni/Madhyamavati, 96, 198, 214, 220
Viriboni/Bhairavi, 88, 145, 149, 210

Yaad ave, 164
Yenpalli kondirayya, 131

About the Author

KESHAV DESIRAJU was educated at the universities of Bombay, Cambridge and Harvard and worked in the civil service. He is a co-editor, with Samiran Nundy and Sanjay Nagral, of *Healers or Predators? Healthcare Corruption in India*, Oxford University Press, 2018. He lives in Chennai and is thinking about upgrading his Telugu before writing about Tyagaraja.